1973 2007

Keeping Competitive in Turbulent Markets, 1973-2007

A History of Royal Dutch Shell

Keetie Sluyterman

Published under licence from Boom Publishers, Amsterdam, initiating publishers and publishers of the Dutch edition.

OXFORD
UNIVERSITY PRESS

2007

Keeping Competitive in Turbulent Markets, 1973-2007 is one of four volumes of the work entitled *A History of Royal Dutch Shell*, written by a team of four authors associated with Utrecht University, Jan Luiten van Zanden, Stephen Howarth, Joost Jonker and Keetie Sluyterman. It is the result of a research project which was supervised by the Research Institute for History and Culture and coordinated by Joost Dankers.

The other volumes are:

Joost Jonker and Jan Luiten van Zanden
From Challenger to Joint Industry Leader, 1890-1939

Stephen Howarth and Joost Jonker
Powering the Hydrocarbon Revolution, 1939-1973

Jan Luiten van Zanden
Appendices. Figures and Explanations, Collective Bibliography, and Index, including three DVDs

Contents

Chapter 1
Coping with OPEC, 1973-1986

Chapter 5
A licence to operate: company response to public scrutiny

Chapter 6
The merger of 1907 taken to its logical conclusion: the birth of Royal Dutch Shell plc

OXFORD
UNIVERSITY PRESS

Great Clarendon Street, Oxford OX2 6DP

Oxford University Press is a department of the University of Oxford.
It furthers the University's objective of excellence in research, scholarship,
and education by publishing worldwide in

Oxford   New York

Auckland   Cape Town   Dar es Salaam   Hong Kong   Karachi
Kuala Lumpur   Madrid   Melbourne   Mexico City   Nairobi
New Delhi   Shanghai   Taipei   Toronto

With offices in

Argentina   Austria   Brazil   Chile   Czech Republic   France   Greece
Guatemala   Hungary   Italy   Japan   Poland   Portugal   Singapore
South Korea   Switzerland   Thailand   Turkey   Ukraine   Vietnam

Oxford is a registered trade mark of Oxford University Press
in the UK and in certain other countries

British Library Cataloguing in Publication Data
Data available

ISBN: 978-0-19-929880-8

Introduction

In 1974 Gerrit Wagner, chairman of Shell's committee of managing directors, proposed that 'a current record should be maintained of Shell's decisions and activities and their background' in what he saw as 'a period of revolutionary change in the oil and energy scene'.[1] He referred to the dramatic events following the actions by the Organization of Petroleum Exporting Countries (OPEC), leading to the first oil crisis in 1973. He considered them such a sea-change in the history of the oil industry that they should be carefully archived for the benefits of later historians. This third volume of the history of Royal Dutch Shell starts at that remarkable moment in the history of the oil industry and has made use of records saved by Wagner's foresight, as well as many other company records.

By 1973 the Royal Dutch/Shell Group had been one of the two largest oil enterprises in the world for more than half a century, in constant competition with the American company Standard Oil of New Jersey (renamed Exxon Corporation in 1972). In volume one of our series Joost Jonker and Jan Luiten van Zanden highlighted how the Dutch-based Royal Dutch Petroleum Company, founded in 1890, and the British-based "Shell" Transport and Trading Company, founded in 1897, merged their activities in 1907. The two parent companies remained separate entities for political, legal and fiscal reasons, but their activities were quickly integrated into one worldwide business enterprise, coordinating the flow of oil from crude oil production in various parts of the world (the upstream business) to transportation, refining the crude and marketing the final products in many different countries (the downstream business). In contrast to the American oil companies, the Group's rise was not based on the existence of crude oil in one of its home countries. Instead, its first access to crude oil came through the British and Dutch colonial empires, giving the Group a very international outlook from the start. Riding the waves of rapid economic growth under the visionary leadership of Henri Deterding, it quickly expanded from its base in the Far East to Romania, Russia, Latin America and the US.

The Group's dual nationality could easily have become a handicap during the First World War, with the rise of nationalism, disruption of trade, and finally the nationalization of Russian oil concessions. But far from falling apart, the Group found new territories for exploration and production to compensate for the Russian losses. During the 1920s, growing particularly fast in the US and Venezuela, it became the world's largest oil business. In its management, a surprisingly diverse group of expatriates played vital roles, some having a strong technological background, while others came with commercial qualities. Though Royal Dutch had a 60 per cent share in the Group against the 40 per cent held by Shell Transport, the Shell brand with its easily recognizable pecten evolved into the dominant brand for the whole Group. In the late 1920s the Group decided to enter the new field of petrochemicals.

After the period of rapid growth, the Group consolidated its position in the late 1920s. Typical of the process of consolidation were the efforts to structure the oil industry by marketing arrangements with the main competitors, culminating in the Achnacarry Agreement of 1928. These arrangements, however, could not prevent overproduction and falling oil prices during the economic depression of the 1930s. In this period the erstwhile formidable leader, Deterding, became an embarrassment for the company. When he stepped down in 1936, he left the internal organization in disarray and vulnerable to infighting at the top. Rising economic nationalism made life particularly difficult for international businesses like the Group, internally as well as externally. Once again the Group lost one of its production areas, when Mexico nationalized its oil industry in 1938. Interestingly, the Group was not particularly eager to look for oil in Saudi Arabia when the opportunity arose for a partnership there, because it was convinced there was no oil to be found, a conviction shared by several others in the industry.

Volume two of this history, written by Stephen Howarth and Joost Jonker, starts with the outbreak of the Second World War, another dramatic moment for this dual national enterprise. Once again warfare, national rivalries and national pride could have caused serious disruption. Nevertheless, although much physical damage took place, precious lives were lost, and some nationalist tensions surfaced among its leaders, the Group as a whole pulled through, and organizationally came out even stronger because senior management succeeded in overcoming their British-Dutch rivalries. However, its position in the industry had weakened somewhat relative to its rival Jersey Standard. During the 1950s and 1960s the oil industry expanded, profiting from and at the same sustaining a long period of global economic growth. Oil overtook coal as the main source of energy, in particular in Europe. The focus of the international oil industry shifted from the American oil fields to those in the Middle East. There, in contrast to the major US oil companies and its British rival Anglo-Iranian (renamed British Petroleum or BP in 1954), Shell did not have a strong ownership position with regard to the low-cost Middle Eastern oil fields, but its long-term delivery contract with Gulf Oil for oil from Kuwait helped to make up the difference. Shell remained a top player in the industry because it had a strong downstream position. It built up a very large fleet and constructed many local refineries that were able to respond quickly and profitably to local demand.

Petrochemicals formed another growth area in this period, and Shell built a series of chemical plants which were impressive in size and innovative research, but extremely erratic in terms of profits.

The post-war expansion and the diversification into chemicals put pressure on the internal organization of the Group, which had been complicated right from the beginning as a consequence of the dual national structure. Directly after the Second World War Shell management began to shape a new organizational structure, which was finally consolidated in 1957-59. The 'matrix' organization was based on profit responsibility at the level of the local operating companies and two central offices in The Hague and London acting in coordinating and advisory roles. Typical of the new structure was the term 'coordinator' for top management positions in exploration and production or chemicals, or for heading regions such as Europe or Africa and South Asia. Though regional and functional management both had a coordinating role, over time the regional voice became the stronger of the two, at least in manufacturing and marketing.

Both parent companies continued to exist separately with their respective British and Dutch styles of corporate governance. Their roles in decision-making, however, were mostly formal, because the Group as a whole was headed by a Committee of Managing Directors (CMD), consisting of the managing directors of Royal Dutch and Shell Transport. The CMD had a collective responsibility and its chairman was not considered to have a stronger voice in decision-making than the other members. Acting as a 'supervisory board' for the CMD was the 'Conference', which included the members of the supervisory board of Royal Dutch and 'non-executive' board members of Shell Transport. The new organizational structure was fine-tuned with the advice of the American consultants McKinsey and Co, but the final result had a strong Dutch flavour with the shared responsibility of board members and an emphasis on consultation and coordination rather than clear-cut delegation. The decentralized organization on the basis of national operating companies furthered the expansion strategy, because the major countries were all eager to build their own refineries and petrochemical complexes.

During the first two decades after the Second World War, by means of joint ownership of large oilfields in the Middle East, and inter-company marketing agreements, the five American oil majors (Chevron, Jersey/Exxon, Gulf Oil, Mobil and Texaco) together with the two European-based oil majors (Royal Dutch/Shell and BP) dominated most of the international oil industry outside the communist areas. One might have expected this dominance to have resulted in high oil prices, but the reverse was the case. The interplay between the oil majors and the oil-producing countries led to increasing crude oil production, and the large supplies of relatively cheap oil kept prices low. However, when the governments of those countries began to realize that they earned less from their own oil than did the governments of oil-consuming countries via taxation, they began to challenge the existing oil regime. At the same time the American oil industry reached its peak production, and began to rely more on imported oil. Developments culminated in the first oil crisis of 1973 – the opening event of this volume.

This volume highlights how the European-based Group faced up to the nationalizations in the oil industry in the 1970s, and how high oil prices cushioned the required changes. The story then moves on to the second challenging period, after the collapse of oil prices in 1986. It explores how the Group responded to innovation in information technologies, and the return of globalization and privatization in the 1990s, with a major organizational overhaul. The book lastly discusses how in the early twenty-first century high oil prices, nationalizations, and alarms about oil scarcity resurfaced. As in the previous two volumes of this history, volume three focuses on five research areas. One of the fascinating aspects of Shell is its worldwide spread in regions and activities, and the changes that took place therein. In this period Shell left some regions, such as Iraq and Venezuela, and successfully entered others, notably the North Sea. It also entered several entirely new business activities, including metals, nuclear energy, coal, and renewable energy, but after a while decided to leave all of them, apart from the renewables. As a worldwide business the shaping of its internal organization was a particular challenge, and forms the second of our research areas. The Group had to try to find the right balance between centralization and decentralization, between coordination through businesses or national organizations, and between the interests of shareholders and other stakeholders, including employees. It had to respond to the rising demands from the general public, customers as well as non-governmental organizations. What will become clear is that successful solutions to deal with the new oil regime of the 1970s were not necessarily suitable for the challenges of the 1990s. To place these Group strategies in context, Shell's performance will be consistently compared with that of its US rival Exxon and its British competitor BP. The competitiveness of Shell is consequently our third research area. The fourth focuses on innovation as a way to improve competitiveness: how and when did Shell try to build up leadership in technology? What were its areas of strength? During the 1970s and early 1980s, technology was used to create growth, but after the mid-1980s it became increasingly important to cut costs. Moving on, the fifth research question concerns the role of politics. Oil and gas were important sources of income for governments but also a cause for concern when energy threatened to become

scarce. Governments and oil companies had their own agendas but also needed each other, which led to a complex interplay, part of which will be discussed in this volume.

In 1971 one Shell personnel manager, writing in the Shell publication *Personnel Management Review* wrote: 'What really happens in that complex of relationships we call "Shell" or the "Group" would keep hundreds of academics busy for years trying to discover and define. We just get on with it, and by and large, it works!'[2] This book touches on many subjects, all of which could be analyzed with the help of specific political, social or economic theories. However, it concentrates on the five research areas highlighted above, and focuses on the broad picture and the main developments with illustrative examples taken from different parts of the enterprise.

This volume is organized with a blend of chronological and thematic chapters. The first chapter discusses the combined impact of the OPEC nationalizations and high oil prices on Shell's oil business. The second chapter moves to the sectors outside the oil industry, namely the Group's entries into metals, nuclear energy, coal and renewable energy, as well as its earlier diversification into chemicals. The third chapter returns to the oil business during the period of low oil prices from 1986 to 1998. Chapter four discusses the internal organization in the context of conflicting demands from employees and shareholders. Chapter five adds the perspective of the public at large, analysing the expectations and criticisms of the society and the company's response. The sixth and last chapter looks at developments during recent years, developments which to some extent are still unfolding, and are therefore more difficult to place in perspective.

Like the earlier two volumes, this one is based on unrestricted access to the internal records of the Group, including the minutes and supporting documents of the CMD and Conference. In addition trade journals, speeches, and company brochures have been consulted. Particularly useful have been the interviews with nearly fifty Shell employees, whose enthusiastic stories greatly enhanced my understanding of their business. There have been only two practical limitations on research, and these affect only the most recent incidents. First, because of unfinished court cases, the issue of the reserves recategorization of 2004 could not be discussed with Shell staff and there was no access to records, regarding the matter except those in the public domain. Second, research at the level of board minutes stopped in 2005 with the unification of the two parent companies into Royal Dutch Shell plc. In concluding any historical work about an organization that is still very much alive and active, it is always difficult to provide a detailed assessment of events approaching the present day. In a few years' time it will be possible to add that assessment.

Acknowledgements

In the course of researching and writing this book I have enjoyed the generous help of colleagues, Shell employees, family and friends, to say nothing of archivists and librarians. It is impossible for me to include each by name. But there are some whose contributions have been so valuable that I wish to record them here. In the joint introduction to the whole work, included in volume one, we have acknowledged the important contribution to our project of the members of the editorial board: our colleagues Karel Davids and Geoffrey Jones, and for Shell, Jeroen van der Veer, Jyoti Munsiff, Adrian Loader and Phil Watts. Their insightful comments greatly contributed to this book. In addition we mentioned the highly appreciated support provided by Pieter Folmer, who has been exceedingly generous with his time throughout the entire life of this project and read all the drafts with great care. One of the many things he did for me was arrange the nearly fifty interviews I had with present and former Shell staff, which gave me valuable insight into the strategic decisions of various business units. A list of their names is included at the end of this volume. These conversations have been one of the great pleasures of writing this book.

I would like to join my colleagues in their great appreciation for the two Royal Dutch Shell archivists in London and The Hague, Veronica Davies and Rob Lawa. Veronica not only took meticulous care of the historical documents but she also shared with me her shrewd appraisals of the inner workings of the company. Rob Lawa made us particularly welcome at The Hague office by arranging (and defending) a study room for us, and he provided us with all the documents we needed despite the fact that his whole archive had to be moved to another building while our research project was ongoing. Dewey White and her staff kindly introduced me to material regarding the lives of expatriate families in their Outpost Archive in The Hague. Piet de Wit provided me with a number of pictures and with relevant information around some of the illustrations. I was delighted with his speed and accuracy. At Shell Oil in Houston I enjoyed and appreciated the help and hospitality of Jack Doherty, and was very grateful for the support we received from Kanada Hardy, Laura Linda and Hector Pineda in tracing the relevant records for us.

I have also greatly benefited from the useful suggestions made by the following present or retired Shell employees who read parts of my manuscript: Michiel Brandjes, Henk Dijkgraaf, Wilbert van Erp, Michael Le Q Herbert, Steve Hodge, Duke Igbuwe, Tim van Kooten, Keith Mackrell, John Malcolm, Karen de Segundo, Peter Vogtländer, Lo van Wachem, and my brother Anton Sluijterman, who moreover was a constant source of information about many of the more technical details of the upstream business. The fruits of their advice are apparent throughout the pages of this manuscript.

I am much obliged to Suzanne Lommers for her assistance in particular with regard to research and social corporate responsibility. Peter Koudijs and Christiaan van der Spek greatly helped with the collection of statistical information.

The outward appearance of this book owes much to the elegant book design by Marise Knegtmans, and the wide-ranging picture research by Nienke Huizinga. Together they aimed at making the visual expression faithful to the text while allowing it to tell its own story. I am much in their debt for the way in which they enriched the reading experience.

Keetie Sluyterman

Coping with OPEC, 1973-1986

From its start in the mid-nineteenth century until the early 1970s, the oil business had been a growth industry. This was particularly true for the 1950s and 1960s, a period of fast economic growth in the western world.[1] The period after the Second World War also signalled the end of the colonial empires of the European countries, including Britain, which would have a large impact on the relationships in the oil industry. The dominance of the oil industry by the major western oil companies, among them Exxon, Royal Dutch Shell, and BP, was no longer acceptable for the oil-producing countries, which were looking for more control over their own resources and for ways of sharing in the process of economic growth. In the late 1960s the oil-producing countries, including Venezuela, Saudi Arabia, Iran, Iraq and Libya, that had joined forces in the Organization of Petroleum Exporting Countries (OPEC), began to feel strong enough to gain more influence over the oil in their ground and derive more economic benefits from it. They could wield their newly found power because in the 1960s the United States had changed from an oil-exporting into an oil-importing country.

This chapter analyses the big challenges arising from OPEC strategies for the oil business in general and for the Shell Group of companies in particular. It explores how the upheaval of OPEC's price and participation policies influenced Shell's access to oil, and the relationship between its upstream and downstream business. Shell's ownership of oil was greatly reduced, which diminished the integration of its activities and forced the different parts of the business to reinvent themselves. The high oil prices, however, sweetened the necessity to engage in structural changes.

[2]

[3]

OPEC takes the lead   In the public perception the post-war
period of rising prosperity finally ended in October 1973, when
access to cheap energy appeared to be the Achilles heel of western
economic growth. The oil-producing countries organized in OPEC
dealt the decisive blow by raising oil prices fourfold between
October and December of that year, while the Arab countries
propped up the price rise with their embargo. The year 1973
became a landmark in the twentieth century. For the ordinary
consumer the oil scarcity and sudden price rise of gasoline was
completely unexpected. The oil industry, however, had seen the
writing on the wall, though it had expected events to unfold later
and more slowly.

Since the late 1950s the oil business had been divided in three
regions: the US oil industry that was protected by import
restrictions; the oil industry in the largely self-sufficient Communist
world; and the oil industry in the rest of the world, which was called
the 'international oil industry'. In Shell's jargon, the latter was
called 'WOCANA', the world outside the Communist area and
North America, in which the Middle East countries were by far the

largest producers. Within WOCANA the seven most important
international oil companies, Royal Dutch/Shell, Exxon, Mobil,
Standard Oil Company of California, Gulf, Texaxo, and BP,
dominated the oil trade, owning 69 per cent of the crude oil in
1970. Together these companies were nicknamed the 'Seven
Sisters'. Of these seven companies, five had American nationality;
one, BP, was British; and one, Royal Dutch/Shell, had dual
Dutch/British nationality. Though the 'Seven Sisters' were still
dominating the industry, they were no longer the only players.
During the 1950s and 1960s other private oil companies, the
'Independents' such as Amerada Hess, Sinclair Oil and Occidental,
had entered the arena, and in 1970 they possessed 23 per cent of
the crude oil, leaving the national oil companies of producing
countries with 8 per cent. In the marketing of oil the seven majors
had an equally dominant position, though no monopoly either. In
1973 the international oil companies marketed 70 per cent of the
international oil (WOCANA) through their affiliates and 22 per cent
via third parties. These third parties were often state-owned
refining operations serving the local market and set up by national

[4]

The Organization of Petroleum Exporting Countries (OPEC) was founded in 1960, with its member countries aiming for higher earnings and a greater say over the oil in their ground. The organization's supreme authority, the Conference, met at least twice a year with delegations normally headed by members' ministers of oil, mines and energy. Seen here from left to right are conferences in Taif, Saudi

Arabia, in 1980; in Abu Dhabi, 1978; and in 1976. During the 1970s prices rose through interaction of the conferences and the markets: ahead of a conference spot prices would creep up in anticipation of reduced production, and afterwards, OPEC members justified increased posted prices by saying they were merely following the markets.

governments to reduce their dependence on the international oil companies. The remaining 8 per cent was marketed directly by producer countries.[2] Through the existence of independents and national oil companies, the oil market had become more complex than in the 1960s, but the role of the producing countries was still limited. This situation was soon to be ended.

As discussed in volume 2, five oil-producing countries, Iraq, Iran, Kuwait, Saudi Arabia and Venezuela had organized themselves in the Organization of Petroleum Exporting Countries (OPEC) in 1960. During the 1960s Qatar, Libya, Indonesia, the United Arab Emirates, and Algeria joined the organization, and Nigeria, Ecuador, and Gabon would follow in the 1970s. The first ambition of the oil-exporting countries was to create a countervailing power against the major international oil companies in order to receive higher earnings from the oil in their ground. Their second ambition was to acquire a greater say over their national oil reserves. In 1968 OPEC issued its 'Declaratory Statement of Petroleum Policy' at Caracas in which it emphasized the inalienable right of oil producers to exercise permanent sovereignty over their natural resources. To secure a greater control over foreign concession holders, it advocated a policy of government participation in the oil industry.[3] Gradually the OPEC countries mounted pressure on the private oil companies. The developments in Libya acted as a catalyst. This country was the first, in 1970, to force the oil companies to accept higher posted prices (which meant higher taxes and higher royalties on oil production), and an increase in the share of profit from 50 to 55 per cent. Shell felt on a slippery slope. Concerned about its worldwide interests, it held out against these demands the longest, but conceded after all other oil companies had given in. Shell's regional co-ordinator Middle East, J. J. de Liefde, later concluded that with hindsight Shell's tough attitude towards Libya was wrong: 'I think we overestimated our importance as innovator or setting examples for others.'[4] Nevertheless, Shell's fear, that the demand of Libya would be followed by more demands elsewhere,

was certainly justified. After the Shah of Iran had demanded a 55 per cent share in profits in 1970, the major oil companies agreed to pay the same 55 per cent to the other Gulf States.[5]

In September 1971 Sir David Barran, chairman of Shell Transport, asked for an interview with the British Prime Minister Edward Heath to discuss the oil supply and demand situation. Shell had prepared a report on 'future energy supplies of the world, excluding the Communist countries', one of the first of their famous long-term scenarios. In this report they concluded that as continued economic progress would entail an increasing demand for energy, the call on Middle East production for the next fifteen years would place this region in a position to control a sellers' market for energy. Barran warned the Prime Minister that this position would enormously enhance the political strength and bargaining power of the existing oil-producing countries,

[5]

[6]

particularly in the Middle East. He did not expect a world energy crisis before 1980, because the oil majors had reached an agreement with OPEC in Teheran in 1971, which would last for five years. But after expiration of this agreement Shell foresaw a rapid rise in the share that producing governments would take of oil earnings.[6] A similar briefing took place in the Netherlands, while a slightly less explicit document was made available for the other European governments. The general managers of Shell operating companies in Europe were encouraged to seek contacts with governments on oil prices, security of supply and related subjects. The Shell board wanted to keep up the reputation and credibility of private industry, because it recognized that the governments of oil-consuming countries were concerned about the dependence of their economies on energy and that some were promoting moves towards more national oil companies.[7]

In 1949 Venezuela took the first step in organizing the oil-exporting countries by approaching Iran, Iraq, Kuwait, and Saudi Arabia to discuss common interests. Held in Baghdad in 1960, OPEC's first conference established it as a permanent intergovernmental organization. Indonesia and Libya joined in 1962 and Nigeria in 1971. Seen here in 1974, from left to right are the Indonesian Minister of Petroleum, Elrich Sanger, at the conference in Vienna; Ezzedin Mabruk (left), Libya's Minister of Petroleum, speaking with Jamshid Amouzegar, the Iranian Finance Minister; and the Nigerian Minister of Petroleum, Ali Monguno, in Geneva.

[7]

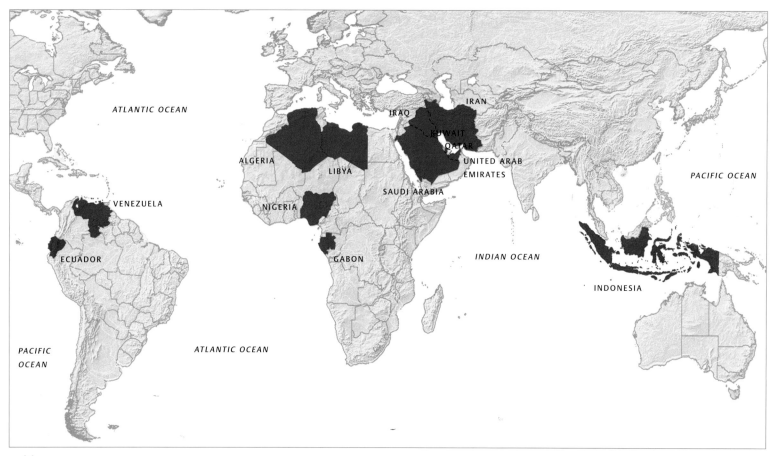

[8]

From the early 1970s the looming 'energy crisis' became a hotly debated topic, in particular in the US. The Shell scenario impressed James Atkins, the US State Department's chief oil expert, who used it in his own 1971 report on the international oil industry through the 1980s. He argued that measures to limit the growth of oil consumption, to raise production and to increase oil imports would be as unpopular as they were costly. The US Department of State should take a leading role in assuring that the American consumers could count on a steady supply of oil at prices the consumers could afford to pay.[8] Since 1958 this country had import restrictions in place, because it wanted to rely entirely on its indigenous oil industry.[9] The growth of their oil production, however, had not kept pace with the growth in energy consumption and from the early 1970s the federal government eased the restrictions on the importation of oil, until the quotas were finally abolished in March 1973. The rising US crude oil imports put pressure on the

international crude oil market and formed a major factor in the evolving oil shock. The Americans were deeply concerned about sustaining the flow of imports.

Their politicians worked hard to create a 'special relationship' with Saudi Arabia and other oil-producing countries in the Middle East. These political manoeuvres worried the Japanese and European governments whose countries were even more reliant on Middle Eastern oil.[10] How to deal with the expected energy crisis? In a Harvard speech, given in the spring of 1973, Frank McFadzean, who succeeded Barran as chairman of Shell Transport, suggested governmental measures along the lines of the pre-war rubber regulation agreements whereby the producing and consuming governments, with the advice of the producing and consuming companies, would set the framework within which the industry would work. He wrote to his board member Michael Pocock: 'Some of the bright boys of planning should be encouraged to shrink their

After OPEC had been established by
Iran, Iraq, Kuwait, Saudi Arabia and
Venezuela in 1960, over the years new
countries joined and two of those left
the organization again after a number
of years: Qatar (1961), Indonesia (1962),
Libya (1962), United Arab Emirates
(1967), Algeria (1969), Nigeria (1971),
Ecuador (1973 till 1992), and Gabon
(1975 till 1994).

horizons from the year 2000 to the period between now and
1980'.[11] Governments, however, tended to act for their own
national interests rather than for the common good, so nothing
came of these ideas. There were also dissidents, who claimed that
oil was in abundance, that the tight supply position was caused by a
'scramble for oil', and that the US predictions of an energy crisis
were a self-fulfilling prophecy.[12] Fulfilled they certainly were.

OPEC countries not only made progress on the front of
imposing higher government taxes and royalties.[13] In March 1972,
the Arabian Gulf countries reached an agreement with the oil
companies over the principle of 'participation' (shared ownership)
by the producer governments in their operations. For Shell this
meant a 25 per cent government participation in their interests in
Qatar and Abu Dhabi.[14] A few months later Ahmed Zaki Yamani,
the Saudi Arabian minister of oil, gave a speech in which he further
elaborated on the theme of participation: What do I mean by the
correct implementation of participation? It is not that the producing
States should simply own 51% of the capital of the companies operating
on their lands. (...) What I mean is that the national oil companies in
producing countries should enter the marketing stages and invest their
surplus revenues in marketing their participation shares of oil.[15]
No wonder the international oil companies were beginning to feel
nervous about their position. In the same speech, Yamani offered a

hand in friendship to the US government and called for a
commercial oil agreement between the two countries, which
would give Saudi Arabian oil a special place in the US. This remark
led to worried speculations at the British Ministry of Trade and
Industry that perhaps the US had closed a special deal with Saudi
Arabia to the exclusion of other nations.[16]

In the meantime public awareness of the importance of
energy and the ultimate limits of oil resources was raised from an
entirely different quarter. The Club of Rome's Project on 'The
Predicament of Mankind' published a widely read report 'The Limits
to Growth', in which it made long-term calculations about the
sustainability of economic growth in the light of population
growth, energy growth and the preservation of the environment.[17]
The report reached a large audience and succeeded in raising
public awareness about the limits of natural resources such as oil
and gas, as well as the possible effects of exhaust fumes on global
warming. Therefore, even without a political fight over access to oil,
the public was getting alarmed about its future scarcity.

In 1973 OPEC's sharp cuts in production created huge distribution problems in the western world, with long queues at service stations becoming a dramatic but common sight. From left to right, customers wait to fill up at a Chevron station in the US and at a Shell station in Assen, the Netherlands, while a station in San Diego, California, offered gasoline by appointment only.

'Equal misery' versus 'my country first'   The fat was in the fire in October 1973, when two events coincided. On 6 October, Egypt and Syria launched a surprise attack on Israel to regain the territory they lost in 1967. Two days after the start of the Yom Kippur war, OPEC held its meeting in Vienna to discuss a higher tax (government take) on oil. Without entering into real negotiations with the oil companies, the OPEC countries increased the government take from $1.77 to $3.04 per barrel, and this was only the beginning.[18] A few days later the OAPEC (Organization of Arab Petroleum Exporting Countries) decided to use the 'oil weapon'. It agreed to cut down the production of oil to support Arab war aims. The first immediate cut of 5 per cent per month would be followed by more and larger cuts. Furthermore OAPEC created discord among the consuming countries by dividing them into four categories of 'friendliness' to the Arab cause, each to be treated differently. On the one end were the 'most preferred' countries, Britain and France, with no set limits, on the other the US and the Netherlands, which were placed 'under embargo'. In between were the 'preferred countries' with 100 per cent of September shipments, and the 'neutral' countries, including Japan, with reduced shipments.[19]

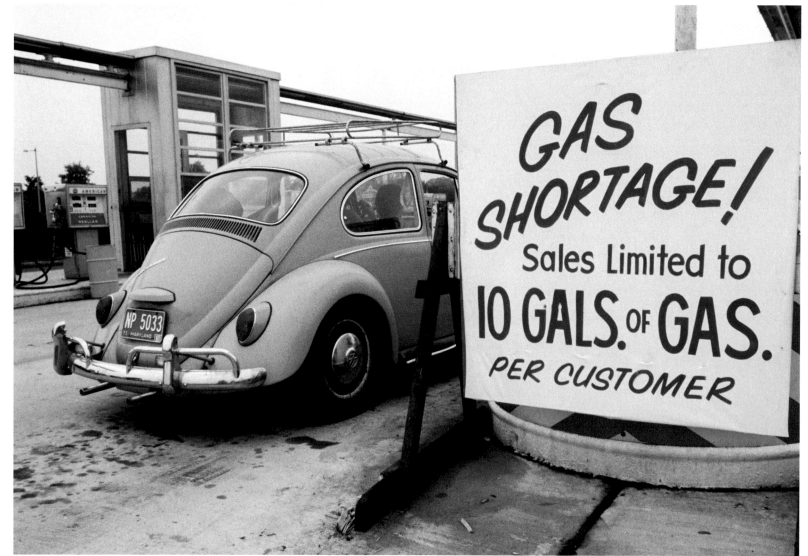

[12]

One service station in Connecticut, US, limited the sale per customer, while another, a Shell station in Boston, Mass., US, had the disappointing message that it was closed.

[13]

The combination of price rises and production cuts sent shock waves through the western world. Suddenly economic growth, taken for granted even by those who criticized it, seemed under threat. The unlimited use of the private car, the most potent symbol of the consumer society, could be nearing an end. For developing countries without oil in their lands, the prospects looked even gloomier. Oil was urgently needed for industrial purposes, for heating, for electricity, but most of all to keep cars on the road. The prospect of scarcity created a panic at the pumps. In the US 'gas lines', the long queues for the service stations of drivers desperate for gasoline, formed the lasting image of the oil crisis. In the Netherlands, the Sundays with bicycles instead of cars on the motorways stuck in the collective memory.

Measures to keep the oil flowing took place at two different levels. At the diplomatic level, governments of the oil-consuming countries negotiated with oil-producing countries. The governments of most oil-consuming countries did their utmost to be on the right side of the Arab countries, to be considered a 'friendly' nation and to receive preferential treatment. If there had to be cuts in oil production, it should not affect the supply in their own countries. For the US the situation was more complicated because it had to choose a middle way between its support for Israel and appeasing the Arab countries. The UK government felt concern about a possible reaction of the US to the oil embargo. In a report to the Cabinet the Joint Intelligence Committee suggested that the US might perhaps consider 'using force to seize oilfields in Saudi Arabia and the Gulf, despite their reluctance after Vietnam to engage in such operations.'[20] Frank McFadzean, chairman of Shell Transport, however, did not think the option of force was very likely, 'given the American leadership crisis'.[21]

[14]

The Dutch government introduced car-free Sundays, starting on 4 November 1973, with the last on 6 January 1974. In the meantime the motor way could be used for bike rides and picnics, though one had to be careful because some traffic was still allowed.

[15]

Wilt u
- eerst bonnen inleveren aan de kassa

en

- daarna tanken

Dank u

AUTO'S/BENZINE, licht gewicht

E 24	BENZINE	E 22	BENZINE
BENZINE	E 23	BENZINE	E 21
BENZINE	E 18	BENZINE	E 16
E 19	BENZINE	E 17	BENZINE
E 14	BENZINE	E 12	BENZINE
BENZINE	E 13	BENZINE	E 11
BENZINE	E 08	BENZINE	E 06
E 09	BENZINE	E 07	BENZINE
E 04	BENZINE	E 02	
BENZINE	E 03	BENZINE	

[17]

At the end of 1973, when it was still unclear how hard the OPEC measures would hit the Netherlands, the government introduced precautionary gasoline rationing for a period of three weeks, starting on 12 January 1974. However, soon it became clear that sufficient crude oil was still available and the rationing ceased on 4 February. At this Mobil service station in the Netherlands the customers were advised to hand in their coupons at the cashier before filling up their cars, thanks.

At the business level, the private oil companies followed their own commercial logic in dealing with the oil crisis. This logic consisted of treating all customers equally. If there had to be cuts in supply, then they should be applied evenly across the board. Shell was one of those who followed the strategy of 'equal misery'. Shell managing directors approved a cut of 12.5 per cent on 1 November 1973 to be applied to all customers, which was increased to 17.5 per cent on 16 November. Thanks to their wide spread in oil resources, they had the ability to draw on non-Arab sources of crude oil, which enabled them to swap oil between embargoed and non-embargoed countries. For instance, the normal stream of Arab crude oil to the Netherlands was replaced by oil from Iran and Nigeria, while part of the Iranian oil for Japan was replaced by oil from Qatar.[22] These swaps demanded a great deal of flexibility from the operating companies, because crude oils differ in quality and the range of products that can be processed from them. The logistics of the allocation processes were complex but the international oil companies used their great experience to handle them, determined to remain involved in the distribution process. What they feared most was being excluded through government-to-government deals.

[18]

In order to safeguard their access to oil, every national government tried to befriend the Arab nations. Seen at left with the Saudi Minister of Petroleum Sheikh Ahmed Zaki Yamani, Britain's Prime Minister Edward Heath was no exception, but to his anger the oil companies took a broader perspective and divided the crude oil equally among their customers. At right in Vienna, on 18 March 1974 six OPEC nations announced the end of their boycott of the US. Algeria postponed this action until June 1974, while Libya and Syria continued their boycott. At the table, left to right, are the Algerian Minister of Petroleum, Belaid Abdesselam; the spokesman for the six nations; and Sheikh Yamani. Seated close by on the right is the journalist Eef Brouwers, editor of the Dutch NOS News. The embargo against the Netherlands continued until July 1974.

The different perceptions of politicians and oil men led to clashes about oil allocation, as for instance in Britain. Because the Arabs considered Britain a 'friendly nation', the British Prime Minister, Edward Heath, insisted on Britain receiving its full share in oil supplies. The oil was all the more needed as a major coal miners' strike was in the making. Heath tried to put pressure on the chairmen of BP and Shell Transport, Eric Drake and Frank McFadzean, when he entertained them to dinner at Chequers on Sunday 21 October 1973. The two chairmen suggested that the UK government should seek agreement through the OECD on a rationing system for imports of Middle East oil. Heath argued that the man in the street would not understand why rationing of oil should be introduced in Britain when the two oil companies based in this country handled volumes of oil that were many times greater than the total British demand. The two oilmen underlined the fact that the operations of the international oil companies, which enabled them to draw on different sources of supply at different times, ensured a flexible response to the growing needs of consuming countries. If the British government gave a directive to them that they must meet British requirements, the producer Governments would probably insist on determining themselves the ultimate destination of their oil, and this flexibility would be lost.[23] McFadzean seems to have explained that he was unable to comply because companies were bound by a web of legal and moral

obligations, and because anyway the Royal Dutch/Shell Group was 60 per cent Dutch-owned. Though BP was 51 per cent owned by the British state, Drake also resisted the request by pointing out that preferential treatment of one country would be damaging for the good relationships within his worldwide company.[24] However, further governmental pressure made Drake reconsider his position. In December 1973 BP agreed secretly to maintain its normal UK supplies.[25] In a reaction to a TV interview of Royal Dutch/Shell's chairman Gerrit Wagner, *The Economist* wrote under the heading 'The Appalling Candour of Gerard Wagner': 'The oil industry, in the person of Mr. Gerard Wagner, chairman of the board of Royal Dutch/Shell, finally admitted, on Dutch television on Tuesday night, what many people knew was happening but would not say aloud: that Shell and the other international companies are sharing their oil out among their customers, so that Britain and France are not getting the full benefit of their pro-Arab policy.'[26] Feelings ran so high that even a liberal journal as *The Economist* sided with the nationalistic 'my country first' view instead of the equal allocation policy of the companies. The French government, too, put pressure on its oil companies, including Shell France, to deliver the normal amounts of oil. Germany, on the other hand, maintained its 'laissez faire' policy with regard to energy.

The situation in the Netherlands was somewhat special, because of the Arab embargo against the country and because

[19]

Rotterdam acted as important transit harbour for Arab oil. Though the Arab countries defended their embargo of the Netherlands as retaliation for the Dutch support for Israel, the Dutch Minister of Foreign Affairs, Max van der Stoel, interpreted the embargo as a more general attack against Western Europe.[27] The Dutch coalition government under the socialist Prime Minister Joop den Uyl discovered that the solidarity of the governments in the European Community in this moment of crisis was very limited. Instead the country had to rely on the 'invisible' hand of the international oil companies, in particular Shell and BP, which rescheduled the crude oil to keep the Netherlands supplied.[28] For transit oil, the embargo was quickly lifted, but otherwise the Netherlands remained under embargo until 10 July 1974. The US embargo had been lifted in June 1974.

It is still under debate whether there was any real scarcity of oil during the last quarter of 1973. The production cutbacks that took place from October through December 1973 amounted to a total lost output of about 340 million barrels. This was less than the inventory built up earlier in that year, so there seems to have been no acute shortfall.[29] However, in the heat of the moment, nobody knew how large the production cuts were going to be or how long they would last. Decisions were taken on the basis of forecasts, and they pointed in the direction of serious future supply problems. In the spring of 1974, however, it became clear that oil was in ample supply. The warm winter, the reduction in consumer demand in response to the high oil price and the failure of the Arab countries to implement in January the increases in their announced production cuts, all worked together to balance demand and supply. By the summer of 1974 stocks were abnormally high for the season of the year. Shell operating companies could have all the oil they wished, provided they could afford it.[30] In 1975 one Shell memo hopefully commented: 'It is common experience that to achieve success is far easier than to maintain it, once achieved. OPEC is finding this out'.[31] Despite the oversupply of oil, the price remained high because of the combination of governments' taxation, royalties and participation.

Though in Europe the blame for the high oil prices was generally placed on OPEC, the international oil companies nonetheless received severe criticism from the public as well as government bodies about their distribution policies. On 21 December 1973 the European Commission launched an investigation to find out whether the international oil companies had supplied the independent distributors in an equitable manner. Their report, published two years later, concluded that their investigations had not revealed restrictive or unfair practices with regard to supplies and prices or towards independent dealers and users. Looking at the whole crisis in a broader context, the report commented that: 'during the crisis the dissimilar actions by member states were aimed at the urgent introduction of measures and gave the impression of an "every man for himself" approach, which was scarcely in the Community spirit. During the same period, because of their international standing and experience, the oil companies made an important contribution to alleviating for the countries of the Community, the serious repercussions on their supplies of the decisions taken by the oil-producing countries.'

The report ended with the final recommendation that the Community should develop a common oil policy.[32]

More so than in Europe, the general public in the United States blamed the oil companies for the high oil prices, despite the fact that the US imports had put pressure on the world's oil supply to start with and that OAPEC embargoed the United States. Because of its large indigenous oil industry it was less obvious that prices in the US would be dictated by events on the world markets. The oil companies' executives had to appear at a hearing before the Senate Permanent Subcommittee on Investigations, chaired by Senator Henry Jackson, who declared that American people wanted to know if this so-called energy crisis was only a pretext to eliminate price competition. He accused the oil companies of making 'obscene profits'.[33] The Federal Trade Commission (FTC) launched a complaint against Shell Oil and seven other major oil companies alleging that they had combined or agreed to monopolize refining. The FTC argued that these integrated oil companies should divest their refining and part of their pipeline operations. The oil companies denied that they had a monopoly position in any part of the supply chain. An amendment in the Senate forcing the oil companies to shed all but one of their major functions – either production, refining, transportation, or marketing – came to a vote in 1975. It failed with 54 to 45 votes, but the US oil industry felt shocked that it had come so close to chaos.[34] The debate about what the oil companies called 'dismemberment' continued with the proposed Petroleum Industry Competition Act of 1976, but this bill did not pass.[35] The oil majors remained integrated companies, but the connection between the different parts changed after the first oil crisis.

'Lifting unknown quantities for an unknown price' Less visible to the general public than the price rises and high profits of the oil majors were the equally dramatic developments in the ownership of oil through the rapidly increasing levels of 'participation' in the OPEC countries, leading to a new relationship between oil-producing countries and the oil companies. OPEC demands quickly rose from the 25 per cent agreed for the Gulf countries in 1972 to 50 per cent host government participation and further, to a share of 90 per cent or even total nationalization. The oil majors, including Shell, lost large parts of their oil reserves, on which they had spent vast amounts of money in exploration and which were the basis for future earnings. Shell's Exploration and Production technical engineers discovered to their dismay that in 1973 non-technical factors, principally host government participation, had been more influential on the Group's oil and gas reserves than achievements in the technical E&P field. They estimated that the Group had lost roughly 50 per cent of its oil reserves and 30 per cent of its gas reserves in just one year, and the end was not in sight.[36] Shell operating companies, used to a long-term planning horizon, were suddenly faced with utter uncertainty while negotiations were going on and demands from governments were stepped up. In the spring of 1974 Dirk de Bruyne, Group managing director, commented that Shell companies had been lifting an unknown quantity of oil (due to the effects of an undecided participation level) at an unknown price, and consequently he had no clear idea of the quarter's results.[37] Even if agreements were concluded there was no guarantee they would last the full period, which made the oil companies wary of concluding them in the first place. There was, however, some light at the end of the tunnel: when the producer governments had huge investments of their own to protect, they might pay more regard to contracts. In 1974 Shell had become resigned to the fact that most of the new exploration ventures had to be undertaken on the basis of production sharing, or in partnership with government, or with government participation.[38]

Most of the mid-1970s were taken up by lengthy negotiations between the oil companies and the governments of oil-producing countries about participations and nationalization. Iran had already nationalized the oil concessions in its country in 1951. While this mainly affected BP, Shell later became involved as a leader (14 per cent) of the Iranian Consortium, established to manage the Iranian state oil company, the National Iranian Oil Company (NIOC), and in March 1973 a new arrangement was concluded in which NIOC became the operator, leaving the Consortium in the role of contractor and consultant. At the same time the Consortium partners succeeded in reaching long-term purchase agreements.

Iraq had nationalized most of the concessions held by the Iraq Petroleum Company (IPC) in the early 1960s. The remaining concessions of the IPC in North Iraq were taken over in 1972. The government of Iraq did not participate in the oil embargo against the Netherlands in 1973, but it nationalized the 60 per cent Royal Dutch component of the Group's 23.75 per cent holding in the Basrah Petroleum Company (BPC) in 1973, and in 1975 BPC was completely nationalized. Libya announced its intention to nationalize the oil industry in 1973, and Shell lost its remaining assets in the Oasis partnership in 1974.[39] In Abu Dhabi, Qatar and Oman, government participation levels rose from 25 per cent in 1973 to 60 per cent in 1974. Complete nationalization followed in Qatar in 1977, and in Abu Dhabi in 1979. The government of Oman remained content with its 60 per cent, leaving considerable incentive to its partners to explore and develop the country's oil resources. Shell's equity interest in the operating company Petroleum Development Oman remained 34 per cent.

The government of Brunei was initially not even sure whether it wanted participation when it was offered 25 per cent by Shell in early 1973. After the fourfold price rise in the autumn of that year the economics of participation improved considerably and the Brunei government informed Shell that it indeed wished to acquire a 25 per cent equity stake in Brunei Shell Petroleum. In November 1974 Shell reconsidered its original offer of 25 percent: 'in view of subsequent developments elsewhere in terms of government participation we now feel that a level of 25 per cent participation is outdated and could be politically vulnerable.' It is interesting to see how quickly Shell adjusted to the new political realities. In 1975 Shell reached a participation agreement with the government of Brunei taking a share of 50 per cent in Brunei Shell Petroleum.[40]

The concessions in Venezuela were under threat as well. In 1971 a law was passed saying that the oil concessions and assets would revert to the state after concession periods began to expire, from 1983 onwards. The rising trend in participations made this time-frame seem too slow, so in 1973 the Venezuelan government started discussions on 'an early reversion of concessions to the state'. Shell companies had worked in Venezuela since 1914. This country was considered an important training ground for managers. Many managing directors of Royal Dutch/Shell had worked in Venezuela during some period of their career. Local staff from Venezuela had been promoted in the hierarchy of Compañia Shell de Venezuela (CSV) and been posted abroad within Shell. Considering its response to the 'reversion of concession', CSV decided that a strategy of 'business as usual' was politically unrealistic. It hoped that a production-sharing arrangement and provision for buy-back oil might be possible.[41] The mood in Venezuela, however, moved towards nationalization of the oil industry, which happened in 1975. Starting from 1 January 1976 operations in CSV's concessions were taken over by a government company, Maraven, under the control of Petroven, a newly formed state oil corporation. Virtually all CSV staff were transferred to Maraven, and A. Quiros, the Venezuelan Shell man, who had been the chief Shell negotiator with the Venezuelan government, became President of Maraven. Similar constructions were put in place for the other foreign-held oil concessions. For the time being, the continued involvement of the oil majors was assured through long-term purchase contracts of crude oil and through service contracts in production and manufacturing.[42]

Progressive demands from the state also characterized Shell's relationship with Nigeria. In 1973 Shell and BP reached an agreement with the Nigerian government in respect of their Shell-BP operations in the country, which gave the government an undivided 35 per cent interest and Shell and BP in return favourable buy-back provisions, but only a year later government participation was stepped up to 55 per cent, reaching 60 per cent by July 1979.[43] This was not the end of the story. One day in the beginning of 1979 the Very Large Crude Carrier (VLCC) Kulu, a Panamanian-registered vessel, moored at Bonny, Nigeria, having been sent by BP to collect a cargo for Rotterdam as part of their normal tanker programme. The Nigerian authorities found a number of South African crew members on board and started an investigation, which revealed that the ship was owned by the South African Marine Corporation of Capetown. Shell was concerned that the Nigerian authorities would react strongly against this breach of their national policy against apartheid in South Africa. The issue seemed to have been settled, but later that year the Nigerian government decided to nationalize BP's 20 per cent share in the venture.[44]

Shell's interests in Kuwaiti oil were indirect through their purchase agreement with Gulf, dating from 1947. This agreement had provided Shell companies with guaranteed quantities of Middle East crude, which in 1974 represented about 10 per cent of the total Shell Group crude stream. However, early that year the Kuwaiti government decided to take a 60 per cent participation in the concession of Gulf and BP via their Kuwait Oil Company, followed in

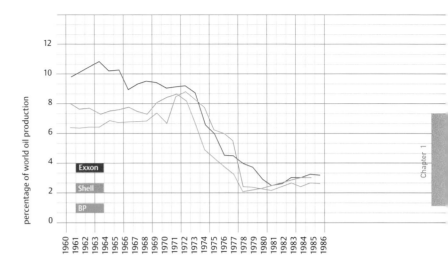

Figure 1.1
Crude oil production Shell, Exxon, and BP, 1960-1986.

1975 by a 100 per cent takeover. Under these new circumstances Shell decided to end its agreement with Gulf, confident as it was of meeting its future requirements of crude through direct deals with the oil-producing countries.[45] Shell had no concessions in Saudi Arabia, but nonetheless followed the negotiations between the Saudi Arabian government and Aramco with great interest, because of the importance of this country in balancing the world's oil supply and demand. While in June 1974 Saudi Arabia was still content with 60 per cent participation, at the end of that year 100 per cent was demanded. In 1976 it was agreed in principle that ownership of all the Aramco assets and rights would be taken over by the government, while Aramco remained the operator with extensive rights to market the produced oil. Though it took till 1990 until the agreements were signed, the deal was actually finalized in 1980 when Saudi Arabia paid compensation for the nationalization.[46] In 1988 the Saudi Arabian Oil Company, Saudi Aramco, was established.

Figure 1.1 shows the dramatic fall in Shell's share in the world's production of oil after 1973.[47] Since 1960 their share had varied between 9 and 7 per cent, but after 1973 it fell to 2 per cent. In the 1980s and 1990s it gradually rose to 3 per cent again. For their main competitors, Exxon and BP, the picture was broadly similar. For some of the years figures about oil production are not available. While negotiations with governments dragged on, oil companies were not always entirely sure how much of the oil they produced was rightfully theirs (the so-called equity oil). The overall trend is clear: the oil majors owned less and less of the oil. If we look at the more restricted international oil world outside North America and the Communist area, then we see a similar shift. In 1970 the seven major companies possessed 69 per cent of the crude oil against only 24 per cent in 1979. The share of other international oil

companies fell from 23 per cent in 1970 to 7 per cent, while the share of the governments of producing countries rose from nothing to 69 per cent.[48] In almost all non-western countries the production-sharing contracts became very popular. Each country developed its own contracts according to its own particular circumstances, but some characteristics were common. The contractor (for instance the oil company) provided the state or state company with technical and financial services and organized the exploration and production. In return the contractor received a certain part of the oil or gas production that resulted from its work. If no oil or gas was found, the contractor would not receive any compensation for its investments made or services rendered.[49]

The events of the 1970s formed a watershed in the history of the oil industry. How little those outside the oil industry realized the importance of the internal changes becomes clear from the following comments of Lord Armstrong, who joined the board of Shell Transport in 1974 after his retirement as head of the British Civil Service: 'I was still used to the old style concession – where it was your oil and you got it out of the ground in your own time and took it away to be refined as you saw fit; you paid royalties and income tax and that was it. Now, of course, the arrangements are much more elaborate with a much higher take by the host governments, and the Shell role changed to one of a management contract in many instances, with long term purchase agreements. Before I joined the board I had not realized the extent to which things had changed.'[50] Gerrit Wagner told students at Rotterdam's

Erasmus University in 1974 that the recent events in the oil industry showed that the idea that the multinational corporation would be a challenge to national sovereignty was just a myth: 'I do not think that we need any other reminder that it is a complete fallacy to suppose that multinational enterprises are organizations that can operate independently of the political, economic and financial conditions established by governments.'[51]

It was very important for Wagner that the outside world should have a realistic and, hopefully, even a positive view of multinational companies. Born in 1916, he had just completed his law studies at Leiden University when the Second World War broke out, which may have influenced his thinking about the supremacy of political powers over business organizations. After working at a bank and the civil service in Rotterdam, he joined Shell in 1946. He developed into a typical all-round Shell manager moving between The Hague and London central offices, and from country to country, including Curaçao, Indonesia and Venezuela, where he met many future Shell top executives. He became Group managing director in 1964, president of Royal Dutch in 1971, and the chairman of CMD in 1972, which office he filled until 1977. After stepping down he immediately became chairman of the supervisory board of Royal Dutch, where he served until 1987. With an interest in history, he liked to look at the long term and the big picture. He engaged in debates with churches and society at large about the role of multinational companies. While a firm believer in free capitalism, he was prepared to listen to its critics, and go out and defend his point of view. After his retirement, he was invited by the Dutch government to chair a committee devising ways in which the government could help invigorate flagging Dutch industry. During his long career he had learned to balance the interests of governments and businesses.[52]

Negotiating skills had been important in dealing with the OPEC governments.

The power of OPEC to dictate the oil market and amass large fortunes seemed unstoppable in the 1970s. Contemporaries started to speculate about the effects this would have upon these countries and the world economy more generally. Even before the oil crisis, in May 1973, the boards of Shell had discussed the prospect of huge, unprecedented amounts of capital flowing to certain producing countries far in excess of their ability for absorption into their own economy. To show the size of the problem it had been calculated 'that the Saudis could purchase a Royal Dutch/Shell Group every year from 1980s onwards from their surplus'.[53] The OPEC members were expected to become rich beyond their dreams, to be able to buy themselves into western enterprises as well as being able to finance new industrial projects to create employment, to improve their infrastructure, and fund national welfare projects. It later turned out that by and large those rosy prospects for the OPEC members did not materialize. Within less than a decade, most OPEC members struggled with unbalanced growth, economic chaos, social unrest, and political turmoil. In some cases, the oil majors were called back in for new investment in exploration and production. However, several of the other prophecies – such as instability of the monetary system, including inflation, and balance of trade problems for the developing countries without oil – came all too true.[54] In their power struggle with OPEC, the oil majors turned out to be tougher, or more flexible, than might have been expected in the mid-1970s.

In their need to adjust to the new circumstances, oil companies were considerably helped by the steep rise in oil prices. This gave them a handsome stock profit to start with and made exploration prospects look very bright. In the face of the OPEC challenge, Shell companies followed three different survival strategies for remaining involved in the oil business. (They also looked for business activities outside oil, but those will be discussed in Chapter 2.) First, they fought for access to the oil they used to own. While the government participations led to an enormous reduction in the Group's oil and gas reserves, much of these 'lost' reserves remained available to Group companies as a result of purchase agreements and the provision of technical assistance. This was particularly true for the first round of negotiations about the participations, when the oil-producing countries still had to fight for the principle of participation and perhaps therefore were willing to make concessions with regard to the marketing of the oil. While the Middle Eastern governments had power over their oil reserves, they still needed the oil majors' distribution networks. In the first wave of participation demands, Shell offered downstream facilities in exchange for access to oil. In 1973 Shell Oil in the US negotiated with National Iranian Oil Company (NIOC) to obtain a long-term supply of crude oil and petroleum products in exchange for manufacturing and marketing assets in the US. Without additional crude oil, these facilities were likely to remain idle in any case. The Group also drew up plans to offer NIOC a share in Deutsche Shell. However, Deutsche Shell did not consider this a particularly good idea, and instead downstream activities in Belgium and Portugal were offered. Nothing came of these negotiations, probably because Shell managers decided that their downstream business was one of their strong points in their relationship with the new owners of the oil. They counted on their lead in marketing experience and refining.[55]

Second, in order to remain an interesting partner for the newly established oil companies of the exporting nations, Shell continued to develop its technological expertise in finding and bringing into production new oil and gas sources. In that sense they responded to the ambivalent attitude of host governments to the oil majors. As the *Petroleum Economist* formulated it: 'the governments are generally anxious to push them out, yet fearful of letting them go.'[56] When Iran turned NIOC into an operator as well as an owner of oil, the former consortium partners set up separate

service companies. The same happened in Venezuela and elsewhere. Without having the benefits of ownership over the oil, the oil majors, including Shell, were anxious to secure the best possible fee in return for their complex services on offer. New rules and customs for rewarding the services of operators had to be thought out and implemented. For the former integrated oil companies this posed new demands on their financial systems, because not only the direct costs, but also the costs of central offices and research had to be included and recovered. From the late 1970s the private oil companies learned that the form of the agreements was relatively immaterial. What counted was the money they could make and the stability of the arrangements.[57] The big question was how long the Middle East would need the expertise and financial strength of the oil majors. In its publications, Shell underlined the importance of its technological skills in combating the energy crisis through developing new sources of energy. Their technical skills could not only secure them a continuing position in the Middle East oil scene, but would also help in moving production outside politically sensitive areas.

This brings us to the third 'survival strategy'. Shell stepped up exploration efforts in non-OPEC countries. In many cases this involved working offshore. It is not that these areas had been ignored before, far from it. But the loss of equity oil in the Middle East gave the exploration and production in other areas a new urgency, while the higher oil prices made offshore projects economically more attractive. In 1976 Shell's exploration activities worldwide covered nearly half a million square miles, of which 60 per cent was offshore. Activities took place off the coasts of Ireland, Spain, Turkey, Malaysia, and Brazil, to name a few areas. Shell Oil Company was also active in the Gulf of Mexico and started with exploration in the Atlantic.[58] It did not participate in the development of the North Slope of Alaska, but it had high hopes of finding oil in the Alaska's Beaufort Sea. One of the most successful exploration and production areas of the 1970s, however, was the North Sea.

[20]   The Brent Charlie platform

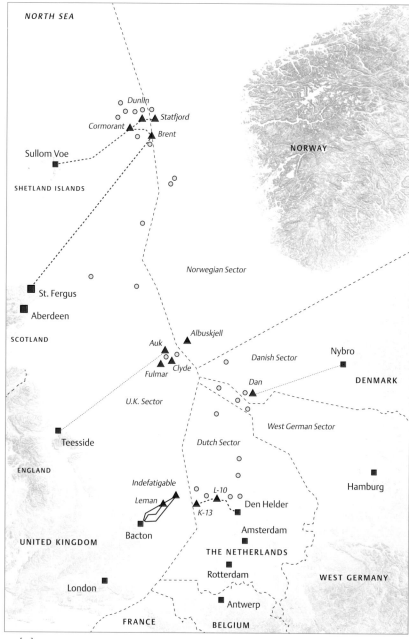

NORTH SEA

Dunlin
Cormorant · Statfjord
Brent

Sullom Voe

SHETLAND ISLANDS

NORWAY

Norwegian Sector

St. Fergus
Aberdeen

SCOTLAND

Auk · Albuskjell
Fulmar · Clyde

U.K. Sector

Nybro

Danish Sector

Dan

DENMARK

West German Sector

Teesside

Dutch Sector

ENGLAND

Indefatigable
Leman · L-10
K-13 · Den Helder

Hamburg

Bacton

Amsterdam

UNITED KINGDOM

THE NETHERLANDS

London · Rotterdam

WEST GERMANY

Antwerp

FRANCE · BELGIUM

[21]

After 1973, high oil prices enabled oil
companies to spend vast sums on
exploration and production in the
North Sea. By 1975, as seen here, the
southern part of the North Sea had
been opened up for gas production,
while a huge oil and gas infrastructure
for the more challenging northern
North Sea was under construction.

...... Tanker route
---- Gas pipeline under construction
---- Oil pipeline under construction
— Gas pipeline
▲ Gas field
▲ Oil field
○ Explorations 1975

Oil production in the North Sea

The rush to the North Sea
started after the 1973 oil shock, when oil prices soared, making the
expensive North Sea activities more profitable, and oil companies
began to shift their exploration expenditures towards politically
safer areas. The compensation money paid by producer
governments also helped to provide further investment in new
areas. Returns in these new areas tended to be lower, but on the
other hand, the new areas were politically more stable. Initially,
Shell employees did not see the North Sea as a particularly exciting
area. The Middle East was the place to be. William Bell, managing
director of Shell UK Exploration and Production (Shell Expro) from
1973 till 1979, doubted whether he was in for a promotion, when the
Coordinator E&P came over to see him in London and tried to
persuade him to leave his very exciting job in the Middle East to
take over a small gas venture in the North Sea. Bell accepted the
job, because he got some hints about the oil finds in the Brent field
in the North Sea, and because 'you don't really have a choice in
Shell anyway and if they tell you: "you are going to go", you go'.[59]

The offshore search for oil and gas in the North Sea began in
the early 1960s, after a vast gas field was discovered in Groningen in
the Netherlands in 1959. While the oil companies were exploring
the North Sea, the governments along the North Sea had their
negotiations on how to divide its mineral rights. Britain succeeded
in getting the largest share of the Continental Shelf. In 1964 Shell
UK established Shell Expro to act as the operator of the 50:50 joint
venture of Shell and Esso, which was established to search for oil
and gas in the UK sector of the North Sea. Initially the oil companies
working in the North Sea relied on their experiences with offshore
elsewhere. For instance, oil rigs and barges from the Gulf of Mexico
came to the North Sea, but they turned out to be too light.
Circumstances in the North Sea were very different. The Gulf of

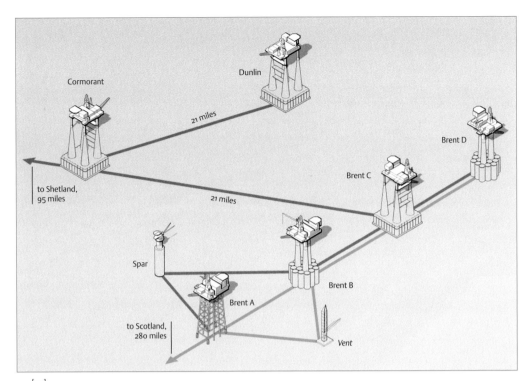

As operator for the Shell/Esso joint venture, Shell Expro developed the Brent field, north-east of the Shetland Isles, with a system of four platforms (Brent A, Brent B, Brent C and Brent D), one floating storage tank (the Brent Spar) and a gas pipeline to Scotland. To carry the oil to Shetland, a separate pipeline system was developed from Brent and the Dunlin field via Cormorant.

[22]

Mexico had its hurricanes but the North Sea suffered from bad weather frequently. Surface currents and trenches required special handling. This enabled the European offshore industry to develop its own designs and service this local market with rigs and platforms.[60]

The first natural gas fields were developed in the relatively shallow southern North Sea, where water depths are around 100 feet. In the mid-1960s the search for oil in the northern North Sea was only lukewarm as production would be difficult and expensive, while abundant cheap oil was being produced in the Middle East. The British government had to nudge BP into applying for concessions in the northern North Sea, and when they were awarded some blocks in the northern basin, they waited for four-and-a-half years before they started drilling. Phillips Petroleum nearly gave up drilling in the Norwegian waters, until it discovered the gigantic Ekofisk oil field in 1969. This find increased the interest of the other oil companies, and BP took up drilling in a block 110 miles offshore of Aberdeen, where a year later it discovered the Forties Field, the first giant oil field in the British sector of the North Sea.[61]

In 1971 Shell Expro announced the discovery of the Auk oilfield, 130 miles south-east of Aberdeen. Shell had also applied for a block further north, in even deeper water in the Shetland area. The Brent field, for instance, was 460 feet deep. John Jennings, who was then chief geologist of the company, remembered that he told R. H. van Nierop, the co-ordinator of Exploration and Production: 'We can only drill there in the summer time. What on earth are you going to do if you find anything? He replied: "you find it, we'll produce it".'[62] In this block, the later Brent field, oil was found in August 1971. However, the discovery well was not tested and the discovery kept a secret because Shell wanted to bid for another block in the northern North Sea with a similar structure, later named the (northern) Cormorant Field. The Group did not want to attract the attention of its competitors. As it turned out Shell offered the astronomical sum of £21 million, while the next highest bid was £11 million by Mobil and none of the others were anything near. The industry was amazed about this large sum of money spent by Shell, and when the second well in this block was dry, and the oil reserves seemed to be very much less than expected, there was some consternation in the Shell camp as well. The rise in oil prices in the autumn of 1973, however, made the Cormorant field suddenly economical again. Therefore work proceeded. As more about the field became known, the reserves rose once

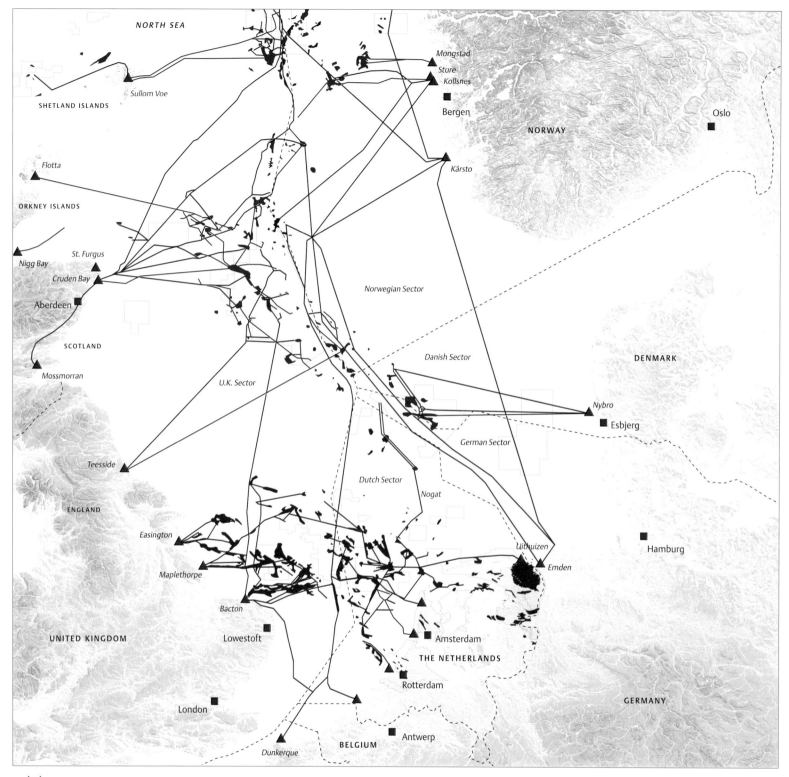

NORTH SEA

SHETLAND ISLANDS

Sullom Voe

Flotta

ORKNEY ISLANDS

Nigg Bay

St. Furgus

Cruden Bay

Aberdeen

SCOTLAND

Mossmorran

U.K. Sector

ENGLAND

Teesside

Easington

Maplethorpe

Bacton

UNITED KINGDOM

Lowestoft

London

Dunkerque

BELGIUM

Antwerp

Rotterdam

THE NETHERLANDS

Amsterdam

Mongstad

Sture
Kollsnes

Bergen

NORWAY

Oslo

Kärsto

Norwegian Sector

Danish Sector

DENMARK

Nybro

Esbjerg

German Sector

Dutch Sector

Nogat

Uithuizen

Emden

Hamburg

GERMANY

[23]

By 2002, the North Sea had become a vast industrial area, criss-crossed with gas and oil pipelines and with platforms, sub-sea manifolds and onshore terminals.

The first Shell/Esso North Sea platforms, such as a Brent A (seen here), were complex steel structures.

 Oil pipeline
— Gas pipeline
 Gas field
☐ Shell interest
🐦 Oil field
▲ Terminal

[24]

more and ended up close to the original estimates.[63] This is a fair demonstration of how perspectives in the industry can change over time.

After the discovery of the Brent and the Cormorant field followed the Dunlin field, also located east of Shetland, in the most northern part of the North Sea. (The names of the Shell/Esso oilfields refer to seabirds.) Shell also participated in the development of oil fields in the Norwegian part of the North Sea, with a 10 per cent share in the Statfjord Field (operated by Mobil and Statoil) and 50 per cent share in Albuskjell, where Phillips was the operator. Shell even had a small share in BP's Forties Fields. In the Auk, Brent and Cormorant fields, among others, Shell was the operator. Shell Expro first developed the Auk field in the central North Sea. This was located in water depth of 270 feet. The circumstances were therefore tougher than in the southern North Sea, but not as challenging as the areas north-east of the Shetland Islands. The development of a single platform with a tanker loading

system went relatively smoothly. In 1975 the first oil to the Auk field was produced.

The Brent field, however, was an entirely different proposition to the Auk. Not only were water depths much greater, but the waves were much higher and the weather circumstances could change completely within a few hours. Fred Chate, involved with the development of Auk and Brent explained the problems with high waves: 'I was down at Brent myself at one time when I experienced a 96-feet wave, now that's something like a 12-storey building coming at you, but fortunately it doesn't seem that way when you are offshore because the time interval between crest and trough is such that the sea seems to rise up rather than come at you in an overwhelming fashion – and of course if you look away from the platform you see the standby vessels going out of sight, you think they have dropped beneath the ocean – you can't see a sign of them, you see them heave up again – it gives you some visual impression of what's coming.'[64]

The Shell/Esso Brent B platform, a Condeep design, was made of concrete and steel. Pulled by five tugs with a combined horsepower of 70,000, the 348-ton platform left its construction site in Stavanger on 4 August 1975 for a 250-mile tow to its destination in the North Sea.

'I don't think anybody really envisaged the scale of what was actually going to hit us.' William Bell

To build a platform and produce oil in such an inhospitable environment was a serious challenge. At the time Shell thought that, considering differences in water depth and weather conditions, developing the Brent field would be about three times as difficult as production in the Gulf of Mexico. With hindsight, it was not three times as difficult but looked more like ten times. It was a huge task. William Bell concluded in 1988: 'I don't think anybody really envisaged the scale of what was actually going to hit us.'[65] This lack of understanding led to long delays and extensive budget overruns. Though Shell had long experience with offshore exploration and production, in Lake Maracaibo in Venezuela, off the Californian coast, in the Gulf of Mexico, and off Brunei, only part of the previous learning was applicable in the North Sea. On the other hand, the learning curve of the North Sea could be put to proper use elsewhere in the Group. For instance, staff of Shell Oil participated in the teams in the North Sea and vice versa.[66]

The initial designs for developing the Brent oilfield were relatively simple with four platforms with oil storing offshore and shipping out by tanker. When the number of platforms from Shell and other operators in that part of the North Sea multiplied, the installation of oil pipelines to the coast became an option. At the beginning, it was not realized that the Brent field contained so much gas along with the oil. Something had to be done with the gas, because long-term flaring was unacceptable for political reasons related to the environment and waste of energy and long-term re-injection was technically undesirable. While work on the platforms was already in progress the designs were changed to include gas treatment, gas re-injection, water treatment, water flooding, gas pipelines, and oil pipelines.[67] The platforms became more like factories than just drilling facilities.

Hitherto, platforms had been made of steel. For production in the northern North Sea, Shell developed gravity platforms, based on concrete. The softer sea bottom was not very suitable for the piling system of the steel platforms, while the concrete platforms could spread their load better. The other perceived advantage of the concrete platform concept was that most work could be done onshore. While the fabrication costs were higher than for steel structures, they were supposed to be cheaper and quicker to install because the modules could more or less be finished onshore. However, this advantage did not materialize. Production in the yards was delayed and as there was a huge pressure to start producing, the modules were towed out incomplete, so that a considerable amount of finishing had still to be done offshore. On top of that came the extra work caused by the changes in designs. Experience with the platform Brent B taught that the number of man hours needed to complete construction work offshore was twice as high as originally planned.[68] Hundreds of people were working simultaneously on the cramped spaces of these platforms, which were like a maze. Jan Memelink, deputy managing director Expro, remarked wryly: 'I must say I always had difficulty in finding them when I was on board, I'd say where are my 400-450 people, you know, I can only see three.' And all these people had to be flown in by helicopter. At the peak of the building period the flight movements of the helicopters were as numerous as the plane movements at Heathrow.[69]

[26]

[27]

Designed and constructed by Anglo-Dutch Offshore Concrete (Andoc), the Shell/Esso Dunlin A production platform was the first concrete platform built in the Netherlands. On 7 July 1976 it began its journey to Norway, for fitting out with production and accommodation units, and reached its final destination at the Dunlin field in 1977.

The redesigns, delays, and extra man hours all led to budget overruns. Inflation did not help either. To add to the woes, industrial relations in Britain were at a low ebb. The winter of 1979 went into history as the 'winter of discontent'. Continued strike actions delayed the work even further. However, the problem of delays and rising costs was not limited to Britain. All oil companies in the North Sea faced the same problem. Norske Shell was confronted with rising costs for the development of the Albuskjell Field, operated by Phillips Petroleum in 1975 and 1976. Though he should have been used to budget overruns by 1979, Group managing director and later chairman of the CMD, Lo van Wachem, found it nonetheless a 'considerable shock' to discover that the costs in the development

of the Norwegian Statfjord B Platform, operated by Mobil and the Norwegian oil company Statoil, had risen by 40 per cent. The Norwegian Parliament instituted an inquiry into the cause of these sharp rises.[70] Fortunately, the high oil prices helped in covering the higher than planned costs.

Delays were not only caused by the situation on the platforms themselves, but were also connected with the efforts to bring oil and gas on shore. Considering the two alternatives of offshore loading for Brent, Cormorant, and Dunlin or going to a protected harbour environment at the Shetland Islands, Shell chose the latter, though on the basis of cost estimates which with hindsight underrated the real costs by a factor of ten. In 1974 Shell UK and sixteen other companies, including BP, Amoco, and Conoco, agreed to build a joint crude oil transportation and delivery system to bring oil ashore from five oilfields to Sullom Voe in Shetland. The construction of the 96-mile pipeline went surprisingly well, even remaining within budget. The facilities in Shetland, however, turned out to be vastly more expensive and took far more time than expected. The Shetland County Council and the Sullom Voe Association put up a very effective fight to protect their environment as much as possible and have their share in the oil bonanza.[71] In 1977 Shell decided to solve the problem of large amounts of gas from the Brent field by bringing the gas onshore via pipelines and building a gas fractionating and storage plant at Mossmoran, Scotland. After a first round of negotiations with the government, Shell received a provisional approval for the project and hoped to commence work in June 1978. Interest groups however raised concerns about nearby radio transmissions, which delayed approval until September 1979.[72] In the meantime, oil production at the Brent fields had to be curbed, until the gas could be transported.

Shell chose a floating storage and tanker loading structure, the Brent Spar, to transfer the oil from the Brent oilfield into tankers while the pipeline structure to bring oil onshore was under construction. Built at Rotterdam with a storage capacity of 300,000 barrels of crude oil, the Spar is seen being floated out from its construction site on 31 January 1975.

[28]

[29]

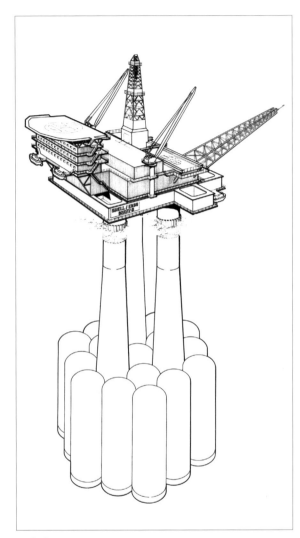

[30]

After the Brent B platform had been placed in its final position, more modules were added in June 1976 (above left), and production drilling began the same year. Whereas the floating Spar storage tank was held in place by six massive anchors, Brent B was the first of a new generation of concrete platforms that could be kept in place by their own weight (above right).

[31]

The Brent C platform, also a concrete gravity structure, was installed in June 1978 and started production in 1979.

The whole offshore industry went through a steep learning curve in the 1970s in the North Sea. 'During the six years I was there we did, with hindsight, most things wrong at the beginning but most things right at the end', concluded William Bell in later years. In the (unnamed) joint venture with Esso in the UK North Sea, Shell Expro was the operator and Esso the non-operating partner. However, when the extent of the developments in the North Sea became clear, and the bills kept rising, Esso became more actively involved. They sent out some specialized people and shared their know-how, including their experiences in drawing up 'no surprise' budgets.[73] After the experiences with the Brent field the building of platforms became more routine. Another interesting learning phase was the underwater production well tied into the South Cormorant platform and a remote-controlled underwater gathering centre, installed in 1982 on the Central Cormorant field at a depth of 490 feet. From the Brent experience the Group also learned in an organizational way, introducing the concept of project management, which turned out to be of great value for the second generation of platforms. Employees were eager to get into a project team, and felt envious if they were not. In Aberdeen the teams put up banners above the front entrances of their hotels, such as 'Huntley Hotel, home of the North Cormorant team'. Workers became so loyal to their projects that they even began to compete with each other. The teams developed the spirit of football teams: Fulmar is the best, North Cormorant is the best. In the end, management had to take care that the overall picture was kept in sight.[74]

[32]

[33]

Further gigantic structures followed. Seen above in 1976 is the base of the Cormorant A platform, which acted as the main pumping station for the entire Brent pipeline system. At left, the Brent D production platform is shown under construction in 1975. Once finished and resting on the seabed, its sixteen cylindrical tanks, 60 metres high, could contain one million barrels of crude oil. The production platform above them was supported by three columns 100 metres high, two of which functioned as drilling rigs, while the third contained a pumping unit.

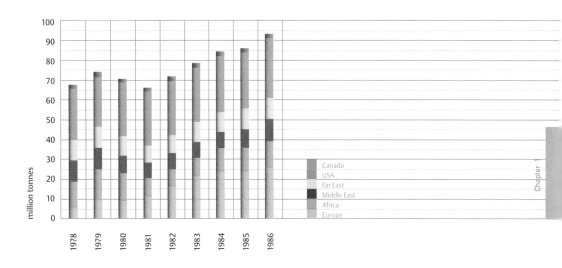

When completed in 1961 at Barrow-in-Furness, UK, by Vickers-Armstrong, the 71,250dwt SS *Serenia* was the world's largest tanker, but much bigger ships soon followed and in 1977 *Serenia* – seen here loading crude oil at the Brent Spar – was converted into a North Sea shuttle tanker by Verolme, Rotterdam.

Figure 1.2
Regional division of Shell equity oil production, 1978-1986.

In 1976 more than 80 per cent of Shell's capital expenditure on oil and gas production outside North America was in the North Sea. This gradually declined to 75 per cent in 1977 and 70 per cent in 1979. In 1982 Shell calculated that it had spent £4 billion on expenditure in the North Sea over the previous seventeen years.[75] Far out in the northern regions of the North Sea a colossal production centre had been built up. One of the pioneers, Ian Henderson, summarized the results thus: 'The last time I was off in the east Shetland basin would be something like February 1977, and there was Brent Bravo which was actually producing, there was Alpha which was still being piled – it was just a jacket. There was Delta which was sitting there in all its glory being hooked up, not yet producing. I went back off again in September 1983, and you could hardly see the water for platforms, the change was so absolutely phenomenal.'[76] How important the oil production from Europe became for Shell, can be seen in Figure 1.2.[77] In 1986 it was the Group's second largest producing area after the USA. Figure 1.2 also shows that Shell Oil kept up its production in the US in these years despite the fact that the US oil industry was past its peak.

One of the reasons for the oil companies to invest in the North Sea was the view that this part of the world would be 'politically safe'. It may have been politically stable, but the governments of western countries were equally inclined to pursue policies of 'national interest' with regard to oil and gas in their territories. In Britain, in 1974 the incoming Labour Party levied a special tax on oil revenues and established a new state oil company, the British National Oil Corporation (BNOC). With this company the government hoped to ensure that the British people would have a real say in the development of their Continental Shelf's riches. Negotiations with the oil companies started. The government soon had to give up the idea of obtaining a majority equity share in the fields already discovered, because public funding did not stretch that far. The oil companies were not prepared to give BNOC any rights in their upstream decision-making without a financial contribution: no say without pay. Nor were Shell and Exxon prepared to accept any involvement of BNOC in their downstream affairs. The discussion then moved towards a 51 per cent share of BNOC in the produced oil. This proposition was not very attractive for Shell and Exxon, because they wanted to use the North Sea oil in their own refineries. After prolonged negotiations, an agreement was reached in which BNOC sold the acquired oil back to the oil companies. BNOC acquired the option to purchase at full market price 51 per cent of all oil from the commercial oil fields under the existing licences. However, at the same time, Shell and Exxon acquired the right to buy back at the same price as paid by BNOC such quantities of the option oil as were needed in their UK refining

01|52

[36]   [37]

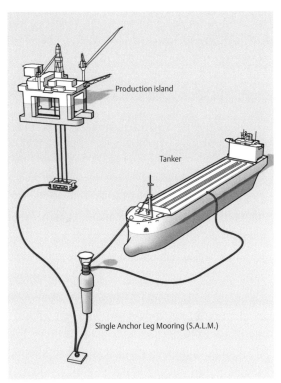

Production island

Tanker

Single Anchor Leg Mooring (S.A.L.M.)

[38]

To collect the oil produced from the Fulmar, Auk and Clyde fields, Shell converted a VLCC into a floating storage unit (FSU), seen at left attached to the 'Fulmar Single Anchor Leg Mooring' (SALM). Resembling a Single Buoy Mooring system but upended (above) onto the seabed, the SALM provided a secure anchor for all-weather loading of crude into the FSU. A shuttle tanker (left) has approached the stern of the FSU to draw off cargo.

and marketing programmes. Basically, Shell UK was neither better off, nor worse off under this arrangement.[78] In handing out new licences, the government also gave BNOC preferential treatment as BP had enjoyed in the 1960s. It came as a shock to Shell to discover that in the next round of the licences (in 1977), in one case Shell Expro would only have a 49 per cent share if it accepted BNOC as a 51 per cent partner as well as the operator.[79]

The British government was clearly determined to set up a fully operational state oil company to profit from the oil boom while it lasted. Before Britain, Norway had set up Statoil as an instrument to give its government more control over oil production and the development of related industries. Statoil participated in all applications and had the right to take over the operatorship at a later date.[80] Participation in oil and gas production looked even more attractive for governments after the Second Oil Shock in 1979.

Second Oil Shock   Had prices been thought high after the first
oil shock in 1973, more was yet to come. Concerns about the future
oil supply and political turmoil in Iran worked together to create a
second steep rise in oil prices at the very end of the 1970s. After
1973 the OPEC countries had succeeded in keeping the oil prices up
even during periods of slack demand through an interaction
between themselves and spot markets. On the spot market goods
are sold for cash and delivered immediately. Each OPEC meeting
was supposed to announce higher prices, so spot markets tried to
anticipate the higher OPEC official prices by higher spot prices.
These higher spot prices then formed the perfect excuse for OPEC
to raise its official prices, as these were only following the market.
The policy worked as long as oil was seen to be in short supply. In
the summer of 1978 US officials were predicting a 'chronic tightness
or even severe shortage of oil supply'.[81]

At the same time the position of the Shah of Iran began to
weaken. In late September the first strikes affected the Oil Service
Company of Iran and NIOC's refinery in Abadan. In the autumn of
1978 widespread strikes and demonstrations brought chaos to the
economy. Shell closely followed developments in Iran, because it
depended on purchases in Iran for about one-fifth of its crude oil
supply.[82] In late November the strikers slowly returned to work and
production was resumed. The problems for the Shah, however,
were far from over. His position became increasingly precarious
after the Ayatollah Khomeini had staged a massive demonstration
in Teheran in mid-December. Strikes in the oil industry were
resumed and output fell below domestic demand. Iranian exports
of oil ceased completely. The service company began to plan the
evacuation of its expatriate staff and their families.

Fear of possible loss of supply increased oil prices on the spot
market. OPEC did not lose this opportunity to raise its prices. In its

Political upheaval in Iran caused a
second shock in oil prices. In December
1978 mass demonstrations took place
in Teheran against the Shah and his
pro-American regime and in support of
the religious leader Khomeini.

[39]

[41]

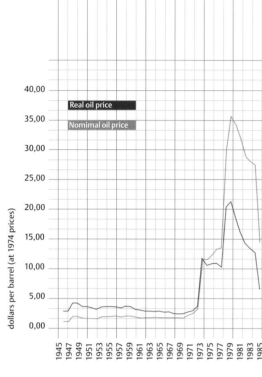

Figure 1.3
Nominal and real oil prices, 1945-1986.

December meeting in Abu Dhabi OPEC noted 'with great anxiety the high rate of inflation and dollar depreciation sustained over the last two years, and hence the substantial erosion of the oil revenues of the Member Countries, and its adverse effects on their economic and social development'. It therefore decided that it was high time to 'correct' the oil price with an increase of 14.5 per cent.[83] But that was not the end. In January 1979 the Shah left his country, and two weeks later Khomeini returned to Iran to take up religious and political leadership. The situation in the oil industry became increasingly unclear. Shell made attempts to maintain contact with NIOC, but in the confusing situation it was difficult to know who was the right contact. In the face of the anti-American emotions in the country, Shell companies concerned with Iran tried to establish a favourable image separate from the rest of the Consortium, but they had no idea whether the Iranian authorities would even be interested in business with the oil majors. They expected them to favour a government-to-government deal. In March 1979 Shell noted that Iran remained anarchic: 'The army appeared to have dwindled away but everyone seemed to have weapons.'[84] The new NIOC management resumed negotiations with the Consortium

members, but on an individual basis. The question was whether Shell companies should be willing to close spot transactions. Would these not add to the scrambling after oil and rising prices? Or would it make no difference as the Japanese and American companies were pushing up the prices with their need for access anyway? Whatever the answer to this theoretical question, Shell companies did not have much choice. They needed the crude for their operations and therefore were an important party in the market, prepared to pay increasingly higher prices to balance their demand.[85] Though not among the hawks with respect to price rises, Saudi Arabia undoubtedly supported the price increases by cutting down its production in January and April 1979. The war of Iraq against Iran, started in 1980, further contributed to production cuts, and high oil prices. The effects of the two oil shocks on the nominal and real price of oil is highlighted in Figure 1.3.[86] The contrast with the long period of relatively low oil prices before 1973 is striking. Both shocks had important consequences for the downstream business of oil companies, as the next sections will explain.

Figure 1.4
Shell equity oil production and total
supply, 1960-1986.

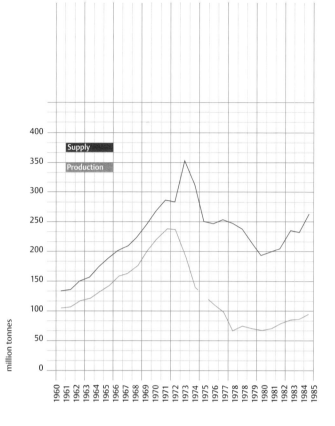

Trading as an activity in its own right   The series of
nationalizations of oil assets and participations of oil-producing
governments before and after the first oil shock brought a partial
end to the integration of the major oil companies. Although they
remained active in all stages of the supply chain, their activities
were no longer fully integrated. In the midst of the negotiations
about participations in 1974, Michael Pocock, Group managing
director, and from 1977 until his death in October 1979 chairman
of the CMD, explained that the objective for Shell companies was
to survive this period whilst keeping intact their downstream
position.[87] As more than half of Shell's employees worked in
the downstream business, this sector was very important in
maintaining employment levels. Pocock had risen through the
ranks via personnel management, and may well have been
particularly concerned about the impact of the upheaval in the
oil industry on employment. His Oxford degree in classics and
philosophy did not seem the most likely preparation for a career in
the oil industry, but after serving in the war he joined Shell in 1946
to work as industrial relations supervisor in Venezuela. He returned
to London to participate in the McKinsey reorganisation, which
underlined the decentralized organizational structure of the Group,
and for the rest of his career he moved between postings in
Venezuela and London. Pocock considered the development of a
genuinely international approach one of Shell's greatest strengths
in human terms, and in his view the wane of hierarchical structures
had been one of the greatest changes in industrial organization. He
was firmly convinced of the rightness of Shell's approach to
decentralize on the basis of geographical units, integrated in
themselves, as was the case in the US and Canada, and increasingly
in the UK as well. Having local authority in place made it easier to
negotiate with national governments.[88]

It is important to note first that the trend towards nationalization
was not limited to the upstream business, because downstream
activities were also affected. In 1975 the government of India
acquired the ownership of the marketing and refining companies
of Burmah-Shell, in which Shell had a 50 per cent interest. This
takeover formed part of the government policy to take control of
all foreign oil companies operating in India. Its price controls
enabled it to squeeze the profits of the private companies, making
continued stay unattractive. In previous years the market share of
Burmah-Shell in India had already gone down steadily because of
the rise of the state company, the Indian Oil Company. The
takeover made at least one party happy: BP was pleased that the
Burmah-Shell agreements, dating back to 1928, were finally
ended.[89] In a number of African countries governments took hold
of (part of) the Shell marketing companies. A special case was
Argentina, where all foreign companies were forced to leave in 1974
and invited back three years later, after the military regime had
decided to restore competition for the state company YPF. In
accepting the return of their nationalized assets, Shell had to
promise, among other things, not to reduce work opportunities for
Argentine nationals.[90]

The nationalizations in the oil industry made oil trading into a more prominent activity for the oil majors. Shell set up Shell International Trading Company (Sitco) in London, seen here in the mid-1980s, as a central division responsible for the co-ordinated procurement, trading and international distribution of crude oil.

[42]

An even more special case was Vietnam. All through the war between Communist North Vietnam and the US-supported South Vietnam, Shell Vietnam had continued its activities, fuelling the war by selling oil to the American and South Vietnamese troops as well as to local traders who knew how to transfer the oil to the North.[91] The question was: how long would the Americans continue fighting in South Vietnam? How long would Shell remain in this war-troubled region? A few weeks before the fall of Saigon, one of the Dutch wives of Shell's expatriate staff noticed, while visiting her American friends, that the coffee was being served out of throw-away cups and only essential furniture was still in place: 'You were not supposed to ask why. Everybody "knew", and still it was a secret. When it was my turn to have the ladies at my home after a game of golf, they looked around with great surprise. They were astonished because all my furniture was still there but they did not really answer my questions. They only said "don't you know?" Of course I told my husband all about it, but his comment was: "Nonsense. Women's talk, you know how Americans can

exaggerate?"' However, soon all Shell expatriates left with their families, leaving only three men behind to organize further procedures. The three missing husbands arrived in Singapore just two days before the fall of Saigon in April 1975.[92]

The nationalizations added to the fragmentation of the former integrated oil business. What did the disintegration mean for the downstream business, with trading, shipping, refineries, and marketing companies? Trading oil had always been part of the operation of an oil company, if only to rectify imbalances between production, manufacturing and distribution. The trading of oil and oil products was also useful to diminish the distances oil had to be transported or to use refineries in the most efficient way. The imbalances between production and refining greatly increased during the early 1970s, as more and more equity oil transformed into long-term delivery contracts. Shell had always been 'short on crude', but this problem became worse. In 1972, of the total amount of oil the Shell companies needed to meet their worldwide commitment, about 60 per cent was covered by production from

[43]

its own concessions. This percentage shrank to 54 per cent in 1973 and even further to 45 per cent in 1974.[93] Figure 1.4 (page 57) shows the increasing discrepancy between Shell's equity production and supply, the difference being made up by trade.[94]

The function of trading became much more important within the organization. Shell had to learn the art of purchasing oil from producer governments. One of its first big deals under the new circumstances was with the Kuwaiti government in 1975. At the same time, Sitco (Shell International Trading Company) was established as a new division of Shell International Petroleum Company Limited, which became responsible for the co-ordinated procurement, trading, and international distribution of oil. By concentrating its acquisition activities in a central agency, Shell could exploit the total purchasing power of the Group and bargain for better deals. Nevertheless, the operating companies were free to make direct deals elsewhere if they perceived more profitable opportunities. Sitco received a double briefing: it had to become a commercial venture in its own right, but it also had to serve the

interests of the Group as a whole. It went off on a flying start: in 1976 Sitco's oil trade amounted to just under 10 per cent of the total international trade in crude. They were buying more than any other organization in the world.[95]

The Second Oil Shock of 1979 led to rising oil prices but also to the cancellation of long-term purchase contracts because of the very wide difference between 'spot' and official prices. As oil prices rose above contract prices, the oil-producing countries were sorely tempted to break existing long-term supply deals and sell their oil at the higher spot prices. This affected in particular the oil majors, which had been able to include long-term supply arrangements in their participation negotiations in the early 1970s. Third party buyers, such as state-owned refineries, which until then bought much of their need from the major oil companies, began to buy on the spot market, or to negotiate directly with the producer governments. The direct marketing of the latter rose from 8 per cent in 1973 to 42 per cent in 1979 of the oil traded outside the communist area and North America.[96] In the past the crude spot

After 1973 Shell was faced with a surplus of Very Large Crude Carriers (VLCCs). A number of those very large tankers were still under construction, and the orders could not be cancelled without paying high penalties.

market, where goods were sold for cash on immediate delivery, had only served to balance surpluses and deficits. Now its role became increasingly important, with oil a commodity to be traded on the spot market like products such as grain.

Shell's trading position changed once again. The loss of crude as a consequence of the Iranian revolution forced Sitco and the other oil majors to use the 'force majeure' clause in their contracts. Sitco cut back on its crude customers with 7.5 per cent to start with. As in 1973, Shell chose a policy of equal misery. At the same time it tried to purchase oil through spot market deals from National Iranian Oil Company (NIOC) as soon as this company had resumed production. The successive deals Shell reached with NIOC illustrate the stiff price rises. In March 1979 Sitco purchased Iranian light for $19.15, in September for $35.65 and in November for $40-45 per barrel.[97] In the meantime the relationship between Iran and the US deteriorated and reached a low point in November 1979, when the skeleton staff of the US Embassy was taken hostage by a group of Iranian zealots in reaction to the admission of the Shah in a New York hospital. After a flawed attempt to rescue them in April 1980, the hostages were finally released on the last day of Carter's presidency in January 1981.[98] In May 1980 Shell received attractive offers from Iran for buying crude oil. Shell was reluctant to accept these offers because of the US sanctions against Iran. Some high officials from the US government put pressure on Shell to heed certain conditions if it valued its interest in the USA, a pressure some of Shell non-executive directors considered a gross interference by a government in the commercial affairs of a company without there being any legal justification for it.[99] In the aftermath of the Second Oil Shock, Sitco lost its long-term supply contracts with Iran and other oil-producing countries. Therefore it could no longer act as the natural supplier of Shell's operating companies, assuring stable supply at relatively low prices. Shell's operating companies began to hunt for oil themselves, while Sitco could only stay in business if it could trade more effectively than the operating companies. Both parties used the spot market as their point of reference. In this same period, a new breed of traders entered the markets, the so-called 'Wall Street refiners', who were not interested in the physical oil but in financial deals. They modernized the oil trade by transferring into it risk management techniques, such as forwards, futures, derivatives, and hedging, from other commodity markets.[100] These different patterns in trading had extensive influences on the marine sector.

Shell's L-class VLCC *Limatula* (seen here under construction at the Odense Staalskibs in Denmark in 1974) was another victim of the age, a short-lived member of the Group fleets.

Completed in 1975, she was superfluous to contemporary needs and was laid up in Brunei Bay until 1977 before being sold in 1981.

[45]

From expansion to contraction in the marine sector

The two oil crises created extensive difficulties for the transport of oil. The tanker market was a volatile business with high losses and swings back to profits. Following the 1973 oil shock, it was decided that in future the Group's Marine Function should be a commercial activity in its own right and not necessarily directed primarily to servicing Shell companies' requirements.[101] Because of the reduction in equity oil, Shell could no longer simply use its own fleet to transfer its own crude to its own refineries. In fact, that had never been the case in the past either, because only part of its fleet was owned, the rest was chartered. For instance, in 1975 no more than 40 per cent of its tanker fleet was actually owned by Shell, though this percentage was expected to rise in the course of the 1970s.[102] The oil-producing governments, stepping up their rights to sell their own oil, also began to influence the transport of the crude oil. Some were considering building up a fleet of their own. Not only that, but the price rise of 1973 had done the previously unthinkable: reduce the demand for oil. In the early 1970s, Shell had expected an important rise in oil demand, and therefore invested in new ships. After 1973 it was faced with a surplus in tankers, in particular in the class of the Very Large Crude Carriers, or VLCCs. As a number of tankers were still under construction, overcapacity would increase rather than decrease in the years to come. Cancellation of new building orders would be too expensive and under the present circumstances buyers were hard to find. The 'Marine Problem', seen to be 'formidable', was tackled through charter arrangements with third parties, 'slow steaming' (keeping the tankers out on sea for longer periods), accelerated scrapping of older ships and the lay-up of tankers.[103] Six of the very large ships, some of them just newly built, were parked in Brunei Bay to wait for better times. When they came back into circulation two years later,

the deterioration of the hulls of these vessels turned out to be greater than envisioned.[104] With an oversupply in tankers the freight rates were at unsatisfactory levels. The decline in demand for tankers continued throughout the 1970s. One factor, adding to the problems, was the fact that 'short haul crude' such as oil from the North Sea increasingly became available. The growing use of pipelines also reduced the demand for tankers. D. R. Skinner, summarizing the Marine Report, explained that the requirement for tonnage in 1978 was only 50 per cent of what had been planned for in 1970.[105]

Though the majority of the competitors seemed to regard their marine function as a service that need not necessarily be on a commercial footing, Shell aimed at making a profit. In practice, however, for most years the activities of the marine sector were loss-making. Not that Shell was not working on the problem, but it was an uphill struggle, a case of 'running to stand still'. Increasing the efficiency of staff offered one way of trying to diminish the losses. One such project was the Dutch 'Project Lange Adem' (Project Long Breath), started in 1976 to optimize social and economic relations on board and on shore. The project aimed to address a number of issues, including the competition from low-wage countries, the technological developments which demanded higher qualified staff and the process of democratization in work relations in the society at large. Revolutionary in the Marine context was the scheme devised to do away with the differentiation between engine room and bridge. The integration of the two groups concerned the various tasks as well as sharing the same mess. A pilot project for 30,000-ton product carriers, started in 1977, reduced staff numbers from 32 to 24.[106]

Losses were not the only problem plaguing this sector. The image of tanker transport, notably of the very large crude carriers,

Most ships end their lives by being sold and broken up for scrap, and many ships from many companies – including numerous Shell ships over the years – have ended up on the breakers' beach at Chittagong in Bangladesh, as happened in 1984 with Shell's aged *Achatina* and *Amastra* (both built in 1958). The much larger but unidentifiable ships seen here were not Shell ships – no Group vessel of that size was sent to Chittagong at that time – but they represent a boom time for the breakers in the middle 1980s.

On 16 March 1978 the wreck of the
Amoco Cadiz (below left) caused
extensive environmental damage on
the coast of Brittany. The ship was not a
Shell tanker, but Shell owned the cargo
and so was seen by environmental
campaigners as being culpable. Protest
posters quickly appeared. In Germany,
with the names Amoco and Esso half-
hidden behind a prominent Shell
pecten (right), the message said 'We
make more than oil', while another in
France (far right) called for a boycott of
'black sea – Shell'. Civilians concerned
about the damage volunteered (below
right) to remove the oil from the
beaches of Brittany.

[47]

61|66

suffered from shipping accidents that caused extensive environmental damage. One such case, which involved oil transported for
Shell, was the VLCC *Amoco Cadiz*, which grounded off the coast of
Brittany in 1978 after a steering failure. The tanker had a full cargo of
Iranian crude. At first a quarter of the oil spilled into the sea. Shell
vessels took up position to take off the remaining crude oil, but
weather conditions made this impossible and the whole cargo
poured out and contaminated the coast. In terms of pollution it was
the worst oil tanker incident up till then, and it received a huge
amount of negative publicity. Shell had chartered the tanker, but the
ship itself was entirely under control of Amoco. Nonetheless, some
fifty ecologists raided the offices of Shell Française in Paris, took
away confidential documents and published them in *Quotidien de
Paris*. The French Consumer's Association initiated a boycott of Shell
Française. Not to be outdone, Shell Française took the Association
to court, demanding (and obtaining) an injunction and interim
damages. Geoffrey Chandler, Group Public Affairs Co-ordinator,
commented wryly that Shell was made into the scapegoat, because
Amoco was not so well known in France.[107] In response to the
disaster, the Intergovernmental Maritime Consultative Organisation
(IMCO) proposed tougher regulations for older ships. Though these
would not be in force until 1982, Shell thought it prudent for its fleet
to act on them and install the necessary improvements promptly.[108]

    The 1979 oil scramble temporarily pushed up demand for
tanker transport and Shell's marine sector made a profit for the first
time since 1973 (and only the fifth time since 1960). There was

[49]

[50]

[48]

some hope that the tide had finally turned. It was also clear that the high price of oil made the relatively high Shell marine costs less of a drawback, but it did not structurally solve the problem of relatively high labour costs. The mood of optimism did not last long. Figure 1.5 compares the development of the tanker fleets of Shell and its two major competitors, BP and Exxon, between 1960 and 1986.[109] (Unfortunately it was not possible to find the relevant data for all years.) The figures include owned as well as chartered tankers, and seem to suggest that Shell and Exxon continued to expand longer than BP. The three companies demonstrated a similar pattern in the rise and fall of their tanker fleets, which continued after 1979.

The high oil price in combination with a general recession during the early 1980s further reduced demand for oil and thus demand for shipping, and the sector went back to losses. The efficiency of the transport was affected negatively by the fragmentation of the oil market. In the period of long-term purchase agreements the transport of oil could be planned in advance and large quantities could be transported at once. With the rise of the spot market transactions, which were inherently short time, the oil movements became less predictable and destinations more varied. On top of that came the losses of supply from Iran and Iraq during the war that broke out between the two countries in 1980. Both had been long-haul crude movements. As a consequence of the war, no fewer than eighty ships were trapped in the Shatt al Arab waterway, which served as the boundary between Iraq and Iran. The oil companies continued to buy oil from Iran and collect it from its largest oil-exporting terminal at Kharg Island in the Arabian Gulf, despite frequent allegations by Iraq that their

[51]

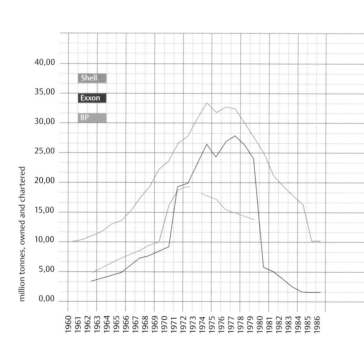

Figure 1.5
Tanker fleets of Shell, Exxon and BP,
1960-1986.

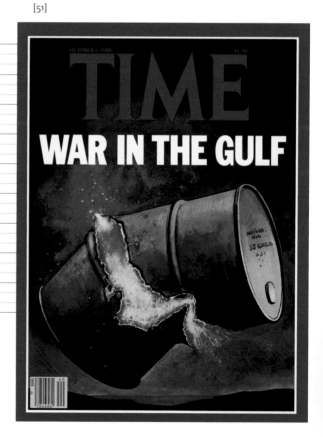

In September 1980 Iraq attacked Iran and war began in the Gulf. At the cosmopolitan port city of Khorramshahr, ten kilometres from the large refinery at Abadan, ships were trapped at the quayside. On 6 October 1980 *Time* magazine's front cover gave an explosive visual summary of the conflict. The war lasted for eight years.

aircraft had attacked the terminal and the tankers loading there. In 1982 Shell received one telex message after another telling about military actions around Kharg Island. From their own masters on the tankers they received different information: the people living there could not recall any major attacks after the first attack at the beginning of the war. Most delays at Kharg seemed to be caused by weather conditions. The lifting of oil under the risky circumstances, however, considerably increased the shipping costs.[110]

[52]

Kharg

When vessel arrives at Kharg no berth is available or port closed owing to
weather conditions, an anchorage is designated by Kharg control approx. 6 to
7' off Kharg East jetty. Total blackout procedures are enforced and seemed to
be very effective, creating an eerie and very sinister atmosphere

Laconica, 11 December 1983

In September 1980 no fewer than eighty ships were trapped in the Shatt-al-Arab waterway, the boundary between Iran and Iraq. Above left, plumes of smoke rise from the burning oil tanks at Abadan, and above right, an Iraqi officer looks across the waterway at the wreck of the Romanian freighter *Olanesti*, attacked by Iranian artillery on 7 October 1980. Nevertheless, during the war oil companies continued to buy crude from Iran whenever possible, loading their tankers at Iran's Kharg Island oil terminal, the largest terminal in the Gulf.

The captain of the Shell tanker *Laconica* described the situation in a telex message to central office 11 December 1983: 'Total backout procedures are enforced and seemed to be very effective, creating an eerie and very sinister atmosphere.'

On 23 November 1983 in a telex press release from Kuwait, the Iraqi Oil Minister defended an attack on oil tankers in Iranian territorial waters as a legitimate action.

[57]

KUWAIT -(AP-DJ)--THE IRAQI OIL MISTER WAS QUOTED TUES-DAY AS DEFENDING HIS COUNTRY'S AIR AND SEA ATTACK ON OIL TANKERS IN IRANIAN TERRITORIAL WATERS LAST WEEK-END. QASSEM AL-ORAIBI TOLD THE INDEPENDENT KUWAITI NEWSPAPER AL-QABAS THAT THE +SINKING OF FIVE (UNIDEN-TIFIED) OIL TANKERS NEAR IRAN+S KHARG ISLAND WAS A LEGITIMATE MARINE ACTION.+

To achieve a new balance between demand and supply in shipping in the 1980s, Shell companies applied the familiar strategies of slow steaming and chartering out to third parties. The number of ships owned by Shell declined further, as did the number of staff. At the same time, new ships were continuously added to the fleet. The VLCCs of the late 1960s and early 1970s were sold or scrapped and replaced by smaller and more flexible new types of tankers which could carry crude oil as well as oil products. In one type of product carrier, the LNG (Liquefied Natural Gas) ships, Shell kept a special interest, because these were usually tailor-made for the various projects. Through selective replacement of older and larger ships, Shell aimed at maintaining a nucleus of modern, cost-effective vessels attuned to the Group's trading needs.

Persistent overcapacity in refining The Group's refineries had expanded through the 1950s and 1960s. By 1970 the Group had 47 refineries. Some were close to the oil production such as the Cardón refinery in Venezuela, others close to long-established consumer markets in the US and Europe or newly developed markets in Africa. In addition, Shell had three large refining complexes, in the Netherlands (Pernis), Singapore, and Curaçao, which acted as 'balancing' refineries. These were able to process different kinds of crude oil into a large variety of oil products.[111] Shell expected the expansion in demand for oil products and refining capacity to continue well into the 1970s. However, in the early 1970s the problem of under-utilization of refineries appeared for the first time. The rise in oil prices further reduced demand, and refineries struggled with over capacity. High oil prices added to the already increasing refining costs as a consequence of rising labour costs and mounting environmental requirements. In 1973 Shell introduced programmes to increase efficiency and save energy. Its operating companies received visits from the 'distillate maximization teams' to find out whether the distillate yield could be improved at low costs, and from the 'energy conservation team' to assess the potential for loss reduction and fuel saving. At the higher oil price, saving energy suddenly became a profitable business, even for Shell companies themselves. A comparative study from an independent American oil consultant, Professor W. L. Nelson, showed that the newer Shell refineries compared favourably with the refineries of seven other major companies, whose identities were not revealed.[112]

The dramatic changes in the oil industry after the first oil crisis had their impact on the amount of crude oil passing through the refineries of the oil majors. Not only Shell, but also its main competitor Exxon, experienced a persistent decline in throughput

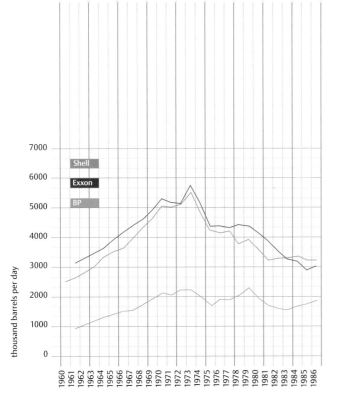

Figure 1.6
Refinery throughput Shell, Exxon
and BP, 1960-1986.

in its refineries after 1973, as can be seen in Figure 1.6.[113] Measured in barrels of crude per day Shell and Exxon were in 1986 back to the level of the mid-1960s. BP, which by 1973 had a much lower throughput than Shell or Exxon, faced a decline after 1973, but then remained with ups and downs at the same level.

The decline in throughput was only half of the story. Apart from increasing efficiency and saving energy, Shell refineries sought refuge in their technological strength by focusing on oil products that delivered a higher value per barrel of crude oil, a process known as 'whitening the barrel'. The lighter products (LPG, gasoline, and naphtha as feedstock for chemicals) had a better profit margin than the heavier products such as fuel oil or bitumen.

It made sense to concentrate on oil products for motorcars and aircraft, because for transport there were few alternative sources of energy. In contrast, fuel oil for domestic and industrial applications could be replaced by coal, gas, or electricity. As a consequence of the rise in prices, demand for fuel oil was dropping, while that of motor gasoline remained steady. Explaining Shell's strategy to a journalist of the American magazine *Forbes*, Dirk de Bruyne, chairman of the CMD from 1979 to 1982, mentioned: 'we foresaw a coming shortage of oil, and that the smart thing to do would be for coal and other forms of energy to take the place of fuel oil. It's a waste of hydrocarbons to put fuel oil in a furnace, umm? The smart thing to do it crack'em to hell and use the products.'[114] Having made his career in Shell via finance, and being an 'unashamed optimist' as he saw himself, De Bruyne enjoyed speaking to financial analysts, one of whom wrote in return that he had 'humanized the Group for us'.[115]

The strategy of 'whitening the barrel' required investment in secondary refining capacity. In the 1970s Shell added a series of thermal cracking units to its existing refineries, followed by hydrocrackers, catalytic crackers, and continous platformers.[116]

In reaction to the nationalization of oil assets in many producing as well as in some consuming countries, Shell also extended its consultative services to third parties. One of the first projects was the building of a new refinery at Cilacap, Indonesia. Shell staff designed the refinery, were involved with the engineering and construction process, and helped to bring it on stream under the supervision of the state oil company Pertamina.[117] In offering technological services to third parties Shell faced a dilemma. On the one hand, setting up new potential competitors was certainly not helping in diminishing the existing problem of overcapacity in refineries. On the other, the services offered a way

From simple to fully complex

Atmospheric distillation

Conversion via
- Catalytic cracking
- Hydrocracking

Vacuum distillation

Deep conversion via
- Coking
- Hydroconversion

White products (distillates)

Black products (fuel oil)

of remaining involved with the oil business in countries where national governments had taken over the oil concessions. For instance, in Venezuela, Shell concluded a contract for technological support to the state company Maraven after it had taken over the Shell manufacturing assets, including the Cardón refinery. In the case of Saudi Arabia the refinery set up in joint venture with Petromin offered Shell irresistible access to crude oil. The 'refinery for access to oil' deal was first discussed in 1975, the contract was closed in 1978, but the refinery and equal joint venture did not come on stream until 1985.[118] Shell's concern that the state oil companies of oil-producing countries would invade their key markets in Western Europe was not entirely unfounded, though it did not happen until the early 1980s. Kuwait was the first to make its entrance by taking over Gulf assets in Scandinavia, Benelux, and Italy. Petróleos de Venezuela SA (PDVSA) acquired downstream assets in Europe as well as in the US, while the Mexican state company Pemex went to Spain. The Norwegian state company Statoil spread its wings in Northern Europe. One could argue that these moves represented a return to the integrated oil company.[119]

The 'invasion' of new competitors increased the already existing problem of overcapacity, a problem made worse after the second price hike, which plunged the world into recession and further reduced oil demand. Shell could no longer escape a serious restructuring programme, starting with 'selective mothballing' and ending with the closure of a number of smaller refineries in Europe, including Ingolstadt in Germany, Teesport in the UK, and Pauillac in France.[120] More dramatic was the sale of the refinery in Curaçao in 1985. The latter was built during the First World War to refine the heavy Venezuelan crude and sell the oil products to the export market. After the nationalization of Shell Venezuela in 1975 the refinery had worked at a loss for most years, partly because of the fall in demand for high-sulphur fuel oil, for which this refinery was particularly suited, and partly because of the divergence between the selling prices of the Venezuelan government and product prices on the free market. Shell preferred to close down the refinery, but realized that this would create major problems for the economy of Curaçao. Furthermore, closure, complete demolition, and clean-up of the site would be expensive and take a

The demand for more refined oil products increased the need for more sophisticated processing, or 'whitening the barrel'. Heavy crude oil feedstock was converted into lighter products by reducing the ratio of carbon to hydrogen, by either removing carbon or adding hydrogen. The carbon-removal route included processes such as coking or thermal cracking. In the 'cat cracking' process, catalysts could be used to speed up the rate of carbon removal. Alternatively, hydrogen could be added, for example in a 'hydrocracker', again with the aid of a catalyst. In the 1980s, at the Pernis refinery in the Netherlands, Shell developed its Hycon process, which could convert an even higher proportion of the barrel into lighter products.

In 1985 Shell decided to close the refinery on Curaçao. After lengthy negotiations, however, the refinery was sold to the government of the Antilles, which wanted to safeguard employment on the island.

[59]

[60]

[61]

long time. It seemed far more sensible to restore the former link between the Venezuelan oil and the Curaçao refinery. Curaçao formed part of the Kingdom of the Netherlands, but with a considerable local autonomy. The late 1960s had seen major riots by Afro-Caribbeans, and for that reason the authorities were concerned about the loss of employment on the island. Under the threat of closure, urgent negotiations took place between the governments of Venezuela, the Antilles, and the Netherlands, which resulted in a transfer of the refinery (plant, property, and equipment) to the Antilles government on an 'as is, where is' basis. The Antilles government concluded an agreement with the Venezuelan State Oil Company, PDVSA, to deliver the crude and operate the refinery, and in October 1985 Shell Curaçao handed over the refinery for the symbolic sum of 1 guilder. Included in the deal was the Curaçao Oil Terminal (COT), built in the 1970s to receive the very large crude tankers. In return for the transferred assets the Curaçao government waived present and future claims against Shell companies and agreed to indemnify Shell companies against future claim legislation for demolition, pollution, and environmental aspects and past taxes.[121] Though in this way Shell had formally bought off its responsibilities for cleaning up the areas around the refinery, environmental campaigners kept looking at Shell as the guilty party in not cleaning up the site after its departure.

'Unprepared and uncomprehending'   At the very end of the oil supply chain comes the most visible part of the enterprise, where consumers experience Shell on a daily basis: the service station. Nothing infuriates customers more than rising gasoline prices, or, even worse, the chance of an interruption of supply. The two 'oil shocks' of the 1970s gave customers much to complain about. In particular the first oil crisis in 1973 came as a genuine shock. As mentioned above, the governments of consuming countries had little appreciation for the 'equal misery' policy of the oil companies during the crisis. As far as the customers were concerned, Shell found that most were 'unprepared and uncomprehending'.[122] How did the Group try to keep its millions of consumers all over the world motivated to use their outlets and to buy their products in the time of rising prices? While the costs of crude oil rose, the marketing organization faced the challenge of recovering the higher prices through their sales of oil products. This was not an easy task, because it required a heightened sense of commercialism. Dan Samuel, introducing the Marketing Oil report for 1973, remarked about Shell that 'the organisation encouraged people to think that money was being made by someone else within the organisation. There was a need for a sharper way of dealing with each other, for avoidance of blurring of issues by package deals, for elimination of over-communication and for

In the early 1970s Shell brought self-service stations ('zelf tank') into the Netherlands. As there was no longer an attendant at the pump, clear pictures were obviously needed (left and far left) to show customers the way to the pump, the shop or the car wash. Female cashiers were smartly dressed (above right) and in this 1972 advertisement (below right), Shell graciously described their role as that of a 'hostess', suggesting hopefully that being a Shell hostess could be the 'most pleasant job for a young woman'.

[62]

[63]

identification of the exact source of profit.'[123] At a time when the profits in the upstream business were under threat, it was all the more important that the downstream business would be profitable in its own right.

For consumers, not quite realizing the amount of tax embedded in the price of gasoline, it seemed an obvious conclusion that the oil companies were making huge profits as a consequence of the OPEC price rises. In fact, the high gasoline tax of European countries formed one of the arguments of the OPEC countries to increase their share in the high gasoline price the European consumers were apparently prepared to pay. The chairman of BP described the oil company as 'a tax collecting agency' for both producer and consumer governments.[124] This is not to deny that the oil majors made huge profits in 1973 – they certainly did – but mostly because they could sell old stocks for higher prices. However, these windfall profits would not last long. Quite the contrary, huge investment would be needed to ensure access to oil in the future. To get this message across in the chaotic period of late 1973 – early 1974, Shell stopped its traditional advertising, and focused on explaining how the world oil situation affected gasoline prices. Consumer governments did their bit to help the consumers by implementing price controls.[125] One of the interesting features of the Shell Group was that there was not one central marketing

[64]

organization, but that the local companies in the various countries were responsible for their own marketing, supported by but not subordinate to the central service organizations. This decentralization was seen as one of the strengths of the Shell Group, but it made the implementation of a joint strategy undeniably more complicated.

The Shell Group worked in several ways to achieve higher efficiency in its marketing operations. Distribution centres were made more efficient through computer technology. Smaller and less efficient retail outlets were closed and more attention was given to larger gasoline stations. The most important retail innovation in the 1970s in Europe and North America was self-service filling stations, a development that was stepped up after the first oil shock. Shell companies thought they had established a lead in the introduction of self-service stations, but they were aware that competitors would follow suit rapidly.[126] Some customers,

however, preferred the personal touch, and in some of Shell's UK forecourts, for instance, the option of personal service remained in place or was even reinstated. In low-wage countries self-service stations were not an issue. In Malaysia personal attention functioned as a selling point. Further efficiency was created through the introduction of credit card payments. In this respect the US was ahead of Europe. While in the US a credit card system was already popular in the mid-1970s, Europe followed cautiously in the 1980s. The promotion of self-service stations tended to have a negative effect on the sale of luboil. Therefore new actions were needed to keep sales up. One of those actions was the creation of quick oil drain units at the service stations, and another was the High Street marketing of luboil.[127]

The regular visits of motorists to service stations made these places ideal locations for additional business. For that reason, local entrepreneurship was encouraged to broaden the income base.

[65]

Self-service stations were also introduced in France and Germany. The service station in Bremen offered an oil change in 4 minutes.

[66]

Most of the motor retail outlets were franchise operations, with Shell as franchiser granting the right to the reseller to display, advertise, and sell Shell products. Depending on the closeness of the business relationship, Shell also provided marketing strategy, advertising support, site operating manuals, and product/service quality control.[128] The franchise structure made it easy to include local activities adjusted to specific local needs. In the early days of motorcars the sale of motor fuels took place at existing drug stores or groceries as additional business. In the 1970s the opposite trend took place, as new businesses were added to the service stations, which first had developed as stand-alone ventures. Initially car-related products and services, like tyres, luboil, batteries and car washes were offered, but soon local ingenuity helped in shaping additional business at forecourts. In 1973 South Africa and Finland experimented with restaurants in collaboration with third parties, while Shell customers in France could cater for their holiday needs.[129] Shell companies sponsored the growth of the 'aftermarket', even though they often only indirectly profited from the sales through more fuel trade. In 1983 Shell marketing made a study of the Shell shops on the basis of the experiences of Dansk Shell, Deutsche Shell, and Norske Shell. The non-auto-related products on sale consisted mostly of items the consumer might pick up on impulse. These included paper products, sweets, drinks, tobacco and toys, but not yet groceries.[130]

The strategy of the refineries to 'whiten the barrel' implied that Shell marketing companies focused their efforts on the lighter oil products, which were also the products with higher margins, such as gasoline for cars, fuel for aircraft, and feedstock for the chemical industry. In 1978 Shell calculated that in the free world outside North America its companies had a joint market share in gasoline of around 17 per cent. In the much more fragmented market of the US Shell Oil had a share of 8 per cent, which gave it a leading position. In the attractive market of aviation fuel for civil transport Shell had a share of 20 per cent. Less attention was given to products and markets that provided little or no added value, and where other energies were likely to displace oil for reasons of either security or economy. Basically, this meant a move away from fuel oil to gasoline. However, it remained essential to find markets for the whole range of products leaving the refineries.[131] Measured in barrels of oil, the sales of oil products of Shell went down after 1973, as shown in Figure 1.7.[132] The same was true for Exxon. Shell halted the decline in the early 1980s and even crept ahead of Exxon. The sales of BP had been considerably lower than those of Shell and Exxon before 1973, but BP kept up its sales much better than its main competitors.

In an organization with an entrepreneurial spirit, each obstacle also offers an opportunity. In the face of high oil prices,

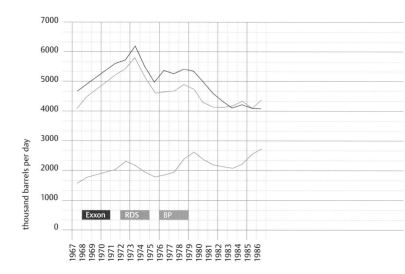

Figure 1.7
Oil products sales of Shell, Exxon, and BP.

[67]

Shell people therefore decided to set up services to help consumers save energy, for instance by insulating their homes. This was not only considered good public relations but was also expected to be profitable. In 1974 France and the Netherlands were the first to provide householders with an insulation service. Industrial consumers formed another group in urgent need of energy conservation. Here Shell Marketing UK studied the possibility of setting up consultancy services. These initiatives helped underpin the Shell image as caring about the efficient use of fuel.[133]

In motor gasolines the challenge for the industry in the 1970s was finding ways of reducing the lead content in gasoline. In the 1920s the industry had discovered that additions of lead led to higher octane gasolines. Those gasolines reduced the knocking noise in the engine and permitted higher compression ratios for improved performance, including faster driving. The motorist loved faster cars and lead became an essential part in the gasoline, until the environmentalists raised concerns about the quality of air and the polluting effect of cars. Legislation in many countries began to demand the reduction of lead in motor gasolines. All through the

[68]

In response to the oil crisis Shell encouraged consumers to save energy. In this Dutch series of advertisements, consumers were told that energy saving meant 'not driving too fast', 'insulating your house properly' and 'turning off the radio if you aren't listening'.

1970s Shell research concentrated on finding ways of reducing levels of lead while keeping driving performance up. Shell Oil had introduced in the US a non-leaded gasoline 'Shell of the Future' as early as 1970. But the consumers did not like it, because the octane level was so low that it negatively affected driving performance. By way of compromise Shell Oil returned to lead, but less of it than before. In the meantime research continued, and in 1974 Shell reintroduced unleaded gasoline alongside its regular and premium leaded grades.[134] US regulation demanded a significant reduction in lead levels for leaded oil from 1974, while industry also introduced unleaded fuel, which by 1986 accounted for 80 per cent of total US gasoline sales. In Europe measures moved slower than in the US. The EC required the introduction of unleaded gasoline in all member states by 1989, while at the same time the maximum lead content was reduced. Consumers were given the choice between leaded and unleaded gasoline to demonstrate their own commitment to the environment. By 1988 nearly 60 per cent of total gasoline sales outside the Communist world were unleaded.[135]

After 1979 and the second oil shock, which increased crude oil prices even further, attention to alternative forms of energy for transport was stepped up. Shell companies were involved with two developments, LPG and sugar alcohol. LPG (liquefied petroleum gas) was a well-known source for heating and cooking (for instance butagas), but as an energy source for road transport it still had a long way to go. On the plus side this fuel had a high octane quality and burned with low exhaust fumes. Therefore it was environmentally more acceptable. The downside was that it needed a new infrastructure and therefore heavy investment in service stations. The high volatility of this source of energy required special (and expensive) handling, storage and transport facilities. In 1979 a considerable growth in automotive LPG was expected, from 1 to 4 per cent of total automotive fuels between 1978 and 2000.[136]

[69]

In order to publicize unleaded petrol, Shell's 'unleaded grand tour' visited service stations around the borders of Wales, including its Dunraven station at Bridgend (left).

It did make some progress in public transport, but otherwise growth was slower than forecast. The most successful experiments with alcohol from sugar as alternative source of energy for cars took place in sugar-producing Brazil. Since the 1930s Brazil had experimented with blends of ethanol from sugar and gasoline, in particular in times when prices for sugar were low. The high oil prices in the 1970s provided another stimulant to use more ethanol. The Brazilian government launched a major National Alcohol Programme 'Proalcool', which required all motor fuels to be alcohol-based. Shell responded by introducing a fuel with 20 per cent alcohol added to the gasoline and one with alcohol only. In the use of alcohol the challenge was to improve drivability of fuels with higher concentration of alcohol. With blends it was important to prevent water from entering the system of storage and distribution, because water could cause the blended alcohol and gasoline to separate.[137]

During the 1970s the long collaboration between Shell and BP in some of their marketing came to an end. Shell wanted to push its own brand without supporting the BP brand at the same time.

Moreover, it seemed that in the UK the agreement had become illegal under the fair trade legislation. Rather than changing the agreement, Shell preferred to end it. Negotiations about separation of the distribution function of Shell-Mex & BP in the UK started in 1971 and led to the establishment in 1975 of two separate Shell and BP marketing entities.[138] In fact, Shell had suggested the split up as early as 1966, but BP had not welcomed the idea. BP used the ensuing negotiations to end the collaboration in other areas, such as in South Africa, via the Consolidated Petroleum Company, another market-sharing agreement of 1928. The collaboration in South Africa was ended in 1975, while the joint marketing organizations in many other former European colonies were ended through nationalizations by the independent governments.[139] Though Shell could proudly point to a marketing presence in more than a hundred countries, in 1985 the downstream sector outside North America was still dominated by north-western Europe both in investment and in sales of oil products.[140]

The government of sugar-rich Brazil promoted motor fuels based on hydrated ethanol derived from cane sugar. The process is shown diagramatically (below), and in September 1979 Shell Brazil introduced such a fuel alongside its more usual fuels (right).

Sugar cane can be used to produce sugar and molasses, but also to manufacture ethanol via a process of fermentation followed by distillation.

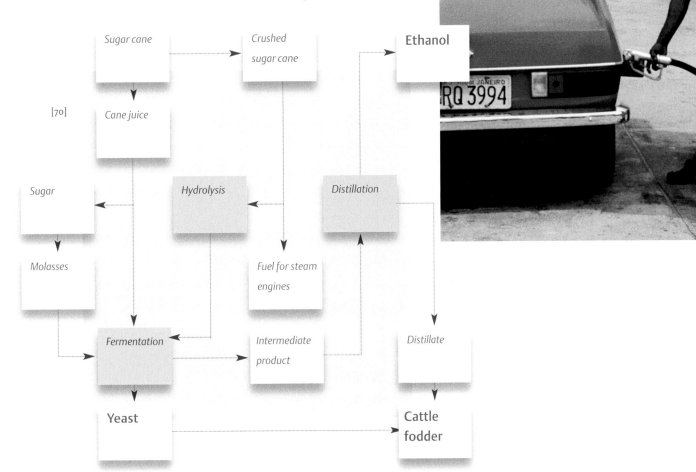

[71]

Production of ethanol from sugar cane

Sugar cane	Crushed sugar cane	**Ethanol**
Cane juice		
Sugar	Hydrolysis	Distillation
Molasses	Fuel for steam engines	
Fermentation	Intermediate product	Distillate
Yeast		**Cattle fodder**

[70]

The marketing of Shell gasoline was based in local marketing companies, because local people were supposed to have the best insights into their own markets. However, being part of a large international organization could be of great advantage in promoting gasoline, and this can be illustrated by the hugely successful 'Come to Shell for Answers' campaign. This campaign was devised by Shell Oil for the US market in 1976 in response to the negative image of the oil industry after the huge rise in oil prices. As the company magazine stated: 'We need all the goodwill we can get, especially at a time when many congressmen are talking about breaking up oil companies.'[1] The campaign did not promote the use of Shell gasoline directly, but invited the public to come to Shell for answers about their automobiles. In little yellow booklets the motorist received tips about car maintenance, the costs of repairs, energy saving, safe driving or first aid on the road. The booklets were included in popular consumer magazines such as *Time, Newsweek,* or *Reader's Digest.* The campaign was backed up by advertisements and TV commercials. More than one billion booklets were printed from 1976 to 1982.[2]

When the campaign in the US became a huge success, many other Shell marketing companies decided to follow the example of Shell Oil, but they adjusted it to their own local markets. Starting in 1977, Shell Nederland Verkoop launched a similar series of booklets under the title 'Shell helpt'. By and large the subjects covered were the same, but the illustrations were different from the US version. In the Netherlands the booklets were distributed via the Dutch postal service to every householder in the country.[3] As a consequence 'Shell helpt' became a familiar slogan (with both positive and negative connotations). In Germany and Austria the motto read 'Wir helfen Ihnen weiter', in France 'Bons conseils', and in Sweden 'Kom till Shell för goda rad'. More countries, including Portugal and Greece, introduced their variations to this theme. As consumers continued to want answers, Shell Oil reintroduced the Come to Shell for Answers campaign in 1990.[4]

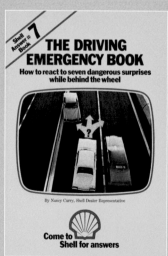

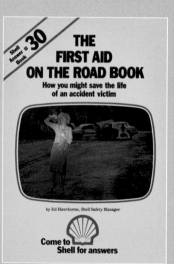

Shell Answer Book #24
THE MORE MILES FOR YOUR MONEY BOOK
How you could cut your gasoline cost by $300 a year - or more.

By Larry Olejnik, Shell Research Scientist

Come to Shell for answers

Shell Answer Book #21
THE DRIVING HAZARDS BOOK
How to open your eyes to potential accidents before they become real

...nnell, Shell Driving Safety Instructor

Come to Shell for answers

SHELL HELPT

...RSONGEVALLEN
...EN OM ZE TE VOORKOMEN?
...ndstofbespaarders?
...er of Normaal?
...erhoud bespaart ook.

...PER AUTORIJDEN
...SPARENDE WONDERMIDDELEN EN WAT ÈCHT HELPT.

Shell helpt
deel 9

Samengesteld in overleg met A.N.W.B., BOVAG en Veilig Verkeer Nederland.

54-RF-39

Hoe uw auto dank zij af en toe een uurtje werk langer meegaat.

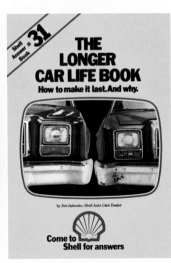

Shell Answer Book #31
THE LONGER CAR LIFE BOOK
How to make it last. And why.

by Jim Jaakoske, Shell Auto Care Dealer

Come to Shell for answers

Shell helpt
deel 10

Samengesteld in overleg met A.N.W.B., BOVAG, Veilig Verkeer Nederland en de Algemene Verkeersdienst Rijkspolitie.

De onbekende gevaren van rijden bij slecht weer.

Shell Answer Book #11
THE FOUL WEATHER DRIVING BOOK
Safety tips you should know when driving in rain, fog and snow

By Bruce Galbraith, Shell Plant Superintendent.

Come to Shell for answers

Shell Oil in the US: acquire and be acquired   Roughly a third of the business of the Shell Group took place in the US and for the most part was looked after by Shell Oil Company. The Dutch holding company Shell Petroleum NV owned 69 per cent of the shares of Shell Oil. Since the Second World War, Shell Oil had developed fairly independently, partly because it was an integrated oil company in its own right, which was exceptional in the Shell Group, and partly as a consequence of the Group's general policy of decentralization, in which the final decisions were made in the operating companies. European companies in general were inclined to give their American affiliates more leeway to act on their own. They considered the American market unique, were impressed by American management techniques and apprehensive of the different legal environment in the US.[141] Nevertheless, the Group and Shell Oil had moved closer together during the 1960s, with many exchanges of staff and trainees as well as research and know-how.[142]

The free flow of people and information became more difficult after minority shareholders launched a suit in 1969, claiming that Shell Oil had been forced to buy Group oil at too high prices, a claim that could not be substantiated. In another claim the Group was blamed for preventing Shell Oil from developing foreign activities of its own to be able to compete on equal footing with its main US competitors. The suit rambled on for years and was finally settled without admission of liability and with approval of Shell Oil stockholders and of the Courts in 1981.[143] For American managers lawsuits were a fact of life and they were not unduly troubled by them. European managers, however, preferred to avoid them. The Group took painstaking care not to seem to influence the management of Shell Oil. The relations between Shell Oil and the Group were covered by a general agreement and a research agreement, which made it possible to exchange research and balance differences with payments.[144] Symbolic of the fact that Shell Oil had a special position within the Group was the fact that Shell Oil used its own variety of the Shell pecten. When the Group moved to a new modern design in 1971, Shell Oil did not follow until 1976, and even then it adopted a slightly different, less abstract design. Normally the Shell Group was very strict in the way its pecten was used.

When the oil production in the US had reached its peak and the country had to rely more and more on imported oil, Shell Oil insisted on starting foreign activities of its own. In 1972 the Board of Shell Oil discussed the option of acquiring exploration rights owned by the Shell Group in the West African countries of Gabon, Senegal, and Gambia. Gerrit Wagner, chairman of the CMD and Chairman of the Board of Shell Oil pointed out for the minutes that Shell Oil could indeed start operations outside the US, even though it might become a competitor of other companies of the Shell Group already working in those countries. That should not in any way restrict Shell Oil in its decisions, which should continue to be made on an independent basis. His personal view, however, was that Shell Oil could best acquire developed oil reserves or supplies rather than 'incur the risks and headaches of exploration in unfamiliar undeveloped areas'.[145] Obviously, the Group was not happy with the situation that its affiliates could be competing with each other in some countries, but it was the inevitable result of the necessary arm's length control. In some cases, as for instance Sabah (North Borneo), Shell Oil had another affiliate of the Shell Group as partner. By 1980 Shell Oil had forty-two international ventures under the name 'Pecten' and in six countries, Syria, Tunisia, Paraguay, the Philippines, Brazil, and Cameroon, it acted as operator. By and large these international activities were not very

Together with Lockheed Petroleum Services, Shell Oil developed sub-sea systems (diagram, below right) to allow oil-field technicians to reach the ocean floor in a diving bell (below left) and then work comfortably in their shirt-sleeves, without the need for diving suits.

[73]

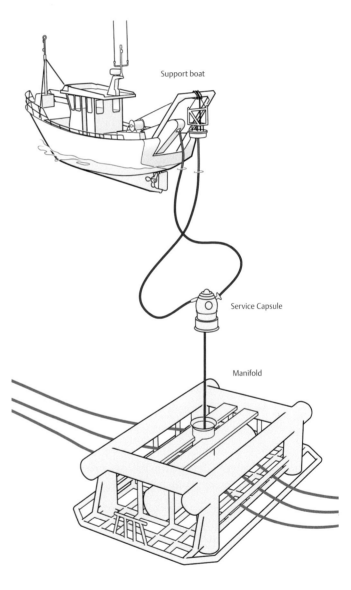

Support boat

Service Capsule

Manifold

[74]

[75]

successful. The best opportunities had long gone, and the rising tide of nationalism mixed with negative feelings towards American politics abroad did not help either.[146] On the other hand, the US still offered interesting possibilities for companies with the right expertise, and Shell Oil had built up considerable expertise in geophysics, offshore development, and secondary recovery.

In the Gulf of Mexico Shell Oil was among the leading producers, as has been discussed in Volume 2. Here exploration and production moved from 'offshore' to 'deep water'. Though depth is relative, the platform Shell Oil built for the Cognac field reached a depth of 1,040 feet, twice as much as the depth of the previous platform. It marked the start of the deepwater production. The steel platform of 1,265 feet was the tallest ever built anywhere in the world up till that time. With the Cognac platform, Shell Oil won the Offshore Technology Conference Award in 1982 for 50 years of innovation in equipment. Together with Lockheed Petroleum

Services Shell Oil also worked on sub-sea systems, which allowed oil-field technicians to reach the ocean floor in a diving bell and then work in their shirt sleeves (instead of diving gear) in the wellhead chamber that was covered over and sealed with the diving bell. Though this system was expensive, it offered possibilities to reach deeper water or produce from fields too small to deserve a complete deepwater platform.[147]

The high price of oil encouraged the industry to get more oil out of existing fields, because it was estimated that in the US on average only 34 per cent of the oil was tapped. The remaining 66 per cent was still in the ground. One of the secondary recovery projects of Shell Oil was Signal Hill in Los Angeles, where during the peak time in 1923 nearly 300 drilling rigs were working at once, producing 250,000 barrels of oil per day. By 1970 production had dwindled to less than 9,000 barrels per day, while the number of wells was still above 200. In preparation of secondary recovery the

With effect from 10 December 1979 Shell Oil acquired the Belridge Oil Company in California for $3.6 billion – the biggest corporate acquisition the world had seen to that date. Shell's enhanced recovery techniques, including steam injection, enabled the 'nodding donkey' pumps to increase production by 26 per cent inside a year, and later to more than double their production.

217 acres of Signal Hill were unified with parties sharing development cost and production units and Shell Oil becoming the operator. The many old and small production and storage facilities were replaced by modern equipment in three central locations. The number of wells was reduced significantly. Only 73 wells remained producing and 53 wells were being used for the injection of water to help the oil move to the surface.[148] In the mid-1970s Shell Oil began to experiment with the next step: tertiary recovery. John Bookout, vice president and later CEO of Shell Oil, explained in 1975 the advantages: 'In the Little Creek Field in Mississippi, for example, we recovered about 25 per cent of the oil in place by primary means. Then, in 1962 we installed a water-injection operation and recovered an additional 20 per cent. Now we have a carbon dioxide injection experiment underway which shows some encouraging results and, if successful, we might recover another 25 per cent – which adds up to about 70 per cent of the oil in place.'[149]

Its leading position in secondary recovery techniques encouraged Shell Oil to bid for the Belridge Oil Company in California in 1979, when it was put up for sale. With oil prices at a record high, the interest of the oil industry in acquiring this company was large, all the more so as President Carter had announced that he would decontrol the price of heavy crude, and exempt such production from his proposed 'windfall profit tax'. Most of the crude oil of Belridge Oil was of the heavy variety. Mobil and Texaco together already owned 35 per cent of Belridge Oil, and were not eager to sell their share. However, the majority owners decided that they wanted a bid for the company as a whole. Industry experts expected the price tag to be in the range of $2 billion or more. Mobil and Texaco jointly bid $1.8 billion for Belridge Oil, but Shell Oil, eager for its bid to go ahead, offered twice as much, an astonishing $3.6 billion. The sum involved made it the largest commercial acquisition up till then. The acquisition added 44 per cent to Shell Oil's domestic crude oil reserves and increased its daily domestic crude oil production by 10 per cent. Shell was prepared to bid as high as it did because it had confidence in its ability to increase production through thermal recovery. This process consisted of heating the crude oil through the injection of steam into nearby wells. The heat made the oil less viscous so that it could be pumped to the surface. Not only was the recovery process expensive, the resulting heavy oil needed more extensive refining than the light variety. As a consequence, this was expensive crude oil. Under the conditions of scarcity of supply and high oil prices in 1979 this purchase nonetheless seemed to make perfect business sense.[150] The acquisition of Belridge Oil drew the attention of the press to the recent successes of the Shell Group. The magazine *Forbes* wrote an article about the Group in November 1980 with a portrait of the directors of Royal Dutch dressed in seventeenth century Dutch costumes on the cover, and posing the leading question: 'Can they overtake Exxon? In revenues, Royal Dutch/Shell is number two in the international game. But this former Cinderella of the Seven Sisters looks like it may soon be the most profitable of them all.'[151]

The relation between Shell Oil and the Group came under renewed scrutiny when the Group decided to invest in coal mining in the US independently of Shell Oil, which had its own interests in coal. Shell's Legal Director, John Hinde, explained that the study of the relation between Shell Oil and the Shell Group would always fall under two headings, the anti-trust laws and the corporate laws protecting the rights of minority shareholders. These two branches of law tended to pull in opposite directions and suggested opposite procedures and disciplines. The corporate law, defending the position of minority shareholders, required that Shell Oil should be independently managed with the Group management keeping at arm's length. Also, the Group or its operating companies (subsidiaries) should not damage Shell Oil's existing business. The anti-trust laws, however, allowed fully owned subsidiaries to work closely together, but expected two independent companies to compete vigorously. How could one compete vigorously with another company and not damage its business interests? In practice Shell always tried to find a middle way between the two sets of laws, and act according to which law in a certain situation was the more relevant.[152] The situation was obviously not ideal, and in 1982 the Group began to think about possibilities of buying out the minority shareholders. It decided not to move as yet because of the uncertain times. However in the Conference the view was in favour of such a move 'recognising that tangible cash flow considerations would never be exceptionally attractive, but that the intangible advantages relating to the Group's freedom of activity in the US – and the protection of our long-term controlling equity – should be considered as of great strategic value'.[153]

On 24 January 1984 Shell Petroleum NV announced its intention to buy the approximately 30 per cent shares of Shell Oil Company not yet owned at a price of $55 per share, or an aggregate price of approximately $5.2 billion. The share price on the New York Stock Exchange moved the day before from $43.50 to $45. The offer of $55 per share was based on the advice of the investment bankers Morgan Stanley & Co, Inc, who considered a price of $53 fair to the minority shareholders. Sir Peter Baxendell, chairman of the CMD, explained the decision at a meeting of the board of Shell Oil two days later. He told the board that the situation was unusual. There were major takeovers of one company by another attempting to acquire control and assets, and there were cases of majorities buying out minorities in order to change the course of a business, make management changes or generally improve, in their eyes, company performance. 'Our offer', explained Baxendell, 'corresponds to neither case. We greatly admire and have the highest respect for the performance, directors, management and staff of this company and have no wish to interfere with current on-going business or the company's apparent direction.'[154] He gave two reasons for the merger proposal. One was the growing importance of the US in all the sectors in which Shell companies were active. The second reason was the possibility of a better integration without the inhibitions arising out of the existence of a minority interest. There would be no changes in the company's management or staff. In accordance with the usual policy, Shell Oil would continue to function as an autonomous unit in the Shell Group of Companies.[155]

Baxendell could promise the management of Shell Oil a great deal of independence because that was the general policy of the Group in any case, and he fully supported that view. 'The top jobs in Shell are, in many cases, with the operating companies and not at central offices,' he mentioned in 1982. After a career in the upstream part of the business, which started in 1946 in Egypt and then brought him to Venezuela, Nigeria and London, he himself had been managing director of Shell Nigeria and Shell UK before becoming Group managing director in 1973, so knew the weight of those jobs from his own experience. He recalled being a 'reluctant repatriate'. It took him a year or two to adjust to life back in the central office in London. He particularly enjoyed the multinational character of the Group. 'It's the thing that makes us different. It picks up the best of the various characteristics, and yet there is a mildly competitive spirit'.[156]

The takeover of Shell Oil fitted in the wave of oil mergers in the US during the early 1980s. The consolidation followed the deregulation in 1981, which lifted protection and increased competition among the majors just at a time that oil demand was dropping. The merger mania started with the colourful T. Boone Pickens, chairman of Mesa Petroleum, buying up stock of Gulf Oil, because he considered the company undervalued. But Gulf management had no wish to be taken over and put up a fight. In the ensuing battle, Gulf management did not succeed in keeping its independence, but it did raise the interest of Chevron and Arco. The battle ended with Chevron taking over Gulf Oil, while Mesa made a fine profit on its Gulf shares. With the takeover of Gulf Oil one of the 'Seven Sisters' disappeared. In the meantime Texaco took over Getty Oil. Mobil bought Superior and BP acquired the 47 per cent of Sohio it did not own. Exxon remained aloof from the merger wave.[157]

In the fighting mood of the moment, the minority shareholders of Shell Oil considered the offer of the Group too low. A committee of outside non-executive directors of Shell Oil hired the investment banker Goldman Sachs, which advised a share price of $80-85. The differences in value estimates reflected different views on the value of proven reserves, the capability to increase reserves and the development of the future oil price. In April 1984 Shell Petroleum came up with a tender offer of $58, three dollars more than the original offer. The minority shareholders, including many Shell executives, were not impressed with this slight rise, and thought it insufficiently reflected the embedded value of their skills and capabilities. The company raider T. Boone Pickens, who was one of the shareholders of Shell Oil succinctly described his view: '$58 is a rotten price. I'm getting screwed.'[158] But his company Mesa Petroleum was heavily exposed through a very expensive exploration programme in the Gulf of Mexico, and he needed cash badly.[159] Nevertheless, many shares were offered and by the end of May 1984 Shell Petroleum possessed 94.7 per cent of the shares in Shell Oil, enough to push ahead with the merger. Various class actions delayed the merger, but in the spring of 1985, the counsel for the largest group of the plaintiffs approached Shell Petroleum for settlement discussions. Greatly helped by the lowering of the oil prices both parties succeeded in reaching an early compromise in which Shell Petroleum paid a further $2 per share. The settlement had to be approved by the court, which described it as 'intrinsically fair and reasonable'.[160] In the light of the 1986 oil price collapse, which will be discussed later, it was probably more than fair. After Shell Oil had been fully acquired by the Group, its autonomy within the Group was kept in place. Shell Oil's management remained accountable to its own Board on which the President of Royal Dutch and the Chairman of Shell Transport continued to serve. The central offices in London and The Hague did not become responsible for reviewing or supporting Shell Oil's budgets and plans, as happened with other subsidiaries.[161]

Conclusion

The Oil Shock of 1973 formed a watershed in the history of the major international oil companies. In two steps their role in the international oil market was transformed. From the First World War till the late 1960s, the oil majors had been seen as fully integrated multinational companies. Though the reality fell somewhat short of this ideal, the integration of their various activities formed part of their competitive strength. The participations and nationalizations of the early 1970s greatly reduced this integration. National companies were nibbling away at their access to oil as well as their access to consumer markets. The 'Seven Sisters' became privileged buyers of OPEC crude, taking large quantities at a slight discount. In the Second Oil Shock they even lost their position as privileged buyers and instead became one of the many parties seeking oil on the international market. By the end of the decade, they saw themselves as suppliers of exploration services and production technology, management consulting, transportation, refining, and marketing.

Under pressure from the governments of oil-producing countries, the oil companies lost most of their control over the crude oil. Why did the oil companies not fight harder to hang on to the ownership of crude oil and why did their national governments not give them more support? The oil companies probably felt vulnerable because they were under heavy public scrutiny as representatives of much disputed multinational companies as well as the 'dirty' oil business. The former concession contracts had been part of a colonial world that was now gone. It therefore seemed inevitable that the old contracts were adjusted to the new relationships between independent national governments and the western oil companies, and the managers of the oil companies realistically adapted their behaviour to the new relations. The US government might have had the military power to intervene, but its difficulties in winning the war in Vietnam made them reluctant to deploy force. Quite the contrary, as it felt an urgent need to increase oil imports, the US government put pressure on its oil companies to go along with the new demands of the oil-producing governments.

It is striking that the major oil companies with their long-term investment in capital intensive production were able to adjust so flexibly and so rapidly to the major changes in their industry. This is even more remarkable when one realizes that the oil majors were not only coping with changes in the structure of the oil business. They also faced stagnating oil production and consumption between 1973 and 1986, while they had been counting on a continuation in growth and had invested accordingly. In the process Shell, Exxon, and BP all saw their share in crude oil reduced considerably. In their efforts to remain involved in the upstream business, they explored and produced oil in more inhospitable environments such as the unruly North Sea and icy Alaska. In the 1980s Shell succeeded in closing the gap with Exxon in oil production. Despite heavy investment in new areas, the big three faced a reduction in all their activities. Their oil production went down, the throughput in their refineries went down and their tanker fleet, both owned and chartered, diminished in numbers as well as tonnage. In the sales of oil products Shell countered the physical decline by focusing on oil products that offered higher value. However, the situation for the oil companies was certainly not bleak in every respect. Thanks to the spectacular increase in crude oil prices, the industry had nothing to complain about in its profitability. Shell remained an important player in the oil industry and succeeded in getting closer to its rival Exxon.

Mixed results of the diversification strategy, 1973-1998

During the 1960s oil prices were low and the governments of oil exporting-countries were pressing for increases in taxes and royalties as well as larger participations in existing oil concessions. Though the Group had no intention of abandoning its core business, it began to look for new areas to continue its expansion course. Could strengths built up in the oil industry be transferred to other sectors, making Shell a more diversified enterprise? The Group was able to offer huge investments with a long lead-time and had experience in solving complex coordination problems. Shell had first diversified its activities in 1927, when it entered the chemical industry, and this had been embraced as a promising new direction, because the chemical industry belonged to the growth sectors of the post-war period. With such a positive example Shell managers felt confident in their ability to engage in new business areas, when the oil industry seemed to reach maturity. In the early 1970s, Shell entered the metals business, and the businesses of nuclear energy and coal. None of these three ventures were a lasting success. The chemical sector, as Shell's oldest diversification, followed a diversification policy in its own right and found this course equally hard going. This chapter will highlight how Shell came to choose its new activities, how it proceeded on an expansion course and why all these ventures brought mixed results at best.

[2]

New ventures and diversification   The rapid economic growth of the 1950s and 1960s had created a feeling among business people that expansion of their companies was self-evident and could be strengthened by careful long-term planning. Futurists would be able to predict the future by imaginative analysis of existing trends. It was the task of professional managers to study the future and use the results as a basis for the company's long-term strategies.[1] Such a strategy would include an analysis of the company's strengths and weaknesses, plus a long-term analysis of its markets, both actual and potential.[2] At the same time the systematic study of the art of managing created the feeling that trained managers would be able to manage every kind of company once they had learned the principles of management.[3] Any degree of diversification of the company was possible if corporate-level managers had the requisite general management skills. As the grass on the other side is always greener, many managers had the feeling that their own line of business was stagnating and that they should move into new areas. The key words of this period were 'new ventures', 'diversification', and 'conglomerates'.

A study of the rise and fall of corporate new venture divisions (NVD) in the US estimated that about 30 of the 100 largest industrial companies in the US used such a division to facilitate new business development in the late 1960s: 'The NVD concept gained popularity almost to the point of becoming a fad', the study concluded.[4] Although the wish to diversify out of what was considered to be a mature industry was the most important motivation for setting up new venture divisions, many managers were also convinced that the large companies in which they worked resisted change and did not know how to turn new research into new business opportunities, despite their large R&D departments. By setting up small new business departments they hoped to

recreate the innovative atmosphere of the small company. A surplus of projected cash-flow and the presence of entrepreneurial managers formed additional factors in explaining the establishment of new venture divisions. However, many of these divisions were short-lived, and by the mid-1970s most of them had either grown and become normal business units, or had disappeared.[5]

Views on the best company strategies at a certain moment in time were very much shared within the industry and in business life generally. Financial journals, trade periodicals, and management literature all contributed to the dissemination of ideas. Large enterprises such as the Royal Dutch/Shell Group and the other oil majors helped spread the ideas and were themselves influenced by them. Shell was among the large industrial companies to set up a new business venture division in 1968. In a very long-term study 'Year 2000' Shell tried to find an answer to the question: 'Is there life after oil?' The oil industry would at some point reach its peak, and very likely had already reached the stage of maturity. The conclusion was that diversification would be useful.[6] Exxon established Jersey Enterprises Inc. (later to be called Exxon Enterprises) to create new businesses and pursue new ventures outside the company in 1965, a few years before Shell.[7] BP created a New Ventures Department in 1974, a few years after Shell. Companies could diversify their activities through product

Group managing director Karel Swart championed the diversification of activities. In late 1974 he visited Shell Coal's operations in Botswana, after the country had granted Shell a seven-year prospecting licence to search for coal, oil shale and radioactive minerals.

[3]

development, for instance on the basis of their own research results, or through mergers and acquisitions. The latter was often the preferred route, because it provided quick entry into a new market and the acquired firm possessed the necessary know-how. However, for companies with important R&D facilities, the research route looked equally attractive, but it required a closer alliance between their research departments and other parts of the companies.

In making decisions about resource allocation, managers found help and inspiration in the portfolio analysis made popular by the Boston Consulting Group.[8] This analysis combined the idea of a product life cycle with the cash-flow cycle. Companies should divide their portfolio into activities at the beginning of their product life cycle and in need of cash and those closer to the end of their life cycle and delivering cash. The advantage of conglomerate companies was that they could manage their cash flows in such a way that the money made by mature products could be invested in new, promising products.[9] In 1971 Karel Swart, the Group managing director coordinating the diversification strategy, referred to a 'theory, which I am prepared to follow part of the way'. He briefly outlined the 'game in a growth industry': 'Invest all your money during the early stages of the upswing. Cash flow is strongly negative but on a small base (...) As the S curve shows more

maturity, i.e. growth shows signs of decline, stop being over-aggressive. (...) Now your race-horse, which you have fed heavily, turns into a cow, i.e. you start milking. Not only do you want your cash back from all those years of negative cash flow, you now want more cash for a new game.'[10]

The diversification strategy raised a number of problems. First, the 'portfolio' strategy advised entrepreneurs to spread their risks by combining products in different stages of their product life cycle. However, that did not necessarily mean that these products would react differently in an economic downturn. In fact, the crisis of the late 1970s and early 1980s affected many industry sectors at the same time. In some cases the problems of overcapacity were made worse by the fact that many firms had invested in the same promising new products. Therefore a spread in activities did not diminish exposure as much as managers had expected. Secondly, large organizations were more complicated to manage than small ones, which increased organizational costs. In various markets large enterprises felt the competitive pressure of smaller and more specialized firms. The question was whether the synergy benefits of the combination were large enough to overcome the rise in organizational costs. Also, the bureaucratic management style of large companies was often not very suitable for small businesses. Lastly, the top management of diversified companies could not possibly possess the specific knowledge of their many and varied subsidiaries. They were disadvantaged when they had to assess the value of investment decisions or the future prospects of firms they were taking over. This led frequently to a rude awakening after the acquisition had taken place.[11] As the discussion of Shell's experiences with diversification will show, many of these general problems turned up in one way or another.

The economic crisis of the early 1980s brought many diversified companies into difficulties. Gradually, conglomerates began to reduce the range of their activities. A study of the diversification record of 33 large US companies over the 1950-86 period revealed that most of them had divested many more acquisitions than they had kept. On average corporations divested more than half their acquisitions in new industries and more than 60 per cent of their acquisitions in entirely new fields. The track record in unrelated acquisitions was even worse – the average divestment rate was 74 per cent.[12] The new management slogans of the 1980s were: 'back to the core business', or 'stick to the knitting'. Companies were supposed to concentrate on their core activities, on what they had traditionally been good at.

In its diversification strategy Shell was caught between two contrasting demands. In order to become another 'leg' on which the Group could stand, comparable with oil or chemicals, the new activity had to be large or have the potential to grow rapidly. How large it should be was not quantified. At the same time Shell was looking for new, innovative projects, where its research could play a decisive role. These ventures were necessarily small with uncertain growth prospects. Shell worked on both fronts, but the two approaches developed more or less independently of each other. The wish for innovative projects led to the establishment of 'New ventures' in research. The ambition for large projects was satisfied by acquisitions and joint ventures. The first substantial acquisition involved the Dutch company NV Billiton Maatschappij, taken over in 1970.[13]

In October 1971 the CMD set up a Panel for Non-Traditional Business (NTB) to keep a close watch over the diversification efforts.[14] Two important large-scale new business initiatives were launched between 1971 and 1973: the diversification into the coal business and the entry into nuclear power. After that, no major diversification projects were undertaken, but the NTB panel remained in existence and in 1974 a New Technology Ventures Division (NT) was set up as secretariat for the CMD Panel.[15] In 1974 the managers were still full of new initiatives. For instance, the road haulage business seemed very suitable, because it was the dominant form of transport in the EEC; it was big, profitable, bound to grow and close to Shell's main business. It was waiting for a new organizational concept, the so-called 'conveyer belt' or 'pony express': by integrating the services of four successful medium-sized haulage firms into long-haul activities. Two firms, one in the Netherlands and one in France, were taken over, but one year later road haulage was abandoned.[16] The seeds and animal feed businesses were other areas considered to possess good growth perspectives. These activities were included in the chemicals sector.

The oil crisis had set in motion an avalanche of articles and studies all hailing the hydrogen economy as the solution to mankind's energy problems. Shell's NT division monitored developments in this field. The reason for the enthusiasm was clear. Hydrogen could be produced from omnipresent water, heat from the inexhaustible sun and, as was thought at that time, nuclear sources. It would be used as industrial and domestic fuel, but also in the transport sector. It seemed to promise a versatile, clean and non-polluting gaseous energy source which, together with electricity, could ultimately supply society's future energy needs. Shell's research laboratory in Amsterdam studied the prospects of such a hydrogen economy. Together with other Shell laboratories, it was involved in fundamental research as well as efforts to develop the commercialization of fuel cell technology for transportation applications. In 1977 the NT division concluded that, due to a reduced rate in energy demand and a lack of resources (people, equipment and capital), the transition to a hydrogen economy would not occur for many decades to come. Moreover, the properties of hydrogen were not thought vastly superior to those of alternatives, such as solar energy. This did not discourage Shell from further research on the possibilities of hydrogen, however, because a very important characteristic of fuel cells was their potential high efficiency. One line of investigation was the fuel cell/battery hybrid. But Shell also concluded that the price of gasoline – apart from taxation – should at least double before the fuel cell car could compete with a gasoline one. Indeed, Shell did not decide to set up a business unit to pursue and develop business opportunities related to hydrogen and fuel cells until it established a new business unit, Shell Hydrogen, in 1999. In the meantime, Shell's NT division, in 1978 named the Non-Traditional Business Division (NTB), moved mostly into the field of renewable energy sources, in particular forestry and solar energy.[17]

Diversification and research   Ambitions for new ventures and diversification had their impact on research, because they put pressure on research and development departments to open up new areas that might become viable businesses in due time. Research in Shell had been the first business function to be separated from the operating companies and be centrally organized in 1946. In the 1960s R&D had contributed to a number of new products and processes, but it was difficult to reap the financial rewards for these innovations because markets did not allow higher prices. For that reason, management began to question research expenditures. There was also a stark dip in the number of inventions that were patented (see Figure 2.1).[18] This reduction was mainly caused by the fact that polymer technology reached the stage of maturity. The number of patent applications remained at a lower level during the 1970s and began to increase again after 1980. In the 1990s the Group tended to form joint ventures or outsource research, which led to the decline in the patent applications. Also the Group reduced its diversification, as will be explained further on in this chapter. The sale of agrochemicals in particular contributed to the reduction in patent applications. In the twenty-first century the renewed interest in research and patent protection of the oil and gas business units could not counteract the declining applications from patents in chemicals after 40 per cent of the sector Chemicals had been put up for sale in 1998.

Figure 2.1
Shell's patented inventions.

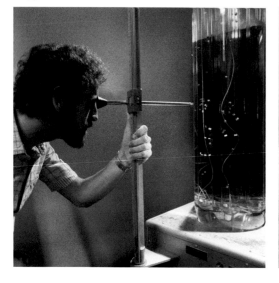

For Shell, research was an important
way of entering new ventures and
keeping ahead of competition.

Measuring the density of polymers in a
density gradient column at the
Polymers Centre in the Shell
Amsterdam research centre (KSLA),
late 1970s.

Research on toxicology of Shell
products in Sittingbourne Research
Centre in Kent, UK, late 1970s.

Cascade trial against the Greenhouse
Whitefly, *trialeurodes vaporariorum*, on
gerbera in Sittingbourne Research
Centre, late 1980s.

In the early 1970s, Shell reorganized its laboratories, reducing the number of locations to increase efficiency and lower costs. The research laboratories of Carrington and Egham in the UK and Delft in the Netherlands were closed, with research and some of the researchers being moved to the laboratories of Thornton and Amsterdam. While the overall research effort was reduced, the research related to the upgrading of products increased. This implied a closer alliance between the laboratories and the businesses. Shell Oil in the US even decided that 'general research' had no value. All research had to be sponsored by one of the operating units. However, the Group as a whole did not follow this way of thinking at that time (though it would reach the same conclusion in the late 1990s).[19] Though the Group kept its general research, the research function and the business sectors became more closely aligned.

Between the mid-1970s till the early 1990s Shell employed around 7,000 people in research in about fifteen laboratories in eight countries. The Netherlands housed the Royal Shell Laboratory at Amsterdam (KSLA), focused on oil and chemical products and processes; the E&P research centre at Rijswijk; and a laboratory in Arnhem for metal research, which formed part of Billiton. In the United Kingdom Shell had a research laboratory at Thornton for fuels, lubricants and product handling and one at Sittingbourne for crop protection, biotechnology, and environmental studies, to name the main fields. Shell Oil in the US had centralized its research for oil and chemicals and processes as well as transportation in the Westhollow Research Centre, Houston, while the Belaire laboratory, also located in Houston, focused on oil and gas exploration and production. More research laboratories existed in Belgium, France, Germany, the US, and Canada. In 1991 Shell opened a research laboratory in Japan, followed in 1995 by a small regional laboratory in Singapore to support the development of oil products adjusted to the special circumstances in this part of the world. The laboratories of Sittingbourne and Arnhem were closed in the mid-1990s following shifts in business interests.[20]

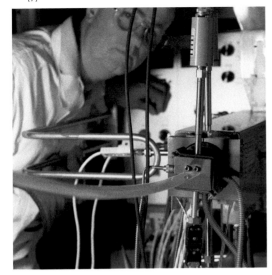

Resins and urethane research with regard to the extrusion of plastic tape (PVC), Shell Amsterdam Research Centre.

Thornton Rotary Cryostat measuring the effects of extreme low temperatures on metals at Thornton Research Centre, UK. This research was important in relation to the LNG technology

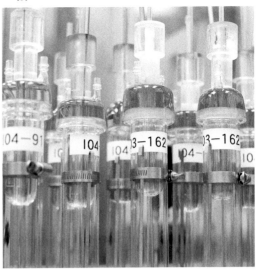

Close-up of oxidation test in Westhollow Technical Centre, Houston, 2004.

Chapter 2

The wish to diversify outside the oil industry had its implications for R&D. A larger part of the budget shifted to non-oil activities during the 1970s, and it came back again in the 1990s when the Group focused its activities. Figure 2.2 shows how the share of oil and gas research in total expenditures decreased from 56 per cent in 1973 to 46 per cent ten years later. In contrast the share of non-oil activities increased over the same period from 4 to 13 per cent. The non-oil activities mainly concerned the diversification into metals and coal. The nuclear research figures were not included because they formed part of a separate joint venture, as will be discussed in the next section. Chemicals remained more or less the same with 32 per cent in 1973 and 35 in 1983. However, in the next ten years, chemical research increased considerably, with non-oil becoming less important and oil and gas remaining at the same level.[21] General research continued at more or less the same level throughout this period.

Figure 2.2
Shell research expenditures, 1973-1993.

General research USA
Non-oil
Chemicals
Oil and gas related

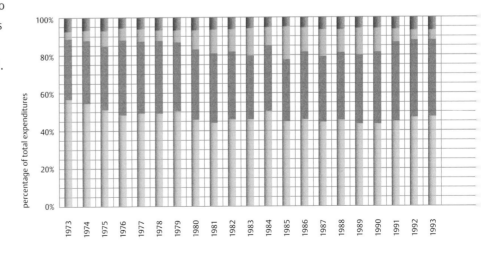

percentage of total expenditures

After 1993 Shell reduced its expenditures on research significantly in response to low oil prices. By 2000 the expenditures were nearly half what they had been ten years earlier. In the general reorganization of the enterprise in the mid-1990s, Shell combined the research and technology to save costs and move closer to the primary user.[22] After 2000 oil- and gas-related research received fresh attention and increasing budgets. The research developments in the twenty-first century will be discussed in chapter 6.

We will now first turn to Shell's main diversification projects, starting with nuclear energy, metals, and coal; then turning briefly to forestry, before ending with the oldest field of diversification, chemicals.

The unsuccessful entry into the nuclear energy business

Just as oil had succeeded coal as the main source of energy in the 1950s, nuclear energy was assumed to overtake oil sometime in the foreseeable future. It was hailed as a plentiful and clean source of energy. The President of the University of Chicago predicted: 'Heat will be so plentiful that it will be used to melt snow as it falls.'[23] Before 1970, electricity demand was doubling worldwide about every ten years and experts anticipated similar growth rates for at least another fifty years. They also expected the rising energy demand to be met by electricity power generated by nuclear reactors. In the 1960s nuclear power seemed to have become economically competitive with other electricity sources. General Electric signed turn-key contracts with utilities for nuclear plants at prices competitive with the cost of coal-fired plants. These contracts underlined the feeling that nuclear power had become commercial. Utilities followed by signing open-ended cost-plus contracts, before the plants ordered earlier were actually producing power.[24] Illustrative of the optimistic mood was the fact that by 1970, while only 4,200 MW of nuclear capacity was actually

The nuclear energy business had three main phases: first, the mining and milling of uranium and thorium ores; second, the chemical conversion and enrichment of uranium (and the processing of thorium) for fabrication into a suitable fuel for a reaction, and the subsequent re-processing and re-fabrication of the spent fuel for further use; third the design, fabrication and engineering of components and plants for the production of nuclear energy.

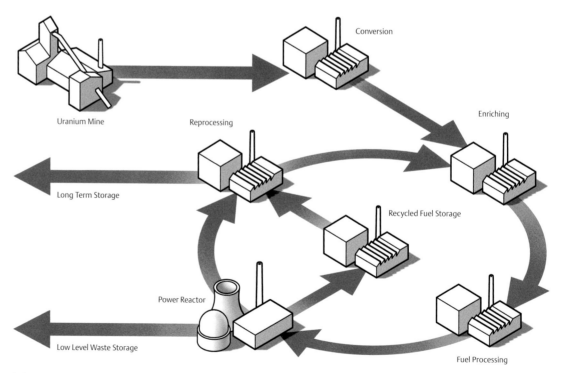

Uranium Mine

Conversion

Enriching

Reprocessing

Long Term Storage

Recycled Fuel Storage

Power Reactor

Low Level Waste Storage

Fuel Processing

operating in the US, nearly twenty times more capacity (72,000 MW) was under construction or on order.[25] Other countries such as Canada, Great Britain, France and Germany developed their own nuclear power programmes, often with different technologies.[26] In 1970, the largest operating plant in the US was only 200 MW in size, but far larger plants of over 1000 MW were already envisioned and ordered. Not only electrical engineering firms like General Electric and Westinghouse were active on this market, but also such oil majors as Exxon and Gulf became involved in the nuclear fuel cycle. Exxon was active in the mining and enrichment of uranium, and Gulf in uranium mining and reactor manufacturing.[27] Was it time for Shell to climb on the bandwagon?

Nuclear energy seemed a very logical new business for Shell. Nevertheless, as we have seen in Volume 2, there were doubts about the attractiveness of this field. Despite the initial conclusion that nuclear energy would not be the right diversification for a private enterprise like Shell, in 1972 discussions began with Gulf Oil Corporation about the possibility of a joint venture in the nuclear energy business; it took shape in 1973. Shell would pay US$190

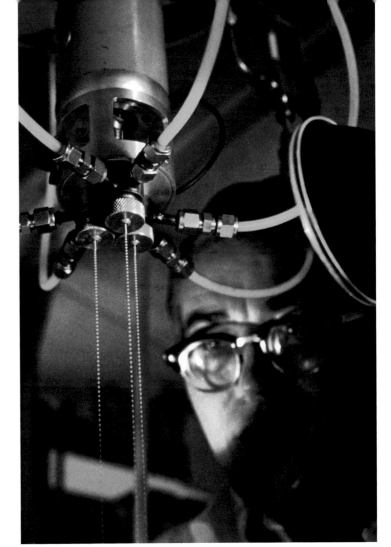

[12]

In 1973 Shell ventured into nuclear power via the General Atomic Company, a joint venture with Gulf Oil Corporation. General Atomic was developing technology for high-temperature gas-cooled reactors (HTGR), nuclear fusion and their peripheral systems. The HTGR was a further development of the gas-cooled reactors using uranium as fuel and helium as coolant. Left: a diagram of the HTGR system developed at Fort St Vrain, Colorado.

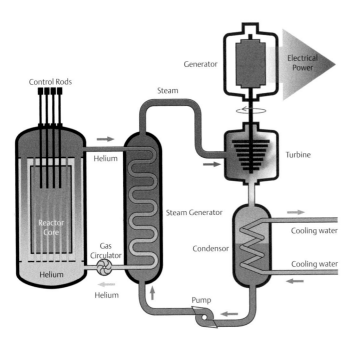

[11]

million for a 50 per cent share in the joint venture to which Gulf Oil would bring its 'Gulf Energy and Environmental Systems' division. This investment would give Shell access to a new type of reactor, the High Temperature Gas-cooled Reactor (HTGR). With its advanced technology this reactor was considered safer than the Light Water Reactor (LWR) that was most frequently used in the US. The first prototype of the HTGR was in the process of being built, and many more reactors were ordered. The joint venture could not hope for exclusivity of the basic patents, because the development was government-funded. Nor would the first prototype, which was being built at Fort St Vrain, Colorado, be competitive with coal-fired power stations at the size of 330 MW, because the minimum competitive size was thought to be about 600 MW. It was hoped that in the beginning profits would come from other activities in the joint venture related to fuel processing. In the middle of the negotiations, in May 1973, the plans for a joint venture had to be announced to forestall any public speculation.

Before the contracts were signed there was a first setback: due to environmental and political pressures two of Gulf's contracted customers, together with quite a number of other utility companies in the USA, postponed their building programmes by two years. As a consequence the production programme of the joint venture would be delayed, but the short-term cash requirements would be lower too. The setback did not end the negotiations, though the signs were not good. The turmoil in the oil business created by OPEC, together with general concerns voiced by the Club of Rome about future energy shortages, seemed to make the diversification into nuclear energy particularly relevant and urgent.[28] However, had Shell waited another year, perhaps it might never have entered this field, because the same oil crisis lowered energy demand drastically.

In November 1973 the new joint venture, with the name General Atomic, could be proudly announced as a great step forward in the history of the Shell Group. In fact, on the request of Shell, there were two joint ventures, General Atomic Company for the US business, and General Atomic International for the international activities. Gulf had contacts with the prospective clients in the UK, Germany, and Japan regarding the HTGR technology. The Shell operating company in the joint venture was Scallop Nuclear Inc. In early 1974 the prospects still looked fine. The Fort St Vrain reactor was intended to go critical at the end of January and full operation was expected in June. As we will see, this information turned out to be vastly optimistic. General Atomic had received ten orders for new reactors. To start with, there were losses, but that had been foreseen, because the first HTGR plants were sold below cost in order to break into the market with this new product. Shell was not entirely confident in the management of General Atomic: it had to transform itself from an R&D company selling concepts into a manufacturing company with a focus on cost control. This required a different type of management, and therefore new, experienced people were brought in. E. J. G. Toxopeüs, who had negotiated the deal with Gulf Oil, relinquished his position as Shell Group Research Co-ordinator to concentrate entirely on the nuclear activities.[29] Despite one setback after the other, he remained optimistic about the ultimate success of nuclear energy and the HTGR technology.

Less than a year after the contracts were signed, however, the joint venture found itself in troubled water. The oil shock had led to higher energy prices, and to a totally unforeseen reduction in energy demand. The utility industry in the US postponed planned growth in capacity. Some utilities even called off their orders with serious consequences for the suppliers, including General Atomic. No fewer than six customers cancelled their orders for HTGR plants

General Atomic Company, California, US, developed an experimental plasma device called Doublet III. The USA Department of Energy and the Japanese Science and Technology Agency cooperated closely on the project, which involved nuclear fusion experiments.

An accident at the Three Mile Island nuclear power plant near Harrisburg, Pennsylvania, nearly led to a meltdown of the plant in 1979. The commotion caused by the accident halted the further development of nuclear energy.

in 1974 and early 1975. To make matters worse, there were delays in the start-up of the Fort St Vrain HTGR plant, and huge overspends in related activities. Shell managers wondered whether Gulf Oil had been misleading them deliberately or whether, to put it more kindly, its joint venture partner had perhaps shown weaknesses in its management of the business. In 1975 the General Atomic partners decided to withdraw from the four remaining contracts with utilities to supply HTGR plants because of technical problems with the start-up of their one prototype at Fort St Vrain. It should

[15]

Candlelight vigil at Three Mile Island nuclear power plant, one year after the accident, to warn about the dangers of nuclear power.

have been operating since 1973, but was still not ready. The decision to cancel the remaining contracts clouded the commercial future of the HTGR technology in the US.[30] Ending the contracts cost money but it also allowed General Atomic to bring down staff numbers and become once again the research operation it had been before. Shell managers raised the question whether technical breakthroughs in this field would not prove to be too costly for private industry to develop. It seemed virtually certain that the world had started nuclear development too soon. General Atomic received funds from the US government to support the research in the HTGR technology, but how long would the support last? General Atomic ordered two studies by two firms of consultants, one dealing with the technical side of the HTGR technology and one with the commercial aspects. They concluded that the basic HTGR concept was sound and had some advantages in safety and environmental respects, but the investments required for the commercialization were so huge that private investors would be unwise to take the lead. Government support would be essential.[31] The construction of the HTGR reactor at Fort St Vrain continued to be dogged with delays and setbacks. The reactor was at last working in 1977, but only at 40 per cent of its design capacity. In 1978 it reached 68 per cent of its design capacity, but then a minor accident caused new delays and instigated further regulations to prevent a recurrence of the accident.[32]

Unfortunately Fort St Vrain was not the only problem area of the joint venture. General Atomic had a 50/50 joint venture with Allied Chemicals in the field of fuel reprocessing. This joint venture, Allied General Nuclear Services (AGNS), was in the process of constructing the largest industrial light-water reactor fuel reprocessing plant in the US, in South Carolina. The capital requirements turned out to be much higher than expected due to inflation and additional safety regulations and environmental protection demands. The construction of the separation facilities and conversion plant went well, but before the plant could start operations, two important issues had to be sorted out: how to manage the disposal of radioactive waste and what to do with the separated plutonium, which could be used in the manufacture of weapons. In the matter of waste disposal the company expected US government funding, and with regard to the plutonium it was hostage to US government policy on the proliferation of nuclear weapons. Some funding was forthcoming, but only for one year. In 1979 President Carter's nuclear non-proliferation policy brought the development of the fuel reprocessing plant to a halt.[33]

In the meantime General Atomic had become embroiled in a number of lawsuits concerning uranium deliveries. Before 1973 Gulf and a mining company with large uranium reserves, United Nuclear Corporation (UNC), had entered into an agreement to supply

In September 1979 demonstrators against nuclear energy in New York posed the rhetorical question: 'Nuclear power the beginning of the end ?' Around the same time Shell decided to move from the building of nuclear power plants back to the research stage, and in 1981 it withdrew completely from nuclear energy.

fabricated nuclear fuel to the utilities. When their collaboration broke up in 1973, the obligations to supply fuel were assigned to Gulf, and UNC undertook to supply Gulf with the necessary uranium for fuel fabrication. Gulf subsequently allocated its obligations to deliver fuel to General Atomic. After 1973 the price of uranium skyrocketed and UNC refused to honour the uranium contracts, arguing that Gulf had mismanaged their joint venture and that Gulf had violated US anti-trust legislation in participating in a uranium cartel. The latter point was eagerly taken up by Exxon Nuclear, which decided not to fulfil its obligations under uranium supplies contracts either. As a result of these refusals to provide uranium, General Atomic could not deliver the fuel to the utilities. In turn these utilities started legal proceedings against General Atomic.[34] Gulf Oil had indeed participated in a uranium cartel, but outside the US with its Canadian subsidiary in uranium mining.[35] Scallop Nuclear had reserved its position in case losses were sustained resulting from shortcomings of Gulf management before the formation of General Atomic. Nevertheless, the litigation and cartel accusations were bound to influence negatively the company as a whole. The cartel disclosures made General Atomic a less attractive partner for US government R&D funding. Added to this were doubts about the viability of the HTGR technology. Though still hopeful about this technology, by 1979 Shell began to think about an exit strategy.

The many financial, technical, and organizational problems of General Atomic were not unique. The whole nuclear energy industry had been vastly overoptimistic about its competitiveness towards other energy sources, in particular coal. 'Nuclear energy is not for the fainthearted', concluded Christopher Flavin from World Watch.[36] Many nuclear power plants completed in the US cost five to ten times as much as originally projected. The nuclear industry had expected to follow the traditional learning curve in which costs would go down as design and construction techniques improved. In fact, construction costs rose steeply, the technical problems in scaling up were greater than foreseen and designs had to be changed in response to safety and health concerns. The final blow to the industry came with the near-meltdown at the Three Mile Island nuclear plant near Harrisburg, Pennsylvania, in 1979. Even though there were no lives lost, the accident brought home the grave risks of nuclear power, and generated a wave of changes in plant design and construction.[37]

In 1976 Shell Nuclear had already decided to return to the R&D stage, and in this context General Atomic had built the Double III experimental nuclear fusion device financed by the US government. Further withdrawal from the commercial industry followed in 1979, when General Atomic agreed with the Public Services Company of Colorado to hand over the nuclear reactor at Fort St Vrain at reduced capacity. Shell Nuclear Inc. also reached agreement with Gulf Oil over the uranium supply and lightwater reactor fuel fabrication business, which in future would be operated for the account and benefit of Gulf Oil alone. Reluctant to give up all contact with the world of nuclear energy, Shell Nuclear continued the partnership with Gulf Oil for another two years, but in 1981 it agreed that Gulf Oil would become full owner of the continuing businesses and programmes of General Atomic. Shell calculated that its nuclear diversification programme had cost around $US 500 million.[38] It had been an expensive learning school.

Entry into the non-ferrous metals with NV Billiton Maatschappij

Shell's involvement with nuclear energy had been a step into unknown territory, a move towards a new technology with exciting but risky prospects. In contrast, metal was an old and tried industry. The acquisition of the Dutch metal company NV Billiton in 1970 represented Shell's first diversification project since its entry into chemicals in 1927. The idea was that Billiton would keep its own identity and would shape and supervise the building up of the non-ferrous metal activities within the Group.[39] Through this takeover Shell wanted to get a base in metals and mining which could be used to develop Shell expertise in this business.

Unfortunately, 1971 was a bad year for metals, with mining and processing capacity well in excess of demand. Shell immediately had a first taste of the cyclical character of the metals industry. This first year of Billiton within Shell was used to formulate long-term plans. Expecting a future increase in demand for metals, plans were made for the expansion of Billiton's mining and processing capacity. A start had already been made with exploration activities in South Africa and Canada. Management assumed that the availability of funds at a time when confidence in the industry was at a low ebb would place Billiton in a better position than its competitors. The company would concentrate on its metal activities and dispose of all unrelated activities. The long-term goal would be for Billiton to become one of the small number of companies that would dominate the non-ferrous metals industry by 1990. The financial targets included a net income attributable to metals of no less than 5 per cent of Group net income by 1990 and a return on investment of 12 per cent or more.[40] In 1972 Billiton was rigorously reorganized. All non-metal activities were sold off. The assets were halved and manpower reduced from 10,000 to less than 5,000.[41]

In 1970 Shell took over the Dutch metals company Billiton, which operated a large bauxite mine in Surinam, seen here in 1975. After the takeover, Shell encouraged Billiton to diversify into a wide range of non-ferrous metals.

For bauxite mining in Surinam, Billiton operated a huge excavator, which dwarfed the people around it.

During the 1970s the Group invested heavily in Billiton, encouraging the company to expand geographically as well as in types of metal. In Surinam Billiton operated one of the largest bauxite mines. It extended its activities in this mineral by participating in an integrated bauxite/alumina project at Worsley in Australia. Another Australian participation was the Windarra nickel mine. Tin dredging took place in Thailand and Indonesia. The company also invested in downstream processing businesses, including a new electrolytic zinc smelter in the Netherlands, a tin smelter in Thailand, and alumina works in Ireland. Even the scrap business was taken on. In all cases, new ventures were entered in combination with others, with Billiton often in the position of minority shareholder.[42]

[19]

Management thought it important to strike the appropriate balance between upstream and downstream activities, because it expected state enterprises to take an increasingly active part in the upstream business.[43]

The new organizational structure of Billiton showed similarities with that of Shell. The overall co-ordination was in the hands of the management of Billiton International Metals BV. This company was the service company with functional divisions, product divisions, and staff services, all intended to advise and service the many operating companies.[44] The operating companies were held by no fewer than five Billiton holding companies, but at the same time they were in many countries embedded in the Shell network of national organizations. The Group's infrastructure undoubtedly helped in achieving Billiton's rapid development. The early losses were seen as a logical consequence of the growth strategy with relatively high head office expenses and research and exploration costs related to potential new business.[45] The positive results of 1979 and 1980 underlined the feeling that Billiton was on the right track. A number of decisions for projects were taken in those two years, including the participation in the Cerro Matoso ferro-nickel mine and smelter project in Colombia, the acquisition of a share in a titanium plant being built in North Wales and a share in a tungsten and molybdenum mine and concentrator in New

In Thailand Billiton engaged in tin dredging and tin smelting, as seen here in the 1980s. In 1975 Billiton became full owner of Thaisarco (Thailand Smelting and Refining Company) on the island of Phuket.

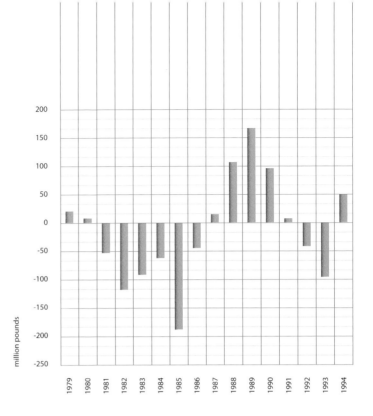

Figure 2.3
Shell Metals earnings
1979-1994.

Brunswick, Canada. In Brazil Billiton participated in an aluminium smelter and acquired a 40 per cent share in the Alumar project to produce alumina and aluminium.

By the time many of the new projects came on stream in the early 1980s, however, the world had plunged into a deep recession. Most metal prices went down as supply outstripped demand. On top of that, many of the new ventures experienced considerable technical problems. Shell's metals operations suffered rising losses, which led to consolidation or termination of a number of old or recently acquired activities. In 1985 tin-dredging operations in Indonesia and Thailand were terminated, the tungsten and molybdenum mine in Canada was closed and the interest in the titanium plant in North Wales was sold.[46] Nearly all liquidations and disposals were in metals other than aluminium, and as a consequence the focus of the Metal Sector moved more and more towards bauxite, alumina, and aluminium.[47] The general mood of malaise was underlined by the suspension of tin trading on the London Metal Exchange in October 1985.[48] Figure 2.3 illustrates how the metals sector ran into losses during the early 1980s and continued to show poor results well into the mid-1980s, at a time when many businesses, including chemicals, had already returned to profits. When finally the tide turned in 1987, it did not take long before the losses reappeared.[49]

After the consolidation and rationalization, it was time to shape a programme for Billiton's future. Comprehensive reviews of all businesses, completed in 1986, failed to identify any fundamental strength or core business as a basis for formulating Billiton's future strategy. Management perceived the short-term need to bring costs down faster than the competition and to improve the quality, reliability and added value of all operations. One concrete suggestion to achieve this high aim consisted of the introduction of 'business centres' with a global approach. Base and precious metal exploration and mining were consolidated in a global 'business centre', and the same structure was applied to marketing activities. With greater emphasis on operations, head office support could be cut back, which resulted in a substantial reduction in office staff. Further cost saving could be achieved by limiting the R&D efforts to the direct support of the businesses. In their discussion of the metals industry environment, Billiton's management pointed out that the most successful companies had been either those with defensible low cost positions or those with significant gold interests.[50] Management seemed to succumb to the lure of gold.

Initially Billiton had no high opinion of gold mining and was reluctant to spend money on it, thinking it too removed from Shell's main business. Their view changed when the bauxite mine in Australia in which Billiton participated turned out to have surprisingly large and financially rewarding volumes of gold.[51] This success inspired management to take up gold mining in Indonesia, Ghana, and Chile.[52] The gold rush, however, did not last long.

The metals business showed a return to profit during the late 1980s, but the economic recession of the early 1990s in combination with high exports from Eastern Europe and the former Soviet Union once again brought lower metal prices and new losses. The new business plan of 1992 concentrated on the upstream business and the related marketing and trading. It reduced the involvement in downstream activities, because those activities continued to be problematical. Though over the years particular effort was made to make the metal works more environmentally friendly, they remained an environmental risk. In early 1992 the metals coordinator Jan Slechte, concluded that 'it was questionable whether the Sector would ever make a financial contribution to the Group sufficient to justify its retention. A complete or partial disposal at the propitious point on the metals cycle might therefore be attractive'.[53] A few months later the South African company Gencor came with a bid for the Billiton metals business.[54] In early 1993 Shell began negotiations. The sale was a complicated and lengthy process, partly because of the many different partners in the various operating companies and partly because of the financing. Finally in 1994 the main part of Billiton was sold to Gencor, while interests in gold mining and exploration in Australia were floated on the Melbourne stock market under the name Billiton. A few remaining interests were sold in 1995.

When the Gencor deal was done, it was time to look back and take stock of more than twenty years' involvement in non-ferrous

[20]

During the late 1980s Billiton became involved in gold mining, after gold had been found in a bauxite mine in Australia in which Billiton participated. In 1989, Billiton acquired a 40.5 per cent interest in the Bogosu opencast gold mine in Ghana.
Left: Worker in the Billiton/Shell opencast gold mine in Ghana.

[21]

Close up of a crucible during a gold
pour in Indonesia in the 1980s.

[22]

Workers engaged in the construction
of the Bogosu opencast gold mine in
Ghana.

metals: overall, profits and losses were about break-even, but the sale of the metals sector did not recover the huge investments made since 1970.[55] Looking back at the end of the Billiton era, Evert Henkes pointed out that while the money invested in Billiton could in retrospect have been better spent, the fact remained that Billiton had been sold as a going concern. Lo van Wachem, former Group managing director and later chairman of the CMD, concluded that the story of Shell's involvement with Billiton was a sad one. Most diversifications by the oil industry had not worked. Perhaps the main lesson to be learned was the necessity of knowing the business in which investment was to be made.[56]

In venturing into metals, Shell had been ahead of its rivals Exxon and BP, but it was not the only oil company that found the diversification hard going. Exxon had some minerals exploration, but did not set up a separate Exxon Mineral business unit before

1980. Expansion followed, but as it went hand in hand with substantial losses, Exxon decided to withdraw from metals in 1986 and gradually sold its assets over the following years. BP started exploring for minerals in the 1970s. In 1980 it made a substantial step forward with the acquisition of Selection Trust, a London-based international mining company with major mineral interests worldwide. Directly after the acquisition BP had to restructure one of the metals subsidiaries acquired in the Selection Trust deal after disappointing results. In June 1989 BP sold most of its metals portfolio, which was easily the largest such of the oil majors, to RTZ (Rio Tinto-Zinc Corporation).[57] Compared to these two competitors Shell stayed in the metal business for a long time, starting early and selling out late.

In the summer of 1973, with the oil crisis looming, Shell stepped up its efforts to become involved in the coal business. Initially the focus was on coal trading. Here, coal loading in the harbour of Rotterdam, the Netherlands.

[24]

Tapping the world's vast coal resources   When Shell

started to think about diversification in the late 1960s, entrance into the coal business did not appear to be its first choice. Perhaps this had to do with the fact that oil had overtaken coal as a source of primary energy. Oil was cheaper to transport than coal, and easier to handle and store. Traditional coal-fired power stations were more expensive than oil-fired ones. It did not seem very logical, therefore, for an oil enterprise to return to this older form of energy. However, coal had one important advantage: the world's coal reserves were many times larger than the oil reserves. Moreover, coal could be used as a raw material for the production of oil products, although the available processes were not yet cost-effective. The latter did not necessarily deter an industry that was used to looking at very long-term perspectives. In 1971 the CMD asked the Coal Taskgroup to investigate taking up coal interests. This decision was influenced by the fact that rival oil companies had already begun to acquire large coal reserves. Shell did not want to be left out. The first investigation concerned the prospects for thermal coals from mine to market and for building up a worldwide reserve base of coal.[58] In the summer of 1973 Gerrit Wagner, chairman of the CMD, decided to make haste with the trade in coal in order to gain experience. The Coal Taskgroup was asked to start trading coal from the US to learn the business by making small mistakes before a large international coal scheme would be set up. The oil crisis in the autumn of 1973 precipitated further action into the coal business. The Coal Production and Trading division was established in 1974 to create opportunities for market entry.[59] When Shell's coal business took shape its organizational structure developed in line with other Shell businesses. Shell Coal International became the service company, providing advice and support to operating companies and co-ordinating transport of coal to international markets. The operating companies, however, were responsible for local developments and operations in their areas.[60] Other oil majors also extended their activities in the direction of coal: for instance BP became active in South Africa, Venezuela, Poland, and Australia, and Exxon in Colombia and Australia.[61]

Naturally wanting its contribution to the coal business to be innovative, Shell turned its attention to technologically advanced transport systems. Long-distance transportation of coal by train was in itself not new, but where large volumes had to be moved from one supply source to a single destination, the 'unit train' concept could be applied. This involved large specialized trains, which were continuously loaded and discharged. Another idea for making transport of coal more efficient and cheaper was the 'slurry pipeline', where very fine, powdered coal was pumped as a suspension in water and then dewatered again.

Two sister ships dedicated to the transport of coal were added to the Shell fleet in 1981, the *Tribulus* and the *Tricula*. Both ships were built by Hyundai Heavy Industries, Ulsan, South Korea.

[26]

In their research laboratories Shell had worked for many years on slurry pipelines and now seemed a good time to press them into service.[62] None of these projects, however, were turned into daily practice.

Shell's involvement with the coal business can be divided in three parts. During the 1970s the business was built up with international coal trading, exploration and production, and participation in coal mining ventures. The 1980s formed a period of consolidation and improvement of the acquired businesses. From 1993 onwards Shell gradually sold all its coal assets. Turning points in this history were the two recessions of the early 1980s and the early 1990s. As its entry port in this new business Shell chose the international coal trade to distinguish itself from the other oil companies, which were mainly active in the US. The international coal trade was for Shell a shorter-term strategy of gaining experience, making profits and establishing contact with major potential customers. The coal service company dealt directly with this part of the activities, and two ships dedicated to the transport of coal were added to the fleet. At the same time Shell encouraged

Shell Australia had a minority participation in the Capricorn Coal Developments (Capcoal). This company developed the German Creek deposit in Queensland, Australia, which contained large reserves of high-quality coking coal. The mine, here pictured in 1983, was an example of underground mining, but the German Creek site also had opencast mining. Right: Coal-related research.

[27]

[28]

The Rietspuit mine in South Africa consisted of opencast mining.

operating companies to start exploration activities in their countries, and exploration was taken in hand in Australia, Indonesia, Spain, South Africa, the US, and Canada. Finding coal was cheap and relatively easy, but the challenge was to find the right quality in the right location and to diversify supply sources. Not all exploration projects resulted in production. Indonesia and Spain, for instance, were abandoned, and plans for coal production in China did not come further than a feasibility study.[63]

Because the route from prospecting to production and saleable coal was time-consuming, Shell decided in 1975 to develop the coal business faster by participating in existing companies. Initially, Shell did not want to become involved with underground mining operations because this required a large labour force, while Shell was more familiar with capital-intensive production. This point of view was quickly amended when Shell companies started to negotiate about participations, because they wanted to keep the options open in case a prospective partner might want to bring its underground reserves into the partnership. The option of working

with local partners made sense because Shell companies had to build up experience in this already well-established field. In some countries, such as Australia, mining regulations prohibited foreign-owned companies from controlling more than half of a project; nor did Australian coal miners welcome the prospect of international oil companies entering their industry. Shell Australia took minority interests in a project to explore and develop the Drayton opencast coal prospect in New South Wales and, among others, the development of the German Creek mine in Queensland. In both cases, the partners were the operators.[64] Other countries where Shell companies built up interests in coal production were South Africa, the USA and Canada. These participations gave Shell access to coal for its international trading operations.[65] Broadly speaking part of the coal from the US and South Africa was intended for Europe, while Australian coal was destined for Japan and Canadian coal for Korea. However, domestic sales remained important too, comprising roughly half of Shell's total sales.

The Shell coal sector achieved rapid growth during the 1970s. The decade was rounded off with the acquisition of a sizeable coal interest in the US.[66] After analysis of US coal companies, the best option seemed to be a participation in the A. T. Massey Coal Company, owned by St Joe Minerals in the USA. It took eight months of negotiations, which resulted in technical audit reports, social and personnel practices audits, as well as extensive financial investigations and a huge pile of legal papers. The result was the formation of a 50/50 joint venture, The Massey Coal Company, in 1980.[67] In the meantime competitors also stepped up their coal

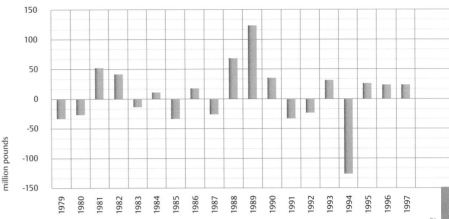

Figure 2.4
Shell Coal earnings, 1979-1997.

production. Exxon, for instance, went ahead with the El Cerrejon coal mining project in Colombia, which was expected to become the largest individual steam coal export project in the world, coming on stream in 1986/7.[68] Shell proudly announced profits for the first time in 1981. However, a year later this sector began to suffer from overproduction, at the very time that many of its mining ventures began to deliver their coal. The problem was comparable with those in Shell's metals business, where the new projects also came on stream at the nadir of the economic recession.

The major coal companies had widened the global spread of their activities. New entrants from diversified oil and gas companies were becoming more significant through large investments and acquisitions. In international coal markets prices for coal fell sharply, reflecting the depressed world economic situation generally and recession in fuel and iron and steel markets in particular. As a newcomer, the Shell coal sector felt the crisis acutely. The following observation in their 1982 coal report is telling: 'Recent experience has shown that coals of lower quality – reserves of which are more readily accessible to newcomers to the industry – are most vulnerable to market downturns'.[69] Shell also seemed to be surprised that sanctity of contracts did not appear to be part of the industry's tradition. So when customers reneged on their contracts, Shell Coal International was left with the off-take obligations. This was in particular true for the obligations related to the Massey Coal Company. To cut losses, planned investments were either re-phased or cancelled and R&D expenditure was reduced.[70]

Against the background of structurally low profitability, the coal sector undertook a study of its competitive advantage. As the industry structure was poor it was unlikely that high profitability could be achieved. Though in theory the sector had the choice between differentiation and a low-cost strategy to achieve competitive advantage, in fact the low-cost strategy was seen as the only realistic option. The sector set itself the target to become a 'Global Supplier', which allowed for some growth under strict cost-control conditions.[71]

The oil price collapse in 1986 put further pressure on the price of coal, making prospects for coal less attractive, but the consequent general economic growth stimulated demand for coal for steel production as well as for electricity generation. In 1988 Shell decided to become more actively involved in the management of mines, particularly in Australia. By that time, the government in Canberra had relaxed the regulations regarding foreign investment and Shell Australia increased its participations, sometimes to 100 per cent. In a number of cases Shell also acted as operator, paying particular attention to safety issues. This led to several industry awards for safety management.[72] However, the profits did not last. Figure 2.4 shows the volatility of earnings from the coal mining sector between 1979 and 1997. (Shell's annual statistical overviews provided no figures for the period before 1979).[73]

From coal to gas to oil

[31]

The oil crisis of 1973 revived interest in the processes of making oil from coal. One such process was developed by Shell and the German firm H. Koppers. Shell set up a pilot plant for the Shell/Koppers coal gasification process at Shell's Harburg Refinery in Germany in 1976, photographed here during the building stage (inset) and two years later (picture left).

More experiments followed at the coal gasification unit at Shell Oil's Deer Park manufacturing complex in Texas (picture right). This unit provided gas and steam to the central power station from 250-400 tonnes of coal burned daily to produce synthetic gas and high pressure steam, 1980s.

One of the interesting possibilities arising from the coal business was the coal gasification process, which produced other hydrocarbon fuels from coal. Various chemical companies and oil enterprises, including Shell, had done work in this field during the 1920s. Germany, with its lack of oil but with ample coal resources, had spent vast sums of money on developing processes to convert coal into oil. The problem lay in creating a process that would be cheap and efficient enough to be able to compete with oil production. In fact, the existing processes did not even come close to meeting this challenge. With the rising oil price in the 1970s the economic challenge became somewhat smaller, which led to renewed interest in technologies to convert coal into oil. Together with the German firm H. Koppers, Shell developed the Shell-Koppers process, combining Koppers' knowledge and experience of atmospheric-pressure coal gasification technology with Shell's high-pressure oil gasification technology. In the gasification process, dried pulverized coal is treated to form synthetic gas, which is primarily a mixture of hydrogen and carbon monoxide. In fact, the mixture consists of about 90 per cent hydrogen. 'If you're not careful you can end up making some very expensive water', Shell's project manager G. J. van den Berg warned in 1980. The synthetic gas can be put to many uses, including as a fuel for power generation.

Following a pilot plant at the Shell research laboratory in Amsterdam, a demonstration plant was set up in Germany in 1976, which operated from 1978 to 1983. Plans were announced for a coal gasification plant at Moerdijk in 1979, but that project did not materialize. However Shell built a demonstration coal gasification plant at Deer Park Manufacturing Complex in Texas. By the time this plant began to operate in 1987, the oil price had collapsed. Though the plant confirmed the high expectations of efficiency and low environmental impact, the economics for expansion were still not right. Shell continued experimenting with this technology, including a demonstration plant at Buggenum in the Netherlands, because of its future promises for clean burning of an abundant resource. At the start of the twenty-first century Shell found parties in China interested in applying this technology to turn some of their abundant coal reserves into synthetic gas.

The knowledge and experience invested in the coal gasification process had further relevance, because similar technologies could be applied to the transformation of natural gas into liquid hydrocarbons that can be used as transport fuels. For this purpose Shell developed its SMDS (Shell Middle Distillate Synthesis) process. The first commercial unit based on this technology came on stream in Malaysia in 1994.[1] The process was useful for turning gas that was far removed from customers into easily transportable oil products. It produced a very clean fuel that could be added to premium motor fuels to reduce the negative impact on the environment, something that was particularly relevant for cars in large congested cities. After the successful application of this technology in Malaysia, Shell designed a much larger gas to liquids plant for Qatar.

By the early 1990s it was time to reconsider the sector's position. Comparison of the Shell coal sector with the performance of selected, major publicly quoted coal companies over the period 1985-90 showed that the Shell coal sector, including its US mining company, ranked seventh in production, fourth in sales, and second in export sales. Clearly, Shell had built up a significant business in coal, as it had set out to do in the early 1970s. The internal 1992 report concluded that the Shell sector was 'established as a market leader in mining and exporting steam coal'.[74] Nonetheless, in the 1990s the Group sold its interests one after the other, and so did the other oil majors. The oil companies found the return on investment in the coal business unsatisfactory, and demand for coal did not rise as fast as had been expected in the 1970s. In as much as companies replaced their oil-fired boilers, they turned to gas-fired technologies rather than to coal. Shell Oil in the US decided to sell its coal-mining subsidiary in 1992, because it had decided to divest non-strategic producing properties. In return it acquired a 25 per cent interest in the purchaser, Zeigler Coal Holding. This share was sold in 1994, resulting in high special charges.[75] Next to go were the coal assets in Canada, again with considerable losses.[76] In 1997 followed the divestment of the mines in South Africa, which actually delivered gains.

By 1997 nearly all coal assets were in Australia, and for that reason Shell Coal became an Australian company. Holding on to the coal business seemed to be worthwhile for implementing a fuels-to-power strategy. The idea was to use Shell's position in coal as a platform for accelerating its entry into 'power', notably into coal-fired generating capacity, in particularly in Asia.[77] The collapse in both international and domestic coal prices in 1998 drove the industry to drastic restructuring. During 1998 and 1999 half of production capacity changed hands in the US. Since 1994 the oil companies BP, ENI, Occidental, Arco, Quaker, and Caltex had all withdrawn from the coal industry, while Exxon, Coastal, and Shell were on the way out.[78] In 1999 Shell management finally decided the coal business did not fit in with its long-term strategy after all. Shell Coal was sold to Anglo-American in 2000. The Group, however, remained interested in the coal gasification technology.

Mid-term review of the diversification process The
three main new business areas Shell entered in the 1970s, nuclear,
metals, and coal, were all abandoned by the end of the century.
None had developed into the 'third leg', comparable to oil and
chemicals, that the CMD had wanted to create in the late 1960s.
The short adventure into nuclear energy had been a mistake,
but one shared with many in the industry. The view that nuclear
energy had become commercially viable was partly based on mis-
information and partly on miscalculation. The forecast high rise in
energy demand did not materialize. In metals Shell achieved some
results with Billiton, but not enough to make good the huge
investments. Being part of Shell did not have sufficient added value.
Coal was the closest to Shell's core business and the Group stayed
with it the longest. Nevertheless, its future was not considered
bright enough for Shell to hold on to coal. Nor was Shell able to
contribute to new transport systems, as had been imagined when
the Shell started its coal business.

Why were the ultimate results so poor? Lo van Wachem,
discussing the Group's diversification policy in 1985, gave some
hints as to why success had eluded them. He mentioned in
particular the setting of unrealistic growth targets in order to
create the kind of size meaningful to the Group.[79] One threat for
successful diversification is a lack of knowledge about the new
business. This problem was certainly mentioned with regard to
the metals business. However, Shell was generally well aware of
its lack of expertise and experience, and therefore left the local
management in place. Still, lack of in-depth knowledge may have
hindered Shell management in making correct assessments of the
quality of the companies they bought or participated in, and the
investment proposals they came up with. The organizational
structure for the new enterprises was copied from the familiar and

[32]

A worker is checking a band-saw at
African Timber and Plywood, Nigeria.
While Shell had tried to grow the
metals and coal businesses quickly into
substantial Group enterprises, the
entry into forestry took place more
gradually. Shell considered forestry
attractive because wood was a
renewable resource. It could be used as
an energy source (biomass), but also as
feedstock for the manufacture of
commercial products. The engagement in forestry was seen as a learning
platform.

trusted oil and gas organization with the division of responsibility
between the local operating companies and the central service
companies, with relatively high R&D and head office costs. The
Shell international network helped in finding easy access to
opportunities worldwide, but this help came at a cost. For instance,
a smaller, leaner head office would probably have been better for
the metals sector, because this was the way other mining houses
were typically organized. The coal sector, too, found its

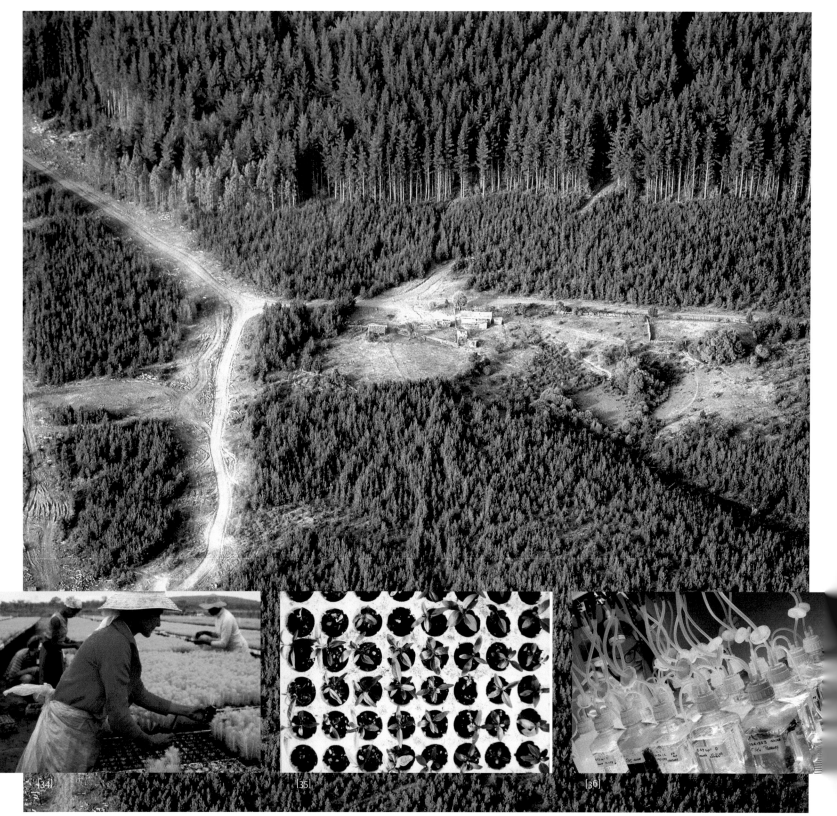

[33]

[34]

[35]

[36]

organizational costs higher than those of its competitors. With modest returns, and little expectation of better returns in the future, shedding the business seemed the most logical course. As we saw, diversification was a general trend in the 1960s and early 1970s, but the fact that so many of the oil companies diversified their activities at the same time very likely formed part of the problem. By moving into metals and coal in a big way, they unsettled these industries and in creating supply far above demand destroyed their own profitability. The oil companies behaved like tourists who by their very presence destroyed the unspoilt places they had come to admire.

Would the outcome have been different if Shell had developed its new businesses more gradually? Forestry, one of Shell's later enthusiasms for developing a new line of business, forms a case for comparison. After its first rather disappointing experiences with diversification (including the high losses of its nuclear energy ventures and the metals business) Shell had decided to continue with exploring new possibilities, but on a much smaller scale. In 1978 it had turned the New Technology Ventures Division into the Non-Traditional Business Division (NTB), intended as a service organization to watch out for new technologies and to coordinate and keep an eye on new business initiatives developed

in the operating companies.[80] Investments were relatively modest and progress was slow, but there were no major failings either. The head of the NTB, Bertus van der Toorn, was anxious to avoid the term 'diversification', because it had come to imply high spending, buying into or acquiring existing companies, or at any rate operating on a large scale. The idea of NTB was that new business should be developed through learning and experience, and therefore NTB used the term 'learning platforms' to describe this approach.[81] Increasingly the focus was on renewable resources, such as forestry, solar energy and biotechnology.

Forestry was considered the most promising of these in the 1980s. Shell operating companies in New Zealand, South Africa, Chile and Brazil became involved in existing plantations or new plantings. Millions of fast-growing pine and eucalyptus were planted. Though this business was far from new, it was new in the Shell context and Shell's ambition was to look at new aspects of it. Brian Jones, head of NTB's forestry division, formulated the Shell target thus: 'In forestry, doing what others have done will not necessarily give us an attractive business. Traditional forestry gives only very modest returns, but there are niches where it is possible to do much better. We know some companies are making over 12 per cent real return, and we intend to be very selective in our

In forestry Shell became involved in various stages of the production process. In Chile it participated in a plantation of 17,000 hectares of Radiata Pine for the sawmill. Left, an aerial view of the plantation, and far right the de-barking of logs at the Santa Fe pulp mill, Chile.

Facing page: from left to right: Nursery for Pine and Eucalyptus, introduced by Shell at the Fazenda Jatoba Forestry venture in Brazil; three-week-old Eucalyptus seedlings in the nursery in South Africa; Forestry research unit at East Malling, Kent, UK.

[37]

investments. For example, we are looking for areas where we can plant fast-growing trees for specific applications. We did an intensive study in Shell Centre as to why some companies in forestry did better than others, and we think we have identified the mistakes.'[82]

Doing better consisted of being able as a large organization to create cohesion between the forestry activities in different countries and having laboratories doing research on micro-propagation. Forestry even brought Shell into the manufacture of pulp in Chile when, in a joint venture with Scot Paper Company and Citibank, it bought a nearly finished pulp mill. The mill was expected to work on the basis of the locally available Radiata pine, but Shell developed a bold and unique strategy of introducing the fast-growing Eucalyptus as an alternative pulping fibre.[83] In 1989 the forestry unit had reached a stage where its size and potential merited recognition as a business in its own right, reporting directly to one of the Group managing directors. It was hailed as the archetype for the 'NTB process', moving from a single platform investment in the early 1980s to a substantial and rapidly develop-ing international business.[84] Further expansion was foreseen, though in 1991 the first divestment took place when Shell South Africa sold its forestry assets because they lacked the 'critical mass' needed to justify investment in a timber processing plant. Further expansion to attain this 'critical mass' was considered impossible because of the limited availability of suitable land and significantly increased land prices.[85] On the other hand, new plantations were established in Paraguay and Uruguay.

Shell concentrated on the establishment and management of high-yield, short-rotation plantations supplying global markets for pulpwood, saw logs and veneer logs. Low prices for wood in the late 1990s as a consequence of weakened demand for wood for the

paper and pulp industry took the shine out of investment in forestry. Evaluating the business, Shell concluded that its forestry business had built up a strong reputation for technology, health and safety, and sustainable development, but net income after taxes had been close to zero, and returns would be well below 10 per cent for the next ten years. 'More importantly, to achieve Shell Forestry's strategy – based on a global fibre offering – significant growth will be required because based on the current Latin American assets alone Shell Forestry will be too small to be a competitive player.'[86] If it came to a choice between further growth, a joint venture, or sale, Shell preferred the last. Though Shell's entry into forestry had been more gradual and on a smaller scale than the diversification into metals, nuclear, and coal, the outcome was not very different. It abandoned the field without having been able to reap the benefits.

Diversification strategies in Shell's chemicals sector

Petrochemicals formed Shell's first diversification away from the pure oil business, and this activity expanded vigorously during the 1950s and 1960s, though by about 1970 some of the glamour of petrochemicals had waned and this sector started to look for diversification of its own. Not belonging to the core business, Shell Chemicals had to defend its position within the oil enterprise each time its financial results were seriously down, which happened only too frequently in the last three decades of the twentieth century. People looked back with some nostalgia upon the spectacular growth of the petrochemical industry during the 1950s and 1960s, when it had been one of the leading sectors in the world economy. The enormous growth of the petrochemical industry was based on technological innovations and on the availability of cheap feedstock. The petrochemical industry in the US mostly used natural gas as source of ethane, propane and butane, which could be cracked to lower olefins. In Europe naphtha, one of the 'middle distillate' products of an oil refinery, was the main feedstock.[87] The products of the chemical industry invaded daily life to such an extent that some observers characterized the second half of the twentieth century as the 'Chemical Age'.[88] People started to wear wrinkle-proof clothes made of nylon and polyester or a mix of those with natural fibres. Washing was made easy by synthetic detergents. Kitchen tables were covered with synthetic laminate such as formica. Wooden furniture could be thoroughly protected with polyurethane varnish. Children amused themselves with primary-coloured plastic toys such as Lego building blocks, while housewives attended Tupperware parties. Those who did not want to combat the fly on the wall with a swat could use Vapona strips instead. A wide range of new medicines and cosmetics became available. The building industry profited from the flexibility and durability of plastics in the form of electrical fittings, water pipes, and insulation. The auto industry used synthetic rubber for car tyres. Packaging based on paper was replaced by plastics such as transparent film. To a large extent, though not entirely, the new synthetic products replaced traditional natural materials such as wood, cotton, silk, wool, rubber, and leather. They also created entirely new products and uses. Shell companies provided many of the chemical building blocks from which these products were made.

In the 1950s and 1960s the petrochemical industry had expanded quickly, and Shell's chemical companies had their fair share in the expansion process. The new products of the chemical industry, in particular plastics, had invaded daily life. With them came new selling methods, such as the Tupperware parties organized for and by housewives to be informed about the benefits of Tupperware. Here a Tupperware party in Le Havre, France, in 1975.

[38]

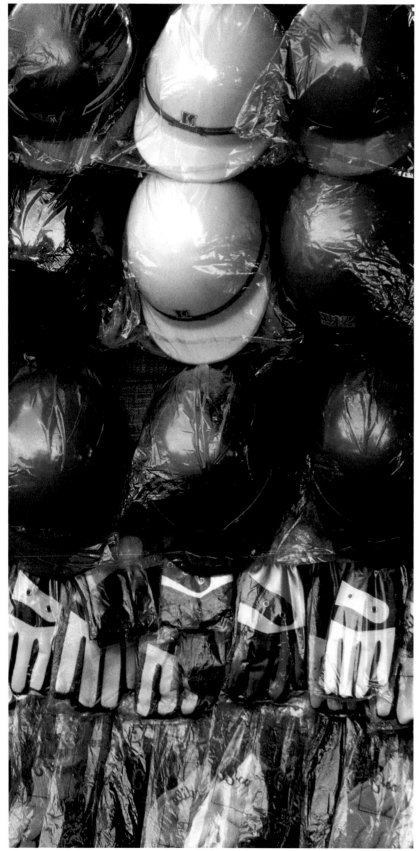

Packaging in paper was replaced by transparent, polypropylene film.

Shell was one of the major players in the petrochemical industry. Measured in sales proceeds, its chemical activities were the largest of the oil majors, and ranked among the twenty largest chemical companies worldwide.[89] In the 1970s Shell chemical activities were concentrated in Europe and the US. In Europe Shell had chemical companies in the Netherlands, UK, France, Germany, to name the four most important ones. In the US the Group owned 69 per cent (after 1984, 100 per cent) of Shell Chemical Company, a division of Shell Oil Company. The Shell Chemical Company in the US was the single most important chemical company within the Group, with a share ranging between 30 and 40 per cent of total Group chemical sales in the 1970s and 1980s. Shell's chemical activities worldwide were often loosely addressed as 'Chemicals'. The Shell companies produced base chemicals such as lower olefins (ethylene, propylene, butylenes, and butadiene) and aromatics (benzene, toluene, and xylene) and higher olefins. These were either sold or worked up into industrial chemicals (such as solvents, detergents and additives), into polymers (including resins, PVC, and butadiene), and into agrochemicals. In the mid-1970s Shell companies were the largest producers of chemical solvents in Western Europe and among the largest producers of polypropylene worldwide.[90] During the 1960s plants had grown in size because large-scale production reduced cost per unit. In the 1950s, for instance, naphtha crackers had capacities of around 50,000 tons of ethylene per year, while in the early 1970s new crackers had a capacity of between 300,000 and 500,000 tons of ethylene.[91] Petrochemical plants posed high demands on capital, but the expectation was that these expenditures would be justified when higher volumes would be met by increasing demands in the future. Profitability seemed just around the corner as soon as the growing supply would be matched by growing demand. In fact, profitability was generally not very satisfactory even in the 1960s because demand was consistently lower than supply. As a result of the growth of the chemical industry in Europe, naphtha was no longer the cheap feedstock it had been in the past. Furthermore, many companies taxed their funds and energies by trying to play a part in the whole range of chemical products.[92] The invasion of the chemical industry by the major oil companies during the sixties had increased the competition and reduced prices. One American chemical company complained about oil companies pricing their products 'like it was a gas war'.[93]

In the early 1970s, even before the first oil shock, growth in demand for petrochemicals slowed just as more new production capacity was being installed. In 1972 Shell's chemical sector undertook a comprehensive review to analyse the strengths and weaknesses of its various activities with the intention of concentrating efforts on those areas where the Group's position and prospects were fundamentally strong, while withdrawing from those areas where the opposite was the case. With the help of an external adviser, the sector developed a planning technique, the 'Directional Policy Matrix' or DPM, to assess the portfolio of activities. All activities were plotted in a matrix on the basis of prospects for profitability and the sector's competitive capabilities. The mood was basically optimistic, so most activities were still considered full of promise, in particular those activities with advanced technology. Some investment plans were delayed and the direct involvement with fertilizers, the first diversification of the Group in 1927, was ended.[94] Shell even published its DPM planning technique, and those who puzzled as to why methods developed for internal use in order to obtain competitive advantage were made available to all, could read the following: 'It would be to the advantage of the industry generally if application of this technique can help other companies to recognize where their strengths and weaknesses lie. There has been in the past a tendency towards imitative and duplicative investment by some companies in certain fields where they have no special position of advantage and this type of investment can be a source of excess production capacity. If this tendency can be counteracted in future, it will not only avoid waste of scarce resources, but will also help the industry to earn the rate of return which it needs, in order to undertake future expansion to meet growing demand.'[95]

The message seemed to be that if all chemical companies would concentrate on the areas where they had a competitive advantage, they would no longer spoil each other's market by creating overcapacity.

As an oil major, Shell could try to find some of its competitive advantage in the 'oil-petrochemical interface': petrochemical plants integrated into large oil refineries had a wide range of feedstock available, which enabled them in principle to make the most of seasonal changes in feedstock availability and market requirement. To play this game to the greatest advantage of both oil refineries and petrochemical companies was certainly not simple, but it held the promise of substantial profits. Inspired by the upheaval in the oil industry, Shell paid particular attention to building plants with maximum feedstock flexibility. The cracker of Shell Nederland Chemie at Moerdijk, which started to operate in 1973, could use either naphtha or gas oil, or a combination of both, for producing ethylene, propylene and butadiene. The ambitions of Shell managers, however, went further. In 1977 they were designing new crackers for the UK and France which would be unique in the way they could switch between three different feedstocks – naphtha, gas oil, or LPG – depending on relative prices and availability. Shell companies were leaders in the development of feedstock flexibility.[96]

At the beginning of the twenty-first century it is hard to imagine life without the products of the petrochemical industry, as the contents of this shed show. The children's toys, the garden chairs, the inside of the mattress, the handles of the wheelbarrow and the hose have all been made of derivatives from petrochemicals, and this list is not complete.

In chemicals, creating new processes can be just as important as inventing new products. SM/PO (Styrene Monomer/Propylene Oxide) and SHOP (Shell Higher Olefins Process) were two innovative processes developed by Shell companies. In 1968 two Shell chemical engineers started research on an alternative way of producing propylene oxide (PO), a colourless liquid used as a chemical building block in a series of products, including polyurethane foams used for furniture and bedding, shoe soles, construction insulation elements and in the automotive industry. The existing processes were either creating huge volumes of contaminated waste water or producing side products that were not in high demand. Thorough research showed that pure silica treated with a titanium compound provided an excellent catalyst for the production of propylene oxide. Economic calculations made clear that the production of propylene should be combined with conversion of ethyl benzene into styrene monomer (SM). The resulting SM/PO process was both cheaper and more environmentally friendly than the older processes.[97] The styrene monomer ended up in products as varied as drinking cups, food containers, car interiors and bridge construction. The first commercial Shell SM/PO plant was built at Moerdijk, in the Netherlands. Plans were drawn up in 1974, but it took until 1980 before the complex plant was in operation.

SHOP was another of those advanced technologies in which Shell sought its competitive advantage. SHOP (Shell Higher Olefins Process) produced linear olefins for a number of uses and in particular for the manufacture of detergents. Before the high rise in oil prices, wax cracking had been used to yield olefins, but in the 1970s this process was no longer cost-effective. SHOP offered a new route because it could use ethylene feedstock. Competitive processes for making higher olefins from ethylene existed, but SHOP offered a greater flexibility and yielded products of higher purity. The first SHOP plant was built near Geismar in Louisiana, US, in 1978. Stanlow in the UK was chosen as the site for the first European SHOP plant to make use of the oil and gas feedstock from the North Sea, which came on stream in 1982. This way Shell could combine optimal integration with unique technology. The SHOP technology gave Shell companies the competitive edge in the detergents intermediate market.[98]

Management of Shell Chemicals also decided to move into new and more specialized areas, either by acquisition or based on in-house research, or both. Animal feed provided a good example of the latter. In 1974 the UK-based Colborn Group, specialist in animal nutrition and health, was acquired. Shell was interested in this company because its own research had found a direct fermentation route for the production of single-cell protein from natural gas. This exciting new technique even seemed to hold the promise of ultimately solving the world's hunger problem, as had pesticides, herbicides and other petrochemicals in earlier years. The idea was to start up a pilot plant and use the protein in compound animal feedstuff. In 1976, however, Shell gave up the project because the economics did not look very promising. Similar research to make proteins from oil was done by some of the other oil majors. For BP, for instance, it marked the beginning of a

[42]

[43]

Plastic products invaded the whole world from the plastic goods market in Mexico, to the plastic bucket seller on his bike in India and the collector of empty plastic bottles in Albania.

[41]

[44]

substantial diversification into nutrition, though it also shelved its protein project later on.[99]

The years 1973 and 1974 showed strong growth in demand and profitability, and the problems besetting the industry did not seem too serious any longer. In their review for 1974 the Shell managers wrote enthusiastically: 'for almost the first time in the post-war history of the Chemical industry, the ability to earn really attractive returns emerged for a brief period. (...) Most chemical plants could be operated close to capacity and there were no spare facilities overhanging the market.'[100] The ghost of an industry in decline had been temporarily laid to rest. The fantastic results of 1974 turned out to be exceptional, because these resulted from industrial customers stocking up, and concerns about overcapacity soon returned in Europe. The long lead times involved in setting up new plants exacerbated the industry's susceptibility to economic cycles. One way of tackling overcapacity was trying to take joint measures in Europe industry-wide, but this option was difficult

because of the risk of being accused of anti-competitive collusion, and because the interests and views of the various chemical companies were not the same.[101]

In the meantime the situation of the chemical industry in the US looked more promising. In 1974 Shell Oil launched a major expansion programme with the ambition of bringing Shell Chemical Company up to the level of the leading eleven chemical companies there. From the fact that oil resources were limited and rising in price, Jack St Clair, president of Shell Chemical, concluded that more of the available oil should go into chemicals. In the long term, that was where the maximum value would be added to the barrel, where the maximum jobs were generated and where the effect on the nation's economy would be realized. Interestingly, he did not discuss the demand side of chemicals, taking it for granted that such useful products would find their way to the customers. To make the best use of the precious and dwindling supplies of hydrocarbon, Shell Oil decided to integrate their refineries and

[45]

The petrochemical industry brought new textiles with strong colours and new characteristics.

chemical plants into a series of manufacturing complexes. This integration took place at Wilmington and Martinez in California, Norco, Louisiana, and Deer Park, Texas.[102] Ernest Werner, Group managing director, felt concerned about the expansion plans of Shell Oil, as he told members of the CMD. The plans assumed that the industrial growth rates for US Chemicals would average 7-8 per cent per year, the same rates as had been achieved during the 1960-70 period. Werner found that assumption 'rather optimistic'. He judged the assumption that prices would remain stable as 'rather vulnerable', and voiced the hope that during the implementation of this major investment plan, progress would be monitored closely with regular re-appraisals against a changing environment, so that the plan could be adjusted if and when required.[103] The legal distance between Shell Oil and the Group was such that Shell Oil did not necessarily have to heed this warning. Expansion plans for the manufacturing complex at Deer Park included a new olefins plant, a multi-unit resins complex and environmental protection and supporting facilities, and in 1979 the projects were completed as

planned, on time and within budget. The general manager of the complex told employees proudly that 'things worked out the way they were supposed to'.[104] Other major projects included the expansion of polystyrene facilities, two polypropylene units, another large-scale Neodol detergent alcohol facility based on the SHOP process, ethylene oxide and ethylene glycol capacity and another plant for herbicides. Shell Chemicals US had achieved its aim of becoming one of the top ten Chemical companies in the US, and the largest domestic arm of any US oil company.[105]

The year 1979 was the best for the Group since 1974. Profits were high and a number of large and technically complicated projects reached their completion. Management, however, had no time to enjoy the fruits of their labour. As in 1974, the high demand in 1979 had partly been caused by stockpiling to forestall further price rises, and therefore Shell management realized that the problem of overcapacity was still very much alive. Indeed, 1980 saw a rapid decline in sales, worsened by the general economic depression, and this was true for Europe as well as the US. As

[46]

customers such as the textile, car, packaging, and building industries ran into difficulties, demand for chemicals went down. The rapid decline in sales in 1980 took the Shell companies by surprise and made management realize that they needed to embark on a radical plan for restructuring the business.[106] The seriousness of problems of the early 1980s can be judged from the capacity utilization of ethylene (the base chemical used as feedstock for many other chemical derivatives), which fell from 80 per cent in 1979 to 55 per cent in 1982.[107]

The financial results of 1980-2 were so poor that Shell even considered the option of withdrawing from petrochemicals. Had the sector become a mature industry which they should leave to others? Should Shell return to its 'core business' of oil and gas? This strategy was rejected because of the size of the chemical operations of Shell companies, their integration with the refineries and the lack of potential buyers. Moving out of chemicals was simply too expensive.[108] However, the losses gave new impetus to discussions within the industry to resolve the problem of over-capacity in Western Europe. The reduction of capacity could not easily be achieved for a number of reasons. Plant modernization, which was essential, often resulted in an increase in capacity. The closure of plants would always be an unpopular measure because of the consequent unemployment, which was hard on those employees who had to leave and demoralizing for those who were allowed to stay on. Some companies were more convinced than others that the reduction of capacity was necessary, or were more prepared to take drastic steps — for instance, national oil companies were reluctant to take action, because they gave high priority to the safeguarding of employment.[109]

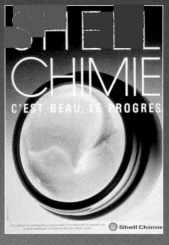

48

In 1987 Shell Chimie in France promoted its chemical products by underlining the progressive character of the chemical industry: 'Progress is beautiful'. In joint venture with Saudi Basic Industries (Sabic) Shell built a refinery and petrochemical complex at Al Jubail in Saudi Arabia.

The poor results in the petrochemical industry were not a problem unique to Shell, but an industry-wide phenomenon. Peter H. Spitz, one of the industry's analysts, posed the probing question: 'How could it be that an industry that fostered so much innovation, produced so many desirable consumer products, and was characterized by such remarkable growth over such a short period of time turned out to be so unprofitable for so many of its participants? Could the companies engaging in this industry have played the game differently, to reap greater advantage from the technological magic they created?'

Writing from the perspective of the mid-1980s, Spitz thought the worst was over because the industry had shown restraint in building up new capacity. In many large chemical companies there was far greater interest in diversification through acquisitions or in entering the production of speciality and performance chemicals that offered higher profit margins than production of basic petrochemicals.[110] Shell companies were among those showing an increasing interest in speciality chemicals.

Moving downstream in the value chain   In 1979, even before the depression of the early 1980s had set in, Anthony Lowe, head of economics and planning of Shell International Chemical Company, reflected on the business strategies of the chemical industry for the 1980s. He was not overly optimistic. With some scepticism he mentioned that individual chemical companies all seemed to follow a strategy of moving towards 'performance' chemicals: 'With, it must be admitted, considerable disillusionment in the boardrooms of chemical companies about the results from and the prospects for heavy organic chemicals and plastics – the bulk commodity end of the industry – virtually every president of every chemical company has assured his shareholders in his annual report that, as a business strategy, greater emphasis will be put on high-margin, high-technology, high-growth specialities, intermediates and other performance chemicals.'[111]

Two years later, in 1981, Lowe's picture of the future prospects of the European chemical industry had become even more pessimistic: 'Against this background of low economic growth, low growth of demand of petrochemicals and plastics, and sizeable manufacturing overcapacity for some years ahead it is impossible to avoid the conclusion that the prospects for the European petrochemicals industry in the '80s are poor unless some remedial action can be initiated in the near future.'[112]

Lowe went on to explain that he did not expect any success from efforts to come to industry-wide rationalization of manufacturing capacity or production quotas in Europe, despite 'dark rumours' that the European Commission would be prepared to initiate some sort of crisis scheme for rationalization of production of petrochemicals in Europe. He considered the chances of unanimous agreement by the Council of Ministers to a scheme for planned scrapping of plants slim, because many private companies were not in favour of regulation of the industry and national schemes would be ineffective in an international industry such as petrochemicals. Moving production facilities to other regions was a possibility, but not without risks. For instance, how long would the high economic growth in Japan continue and on what terms and conditions would European investors be accepted in Saudi Arabia? With regard to the strategy of moving into speciality chemicals, Lowe had some pertinent questions: what is the connection with petrochemicals, and is it not dangerous to assume that speciality chemicals are inherently profitable? After all, research costs were high and success was not guaranteed. He warned against the strategy of concentrating on the more profitable product lines, given the nature of co-production of products in the conventional petrochemicals complex. He ended his address by admitting that he could not pinpoint universal panaceas to remedy the problems of the European industry as he foresaw them, though perhaps some individual companies would be able to develop successful strategies. Indeed, the problems of the European chemical industry would turn out to be very persistent with each hopeful recovery crushed by another cyclical downturn.

The disappointing results of petrochemicals in the early 1980s inspired many chemical companies to focus on speciality chemicals such as catalysts, luboil additives, oil field chemicals, and agrochemicals. There was no precise, widely accepted definition of speciality chemicals. It was more about the product–market combination than the products themselves. Whereas commodity chemicals were purchased in large volumes on the basis of specification, and with price as the overwhelming consideration, speciality chemicals were purchased in small quantities on the basis of performance, and with service as an important factor. Achieving success in specialities required a different set of skills from those required in conventional petrochemicals. Engineering and operations were key aspects for petrochemicals, but speciality chemicals relied heavily on marketing and product development, and companies producing them tended to be small, flexible organizations with emphasis on R&D and marketing, compared with the large petrochemical firms. The total sales of speciality chemicals were considerably smaller than sales of conventional petrochemicals, but in the 1980s high growth rates for speciality chemicals were expected, as well as a high return on capital employed.[113] Most petrochemical manufacturers, including Shell, moved into speciality chemicals. It was foreseen that Europe would not be able to compete with Middle Eastern production of base chemicals because of the latter's easy access to cheap feedstock. However, Europe could hope to continue to compete in higher technology products, such as speciality chemicals, where quality and performance were paramount.[114] Shell was well aware that various Middle Eastern countries were planning to build petrochemical facilities, because Shell Oil was involved with one of these plans, the building of a chemical plant in Jubail, Saudi Arabia. The plant was a joint venture between Saudi Basic Industries (Sabic) and Shell Oil, and received the name Sadaf, Arabic for 'sea shell'. Negotiations with the Saudi Arabian government had started in 1976 and a decade later the plant was fully operational.[115] Saudi Arabia had formed similar joint ventures with other oil companies, as for instance with Exxon. By partnering with Sabic, the oil companies created possibilities of channelling the Saudi exports through their own distribution networks.[116]

Not only were speciality chemicals seen as requiring more intensive knowledge, they were also considered to be less affected by cyclical variations than base chemicals. But, despite the many advantages, Shell harboured some reservation about the wisdom of moving further into speciality chemicals, including agrochemicals, because these products needed extensive innovative research. Was the Shell organization and culture geared to these needs? In 1983 a study was undertaken with the help of outside consultants to shed light on this. The study found that success in speciality chemicals required leadership in markets, access to world markets, market-driven R&D, and a centralized culture and organization. Obviously, the decentralized Shell organization and culture were not compatible with some of these demands. That did not deter management of the Chemical sector from proceeding on this path, but they voiced a preference for moving ahead through acquisitions in selected areas and considered the option of taking over a major multi-product company.[117] In its wish to acquire speciality chemicals Shell was not alone: BP Chemicals took over a number of companies in the materials business, focusing on ceramics and thermoplastic composites, and Exxon Chemicals acquired interests in the areas of water-treatment and oil-field recovery chemicals.[118]

One of Shell's representatives is seen advising an onion farmer on the use of Ripcord in Indonesia in 1982.

[50]

[51]

Despite concerns about the use of pesticides, herbicides and insecticides, Shell was active in this sector until 1993. However, it stepped up toxicological research to assess the impact upon the environment as well as on the individuals producing and using the chemicals. It also had an extensive research programme to develop new pesticides that were more selective and therefore could be applied in smaller amounts. In addition Shell provided instructions to help users handle the products properly. However, stricter governmental regulations gradually banished many of these agrochemicals.

Above: Local Shell Chemical distributor of insecticides in El Salvador.

Two packages of Shell pesticides, produced by Agrishell, Shell France, the herbicide Bladex and the insecticide Fastac.

Shell had already some activities in this field of speciality chemicals, including catalysts and agrochemicals. Catalysts were a logical business for Shell because it used them widely in its own oil, gas and chemical facilities. It possessed valuable know-how thanks to its expertise in refining and its research capabilities in oil and chemicals. Growing demand was foreseen because of the high price in oil and the drive for energy saving in production processes. The application of catalysts improved the yield and made it possible to use lower temperatures in production processes and thus save energy. Environmental concerns also added to the rising demand, because catalysts could be used to remove impurities like sulphur from refined products. With the increasing emphasis on protecting the environment the demand for such catalysts was growing. Initially Shell Oil in the US manufactured the catalysts needed in the Shell operations, but when demand in Europe increased, Belgian Shell set up a catalyst plant in Ghent in 1981. Two further plants followed, which served Shell affiliates as well as third parties.[119]

[52]

Mixed results of the diversification strategy, 1973-1998

With fish cages in a rice paddy experiments were carried out in Indonesia to examine the effects of the insecticide Fastac CS on the growth and productivity of common carp.

[53]

Of even older origin within Shell were the agrochemicals. In the 1980s Shell ranked fourth among the world's agrochemicals producers, with two important centres of research in this field: Shell Development Company's Bioscience Centre in California and Sittingbourne Research Centre in the UK. They developed products such as Azodrin for protecting cotton against mites, and the weedkiller Bladex. Since the 1960s it had become increasingly clear that agrochemicals could have detrimental effects on the environment as well as positive effects on food production and health. This industry found itself caught between the conflicting demands of improving agricultural production while safeguarding public health and the environment. Focusing on the positive aspects of agrochemicals, Shell had been slow in acknowledging the full extent of the negative impact of chemicals such as aldrin and dieldrin.[120] The launch of the insecticide Fastac in 1983 was a step in the direction of combining a high activity and broad spectrum of control with reduced environmental effects.[121] In 1986 Shell Oil in the US decided to sell its agrochemicals to DuPont, partly because of disappointing results, partly because it foresaw

rising risks of litigation. However, Shell companies outside the US did not follow this example. They still had confidence in their agrochemicals business and in the ability of research to ease the problem of toxicity in the longer term.[122] Other speciality chemicals on which Shell companies focused were two products close to their own operations: additives for luboil and oil field chemicals for enhanced oil recovery.

The oil price collapse of 1986 changed the relative values of the specialities compared to base chemicals: with lower oil prices the threat of the Middle East was no longer so serious, and in addition, the production of base chemicals profited from the lower feedstock prices. For some specialist products sales prospects became less encouraging. For instance, with low oil prices the enhanced oil recovery chemicals were suddenly less in demand. Many of the enhanced oil recovery projects were postponed as they were no longer profitable. Nonetheless, Shell companies continued to invest in speciality chemicals. The lower oil prices would contribute to economic growth more generally which would benefit all chemical activities. More takeovers followed, including

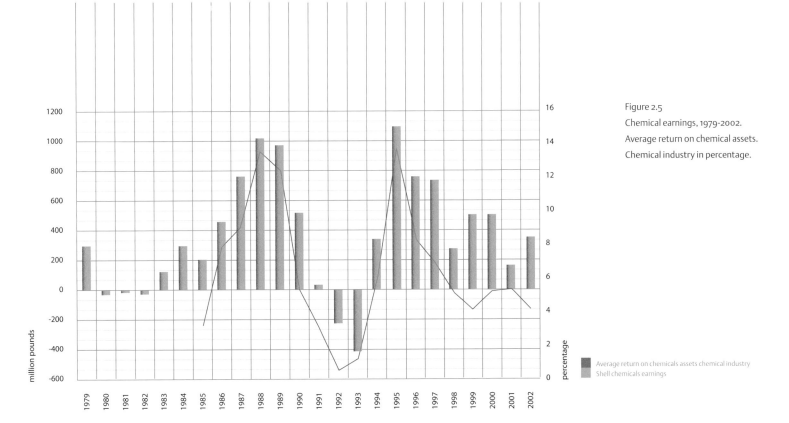

Figure 2.5
Chemical earnings, 1979-2002.
Average return on chemical assets.
Chemical industry in percentage.

Average return on chemicals assets chemical industry
Shell chemicals earnings

the German agrochemicals firm, CelaMerck, paid for with the profits from base petrochemicals, which soared in the late 1980s. Once again the future for chemicals looked bright and new investments were planned. Shell expanded in many directions. The sharp rise in oil prices as a consequence of the first Gulf War, gave the chemicals one more excellent year in 1990, but in 1991 the tide turned yet again as another economic crisis negatively affected this sector.

Figure 2.5 highlights how volatile earnings were, and how serious the situation was during the early 1990s. (Figures before 1979 were not available).[123] Shell's earnings are compared with the average return on assets in the chemical industry as a whole (chemicals companies as well as the chemicals sectors of oil companies) to illustrate how much the ups and downs were part of the general cycle of the industry. The losses in the base petrochemicals did not come as a surprise, because this part of the business was known for its volatility. But, unfortunately, the speciality chemicals, which were supposed to be more stable, gave poor results as well. Why did this sector fail to perform satisfactorily

for Shell? One tentative answer might be that the decentralized organizational structure was not ideal for this kind of business, as had been found in the 1983 study; but at the time the prospects seemed so attractive that Shell chose to ignore the results of its study. The chemical companies with whom they were competing certainly had more centralized organizations. Also, the marketing and culture for specialized products was quite different from that for bulk chemicals. Furthermore, the strategy of growing through takeovers was risky, because companies normally do not sell their crown jewels. In this context Shell's co-ordinator for Chemicals, Peter Vogtländer, concluded that the speciality business was only profitable if the business was substantially better than that of competitors. Efforts to acquire or develop a profitable business were both costly and time consuming.[124] If moving downstream in the value chain was not the answer to making the results of Shell chemicals less volatile, then what should be the next strategy?

'Strong restructuring with bold mergers'   The oil and petrochemicals consultant Roger Langley told the industry in 1993 not to expect a miraculous recovery. If the earlier cyclic features were to repeat themselves, the least efficient plants would be closed and there would be a recovery in demand in 1994-5, but he prophesied that neither was likely to happen. He recommended 'strong restructuring with bold mergers'.[125] In fact, demand picked up after 1995, showing how difficult it is to foretell the future, even for industry experts. Evert Henkes, head of Shell Chemicals International commented in 1996 on the returning problem of surplus capacity: 'One suggested strategy to cope with this is contra-cyclical investment, but this has proved to be an extraordinarily difficult thing to do in the petrochemicals cycle, possibly because the "cycle" may not be so predictable after all.' He added: 'There is a question as to whether it's a cyclical business, or whether it's a volatile business.'[126] Whatever it was, it certainly was difficult to make sufficient money out of chemicals over the cycle. This was unfortunate, because in the 1990s shareholders in the US and Europe became increasingly vocal, pressing management to achieve high returns on investment. Targets of 12 per cent or more return on average capital employed were difficult to realize in a capital-intensive industry such as petrochemicals. As a consequence, companies tended to be very critical towards 'under-performing assets', selling units off or closing them down.

In the 1990s Shell strategies were mostly shaped through buying and selling companies and business units. There did not seem to be time for internal growth or gradual transformation. Companies were bought, merged and divested again. In this Shell was not alone. As *The Economist* wrote in 1997: 'European chemical companies are splitting and recombining faster than molecules in a catalytic cracker'.[127] Following the bad results of the early 1990s, management of Shell Chemicals decided that a more selective and focused approach was needed. The 'select and focus' strategy placed the emphasis back on the core petrochemical business, but it did not dismiss all specialized business and it kept the door open for new developments. The portfolio of businesses remained under constant review, and management's views on what should be developed, maintained for cash, milked for profit or sold changed frequently in response to changing circumstances.[128]

Behind this restructuring strategy were two main drivers. First was the enormous pressure, referred to above, of reaching a return on average capital employed of 12 per cent or more. One might wonder whether the target was not unrealistically high. In 1979 it was calculated that between 1959 and 1979 the average return on capital in Shell's chemical sector (excluding the USA and Canada) had been 6.4 per cent.[129] Realizing more than twice as much was a tough target, to say the least. Because many activities did not earn that much money they were continuously candidates for divestiture. Research was under constant pressure to become more focused and reduce expenses. The development of in-house technology only occurred where this provided a clear advantage over out-sourcing.[130] The second driver was the globalization of markets. Companies responded by concentrating on products in which they could create a global position. Becoming market leader worldwide was the ultimate goal. This strategy implied cutting down the portfolio, because it was impossible to achieve leadership in a large number of products. Small businesses had to go because they could not achieve 'critical mass'. In the 1970s the supposed synergy between different activities and products had been a powerful argument to spread the net wide. This was no longer seen as a valid argument: each line of business had to prove its value independently, and many did not stand the test. However, it would be wrong to suppose that the globalization strategy only led to a reduction in the activities. It also led to new business initiatives in Asia.

In the constant process of restructuring of the 1990s, Shell first divested its agrochemicals business, including the recently acquired CelaMerck by selling it to the American Cyanamid

'European chemical companies are splitting and recombining
faster than molecules in a catalytic cracker'. *Economist, 15-02-1997*

Company in 1993.[131] Next to go were the fine chemicals, mostly
intermediates for pharmaceuticals or the speciality chemical
industry. These were sold in 1996 to Inspec plc., a young company
formed in 1992 as a result of the sale of an existing BP business.[132]
Clearly BP was following a comparable divestment policy. Shell did
not divest all speciality chemicals, however. Two were kept: the
catalysts and additives businesses. The catalysts business in Europe
was combined with that of Shell Oil.[133] Because leadership
positions were considered of utmost importance, Shell did not
want to continue with the additives business on its own. What was
needed was 'critical mass' to make an impact on the market. The
best way to achieve this critical mass seemed to be the formation of
a 50/50 joint venture, incorporating the additives businesses of
Shell companies and those of Exxon. This choice was surprising
because of the strong links between additives and the lubricants
business, where both parties were fierce competitors. The joint
venture would therefore require Chinese walls between the
respective research competences of Shell and Exxon. The deal was
agreed upon in 1996.[134]

Illustrative of the policy of restructuring through bold
mergers was the history of Shell's polyolefin business. In 1992 Shell
started discussions with the Italian company Montedison to merge
their worldwide polyolefins interests on a 50/50 basis. The
combined business would have a market share of approximately 19
per cent of world polypropylene sales. In Western Europe the
market share would be 25 per cent and in North America between
25 and 30 per cent. Shell would become the manager. Montedison
would contribute the chemical business of its Himont subsidiary
and Shell companies certain polypropylene and feedstock
businesses. The joint venture would mean a saving on research and
development costs. Shell Chemical in the US, in particular, would

benefit from the combination through feedstock integration.[135] As
negotiations evolved it became clear that Shell Chemical could not
participate in the joint venture because of arrangements with
Union Carbide. In 1988 Shell Chemical and Union Carbide had set
up a polypropylene joint venture facility at Seadrift, Texas, in which
a successful Shell Chemical catalyst SHAC was combined with
Union Carbide's Unipol process and international licensing
experience.[136] Union Carbide was unwilling to terminate this joint
venture. The next hurdle was a restructuring of Ferruzzis Finanziaria
and Montedison, which required the banks' acceptance before a
merger deal could proceed, but in December 1993 an agreement
with Montedison was signed. Nevertheless, before the new joint
venture under the name Montell could become operational, the
cartel authorities in Europe and the US had to finish their inquiries
into the planned merger. In early 1995 agreement was reached, and
nearly three years after the start of the negotiations Montell finally
took off.[137] Just two years later Montedison decided that
petrochemicals were no longer part of their future strategy. Shell
was prepared to take over their 50 per cent share because the
acquisition would be a significant step towards realizing their
chemicals vision of becoming the leading global petrochemicals
company; it was also considered useful with regard to future
alliances and restructuring of the chemicals portfolio. In the annual
report of 1997 the acquisition was praised with the following words:
'In 1997 the venture's ownership passed entirely into the hand of
Shell companies, thereby demonstrating their belief in the
development potential of polypropylene and their determination to
remain the world leader in the production and marketing of this
thermoplastic.'

According to its new CEO, Peter Vogtländer, Montell was a fantastic business, an acknowledged leader in technology, substantially larger than the competitors and much more global. What really puzzled him was why such a strong business could not achieve satisfactory results.[138] It went against all managerial wisdom, which suggested that good results came from being the undisputed market leader. However, after having achieved its initial goal of world leadership with Montell, Shell management decided that being the number one in this business was not so attractive after all, because it also meant being very exposed. After only one year of 100 per cent ownership, in 1998 disappointing financial results led to the decision to put 50 per cent of Montell up for sale as part of a large restructuring plan.

The restructuring of 1998 was as bold as the Montell merger. In 1997 Shell Chemicals had presented its business plan 'building on basics'. With the use of the Directional Policy Matrix, developed by Shell in the early 1970s, this plan examined once again the portfolio of businesses to find out in which of them Shell could hope to achieve 'leadership'. By 'leadership' the authors meant 'the possession of a sufficient sustainable competitive advantage to deliver robust financial performance'. The position of competitors was analysed to determine where Shell could hope to find its competitive advantage. The study saw base petrochemicals and intermediates as the foundation of the future portfolio,

recommended the purchase of the 50 per cent share in Montell, and proposed the divestment of PVC, synthetic rubber and polybutylene. A number of more specialized products should remain. The study followed the decision taken earlier that year to turn Shell Chemicals into a global company, including the activities in the US. All product business units became responsible for their own global profit and loss accounts, which made it possible to take decisions on the basis of the global perspective of the various business units. The creation of global product business units made it easier to carve out specific activities and sell them.[139] But which should be sold and which kept? When Shell's chemical business was still in its early phase, in 1961, management had discussed its future, considering a choice between focusing on large-volume base chemicals; on small-volume new to be discovered products; or on the manufacture of end-products. At that time management was not in favour of limiting the business to base chemicals.[140] Thirty-seven years later, however, the discussions on the future portfolio culminated in the tough decision, taken in October 1998, to go 'back to basics' and dramatically reduce the chemicals business activities outside the base chemicals and intermediates. No less than 40 per cent of the chemicals business was put up for sale. This included finding a joint venture partner for the 50 per cent of Montell that Shell had acquired the year before.[141]

A special divestment team was set up to deal with the sale of the product business units that were marked for divestment. With regard to the 50 per cent share of Montell an agreement could be reached with BASF in 1999 which also included Elenac, the joint venture of all European polyethylene activities of Shell and BASF established in 1998. The new venture proceeded under the name Basell.[142] Apart from diminishing its exposure in polyolefins through this joint venture, Shell also divested various businesses in

In the 1990s the chemical industry restructured constantly, and so did Shell. In 1995 Montedison and Shell combined their polyolefin businesses in the joint venture Montell. Two years later Shell became full owner and soon after started negotiations with BASF about a joint venture of their polyolefin businesses, which led to the formation of Basell. The picture shows Montell's Giulio Natta Research Centre in Italy in 1997.

the groups of polymers — including PVC, general-purpose rubbers, thermoplastic elastomers, and resins — in the late 1990s, because these activities were not in a leadership position.[143]

In some cases new developments pursued in the 1990s were abandoned again in the reorganization of 1998. This was true for both polyethylene terephthalate (PET) and Carilon. In 1989 Shell had built the first PET plant in Italy to produce tough, light and transparent, recyclable packaging material. It was used in the bottling industry, replacing glass with plastic bottles. Shell was not the first in this market, where polyester producers had already a strong position, but it hoped to compete on the basis of Shell's different technology. In the early 1990s PET resins for packaging were seen as one of the sector's promising new developments targeted to grow for profit. As sales were rising, expansion of capacity in the US, UK, and Italy took place to keep up a leading position, but Shell's optimism about PET did not last long. In 1997 it was decided to divest PET, because it was, after all, not in a leadership position. In fact, the losses were serious and it was difficult to find a buyer, let alone make money out of the sale.[144] Another promising new venture, based on Shell technology, turned out equally disappointing. The new polymer under the trade name of Carilon, developed and heavily patented by Shell, was expected to have competitive manufacturing costs, but Shell proceeded carefully with a pilot plant at Moerdijk before taking further investment decisions. Carilon belonged to the engineering thermoplastics, which found their way into automotive, electrical, and industrial and appliance markets. However, the manufacturing costs were high compared to bulk grade nylon and the major chemical companies had competing products. The first Carilon plant was built in 1994. For a few years Carilon functioned as a positive example of new products developed by in-house research,

but in 1998 it was on the list for divestiture. Nearly thirty companies were contacted to buy Carilon but none was interested. In the end Shell had to close it down.[145]

Even Shell's successful high performance thermoplastic elastomer, Kraton G, was sold. This product was used in applications where an attractive feel, flexibility and durability were needed, for instance the handgrip of screwdrivers and bicycles or the housings for car gearsticks or the teats of babies' bottles. For many years, Shell only manufactured Kraton G in the US, where production had started in 1974. As demand increased, Shell decided to come to Europe with this exciting product. In 1992 the building of a Kraton G plant in Berre, France, was announced and within thirty months it was ready for production. 'We had high expectations that the product would perform well and it has. The technology is very versatile and lends itself to a great deal of further development,' Peter Boorman, head of Shell Chemicals European thermoplastic elastomer business, remarked in 1994.[146] Nevertheless, in the big sale of 1998 Kraton G went together with the rest of the elastomer business. As a consequence of the drastic reorganization of 1998 staff numbers in the chemicals sector went down from 21,000 in 1997 to 10,000 in 2000.[147]

Back to basics In the future Shell would concentrate on the core products in petrochemicals: the major cracker products, petrochemical building blocks, and large volume polymers.[148] What had happened in the meantime with these base chemicals, the production most closely related to the oil refineries? As discussed above, Shell made efforts in the early 1980s to reduce production capacity, in particular ethylene capacity in Europe. Competitors had done the same. For instance, the ethylene capacity in Western Europe went down from 17 million tonnes in 1980 to 14.7 million in 1990, a reduction of 14 per cent. The reduction, however, was unevenly spread over the industry. The oil majors and chemical companies had reduced their capacity considerably, while the national oil companies from consumer countries had somewhat increased theirs. After 1990 all groups once again enlarged their capacity, while Shell capacity already increased after 1985.[149] This increase partly resulted from improving existing plants and removing bottlenecks, and partly from new capacity coming on stream. Related to the oil and gas production in the North Sea, Shell and Esso had built a jointly owned ethylene cracker in Mossmorran in the UK, which came on stream in 1985. At the same time the older ethylene cracker and some derivative plants at Carrington in the UK were closed. In Europe efforts were concentrated on higher efficiency and the reduction of the workforce. One way of increasing efficiency was to

After 1998 Shell Chemicals went back to basics, concentrating on base chemicals. Control room at the Shell Pernis COD plant, manufacturing solvents, in 2006.

[55]

change the organizational structure from one based on national organizations to one based on business units. The feeling was that competitors such as Dow Chemicals could move more quickly and had lower costs because they could direct centrally all activities within Europe. After extensive study the European chemical activities were brought together under the co-ordination of Shell Chemicals Europe in 1994. Shell Chemicals Europe managed the largest petrochemical business in Europe, with 7,000 staff spread throughout eighteen operating companies. It included twelve manufacturing sites in seven countries.[150]

During the 1980s the Asian countries, and in particular Japan, displayed rapid economic growth, which was looked upon with envy by the US and Europe. Asia seemed to be the place where things happened, where one had to be. This was also true for the chemical industry. The move away from the USA and Western Europe can be illustrated by developments in the key petrochemical product ethylene. In 1970 the USA and Western Europe had respectively 45 and 37 per cent of world ethylene capacity (excluding the Communist bloc), Japan had 13 per cent and the rest of the world a mere 5 per cent. In 1990 the figures were respectively 35, 28, and 11 per cent for USA, Western Europe, and Japan, while the rest of the world had no less than 26 per cent.[151] After 1990 this trend continued, with increasing shares for the Middle East and Asia, in particular China.[152]

Shell managers too decided that it was desirable for the chemicals sector to gain access to the Asia/Pacific region, and in 1987 they started negotiation with the government of Singapore to take over their shares in a large petrochemical complex in Singapore as part of their privatization programme. The other partners were various Japanese consortia, including Sumitomo. Agreement was reached in 1989. Shell did not see this participation as a portfolio investment, but wanted to play an active role in management.[153] In 1994 Shell decided to make a major investment in this area by building a second integrated petrochemical complex in Singapore consisting of an ethylene cracker, polyolefins plants, and an SM/PO plant based on Shell technology. Though the domestic market was small, high demand was expected in regional markets. A similar SM/PO plant was built in Moerdijk, in the Netherlands, also in joint venture with BASF, to be integrated with the older SM/PO unit.[154] In the early 1990s the question arose whether the rapidly expanding industrial base of southern China might offer serious competition to centres like Singapore. Shell concluded that it was best to be present in both places and started a feasibility study into a refinery and petrochemical complex in the Guangdong province. Since the early 1970s Shell had been involved in selling its chemical products to China. The China Nanhai project took a long time to study and negotiate. Finally in 2000 agreement was reached to set up a 50/50 joint venture between Shell Chemicals and the China National Offshore Oil Corporation (CNOOC) to manufacture and sell a range of petrochemicals, principally intended for the Chinese domestic market. It included an SM/PO plant.[155] Production in the Far East was considered particularly attractive because of its large potential markets. Figure 2.6 shows that for many years the sales of Shell Chemicals were focused on the US and Europe. Recently, however, Shell's sales in the Eastern Hemisphere have increased, while those in Europe have fallen.[156]

Figure 2.7 summarizes the oil and non-oil earnings of Shell for the 1975-2002 period.[157] The chemicals sector had a marked influence on the total results of the group. The earnings and losses of the other non-oil activities in total, however, were modest compared to the results of the oil activities.

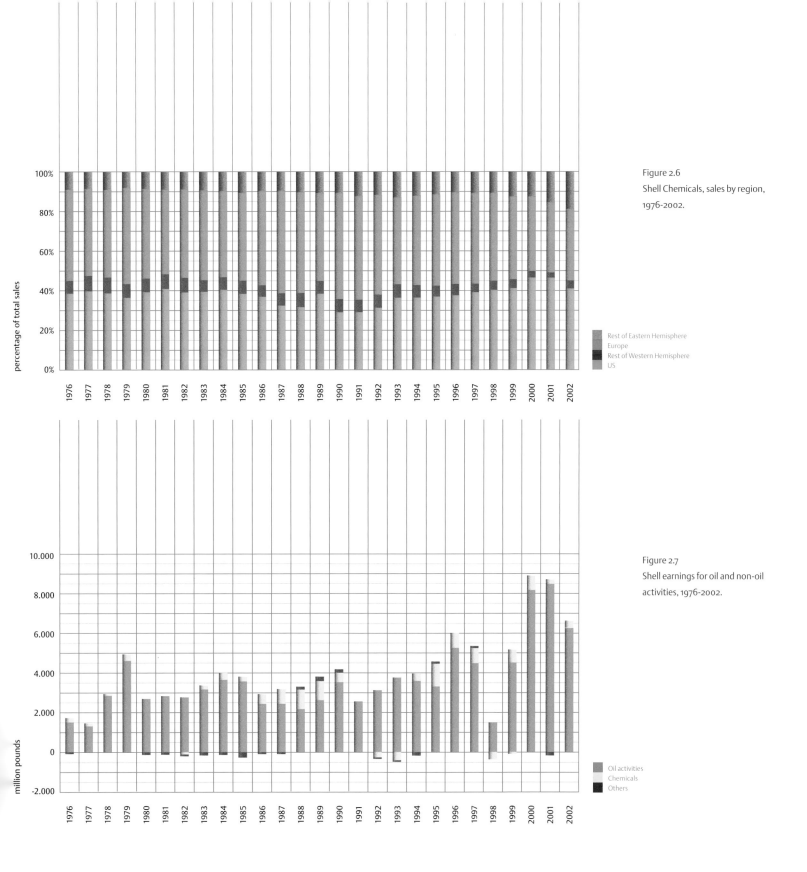

Figure 2.6
Shell Chemicals, sales by region,
1976-2002.

percentage of total sales

Rest of Eastern Hemisphere
Europe
Rest of Western Hemisphere
US

Figure 2.7
Shell earnings for oil and non-oil
activities, 1976-2002.

million pounds

Oil activities
Chemicals
Others

[56]

Conclusion In their attention to the possibilities of diversification Shell managers initially responded to the general business philosophy of the day, which prescribed that one should strengthen one's company by engaging in other fields. This general motivation led to the entry into the metal business. When the oil business came under pressure from oil-producing countries and oil prices began to rise, a move into other sources of energy, such as nuclear, coal, and later forestry, seemed to be particularly relevant for an oil company. Looking back on thirty years of diversification one is struck by the tireless energy of Shell employees in looking for new fields, new products, new processes or new ways of doing business. After each setback they tried again with undiminished confidence to do better next time round with hopefully greater financial rewards. Not only did Shell enter new industries, but it also wanted to contribute added value in the form of innovative research results or novel marketing approaches. The chemicals sector also spread its wings in many directions, some of them based on unique Shell technologies. By 2000, however, the activities in metals, nuclear, coal and forestry, so optimistically and perhaps naively embarked upon, had been divested. Some of them had brought positive earnings, but most had not. The chemicals sector had returned to base chemicals and a selection of derivatives and polymer. However, it had become geographically much more varied, so not all initiatives were lost.

The result of all the comings and going discussed in this chapter was that many employees and countries had mixed experiences with Shell. High hopes for new employment or new businesses in their country turned into disenchantment when Shell decided to leave again. Indonesia is an example of how the continuously changing ambitions affected this country. Shell embarked on tin dredging and gold mining and withdrew again, it took on coal exploration and shared in coal production and left the field again, each time accompanied by job losses, leaving the staff discouraged.[158]

In the mid-term evaluation of the diversification process, we concluded that part of the frustration with the diversification process may have lain in the unrealistic expectations of the growth that could be achieved and the financial benefits that might accrue. The decentralized organizational structure of Shell offered an advantage when entering a new field worldwide, but it increased the operating costs, making the new ventures less competitive compared to smaller companies in the field. The fact that all the oil majors followed more or less the same diversification strategy brought a serious risk of making the target businesses overcrowded and less profitable. The chemicals sector wrestled with high volatility in its results, which demanded from management considerable conviction in periods of economic downturn to hang on to its business. With hindsight we know that the petrochemical industry faced an uphill struggle in the last quarter of the twentieth century, because the fundamental discoveries had already taken place in products as well as processes. In most cases companies had to be content with increasing efficiency of their processes and improving the performance of their products. The key to understanding Shell's disappointing experiences with the diversification can probably be found in Werner's comment of 1971: 'I do not know of any important other business but Oil combining low labour and high capital with a high rate of return. "There simply is no other business like the Oil business".'[159] None of the new businesses could compare in profitability with the oil sector. The target of 12 per cent return on average capital employed was simply too high, the yardstick frustrating for management. Shell came to the logical conclusion that it should focus its energies on its core business. Petrochemicals, however, being closely related to the core business, remained part of the Group.

Adjusting to a world of low oil prices and global markets, 1986-1998

The year 1986 marked the beginning of a long period of low crude oil prices, which lasted till 1998. The OPEC cartel did not disappear but it was unable to keep prices up, because oil supply outstripped demand. The fall of the Berlin Wall in 1989 heralded the collapse of communist regimes in Eastern Europe and the political disintegration of the Soviet Union. Capitalism seemed to have demonstrated its superiority over communism. While during the 1960s and 1970s government influence on the oil industry had been on the rise, now the ideology of the free market dictated a more modest role for governments. Liberalism and globalization combined in increasing competitive pressure on the oil industry, leading to sustained efforts to reduce costs and increase operational flexibility.

This chapter explores how Shell's upstream and downstream business fared during the period of low oil prices. The low prices gave customers more clout over the industry, underlining the importance of marketing. Shell countered the increasing competition from national oil companies from oil-producing countries on the European and American markets by seeking new markets in Eastern Europe, Latin America and Asia. In exploration and production the focus was on cutting costs by the application of the newest technology, by making the most of existing opportunities rather than through greenfield ventures, and by creating access to major resource holding countries. In its long-term scenarios Shell identified gas as the energy source of the near future, the clean and versatile energy source that could act as a bridge between declining oil production and the renewable energy of the distant future.

In 1989 the Berlin Wall came down, soon followed by the collapse of communist regimes in Eastern Europe and the political disintegration of the Soviet Union. Finally people from Eastern Europe could travel freely to the Western European countries, and many of them did so by car. Some were even helped by the border guards to keep their cars – often the well-known East German brand Trabant – moving forward.

[2]

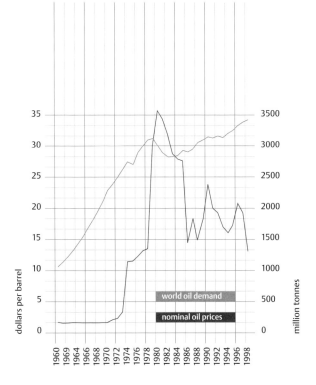

Figure 3.1
Crude oil prices and world oil demand,
1960-1998.

Oil price collapse   More shocking for the industry than the oil price rises in 1973 and 1979, was the oil price collapse of 1986. Though oil prices had come down slowly from their 1979 peak in the early 1980s, they remained fairly high until January 1986. The OPEC producers found it increasingly difficult to defend the high oil prices achieved in 1979. On the one hand, customers had responded to the high oil prices by reducing demand, in particular for non-transport fuels. They had also become more energy-conscious and devised methods to use energy more efficiently. On the other hand, the oil companies had opened up new production areas outside the OPEC countries. The rising production in non-OPEC countries, including the North Sea, changed the scarcity of oil into a glut. The only way in which OPEC producers could harden the crude oil price was by reducing their own production, but in the previous years their governments had become used to spending their oil dollars lavishly, and therefore it was difficult to accept lower incomes from oil, all the more as their oil revenues had already come down because of inflation. The OPEC countries found it hard to close ranks. This led to the marked fall in prices from December 1985 onwards.

Figure 3.1 highlights the movement of crude oil prices and world oil demand between 1960 and 2002.[1] It shows the huge volatility in prices in particular between 1970 and 1990. The two price hikes of 1973 and 1979 pushed up the oil prices to unprecedented heights, but the price fall in 1986 was equally spectacular. The situation was even more dramatic than the annual figures reveal. The WTI (West Texan Intermediate) future market reached a peak of $31.75 per barrel on 20 November 1985, and over the next few months prices dropped as low as $10 per barrel.[2] The price of Brent crude fell from $26.30 per barrel in 1985 to the meagre sum of $9 per barrel in July 1986.[3]

For insiders the oil price collapse did not entirely come as a surprise, because in the years after 1979 prices had come down gradually. Since the late 1960s, Shell used scenario planning to anticipate the need for changes. In mid-1985 the Committee of Managing Directors (CMD) asked the planning department to study the effects of an 'Oil Price Collapse' (OPC) scenario. For different price scenarios the short-term and long-term consequences were calculated in great detail. In December 1985 Arie de Geus presented the results of these calculations to the Conference. The report concluded the Group was in a strong position to face a short-term collapse in prices: 'Our analysis so far suggests, however, that if oil prices do not collapse for a prolonged period below $10 per barrel the Group would have significant room for manoeuvre relative to many competitors.'[4] As a consequence of this preparatory work, the Group was able to act quickly when the oil prices started to fall rapidly in December 1985 and the first half of 1986. As we will see later in the chapter, Shell was determined not to overreact and risk long-term growth prospects, because it expected prices to rally within a few years.

The low oil prices were good news for oil-consuming countries, bad news for oil-producing countries, and mixed news

In 1988 the war between Iraq and Iran came to an end. Crowds of Iraqis gathered at Baghdad stadium to celebrate the ceasefire.

For the Iraqi people the peace did not last long, however. In August 1990 Iraq invaded Kuwait, causing a stark but short-lived oil price rise. As a consequence the gasoline prices in the US rose immediately (picture top right). In February 1991 a US-led coalition forced Iraqi troops out of Kuwait. Retreating Iraqi troops set many oil wells on fire.

for the US, which was both producer and consumer. The vice-president of the US, George Bush, visited Saudi Arabia to encourage them to take measures to stop the price fall, because low prices would cripple the domestic American energy industries, with serious consequences for the nation.[5] In December 1986 the OPEC countries succeeded in stopping the price fall, and maintaining the price in the range of $17 to $19 per barrel. A ceasefire between Iraq and Iran in August 1988 did not upset the oil prices. The invasion of Kuwait by Iraq in 1990, however, caused a stark but short-lived price rise. The invasion was followed by intense international negotiations about how to react to the challenge posed by Saddam Hussein. In February 1991, a US-led coalition came to the defence of Kuwait and forced Iraq out of Kuwait. Interestingly, crude oil prices went down as soon as the counter-attack began. They remained at a low level all through the 1990s, with a nadir in 1998, when crude oil prices dipped below $10 dollar per barrel.

[3]

[4]

REG. UNLEADED | SUPER REGULAR | SUPER UNLEADED

1 1 3 9/10 | 123 9/10 | 132

SHELL | SELF SERVE | GASOLINE

[5]

[6]

Adjusting to a world of low oil prices and global markets, 1986-1998

Globalization and Liberalization

Since the early 1980s, the globalization of markets had been prophesied. One of the first to use this expression was Theodore Levitt, who wrote in 1983: 'A powerful force drives the world toward a converging commonality, and that force is technology. (...) The result is a new commercial reality – the emergence of global markets for standardized consumer products on a previously unimagined scale of magnitude. (..) Gone are accustomed differences in national or regional preference. Gone are the days when a company could sell last year's models – or lesser versions of advanced products – in the less-developed world. And gone are the days when prices, margins, and profits abroad were generally higher than at home. The globalization of markets is at hand.'[6]

The word globalization caught the imagination and quickly became a household name for all kinds of developments, ranging from the creation of a world market in consumer goods and companies who plan their production facilities on a worldwide basis, to international capital markets, cross-border alliances and mergers and growing foreign direct investment. Whether globalization was something new, whether it really took place, and whether it was a positive or a negative phenomenon remained under discussion for the rest of the century.[7] Shell certainly prepared itself for competition on global markets. Since the Second World War the oil industry had been divided into a communist and a non-communist area. This division disappeared after the collapse of the Soviet Union and the regime changes in many Eastern European countries. Though the political and economic situation in the former Soviet Union remained unstable, their large reserves of oil and gas offered enticing opportunities for exploration and production. Another big country, China, which had opened up in the late 1970s, started negotiations with foreign companies about investing there.

Market liberalization, including deregulation, reduced protectionism and, in some cases, diminishing government participation, characterized the 1990s. How did this trend influence the oil industry? John Jennings, Group managing director, commented in 1994: 'In today's globalised business world, whether in the unrepentantly Capitalist systems of the G7 countries or in the more hesitantly emerging nations, one of the catchphrases is 'the market will decide'. That may be so, but I think if we are honest with ourselves, many now-senior managers in the energy industries would say that we have spent much of our careers dealing with markets which are seriously imperfect. For example, governments and their utilities have controlled large parts of the entire power generation chain.'[8]

Politics remained important in the oil industry, but many governments privatized their national oil companies, and some deregulation of energy markets took place. Though Jennings did not expect a global free market in energy, he noticed that not only the US and the UK, but also countries such as China, Russia, India, Argentina and Chile, had adopted free-market reforms as objectives and were on their way to implementing them through privatization and deregulation programmes. Europe made a start with the abolition of national energy regimes. The Middle East governments clung to their national oil companies but began to invite foreign oil companies back in.

Upstream wrestling with low oil price   High and low oil prices had different influences on different parts of the oil business, as can be illustrated by comparing the movements in crude oil price with investment in exploration and production on the one hand, and manufacturing and marketing on the other. Figure 3.2 (see page 164) summarizes Shell's investment policy during periods of high and low oil prices. (Prices and investments are measured at 1974 levels, and are thus adjusted for inflation).[9]

During the period of low oil prices in the 1960s investment by Shell companies in exploration and production was relatively low, while investment in manufacturing and marketing was high. After the first oil shock of 1973 the picture changed dramatically with investments in the upstream business going up, and those in the downstream going down. High crude oil prices were favourable for exploration and production because they boosted profits as well as prospects, and both encouraged further investment in this sector. For the downstream business the consequences of high crude oil prices were more mixed. High crude oil prices led to higher prices for oil products, but the increase was probably not enough to compensate for the more costly feedstock. Moreover, high prices in oil products reduced demand. After the oil price collapse of 1986 the picture changed once more, with upstream investment going down and downstream going up, though not as much as one might have expected. It is clear that in the upstream part of the business there was a much closer link between investment and crude oil prices than in the downstream part. Low oil prices were downright disadvantageous for upstream, but had more varied consequences for the downstream business. The story of the downstream business will be told later on in this chapter. First, the focus is on the hard struggle of exploration and production to adjust to the fall in oil prices and their continued low level during the 1990s.

Because of its scenarios Shell had already envisioned a world of cheap oil, and as soon as the collapse occurred the Group immediately put a number of very expensive exploration projects on hold. In 1986 Shell did not expect the oil prices to remain very low for a long period. Though it put the brake on expenditures in exploration and production in the short term, it did not want to

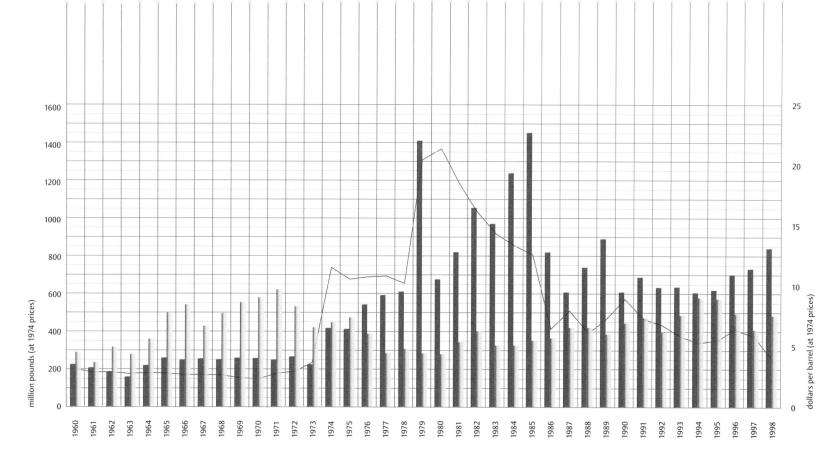

Figure 3.2
Crude oil prices and Shell's investment
policy, 1960-1998.

forego medium-to-long-term investment opportunities. However, by 1988 Shell top management was convinced the oil price would remain low for the coming years. John Jennings, then head of E&P, believed that sustained price rises above $20 per barrel were unlikely.[10] Though the price rise in 1990 seemed to prove him wrong, this rise turned out to be short-lived, only caused by the political situation in the Middle East. For the rest of the 1990s, the price of oil remained low. Moreover, the oil fields in the North Sea and Oman were beginning to mature, which meant incurring higher costs to produce the remaining oil. How did Shell's E&P counter this situation?

New technological solutions offered one way of tackling lower incomes and rising production costs. Over the years the oil industry, including Shell, developed many initiatives in this direction with major technical successes and breakthrough performances. Three-dimensional seismic technology was the single most important technological breakthrough in the last quarter of the twentieth century. With the help of high-speed

Success in oil and gas exploration and production depends largely on the quality of knowledge about underground rock formation. The more sophisticated the knowledge the higher the success rate in exploration, while better insight into reservoirs of oil and gas hugely supports oil and gas production. The three-dimensional (3D) seismic surveys, developed during the 1980s, played an essential role in acquiring better insight into underground rock formation and reservoir behaviour.

The first step in making 3D seismic surveys consisted of creating vibrations in the surface by a bang. Seismic vibrations trucks, such as those shown above in the Omani desert, created vibrations on the ground by moving a heavy weight up and down. The signals were picked up by geophones and stored. The stored information was then sent to computers, which were provided with special software to manipulate the information and finally turn the signal into a three-dimensional survey of the underground terrain. The results could be printed out as a two-dimensional map, but also shown in three-dimensional computer images. In the picture (middle), the colour blue stands for water, green is gas and red is oil At the computer the layers could be rotated, and the reservoir characteristics assessed from different angles.

[9]

[10]

[11]

[12]

Adjusting to a world of low oil prices and global markets, 1986-1998

[13]

Horizontal drilling, seen here left, has been known since 1929, but its special value became apparent with the discovery of oil fields in tight strata of low permeability, such as chalk and limestone. Because in such fields oil does not flow easily, with normal vertical drilling only 5-10 per cent of the oil would be produced. Horizontal drilling, however, could intersect natural fractures, or even link up separate parts of a reservoir. In the mid-1980s this technique became in use in the industry. Shell played an active role in the development of this technique.

Exploration drilling at Colorado Creek in Guatamala with the slim-hole drilling technique in 1992. Slim holes are much cheaper and have less impact on the environment than conventional drilling.

computers and advanced software geologists were able to manipulate vast quantities of geological data generated by an exposion or a bang on the earth's surface. From the vast amount of data they could build three-dimensional images of the structures of an oil basin, enhancing their understanding of the oil and gas reserves. This enabled them to drill exploration wells more accurately, design new facilities effectively and optimize the use of the installed infrastructure. As a result of faster computers and better software, calculations that took months in the past, could be finished in a matter of days. In the late 1980s Shell stepped up its efforts in 3D imaging. Before 1985 Shell's operating companies (outside North America and excluding partner operated surveys) covered less than 4,000 square kilometres per year with 3D seismic surveys, but in 1990 they covered 16,000 square kilometres on land as well as sea.[11]

An astonishing new technology allowed wells to be drilled which deviated from vertical to the horizontal, the so-called horizontal wells. Oil that normally would be by-passed by conventional drilling could be reached by horizontal drilling. Though horizontal drilling was more expensive than conventional drilling, these higher costs were easily offset by improvements in productivity and increases in production. Drilling costs could be reduced by drilling smaller holes, so-called 'slim hole drilling'. This technology made it possible to drill wells as small as 4 inches in diameter up to 5000 metres. This new technology allowed a whole series of reductions in rig size, location area, casing, drilling mud, cement and transport, which all contributed to lower costs. As drilling often accounted for more than half the costs of exploration and field development, reducing these costs was of vital importance in a period of low crude oil prices. It also had environmental advantages, because it resulted in less mud and fewer cuttings.[12] Improvements in design led to platforms that were smaller and lighter and needed fewer people to staff them. Unmanned platforms were commonly used to develop smaller accumulations.

[14]

Adjusting to a world of low oil prices and global markets, 1986-1998

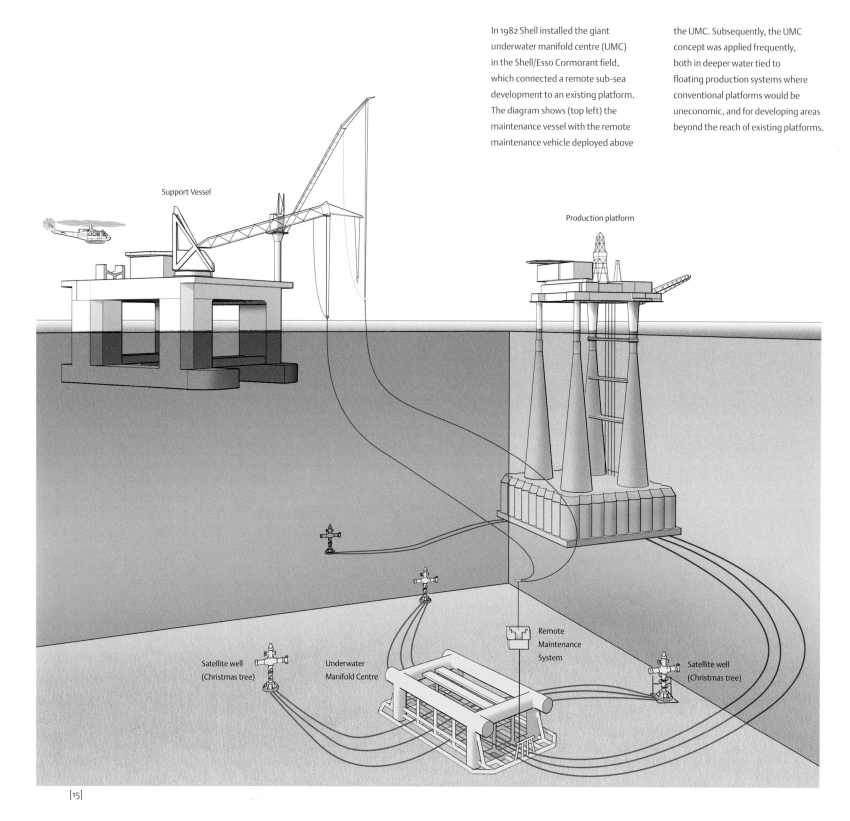

In 1982 Shell installed the giant underwater manifold centre (UMC) in the Shell/Esso Cormorant field, which connected a remote sub-sea development to an existing platform. The diagram shows (top left) the maintenance vessel with the remote maintenance vehicle deployed above the UMC. Subsequently, the UMC concept was applied frequently, both in deeper water tied to floating production systems where conventional platforms would be uneconomic, and for developing areas beyond the reach of existing platforms.

Support Vessel

Production platform

Satellite well
(Christmas tree)

Underwater
Manifold Centre

Remote
Maintenance
System

Satellite well
(Christmas tree)

[15]

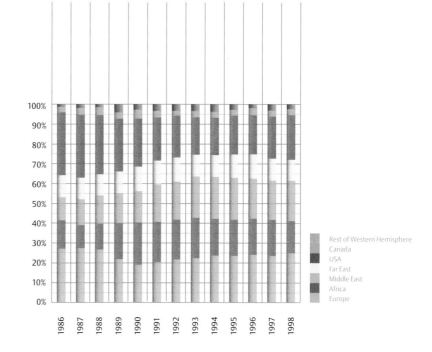

Figure 3.3
Regional division of Shell equity oil production, 1986-1998.

	Rest of Western Hemisphere
	Canada
	USA
	Far East
	Middle East
	Africa
	Europe

Tension leg platforms, floating production and storage vessels, and sub-sea manifold hubs made it possible to reduce substantially the very high costs of exploring and producing in ever deeper water.

In the battle with low oil prices, Shell further tightened its criteria for new investment and focused on more intensive exploration of existing oil provinces. In 1991 there still appeared to be an adequate supply of opportunities. As a consequence of the energetic exploration in the 1970s and 1980s, by 1992 Shell's equity reserves had risen to the pre-nationalization levels of the late 1950s, no mean achievement.[13] This was all the more remarkable, because few new oil provinces had been discovered by Shell or its competitors during the period of high oil prices and hectic activity in the early 1980s, and under the present circumstances it was even more difficult to find a significant source. For that reason Shell treasured the small 'bread and butter' discoveries in its existing producing areas.[14] In 2001 Andrew Wood, head of Global Exploration, gave the following description of Shell's capabilities and choices: 'Shell people and technology are good at making the most out of mature producing provinces. During the 1990s Shell proved to be very good at exploring in its own back yard. (...) In terms of Shell's ability to replace its reserves, we add a lot more through reserves revisions than our competitors. It is also a reflection of the fact that Shell tends to be relatively conservative when it comes to booking reserves before a discovery is developed,

but allows the reserves estimates to grow over time as we gain confidence in a field.'[15]

A third option for Shell to solve the problem of higher cost and lower prices was finding upstream opportunities in major resource-holding areas in the Middle East, like Saudi Arabia, Iran and Iraq, or in the countries of the former Soviet Union. The OPEC strategy of raising oil prices in the 1970s had created the ironic situation that the major oil companies had produced the expensive oil first while the cheap oil of the Middle East remained in the ground. Shell expected that continuing low oil prices would shift the focus of the oil industry back to the Middle East as low cost producer, and it was eager to re-enter this area.

Figure 3.3 highlights the regional division of Shell's crude oil production.[16] The importance of oil production in the North Sea and the USA diminished, while Africa and the Middle East became more important. In sum, three responses of Shell (and its competitors) to the low oil price regime were identified: new technologies, more intensive exploration of existing oil provinces, and finding upstream opportunities in major resource-holding areas. The combined effect of these three responses will be illustrated by looking in more detail at a number of Shell production areas, including the North Sea, Oman, the USA, and Russia. Nigeria will be discussed in chapter 5.[17]

Adjusting to a world of low oil prices and global markets, 1986-1998

Accidents bedevil the

Page 170

Building of the huge eight-legged Tern steel jacket in the mid-1980s. Installed in 1988, it was the largest barge-launched structure in the North Sea. Vertical piles were used to pin the structure to the seabed. Crude oil from Tern was to be exported via North Cormorant into the Brent system for delivery to Sullom Voe (Shetland Isles).

Page 171

The Eider production platform was built to be a satellite of two neighbouring platforms, North Cormorant (already on stream at the time), and Tern. It was the first oil production platform in the North Sea to be designed for unmanned operation. The first-stage processing of crude would take place on Eider, and partly processed oil would be piped to North Cormorant for final treatment, 1987.

Work in the offshore industry can be very challenging, such as work involved on the riser, the part of the drill shaft that is above the seabed, pictured here.

[18]

North Sea: high costs and safety concerns

The development of the oil fields in the North Sea had been greatly furthered by high oil prices in the 1970s. New fields came on stream and, despite production delays and budget overspends, the industry was booming. However, the price fall in 1986 suddenly changed prospects for new fields. In April 1986 Shell decided not to go ahead with the development of the Gannet field, which was already in an advanced planning stage. First, a more cost-effective design had to be conceived. A careful reappraisal of the entire design succeeded in achieving a reduction of no less than 40 per cent in the project's cost.[18] For the development of the Gannet field Shell built one central processing platform linked to four satellites. These satellites were not unmanned platforms, but sub-sea wellheads, tied back into Gannet's central platform over distances up to ten miles. Oil from the Gannet complex could be exported through the Fulmar floating storage unit, and the pipeline from Fulmar to St. Fergus in Scotland provided transport for gas.[19] The complex was up and running in 1992.

In the late 1980s production in the older fields became more difficult as the easy oil had been creamed off. To make matters worse, the Piper Alpha disaster, causing the deaths of 167 people, raised serious concerns about platform safety. In 1988 the oil platform Piper Alpha, operated by the Occidental Group, caught fire following a gas explosion, which led to the worst accident in offshore oil history. Shortly before this accident, there had been an explosion on the Brent Alpha platform operated by Shell Expro. All parts of the Brent Alpha safety systems, including gas detectors, deluge systems, and personnel mustering had operated correctly. Moreover, thanks to the design of the platform, the force of the explosion had directed itself away from the structure.[20]

North Sea

In 1988 the platform Piper Alpha, operated by the Occidental Group, caught fire, which led to the worst accident in offshore oil history, causing the deaths of 167 people. The disaster raised serious concerns about platform safety in the North Sea.

[19]

Nevertheless, safety measures came under renewed scrutiny, as more accidents increased concern about the first generation of offshore platforms. A floating storage system broke loose in a storm at the Shell-operated Fulmar system in 1988, and there was an explosion at the Brent Delta platform over the New Year's holiday. In 1989 a gas explosion damaged the Shell-operated Cormorant Alpha platform. Ironically, the gas leak took place during installation of an emergency shutdown valve which was itself part of a safety upgrade taken after the Piper Alpha disaster. Fortunately, nobody was hurt, but the interconnected Brent pipeline system once again had to be shut down.[21]

Shell Expro combined the improvement in safety and integrity of its platforms with a massive project to redevelop the Brent field for low pressure operation. This involved management of, and production from, moving oil rims, never before tried on such a scale anywhere in the world. Basically, production shifted from a focus on oil to one on gas. Because of this new development, the Brent field offered a second exciting learning process about reservoir management and well engineering. Problems which arose on the way could be tackled effectively, so that the Brent Redevelopment Project could be applauded as a major technical achievement as well as an economic success. Overall the project met or exceeded all the original targets for value generation.[22] In one respect, however, the Brent project did not meet its target. The decision to decommission the Brent Spar storage buoy caused a huge public outcry, which will be further discussed in chapter 5.

In the early 1990s Shell carried out a refurbishment programme on the Brent platform following modern safety standards, which included the installation of accommodation units set apart from the production units. Left, the hook-up of the accommodation unit at Brent B, right the positioning of the top section of new drilling equipment set on Brent C.

[21]

Exploration efforts continued to be met with considerable success, but the average discovery size dropped. West of Shetland in the Atlantic, two major new fields, operated by BP, constituted new challenges in finding ways of working in deep and turbulent water at production and operating costs that were justified at low oil prices. For the Foinaven deep-water oil field Shell and BP hoped to hasten the whole process from discovery to production by relying heavily on a strategy of alliances with contractors. It consisted of a combination of a floating production, storage, and offloading unit with sub-sea manifold hubs. Stretch targets with regard to budget and schedule terms could not be met, but production performance was good after the project was finished.[23] In the late 1990s Shell tried to upgrade its portfolio by swapping assets, selling assets that did not offer sufficient return with low oil prices.

For Shell, Oman is an important production area through its participation in the company PDO. Left, pipeline construction, and below, the main gate at Rima, both in the interior of Oman. The logo of PDO represents a fossil as a symbol of the search for oil.

[22]

[23]

Oman: from expanding production to struggling with maturing oil fields

Shell's activities in Oman provide another example of making the most of maturing oil fields. As oil production has a natural tendency to decline, ever more sophisticated strategies have to be applied to boost it. In Oman Shell is operator and private shareholder in Petroleum Development Oman (PDO). A year after the first oil price shock in 1973, the Omani government acquired a 60 per cent interest in PDO, with Shell's share becoming 34 per cent. In other respects as well, the company became more locally embedded. In 1980 PDO introduced a new logo, representing a fossil as symbol of the search for oil, to strengthen the company's local identity. Furthermore PDO was established as a locally registered company. A far more significant contribution to the local character of the company was the employment of local staff. In the 1980s, the replacement of expatriates by Omanis at all levels within the company became official company policy. In 1988 half of the staff were Omani and by 2000 this had risen to 84 per cent. The programme provided training programmes for local staff and supported local business through its purchase policy.[24]

Figure 3.4 tells the story of PDO's oil production in a nutshell.[25] After years of exploration in north Oman, oil in commercial quantities was discovered at Yibal, Natih, and Fahud in the early 1960s, as was explained in volume 2. The first regular exports took off in 1967. In the early years production rose quickly to a level of about 300,000 barrels per day. From 1976 onwards, however, the oil production from the primary development in the north began to decline. To stop the drop in production in the older fields, PDO

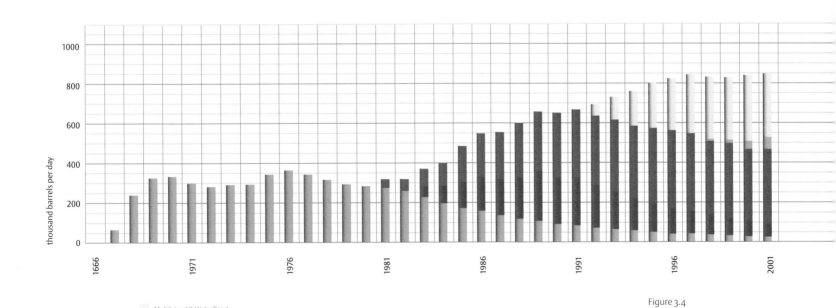

Figure 3.4
'Waves' of development in oil production of PDO.

Multilateral & Waterflood
Infill drilling South & Central
Primary development South & Central
Infill drilling North
Primary development North

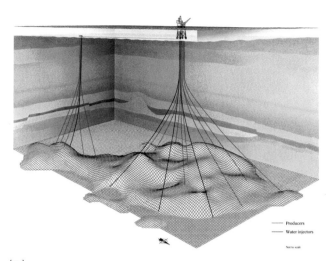

[25]

For much of the oil production in Oman it was necessary to use water injection. The diagram displays the principle of water injection and shows how this reservoir needs some highly deviated production and injection wells.

began to implement plans to increase water and gas injection. In the meantime PDO had been active in building up production facilities in central and south Oman, including a 445-kilometre pipeline from Marmul to Qarn Alam, linking the North and the South Oman oilfields. In 1980 the first oil from the south was delivered. Production returned to the level of 300,000 barrels per day and then began to grow rapidly.[26]

　　Much of the Oman oil in the south and centre is heavy and therefore special treatment is needed to get the oil out of the ground. In the 1980s PDO developed several pilot projects to test enhanced recovery methods. Even with injection of water, the ultimate recovery rate for the Marmul field in the south would be less than 15 per cent because the water tended to pass by and under-run the oil. However, if water could be 'thickened' by mixing it with polymer, higher production could be expected. Injecting steam could be another way of increasing production. In the Qarn Alam field in the centre of Oman the primary recovery would

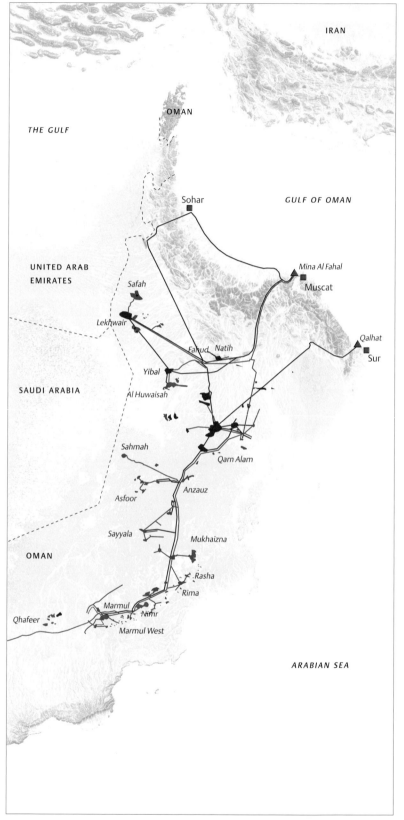

[26]

Map of Oman

— Gas pipeline
◣ Gas field
— oil pipeline
◣ Oil field

In August 1994 PDO moved a rig from the southern desert base at Marmul through the Qara Mountains to the plains around Salalah.

[27]

produce less than 2 per cent of the oil in place. For this field PDO devised a pilot test to inject water that was twice as hot as water boiling at normal atmospheric pressure to make the rocks 'water wet' instead of 'oil wet' and thus release the oil. PDO decided to develop these three pilot tests for hot water, steam, and polymer during the 1980s. It was anticipated that large-scale projects would follow to sustain oil production levels in Oman at the end of the century and into the next.[27]

Then came the oil price collapse in 1986, which necessitated a major revision of the work programme and very sharp cutbacks in capital expenditure, operating expenditure, and manpower levels. The polymer flooding pilot project proved an outstanding success, and steam soak and hot water injection tests gave good results, but the real challenge consisted of reducing the costs of enhanced oil recovery, so that they would be competitive at oil prices below $15 per barrel. For the time being, such a sharp reduction in costs was not feasible and therefore interest in these projects waned as the low oil price regime continued through the 1990s.

Fortunately, another technological breakthrough came to the rescue: the company boosted oil production by perfecting the technique of drilling horizontal wells. For instance in the Nimr field thirty new horizontal wells increased production by 30 per cent and succeeded in identifying an extra 102 million barrels in reserves in

1993. The use of three-dimensional seismic surveys enhanced the hit ratio in pinpointing additional finds and reserves. PDO concluded in 1991 that it had achieved 20 per cent cost savings by drilling slim holes as opposed to conventional wells. The target was a saving of up to 50 per cent. Infill drilling formed a cost-effective way of adding to production, while water flooding also helped to augment production. All this resulted in an increase of oil production from 550,000 barrels per day in 1986 to a peak of 846,000 in 1997. Unit operating expenditure went down from $1.42 in 1993 to $1.33 in 1997.[28] The company expected this trend of rising production to continue in the twenty-first century. However, after 1997 higher production targets could no longer be met. Worse, production began to decline.

After struggling for a few years with production targets that could not be met, PDO management rigorously lowered its targets for 2003 and started extensive field studies to increase its understanding of the mature producing reservoirs. As a result of the studies, management revived the enhanced oil recovery projects that were laid to rest in the 1990s, but became attractive again when oil prices started to rise after 1998. By 2005 the introduction of steam injection at Fahud, miscible-gas injection at Yibal and polymer flooding at Marmul all contributed to reversing the decline in oil production in PDO.[29]

Despite their inhospitable climate and
sensitive environment, the seas around
Alaska attracted many oil companies to
explore for oil. In the 1980s Shell Oil had
high hopes of finding oil in the Beaufort
and Chukchi Seas, off Alaska, where it
acquired extensive exploration rights.
It built a gravel island, Seal Island, to
accommodate drilling equipment,
while reducing the environmental
impact of the exploration drilling.
Though some oil was discovered, the
amounts were not large enough to
justify production.

[29]

US: struggling with high-cost oil   Shell Oil in the US
possessed many mature oil fields, including the heavy oil of the
Belridge Oil Company in California, purchased in 1979. In 1987 no
less than 58 per cent of Shell Oil's US crude oil production needed
enhanced recovery methods, such as steam injection or carbon
dioxide flooding.[30] Not only was the heavy oil expensive to
produce, it was also expensive to refine, while in times of declining
oil prices the heavy oil and residual fuel tended to fall in price even
more than lighter fractions. Moreover, heavy oil had a greater
negative impact on the environment. The acquisition of the
Belridge Oil Company had greatly expanded Shell Oil's domestic
energy resource base. Looking back on his ten years in office as
CEO of Shell Oil, John Bookout explained in 1987 that the Belridge
purchase accounted for about 60 per cent of the company's
acquisition spending over that period. After the oil price collapse
of 1986 Shell Oil had stayed the course, and, in contrast to its
competitors, not embarked on major programme cuts or large-
scale enforced redundancies. As a consequence, oil production and
oil reserves continued to grow, but income in relation to capital
invested declined.[31] After disappointing financial results in 1990
and 1991, the focus shifted to upgrading capital and costs structure
through selective acquisitions, exchanges and divestment. Staff
numbers went down from 32,000 in 1990 to 22,000 in 1993. Shell
Oil had not had such a low staff count since 1932, the nadir of the
Depression years.[32] After the possibilities of cutting costs had been
exhausted, Shell Oil decided in 1995 to combine mature upstream
assets in West Texas and New Mexico with those of Amoco to
create further cost savings. A similar arrangement was made with
Mobil with regard to the mature oil fields in California.[33]

Because all easily accessible oil in the US had long been discovered, new developments had to take place in frontier regions, in the Arctic conditions of Alaska, the unexplored waters of the Atlantic or in the deep-water of the Gulf of Mexico. With exploration in the Beaufort and Chukchi Seas in Alaska, Shell Oil entered a frontier area, which not only had a forbidding climate but also a sensitive environment. For that reason, Shell Oil built a gravel exploration island in the Chukchi Sea to reduce environmental damage. In 1990 two exploratory wells were completed and another started. After a fourth well in 1991, the results were not considered hopeful enough to continue the exploration efforts. Nor had Shell Oil any success in the deep-water Mid-Atlantic, off New Jersey, despite its experience in deep water exploration.[34]

Shell Oil had a long tradition of offshore exploration and production. The first platform built in 1947 was in 6 metres of water, in 1970 a depth of 114 metres was reached, and in 1988 Shell Oil installed the world's largest offshore steel construction, the Bullwinkle drilling and production platform, in 412 metres of water. To give this water depth some context: the Eiffel Tower in Paris is 318 metres high. The successful start-up of production of oil and gas in 1989 stimulated Shell Oil in developing even more ambitious plans. The Auger field, also in the Gulf of Mexico, had a record depth of 870 metres, twice that of the Bullwinkle field. For the development of the Auger field, Shell Oil chose the concept of a tension leg platform, first tried out by Conoco in the Hutton field in the North Sea.[35] Production from this field started in 1994, and yielded oil faster and in larger quantities than planned. Already in 1994 the field produced 55,000 barrels per day from seven wells, while the planning target had scheduled 46,000 barrels per day from thirty-two wells in 1996. As a consequence Shell Oil planned more tension leg platforms at even greater depth. The Mars field – the largest discovery in the Gulf of Mexico for twenty-five years – was brought into production using a tension leg platform in a record water depth of 890 metres. The Ursa tension leg platform

In the Gulf of Mexico Shell Oil was a major player. With its Bullwinkle drilling and production platform it reached a record size in steel jackets, here on its way to the Gulf in 1988, to work in water 400 metres deep.

reached a world record water depth of 1,204 metres. For natural gas in an even deeper field of 1,650 metres, the Mensa field, Shell Oil built a sub-sea wellhead, which started production in 1997.

Shell applied the learning in deep-water production from the Mexican Gulf to other deep-water exploration and production in West Africa, South-East Asia, and North-West Europe. In 1997 Shell decided to concentrate its deep-water experiences in a separate company, which focused on developing deep-water fields quickly. Shell Oil people brought to the venture expertise in the areas of tension leg technology and a 'portfolio' approach to the project management, whereas other Group employees outside the USA contributed valuable experience in relation to floating production and storage vessels and other sub-sea work. The objective was to ensure that Shell companies were selected as preferred partners for deep-water development opportunities worldwide, for instance in deep-water acreage in various areas along the western coast of Africa, Brazil, and the South China Sea.[36]

Gulf of Mexico

▫ Shell interest
■ Gas field
■ Oil field

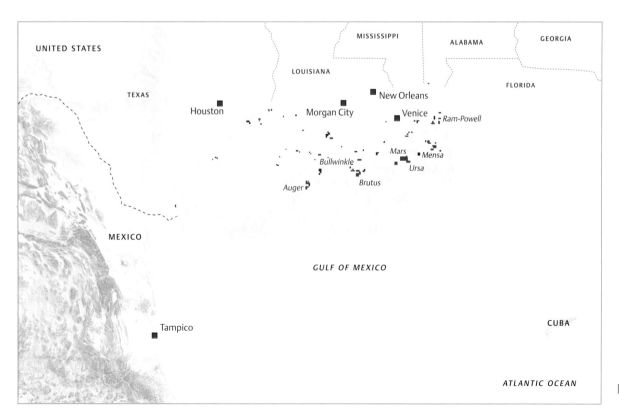

[31]

The next step in enabling production at even greater depths involved another technology, the tension leg platform (TLP). The technology was pioneered by Conoco in the North Sea and the Gulf of Mexico off Louisiana. It was warmly embraced by Shell Oil, which used it for five platforms in the Gulf of Mexico: the Auger, Mars, Ram-Powell and Ursa. While the Augur, which started production in 1994, stood in water 872 metres deep, the Ursa reached first production in 1999 in a water-depth of 1204 metres.

[32]

[33]

A TLP consisted of a semi-submersible type of platform, anchored to the seabed with vertical, taut steel cables. A group of tethers or tendons at each of the structure's corners was called a 'tension leg'.

Left: Pipes and supports beneath Shell Oil's Augur drilling platform in the Gulf of Mexico in 1995; right: Worker on the Brutus, Shell's fifth tension leg platform in the Gulf of Mexico to develop the Green Canyon Block in 909 metres' depth of water. Although similar in size and configuration to Shell's Mars and Ram Powell TLPs, the Brutus was especially designed to serve as a hub for sub-sea developments in the surrounding area. Production started in 2001.

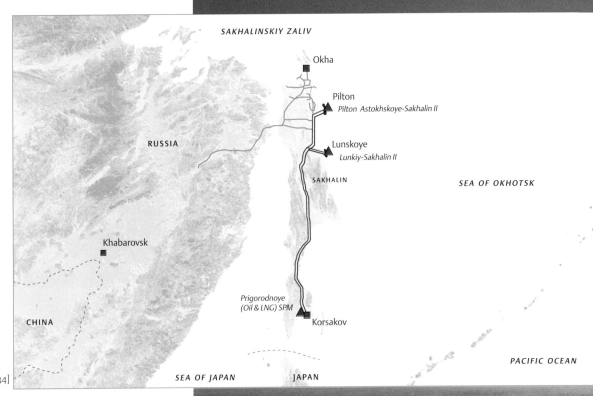

SAKHALINSKIY ZALIV

Okha

Pilton
Pilton Astokhskoye-Sakhalin II

Lunskoye
Lunkiy-Sakhalin II

RUSSIA

SAKHALIN

SEA OF OKHOTSK

Khabarovsk

*Prigorodnoye
(Oil & LNG) SPM*

CHINA

Korsakov

PACIFIC OCEAN

[34]

SEA OF JAPAN   JAPAN

Shell participated in the joint-venture
company Sakhalin Energy, established
to develop oil and gas production off
the Russian island Sakhalin. In 1999 it
began producing oil from the Pilton-
Astokhskoye field with the Molikpaq
platform, seen on page 03/192. The
Lunskoye A platform, shown on page
06/398, will produce gas from the
Lunskoye field. The Sakhalin II project
involved the building of a large LNG
plant at the ice-free Aniva Bay in the
south of Sakhalin Island. The
construction of the LNG plant at
Prigorodnoye, in the south of Sakhalin
Island, is shown on page 06/400-403.
The LNG plant will receive gas from
production facilities in the north of the
island. Some 160 LNG ships a year will
dock at Aniva Bay when the project has
become fully operational.

Chapter 3

Upstream opportunities in major resource-holding countries

One of the options for Shell for solving the problem of higher production costs and lower oil prices was finding upstream opportunities in major resource-holding areas in the Middle East, like Saudi Arabia, Iran and Iraq, or in the countries of the former Soviet Union. By entering Russia, Shell would gain access to potential large oil and gas reserves, but producing these resources was neither easy nor cheap. The Middle East was still the only region with abundant and cheap oil. In a world of low oil prices and increasing competition, Shell had all the more reason to try and get access to the oil in countries in this region. In 1986 about 50 per cent of the world's proved oil reserves were in Saudi Arabia, Kuwait, Iran, and Iraq.[37] Entering these areas for oil production, however, remained a distant prospect during the 1990s. Even though Shell had a refinery in Saudi Arabia in a joint venture with the Saudi government, it did not succeed in turning this activity into an opportunity for oil production in the kingdom. While the war between Iran and Iraq continued until 1988, there was little appetite to enter either of these countries. After the invasion of Kuwait and the resulting war against Iraq, this country was basically a no-go area. In Iran the prospects looked somewhat better. Here Shell set up a partnership with British Gas, Petronas Carigali, and Gaz de France to study the possibilities for export of gas from the South Pars in Iran to Pakistan. This study demonstrated the commercial viability of the project, but was it politically advisable? Shell felt that US sanctions, actual or threatened, hampered its possibilities of entering Iran. In mid-1997 Iran wanted to go ahead with the project, while Shell still hesitated, because of political sensitivities. The CMD did not want to proceed unless this proposal received support from key countries. Shell deferred further action to the future, hoping for a move towards a more moderate regime

The first successful project of Sakhalin Energy consisted of oil production from the Molikpaq platform at the Pilton-Astokhskoye field. Production in waters that were frozen for half of the year started in July 1999.

[37]

[38]

The Russian island of Sakhalin
traditionally had some onshore oil
production, but the Russian
government preferred the
international oil industry to develop
the more challenging offshore oil and
gas fields. Above, a worker at Sakhalin
island onshore oil fields, and, left, oil
field workers in Siberia in 40-below-
zero temperatures. Right: Oil fields in
Baku, Azerbaijan in 1997.

[39]

in the country.[38] Indeed, a year later political developments in Iran seemed to warrant a more active approach, and all Shell businesses started to make plans.[39]

Even before the end of the Cold War, Shell's E&P management considered access to the large oil and gas reserves of Russia as one of the key issues for future growth in oil production. However, the obstacles to investing there were formidable. Russia was inclined to encourage foreign oil companies to explore the technically more challenging fields with high operating costs and large distances to markets. Even more of an obstacle was the lack of legal and fiscal structures. In 1992 Shell wrote in its annual report with some exasperation: 'Attempts to develop major oil and gas exploration and production projects in Russia have yet to result in

finalized agreements, but not for want of effort on our part.'[40] At the same time Shell could announce the first step in the desired direction, because it had acquired a 20 per cent interest in a consortium investigating the development of oil and gas reserves offshore at Sakhalin Island. Being on the periphery of Russia was seen as an advantage, because this project would be less vulnerable than others to export bottlenecks and to the transportation monopoly of Transneft.

Despite the fact that Sakhalin Island is in the far east of Russia with a harsh climate by West European standards, Shell found there was no shortage of expats eager to take part in this adventurous project. One Shell spouse described the experiences of living on Sakhalin Island during the mid-1990s: 'Two years after our initial

The oil industry in Baku, Azerbaijan, 1994. In the 1990s Shell together with other oil majors tried to get access to countries with major oil and gas reserves, including the countries of the former Soviet Union. During the early twentieth century Baku in Azerbaijan had been the centre of a thriving oil industry and oil production was still going on in the 1990s. In 1995 Shell missed the opportunity to participate in the Azerbaijan Consortium, but in 2000 it acquired a 25 per cent interest in the Inam licence in the Caspian Sea, off the shore of Azerbaijan. Shell also participated in the Caspian Sea Consortium developing the Kashagan field.

visit here, we still find Sakhalin, an island in the far east of Russia, a unique posting: a life of extremes in both climate and daily living. Their standard of living, by Western standards, is very low. Inflation is rampant and people have to be enormously resourceful. On their side is an unspoilt landscape full of rivers, rare plants and birds, and abundance of salmon in the summers, exotic mushrooms, berries of all types and wild bears. (...) There is nothing green for anyone in midwinter when the temperature drops to –30° C, but we have a large greenhouse as of this year. The pleasure of otherwise unavailable vegetables is indescribable. From January we enjoy long cross-country ski trails, and in February, Sundays can be spent ice-fishing. (...) There are times when the cup is brimming over and others when it's difficult to reach the drops at the bottom.'[41]

The enthusiasm of the oil industry for the development of oil and gas off Sakhalin Island was considerable. No fewer than three projects were being developed at the same time. Shell participated in Sakhalin II, an oil and gas development for which the participants had set up the joint venture Sakhalin Energy. The participants at that time included the contractor McDermott International, Marathon Oil, Mitsubishi, Mitsui & Co, and Shell. Sakhalin I was largely an oil development with some associated gas with several Japanese participants and Exxon as partners. Sakhalin III comprised Texaco, Mobil, and Exxon. By 1994 Sakhalin II was the most advanced of the three projects.[42] Sakhalin Energy declared Commencement Date under the Production Sharing Agreement in June 1996 in order to avoid the risk of losing its rights.[43] The Russian Federation actively supported foreign investment in the oil industry by introducing federal laws on underground resources and on production sharing agreements between 1992 and 1999.[44] The western oil companies were also looking at opportunities to acquire Russian oil companies, which were being privatized. Shell, for instance, considered the acquisition of Rosneft, or

parts of it, in 1997-8. So bold a step, however, was not taken.[45]

In the early 1990s Shell opened new representatives offices in countries of the former Soviet Union, such as the Ukraine, Kazakhstan, and Azerbaijan, the old oil region with the capital Baku, to pursue options in these regions. For instance, in 1994 the possibility arose of acquiring part of the interest of SOCAR, the State Oil Company of Azerbaijan, in the Azerbaijan Consortium, led by BP and Statoil. However, the deal did not materialize.[46] In 1996 Mark Moody-Stuart described the failure to gain access to Azerbaijan as the 'major regret of 1995'. Members of the Conference discussed the reasons behind this failure. Lo van Wachem argued that major 'visionary' opportunities often needed individual 'champions' rather than committees to promote them. Cor Herkströter replied more cautiously that 'the difficulty was that such champions tended to be more often wrong than right, and that their "vision" came at a price.'[47] This exchange is remarkable in the light of later discussions about the value of decisions made by committees versus the merits of one CEO.

Because of the large size of the projects and the huge risks of operating in politically unstable regions, the western oil companies preferred to work together in consortia. One such consortium was the Caspian Sea Consortium working in the North Caspian Sea to explore the Kashagan field. Here the joint venture partners consisted, apart from Shell, of Agip, British Gas, BP/Statoil, Mobil, Total, and Kazkhoil. Shell had not been able to enter the AIOC Consortium, exploring the Tengiz field in the Caspian Sea, and therefore was all the more eager to participate in the Kashagan field.[48] While Shell undoubtedly had made some progress in its efforts to access oil in major resource-holding countries, much more had to be done before a real impact could be expected.

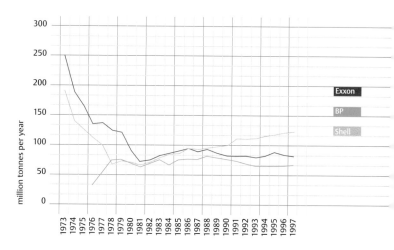

Figure 3.5
Equity oil production Shell, Exxon, and BP, 1973-1997.

Figure 3.6
Proved oil reserves of Shell, Exxon, and BP, 1982-1997.

Shell's crude oil production and reserves in a period of low oil prices   Assessing Shell's three upstream strategies of countering the low oil prices, we can conclude that two were successful and one still mostly a future promise: production costs had come down as a result of technological improvement and innovation, and Shell had made the most of existing oil production areas. The third strategy of gaining access to major resource-holding countries remained to a large extent in the negotiating stage, though in the countries of the former Soviet Union real progress had been made by 1997.

Despite the low oil price, Shell gradually increased its equity oil production from 95 million tonnes in 1986 to 122 million tonnes in 1997. In contrast, both Exxon and BP struggled with slowly declining oil production after the oil price collapse of 1986, as can been seen in figure 3.5.[49]

The oil production, to a large extent, resulted from the exploration successes in the past. To secure future production, reserves had to be increased continuously, but that was not easy to achieve in a period of cost-cutting as a consequence of low oil prices. Initially, Shell had kept up its exploration efforts, and as we can see from figure 3.6 its proved oil reserves continued to grow till 1990.[50] Between 1990 and 1994 Shell reduced total exploration expenditure by some 35 per cent. Part of this reduction had been achieved by applying advanced technologies, and as such was a good sign. But Shell also had been less active in pursuing oppor-tunities. For instance, in 1994 a total of eighty-nine exploration wells had been drilled, the lowest number for ten years.[51] Moreover, in the early 1990s Shell companies had not been particularly successful in greenfield exploration and for that reason had been advised by the CMD to concentrate more on exploration close to existing production fields.[52] In the E&P self-appraisal of

1996, A. J. Parsley, then director of new business development in E&P, admitted that Shell perhaps had taken a too rigidly 'mechanistic' approach to evaluating the risk/reward balance in exploration opportunities. A concern with precision had militated against a sufficiently business-like approach, as had the 'over-cautious tendency always to look for "ways back" when exploring new possibilities'.[53] While Shell had built up new proved reserves rapidly during the 1980s, the low oil prices and its cautious approach resulted in a slowdown during the 1990s. Shell was certainly no exception in the oil industry. The proved oil reserves of Exxon and BP were basically flat through the 1990s, as figure 3.6 shows. Shell's competitive position in 1997 looked strong enough to create future production growth and remain an industry leader through organic growth rather than a merger or large acquisition.

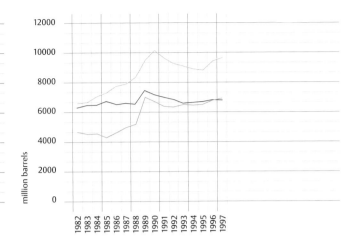

million barrels

downstream business. Figure 3.2 (see page 164) compares Shell's

The downstream business in a world of low oil prices

While the upstream business struggled with low oil prices, the downstream business did not benefit as much as could have been expected. As mentioned earlier, for the upstream part of the business high crude oil prices are more advantageous than low oil prices, but for the downstream business the relationship is more complicated. High crude oil prices led to higher oil product prices, but with some delay, and the rise did not always sufficiently compensate for the higher prices in feedstock. Also, the higher prices of oil products reduced demand, because of the negative effect on economic growth and because people tried to use expensive energy more efficiently. Low crude oil prices meant that refineries and marketing had cheaper input, but they also felt pressure on their margins. The lower oil prices were caused by ample supplies of oil, and this encouraged new entrants into the refining and distribution of oil products, which increased competition. On the other hand, lower oil product prices could stimulate demand. For all these reasons it was not clear-cut whether Shell's downstream business would profit from lower oil prices, and whether it should step up its investment in its

downstream business. Figure 3.2 (see page 164) compares Shell's investment in the upstream (exploration and production) and downstream business (manufacturing and marketing). It shows that in the face of volatile oil prices, the downstream investment remained fairly stable. In the period of low oil prices during the 1960s, investment in manufacturing and marketing was indeed high, and after the rise in oil prices in 1973, these went down somewhat. After the oil price collapse in 1986 investment in manufacturing and marketing went up again till 1995, as one might have expected, but then it diminished while oil prices were still low and the physical world oil consumption was slowly but steadily rising. Equally telling of the shift between upstream and downstream are the figures of the earnings of both parts of the business for the period from 1980 onwards, highlighted in figure 3.7.[54]

During the period of high oil prices, earnings from exploration and production were much higher than those in manufacturing and marketing, but this dominance greatly diminished after the oil price collapse. In four years, 1988, 1989, 1994, and 1998, earnings from manufacturing and marketing even surpassed those in exploration and production. Downstream became once again, as it had been in the 1960s, a respectable part of the business. Measured over the whole period 1980-1998, the upstream business delivered 60 per cent of the combined earnings.

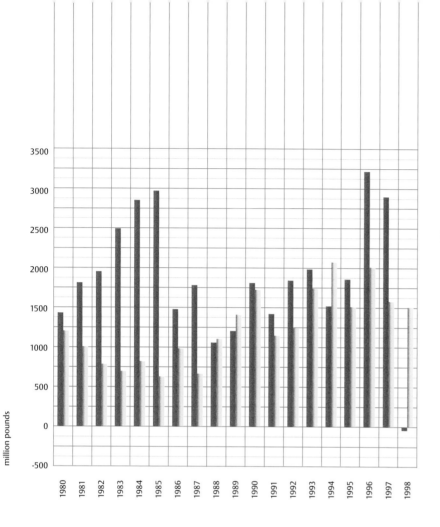

million pounds

■ Exploration and production
□ Manufacturing and marketing

Refineries: New Look, new countries, and exit strategies

The Shell refineries in Europe and the US had greatly expanded during the optimistic 1960s, and struggled with overcapacity all through the 1970s and early 1980s, as discussed in chapter 1. They finally seemed to have turned the corner by the end of the 1980s. The fall in oil prices led to improved margins for the refineries and with demand for oil products on the rise the prospects for the Shell refineries began to look healthier. In the late 1980s about 70-80 per cent of Shell's refinery capacity in Europe covered the Group's core business. Exports and processing for third parties accounted for the remaining refinery capacity utilization.[55] Shell had a legacy of many small and relatively old refineries in Europe, which had to be updated continuously. In 1987 Shell companies had an equity stake in no fewer than fifty-three refineries, of which eighteen had a start-up date prior to the 1970s and half of those were constructed before the war.[56] Therefore, an investment programme was launched to give some refineries a 'New Look', while contemplating the closure of other refineries. The 'New Look' programme aimed at a 20 per cent reduction in hardware cost and at least 30 per cent improvement in fuel

Figure 3.7
Earnings of Shell's upstream and downstream businesses, 1980-1998.

In the late 1980s Shell Singapore extended its refinery at Pulau Bukom with a long residue cracking unit. Similar units were also attached to the refineries in Stanlow (Britain), Berre (France) and Geelong (Australia).

economy.[57] New technology appeared in the long-residue cat cracker at Stanlow, England, the cat cracker revamp at Berre, France and the long-residue cat cracker at Singapore. The long-residue cat cracker at Geelong, Australia, came on stream in 1991. The application of a new family of hydrocracking catalysts took place at Singapore and Whangerei, New Zealand.[58]

The late 1980s saw the introduction of Shell's 'Hycon', a hydrocracker using the newest technology. Commenting on its location at Pernis, Jeroen van der Veer likened it to 'a supermodern bathroom in an old canal house'.[59] It took a number of years to get the Hycon working to specification. In the meantime, the Per + project, launched in 1992, added three more enormous plant complexes – a gasifier, a hydrocracker and a heat and power co-generating plant –, and upgraded some existing units. The renovation and innovation programme turned Shell Pernis once again into a 'state of the art' refinery. The investment sent a powerful message to employees and the industry that Shell had confidence in the future of the refinery. However, as a consequence of automation fewer and fewer employees were needed to shape that future.[60]

Shell invested heavily in conversion capacity to upgrade the oil products from heavy fuel into lighter products such as gasoline. At the time it seemed a smart move to concentrate on products with higher value. In the mid-1990s, however, Saudi Arabia changed its crude oil marketing strategy in response to production restraints. It discouraged the sale of heavy crude in favour of light crude to maximize its revenue. Suddenly the European refiners, including Shell, had more conversion capacity than they needed.[61] The new investments did not earn sufficient money and the return on investment for Shell manufacturing plummeted. Other factors contributed to the poor results. As mentioned above, new refinery

[42]

capacity was built up in other regions, in the producing countries of the Middle East as well as in the new growth markets of Asia. Shell operated refineries in Japan, Malaysia, the Phillipines, Saudi Arabia, Singapore, and Thailand, and was interested in building one in China, which, however, did not materialize.

With modest growth prospects in Europe and the US, most of the Shell refineries there seemed in the wrong place at the wrong time. The heavily capitalized refineries dragged down the return on capital employed of the downstream business. As the Group managing director for Oil Products, Paul Skinner, concluded in 2000: 'The blunt fact is that most refining investments over the past twenty years have not delivered an adequate return.'[62] This was a serious issue, because return on investment rated highly with the industry analysts in the 1990s. Would it not be better to get rid of the refineries altogether? By the mid-1990s Shell's supply capacity of white oils significantly exceeded its demand for

In 1990 Shell Singapore opened its long residue catalytic cracking unit in Pulau Bukom, Singapore. The new unit lowered production costs, increased the flexibility of the refinery to match supply and output, and enabled it to produce more products with high added value, such as lead-free gasoline.

branded white products in Europe. Supply cover amounted to almost 120 per cent of Shell-branded sales volumes. Shell considered a lower level of refinery cover, circa 80 per cent, more than enough to ensure supply security and allow for more profitable deals on the spot market. Therefore it developed alliances or exit strategies for the Cressier, Berre, Shell Haven, and Pernis refineries, which continued to show a poor return on capital.[63] However, willing partners were not easy to find. Some refineries, like Cressier, were sold, others, like Berre, reduced in size. Shell Haven ceased operations. Pernis, one of Shell's largest refineries, remained in business. In the US the refineries became part of an alliance with Texaco, as will be discussed later.

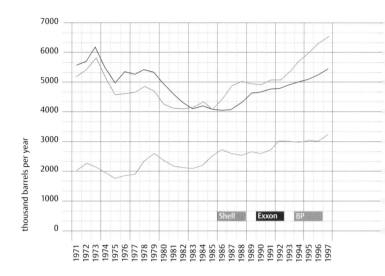

thousand barrels per year

1971 1972 1973 1974 1975 1976 1977 1978 1979 1980 1981 1982 1983 1984 1985 1986 1987 1988 1989 1990 1991 1992 1993 1994 1995 1996 1997

Shell   Exxon   BP

Wooing the customer   Low crude oil prices were a result of overproduction. In a climate of oversupply, customers had to be wooed again. Shell sales of oil products in thousands of barrels per day increased steadily from 1986 onwards after the gradual decline since 1973, as figure 3.8 shows.[64] Exxon and BP succeeded in increasing their sales too, but less than Shell.

For oil products the customers were increasingly the users of transport oil, because during the period of high crude oil prices the use of oil for other purposes had been discouraged. Electricity companies had turned to gas or nuclear energy, industry had changed from oil to gas, and household heating had also moved from oil to gas. For cars and trucks, however there was still no viable alternative to gasoline or diesel, apart from a modest role for LPG. Aircraft and ships were heavy users of oil-based products. The latter customers were business-to-business relations, and they were increasingly served on a worldwide basis. The market for cars and trucks, however, was traditionally very local. The key question was whether these markets would become increasingly global and whether this would give Shell with its worldwide retail network a competitive advantage. In 1986 Shell concluded that markets were becoming more transnational and management of brand distinctiveness across national boundaries was becoming more important.[65]

According to the company strategist Michael Porter, professor at Harvard Business School, companies which wanted to increase their competitiveness had to make a choice between three basic strategies: being a low-cost producer, following a differentiation strategy, or focusing on niche markets.[66] While Porter helped find the competitive strategy that fitted the specific business unit, his colleagues, G. Hamel and C. K. Prahalad, underlined the need to identify, cultivate and exploit the core

competence of the corporation. From focusing on core business, the companies should move to consider their core capabilities and broaden their activities again, building up new capabilities and being the first to change the rules for the industry.[67] These theories were well known in Shell, judging from the vocabulary managers used to describe their choices. For Shell, trying to be a low-cost producer was not an obvious choice, as Bill Bentley, Shell's supply and marketing coordinator explained: 'If we are not the lowest-cost operator in our industry – and I suggest that long-established Shell culture does not easily lead us in that direction – then we have to ensure that we have a business portfolio of a range and quality that marks us out from the generality of our competitors.'[68] The differentiation strategy was therefore the preferred one. To create brand distinctiveness, Shell launched two new brands on the basis of new technology and supported by heavy advertising, Helix motor oil in 1985 and Formula Shell gasoline in 1986. Interestingly Helix was not sold under the name of 'Shell Helix', but just as 'Helix' (from Shell), to position the product as something special. Added to this was the innovative pack, designed for customer convenience, to underline Helix as a 'personality in its own right'. The word Formula in the new brand for gasoline was chosen for its

Figure 3.8
Oil products sales of Shell, Exxon, and
BP, 1971-1997.

This floating Shell station serviced the
fishing fleet at Sandakan, on the east
coast of the Malaysian state of Sabah,
in 1991.

[43]

[45]

[46]

Products of Shell normally carried the Shell name, or variations on the name such as Shell Super Plus Motoroil, here in use at a Shell branded retail outlet in Jeddah, Saudi Arabia, in 1986. To create brand distinctiveness, Shell launched two new brands on the basis of new technology and supported by heavy advertising. The gasoline Formula Shell, introduced in 1986, had Shell as part of the name, as was usually the case. In contrast, the motor oil, launched the year before, carried the name Helix, and seemingly as an afterthought it was also called 'a product of Shell'.

scientific connotations. Also, it appeared unchanged in many languages, which was important for international advertising. In the UK, Formula Shell was launched with the punchline: 'From today not all petrol is the same.'[69] The launch of Formula Shell in Europe resulted in higher sales. This early commercial success, however, became qualified when it appeared that in a small number of cars the new gasoline caused inlet valves to burn. Negative publicity was inevitable, though the damage occurred in only four countries, Denmark, Norway, Malaysia, and the UK. It took Shell technical experts in collaboration with the motor manufacturers more than a year to establish the cause of the problem. In the meantime, the Formula Shell brand was withdrawn from a number of markets, including the UK. Once the problem had been identified, the product was reformulated and relaunched, in some markets under a new brand. Lessons learned from the introduction problems with Formula Shell included the decision to forge closer links with the motor manufacturing industry in developing new products.[70] In 1996 Shell teamed up once again with Ferrari in the Formula One races.

FORMULA Shell

In 1985 this huge Helix Balloon was used to advertise Helix as a personality in its own right, just Helix - which was a replacement for Shell Super Plus Motoroil. Inset: Advertising material at Shell retail sites in China.

Chapter 3

[49]

[50]

[51]

[52]

In 1992 the Group developed a new Retail Visual Identity (RVI), to be gradually introduced all over the world, though not in the US, which had its own service station design. The visual identity included all elements of modern service stations, pumps, forecourts, canopy, service bay, car wash and – naturally – shops. The warm inviting colours were supposed to give customers a safe and welcome feeling, in particularly if they were driving out in the rain by night. Clockwise: Service station at Corcovado Mountain, Brazil by night, the Phillipines, Corcovado Mountain by day, and Cairo, Egypt.

The sale of differentiated products ultimately rested on the strong brand image of the Shell pecten, as one of the industry's most widely recognized marketing symbols. But even well-established brands need an overhaul once in a while, together with other expressions of company identity. Shell Oil introduced a new design for its service stations, called Silverado, in 1988. The yellow of the Shell pecten was the 'key color in the Silverado system, the sun around which all others revolve'. But red was used more sparsely than in the Shell service stations outside the US. Instead light and dark grey served as supporting colours to provide 'a neutral field for strong contrast'.[71] It was illustrative of Shell Oil's independent position within the Shell Group that it was allowed to hang on to a markedly different design of service station, even after the Group had bought out the minority shareholders. Also its design of the Shell pecten remained somewhat different until 1998. Market research in the late 1980s into the public perception of the 'visible manifestations' of the various majors (in particular the general impression of the service stations) in the world outside the US indicated that Shell was viewed as more friendly than other companies in the study, including Exxon and BP. Its image, however, was slightly less 'modern' than that of BP, though at par with Exxon in this respect.[72] Shell's marketing managers concluded that there was room for improvement but no need for drastic changes. They set up an international project team with representatives from eight key operating companies to come up with new design ideas.

After four years of study a new Retail Visual Identity (RVI) was ready to be launched. It combined simplicity with warm welcoming colours. The former two-dimensional design gave way to a three-dimensional system, which included architectural and graphic design, full dimensions, materials, colour, and construction details to create a genuine international consistency. The cost of designing the new visual identity ran into some millions of dollars, but the actual transformation of the 40,000-strong worldwide network of retail outlets would be many times more expensive. For that reason, Shell did not opt for a simultaneous implementation at all its sites worldwide. Instead it chose a gradual approach, implementing the new design through the normal capital and

[53]

maintenance budgets.[73] In a gradual process all Shell retail outlets outside the US were redesigned. At the end of 1993 some 1,100 sites had been converted to the new Retail Visual Identity in over 40 countries, in 1994 this number had increased to 3,000 sites in 50 countries and by 1996 over 16,000 sites in some 100 countries featured the new Shell design and layout.[74]

'Oil faces a paradox', remarked John Jennings in 1994, 'we know that it is a finite resource, but currently there is a substantial surplus of supply capacity. The overhang of production capacity in OPEC will dominate the market for some years to come.'[75] This easy supply situation created an opportunity for new entrants in the oil retail business, including the hypermarkets. They sold

gasoline as part of their total 'customer offer', which meant that they could, if they wished, offer it at somewhat lower prices to attract customers to their stores, and take the profits on the sales of groceries and other products, though they had to face stiff competition in their normal business as well. In the UK and France hypermarkets were highly successful in increasing their market share in gasoline sales. The competition from hypermarkets was not restricted to Europe, but also took place in Australia, Malaysia, and Japan.[76] Shell tried to tackle this competition by driving operating costs down, by loyalty programmes and by offering differentiated products for which customers might be willing to pay more. One of these differentiated products was a cleaner gasoline

The car wash of a Shell Oil service
station in Dallas, US.

for the environmentally conscious consumer. Though customers appreciated cleaner products, their positive reception was not translated into a willingness to pay more for these products, unless they also offered better driving performance.[77]

Another way of tackling the competition from hypermarkets included a more active stance in non-fuel retail. Since the 1970s Shell had used its forecourts for additional commercial activities, ranging from car washes to shops and restaurants, but their dealers handled most of these activities. In 1996 Shell decided to make a concerted effort to promote the non-fuel business as part of its own business. Alongside the Select stores, other prototypes would be developed. Shell companies had the customer flow and the real estate for a successful convenience store operation. Now was the time to realise this potential and create a new source of income, which could share the financial burden of the forecourts with the fuel retail. In Australia, approximately 75 per cent of Shell's retail income was attributable to non-fuels retailing, so there were huge possibilities. For the plans to work it was essential to move forward on a global basis with prototype ventures. These included global purchasing by Shell of confectionery, tobacco, and beverages. Learning how McDonalds transacted its business, Shell concluded that it should avoid delays by opening new stores in the standard format and then fine-tune them in response to customer reaction.[78] The new strategy met with some success, in particular in Canada, but overall growth in non-fuel sales turned out to be slower than expected, and as a consequence the activity was considered to be overcapitalized.[79] In a business environment in which the return on capital dominated decision-making, over-capitalization was an unforgivable sin.

If the non-fuel retail was not solving the problem of increasing competitiveness, then there always remained the

instrument of cost cutting. In the highly competitive market in the US Shell Oil decided in 1996 to create savings through combining its downstream activities with those of Texaco. During the second half of the 1980s, Shell Oil had been the US top gasoline marketer and in 1990 it was the first company to market a reformulated gasoline, SU2000E, especially designed for the nine metropolitan areas which the federal government had identified as having the nation's most severe ground-level ozone problems.[80] Compared with its competitors, Shell Oil's portfolio of refining and marketing interests in the US continued to perform well in the 1990s, but it was only achieving a return on capital of between 8 and 10 per cent, compared with a target of 15 per cent. The industry average was about 7 per cent, and even the strongest competitor was not making more than 12 per cent, but Shell Oil was determined to become the low-cost leader of the US. A joint venture with Texaco seemed to offer the prospect of achieving just that through realizing the many identified synergies: 'The venture would be designed to enhance the value of both the Shell and the Texaco brands, which would each be subject to formal license agreements, with annual reviews and appropriate remedies in case of failure to maintain standards.'[81]

For both parties it was important to keep their brand presence in the US market, and both parties wanted to be involved in operating the joint venture. Moreover, Texaco already had a joint venture with Saudi Refining, a subsidiary of Saudi Aramco, in the east of the US. As a consequence the organization structure of this collaboration between Shell and Texaco for the US market became fairly complicated. Set up in 1998, the alliance consisted of two joint-venture organizations and two service organizations: Equilon Enterprises combined the refining and marketing activities of Texaco and Shell Oil in the mid-western and western US, while

US

1963   1976

A brand is an important intangible asset for a company. It is a name, sign or symbol that identifies the origin of a particular group of products or services and differentiates them from those of competitors.[1] In the case of Shell the business name and the brand name are the same, and the reputation of the company and most of its products are therefore inextricably linked. Its symbol, the pecten, has already been in use for more than a hundred years, making it unique in the world of brands. The Group's marketing department were the guardians of the Shell brand. Shell's strategy was to renew its emblem (the Shell pecten) and other visual manifestations gradually, thus keeping them fresh while retaining recognition. In the late 1960s Shell Marketing invited the Compagnie d'Esthétique Industrielle (CEI), the Paris agency of the American designer Raymond Loewy, to make a new design for its service stations and its pecten. Loewy produced two versions for the pecten, one lettered and one unlettered, and the unlettered was chosen. Introduced in 1971, the new pecten had a bold, modern feel, and, gradually spreading as part of the routine renewal of service stations, it became a 'symbolic logo', because it needed no name. Typical of the decentralized organizational structure of the Group, operating companies were invited to convert to the new design and most of them did, but not all. For instance, Shell Oil in the US chose to stay with its existing emblem, though it moved closer to the new Shell pecten in 1976.[2] In the mid-1970s Shell marketing managers formulated a general statement of philosophy, in which they underlined the need actively to protect Shell's brand strength and distinctiveness over the long term. They argued that the performance of Shell gasoline must be at least equivalent to that of its major competitors in each market, because the brand should guarantee quality and reliability. When Shell began to engage in activities outside the oil industry in the 1970s, the question arose whether those activities, such as metals, nuclear, and coal, were allowed to use the Shell brand. Though the surveillance of the use of the Shell brand remained part of the mandate of Marketing, the CMD set up a cross-business brand identity committee to advise on the use of the Shell name and brand in new businesses.[3]

In the second half of the 1980s marketers in general became more interested in brands and brand management: brands that were well known and highly appreciated by consumers represented considerable value.[4] At the same time the financial markets began to underline return on capital as the most important measure to compare company performance, and the brand stood for a source of income that was not based on physical assets. The Shell keepers of brand and trade marks more generally defended the value on two sides. On the one hand, they registered brand, trade marks, and in some cases the use of red and yellow in all relevant countries and protected them against counterfeiters. On the other they tightened internal guidelines for the use of the emblem and the word 'Shell'. It was not permitted to form composites with the name Shell, or to write anything in the emblem or across the emblem. Neither was it allowed to change the form or colour of the pecten.[5] When Shell updated its service stations in 1993, the existing pecten design, then already twenty years old, remained basically unchanged.

Because the Shell emblem had developed into a widely known

symbol, certainly in the western world, critics frequently distorted the pecten to make their point. Sometimes the critics used familiar Shell slogans such as 'you can be sure of Shell', or 'Shell helpt' to ridicule or criticize the company. English- language journalists frequently and boringly presented bad news under the heading 'Shell shock'.

In 1996 Shell started to measure the strength of its brand. Because the criteria changed frequently, it is difficult to show how the strength of the brand evolved over time. Strong brands were expected to have a high level of unprompted awareness. The research action standard set was that more than 80 per cent of the respondents surveyed should be aware of the brand. Shell brand tracking research over 1996 in fifty-two countries around the globe (outside the US) showed that, in two-thirds of those markets, unprompted awareness was higher than 80 per cent. Not surprisingly, in the Netherlands the awareness was close to 100 per cent. It was also determined that strong and profitable brands should be expected to have brand preference shares in excess of 20 per cent. Again, this was true for the Shell brand in two-thirds of

the countries. In more than thirty of fifty-six countries, the Shell brand was in first or second position as regards brand preference ratings amongst its competitive set.[6] The study confirmed Shell's strong position in the downstream business, but it also showed that there was a challenge ahead in the remaining one-third of the countries. Global research in 2005 (including the US) highlighted that the Shell brand ranked higher than that of BP, Esso, or Mobil in terms of both awareness and preference in those markets where Shell had a presence. What did the brand tell the consumers, in particular the motorists? Two-thirds of the users thought that Shell was a brand they could trust and that stood for high quality fuels.[7] Indeed, the international success of global brands, such as the Shell brand, led consumers to associate them with better manufacture and more innovative products than local brands.[8] In the twenty-first century Shell has continued to guard its brand carefully. As *Shell World* wrote in 1990: 'Oil wells dry up. Tankers rust and people die, but brands and trade marks live on.'[9]

[55]

[56]

Motiva Enterprises included the refining and marketing businesses of Shell Oil, Texaco and Saudi Refining in eastern US. Motiva and Equilon set up two jointly owned service organisations, Equiva Services for administrative and professional support and Equiva Trading as a trading unit.[82] Savings were foreseen, but did not materialize. In fact, the opposite happened. The operating structure added more costs than the planned synergies obtained, which might have been avoided if the parties had followed the E&P model of working with one operator. However, the merger movement of the late 1990s came to the rescue of Shell Oil, as will be explained in chapter 6.

While struggling in the established markets of western Europe and the US, Shell identified new countries and markets in which it wanted to try its luck. Lubricants and retail normally spearheaded the entry into new markets. The fall of communism opened new possibilities for marketing in Eastern Europe as well as in the former Soviet Union. For the time being, Shell concentrated in the former Soviet Union on exploration and production activities, while it adopted a 'wait and see' strategy for downstream. In Eastern Europe retail opportunities were actively sought. The short-term objective was to have an operating company in each country, high-calibre local Shell staff, and the establishment of the Shell brand and reputation.[83] Shell had never entirely left these

When the markets of the middle and eastern European countries were opened to private capital after the fall of communism, the Group had to start from scratch in promoting the Shell brand. A tried and trusted way of publicizing its brand was through participating in a rally, such as the Rally of Romania in 1994.
Middle: Eager buyers in a Shell Select shop in Hong Kong.
Right: Interior of a select shop at a Shell retail outlet in Thailand, which actually could have been anywhere in the world.

countries, and therefore could immediately grasp the new business opportunities. In Hungary, where Shell products had been traded since 1960, a joint venture with Interag was concluded in 1989 to expand the automotive retail sales. By 1992 the joint venture had seventy-five service stations in Hungary and a year later Shell acquired the remaining 23 per cent interest from Interag. Deutsche Shell quickly moved forward in east Germany, opening its sixtieth service station in 1992. In that year the first Shell service station in the Czech Republic was opened. In the next few years Shell introduced retail sites in ever more Eastern European countries, including Bulgaria, Lithuania, Estonia, Slovakia, Poland, and Latvia. New retail market entry initiatives were also being pursued in South and Central America, because economic growth and liberalization offered new opportunities for private business. For instance, Shell established retail networks, including Select stores, in Peru and Ecuador, following deregulation in 1993.[84] All these markets were

fairly small and fragmented, and therefore needed a very focused approach to become profitable.

The really exciting markets were the large potential growth markets in India and China. Shell's entrance into the Indian automotive retail market consisted of a joint venture to blend and market Shell-branded lubricants, set up in 1994. Shell Chemicals had visited the Canton Fairs since the early 1970s and following China's 'Open Door Policy' of the late 1970s other Shell businesses became interested in finding a foothold in the large Chinese market.[85] Shell engaged in offshore production and crude oil trade, and gradually built up a marketing organization with oil products such as lubricants, bitumen, and liquid petroleum gas. In China the marketing encountered a real challenge, because the Shell pecten was not yet a familiar symbol.[86]

Shell often used the sale of lubricants to explore new markets or re-enter old markets, followed by the opening of retail stations. For heavy diesel trucks Shell developed a special lubricant, Rimula Oil, that found its way into the growing consumer markets of China, together with Rotella SX and Shell Super 2000. Below: an advertisement for Shell lubricants in India from 1994.

[59]

Learning to play the global game in downstream

During the 1990s the world became increasingly interconnected. Globalization and liberalization went hand in hand, creating a much more competitive environment across borders. Shell downstream companies responded with two important organizational changes. Firstly, a greater emphasis was placed on the coordination of the three business entities, manufacturing, marketing, and trading & shipping, in order to optimize the total results rather than the individual results. Secondly, the traditional country-by-country approach was superseded by a regional and global approach while maintaining the traditional decentralized structure. From being European-focused, the downstream business aimed at building up equal strength in the three major regions, Europe, the Americas, and the Far East, and from there it developed into one global business approach. Shell's oil products division tried to reap the benefits of a global network, while sustaining a local presence. A local approach to the customer was considered essential, because customer taste and preferences continued to be firmly local-specific. This was true of food and drinks, as one might have guessed, but preferences in gasoline showed important local differences too.[87]

In the globalization of the downstream business, trading and marine had taken the lead. In the 1970s, Shell had set up a separate trading unit, Shell International Trading Company (Sitco), which developed into one of the biggest oil trading companies in the world. Crude oil trading in the 1980s underwent two important changes. First, after the second oil crisis, many long-term contracts were replaced by short-term contracts or spot market transactions. The other major change was the introduction of future contracts in crude oil at the New York Mercantile Exchange (Nymex) in 1983.[88] The International Petroleum Exchange, part of the London Commodity Clearing House, quickly followed the Nymex example by introducing futures contracts for gas oil and Brent crude oil. The Singapore International Monetary Exchange (SIMEX) established a third futures market in 1989. In trading, high or low oil prices per se are not the issue, but traders thrive on price volatility. In the 1980s techniques from the stock market entered the oil trading business through the participation of the 'Wall Street Refiners', the financial and investment community, which had already been operating extensively in other commodities. They brought risk management techniques to the oil markets. The trading floor in Shell Centre in London became an exciting place with phones ringing incessantly and screens flashing and bobbing about like the lights on pin-ball machines. Everybody had to be highly motivated to withstand the pressures and the unsociable hours involved. Few could enjoy undisturbed evenings or weekends. Staff were young and turnover was high. Sitco's president Silvan Robinson called this trading the 'sexy part of the business'.[89] Other parts of the business included the trade in oil products, aviation fuels, and bunker oil for the marine, not to forget the less spectacular but equally essential back-office work of the documentation and transportation staff and the financial division.

Crude oil trade took place in different markets with three different markers: West Texas Intermediate (WTI), Brent and Dubai. The OPEC producers insisted on determining the destination of their crude. Therefore, this oil was non-tradable. The North Sea crude, with the Brent oil price as marker, could be traded freely, and here Shell had an important position. The US market had small physical amounts of oil but lots of paper trade (in contrast to the 'wet oil trade', which is trade in the real product).[90] Between these different markets were obvious linkages, and traders took advantage of differentials between the markets. They had to be quick to be the first to spot the differences, before that window of opportunity closed. Sitco, as the central organization in Shell, aimed at finding the best markets for Shell's equity production, or buying as cheaply as possible on behalf of Shell refineries and adding value by trading on its own account.

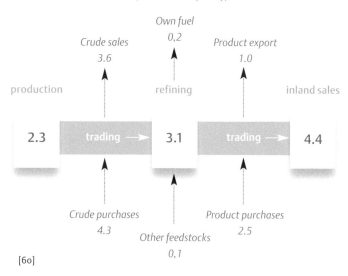

Hydrocarbon flow
(million barrels per day)

Own fuel
0,2

Crude sales
3.6

Product export
1.0

production   refining   inland sales

2.3   trading →   3.1   trading →   4.4

Crude purchases
4.3

Product purchases
2.5

Other feedstocks
0,1

[60]

When the Far East showed strong economic growth, Shell set up a separate trading unit for oil products within Shell Singapore, the Shell International Eastern Trading Company (Sietco), in 1991.[91] In a way, this move towards regionalization was surprising in the light of the globalization. Paul Skinner, then president of Sitco, gave the following explanation: 'It was clear that, as far as the Far East is concerned, it would be better managed by people operating off a large refining base in the region, who understand the mechanics of local markets, the preferences of customers and are available in the time zone to serve better the requirements of those customers.'[92] It is a fair illustration of the challenge of being both local and global. Sietco was modelled on Sitco with one exception: the marine activities were included. The combination worked well and in turn inspired a closer collaboration between Sitco and Marine in Shell.

Like the refineries, the marine sector had expanded vastly during the 1960s and new tankers, ordered in these prosperous times, came into service in the mid-1970s. By then circumstances had changed dramatically. The problem of overcapacity haunted the marine sector well into the 1980s, causing heavy losses. Shell's marine sector was bearing the burden of twenty-five year charters, which still had not expired.[93] In the heavy international competition, the Shell shipping companies in Europe struggled with high

manning costs compared to shipping companies sailing under some other flags. In 1986, Shell decided that only drastic measures could bring the marine sector back into profits. The Dutch fleet reduced manpower levels. The UK fleet chose a more radical solution: all sailors stopping being Shell-employed sailors. They were made redundant and received a severance package. A third-party manning company was established in the Isle of Man with all seafarers being offered a new job under the terms and condition of that company. Obviously, these terms and conditions were less attractive than those they were used to. These measures came as a shock for those concerned, if only because the marine staff had such a distinctive business culture, with a pride in their profession and strong sense of loyalty to the Group. Many sailors were deeply disillusioned by Shell and 35 per cent chose retirement. It was some consolation that in 1990 the name of Shell was restored to the sailors as the manning company was renamed Shell Marine Personnel (Isle of Man) Ltd.[94]

The restructuring came at a time that demand for charters was rising as a consequence of low oil prices and additional long-haul crude movements. Moreover, the shipping industry benefited from lower bunker prices.[95] Just as the industry was beginning to feel more optimistic, a huge oil spill with long-term consequences occurred. The oil tanker *Exxon Valdez* grounded in Alaskan waters on 24 March 1989, spilling 240,000 barrels of crude oil in one of world's most protected areas. The oil spill caused widespread environmental damage that made the world acutely aware of the risks involved in large-scale oil transports. The tanker was not an old ship, but nevertheless the disaster stepped up a debate about the age of ships and about the benefits of double-hull tankers. The disaster also set the oil companies thinking about the risks and benefits of their tanker operations, because oil spills could involve costly clean-up exercises as well as costly legal proceedings and claims. This was particularly true for the US, where courts could award punitive damages and ship-owners faced virtually unlimited liability in the event of an oil spill. Shell shipping companies decided to stop carrying crude oil in their own tankers to US ports, with the exception of the Louisiana Offshore Oil Port.[96]

As a consequence of the *Exxon Valdez* disaster Shell reconsidered its whole strategy with regard to its Marine sector. While the second half of the 1980s had been focused on cutting costs to raise profitability, after the disaster the issue of exposure from oil spills took centre stage. 'Major oil companies feel particularly exposed as they will always be seen as potential targets however remote their connections with a spill', argued Ian McGrath, Shell's marine coordinator. He added: 'There is an expectation in society that an oil company should meet the cost of the clean-up and damages arising from an oil spill, irrespective of whether it has any responsibility or potential liability.'[97] Realizing that the oil companies would be held responsible for oil spills, whether they were the ship owners or the cargo holders, Shell concluded that they could best transport their own cargoes to diminish exposure. Logical though this 'Group Oil On Group Ship' strategy sounded, it was difficult to combine this restriction with an efficient and cost-effective movement of tankers and cargoes. Shipping needed to be flexible. Therefore Shell decided that voyage charters would still play a role, but the marine sector would become more active in setting industry standards and checking the quality of the ships they hired. From a system of blacklisting unsatisfactory ships, they moved to an approval system identifying good-quality ships. At the same time, the number of owned ships was gradually reduced to a core fleet of around fifty tankers, enough to maintain marine expertise.[98]

The reduction in the Shell fleet called for a change in the structure of the marine sector. In the 1960s, Shell had four national shipping companies under the Dutch, German, French, and British flags, and a central organization to manage about 300 oil ships. In 1992 there were only sixty-nine oil ships and still five organizations to manage them. This disparity obviously needed to be addressed and in 1994 the operational management of all the international fleet together with the vessel trading and services were all combined in one single company, Shell International Shipping (SIS), based in London. Despite its smaller number of vessels, SIS remained one of the largest fleets of oil and gas vessels in the world. Initially, the marine presence in the Netherlands, Germany, and France, as well as the Isle of Man and Cyprus were retained to recruit and contract seafarers in the unified fleet.[99] But in 1995 the manning of the fleet became centralized in Shell International Manning Services, located in Singapore with administrative services provided from the Isle of Man. This international manning company employed seafarers of all nationalities on internationally competitive terms and conditions.[100] Within Shell Shipping, the actual shipping became less important while the delivery of services to Shell companies and third parties increased in importance. Jan Kopernicki, vice-president of Shipping, summarized its tasks simply as: 'we busy ourselves with all that floats and gets wet'.[101] Even before this final international integration had taken place, Shell shipping and trading were combined into one company, Stasco, short for Shell Trading and Shipping Company. The two activities were closely related, in particular oil trading and freight trading, for which both speed and timing were essential.[102] The convergence of the two companies also acted as a pathfinder for a review into the role of the Group service companies, which will be discussed in chapter 4.

S hell's focused thinking about scenario planning began in the mid-1960s, when E&P management realized they routinely assessed technical risks when they had to make investment decisions, but did not include the political and general risks. Therefore they asked Jimmy Davidson, head of Group planning division, whether it might be possible to incorporate political and general risks in upstream investment evaluation.[1] For the oil industry the rising ambition of oil-producing countries formed an obvious political risk. In the early 1970s the Shell planners, headed by Ted Newland and later Pierre Wack, foresaw a tension between the increasing demand for energy and the desire of Middle East countries such as Saudi Arabia to preserve their resources. As a result oil producers would acquire the upper hand over buyers and prices would rise rapidly.[2] Shell urged western governments to take precautionary action in case of an oil shortage. Though governments did not take action until the first oil crisis of 1973 unfolded, Shell realized the value of planning and in particular of scenario planning. This technique analysed the major forces at work, how they related to each other, and what the possible consequences could be. Scenarios did not forecast, because the future was deemed to be unpredictable. Instead several different futures were sketched out, and each story had its own internal logic. The stories started with things that seemed to be fairly certain and moved forward to more speculative developments. Managers were invited to think about several options and prepare for them, so that they would not be taken by surprise.

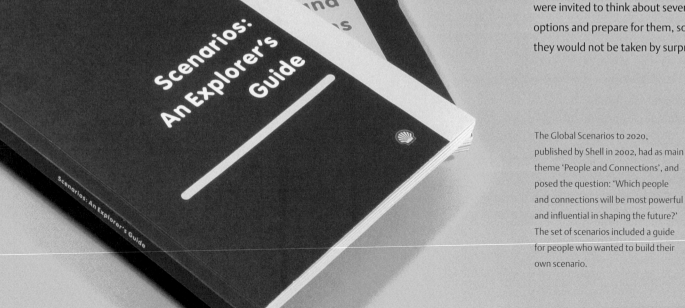

The Global Scenarios to 2020, published by Shell in 2002, had as main theme 'People and Connections', and posed the question: 'Which people and connections will be most powerful and influential in shaping the future?' The set of scenarios included a guide for people who wanted to build their own scenario.

Initially the scenarios were developed by a Shell team in collaboration with outside experts to support the CMD in its long-term decision-making. In the 1980s Shell managers became more actively involved in discussing the scenarios and were required to plot their own plans against the scenarios. Apart from the general scenarios more focused scenarios for specific regions, countries, and business sectors were also developed. While outside experts played an important role in thinking through the political, economic, and social developments, internal Shell employees were deeply involved with the business and energy scenarios.

The general scenarios often told two contrasting stories, both of which were given engaging names. The scenarios in the mid-1970s, developed with the help of Herman Kahn and his Hudson Institute, contrasted the 'Belle Epoque' with the 'World of Internal Contradictions'. The 'Belle Epoque' stood for high economic growth, while the 'World of Internal Contradictions' brought stagnation. The theme of economic growth or lack of it remained high on the agenda with the scenarios in the 1980s, and some optimism about future growth returned to the scenarios. The scenario of 1989 explored what a 'Sustainable World' would look like.

The scenarios of the 1990s were based on the vision that the forces of globalization, liberalization, and technology would shape change and integration. With names such as 'New Frontiers' versus 'Barricades', 'Just Do It' versus 'Da Wo (Big Me)', and 'New Game' versus 'People Power', the global scenarios contrasted different kinds of economic organization, with liberal free market capitalism on the one hand and the cooperative and more collective forms of organization on the other.[3]

Did the scenarios help Shell reach more accurate decisions or reach them faster? On the one hand, scenario planning meant that the rise of the oil prices in the early 1970s was not entirely unexpected by the Group, and the scenarios stimulated Shell marketing to focus Group refineries on transport fuels rather than fuel oil. Work had been ongoing on the options if oil prices fell in the mid-1980s, and Arie de Geus argued that as a result of scenario planning Shell moved quickly (though not faster than BP) to establish a comprehensive trading floor as a result of the scenario thinking.[4] But on the other hand, by signalling the possibility of very fast growth in electricity demand, the scenarios also led to the Group's engagement in nuclear energy. Likewise, they signalled the possibility

that coal would fill the energy gap in the 1990s, and thus justified Shell's entry into the coal business. Though Shell entered these fields quickly, neither nuclear nor coal turned out to be particularly successful. Again, in the late 1970s the scenarios pointed out the enormous potential for change in China and Russia, and Shell's scenario planner Peter Schwartz remembered how in the early 1980s he and his team began to study the economic policies of the 1920s in the Soviet Union, a study which led to the view that a more liberal economic policy might be close at hand. This view underlined the understanding that oil prices would come down in the near future and made Shell look at certain investment decisions more critically than it otherwise might have done.[5] Yet, though the scenarios had noted the growing importance of environmental concerns, they could not prevent the decision to sink the Brent Spar unleashing a major public outcry. The scenarios did not and were not supposed to foretell the terrorist attack on the US on 11 September 2001, but as early as the mid-1980s the scenarios about the Middle East signalled rising Islamic fundamentalism as a matter of serious concern.[6] In the 1990s the leaders of Shell frequently used the scenarios as basic material for the many speeches they

were expected to give. Interestingly the possibility of a strong rise in oil prices at the beginning of the twenty-first century was not included in any of the scenarios of the late 1990s, though prices were expected to rise substantially later in that century. In short, the most positive contribution of the scenarios was that they forced management to think flexibly about the future and to be critical of established routines. With hindsight, they told as much about the period in which they were written as about the future they were supposed to reveal.

The discovery of the gas field in Groningen in 1959 turned the Netherlands unexpectedly into a resource-rich country. The Dutch government showed itself as eager as the OPEC governments to profit from this natural resource, and it encouraged the use of natural gas by households and industry alike. To that purpose the whole country became covered by a dense gas infrastructure built during the 1960s and early 1970s.

Rise of natural gas: Groningen, North Sea, and LNG

One of the most remarkable developments of the 1990s was the rising importance of natural gas in the total activities of the Group. Gas developed into the Group's second core business, surpassing its chemical interests. The two stepping stones for Shell's gas business, the Groningen gas field and the development of LNG, had been laid in 1959. In that year Shell found the Groningen gas field in the Netherlands, which turned out to be of such impressive proportions that comparisons were made with Saudi Arabia. The Dutch government had left oil exploration and production in the Netherlands to Shell and its partner Esso (Exxon), working together in the Nederlandse Aardolie Maatschappij (NAM). However, the state became closely involved in the development of this huge gas field. The Dutch government was as eager to profit from its natural resources as the governments of the OPEC countries. The Groningen concession was given to NAM, but the cost of production and the revenues from the sales of gas were accounted for in the newly established Maatschap Groningen, in which NAM had a 60 per cent share, while the Dutch State Mines (DSM) held 40 per cent for the Dutch state. Because the Maatschap was also taxed at the upstream tax rate, the state collected around 70 per cent of the profits. On top of this, a 'windfall tax' mechanism was introduced in 1975 under which the government's take could rise to 85 per cent; this was brought to a maximum of 95 per cent in 1979. The Maatschap Groningen sold the gas to Gasunie, a company established in 1963 in which Shell and Esso participated for 25 per cent each and the state for 50 per cent, 10 per cent directly and 40 per cent via DSM.[103] In the 1960s Gasunie built an extensive natural gas grid in the Netherlands. Households turned in huge numbers from coal and fuel oil to natural gas for heating and cooking, because it was clean, easy to use, and cheap. The government

[63]

[64]

[65]

encouraged industry to use gas, which was in ample supply, and large export contracts were concluded, because nuclear energy was expected to replace gas in the foreseeable future. In 1970 the Netherlands supplied 92 per cent of Europe's internationally traded natural gas.[104] In addition, the Groningen gas find marked the beginning of exploration and production in the North Sea.

After the first oil shock of 1973, the Dutch government decided to reduce the depletion rate of the Groningen gas field to preserve the gas for future generations. It limited the export of gas, while other countries such as the Soviet Union, Norway, and Algeria began to supply the European export market. With an export of 50 billion cubic metres (bcm), the Netherlands had a share in Europe's internationally traded gas of 76 per cent in 1975, but twenty years later, with a volume of 40 bcm, its share was only 10 per cent. While limiting the export of gas, the Dutch government encouraged exploration for other gas fields in Dutch territory. No second field of the size of Groningen was discovered, but a number of small fields, onshore and offshore, were found and came into production. The Groningen gas field was not only huge, but it also had a special geological structure, which made it possible, after substantial investment in wellhead production capacity, to vary production according to summer or winter demand. This flexibility in production led to the government policy to reduce the production of the Groningen field and give priority to exploiting smaller gas fields first. Gasunie contracted all the gas produced from the small fields, while Groningen became the swing supplier. This policy greatly stimulated the search for and production of gas in the Dutch part of the North Sea in which NAM played a vital role.[105]

The second significant development in 1959 was the construction of the first ship that could transport liquefied natural gas, the *Methane Pioneer*, belonging to Constock International

To ensure uninterrupted natural gas deliveries to the Dutch industry during periods of peak demand in wintertime, Gasunie built an LNG peak shaver tank at the Maasvlakte in the Netherlands in 1977.

[66]

[67]

[68]

Methane Ltd. The challenge in transporting gas in liquid form
(LNG) was that it had to be deeply refrigerated to an astounding
temperature of minus 165 ° C. Understanding the future prospects of
LNG shipping, Shell acquired a 40 per cent interest in Constock.[106]
It then went on to develop its first major LNG project in Brunei for
contracted customers in Japan, which turned out to be a technological as well as financial success. In December 1971 Shell delivered
its first shipment of LNG to Japan.[107] The LNG technology offered
the key to the gradual end of the practice of flaring associated gas.
Malcolm Brinded remembered its beneficial impact on Brunei: 'I
lived in Brunei in sight of the plant for 5 years from 1975. In the first
year, there was effectively no night sky where we lived. It was so
bright that you could easily drive along the beach at night, lit solely
by the flares. Within a couple of years all that changed. LNG exports
transformed the economics of installing small gas gathering and
gas compression plants all along the coastal oil fields and one by
one effectively all the flares went out, with all the associated gas
being gathered and exported.'[108]

After the exciting breakthroughs of the 1960s, the 1970s and
1980s offered more of the same. Between 1975 and 1991 the gas
sales in volume of the Group remained more or less at the same
level. However, this did not mean that nothing happened. Quite the
contrary, continuous new initiatives were necessary to keep sales
going. Shell focused its attention on the development of gas in the
North Sea and putting together LNG projects. The Netherlands
formed the backbone of Shell's gas sector in sales as well as in
earnings. After the first oil shock in 1973 the oil companies,
including Shell, stepped up their efforts to find oil and gas in the
North Sea. As discussed in chapter 1, the Brent field turned out to
have considerable amounts of associated gas. This was a mixed

blessing because collecting the associated gas made the construction
of the platforms more complicated and more expensive. But the
alternative of flaring the gas was not environmentally acceptable, and
therefore a Brent gas system was put in place, which began to deliver
in 1979. In the 1960s Shell and others had already discovered gas fields
in the southern North Sea, but the low gas prices paid by British Gas
did not encourage further exploration of this area until the mid-
1980s.[109] In the Norwegian part of the North Sea Norske Shell had
a share in the Albuskjell field, which began to deliver in 1979.

The most challenging gas find in the North Sea, however, was
the Troll field, off the Norwegian coast. From seismic surveys made
in 1971 geologists from several companies had identified a 'flat spot'
in block 31/2 and its neighbouring blocks 31/3, 31/5 and 31/6, which
pointed in the direction of a major oil or gas field. When block 31/2
was put on offer in 1978 many companies were interested, despite
the fact that the depth of 350 metres of water and the long
distance to markets made it a very demanding project. There was
also the risk that much of the field would lie in neighbouring blocks
and that these would be awarded to other parties in one of the next
rounds, which indeed happened. In the fourth licensing round Shell
placed other blocks at the top of their list and gave block 31/2 a
priority four, but it was prepared to take 31/2 in combination with
another block. Shell was awarded the licence for exploration, but
under very strict conditions. According to Norwegian policy at the
time, large interests were reserved for the national oil industry,
including a 50 per cent share for Statoil, and while Norske Shell
became operator for the exploration, it had to accept that the
government reserved the right to transfer operatorship to Statoil
during the production phase. The first well, drilled in July 1979,
established a massive gas and oil field. The gigantic task of bringing

Right: After the production of natural gas on land or at sea, the next step in any LNG project is the refrigeration of the gas to minus 1650 C. Now in liquid form, it is stored, loaded, and shipped to its overseas market. In the receiving country, the LNG is stored again pending its regasification and distribution to consumers.

Left: During the 1970s and 1980s the oil industry learned to produce oil and gas in ever deeper waters by building ever taller platforms. Among the tallest platforms was the concrete gravity base structure built to develop the Troll field, off the Norwegian coast, here seen as an artist's impression next to Tower Bridge in London.

[69]

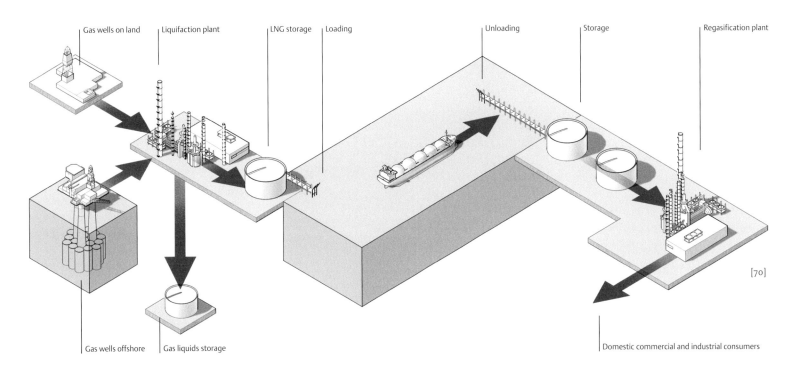

Gas wells offshore | Gas liquids storage

Domestic commercial and industrial consumers

[70]

Chapter 3

the oil and gas to consumer markets could begin. Norske Shell in partnership with Statoil developed the gas field, while Norsk Hydro brought the thin oil layers beneath the gas into production.[110]

While the discovery of the Troll field was potentially very important, it was expensive to develop. Long-term sales contracts were needed to justify the huge investments necessary to produce and market the gas. In 1979 this problem seemed surmountable, but by the time Statoil, as principal negotiator, was ready to sign a sales contract with a consortium of European gas buyers, the oil price had collapsed. The sellers' market had changed into a buyers' market. Nevertheless, John Jennings recommended the deal to the members of the Conference, explaining that the Troll field was unusual for many reasons. The gas fields were large and in very deep water. The platform that would be built for the first phase of the development would be the largest construction of this type and the gas sales contracts were for an exceptionally long period of thirty-five years. Last, but not least, the project was of strategic importance for Europe as it would be the only indigenous source of gas that could be a real alternative to Russian sources, apart from the Groningen gas.[111] In 1995 the giant concrete platform A, the tallest structure ever moved, was towed towards its final resting place and work began to prepare it for production. Finally in 1996 the gas from Troll began to flow from the onshore processing plant

at Kolnes, near Bergen, to customers in six European countries. It took sixteen years to bring the Troll field into production, but it is expected to serve European gas customers for fifty years.[112]

Long lead times were not just typical for the North Sea gas projects but also characterized the LNG projects. Another shared feature was that long-term sales contracts preceded the building up of the facilities, which contrasted sharply with the custom in oil production and marketing. After its success with the Brunei LNG scheme, Shell developed many more projects, though not all materialized. In 1976 Brunei was the largest individual source of LNG supplies with Algeria and Libya (not Shell projects) in second and third places respectively. Shell expected a strong growth in LNG and was involved in negotiations relating to proposed LNG projects in Australia, Nigeria, Qatar, and Sarawak. As Shell had only small shares in many of the new projects, Group companies had to 'run to stay still'. Shell did not go ahead with the LNG project in Qatar at that time and the Nigeria LNG project had to be postponed several times, but the LNG project in Malaysia proceeded according to plan with the commencement of LNG shipments in 1983.[113]

In the meantime the safety of LNG became a major public concern. An unpublished report on the hazards of importing LNG via Rotterdam had been prepared by the Dutch institute TNO. In

In projects such as the Australian North West Shelf, where Woodside Petroleum was the operator working on its own behalf and that of joint ventures including Shell, LNG technology made it possible to bring gas from remote fields to consumer markets.

1978 a book *Time Bomb* appeared with the object of revealing to the public 'the truth about the newest and most dangerous energy source, liquefied natural gas'.[114] Shell responded by dismissing the claims and stepping up its own research in the field of safety, in particular into risks involved in the long-distance transport. In the late 1970s it devoted the considerable sum of £4 million to tests at sea with separate instantaneous and continuous spills of refrigerated LNG, some of which were ignited. The results of these tests were given to a group of scientists. Shell hoped in this way to obtain planning permission for the building of new LNG terminals in Europe. Over the years safety research continued, though Shell could point out in 1994 that in its thirty-year history, the international LNG trade had an excellent safety record with no major incidents recorded in some 15,000 voyages.[115]

One of the major gas developments took place in Australia, off the north-west coast, in an area known as the North-West Shelf. This was another area of both oil and gas production, and Shell was among the major investors. As happened elsewhere, a joint venture was set up for the exploration and production, but its structure was complicated and involved frequent inter-company manoeuvring. In the North-West Shelf LNG project six partners were involved, each with a one-sixth share. The six participants were Shell, BHP, BP, Chevron, Woodside, and MiMi, a joint venture between the two Japanese trading houses Mitsui and Mitsubishi. To complicate matters, Woodside Petroleum, who was the operator, was a small publicly listed Australian company, in which Shell and BHP each had a 21 per cent stake. Concerned that Woodside would not be able to meet the increasing financial demands for the next phases of the LNG project, Shell and BHP decided to make a bid for Woodside's remaining shares in order to increase their share to at least 70 per cent. Despite criticism that the offer price was too low, Shell and BHP received enough acceptances to increase their share

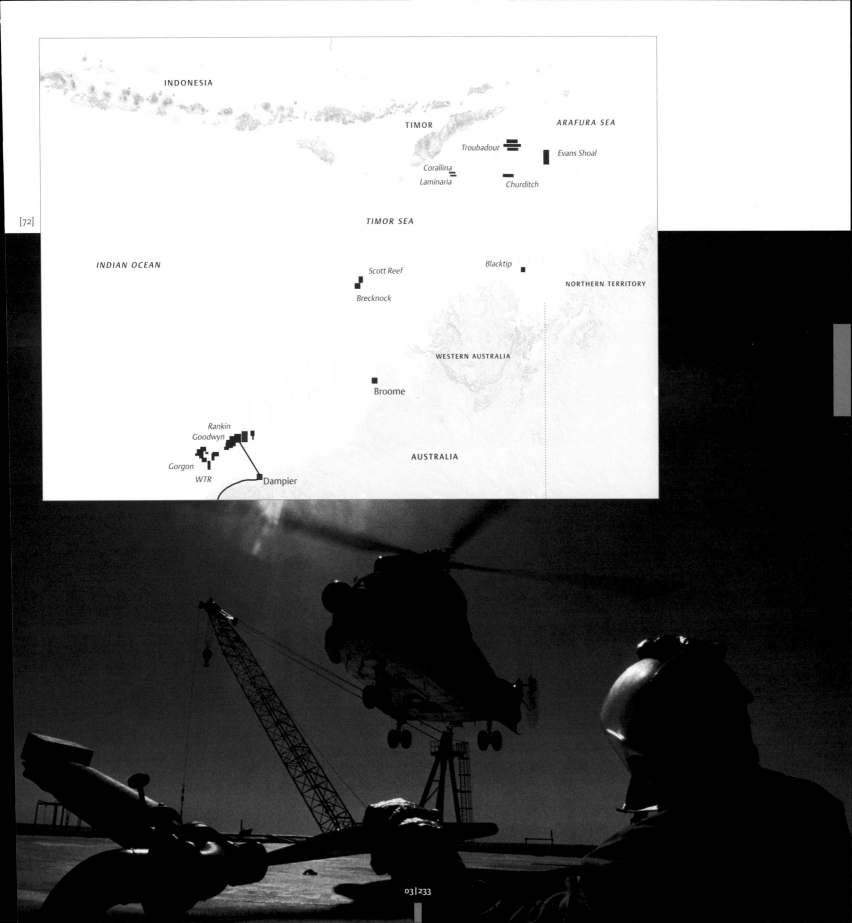

INDONESIA

TIMOR

ARAFURA SEA

Troubadour

Evans Shoal

Corallina

Laminaria

Churditch

TIMOR SEA

INDIAN OCEAN

Scott Reef

Blacktip

NORTHERN TERRITORY

Brecknock

WESTERN AUSTRALIA

Broome

Rankin

Goodwyn

Gorgon

WTR

Dampier

AUSTRALIA

[73]

Transport of LNG took place in specially designed ships with their characteristic shape, usually in the form of a set of spherical tanks. Here are two tankers dedicated to the North West Shelf project in Australia, one going out laden with cargo, and one coming back to take on a fresh load.

to 80 per cent.[116] The first shipload of LNG sailed to Japan in 1989, ahead of schedule. During the 1990s more LNG trains were added as the Goodwyn field was being developed.[117] The gas project lead times were not only long but also became longer over time. It took nine years to develop and build the Brunei-Japan LNG scheme, seventeen years for the Troll gas project and eighteen years for the NW Shelf Australia LNG scheme.[118]

While the oil price collapse of 1986 had a marked influence on the oil industry, the gas sector felt the impact much more slowly, because the long-term sales agreements retarded the effect. Shell was certain that future results would come under pressure and that it might be necessary to compromise on prices and profitability in order to protect market positions. However, it expected its natural gas sector to remain a major generator of funds for the Group in the long term. Indeed, the gas businesses demonstrated considerable resilience.[119] Shell remained committed to expand its gas business, but to survive in a world of lower gas prices, it was essential to get costs down whilst preserving safety. For instance, in Shell-advised LNG ventures a reduction in operating costs of 45 per cent over the period 1990-99 could be achieved.[120]

New gas plays   In the 1970s and 1980s the attention of oil companies had been focused on oil rather than gas, but that changed in the 1990s. In its long-term scenarios, published in 1986, Shell looked at the energy markets from the perspective of 'lifecycles' of energy resources over a period of 200 years. It was clear that wood had given way to coal, and coal in its turn had given way to oil. Though the conclusion was not yet firmly drawn in these scenarios, the implication was already there that in due time oil would be overtaken by gas.[121] This was indeed the message of Jeroen van der Veer in 2002 for a group of investors in Qatar. He argued: 'If coal fuelled the nineteenth century and oil was the fuel of the twentieth, gas is destined to be the fuel of the twenty-first.'[122] The Shell gas planning scenarios from 1992 had already concluded that under their two different scenarios of 'sustainable world' or 'global mercantilism', the demand for gas would increase, but in the first scenario even more than in the second. One of the great advantages of gas over oil was that it was a cleaner energy source, and this was particularly apparent in power generation. Emissions of carbon dioxide from gas combustion were less than half that of coal and 70 per cent of oil. Moreover, no sulphur dioxide was released and the emissions of nitrous oxides were comparatively small. Since the publication of the Bruntland report on sustainable growth in 1987, Shell expected governments to become more active in introducing legislation to limit or tax emissions.[123] In the early 1990s the Group companies together were the largest seller of natural gas in the world, excluding the 'captive market' of the state entities. Considerable growth could be achieved in the 1990s, as is clear from figure 3.9 (see page 236), which highlights Shell's gas sales between 1971 and 1997, as well as figures for Exxon and BP.[124] The figures for Exxon relate to gas sales for the period 1971 till 1979 and to gas production from 1980 onwards, and are therefore unfortunately not entirely comparable. The Shell sales of natural gas show a steady rise from 1990 till 1997.

In particular growth in gas use for power generation was expected to rise at the cost of coal, because of environmental concerns. In 1983 Shell had concluded that there was little option for gas in power generation, because nuclear and coal-fired stations

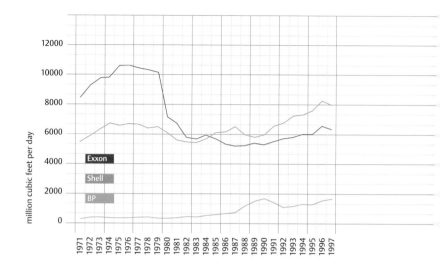

Figure 3.9
Natural gas sales, Shell, Exxon,
and BP, 1971-1997.

would take the major share of the market. In 1988, however, Shell felt less certain about how the power generation market would develop. A year later it was convinced that gas would increasingly be used for power generation and that the European Community would relax its rules concerning the use of gas for this purpose, which it had discouraged since the first oil crisis of 1973. One of the reasons why Shell foresaw a greater use of gas for power had to do with high expectations of a new technology, the gas combined cycle technology, which would make it possible to generate electricity more efficiently at lower costs, according to Shell.[125]

While Shell predicted an increasing demand for gas for power generation, it had no ambition to become involved in power generation itself. At least, that was the opinion voiced in the Conference in 1994. By 1997 this view had changed, when Walter van de Vijver presented his 'fuels-to-power' strategy to the Conference as a way of increasing the gas sales. It expected to sell both LNG and pipeline gas to newly built gas-fired power stations. The first move to realize this strategy consisted of taking a 50 per cent share in InterGen, a company of Bechtel Enterprises and a major international developer of private power projects. Though InterGen was an American company, all projects were outside the US and still under construction.[126]

With regard to liberalization of markets, Shell sent out mixed messages. On the one hand it formed Quadrant Gas Limited to gain access to gas marketing opportunities within the UK.[127] And in general it supported the idea of competition and free market access. J. R. Williams, Natural Gas and Coal coordinator in 1993, argued that the prospect for long-term developments, particularly those seeking to export to Europe, should be enhanced by free trade – not hampered by restrictive national or supra-national energy policies – and by fair competition. On the other hand, he

explained that the security of supply relied on continued investment in long-term projects and that these investments would only be forthcoming when sales were ensured through long-term relationships and agreements.[128] Certainly Shell was not in a hurry to change the 'Gasgebouw' in the Netherlands that had been a source of steady income for many, many years.

In the meantime, gas markets in the US, which for decades had been tightly controlled, were increasingly deregulated. In the mid-1980s Shell Oil in the US hired McKinsey to formulate a gas strategy at the time when Jeffrey Skilling was one of their consultants. McKinsey wrote a study report with novel ideas on how to make money in gas merchandizing after controls had been eliminated. Shell Oil, however, did not follow up the ideas and shelved the report. Skilling, on the other hand, liked his ideas so much that he went to another company, Enron, where he put them into practice.[129] Enron was formed in 1985 from the merger of two regional pipeline utilities. It achieved impressive growth by making optimal use of the opportunities which arose out of the deregulation of the American gas market and which it actively promoted. In 1994 *The Economist* wrote an article about Enron with the heading: 'An obscure Texas company has dazzled the stock market. So far', and in a later article *The Economist* explained how it worked: 'In the traditional regulated market, utilities were monopolies with fixed prices: they hired engineers to build large reliable plants. In Enron's world, the engineers have been replaced by theoretical physicists trained in portfolio analysis; the reliability is engineered on the trading floor, where young traders price and strike deals with customers in something like 90 seconds. By pooling these customised contracts, Enron believes it can hedge its financial risk while delivering power at a competitive price.'[130] Discussing the competitors in the Conference, Henk Dijkgraaf, Natural Gas coordinator, mentioned that: 'Enron constituted an entrepreneurial, nimble-footed and formidable competitor, although it currently lacked access to LNG.'[131] Shell people were intrigued by the sudden rise of this rival, but did not quite understand how it could be so profitable. With hindsight we know that Enron was unable to sustain its growth in the late 1990s without accounting scams, but during the 1990s it was seen as a remarkable innovator, and an example for others.

In an effort to find similar profits in a gas pipeline play, Shell Oil formed the gas trading company Coral Energy as a joint venture with Tejas Gas Corporation, a publicly traded natural gas pipeline company, in 1995. The next step consisted of the acquisition of the midstream gas business of Tejas Gas in 1997. This acquisition was one of those unfortunate investments that went wrong from the very beginning. From 1994 Shell Oil had gone through a process of transformation to create an environment in which people had more freedom and more accountability. 'Today, we're asking people to innovate and take risks, understanding that not every innovation will be successful, and that the ability to tolerate and learn from mistakes is one of the hallmarks of an innovative culture', explained Philip Carroll, CEO of Shell Oil in 1997.[132] The original plan had been for Shell Oil to merge its midstream assets with those of Tejas, but in September 1997 the views changed and the preferred route

became one where Shell Oil was to purchase 100 per cent of the Tejas shares at a considerable cost, while leaving the existing Tejas management in place. According to Shell, this management exhibited little cost-consciousness, concentrating on future deals and not on current operating performance. The return on investment and other indicators were on a downward slope by mid-1997, but Shell Oil management and its negotiators appeared to have ignored the trends, despite the fact that Price Waterhouse had performed a two-month-long due diligence operation. Soon after the purchase, Tejas Gas was restructured and part of the assets were sold. US$1.6 billion of the US$2.9 billion acquisition price were written off within a three-year period.[133]

One of the big problems of gas is that it is expensive to transport, while many gas fields are far removed from consumer markets. LNG processing and transport as well as long-range pipelines required heavy investments. Therefore, Shell developed an alternative solution to finding markets for remote gas, the 'gas to liquids' (GTL) technology. This is another name for the Shell Middle Distillate Synthesis, explained in chapter 2. In 1984 Shell decided to build up an experimental GTL plant in a country where gas was abundant. The plant was set up in Bintulu, Malaysia. After delays the first products arrived in 1994. Initially, the idea was to serve the local market, but the quality of the product turned out to be so clean that it was instead used to enhance the fuel quality for markets that were prepared to pay a premium.[134] With costs coming down and prices for quality products going up, the innovative GTL technology became commercially feasible. In 1997 Shell planned a larger GTL plant as a way of achieving access to a major resource holder. One of the options under consideration was a plant in gas-rich Qatar, which became a reality in the twenty-first century.

LNG carrier of the North West
Shelf project in Australia.

Conclusion   After the nationalization of many of its oil concessions during the early 1970s, Shell had been able to find and produce new sources of oil and gas under more difficult circumstances, helped by the high price of oil. In the 1980s it succeeded in closing the gap with Exxon and this trend continued after the oil price collapse of 1986. Though measured in 1974 prices Shell reduced its investment in exploration and production after 1986, it did not cut back as heavily as some of its competitors. As a consequence, production of oil and gas continued to grow, making Shell the largest producer amongst the traditional oil companies. In 1989 Shell had overtaken Exxon in production as well as reserves. When oil prices continued to remain low during the 1990s, cost-cutting became inevitable, all the more so as shareholders became more demanding. The focus shifted from production to profitability, as will be discussed in the next chapter, and Shell adapted successfully. In August 1997 the American journal *Fortune* hailed Royal Dutch/Shell as the most profitable enterprise in the world, and for the third consecutive year it led *Fortune's* list of Global 500 companies ranked by total profits.[135] New technologies had helped to reduce costs of exploration and production, while at the same time developing ways of accessing oil that had been previously considered out of reach. In the upstream sector Shell made the most of maturing oil fields. The conviction that oil prices would stay low into the next century made Shell very strict in assessing and accepting future projects. Therefore profitability had come at the cost of future growth prospects. Yet, at the same time consistent efforts were directed towards creating opportunities for entering major resource holding countries. Though not without promise, these were very long-term strategies.

Shell's success story of the 1990s was the impressive growth in the gas business, moving ahead of competitors in natural gas sales and in the development of fuel transformation technologies, in particular the production of oil liquids out of natural gas. The downstream sector had profited from low oil prices. Traditionally strong in marketing, Shell had passed Exxon in the sale of oil products in 1986 and it remained ahead of the competitors during most of the 1990s. After more than twenty years it had finally come to grips with its overcapacity in refining, a legacy from the 1960s. A similar problem in marine had been countered by drastic measures, which had transformed the marine sector from shipping to services. The downstream business had other trends to worry about, such as liberalization of markets and a trend towards globalization, which formed a challenge for an enterprise whose strength was traditionally based in its decentralized structure. How Shell worked to adapt its organizational structure to the new challenges will be discussed in the next chapter.

Motivating staff and satisfying shareholders, 1973-1998

Increasing pressure from shareholders and globalization of markets led to changes in business outlook which motivated Shell to reconsider its internal organizational structure. The big reorganization of the mid-1990s is the central event in this chapter. It is, however, embedded in a more general discussion of the Group's personnel policy, the role of management, and the influence of shareholders. During the period of rapid growth after the Second World War, Shell had built up a solid personnel policy and organizational structure in which management had a strong position in deciding the future of the company. The question was how long these structures would remain appropriate in different business environments. During the 1970s employees demanded more freedom to shape their own work and greater involvement in business decision-making. During the 1980s the shareholders began to express their points of view about company policies more strongly. The Group regularly reviewed both the staff policy and internal organization, and made minor adjustments and improvements. Making more radical changes, however, was difficult, because there was a close link between the staff policies, in particular recruiting and career advancement of management, and the internal organization and coherence within the Group. The final overhaul of the matrix structure in the mid-1990s therefore was an unsettling process. Started off as a 'Central Offices Review', it turned into a 'Transformation' process that aimed to make structures simpler and managers more accountable for their financial results. In the short run it encouraged individual performance and reduced Group loyalty. Drastic though the reorganization of the mid-1990s was, it did not deal with two remaining elements of the past: the Committee of Managing Directors (CMD) and the dual nationality through two parent companies.

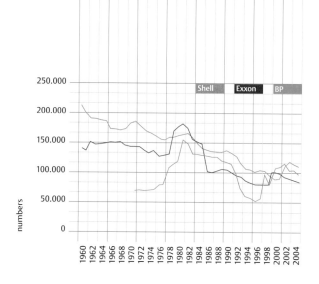

Figure 4.1
Number of employees at Shell, Exxon,
and BP, 1960-2005 .

Managing a large workforce

During the 1950s Shell had grown into a vast international enterprise with at its peak some 260,000 employees. Though numbers decreased in the 1960s, by the early 1970s Shell still employed a large international workforce of between 150,000 and 180,000 people, spread out over some hundred countries. About two-thirds of employees worked outside the two home countries of the parent companies. During the last quarter of the twentieth century Shell's staff numbers showed a steady decline, though the workforce remained substantial. The same was true for its main rival Exxon, while the size of BP's workforce displayed some considerable ups and downs. Figure 4.1 shows how the total numbers of employees of Shell, Exxon, and BP developed from 1960 to 2005.[1]

The overall figures conceal different patterns of growth and stagnation in the various sectors as described in the previous chapters. In the downstream and chemicals business the numbers of employees declined because of long-term overcapacity. In the upstream business nationalizations in some countries alternated with new opportunities in others. Added to that, productivity had risen, making it possible to do the same amount of business with fewer people. The rise in staff numbers during the second half of the 1970s was related to the diversification policy of the three oil companies. The steep rise in staff numbers of BP in 1978 was caused by the increase of BP's shareholding in the American company Sohio to 54 per cent, leading to the consolidation of Sohio's figures. The gradual abandonment of the diversification strategy, the long period of low oil prices, productivity rises as a consequence of computer technology, and the policy of outsourcing, all caused further reductions in staff during the 1990s. Interestingly from 2001 the number of Shell employees began to increase again as a response to a growth policy.

Personnel policies in the Shell Group were largely locally determined. The organizational structure introduced in the late 1950s had the principle of decentralization as its basis. The local operating companies and their managers were responsible for the business results, and reported to the regional coordinators, while the functional coordinators at the two central offices gave advice and formulated general company policies. With regard to human resource management the Personnel Coordinator with his staff dealt with general strategies, gave support to operating companies and looked after the recruitment and development of a core group of staff, in particular the international staff. The local operating companies looked after their own staffing needs and had their own policies adjusted to national customs and regulations, but in line with general Group policy. Their top management was recruited centrally, but some of the local staff also became part of the group of expatriates.[2]

Group personnel policy found its expression in guidelines, the so-called Personnel Management Guides. These guides discussed a large number of issues ranging from the standard questions such as training, planning and developing manpower, and retirement benefits to more fashionable discussions such as employee participation, equal employment opportunity, and social performance. The Group's Statement of General Business Principles from 1976, which will be further discussed in chapter 5, recognized the following responsibilities of the Group to employees: 'To ensure that employees have good and safe conditions of work, good remuneration and retirement benefits; to promote the development and best use of human talent and potential and to encourage employee involvement in the planning and direction of their work, recognizing that success depends on the full contribution of all employees, who in turn must be fairly treated.'[3]

Shell valued its reputation as a good employer. It also approached its staff policy in a systematic way. Its personnel department, Group Personnel, kept in touch with developments in the social sciences and made use of social theories in their own internal reports. These theories were confronted with the routines and practices that had developed in the Group over time.[4]

'Growing your own timber'   Typical of Shell's personnel policy in the 1960s and 1970s was its long-term view. Staff were recruited and trained with the idea of keeping them in the organization for the rest of their working lives, as long as they functioned satisfactorily. From today's recruits would come the future senior management. For this reason particular care and attention was given to the selection, assessment, and development of potential managers. Within Shell this policy was termed 'growing your own timber'. Managers were defined as those holding jobs in the 'lettered category', above job group 1. Shell had job categories ranging from 15 to 1 and then four lettered categories ranging from A to D. After that came the 'unclassified category', the highest positions in the Group.[5] Just as businesses were used to making long-term plans, Shell Personnel developed programmes to follow the long-term requirements for managers: what kind of quality, which nationality and how many managers would the Group need in fifteen years time?

For its management the Group recruited predominantly among university graduates with a focus on chemistry, chemical engineering, mechanical engineering, and furthermore mining engineering and geology. In the 1970s MBA students made their entrance into the Group, but 70-80 per cent of new recruits had technical qualifications, in response to the requirements of the businesses. About 80 per cent were either Dutch or British.[6] Because of the largely technical background of its recruits, Shell gave special attention to social issues in its management development programmes in order to create 'well-rounded' managers.

To be able to fill future managerial positions, it was important to recruit graduates with 'high potential'. G. A. Wagner, Group managing director, explained in 1970 that industry could no longer

'Helicopter Quality': 'a man's ability to look at a problem from a higher vantage point and shape his work accordingly on the basis of a personal vision'

The CEP or Current Estimate Potential played an important role in career planning in Shell. Employees destined to reach the higher ranks in the organization moved quicker through the job groups than the others and attained more responsible positions at an earlier age. This system was also used in some of the companies in which Shell was a partner, such as PDO in Oman, as the CEP card, seen right, shows.

Have a break:
Shell people in the 1970s.

rely on the traditional ways of identifying and training managers in an ever more complex social and economic environment: 'we can no longer expect that high quality executives will emerge merely by chance, personal drive or natural buoyancy, like cream rising to the top of the milk'.[7] Instead selection should be objective and scientifically based. Careers should be judiciously planned and developed. In order to achieve this scientific base, Herman Muller, a Shell executive with extensive experience within Shell, had been asked in 1966 to identify the qualities which enabled people to fill senior positions successfully. He wrote a dissertation about the

[2]

ENGINEERING FUNCTION

Process Engineering - Development template

TYPICAL DEVELOPMENT PROFILES

YEARS	Age	CEP 3	CEP 2	CEP 1	LC
1	24	JGG	IP PERIOD	IP PERIOD	IP PERIOD
2	25	PRODUCTION OPERATIONS (OPTIMISATION) JGG	JG5 PRODUCTION OPERATIONS (OPTIMISATION)	JG5 PRODUCTION OPERATIONS (OPTIMISATION)	JG5 PRODUCTION OPERATIONS (OPTIMISATION) + LDSC
3	26	LDSC	LDSC	LDSC	CONCEPT ENGINEER
4	27		CONCEPT ENGINEER	CONCEPT ENGINEER	JG4
5	28	CONCEPT ENGINEER			PROJECT ENGINEER
6	29		PROJECT ENGINEER	JG4	
7	30	JG5		PROJECT ENGINEER	BROADENING ASSIGNMENT HSE CONTRACTS or AUDIT
8	31	PROJECT ENGINEER	JG4 SENIOR CONCEPT ENGINEER		JG3
9	32			BROADENING ASSIGNMENT HSE CONTRACTS or AUDIT	HEAD OF PROJECT
10	33				
11	34	JG4	BROADENING ASSIGNMENT HR, HSE or TKL	JG3	BROADENING ASSIGNMENT ECONOMICS
12	35	PRODUCTION OPTIMISATION		HEAD OF CONCEPTS	
13	36		SENIOR CONCEPT ENGINEER	BROADENING ASSIGNMENT ECONOMICS or OPERATIONS	JG2
14	37				ENGINEERING TEAM LEADER
15	38	SENIOR CONCEPT ENGINEER		HEAD OF PROJECTS	
16	39		JG3		
17	40	SENIOR CONCEPT ENGINEER	HEAD CONCEPT ENGINEER	JG2	BROADENING ASSIGNMENT OPERATIONS
18	41			ENGINEERING TEAM LEADER	
19	42				JG1
20	43	SENIOR PROJECT ENGINEER	HEAD CONCEPT ENGINEER & CFOH Side Kick	BROADENING ASSIGNMENT OPERATIONS, HSE or CONTRACTS	ASSET MANAGER
21	44				
22	45				
23	46	JG3	JG2	JG1	LCA
24	47	SENIOR DISCIPLINE ENGINEER & CFOH SIDE-KICK		ETL + CFOH	ASSET MANAGER & FUNCTIONAL RESPONSIBILITIES
25	48				
26	49	HEAD OF PROJECTS	ENGINEERING TEAM LEADER	ASSET MANAGER	
27	50				
	50+				

NOTES 1 Cross Postings will be pursued where available. Exposure in other OU should, where practical, match above profiles

[3]

search for the qualities essential to advancement in a large industrial group. His supervisor, D. J. van Lennep, professor in industrial psychology at Utrecht University, acted as a consultant. The study applied to a much wider group than managers alone and formed the basis of a method for appraising the potential of staff in Shell.

Muller (and presumably Shell) had four objectives with this study. The first was to establish 'the qualities which appraisers in Shell appear to have in mind when they differentiate between promising and less promising men'. The study built on practices that were already established within the Group. The second objective was to assess whether the managers indeed possessed the identified qualities. The next step in the research should have been to predict the possibilities of advancement of younger men, presumably on the basis of the identified qualities, and lastly to establish the validity of these predictions. Of the four objectives, only the first one was realized in the dissertation, which was published in 1970. That means that the study confirmed an existing practice, giving it an academic backing and a useful terminology.

The Shell practice, confirmed by Muller's study, consisted of assessing new recruits (often university graduates) on a number of qualities and then ranking them according to their 'ultimate potential', which was 'the highest job group a man may be expected to reach'. The most important criterion for advancement turned out to be the 'Helicopter Quality': 'a man's ability to look at a problem from a higher vantage point and shape his work accordingly on the basis of a personal vision'. Of the total of twenty-seven qualities formulated and tested, three others were considered closely related to the Helicopter view: the power of analysis, imagination, and the sense of reality.[8] Together Shell summarized those four qualities as 'HAIR'. They played an important role in the assessment of recruits and development of future managers.[9]

Even after identifying the qualities that make good leaders, it was not easy to determine who of the high-potential recruits would really make it to the top. Only a few recruits would be so outstanding that it was immediately obvious they could go a long way. Some would show great promise at the start of their career, but fail to live up to that promise. Others might not look outstanding at the start of their career, but turn out to be excellent leaders later on. Therefore Shell continued to assess a fairly large group of promising young managers during the early years of their work to discover how they developed over time. The supervisors would assess how far the future manager would ultimately rise in the organization by determining this person's current estimate potential (CEP). The CEP could go up or down, depending on how well that person developed. In the late 1970s this management instrument became more democratic in the sense that it became customary for the supervising manager to discuss, in broad terms, his estimate of the CEP with the person concerned. The idea behind this openness was that the manager would feel personally responsible for the assessment and development of his staff. However, the fact that employees were told about their CEP made a downward adjustment somewhat more difficult. At the same time the boss of the manager was also included in the assessment

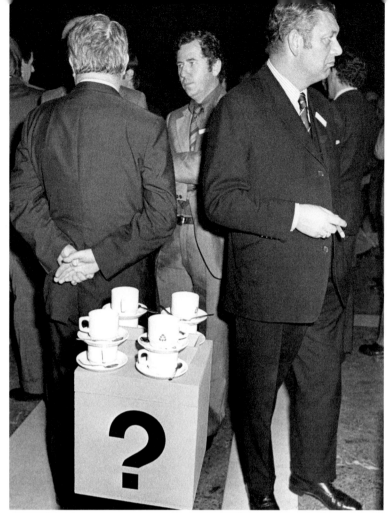

[4]

[5]

process, and the whole system of appraisals and reappraisals became a continuous process as well as a ranking process in which the relative merits of staff were compared. The career patterns that resulted from this system tended to start on a shallow curve in the beginning and then steepen up in later years. One had to be patient. The Group Personnel Coordinator Terry Gerald argued in 1977 that the Shell system ensured that few people 'burned themselves out' and that there were few cases of 'over-promotion'. The system also allowed 'timely, tactful and non-disruptive adjustments in cases where people fail to live up to early expectations – while at the same time making allowances for "late starters"'.[10]

Reaching the levels of higher management had the advantage of becoming eligible for special rewards. Incentive schemes belong to the reality of business life, but appreciation differed over time. In 1970 the Management Development

Committee in Shell discussed the Incentive Award Scheme that had been introduced in the late 1960s. Some senior managers commented that they did not like the word 'incentive' as it implied they would not be motivated without such a scheme. They preferred the phrase 'reward for excellent performance'. Others were critical of the whole idea behind incentive schemes: 'The typical ultra-competitive American-type extreme individualist is by many people no longer envied but pitied.'[11] The name of the scheme was indeed changed into 'Senior Management Award Scheme'. Though some coordinators had their doubts about the desirability of any management award scheme, it was considered impossible to abandon it as long as the competitors had similar schemes. There was a warning note, however, against local award schemes: 'It was suggested that by using return on capital as a basis for distribution between companies there was a danger that some

[6]

Conference of Shell marketing in 1975.
Attendees are reading the special goals
issue, but some questions still need
answers.

chief executives might be loath to take on commercial transactions
which were necessary for overall Group reasons but which reduced
their own profitability.'[12]

Not all shareholders liked the idea of incentives for top
management. At the Annual General Meeting of Shell Transport in
1972 one of the shareholders opposed the proposed Share Incentive
Scheme, commenting that senior executives in Shell companies
were already paid well enough and that if they felt that they could
not give their best without a Share Incentive Scheme they should
be replaced. Rather the board should consider schemes that would
benefit all members of staff, perhaps in the form of putting staff
savings into a trust fund. A vast majority of shareholders, however,
supported the board's proposal.[13]

During the 1970s those working in Britain experienced what was called 'salary compression'. The salary differentials between different levels of staff lessened, partly because of direct government action, including taxation, and partly through trade union pressure. Social conscience also played a role.[14] Indeed, salaries in the UK were lower than in most other western industrialized countries. In 1978 the Shell Personnel Coordinator, Terry Gerald, criticized what he called 'frequent, politically motivated suggestions, which were based on over-simplified comparisons and ignored both the effects of progressive taxation and the concept of life-time earnings, that managers were over-paid in relation to workers'.[15] While Shell supported salary differentials, these were mostly based on classification of the jobs. Salary rises came with steady progression through the various job groups.

During the 1960s the management of large industrial companies had developed into large bureaucracies not unlike government departments. The managers, through their long-term planning and professional management techniques, seemed to be able to guarantee the longevity of their companies. Not only that, the large multinational companies and their managers were seen as exercising an important and not always beneficial power in society, as will be further discussed in chapter 5.[16] However, the power of management, real or imagined, did not remain unchallenged. First employees and later shareholders demanded more say in the development of their companies. Developments in Shell mirrored these general trends.

Industrial democracy   Lack of economic growth during the 1970s meant that employees could no longer expect the salary rises of the 1960s and also that they had fewer chances for promotion. Trade unions therefore devoted more attention to non-material gains, such as workers' participation in management, also termed 'industrial democracy'. Collective bargaining remained in place, but trade unions wanted more influence for employees on important managerial decisions in individual enterprises. They reasoned that shareholders were not the only ones with a 'stake' in the company. What happened to their company, and thus to their jobs, was even more important for employees than for shareholders, and therefore as 'stakeholders' employees too should have a say in important strategic decisions. This demand for industrial democracy was predominantly a European movement and the content differed in the various European countries. In the mid-1970s discussion focused on the representation of employees at the board level. In 1974 the German government proposed legislation that would provide for 50 per cent worker-participation in the Aufsichtsrat (supervisory board). German companies, like Dutch ones, had a two-tier board system with a board of managing directors and a supervisory board. The employee representatives would be nominated by the trade unions. The bill became law in 1976.[17] This German model of co-determination was discussed at the European level. Shell companies were not opposed to trade unions but were against co-participation via trade union representation. In the event of co-determination, representatives of Shell workers should represent all levels of staff. Shell argued that parent companies located in the EEC should be excluded from the system and that shareholders should appoint the management of subsidiaries.[18] They were therefore pleased with the provisions enacted three years earlier in the Dutch Company Law of 1971.

In Dutch law works councils received the same rights as share-holders regarding the nomination of members of the board of supervisory directors in limited liability companies above a certain size. The main power of the board was the appointment and dismissal of the board of managing directors. According to the new law, the members of the board of supervisory directors nominated themselves by a system of co-option. However, the works council, the shareholders' meeting, the board of managing directors and the board of supervisory directors were all allowed to propose nominations for the board of supervisory directors. Both the works council and the shareholders' meeting had the right to veto a nomination. Shareholders were no longer considered more important than employees.[19] When the holding company of a multinational group was Dutch, the holding company was exempted from the worker representation scheme if the majority of the employees of the group worked abroad. The Dutch subsidiaries of the Group were not exempted and had to adopt the scheme, but with one important modification: the appointment of the managing board of the subsidiary and the adoption of its accounts were not matters for the supervisory board of the subsidiary as would be the normal case, but for the general meeting of the shareholders, i.e. for the parent company.[20] These provisions met important needs of the Shell Group. It was vital for the functioning of the whole international Group that the parent companies would maintain their role in the appointment of senior managers and in decisions about large-scale investment. The circulation of international staff throughout the Group via senior management positions formed an essential element in steering the Group. Moreover, Shell wanted to avoid any possibility that the employees of one particular country would dominate its international business. This would cause resentment and possible retaliation from other national groups or governments. Very likely it would also reduce the confidence of international investors.[21]

While the arrangements in one of two home countries, the Netherlands, were fairly satisfactory for Shell, those in their second home country, Britain, threatened to become unfavourable. At this point in UK history, trade unions were very strong and active. In 1975 the Labour government had appointed a Committee of Inquiry, chaired by Lord Bullock, to advise on questions relating to representation at board level in the private sector. The Committee was asked to accept as point of departure the need for a radical extension of industrial democracy in the control of companies by means of representation on boards of directors and the essential role of trade union organizations in this process.[22] The Committee came to the majority conclusion that the relationship between capital and labour needed to be put on a new basis.

Representatives of employees should be given a real share, and not a sham or token one, in making strategic decisions about the future of an enterprise. In practical terms the Committee proposed that representatives of the employees would become members of a reconstituted unitary board, rather than introducing a supervisory board.[23] The Committee considered whether it should follow the Dutch example and suggest a special position for multinationals, including British-based ones. It concluded, however, that it would be unjust to exclude some employees in the United Kingdom from representation at board level just because they worked in a group which had employees overseas. Certainly their interests would not be served with representation at a lower level only, because the top board would take the strategic decisions about how resources should be allocated amongst all subsidiaries. These kinds of decisions could seriously affect the situations of employees.[24]

The chairman of Shell Transport, Michael Pocock, who promoted the concept of professional management attuned to the needs of a changing world, voiced his displeasure with the Bullock report in no uncertain terms at the Annual General Meeting in 1977: 'It is difficult to find polite things to say about this report – certainly the Majority Report. Of course, the terms of reference were loaded, but even so the recommendations are extremely biased. Those who signed the Majority Report were predominantly academics – armed with untested theories and misleading examples from other countries, but seemingly innocent of the experience of actually managing a business in the UK – and trade union leaders – who are no doubt dedicated to furthering what they see as the interests of their own members, but dedicated also to a further massive shift of power over corporate decisions into union hands. (..) There is no way in which the control of international operations and a wide range of international investment decisions by representatives of UK employees – or indeed of any national group where ever located – would be acceptable to overseas governments, to our partners in other countries, or to Shell employees worldwide.'[25]

With a change in government in Britain, the issue of industrial democracy disappeared from the agenda. Within the European Community several draft proposals for employee co-determination, including the Fifth Directive on company law, moved through the various bodies of the European Parliament during the 1980s, but their progress was considerably slowed down by resistance put up by employers. Shell companies contributed to the debates on the basis that individual employee involvement and in-house consultative bodies should be encouraged. However, co-determination legislation was seen as a threat to the international status of the parent and holding companies. Nevertheless, Shell management realized the logic that cross-border consolidation of business would in due time be followed by cross-border consultation.[26]

Towards a new Shell culture The industrial democracy movement demanded more influence by employees at board level. But employees also wished for more influence in their own direct work environment. Shell's Personnel Report of 1973 explained that society and the needs of its members were changing: 'People are no longer grateful for the opportunity to work, and work must therefore be made more challenging in itself. Managements, moreover, must be attuned to the increasingly vocal demands of employees for involvement in the work process'.[27] These changes in society seemed to demand organizations that were less hierarchical and more organized from bottom up. To a certain extent the wish for more decentralized authority fitted with changes in the oil industry. The greater role national governments began to play in their national oil industry reduced the integration of the activities of the oil majors such as Shell. In reaction, Shell expected its downstream operations to act more independently and take responsibility for their own profits. At the same time, society expected greater social responsibility. These two sets of demands required a different attitude from managers.

In 1978 Shell Personnel set up a study team to analyse external changes and develop the appropriate Shell response. The report concluded that 'survival in a highly competitive, fast-changing world requires managerial staff which is commercially minded, profit oriented, aware of social and political constraints yet flexible and willing to take risks'. Did Shell have these ideal managers? Not yet, as the study team concluded in its report 'Stepping stone to a new Shell culture'. In this report, they explained that in the integrated business, overall business decisions were largely taken at the very top of the managerial pyramid. Only the top managers could see the total picture and they depended on consistency in information flows and procedures throughout the Group to make their decisions. The various links in the supply/demand chain were functionally organized with relatively clear and simple objectives, such as cost minimization or volume maximization. For lower levels of management profit-orientation was impossible, because it was difficult for them to know how their jobs related to the local company's profits or to Group profits. The required consistency in the Group through rules and regulations limited their flexibility, while increasingly they were expected to be in tune with the local and regional environment. The report described the Shell management style in the 1970s as characterized by performance orientation rather than profit orientation. Loyalty was to a function, not a business. Even senior managers accepted that they were only 'small cogs in a large complex gear chain'. They eagerly accepted risks related to technical innovation but were averse to commercial risk-taking. Motivation was through promotion and career prospects.[28]

What the report on the Shell culture basically argued was that the ambitions of Shell staff were geared towards growth and technical performance more than towards profitability. The economic stagnation and rising employees' expectations, however, required a different Shell culture. The Shell task group working on this issue started with the recommendation to move away from the large centralized structure towards smaller and more decentralized business units attuned to the market place, because this would stimulate greater commercial awareness, flexibility, and motivation. With fewer growth opportunities staff could not be motivated by the prospect of loyalty being rewarded with career advancement in the course of time. In fact, the report called this the 'promotion syndrome' in Shell. Staff in Shell had been led to believe that reaching their 'ultimate potential' was almost the most important thing in life. But there were other ways of rewarding and motivating people. Employees would be easier to motivate if they could see the results of their efforts and were rewarded according-ly. Shell was found to have too many procedures which discouraged creative policy thinking in the operating companies. Therefore, the task group recommended that a premium be placed on imaginative and commercial management coupled with a higher degree of social and political awareness: 'There is a need to create a climate which values creativity higher than conformity, which allows risk-taking and rewards the maker of legitimate error higher than those who have never made a mistake because they have never taken a risk'.[29] This more imaginative management was in particular needed to realize the diversification process.

To counter unemployment in European countries, the European trade unions developed initiatives to reduce working hours and share existing work more equally among the workforce. One of those initiatives entailed the introduction of a five-shift system in refineries. Such a system would offer a better work/life balance for refinery workers and create more employment. However, it would also be more costly and reduce the competitiveness of the European refineries. The trade unions in the Netherlands decided to make the Shell refinery at Pernis the focus of their action for a five-shift system in 1979. The trade union FNV called a strike, and many of its members responded. On 24 September 1979 the unions closed the gates (left). However, of the 5,000 employees in Pernis, only 2,100 were members of FNV. Many of those outside the union, and in particular middle and higher management, disagreed with the strike. Even among the FNV members there were those who could not imagine a strike at Shell because there had never been one in the past. The next day they demonstrated against the strike with banners reading 'hands off' and 'our production has to be

[7]

resumed' (right). Those willing to work broke the picket line with the support of senior management. All employees went back to work and in the ensuing negotiations realized a form of five-shift system.

[8]

The report not only spoke of a new culture, but also of the need to 'release' people. This, however, was not easy in a situation in which unemployment was already a societal problem and Shell companies felt they had a societal responsibility. Here Shell had to move very carefully. It is not quite clear what happened with the report once it had been finished. The report had been made by the downstream sector in Europe, and had particular relevance for this sector as it had to face up to reduction in demand and overcapacity.

Staff in exploration and production also experienced significant changes in their role in the 1970s. In many traditional areas, they saw their influence reduced through nationalizations. In cases where the Group kept on acting as service provider, the expatriates who remained in their jobs had to learn to adjust to different relationships, less directing and more serving. National governments also insisted on the employment of more local staff in managerial positions. Many countries were no longer willing to give work permits to inexperienced expatriates. This affected the Group policy of sending promising young staff overseas for learning purposes. It made its key strategy of rotating its international staff more difficult to realize. One way of addressing this problem was through 'cross posting', sending local staff abroad in exchange for the inclusion of overseas staff locally.[30]

The theme of corporate culture received renewed attention in the early 1980s, when a small working team studied the concept itself as well as Shell's corporate culture. In May 1982 the team presented its findings, well before the book by Peters and Waterman, *In Search of Excellence*, caused a boom in management literature on corporate culture.[31] Apparently, the team working on this subject had experienced some scepticism, because in the accompanying note of the final draft the author commented: 'The real question is whether one believes that "corporate culture" is more than a fashionable planner's concept, whether one can do something about it, and whether Shell needs it.' Describing the Shell culture was not easy, because the different businesses and the operating companies in various countries all had their own culture. However, one could presume that the Group had one dominant culture, and that would be a mix of Anglo-Dutch characteristics. The report mentioned that various analysts (not named) suggested that the Anglo-Dutch combination was a harmonic and productive one. The British element represented the language link with the world, the contacts with the City, the appreciation of trade and diplomacy. The Dutch element emphasized the role of technology and technologists, and reflected a preference for principles rather than prestige. The Dutch analyst Peereboom was given the opportunity to try and discover 'the true nature of Shell'. To this purpose he interviewed a large number of people ranging from shop stewards to members of the CMD. At the end he could not point to something special, something very typically Shell. The report summarized his findings: 'He found that the company operates in a very common sense type of way, and that employees accept the facts of corporate life without too much dispute. The company is well-managed, and is truly international. It is concerned about its image; employees are generally mobile and have a strong sense of loyalty.'[32] Perhaps a non-Dutch analyst might have found some elements of the corporate culture specifically Shell or specifically Dutch.

The study team argued that Shell employees themselves would see Shell's identity in the light of its commercial tasks: 'In this perspective, its culture is dominated by a long tradition as a worldwide integrated exploration-to-customer company. The resulting culture is based on volumes, on "streams", on technology-push rather than market-orientation.' Here the report referred back to the above-mentioned study of 1978. The average Shell employee saw Shell as a fair and decent employer, as a company that cares about its image and wants to be seen as a respectable organization. Two long quotes serve to illustrate the report's interpretation of the internal view on the company: 'The company can be sensitive and diplomatic; conflict is not appreciated, consensus is. There is no tradition of centralized strong-arm leadership, and the Group can therefore afford to be decentralized. Top management do not have a pronounced image which is well-known throughout the company. There is little desire to re-evaluate the past and to identify who is to blame for mistakes. Mobility and loyalty are rewarded. Decision-making implies looking for 'common ground'. There are many checks and balances, and adaptation to change is slow unless in times of crisis. The observation that Shell is dominated by engineers and accountants, is probably valid and relevant. (..) Because Shell is big and powerful, there tends to be a climate conducive to complacency and arrogance. It sometimes seems that the company behaves amoeba-like, and lacks determination. The company as a whole tends to be introvert and locked into itself, so that it appears to be insensitive to its environment, with little genuine commitment to the outside world. In some respects, the company shows 'club'-characteristics, comfortable, afraid of feelings, and slightly hypocritical. Decision-making is often based on trade-offs, on artificial conformity, on 'consensus by default'. Shell's corporate culture thus appeals to those who want a combination of security and ambition. There is a tendency to 'maintain' and preserve. Emphasis is often on tactics rather than on strategies.'[33]

Though the report did not present clear recommendations, it suggested that the culture should move away from the well-oiled machinery of the large bureaucracy to become more entrepreneurial. If the future would bring 'turbulent times', and that seemed highly likely, employees should be given the opportunity to engage in new developments, to innovate, to take risks, and make mistakes.

Both reports, discussed above, underlined that the Shell culture was based on 'technology-push' rather than market-orientation. However, during the 1970s and 1980s Shell moved ahead of its competitors, displacing Exxon as the world's largest oil company in 1989.[34] Shell managers must have done something right and must have had some considerable understanding of the markets to achieve this position. Nonetheless, a Shell study in 1989 once again sent out the clear message that managers were not sufficiently geared to the market. The Shell culture was seen as polite and fair, although predictable and consensus oriented. This strong sense of loyalty, the report argued, made the organization averse to change. While being professional and well organized, Shell lacked the personal accountability that could drive staff in a motivational sense. It needed a sense of urgency and leadership and a clear vision of where the company wanted to be.[35] Interestingly none of the three reports on Shell's culture discussed the lack of women in higher managerial positions and its possible consequences for the corporate culture.

The lack of women in higher managerial positions in Shell The question whether Shell should assist high-calibre women to develop satisfactory careers within Shell had already been under discussion in the mid-1960s. The Personnel Department did not consider special support the right way forward, because it feared that this might be counterproductive. It favoured complete equality between men and women.[36] In 1970 a report was published about the employment of women in the London service companies. Shell wanted to know whether optimum use was made of available female staff. The resulting report concluded that the Group incurred a loss because it under-utilized the potential of women. It also found that the motivation of women towards a career tended to be profoundly different from that of men. For most women during their twenties and thirties careers were not a primary long-term goal, whereas in their forties or after marriage and the all-embracing early commitments to a family, women were prepared to embark on a career with determination and energy at a time when many men have passed their zenith . This, the report stated, should be used to advantage.[37]

Progress in advancing the careers of women in Shell was slow. In 1973 the Shell personnel staff member D. N. Leich wrote to the Personnel Coordinator Sir Richard Meyjes that a workshop dealing with this issue found that women with potential for more senior jobs should be promoted urgently, because the present situation with only three women in over 1,000 top managerial positions (the so-called letter category positions) was unacceptable and untenable: 'If these figures were more widely known it could attract most undesirable publicity, particularly given the present prospect of legislation in the UK on the whole subject of discrimination against women in employment.' Coordinators and independent Division Heads were advised to develop women within their organizations to senior positions in 'significant numbers' within a period of three to five years.[38]

The expectation that the government in the UK might introduce legislation was based on developments in the US.[39] The Shell personnel staff member Ria Endert-Baylé paid a visit to the US to study the matter and concluded that the situation in the

Netherlands in the 1970s was comparable to that in the US ten years earlier. Since that time legislation in the US had made a difference. The Equal Pay Act of 1963 and Civil Rights Act of 1964 enabled women and organizations to file charges against employers. An Executive Order from 1972 made it imperative for companies that wished to bid on – or keep – federal contracts to establish affirmative action programs that ensured equal promotion and placement opportunities for women in all ranks.[40] A Shell report from 1974 mentioned that the greatest opportunities for Shell women to reach senior positions appeared to be in Shell Oil because legislation and pressure groups in the US had obliged the company to develop a quota system for ensuring that there would be a number of women in the senior job groups.[41] Apparently regulation helped to promote female careers, but Shell preferred the voluntary option: 'Warned by developments in the US, we should make better use of women's talents without government pressure.'[42]

The early 1970s, however, were not the best of times for making a move to lessen discrimination against women in the service companies. Listing the pros and cons, an internal memo mentioned under the cons that giving special consideration to women at a time when job opportunities were shrinking for men would give the men a 'further cause of resentment'. Were there no other more pressing problems to tackle? In the pros it counted the wish to uphold the good name of the Group as an employer and the need to anticipate legislation in defence of women's interests in industry, but also the fact that women brought their own unique talents and skills which were invaluable to business.[43] Richard Meyjes did not think that the position of women in Shell was worse than in other major companies in Europe, but he agreed that the

Katharine Whitehorn exercises her sharp wit and her sharp pen to ask our readers (mainly men) . . .

SO WHY ARE YOU SO SCARED OF WOMEN?

I once had lunch with an industrialist who said if women didn't get on in business, it was their own fault. If women, he said, were better mothers, then there wouldn't be so many insecure middle managers who felt threatened every time an able woman was around.

It's a theory not much more daft than most of the clubmen's consensus of why women aren't up to it. They tell each other women get moody by the month—which they do, and can predict and take pills for: men, who have mood swings too (as anyone who lives with one realises) have to relate their ups and downs to something 'objective' like the price of copper or the alleged performance of the sales force—much more dangerous.

They tell each other women don't take their careers seriously, neglecting the fact that by 1980 one woman in five will be the sole breadwinner of her family—not to mention the screams of pain that go up from the husband of any career girl who actually shows signs of staying home and warming the slippers.

An unstable work force? Wrong—biggest absenteeism is among single men under thirty, who presumably aren't staying home to sponge down the children's chickenpox.

Mind you, I think we do make the mistake of using the family as an excuse—we ought to say we have a conference in Birmingham, the way the men do when they want a day at the races (or am I being told men never go racing weekdays?).

Women do knock off to have babies from time to time, but an enlightened firm—one that will pay a man three months' salary while he has a slight coronary brought on by drinking and smoking—can usually stand financing a slight case of pregnancy brought on by other indulgences. And Unilever's Marketing Division, which doesn't take on people trained elsewhere, reckons it gets more mileage out of the women it trains than the men (haven't stopped taking on men, though. Funny).

What women are really up against is the fact that they have to make it in a tribal culture that wasn't built to include them. This hasn't much to do with what the job actually *is*, but a lot with what men think it is.

Graham Cleverley, in his brilliant book *Managers and Magic*, shows how a good many of the rituals of modern business, ostensibly concerned with making money, are actually there to reinforce the *mana* of the tribal chiefs involved. And he equates the subliminal terror of the business man (subject, like actors and gamblers, to a greater dependence on luck than is comfortable) with the fear of being contaminated by femininity—by weakness—felt by primitive warriors.

The man who says 'never buy shares if there's a woman on the board' reminds him of the tribesman who, finding that a menstruating woman had walked across his blanket, killed her and died of fright within a fortnight.

Women provide—or they could—a different angle from the traditional male one. This is the last thing most of them want, innately conservative as they are (you doubt it? Look at their clothes. That lapel hasn't been fastened since about 1790, and where's the forthright modern thinking behind the *tie*?). Still, times are changing: a few women kicking about the place might be as good a way of jolting the executive from its long company sleep as any.

In the unlikely event of any firm actually wanting to boost women in management, I'd suggest concentrating on three main things. First, expectation. I interview for Civil Service boards and the girls straight out of college have confidence and an exact idea of their worth—but sometimes we see the same sort after five years of ordinary work, and they aren't nearly so good, because not enough has been demanded of them. They have been handed the soft options, not tried out on the tough jobs, never left with the buck.

The first few years of anyone's working life are crucial. And some of the things people complain about, like a tendency to take things personally (my male bosses are always doing this) can be ironed out at this stage if a girl is working under some tough Kojak who says 'don't give me that, sweetheart'.

You remember that experiment they did in California schools? Told the teachers that a random set of names were the ones the tests showed were brilliant. In three years these ones *were* the brightest, because it had been expected of them.

Second, flexibility. A woman's life pattern may not be the same as a man's—which doesn't mean it's worse. You know the company man who spends his twenties finding out how the company likes it done, his thirties doing it, and his forties wondering why they didn't promote him? A career progress that doesn't consist of simply moving up one company rung per year might be all to the good. Five years in the hell of family life would well equate to the same time down-table in head office, just as in Britain, after the second world war, they allowed five years as a serving officer to equal two whole terms at an Oxbridge college.

Flexitime, re-training, cross-posting, consultation before sending someone off to one of two nearly equivalent jobs—these things can make all the difference between using women efficiently and having them pack it in.

And, most important of all, habit. Most men don't consciously choose the third option to the old question 'Do you want women in the club?' Answer Yes or No or Good God No. They simply think 'what sort of man do we want for the job?'—not what sort of man or woman; they expect business gatherings to be gatherings of men because that's what they're used to.

It's no accident that the countries where they've had a woman premier are in cultures where they're accustomed to bossy old grandmothers so it doesn't strike them as odd. This is why it's worth having a token woman at any level—even, I'm tempted to think, a stuffed dummy (and if

the dummy never opened its mouth or contradicted the chaps in any way it would, if social life's anything to go by, be thought immensely discerning and wise). But once the shock is past, it's the *second* woman that counts.

You remember when you were a little boy, and your mother told you to hold your cut finger in the water and count five—then hold it there and count ten—then fifteen . . . and there, it didn't hurt so badly after all, did it? □

This is International Women's Year. In our next issue 'Shell Magazine' will be publishing the views of a number of Shell women around the world, including their answers to the question: 'When do you think you will see a woman as general manager of your company?'

Katharine Whitehorn, one of Britain's most well known—and wittiest—woman journalists has been a keen observer of the changes in society in the sixties and seventies, writing and broadcasting, with a regular column in 'The Observer' newspaper. She has served on official committees on the social effects of television, on the age of majority for young persons and is now a woman's voice on the Board of the British Airports Authority.

11

[9]

In the 1960s Shell's personnel managers began to consider the lack of women in higher managerial positions as an issue that needed to be addressed. This situation, however, turned out to be very difficult to remedy. *Shell Magazine* used the International Women's Year of 1975 to ask Shell managers the searching question: 'Why are you so scared of women?'

recruitment of women of the necessary calibre and their subsequent promotion to the highest level in Shell companies was unsatisfactory. Special action was clearly needed. Though efforts to increase the number of women in senior positions in the UK and the Netherlands were stepped up, by 1974 there had been no significant progress.[44] The Personnel Report for 1975 admitted that more continued pressure and persuasion would be needed before 'our managers accept women as equal candidates to men for senior jobs in our general commercial business'. And a year later the report

complained again that prejudices against women managers still existed. In 1973, out of 245 letter-categorized jobs in the London service companies only two were occupied by women. Five years later the number of letter-categorized jobs had risen to 278, but still only two were occupied by women.[45] Perhaps discouraged by the lack of progress the personnel management let the issue of promoting women slip from their radar screen during the recession of the early 1980s.

In the second half of the 1980s personnel managers stepped up their efforts to recruit more women and members of minority groups. In 1991 Shell hired an external expert, Dr. L. Mee-Yan Cheung, to evaluate Shell International's Graduate Recruitment Programme with respect to equal opportunities. The report posed the difficult question: 'Is Shell's recruitment practice discriminatory?' And the answer was 'no' and 'yes'. Shell did not discriminate specifically

In the 1960s women in western countries clamoured for equality in pay and career opportunities. A huge demonstration in New York City in 1970 demanding that women join forces used the same slogan that Marxists had to encourage the labouring classes to unite worldwide. Inset: women in France demonstrating in 1982 against part-time work and for the liberation of women.

against members of ethnic minority groups or against women. Their graduate recruitment activities in their various forms did not contain any directly discriminatory practice. But the recruitment and selection process, though without explicit or malicious discriminatory intentions, excluded many suitable candidates who came from outside the traditional pool of Shell recruits. Shell's culture placed a heavy emphasis on high academic achievements and clubbability in certain functions. The report cited a recruiter who commented on 'a bias towards students who have a cosmopolitan view of the world, who have a very up-to-date awareness of world current events, and who are highly articulate and enter confidently debates at interviews and into discussions in groups'. These students tended to come from privileged backgrounds. The report concluded that minority groups and women had fewer chances of being selected because of Shell's narrow definition of a person with high potential. Shell did not in an organized conspiratorial manner explicitly bar specific social categories from recruitment or promotion. Statistically, however, certain social categories were clearly excluded. Shell's various established practices and ethos apparently had a disproportionately adverse impact on minority groups. The role of Shell's corporate culture should be critically examined, advised the report.[46] In its Annual Report for 1991 Shell underlined its commitment to equal opportunity policies. Whether any specific action followed, however, is not clear. These matters were certainly not top priority during the reorganization of the service companies and the enterprise as a whole in the mid-1990s. It was not until the late 1990s that the CMD started to consider introducing targets for the number of women in higher managerial positions. One such target referred to 20 per cent of women in top management by 2008, which was a tall order because in 2000 that percentage was no more than 7.8. [47]

[12]

Expats: life on the move

The core group of employees essential in maintaining cohesion within the Group was a cluster of about 10,000. Approximately half of those were working outside their own countries. They were responsible for upholding the Shell culture and values throughout the business empire. In order to achieve this cohesion it was considered important that the expatriates circulate around the globe, moving from one posting to the next. In 1981 *Shell World* compared the present with an undated past: 'In the early days discipline was tougher, hierarchy more rigid, overseas assignments long and the regions in which expats worked more uncomfortable. It was a man's world.'[48] In the 1970s it was usual to move staff to a different assignment every three to four years. For staff with ambitions it was important to become part of this internationally mobile workforce because it marked the way up to the top. It was unusual in Shell to reach one of the top positions without serving in at least four different countries. All Shell businesses used expatriates, but in 1986 the majority of them worked for Exploration and Production. Shell was unique in the large number of expatriates it used. None of the other international companies had so many expatriates.[49] Furthermore, Shell had a policy of keeping families together or at least keeping couples together.[50] Therefore whole families had to be moved around the world frequently.

Left, bachelor apartment in camp Rimi in the interior of South Oman. Right, two expat wives shopping at the local market.

[13]

The Shell Personnel Department had a whole set of routines and rules to deal with these moves. Because the assignments abroad formed part of career planning, it was customary in Shell that bosses moved their staff according to the needs of the business and the stage of the individual's career. Staff had little say in the matter, and spouses had even less influence over their own lives. Many memories of Shell spouses start with: my husband phoned to tell me that we have to move to Brunei in three weeks, or we are on transfer to Japan. Or worse, destinations could change before take off. One family was supposed to go to Curaçao, then to Argentina, but ended up spending several years in London. From there they should have gone to Nigeria, the furniture was already packed, the house empty, the farewell parties given, but the work permit did not materialize. They did not move to Nigeria after all. The next posting turned out to be Budapest.[51]

Expatriation had its attractions and drawbacks. Living abroad was an adventure, away from the predictability of life at home, but also away from family and friends. Climate conditions could vary from tropical heat in Brunei to the cold winters of Alberta and from the rainy weather in Aberdeen to the desert in Saudi Arabia. It was part of the Shell practice to give business visitors, temporary assignees, and expatriates an allowance to equip themselves with appropriate clothing if they had to move to areas where the climate was fundamentally different from that of their base country. In 1977 Group Personnel, however, realized that the 'outfit allowance' had become too restricted, in a way too paternalistic. As a consequence of increased air travel, the introduction of air conditioning and changes in clothing fashions the clothing needs had changed, while at the same time staff had other personal expenditure associated with moving overseas. In future expatriates received a 'settling in'

[14]

[15]

[16]

Expatriates often had access to attractive company clubs with restaurants, swimming pools, and other sport facilities, such as the PDO club at Ras al Hamra, Oman. The clubs offered leisure after work, or an opportunity for partners to enjoy themselves during the day. In the 1990s it became increasingly clear that partners wanted more from Shell. Many preferred to have jobs of their own, or at least some possibilities to further their future job options.

Training was and is an important aspect of human resources policy. Far right, the trainee geophysicians in Cody Wyoming in 1978, and right, the training at the Shell Research Centre in Amsterdam in 2006.

allowance that could be spent more flexibly according to their own needs and preferences.[52]

Housing conditions for expats were often luxurious compared to those at home. Depending on the posting, domestic help was easy to get. Those working for Exploration and Production often went to fairly isolated places where Shell had built a compound for its staff. Here a special kind of social life blossomed. Some loved it and others hated it. One spouse described her own mixed feelings thus: 'Can anything be more beguiling than the prospect of spending a few years living beside a tropical beach in a bungalow nestling among the palm trees? With a golf course on your doorstep, a swimming pool, tennis courts, a jungle backdrop and above all peace and quiet away from the hustle of city life? This idyllic situation does exist and is to be found at Taman Kidurong, home for the families of the staff of the Shell MDS project in Bintulu, Sarawak. Life here is good, but there is another side to this scenario. (..) There is a strong sense of isolation since the only way in and out is on the turbo-prop Fokker Friendships which fly to and from Kuching via Bintulu's small airport which sits bang in the middle of the shopping centre. The small expat community can be very claustrophobic, and for such a group to work requires efforts of quite heroic proportions at times. (..) Then, there is almost no opportunity for the wives, some of whom are highly qualified and have given up good jobs to follow their husbands, to find an outlet for their talent. This explains the often frantic involvement in

[17]

[18]

bridge, golf, tennis, swimming, painting, sewing and other group activities, all providing an antidote to boredom, but sometimes seen by the outside as further proof of the indulgent lifestyle that the expatriate seems to enjoy.'[53]

Expats working for Marketing were normally based in the big cities and as they did not live on a compound they tended to mix more with the local population. Arriving in Rio de Janeiro in 1983, and temporarily living in a hotel, another Shell wife wondered how she would cope. She had learned about Brazil in advance, already starting to speak and understand the language. She made plans to write, to weave, and to follow all sorts of interesting new pastimes. But she had not counted on 'the sinking feeling' that she got when her husband set off to work each morning, and she was left to face a day with little or no structure. Nor was she prepared for the frustrations of being a full-time mother. But after a while she settled in, finding interesting work to do. She even threw out all her European summer clothes in exchange for the more colourful Brazilian dresses.[54]

The clashes of different cultures could be a source of inspiration as well as irritation. Because it was important that managers understood the cultural and social environment in which they were working, they (and their spouses) received special training before moving to a new assignment in a different country. Awareness of cultural differences was extra-important when working for a foreign organization in which Shell companies had

only a minority interest.[55] No wonder that personnel managers were interested in the academic research done by Geert Hofstede, who became professor at Tilburg University and subsequently at Maastricht University in the Netherlands. His attempts to 'draw a cultural map' of the world found its way to Shell's Personnel Management Review as early as 1981. Hofstede argued that management theories did not have universal validity. Managers moving abroad therefore had to familiarize themselves with the host country culture. That in itself was nothing new for Shell managers. What they thought interesting in the work of Hofstede was his effort to submit cultural differences to a rational analysis based on statistical data and theoretical reasoning. He classified countries according to four dimensions: hierarchy, individualism, uncertainty avoidance and 'masculinity'. With the help of these 'maps' companies would be able to predict the cultural difference between subsidiary and parent company. Then they could decide to what extent they wanted to adapt to local culture or try to change it.[56] Shell used the work of Hofstede and his followers, including Fons Trompenaars, in training its expatriates.[57]

The group of expatriates was not just made up of British and Dutch nationals. Already after the Second World War Shell had started a policy of 'regionalization'. A Shell report from 1959 defined 'regionalization' as the term used within the Group 'to denote the recruitment, training and promotion of locally employed staff capable of assuming executive responsibilities, of

[19]

Curious, but shy. Children in Quriat, Oman.

sharing in the management of their local company, and, where their abilities justify it, of entering the ranks of the Group's world-wide service'.[58] This policy of training local people with high potential and including them in the international workforce initially met with considerable success. In 1960 of the group of 4,800 expatriates 13 per cent had another nationality than British or Dutch and in 1970 this had risen to 22 per cent.[59] However, during the 1970s not much progress was made in diversifying the group of expatriates further. In 1980 still no more than 22 per cent of expatriates were other than British or Dutch. During the 1980s this percentage had risen somewhat, reaching 26 per cent in 1988.[60] The expatriates formed part of the larger group of about 10,000 employees whose careers were centrally planned. In 1976 47 per cent of this group were British, 33 per cent Dutch, and 20 per cent other nationalities. In 1985 the British and Dutch share in the core group was even larger, with British 54 per cent, Dutch 31 per cent, and others 16 per cent. The combined British/Dutch share therefore increased from 80 to 84 per cent of the core group.[61] Clearly, more concerted effort would be needed to make the core group of employees more diverse.

The successful collaboration of British and Dutch employees in Royal Dutch Shell has often been used as evidence that the Dutch and British business cultures are attuned to each other. In staff magazine *Shell World* of 1982 the editors posed the question: What do Shell people themselves think? They quoted the then president of Royal Dutch, Dirk de Bruyne, who commented: 'The British and Dutch characters are complementary. The Dutch are methodical and precise. The British are inventive and can improvise better than we can. The two mix well together. On the other hand the Dutchman can be blinkered and pig-headed while the British sometimes try to muddle through'.[1]

Shell World invited employees to give their views, but only a few responded, more of them Dutch than British, and the published reactions related only to the use of language. A British employee complained that while staying in the Netherlands he had no chance to learn Dutch because Dutch people preferred to speak English. A Dutch employee commented that it was a safe generalization that the British tend to speak better English than the Dutch do. As the Group's language was English, this was somewhat unfortunate for the Dutch: 'Yet both seem to find it more natural to utter "sweet nothings" in English and to swear in Dutch'.[2] The reluctance to discuss British – Dutch national differences might have two reasons. Firstly, neither side wished to offend. Secondly, and more importantly, Shell people knew so many different British or Dutch people that easy stereotyping was no longer possible, because in most cases it simply did not apply. One area, however, that was often cited as a difference, was British circumlocution and Dutch plain speaking. Both parties also played with this difference, for instance if a British person wanted to say something bluntly, it would be introduced with the words: 'today I will express myself in the Dutch way', and then it would be considered acceptable.

Asked about differences between the Dutch and British employees within the Group, two long-career Shell managers, Rob Routs, CEO of Oil Products and Malcolm Brinded, CEO of E&P, argued that these were more related to differences in professional background and recruiting policy than to national background.[3] Because of the historical divisions of labour between the London and The Hague offices, the London central office looked after finance and marketing and as a consequence recruited more commercial people and people with MBAs from the pool of British graduates. In contrast, The Hague central office looked after manufacturing and E&P, and tended to recruit more Dutch graduates with a technological background. The British managers tended to outnumber the Dutch in finance and marketing, and the reverse was true in manufacturing, while E&P was more equally mixed. In the core group of management British staff outnumbered Dutch staff. In order to keep a balance between both sides in the Group, the human relations department and the CMD guarded the division of senior positions. Though in principle the best person should get the job, it was also considered important to watch over the balance between Dutch and British nominations.

It would be wrong, however, to see the Group as no more than a Dutch - British collaboration. Because initially neither of the home countries produced oil, the Group was internationally active from the very beginnings. Right from the start many nationalities mixed at all levels, and this international mix remained a leading characteristic of the enterprise. Mark Moody-Stuart, chairman of the CMD, remembered that he never worked in an office with fewer than seven nationalities.[4] Nonetheless, Dutch and British males still dominated in higher managerial positions, and from the late 1990s Shell's human relations department made a concerted effort to increase diversity. As a consequence in the early years of the twenty-first century both the number of women and the number of non-Dutch and non-British nationals in higher managerial positions increased.

In 1986 Sir Peter Baxendell, retired Chairman of the CMD, gave a speech to the INSEAD International Human Resource Management Symposium, in which he neatly summarized the Shell policies up till 1986, the period of high oil prices. The human resource management of Shell consisted of four main elements. Employees were expected to stay at Shell for the whole of their career. Bonuses played only a minor role in motivating staff. The organization was decentralized with profit responsibility at the level of operating companies. A fairly large group of expatriates moved from one assignment to the next and thus played an essential role in creating coherence in the vast, regionally spread-out Group. All these elements came under pressure when low oil prices increased international competition and rising demand from investors placed cost cutting high on the agenda.[62]

Low oil prices and vocal shareholders In the 1970s Royal Dutch and Shell Transport together had about a million shareholders. This number went down to about 900,000 in the 1980s and stayed at that level during the 1990s. More than 95 per cent of Shell Transport shares were held by shareholders in the UK. However, the Royal Dutch shares were more internationally distributed, as is shown in table 4.1.[63] During the 1980s American ownership of Royal Dutch shares increased, while shareholding in Switzerland and France became less important. In part, the increase in American ownership by 1985 can be explained by the fact that in that year the Group bought out the minority shareholders of Shell Oil. Quite a few Shell Oil shareholders subsequently bought Royal Dutch shares. We may assume that as a result of this shift the voice of the American shareholders and their point of view became stronger and that of the continental European shareholders weaker. With the Shell Transport shares mostly in the hands of British shareholders, Group management was fully exposed to the pressures of the Anglo-American financial markets.

When the CMD decided to diversify outside the oil industry in the late 1960s it argued that a company had a life of its own and that senior management had the mandate to manage share-holders' funds in such a way that the interests of employees as well as shareholders and the community at large were taken into account. Shareholders did not necessarily come first.[64] This point of view continued throughout the 1970s, as illustrated by a quote from the Annual Report of 1979: 'Shell companies recognize interrelated responsibilities in business – to shareholders to protect

Table 4.1
Geographical distribution by
percentage Royal Dutch shares.

	1970	1975	1980	1985	1990	1995	1999
UK	4	3	5	4	1	1	3
Netherlands	33	39	33	27	36	40	46
US	25	15	21	39	37	40	38
Switzerland	18	23	25	18	17	11	8
France	15	11	9	8	5	4	3
Rest	5	9	7	4	4	4	2

and provide a return on their investment; to customers for quality, price and service; to employees in recognition of their contribution; and to society for the conduct of business in accord with good citizenship and proper regard to safety and the environment. To discharge those responsibilities, Shell companies must stay in business – and no company can stay in business without adequate profitability.'[65] Profits were seen as necessary for Shell companies to stay in business, but not as a goal in themselves. In 1976 Shell distributed leaflets among its employees with the key points of the Annual Report. It explained how the business was doing and where the money went. The tables showed that from every £100 of total revenue, governments received £59, employees £6 and the shareholders only £2.[66] The rest was for operating costs, purchases and reinvestment. The message was clear: the company was not working for its shareholders alone but for all the relevant stakeholders.

In the early 1980s financial raiders in the US demonstrated that they could and would make or break a company if management did not achieve the perceived maximum share price. The financial raiders did not see the company as a personality with a life of its own to be led by managers in the interest of a large group of stakeholders. For them it was a bundle of assets to be managed to the best advantage of the investors. The emphasis on assets made the 'return on assets' an important criterion for judging the success of a company, together with the market price of shares. Influenced by the financial raiders, shareholders became more critical of the performance of managers. They could raise their voice louder because they were no longer only a large and anonymous group of individuals but consisted in part of strong institutional investors such as pension funds. The American journal *Harvard Business Review*, well read in business circles, asked CEOs the question: 'What's the difference between current stock price and maximum

In 1976 Shell presented the key points of its Annual Report in an additional leaflet to explain how shareholders received no more than a small portion of the total revenues. The approach was markedly different from the emphasis on 'creating shareholder value' in the 1990s.

[21]

Chapter 4

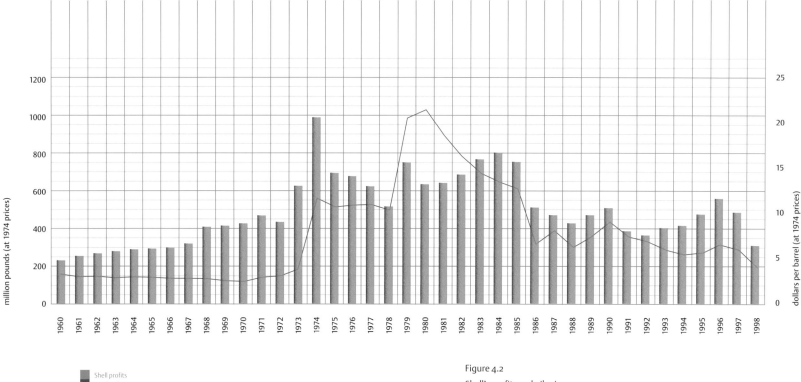

Figure 4.2
Shell's profits and oil prices
1960-1998.

Shell profits
Crude oil price

share price? Answer: Maybe your job'.[67] CEOs were encouraged to manage the 'value gap', the difference between the market price of a share of a company and the value of that share if the company was managed for the maximum share price possible at that time. The idea was that for most companies this value gap was considerable, and that shareholders should pressure management to become more enterprising. The article outlined three strategies to bridge the value gap: improving operations, including cost reductions and reduction of overheads; the use of leverage in the capital structure; and the sale of assets that were 'less valuable to the current company owners'.[68]

In the Annual Reports of Royal Dutch and Shell Transport the shift towards more explicit attention for shareholders was noticeable. For instance, the report of 1988 mentioned 'the endeavour to maintain profitability to provide value to shareholders'. However, the other stakeholders were not forgotten either. In 1984 the return on net assets was mentioned in the introduction for the first time and in 1993 return on capital had become 'our key profitability criterion', which invariably needed to

be improved.[69] Shell followed two of the three strategies *Harvard Business Review* had outlined. Underperforming assets were put up for sale, including most of the assets acquired in the context of the diversification strategy, as discussed in chapter 2. How from the early 1980s onwards cutting costs and reducing numbers of employees would become a way of life, will be discussed later on in this chapter.

It was unfortunate for the oil industry that shareholder pressure increased just when oil prices went down, making it harder for management to please the shareholders. Figure 4.2 highlights the movement in Shell profits and oil prices at 1974 levels, so corrected for inflation. In the period of high oil prices, between 1973 and 1985, Shell made substantially higher profits than in the period of low oil prices in the 1960s as well as in the second period of low oil prices from 1986 to 1998.[70]

Though Shell's profits (at 1974 prices) were lower after 1986, in nominal prices they continued to remain fairly high, apart from the dramatic fall in 1998. In figure 4.3 Shell's net income in nominal prices is compared with that of Exxon and BP on the basis of figures

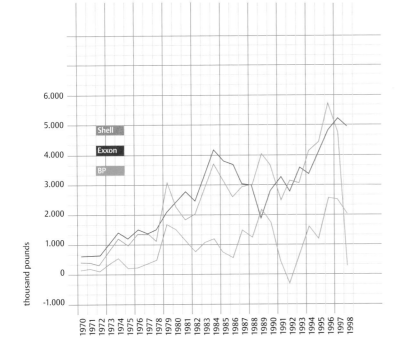

Figure 4.3
Net income of Shell, Exxon, and BP
1970-1998.

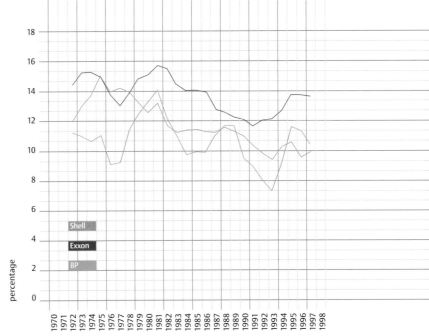

Figure 4.4
Shell, Exxon, and BP's ROACE
five-year moving average
1970-1999.

published in annual reports.[71] Because of differences in accounting standards, the comparison can give no more than an indication. For most of the time the results of Shell and Exxon were very close, with Shell in the lead during the late 1980s and early 1990s. However, in 1998 Shell results plummeted, while those of Exxon and BP remained more or less on course. The dismal performance of 1998 was in part caused by the sharp fall in oil prices below $10 a barrel. Earnings excluding special charges were 36 per cent lower than the year before. More important were the special charges of $4.2 billion for restructuring, redundancies, and writing down asset values. The latter included heavy oil producing assets in the US and certain assets from the recently acquired Tejas Gas Company, discussed in Chapter 3. The restructuring involved a major part of the chemical activities.[72]

As mentioned above, in the 1980s, return on invested capital became an important ratio to measure and compare company performance. Shell used the ratio return on average capital employed (ROACE). Each year Shell made an internal report comparing the performance of oil majors. For this purpose the compilers of the reports used the annual reports of competitors and internal sources for Shell. To some extent the figures were adjusted to make them more comparable, but complete comparability could not be achieved. Therefore, the writers warned the readers to use the figures with care. Because the figures were used internally by Shell and thus played a role in their decision-making process, it is interesting to see how management viewed the position of Shell among its competitors. Differences in accounting standards, in particular the way they measured price changes in stock, had an influence on the results of individual years, but should average out with the use of five-year moving averages, as has been done in figure 4.4, which highlights the ROACE for Shell, Exxon, and BP over the years 1970-99.[73]

Two conclusions stand out. Exxon's ROACE was the highest for most years, and in particular in the period of low oil prices. BP's ROACE was lower than that of the other two for most of the time, but rose quickly in the mid-1990s. The second conclusion is that the trend in ROACE was downwards for all three companies, with BP showing the greatest volatility. In 1975 Shell compared its organization and results with Exxon. The internal study concluded that Exxon's strength was rooted in its financial power. Its low gearing, consistent earnings growth, and high dividend payout, had given it the highest reputation in the investment community. This strong position was based on its ability to take advantage of major established opportunities, including Venezuela, Aramco, North Sea gas and oil, and the Alaskan North Slope. The company focused on upstream to a larger extent than Shell did. Because after the Second World War Shell had a weaker position in the upstream than Exxon, it had been more careful to develop the downstream sector, concentrating on special products, a whiter barrel and higher profits areas. Exxon management was described as 'sound, thorough, hierarchical and professional'. It was also organizationally more centralized than Shell. The study posed the question whether such a highly centralized management system could efficiently respond to 'today's changing world environment'. However, it concluded that until demonstrated otherwise, Exxon must be assumed to continue to be the Group's most formidable competitor.[74] Exxon was able to earn a similar income with a smaller amount of capital. The gap became smaller during the 1980s and then widened in the 1990s. In 1993 Shell made another comparison with its rival Exxon. The good news was that, with regard to the relative workforce efficiency of Shell employees compared to those of Exxon, a stark improvement had been achieved. In 1970, an Exxon employee was regarded as 57 per cent more efficient than his Shell counterpart (in terms of barrels per day per man) but by 1993 the gap had closed to 6 per cent. Shell's ROACE, however, had been two percentage points lower than that of Exxon over the past ten years. Exxon managed its assets more aggressively than Shell. In particular Shell's record in all sectors in the US had been consistently worse than Exxon's by a large margin.[75] The steadily declining ROACE of Shell as well as the fact that Exxon managed its assets better, led to a series of internal reorganizations in Shell, which will be discussed in the rest of this chapter.

SCORE (The Service Companies Operations Review Exercise)

During the economic recession of the early 1980s many companies critically reviewed their operating costs with special focus on the costs and benefits of their headquarters. Though Shell was still making comfortable profits, its return on average capital employed showed a decline after 1979, as mentioned above. Moreover, the demand of Shell's operating companies for services from the service companies was changing because of changes in the oil industry itself. Operating companies had reduced their own costs and in their efforts to reduce these costs became more critical of the overheads charged by the service companies. First the units in the service companies themselves had been asked to devise ways of cutting costs, but the units failed to provide any substantial savings. Therefore the CMD engaged the consultant McKinsey & Co to act as an 'outside catalyst'.[76]

McKinsey had developed a participatory method to assess whether headquarters added sufficient value. The McKinsey method was inspired by Parkinson's Law that bureaucracies tended to grow if left to themselves: 'Work expands so as to fill the time available for its completion' and 'an official wants to multiply subordinates, not rivals'. In periods of expansion of the business headquarters expanded equally, but during periods of stagnation or contraction they tended to remain level or decline more slowly than revenues. To trim costs effectively, yet avoid undermining staff morale, McKinsey had developed the Overhead Value Analysis (OVA). Traditional cost-cutting exercises focused on individual working habits or functions. OVA looked at end-products, such as reports or analyses. It brought users and suppliers together to compare the value to the costs of each product. All members of staff were invited to look critically at their activities and decide to which extent these really added value. Perhaps those quarterly reports were superfluous, or maybe they could do with two estimates instead of three?[77]

The process worked 'bottom up'. The idea was that members of staff would feel more motivated to find cost-saving measures if they were involved in the process. However, staff realized that at the end of the day their numbers had to go down. The Central Staff

[22]

[23]

In the 1990s, executives felt pressure from shareholders as well as from non-governmental organizations such as Greenpeace, but the demands of the two groups did not necessarily match. Above, a demonstration of Greenpeace at the Royal Dutch AGM in May 1997 and below, Greenpeace at the Royal Dutch AGM in May 2000.

Council in The Hague therefore looked closely at the job changes and the redundancy packages. The exercise encouraged voluntary early retirement, and apparently many members of staff felt inclined to consider it, because more than 900 people asked for personal financial information on the consequences of early retirement.[78] The SCORE exercise took longer than expected, because so many people were involved. Evaluating the process, I. H. Wilson from Organizational Services remarked that most people, if asked publicly 'What did you do in the great SCORE war', replied that they had defended all the work they were currently doing. In private, however, they admitted that the exercise had been useful in getting costs down.[79] Group Personnel, for instance, identified overall savings of 21 per cent. These savings were typical for the service companies as a whole.[80] With hindsight, SCORE was no more than an overture to the reorganization of the mid-1990s.

The matrix structure reaffirmed   Two years later, the oil price collapsed and once again costs had to be reduced. Lo van Wachem wrote to Coordinators and Independent Division Heads that he recognized that coming so soon after SCORE and similar exercises in many operating companies this exercise would require careful management. However, Group companies should either be among the low-cost operators or, if not, have a good business reason for not being so. Shell managers should keep in mind that competitors had already announced measures to cut costs. BP, for instance, announced in August 1986 that a reduction in costs of 20 per cent had to be achieved by the end of 1987. According to information at Shell, BP planned a renewed attempt to divide the headquarters yet more clearly into three different parts: corporate, service, and businesses. The corporate part, which might ultimately come down to some 400 people, did not have its costs charged out. The service part would be obliged to live entirely on proceeds received from the businesses to whom the services were provided. The businesses would as before charge their own costs against the business. The regional axis would remain weak. These were the plans of BP.[81]

The key question was: should Shell follow a similar route? Had the outside world changed in such a way that the internal organization, so successful in the past, needed to be adapted? To a large extent the organizational structure of the service companies was still based on the reorganization of 1957-59, which introduced

Before the arrival of desktop computers, secretaries fed information to the large mainframe computer via terminals.

[24]

the matrix structure with businesses (operating companies), functions (exploration and production, manufacturing, marketing, chemicals, legal, personnel, etc.) and regions. However, it would be wrong to assume that the structure had remained unchanged ever since. As a consequence of the diversification policy of Shell, the matrix structure became even more complicated with the development of business sectors, such as metal and coal alongside the traditional oil and chemicals sectors. In many countries Shell was active in various sectors. In 1977 it was decided to nominate a Shell representative in each country, who would be responsible for the harmonization of all Shell activities in the various business sectors in that country in consultation with the Regional Coordinator. The Shell representative would prepare and submit a Country Plan to the service companies and handle general matters of common concern to all business sectors, including government, public, and employee relations.[82] At the same time, the Regional

Coordinators Oil were converted into Regional Coordinators for all Group activities in that area and a Shell representative was set up in each country. As R. H. T. Hingston, Head of Organizational Services, explained in 1986: 'this move, far from being, as some people think, chipped on the tablets of stone by Deterding and Samuel, was the response of an oil company to its new status as a company with several business streams. It is this line with a Shell Representative at one end and a Regional Coordinator at the other that most markedly distinguishes us from competitors like Exxon and BP.'[83]

He argued that now the time had come to make a choice between evolving the existing organization further, or creating something entirely new: 'Is evolution enough or does the environment tell us we must try to arrange a beneficial mutation?'.[84] The expansion of the information technology and communications systems, leading to the development of a truly global business environment, formed the most pressing challenge

PDO had its own translation section to translate English into Arabic and vice versa at Mina al Fahal in Oman. Company magazines appeared in two languages, with the English version moving from left to right and the Arab version from right to left, with the two meeting right in the middle.

[25]

for the matrix structure. Another question under discussion was the planning system, which was expensive, elaborate and partially overlapping with other evaluations. One of the suggestions for improvement included the introduction of targets for the individual businesses. This represented a shift in managerial style, because control of Group standards, which was more or less automatic under resource management, was lost in a target-setting approach.[85]

For the first time in Shell's history all the Coordinators and independent Division Heads of the service companies came together in September 1986 to discuss the role of the service companies. More meetings followed in 1987. This process became known as the 'Haslemere exercise'. It ended with the drawing-up of a document in which the principles of the matrix structure were reconfirmed. The CMD accepted these conclusions. On 3 November 1987 Van Wachem wrote to the Coordinators and

independent Division Heads that the CMD supported the following two related principles:

a The operating companies should continue to be the basic business unit of the Group

b A matrix organization in the service companies continues to be the best structure for enhancing the performance of the operating companies and securing their status.

The CMD was aware that the matrix needed constant house-keeping and it wished to encourage and maintain initiatives to reduce bureaucracy and duplication of roles and tasks. The changes, however, should not be sudden or disruptive but rather evolutionary, pragmatic, and segmental.[86]

Here ended the first round of reflection on the need for a new organizational structure. It basically confirmed the nationally-based decentralization that had been such an important element in the history of the company. Van Wachem passionately believed in

For many people at Shell work takes place in offices behind computers rather than on an offshore platform or on location in the middle of the desert. Shell Trading at Shell-Mex House.

[26]

the great value of devolved management responsibility resting in the national operating companies: 'The local operating company, be it Deutsche Shell or Shell Chile, is the cornerstone of our operations as we believe that local management is best placed to make the most appropriate decisions in the local business environment', he told the members of the German Society of Business Economics in 1992.[87] But diversity has to go hand in hand with unifying forces. The expatriate postings formed one of the important factors in creating unity. He told his audience: 'In working abroad, an expatriate brings to the host country a set of values stemming in part from his upbringing, in part from his experience. Assimilating the values of the host country, he achieves a synthesis of inestimable value to the business. And in the aggregate, the extent to which many of the senior managers in Shell are personally acquainted with one another is a source of great cohesion allowing many problems to be resolved more quickly and amicably than might otherwise be the case.'[88]

Expatriation therefore served two important goals. It made managers more aware of the value of cultural differences and it created a core group of managers who knew each other and could rely on each other. Foreign postings formed an essential part in career advancement and in sharing knowledge and expertise throughout the Group. As Van Wachem explained on the same occasion: 'It is comparatively rare for people to achieve senior positions in the Shell Group without having worked abroad and it is also unusual for the board of a Shell Company not to have at least one expatriate on it.'[89]

Lo van Wachem himself was a good example of this kind of career. He was born in Indonesia in 1931, where his father also worked for Shell, and graduated as a mechanical engineer from the Delft University of Technology in 1953. After a traineeship at the Bataafsche Petroleum Maatschappij in The Hague he went to

Shell Mexico City office, 2004.

[27]

Venezuela and stayed there until 1963. Further postings in Nigeria and Brunei followed, then a short stay in The Hague, again to Nigeria and back again to The Hague. In the meantime he moved into the lettered job categories and up to the unclassified one, to become chairman of the CMD from 1985 till 1992. And after retiring as president of the Royal Dutch Petroleum Company in July 1992, he was immediately appointed chairman of the supervisory board of Royal Dutch. His long career at Shell, his wide-ranging experience abroad, his professionalism and his strongly held convictions made him into one of the most influential people in the history of Shell. The board of directors of Shell Oil praised him as being 'renowned as a leader and statesman', words reminiscent of his predecessor John Loudon.[90]

The career of his successor Sir Peter Holmes, chairman of CMD from 1992 to 1993, revealed a similarly long series of expatriate positions. His parents had been expatriates, and he

himself lived abroad for most of his life. He served in the Korean war, read history at Cambridge University and had a passion for mountaineering alongside many other interests. He came to Shell in 1956, went to Sudan, then to Lebanon, where he learned Arabic, which stood him in good stead when he accepted a posting in Libya and again later on in his career when he became the Group's representative in that country. After a posting in London, he became managing director of Shell-BP Petroleum Development Company in Nigeria in 1977, a country that fascinated him so much that he wrote a book about it. In 1982 Holmes was appointed Group managing director and from 1992 till 1993 he served as chairman of the CMD. On his death in 2002 the British newspaper *The Independent* wrote about him: 'The oil industry has produced some dominant figures at the top, but few cultivated ones and still fewer corporate mavericks. Peter Holmes, who headed Shell Transport and Trading between 1985 and 1993, was both.'[91]

The Royal Dutch/Shell Group of companies had no American-style CEO. The highest office in the enterprise was that of chairman of the Committee of Managing Directors (CMD). That chairman could be either the president of Royal Dutch or the chairman of Shell Transport, and in the CMD he (all chairmen were male) was considered to be first among equals. In interviews, any CMD chairman would underline that he was acting as a team member. His authority within the CMD depended on his leadership and charisma, not on formal power. From 1972 (when Wagner took office) till the formation of Royal Dutch Shell plc in 2005, the Group had ten Chairmen, which means that on average each person remained in office for little more than three years. Lo van Wachem served the longest term with seven years. Even those seven years marked a stark contrast with the early years of the Group, when Henri Deterding was in a leadership position for more than thirty years.

Table 4.1 lists the names of the chairmen, their years in office, their university degrees and the countries in which they worked. There seems to have been a tacit understanding that the chairmen would in turn come from the Dutch or the British side of the company. The only exception was the nomination of Phil Watts after Mark Moody-Stuart stepped down. Watts was also an exception in another respect, in 2004 being the first chairman who left the company after having lost the confidence of the boards. Michael Pocock remained in office for a shorter period than planned because he died from a heart attack at the age of fifty-nine. Dutch and British chairmen alternated, but the Dutch stayed in office longer

Gerrit Wagner

[28]

Michael Pocock

[29]

Dick de Bruyne

[30]

Peter Baxendell

[31]

Lo van Wachem

[32]

in office	university degree	main field of expertise	postings in countries outside UK and Netherlands
1972-1977	law, Leiden	General management	Curacao, Venezuela, Indonesia
1977-1979	classics and philosophy, Oxford	Personnel	Venezuela
1979-1982	economics, Rotterdam	Finance	Indonesia, Italy, Germany
1982-1985	petroleum technology at the Royal School of Mines in London	Upstream	Egypt, Venezuela, Nigeria
1985-1992	mechanical engineering, Delft	Upstream	Venezuela, Brunei, Nigeria
1992-1993	history, Cambridge	Downstream	Sudan, Lebanon, Persian Gulf, Libya, Nigeria
1993-1998	economics, Rotterdam; accountancy, Rotterdam	Finance	Switzerland, France, Germany
1998-2001	geology, Cambridge	Upstream	Spain, Oman, Brunei, Australia, Nigeria, Turkey, Malaysia
2001-2004	geophysics, Leeds	Upstream	Indonesia, Norway, Nigeria
from 2004	mechanical engineering, Delft; economics, Rotterdam	Downstream	Curacao, USA

during the 1972-2005 period. Though this outcome must have been accidental, the division in time between Dutch and British leadership exactly reflected their 60-40 per cent shares in the Group.

In contrast to earlier periods, in these years every chairman had a university degree. Nevertheless, it is striking how varied the backgrounds of those ten men were. Pocock and Holmes represented the British tradition of having a general education at a prestigious university rather than an industry-focused one. Pocock studied classics and philosophy at Oxford and Holmes graduated in history from Cambridge. The other three British chairmen followed studies that were more logical in the context of the business. Baxendell had a BSc degree in petroleum technology from the Royal School of Mines in London, Moody-Stuart a doctorate in geology from Cambridge University and Watts graduated from Leeds University with a BSc in physics and MSc in geophysics. Of the five Dutch chairmen, one, Wagner, studied law in Leiden, while two, De Bruyne and Herkströter, graduated in economics at Erasmus University Rotterdam. Herkströter also qualified as a chartered accountant. Van Wachem and Van der Veer graduated as mechanical engineers from the Technical University Delft, while Van der Veer earned a second degree in economics from the Erasmus University Rotterdam.

In oil companies the exploration and production side is often considered the heart of the business, and managers working in the upstream business are most likely to reach the top. The background of the ten chairmen, however, was remarkably varied. Four were indeed upstream men, but two came from the downstream side, two from finance, one from personnel management and one had a more general management background. All chairmen worked

Peter Holmes

Cor Herkströter

Mark Moody-Stuart

Phil Watts

Jeroen van der Veer

[33]

[34]

[35]

[36]

[37]

[38]

Moody-Stuart

their entire career for Shell, with the exception of Herkströter, who started his career in Billiton before this company was taken over by Shell in 1970. However, he too worked for a long time in Shell before reaching the top. All had spent a large part of their career outside their home countries. They all worked in the Netherlands as well as in the UK, but they also had postings outside those two countries. Those who started their career after the Second World War went to Indonesia or Venezuela or both. In later years an assignment in Nigeria was a good way of moving up the career ladder. Interestingly Jeroen van der Veer was the first chairman who had a posting in the US.

In 1987 the American journal *Fortune* commented that: 'In the boardroom at Royal Dutch/Shell, chairmen come and go. And hardly anyone, including people who make it their business to track such things, even notices.' It explained that nobody took notice because the company was run by committees and whoever was at the top, they just carried on being good at what they were doing.[1] Management

[39]

by committee seemed to guarantee continuity in company management and strategy. During the dynamic 1990s, however, change was considered more important than continuity, and personal leadership seemed to offer a better chance for far-reaching change than committees. As a consequence, the Shell structure of collective responsibility was considered to be slow, elaborate, and insufficiently transparent. With the unification of 2005 Shell introduced the Anglo-American-style CEO who can be held personally accountable if things go wrong. As Jeroen van der Veer, Shell's first CEO, commented cheerfully: 'My head is on the block.' But he also underlined that he was in it for the long term.[2]

[41]

Holmes being interviewed for Shell World in 1992.

[40]

After stepping down as chairman of the CMD in 1977, Wagner immediately became chairman of the supervisory board of Royal Dutch, where he served until 1987. Wagner is seen here chairing two AGMs of Royal Dutch, left with Van Wachem as president, and right with De Bruyne as president.

Career planning and visible recognition of excellence

At the same time as the internal organization was under review, external researchers were hired to investigate the system of staff appraisal used in Shell. The study concluded that the concept of Current Estimate Potential (CEP), which pervaded the Shell culture, had proven most useful in career planning. However, they agreed that some aspects of 'business orientation' should be added to the traditional HAIR qualities. To this purpose they did pilot studies within Shell with two additional qualities: 'business sense' and 'achievement orientation'. With some modification the CEP concept remained in place. The study also advised that greater emphasis be placed on target setting and performance review. Another pilot study confirmed that target setting worked well if senior management developed a clear vision statement and if the targets were set in a participative process.[92] From target setting and performance review, it was a small step towards the linkage of pay to performance.

Concerns of Shell's Personnel Coordinator during the 1970s that salaries might become too equal turned out to be premature. During the 1980s the opposite movement took place and salary differentials widened. Young urban professionals with MBAs were able to earn high incomes at an early age. The City of London, for instance, offered promising young professionals, such as oil traders, investment analysts, and computer analysts, salaries that Shell did not match. In fact, the Personnel Coordinator, G. F. Peccioli, wondered whether Shell was still attractive enough for the best recruits. Were these high flyers still willing to come and work in what was being considered a 'sunset industry'? Moreover, the size of large companies, such as the Group, appeared to be an inhibiting factor in attracting excellent recruits. Many young recruits resigned because they found the Group too bureaucratic.

As Shell was not in the habit of recruiting experienced senior staff, getting the right number and quality of recruits was considered vitally important for the long-term provision of senior management.[93]

Management in Shell companies outside North America had generally been reluctant to differentiate much between individual financial rewards on the basis of performance. During the mid-1980s, however, Shell operating companies felt they had to change their policy in this respect, because young high-potential people wanted to see an immediate, tangible recognition of their efforts instead of waiting patiently to be moved upward in the hierarchy, as they had done in the past.[94] The times demanded visible recognition of excellence. A growing number of operating companies reinforced the linkage of pay to performance. The acceptance of performance-related remuneration also implied greater differentiation between individuals, and that was a trend that increased during the 1990s.[95] In 1994 the Human Resources (HR) department successfully proposed the introduction of variable pay through a Group-wide scheme applicable to all letter category staff 'as a means of creating alignment with business objectives for the management cadre of the Group'.[96] This time no indignant shareholder argued that staff who were not motivated without extra money should be replaced. However, the question was, could individual performance really be measured adequately in an organization that was so strongly based on cooperation and shared responsibility?

TINA and Service Companies Review In the early 1990s the Shell global scenarios highlighted two important changes in world history. The collapse of the Soviet Union brought to an end the framework of international affairs in place since the Second World War. At the same time the world realized, according to the scenarios, that authoritarian political regimes and centrally planned economies simply did not work. In the rich countries as well as in Latin America and Asia, privatizing and deregulation were the order of the day. Political liberalization went hand in hand with economic liberalization. But liberalization could evoke two responses: it could be embraced or it could be resisted. From these observations, Shell painted two scenarios in 1992: New Frontiers, and Barricades. In New Frontiers, political and economic liberalization created enormous upheavals as markets and societies dismantled long-standing barriers, and poor countries began to claim a larger role for themselves on the world stage. In Barricades, people resisted liberalization because they feared they might lose what they valued most – their jobs, power, autonomy, religious traditions, and cultural identity. Two years later, in 1994, the Shell scenarios concluded that the powerful forces of liberalization, globalization and technology were there to stay. No alternative economic or ideological model could compete with the emerging global consensus about the value of open markets and the necessity for macroeconomic prudence. The scenarios concluded that the world had learned in the 1990s that 'There Is No Alternative' to adapting to these powerful forces: 'TINA is a rough, impersonal game, involving stresses and pressures akin to those of the Industrial Revolution. Under these pressures, some people will do well – the knowledge elites, for example, who can seize opportunities whenever and wherever they arise. But others, who are not so entrepreneurial or well educated, feel the pressure of job insecurity, and income inequality grows in almost all developed nations. Precisely because "There Is No Alternative", people in many parts of the world fear a growing loss of control over their destinies and also fear that the lives of their children will be more difficult than their own.' Refusing to play the game, however, was no alternative in the vision of the Shell scenarios. 'The issue is, therefore, not whether a country or company can refuse to play the game – but what is the best way to play it? What are the strategies necessary for success?'[97]

Under the pressure of the forces of liberalization, globalization, and technology, the dynamics of the business had changed. New companies, in particular the internet companies, showed double-digit growth. On top of that, new competitors entered the arena: the 'low-cost, nimble-footed' competitors such as Enron. Was the Shell Group still in tune? Cor Herkströter, who became the chairman of the CMD in 1993, had his doubts. He had joined Shell in 1970 through Shell's acquisition of Billiton. With a background in economics and accountancy, he served in a mix of financial and general management positions, including managing director at Deutsche Shell, before becoming Group managing director in 1989. Looking at the return on average capital employed over the last ten years, he concluded that Shell's performance had been less than satisfactory. Major cost cutting and reduction in numbers of employees had not resulted in sufficient savings. Apparently it was not enough simply to attempt to do the same with fewer people. The structure of the service companies needed a thorough overhaul.

Herkströter asked Group Planning to organize an 'away weekend' at Hartwell House in April 1994, where invited coordinators and chief executives, including those of Shell Oil (USA) and Shell Canada, gathered to discuss future economic developments and the role of the service companies. He invited the CEO of Shell Oil, Phil Carroll, to talk about the turn-around achieved in Shell Oil after the dismal results of 1991. According to Carroll, winning companies in the twenty-first century must be able to create order out of complexity, understand both the uses and limitations of technology, think differently from competitors, adopt a distinctly up-tempo beat and tap the talents of all their people. He wanted Shell Oil to become the 'premier company in all industries'. Five characteristics – belief in people, trustworthiness, excellence, innovation, and a sense of urgency – had been identified as core values of the company. Based on the new vision and values a new, more entrepreneurial business model had been developed and as a consequence business results improved. The introduction by Phil Carroll had an obvious message for the top Shell managers present: you can achieve the same if you follow a similar route.[98] The meeting concluded that the need to secure better overall results had structural and organizational implications. The CMD set up a team to review the role of the service companies and enlisted the support of two consultants from McKinsey & Co.

The Review Team had intense debates and many meetings with senior management in the autumn of 1994. Basil South (Head of Organizational Effectiveness in HR) kept a diary of the review process, which gives a lively picture of the process. He described a meeting in the Netherlands in October 1994, where the team and McKinsey prepared a presentation of its findings so far and the 'aspirations for the corporation' and the way ahead for CMD: 'When Cor Herkströter came at 16.30, he was not too impressed by some of the tone of the interview feedback – questioning the value of technology and the lack of strategy – nor by the woolliness of the "aspirations"'. This feedback led to the rewriting of the script over the weekend by Henk Dijkgraaf and the subsequent week's work.

Interviews by the Review Team with people in the organization highlighted a number of concerns. The first concern was that the central offices, which since the reorganization of 1957-9 were divided into separate service companies, acted as advisers to the operating companies as well as shareholder representatives on

In 1994, Cor Herkströter, chairman of the CMD, decided to review the internal organization because costs were considered too high in a world of low oil prices and intensive competition. After extensive studies the time had come for him and a group of senior managers, in March 1995, to inform the assembled employees in Shell Centre, London, about the planned reorganization.

[42]

Motivating staff and satisfying shareholders, 1973-1998

behalf of the holding companies. The distinction between those two roles was not always sufficiently clear. Therefore, the existing confusion of roles between that of a service provider and that of a shareholder had to be removed. Moreover, the services provided were not always those needed by the business. Service providers were regarded as dictating to the operating companies and as charging excessively for services, some of which were not desired by operating companies. The many checks and balances were considered both excessive and ineffective. The service companies did not display an adequate performance ethos and they showed a lack of direction.[99] The concerns reflected the changing views in society more generally about the importance of markets and the need to become more responsive to shareholders' demands and expectations. Steering the company on financial performance had to become as important internally as it had become externally. When John Jennings described the Service Companies Review at a press conference in the City of London in November 1994, the *Financial Times* commented that 'the company gave a positive and reassuring performance and focused on hefty cost-cutting'. A UBS broker's report wrote upbeat: 'buy'.[100] Redesigning and cost cutting to raise the dividend for the shareholders was what the financial markets expected from companies.

It was expected that reduction of the number of organizational layers would reduce costs and make the organization more flexible and responsive to the market. But the trend towards globalization seemed to demand more drastic changes in the whole organization. The operating companies, in particular those in the downstream sector, had already taken initiatives to cluster some of their activities and seek collaboration over national borders. With these initiatives in mind, the Review Team came up with a proposed new structure for the central offices. The principle of decentralization would remain.

Executive authority would reside with the operating companies or, if clustering had taken place, the operating units. The operating companies would remain the 'building blocks' of the Group, but they would be defined according to their business instead of their nationality. The emphasis in the central offices would shift away from the national and regional organization towards five worldwide businesses (except for North America): Exploration and Production, Oil Products, Chemicals, Gas, and Coal.

John Jennings came up with the idea of executive committees for the businesses, later called Business Committees, which would take over the representation of the shareholder from the regional organizations.[101] These committees would work as teams with collective responsibility and a member of the CMD as non-executive chair. Each committee would contain three to five of the most senior executives of the business and two service providers, one responsible for research and technical services and one for strategy and business services. The Business Committees were responsible for strategic, long-term decisions and those with international implications. The operating companies or operating units looked after their individual operations, the day-to-day management. The regional organization would disappear, though some regional elements would remain. The reorganization of the central offices in The Hague and London did not involve Shell Oil or Shell Canada. For Shell Canada the reason was simple: there were still outside shareholders. Shell Oil, however, had been fully owned by Shell since the mid-1980s, but its operations were still not integrated. Within Shell Oil, managers wondered why the rest of the Group did things differently and pointed out advantages which could be gained from increased standardization of systems and practices.[102] Whether the Group or Shell Oil had to change, however, was not quite clear. As a step forward in closer collaboration, representatives of Shell Oil would attend the meetings of the Business Committees.

During the review process, it became clear that these organizational changes would involve the whole Group, not just the service companies, but the implications for the rest of the organization would be discussed and decided upon at a later stage. First the role of the central offices needed to be redefined. Their activities could be divided into three parts:

1 a small corporate centre to support the CMD and the holding companies
2 business organizations to support the Business Committees each with worldwide responsibility (except North America)
3 professional services units to provide general services such as Human Resources, Finance and Legal advice to their customers, the operating companies, in response to requests from their customers and against market-based prices.

The proposals of the Review Team were extensively discussed in the Conference and by the senior management in special meetings organized by the CMD. In the Conference, former members of the CMD raised concerns about national representation. Van Wachem underlined that Shell companies must continue to be seen as loyal corporate 'citizens' of the countries in which they operated and Holmes remarked that the role of national operating companies and the devolution of responsibilities to national CEOs had been a key feature of the Shell Group to date. Herkströter reassured them that any changes in this regard would be incremental and occur over a fairly long period of time. The Review Team was aware of the importance of striking the right balance between overly-powerful operating companies forming 'national baronies' on the one hand, and overly-dominant businesses creating 'business baronies' on the other.[103] Senior management, brought together in Hanbury Manor to discuss the proposals, voiced many concerns, including concerns about the cross-sector coordination in the new organization and about the reduced role of the country representative. Would governments and third parties still know who 'spoke for Shell' in their countries? There was also a warning note that the transitional phase had to be handled with care, because the experience of other companies that had restructured showed that morale could be badly affected with the result that good people would leave during the transition period.[104]

Finally, on 29 March 1995, Herkströter presented the plans to staff. In his speech entitled 'Right for the times and right for Shell', he told his audience that the organizational changes would be radical and have a 'significant impact on all of us'. They would change the way in which Shell people worked and interacted and, yes, they would also lead to job reductions. But the organization would become simpler, cheaper, and more effective. The intention was to create a work environment where the full potential of Shell employees could be released: 'We want them to feel motivated by greater accountability and increased clarity of roles. We want to emphasize professional competence and results orientation, both for the satisfaction and development of our staff, as well as for the success of the Group's business.'[105] On 19 April 1995 the Review Team sent its 'Transition paper' out to Coordinators and independent Division Heads. This marked the end of the planning period and the start of the implementation period. A Transition Team took charge of this next step and the new organization was to take effect from 1 January 1996.[106]

Employability versus loyalty   The reorganization was not just about doing things differently, but also about cutting costs. As Herkströter acknowledged in the Conference: 'a substantial reduction in the numbers of staff employed in the Central Offices was being sought.'[107] With the new organization in place, it was expected that staff members could be reduced by 30 per cent.[108] First the leading positions for the new organization were filled, then the other positions, and for those who would no longer have a place, a redundancy package was arranged to sweeten the departure. By the end of 1995, 500 of the planned 1,400 job losses had already been achieved through transfers and natural turnover, but 900 more had to follow.[109] In February 1996 the staff of central offices had been reduced by just under 27 per cent.[110] More than a quarter of the staff had been made redundant. This was a drastic measure with far-reaching consequences. In a short period of time a great deal of experience left the organization. But it also created a different atmosphere. With fewer senior management levels and more delegation of authority to those closer to the customer, lower management jobs became more challenging, requiring more accountability. At the same time, loyalty to the company was no longer expected nor rewarded. In its Annual Report for 1994 Shell explained the new relationship between large companies and their employees. In all major companies the numbers of employees had gone down over the last twenty-five years, and Shell was no exception. This trend was likely to continue, and therefore more people would have to be 'released' in the future: 'Without the promise of long-term job security for all, innovative payment structures are needed to reward high-level performers, and training and development of skills which increase the individual's value become ever more important.' Caring for staff included making sure that 'those released are well qualified by their job experience, appropriately treated financially, and helped to find alternative careers'. It was the task of companies to develop a highly capable, flexible and forward-looking workforce, and governments should make redundancy easier rather than more difficult.[111]

This new policy clashed with the previous long-term personnel strategy of 'growing your own timber', which some critics described as 'creating your own dead wood'. People who on the basis of the CEP could have expected to rise to the level of the 'lettered categories' were simply made redundant. Though the whole system of CEP was never officially abandoned, its role was greatly reduced in practice. The rise of the internet made possible a more direct way of posting jobs and applying for them. Staff were encouraged to look for jobs on the Shell intranet and apply for them directly instead of waiting to be moved around by their bosses, a system called 'open resourcing'. Some hailed the new system as the end of paternalism, others were less happy because the system seemed to reward drive and ambition more than technical expertise. The open resourcing also ended the disciplinary effect of 'godfathers'. In the old system the functional bosses played an important role in moving staff up the career ladder and therefore it was important for staff to seek approval of these bosses. From the perspective of the enterprise as a whole, the system of open resourcing was less able to make sure that the right persons would be available for the jobs in which their specific

FORWARD ON THE ROAD TO RENEWAL

Where we've been...

LEAP
Global CHEMICALS
GLM
SEOP
SHELL WIDE WEB
FRD
PSUs

BFI
Learning Centers
BUSINESS FRAMEWORK
Balanced Scorecard
SSI
Variable Pay
Operations Excellence
BUSINESS PRINCIPLES

Service Review
VCP
CAS
Open Resources
CLUSTERS

Where we are...

CUSTOMER FOCUS
CORPORATE IDENTITY
SHELL Capital   Aquisitions
New Ventures   SLC   REPUTATION
GAS   SHELL IN SOCIETY
RUSSIA   New Graduate Recruiting
CAMISEA   Transformation Journey
BUSINESS WEEK   PLAN CONTRACTS
SHELL LIFE
Engagement SKILLS   Renewables SECTOR
Service SURVEYS
DIVERSITY   CORE PURPOSE

Where we're going...

BOUNDARYLESSNE
SHEPHERD LEADERSHIP   GROWTH   Know Man
15% ROACE   DISTRIBUTED STAFF
LEARNING CULTURE   Learning Process
SAPY/3   Renewables   Results
TWO-WAY COMMUNICATIONS
Supply Chain Management   Break through PERFORMANCE
NETWORKS   ORGANIZATION ALIGNMENTS
CULTURE AS GLUE   DOING WHAT WE SAY WELL DO
HR Guiding Principles   Group-wide SURVEY
Functional Excellence   CONFIDENCE

Illustrating the journey at every stage through the past, present and future.

[43]

The reorganization of the service companies marked the beginning of a more extensive process of transformation. As illustrated in *Shell World*, by 1998 the organization seemed to be half-way towards the final goals of a 15 per cent return on capital and a 'boundaryless' world.

qualities were most needed. The new system did not bring an end to the feeling that you needed support higher up in the organization. Tellingly, when E&P reduced its staff significantly in 1999, those who lost their jobs felt their cases had not been well represented in 'The Hague'. The spouse of one recipient of the severance package wrote about her husband's reaction: 'He felt he had been unfairly dismissed, that it was an attack on his personality and that the people who represented him did not fight for him'. Another spouse commented about his wife's redundancy: 'It was an enormous shock to us both. Janny felt very bitter about it and thought she had not been properly defended by our representatives in The Hague'.[112] Losing their jobs was particularly difficult for expatriates, because they often had uprooted their family life to accept a post outside their own country. It may have come as an extra blow, because in the 1990s Shell had tried hard to make expatriation more attractive for employees and their families.

The position of expats under pressure   What remained in the reorganization of the mid-1990s was the system of expatriates and, in particular, the policy of cross-posting staff.[113] The system, however, was not without problems. In the first place, the use of expatriates was expensive. These higher costs had to be defended to joint-venture partners, all the more as Shell made more use of expatriates than other companies did. But there was the added problem that employees were less willing to accept expatriation. The life of the expatriates had lost some its glamour when international travel became easy and affordable to many. To find out why staff were becoming less mobile, E&P commissioned a major survey by an independent survey organization. Spouses received a separate questionnaire on which to give their views. The overall response was 70 per cent, which was very good. The survey made clear that two societal factors were limiting mobility: changing attitudes towards gender roles and changing views on boarding schools. Parents no longer wished to send their children off to boarding school when they were ready for secondary education. Spouses often wanted to pursue their own careers, and if they followed their partners they wanted to be able to do some meaningful work in the new host country. The vast majority of staff and spouses were by and large content with the expatriate experience. Illustrative of a general trend towards more individual choices, staff and spouses voiced a preference for less prescriptive expatriation packages and more flexibility and freedom of choice.[114] The Shell spouses, including Judy Moody-Stuart, decided to act on these findings by creating their own network, Outpost, funded by Shell and housed in The Hague central office. Supported by an increasing number of local information network centres, Outpost provided practical information on everyday life in the countries where Shell expatriates were posted. The information network used the experience of spouses to inform and support the next generation of spouses.[115] The survey had made clear that more attention should be paid to finding jobs for spouses or creating opportunities for them to increase their professional skills through further education. Shell Human Resources responded by setting up the Spouse Employment Centre in 1995. It was not a job agency, but it helped partners to explore their options and identify work, paid and unpaid, as well as educational opportunities. Moreover, initiatives were launched to provide secondary schooling for children in their own language. In the past Shell had preferred to keep the family together, but as a result of the survey it accepted that is some cases 'unaccompanied assignments' or commuting between the offices in The Hague and London would be feasible. The survey also made clear that the assumption that Europe was an easy location to live in was not necessarily true, so expatriates arriving in the UK or the Netherlands needed more assistance. One other of the many actions following the survey was better support for those returning to their base country, because this could be a 'culture shock' in its own right.[116]

During the 1990s the group of expatriates became more international. In 1988 no more than 26 per cent of expatriates had nationalities other than Dutch or British. In 2001 this percentage had risen to 37. Of the group of 5,500 expatriates that year 33 per cent were British, 30 per cent Dutch, 14 per cent other Europeans and 23 per cent other nationalities. In another respect the group also became more diverse: the number of female expatriate employees in Shell doubled from 4 per cent to 8 per cent (excluding Shell school teachers).[117] This arose in part from focused efforts to promote diversity within Shell.

LEAP and Transformation   After the new organization had been designed and discussed in the various committees, it was time to start the actual process of transformation. To this purpose the CMD enlisted the advice of another set of consultants. With their help, the Transformation Team created a video presentation, 'The New Shell', in which the CMD explained the why, what, and how of the transformation. All senior managers were encouraged to tell the following Shell storyline: Why do we need to change? Because there is a need for breakthrough performance in an increasingly competitive world full of opportunities. What do we want to be? Top performer of first choice. How do we intend to do it? Through energized leadership, customer focus, and unleashing talent at all level. What is necessary is a real transformation. Shell people would still need integrity, professionalism, respect for individuals, the long-term view, and pride in Shell (but without arrogance). However, what had to change were excessive internal focus, tolerance for under-performance, analysis paralysis, bureaucracy, diffuse accountability, and obsession with consensus. The behaviour that the transformation process wanted to encourage consisted of real customer focus, adding value through leveraging the diversity of people, active external focus, commitment to profitable growth, actively seeking breakthrough performance, individual excellence within high performing teams, real commitment to targets. Through a programme of communication meetings and action-oriented workshops the employees in the central offices had to learn this new behaviour.[118]

The CMD formed a leadership project LEAP (Leadership and Performance) to facilitate the transformation process and create a 'leap' forward in growth and financial results. The businesses were encouraged to set themselves high 'breakthrough' targets. For instance, Oil Products aimed to achieve a growth target of 12 per cent per year and a 20 per cent return on capital employed by 2000. To realize higher performance, LEAP introduced a management technique developed by Larry Selden, a Columbia business school professor, called 'Moving the Dot'. He taught people to track their time and figure out whether what they were doing succeeded in 'moving the dot' on a graph of growth and returns to the north-

east. If the dot moved in this direction, it meant that their work contributed directly to the growth of returns and the growth of margins. As Steve Miller, Group Managing Director, explained in 1997, encouraging new leadership and 'dot moving activities' were necessary to keep the transformation process on track: 'Going through the kind of profound change we are undertaking inevitably leads to a period of as much as three years in which the old culture and the new are in competition for dominance. It's a continuous struggle. In our case I'd say that a lot has been achieved and a lot of enthusiasm for change has been generated, but I also know that there will be times when the "old" status quo is in a commanding position, and that means that to create change requires a lot of positive energy.'[119]

How did the employees of the central offices feel about the new Shell? One in four had left, more or less voluntarily, during the past few years. Did the message of the new Shell inspire them? In September 1996 the employees received the first Transformation Survey to voice their view on the process. Asked whether the transformation had generated an enthusiastic commitment, 63 per cent gave an unfavourable response and only 15 a favourable one. Nevertheless 53 per cent agreed that the changes were moving Shell in the right direction. Perhaps the lack of enthusiasm had also to do with the fashionable language of the management consultants, which did not appeal to sceptical academics, many of whom worked in Shell. Evidence of their scepticism is the response rate to the question: 'How successful do you think your business is currently being in achieving breakthrough performance?' Not very, replied 58 per cent. To the same question about 'energized leadership' 61 per cent did not think their business was very good, and for 'unleashing talent at all levels' the negative response was 64 per cent.[120] In the US magazine *Fortune* Hans van Luijk was cited as an example of a

Understanding change to be a continuous process, the CMD organized increasingly large Group Leadership Meetings (GLM) to transmit the message of transformation and energize the leaders. In 1997 130 delegates visited the leadership meeting in which they concluded that the core purpose of Shell was 'Helping People Build a Better World'. Left, Gary Steel of LEAP (Leadership and Performance) standing with Cor Herkströter at one of the GLM sessions; right, Leslie Mays, diversity director at Shell Oil, US, at a voting session.

[44]

positive change in behaviour: 'Many say the most transformed executive is Hans van Luijk, Shell's chief research and technical director of the downstream business (refineries and gas stations). "This guy was a cold technocrat", says consultant Mirvis. "Now he is warm and a leader". Maybe, but Van Luijk himself resists notions that he has changed: "I am not a fool", he says. "If everybody around me speaks Russian, I speak Russian. But emotionally, I still struggle with these silly games on leadership".'[121]

Those who did not agree with some of the new initiatives also felt that their point of view was not taken seriously and that they were seen as part of the 'old culture', those who wanted to block progress.[122]

To increase the number of managers in tune with the new Shell, the CMD organized ever larger meetings of the senior management. The first ad hoc Leadership Meeting in 1994 consisted of about seventy-five people, while the General

Leadership Meeting in 1997 included 130 managers.[123] Of even larger proportions was the first Business Week in Maastricht in 1998, organized to drive through the transformation and achieve the 'change in mindset' needed for the new Shell. Here 550 senior managers gathered for a 'high-energy, action packed' week. Each of the businesses had two days in which to discuss its ideas to move the transformation forward. During the final day, called 'Delivery Day', they presented their plans to each other. Apart from serious talk, playful elements had been included. Afterwards, *Shell World* enthused that this event would go down as a landmark in Shell's history. (And it may well do so, but for different reasons.) It described how Phil Watts of the CMD, arrived on stage in a spaceship, wearing a silver space suit and helmet, and told the audience: 'I have seen the future and it was great.' It related how the CMD joined the delegates in a mass performance of the dance, the Macarena.[124] After reading the description of the events in *Shell World*, a retired Shell man wrote a sharp letter to the editor about

[45]

the 'goings on' at the meeting, telling how he had immediately called his stockbroker with instructions 'to sell Shell Transport & Trading while there was still time'. He ended his letter with a dig at management consultants: 'In the meantime we have not only Henri Deterding turning in his grave but also a dizzy Marcus Samuel looking down on all this and wondering if their successors are mad or just victims of the current fashion for senior politicians and business managers to make fools of themselves at the behest of their counsellors and spin doctors.'[125]

Mark Moody-Stuart, the incoming chairman of the CMD, had some reservation about the Business Week too, but for quite another reason. He had the impression that too many managers were still not involved in the transformation process. He was well aware that, being male, British, a Cambridge graduate and a long-term expatriate, he himself fully embodied the traditional characteristics of Shell senior managers. After joining Shell in 1966 as a geologist, he had worked in E&P in Spain, Oman, Brunei,

Australia and the UK. After a second term in Brunei he went to Nigeria, followed by posts as general manager in Turkey and Malaysia. In 1990 he became E&P coordinator, and a year later Group managing director. In his view the transformation process should make Shell people take responsibility for contributing to a stable and prosperous society. The Group itself should become more diverse: 'What we want are different ways of thinking from people with different backgrounds which reflect our customer base and the values of the world we work in. Variety makes good commercial sense and there is inherent value in diverse thinking'.

However, he also wanted Shell managers to listen to customers and improve financial performance. And he added to his wish list: 'I want to make sure that we have pride and excitement in the organization and a sense of belonging'.[126]

The process of organizational change continued. In the service companies the emphasis had been moved from nations and regions towards the business sectors. The next logical step was to globalize the business sectors, get rid of the 'national baronies' and integrate Shell Oil more fully into the business sectors and the service organization. In 1998 Paul Skinner, a later member of the CMD, argued that the interests of Oil Products would be best served with one global organization with an Executive Committee and a fully accountable CEO, instead of the consultative Business Committee with a non-executive chair.[127] What consequences, if any, would such a structure with CEOs for the main businesses have for the CMD? Should the CMD change too? After studying the problem, the CMD consciously rejected a conventional structure with a Group CEO, a Managing Director for each main business, and a Finance Director, because it believed that in an organization of the size and complexity of the Group the checks and balances and wider input of a collegiate CMD added more value. In the Conference Van Wachem and Aarnout Loudon voiced their doubts. Van Wachem stressed that 'a business model having CMD on top of CEOs would be artificial and unsustainable in the longer term', which turned out to be true. Loudon warned that 'appointing CEOs for each business and then having the CMD organizationally on top of them would be asking for trouble'. Arguing in favour of a CEO, Watts told the Conference that the present structure of Business Committees only worked in good times. As soon as tough decisions had to be taken, a CEO was needed, and if such a person was not in place, the chair would end up by acting as CEO.[128] For Oil Products the CMD did indeed introduce the new structure and nominated a CEO. The introduction of a similar structure for E&P was postponed because the position of CEO was already 'de facto being filled by Watts'.[129]

In the second half of the 1990s, top management kept urging staff to step up their efforts to achieve more efficiency and higher performance levels with slogans such as 'LEAP', 'Meeting the Transformation Challenge' and 'Striving for Breakthrough Performance'. Staff were challenged by devolved responsibility, energized by the assurance that they were allowed to make mistakes, offered bonuses for performance. But it did not make them any happier. The Shell People Survey, rolled out in April 1999 to almost 90,000 employees across 130 countries showed low morale across the Group. The response rate was high, 70 per cent, and that showed that employees cared and wanted to have their say, and that in itself was considered by management as a positive sign. But, as Mark Moody-Stuart commented: 'Most of you feel that work pressures are excessive'.[130] Interestingly, the Shell long-service people were less positive than new people. The makers of the survey commented that this outcome was most unusual.[131] It seemed to suggest that many of the older Shell staff members were still unhappy about the recent changes. At the time of the survey, the oil industry was facing very low world oil prices, and all operating companies were involved in cost cutting and shedding unprofitable assets. The survey of 2000 showed a small increase in the favourable perception of 'leadership' and 'Shell in society', but a deterioration in perceptions of 'customer focus', 'work life balance', and 'performance reward'.[132] There was a particular problem with the combination of bonuses and short-term assignments: when things did not go according to plan, the managers who took the decisions in the first place were no longer in place 'to pick up the bill'. When interviewing Mark Moody-Stuart, the *Financial Times* wanted to know whether the 'new Shell' had become more investor-friendly, or if it was waiting for the present fashion for shareholder rights to pass. 'It is true, most people in the Group don't get out of bed in the morning saying they are off to deliver shareholder value', and he added the observation from a senior colleague: 'The graveyards are full of analysts who have recommended selling Shell shares.'[133]

The structure of two parent companies   The critical attitude of financial markets towards the performance of companies, as mentioned earlier, resulted in more questions being asked about the corporate governance of companies. The structure of the Group with two parent companies based in two different countries was seen to be very complicated, and the financial analysts did not like it because they found it difficult to see who exactly could be held responsible. Internally it was a recurring issue that the shareholding was not divided equally. As Malcolm Brinded, Group managing director, commented: 'Every decade or so Shell Transport would ask for the 60-40 ratio to be changed, and Royal Dutch would rebuff it'.[134] For instance in the 1970s this issue had come up again. In 1972, the UK had introduced a new tax law, the 'Advance Corporation Tax', which effectively gave shareholders a credit for tax paid by a company. According to Royal Dutch this tax credit should be included in the calculation of the after-tax Group income which was to be divided 60:40; in other words Royal Dutch maintained that Shell Transport received too great a share of Group income. Shell Transport disputed this and the two disagreed how to resolve the issue. In addition Shell Transport was affected by UK-government imposed dividend restraint. This led to a situation in which Shell Transport amassed funds because it could not distribute dividends and received a share of Group income that Royal Dutch considered too high. The amassed funds could not be used for business purposes either, because Shell Transport as a parent company did not engage in business directly.[135] The issue took a long time to resolve, and during that period Shell Transport identified an interesting option: in 1977 Michael Pocock, chairman of the Board of Directors of Shell Transport, informally asked Gerrit Wagner, president of Royal Dutch, whether 'Shell Transport might use its surplus funds for the purpose of increasing its 40 per cent

interest in the Group.' Wagner replied that he could not imagine on what grounds this would be acceptable to Royal Dutch but 'he would certainly study a detailed proposal to that effect and submit it to the Board of Management and the Supervisory Board.'[136] After these discouraging words, Shell Transport probably did not pursue the idea. In any case, the 60-40 ratio did not change, and the tax issue was resolved between the two parent companies without having to go to court.

The two parent companies had their own boards, and these discussed issues of remuneration, stock options and dividends. Most other discussions relating to the running of the Group took place in the CMD and the Conference. The meetings of the boards of the parent companies simply confirmed that particular questions had been discussed in the Conference, with the decisions being taken by the holding companies. Therefore, did the division of ownership between the two parent companies really matter? For running the Group it was not particular relevant and most employees would be totally unaware of any discussions about shareholding. However, for the non-executive members of the Shell Transport board and the members of the supervisory board of the Royal Dutch it became more important when financial markets demanded greater clarity of their roles and responsibilities. Responding to the recommendations of the Committee on Corporate Governance in the Netherlands, the Boards of Royal Dutch clarified their responsibilities. In the Annual Report of 1998 they included the following sentence: 'The Supervisory Board is responsible for supervising the policies of the Board of Management and the general course of business of the Company and the Group and further advises the Board of Management.'[137] This particular sentence, which remained in the yearly reports until 2005, was not found in the *Annual Report* of Shell Transport. It made clear

[46]

that the ultimate responsibility for the strategy of the Group lay with Royal Dutch and its Management and Supervisory Boards.

During 1998 and 1999 both the structure of the CMD and the Group structure with two parent companies were studied and a number of proposals brought forward. The Conference, however, advised that more time was needed to digest the proposals.[138] In 1999 Moody-Stuart, chairman of the CMD, summarized the findings in a note for the Conference. He noted the desire to facilitate acquisitions by using shares, and the fact that the outside world found the Group structure complex and opaque. He presented three options with increasing degrees of coordination. The first step might be the conversion of Shell Transport shares to the euro, paying dividends in euros, and changing the names of Royal Dutch and Shell Transport to Royal Dutch Shell NV and Royal Dutch Shell plc. The next step could bring common boards for Royal Dutch and Shell Transport. Finally a merger could be considered with Royal

Dutch buying all Shell Transport shares. Though the note was intended for information only, Van Wachem stated in the Conference that 'none of the proposals would serve the interests of Royal Dutch shareholders, not even the full merger, because their weight in the controlling parent company would be diluted.'[139] Mark Moody-Stuart felt that in his whole career he had never been closer to being dismissed than at that particular moment when he had tried to change the dual parent company structure.[140] For the time being, the plans for restructuring were shelved.

Since the CMD had been introduced in the 1950s, its chairman was the first among equals and not a CEO. However, in the late 1990s the leaders of the business units became CEOs of the units, and therefore the question arose whether the position of chairman of the CMD should evolve into that of a CEO. In December 2000 the nomination of the next chairman of the

[47]

CMD had to be decided and the chairman of the Supervisory Board of Royal Dutch, Lo van Wachem, explained in the Conference that because both parent companies felt comfortable with the structure of a collective CMD the need for detailed formal appointment procedures had never arisen.[141] He was aware that some members of the Conference felt uncomfortable with the notion of a collective CMD, because it was seen to be cumbersome or old-fashioned and lacked clarity. However, should the Group wish to move to an executive Chairman/CEO, the Royal Dutch Supervisory Board would demand the right to appoint that CEO. Such a CEO would be accountable to the Royal Dutch Supervisory Board: 'Bearing in mind Royal Dutch's 60 per cent interest, Royal Dutch would have to be in that position in order to discharge its fiduciary duty under both Dutch company law and international corporate governance rules.'[142]

One might wonder why Royal Dutch over the years insisted on its majority position and the rights that came with it. According to Jeroen van der Veer, the last President of Royal Dutch, it was a matter of self-preservation: 'if it would have been a 50/50 division, the British culture, which is more dominant than the Dutch one, would have made it an almost full British company over time (rather than a 50/50 one).'[143] In other words, in order to achieve an equal balance of influence, Royal Dutch needed a majority over Shell Transport. The need may have been felt because in the core group of management British staff easily outnumbered Dutch staff.[144] When the structure of the parent companies was finally changed, as will be discussed in chapter 6, it would not be a simple adjustment of the shares, but a total unification.

[48]

Conclusion In the period of economic growth and the expansion of the oil industry Shell had built up a solid personnel policy based on the long-term perspective. Key concepts were the lifetime career prospect, limited use of bonus systems, decentralization and coherence through the circulation of expatriates. To stimulate this circulation, each assignment lasted no longer than three to four years and supervision was extensive because the postings were part of the system of training and career advancement. The internal organization was based on a three-dimensional matrix structure with businesses, functions and regions. The structure required an intricate interplay between senior management and resulted in many checks and balances as well as many management layers. Decision-making tended to be collegiate.

The prospect of long-term employment was not limited to management but encompassed all staff. The 'Shell way of doing things' included care for local staff according to local circumstances, but with proper regard for central rules and standards. The stagnation in refining and chemicals of the 1970s required adjustments, but profits in the upstream business cushioned the problems of overstaffing. Also, in Europe employees demanded greater involvement in the company at various levels, including board level. In some countries they succeeded in strengthening their position, but in the 1980s this process stagnated. Instead, shareholders became more active and challenged the dominance of managers. In the Shell culture there was a strong commitment to technological excellence and understanding of local markets, but shareholders expected management to focus more on profitability. Rising demands of shareholders came at a time that oil prices were low, increasing the pressure on management.

After the oil price collapse of 1986 Shell profits went down to a structurally lower level. Adjustments were called for, but Shell was slow to adapt. Perhaps this can be explained as the 'dialectics of progress'. The matrix structure and the personnel policy formed a coherent whole; change one part and you had to change everything. Therefore, at first all initiatives for change, in the matrix, in career advancement (CEP) and in the payment systems, led to adaptations rather than radical reforms, until the review of the service companies in 1994 initiated radical change. The transformation process did not go smoothly because the former coherence was lost before a new one could be built up. For example, the system of performance-related payment did not fit with the collegiate decision-making so pervasive in the Shell culture. The devolved responsibility to lower levels clashed with the old system of short-term assignments, because managers were often no longer there to face the consequence of their own decisions. The concept of 'employability' did not go down well with employees brought up to expect lifetime employment in exchange for lifetime loyalty. The many rounds of redundancies reduced morale. Many employees felt diminished rather than energized.

Because of the stark contrast between the new and the old Shell culture, change took a long time to realize. Top management proceeded slowly because it did not want a radical break with the successful past. Initially the transformation process seemed on track with rising profits. In 1998, however, profits went down dramatically and Shell lost position towards its main traditional rivals in particular because it did not participate in the merger boom, which will be discussed in the next chapter. It prepared itself for a world of low oil prices. It could have survived a further drop in prices to US$8 dollar per barrel. Instead, oil prices started to rise, once again creating totally different prospects and challenges for the oil industry.

Chapter 5

A licence to operate: company response to public scrutiny

Over the years, Shell always had its fair share of public scrutiny and outright criticism, but its place in the world was much more heavily contested over the last three decades of the twentieth century than it was earlier. The combination of confrontational post-colonialism in some parts of the world and forceful environmentalism put it on the defensive in many places. Shell had to respond to its critics and to accommodate at least some of their points of view while still pursuing its business objectives. Shell companies experienced double scrutiny as they were in the oil business as well as part of a multinational group.[1] The Group considered a good reputation of vital importance for attracting good staff, finding customers for its products and dealing successfully with governments. This chapter discusses some of the many different criticisms raised by the public and Shell's strategies to address these issues. Basically, the public concerns revolved around the alleged economic and political power of multi-national companies, the influence of the oil industry on the environment, including oil spills and worries about energy shortages, and its presence in countries with oppressive regimes. Issues that had a clear impact on Shell's public relations strategies will receive particular attention, including the failed oil boycott of Rhodesia, Shell's controversial presence in South Africa, the protests against the planned sinking of the Brent Spar, and the environmental and human rights concerns in Nigeria. The issues changed over time as the business environment shifted, but overall public scrutiny and criticisms toward Shell intensified. With media offering more and more news in real time, public emotions could run high, and as a consequence attacks on companies became emotional and more widespread. Accordingly Shell stepped up its efforts to respond effectively to defend its reputation in order to keep its 'licence to operate'.

Ignoring attacks 'at our peril' 'The ability to operate' depends on Shell's reputation and this reputation is under constant attack, warned Geoffrey Chandler, Shell's Trade Relations Coordinator in 1972, when he gave a talk to staff in the Central Offices in London and The Hague. What Shell did affected the lives of many people in developed and developing countries. Education throughout the world had spread and deepened, and with it the scrutiny and criticism of Shell's operations had grown. Speed of communication had accelerated. Therefore, what Shell did in one country would immediately be known in other countries and throughout the world. Chandler posed the question whether these attacks mattered to Shell. His answer was an emphatic Yes: 'We ignore them at our peril.' And he explained the importance of a good reputation: 'We sell products because people have confidence in them, not just because they are good. We recruit good people because they know enough about us to think we are worth working for. We keep the loyalty of good people because they can take a pride in Shell. We are allowed to operate freely to the extent that people understand what we do and believe that we have a useful service to offer. And that is what reputation is about.'[2]

The good opinion of consumers, employees and the general public were seen as essential for the successful running of the business. For a good reputation two things were needed: first, good policies and good performance, and second, communication. Chandler saw providing reliable information as the key to building up a good reputation. The CMD considered Trade Relations (in 1976 changed into Public Affairs) an essential business function, entrusted to a coordinator reporting directly to the CMD. The department had the task of communicating with governments, the

To improve the removal of traces of oil from its waste water Shell Pernis opened a new waste water purification plant in 1979.

general public, and Shell employees. This chapter focuses on the communications with the general public.

What kind of attacks were the Shell companies experiencing in the 1970s? There were many general criticisms and they came from a wide range of sources. First, there was public concern about the power of large companies, inspired by popular academic writers such as John K. Galbraith. In his book *The New Industrial State* he argued that the ideology of market capitalism with perfect competition was a myth. Instead, planning had become all important. The large companies controlled the markets they were supposed to serve and bent the consumers to their own needs. In the large companies ownership was separated from management. The power and initiative were located in the technostructure, the group of scientists, engineers, economists, accountants, and other specialists who collectively made plans for the future of the company. Because the companies deployed giant units of capital in technology-intensive lines of production, they had to plan production long-term into the future. The state supported the planning of the large companies by providing what they were unable to finance themselves: the newest technology via military spending and highly trained employees via education.[3] Critics termed this alliance 'the military-industrial complex'. Consumers did not have as much free choice as they thought, because advertisements, 'the hidden persuaders', manipulated consumer demand.[4]

Many writers critical of capitalism opted for changes within the system, for instance the introduction of more regulations. The neo-Marxists, however, attacked the capitalist production system itself. Multinational companies formed the basis of the era of late capitalism and the main instruments of the exploitation typical of the post-war neo-colonial structure.[5] In their attacks on the world

imperialist system large enterprises such as the Shell Group were obvious targets. One group of scholars particularly focused on the international role of multinational companies in furthering or halting economic development in less developed countries. Optimists underlined the advantage of the transfer of technical knowledge by multinational companies and the fact that they were building infrastructure. Pessimists, however, pointed to the dependence of developing countries on decisions taken elsewhere and on the fact that the transferred technical knowledge was not the kind these countries needed. They argued that the infra-structure was limited to the needs of the multinationals and that the economic development took place in export sectors with little positive effect on the rest of the economy.[6] Churches were also very critical of multinational companies. Geoffrey Chandler remarked in 1977 that the World Council of Churches was now focusing its 'attack' on multinational companies. The Council was claiming, inter alia, that the multinationals were exploiting cheap labour and that they were 'agents of underdevelopment'. It seemed that the Council was also making a political attack on the market economy.[7] Shell employees who also happened to be church members felt like outcasts. In an address to the World Council of Churches, Chandler explained his frustration: 'I am asked to believe that I and my colleagues – who range from people in simple jobs to distinguished scientists of international repute – are parties to a cheap conspiracy to defraud the poorer nations of the world.' He tried to convince the Council that in fact multinational companies had a useful role to play in a new international economic order.[8]

The 1960s also saw the rise of the environmental movement, which considered big business as a main contributor to the problem of pollution. The rapid post-war industrialization of many of the developed countries had a noticeable impact on the quality

of water and air. The oil companies Shell and BP, realizing pollution had to be taken seriously, set up the foundation CONCAWE (Conservation of Clear Air and Water, Western Europe). The industry took measures to counter the problems locally for the people living around the factories. Shell Pernis, for instance, built a chimney 213 metres high under the motto 'the sky is the limit'. The chimney, finished in 1968, was a success for the people living close by, but it only moved the air pollution further away, as soon became clear. Therefore it was equally important to clean up the emissions.

Reducing levels of sulphur had been one of the targets as early as the 1950s.[9] In the Yokkaichi refinery in Japan Shell developed a new process for removing sulphur from the gases of the sulphur-recovery units. In the US Shell Oil turned the removal of sulphur into a profitable business by finding a market for its sulphur and Shell Canada did the same. In the oil industry oil spills, gas flaring, pollution from tanker cleaning in mid-sea, and incidents with tankers caused particular environmental problems. Shell took a leading role in the foundation of the International Petroleum Industry Environmental Conservation Association in 1974, which had the objective of keeping in touch with national governments and providing them with sound technical and economic bases for legislation.[10] Acknowledging the need for environmental measures, the industry wanted to further international coordination in order to create a level playing field for the oil companies. From the mid-sixties onwards, the public became increasingly concerned about the use of agricultural chemicals and about the exhaust fumes of cars. Shell responded by including these concerns in their research programmes and by providing toxicological information for the general public, including Shell's point of view on these issues.[11]

[4]

The pollution of the environment formed part of a wider discussion of where mankind was heading. How long would the earth be able to support both population increase and economic growth? A group of independent scientists gathering in Rome in 1968 decided to study the 'predicament of mankind'. In 1972 they published the report 'The Limits to Growth', in which they concluded: 'If the present growth trends in world population, industrialisation, pollution, food production, and resource depletion continue unchanged, the limits to growth on this planet will be reached sometime within the next hundred years. The most probable result will be a rather sudden and uncontrollable decline in both population and industrial capacity.'[12] The report argued that there was still time to change the trends, but immediate and concerted action was called for to direct society towards goals of equilibrium rather than growth. It would be necessary for the present generation to reduce pollution, increase energy efficiency, find alternative sources of energy, level off population growth, and divide resources more equally between developing and developed nations. Though the report did not put the blame on any specific institution, it was clear that its message had implications for resource industries such as the oil industry.

On top of the generally negative image of 'big business' in many circles came the first oil price shock of 1973. While the western oil companies were fighting for their continued existence in the teeth of nationalization of their concessions in oil-producing countries, the general public focused on scarcity of supply and rising petrol prices. Oil companies in the various western countries were blamed for not putting national interests first. When they succeeded in securing supply, the public began to question the spiralling profits of the oil companies. They were accused of collusion to create these high oil prices. The European Community decided to investigate the behaviour of the oil companies during the period of the oil embargo, discussed in chapter 1. The commission of investigation concluded that the contraction in supplies had been the result of production cuts ordered by the producing countries and of their embargo directed at the Netherlands and the US. An analysis of the various systems and levels of transfer prices did not reveal any concerted practices among the oil companies. In fact, the oil companies, because of their international standing and experience, had indisputably made an important contribution by easing the supply situation created by the producing countries. The report concluded by pointing out that the crisis had highlighted the power wielded by these large oil companies and the limitations of any attempt at state intervention. But it hastened to add that the producing countries had progressively achieved a transfer of power

to their own advantage.[13] Though this report cleared the oil companies of the charges of collusion, the public remained unconvinced in
the face of high petrol prices.

High oil prices, however, boosted energy savings and led to a
decline in CO_2 emissions much more effectively than the climate
policies of the 1990s.[14] The Group encouraged the public to be
more careful with energy and achieved considerable energy savings
in its own operation. Obviously, the high oil price made investments in energy reduction very rewarding. The accusations of
causing high oil prices returned after the second oil shock in 1979.
Interestingly, in the European countries the public recognized that
the escalation of oil prices stemmed from the OPEC countries and
not from the oil majors. In the USA, however, the public image of
the oil companies was markedly worse than in Europe. Here the oil
companies were blamed for the gasoline shortages and rising oil
prices.[15] The industry itself felt constricted in its function by the
many rules and regulations. Shell Oil complained in its Annual
Report of 1978 about the major obstacles industry had to face in the
US: 'We as a nation have produced, through the political process,
legislation and regulations on behalf of consumer protection,
worker safety, clean air, clean water, pristine wilderness, better
mileage, small businesses, endangered species of plants and
animals, and so on. While well-meaning efforts to create and
manage the optimum solution for each of these issues through
federal, state and local regulations were underway, many people
lost sight of the larger picture. The results have been overregula-
tion, which threatens the health of the total society and its
economic processes and is a particular concern to the energy
industry.'[16]

The critical inspection of the oil industry did not stop at the
national level.

Statement of General Business Principles   The
combination of general scrutiny of multinational companies and
more particular scrutiny of the oil industry led to quests for
information by international bodies. The UN Commission on
Transnational Corporations set up an Information and Research
Centre on transnational companies. Shell's Trade Relations report
from 1975 mentioned that 'transparency' had become a key word
to describe the general requirements of governments and stated
that '.. in principle, subject to appropriate safeguards and definition
of objectives, we are in support of better information as a means of
dispelling mythology'.[17] At inter-governmental level the Organization for Economic Cooperation and Development (OECD)
prepared guidelines on multinational companies. Shell welcomed
these guidelines, published in 1976, because they formed a first
step towards internationally agreed standards of business
behaviour. They were seen 'as representing generally realistic
recommendations'.[18]

The Shell Group also developed its own internal guidelines.
Formulating a general statement of business principles was not
easy for a Group which valued the managerial autonomy of its
operating companies. Indeed the business principles of 1976 were
seen as guidelines. Certain practices were allowed to vary between
countries. However, there could be no modification of standards on
such fundamentals as attitudes to bribery and the integrity of
accounting records. In presenting the guidelines to the Shell
companies, the Regional Coordinators reminded the managers of
the operating companies that frequently Shell employees themselves were among the critics of the Group, and this should be
considered as an asset, because the attitudes and values of Shell
staff were often a mirror of those of the societies in which Shell
companies worked.[19] The guidelines outlined in the Statement of

[5]

In 1985 PDO set up the Marmul Desert Agriculture project as a gift from the company to Oman. Approximately 110 hectare of desert near Marmul was irrigated with ground water to produce hay for the local community. It also tested the potential to grow other crops.

General Business Principles were not new, but they were put together for the first time in 1976.

The Statement did not debate issues, but clearly responded to criticisms raised by certain groups in society. To those who accused companies of having the maximization of profits as their only goal, the Statement opened by making clear the wide-ranging vision of the Group: 'The objectives of the Royal Dutch Shell Group of Companies are to engage efficiently, responsibly and profitably over the long term in the oil, gas, chemicals, coal, metals, and related businesses, and to play an active role in the search for and development of other sources of energy.' In addition to the duty of protecting shareholders' investment and providing an acceptable return, three further interdependent responsibilities were recognized, those to employees, to customers, and to society. Profitability was seen as a condition of carrying out these responsibilities and of staying in business. To those critics who wanted to give the state a more prominent role, Shell upheld its belief in the market economy. Though Shell companies worked in a wide variety of environments over the nature of which they had no power, the Group stated that over the long-term the community would be served most efficiently in a market economy. Referring to the rising voice of people who wanted Shell to leave South Africa, the Group stated that Shell companies should endeavour always to act commercially, operating within existing national laws in a socially responsible manner and to avoid involvement in politics. The Statement underlined this point further by explaining that: 'Decisions, and particularly investment decisions, should be based on commercial criteria and not aim at influencing political causes or the pattern of particular societies. The latter are the concern of individual citizens and governments and not companies.'

Considering grants and general community projects, the Statement once again argued that conducting the business efficiently was the main responsibility of Shell. 'In addition the need is recognized to take a constructive interest in social matters not necessarily related to the business.' Shell companies had to adhere to strict principles relating to the legality of payments made by them and to the integrity of all accounting records. The offer, payment, or taking of bribes were unacceptable practices. The Statement concluded with the recognition that the activities in which Shell companies were engaged had their impact on national economies and individuals. For that reason, full relevant information about these activities was given to legitimately interested parties, both national and international, subject to any overriding consideration of confidentiality proper to the protection of the business and the interest of third parties.[20]

Other oil companies came out with comparable policy statements. For instance Exxon gave a booklet to its employees dealing with ethics and responsible behaviour. Interestingly, the Exxon document focused more on the individual employee rather than the operating companies. Starting with the policy on business ethics, the office of the chairman wrote: 'The policy of this Corporation, as stated by the Board of Directors years ago and reaffirmed by the Board at its September 1975 meeting, is one of strict observance of all laws applicable to its business.' Staff were addressed personally in the following manner: 'An overly-ambitious employee might have the mistaken idea that we do not care how results are obtained, as long as he gets results. He might think it best not to tell higher management all that he is doing, not to record all transactions accurately in his books and records, and to deceive the Corporation's internal and external auditors. He would be wrong on all counts. We do care how we get results.' Despite

At the request of Sheikh Qaboos Bin Said, the Sultan of Oman, Shell started the ORYX project to reintroduce the Oryx to one of its former habitats in central Oman in 1976.

[6]

[7]

Safety sign for construction workers building the Shell Tsukuba laboratory in Japan in 1991.

Right: Warning for a newcomer in the refinery in the 1970s.

using the male form of address in this document, the company advocated a policy on equal opportunity for individuals, 'regardless of their race, color, sex, religion, national origin, age, physical or mental handicap, and veteran's status'.[21] Incidentally, this last clause was absent in the Shell statement. Instead, the Shell statement mentioned the responsibility of the Group 'to promote the development and best use of human talent and potential and to encourage employee involvement in the planning and direction of their work'. This was a response to the requests in some European countries for employee consultation and democracy.

The Statement of General Business Principles was initially intended for internal discipline, though the document could be made available to interested parties who might ask for it explicitly. The business principles have been freely available to the public since 1981. In addition to the business principles, Shell developed a set of internal guidelines on safety, occupational health, and environmental conservation matters. Safety performance was monitored regularly. All accidents were evaluated with lessons included in the Shell companies' code of practice. The prevention of accidents constituted a critical factor in the design and operation of Shell installations. To reduce accidents through human error, Shell

[11]

Over the years safety measures in Shell operations became more stringent, as can be judged from more elaborate clothing and other ways of covering the body to shield it from dangerous impacts or substances. Managers had the responsibility to reduce the number of accidents among their employees. Through signs employees were told to take safety seriously, but Shell companies also organized regular training programmes to make employees more safety-conscious.

introduced training programmes to increase the safety consciousness of staff.[22]

In 1976 Shell's Department of Trade Relations commented on the fact that the general public as well as younger members of Shell companies expected large organizations to be accountable to the community not only in financial terms but also in 'social performance'. The area of corporate social responsibility included the attitude to environmental conservation, the treatment of employees, service to customers, grants and other forms of community involvement. Many of the Shell companies had social programmes, depending on local circumstances and customs, but these activities were not centrally coordinated. Within the Group Shell Oil already had considerable experience in formulating specific objectives to achieve improvement in the sphere of corporate social contribution.[23] From 1978 onwards the Shell Group began to report on its contribution to society in its annual reports. The social programmes had a strong focus on educational activities. For instance, operating companies in Australia, Brunei, Japan, Malaysia, and Nigeria enabled students to follow education in the UK. The Pilipinas Shell Foundation supported projects to give young people from poorer parts of the country practical training to

FORESTRY SAFETY RECORD

ACCIDENT FREE WORKING DAYS

ACCIDENT FREE
DAYS WORKED   69

TARGET   90 DAYS

DATE OF LAST
ACCIDENT   30.11.87

BENZ
KUPHE

SAFETY **CBR** PERFORMANCE
1991

HOURS WORKED AT END OF   APRIL   918708

LOST TIME INJURY FREQUENCY   2.1

DAYS SINCE LAST ACCIDENT   24

17

To encourage safety-consciousness, billboards kept track of accidents and promoted accident-free hours and days. Clockwise from bottom left: inset, the April 1991 safety performance at the Ghanaian CBR gold mine (Canadian Bogusu Resources, which Billiton acquired); main picture, working towards a forestry safety target in 1988; a record achieved at Geelong, Australia in 1969; and the Dutch inland waterways fleet in 1978. Only 3 accidents so far, and 175 accident-free days of work.

increase their opportunities in finding work. In developing countries Shell introduced courses aimed at improving farming methods, including the accurate and safe use of agrochemicals and small farm business management. Since 1970 Shell UK gave donations to the Intermediate Technology Development Group, which specialized in designing agricultural machinery to be used and produced in developing countries. Shell Brasil supported a forest ecological study in Brazil. But not all projects were focused on developing countries. In 1982 Shell UK started the 'LiveWIRE' scheme to help young people set up a business on their own. Deutsche Shell had a series of activities around children and traffic, including a project to teach children how to behave in traffic, and support for scientific studies of accident proneness among young children. Shell's social activities included the sponsoring of sports and arts, as for instance the annual fun mass jog in Singapore. Shell Canada sponsored an exhibition of Inuit and other native Canadian artefacts to mark the 1988 Winter Olympics. These sports and cultural activities, however, had a somewhat lower priority than education and the environment.[24] Compared to the sums involved in the real business activities the social funding was no more than the icing on the cake, though it was considered progressive at that time.

Shell followed the approach of the 'accident pyramid', arguing that one fatal accident was the tip of the iceberg. For instance, 100,000 unsafe practices could lead to 10,000 near misses, to 1,000 non-life threatening incidents, to 100 life threatening incidents, and then one fatal accident. The prevention of accidents therefore had to start with examining the daily routines. In order to reduce the number of accidents Shell considered it equally important to include safety measures in the design stage for new equipment and facilities.

Chapter 5

In 1976 the past came to haunt the oil industry in the form of critical questions about the handling of the boycott against Rhodesia after the government of Southern Rhodesia, representing the white settler community, had unilaterally declared its independence from Britain ten years earlier. On 11 November 1965 Prime Minister Ian Smith had signed the declaration of independence from Britain and that country had responded with a boycott against Rhodesia, expecting the Smith regime to collapse within weeks. When this did not happen, oil companies were blamed for supporting the regime by continuing to sell oil products.

[19]

Oil supplies to Rhodesia

The reputation of the oil industry was just recovering from the low level it had reached during the first oil price shock, when the question of oil supplies to Rhodesia (Zimbabwe) grabbed the headlines in 1976. This was particularly true for the press in Great Britain. For the unfolding of this story we have to go back in time to 1965, when the government of Southern Rhodesia, representing the white settler community, declared unilaterally its independence from Britain.[25] The British government did not want to bring Rhodesia back into the British Commonwealth of Nations by force, but expected to bring the regime to its knees in weeks rather than months through the sanctions weapon. On 20 November 1965, the UN Security Council called for non-mandatory selective sanctions, including an oil embargo, to end the rebellion. Britain introduced oil sanctions, making it illegal for UK-registered companies or UK citizens to supply oil to Rhodesia, or to intermediaries thought to be involved in supplying Rhodesia. Virtually all other UN members introduced similar legislation, but tellingly not South Africa or Portugal with its colony Mozambique. In response to the sanctions, the international oil companies stopped their deliveries to the Mozambique port of Beira with its pipeline to their Rhodesian refinery at Umtali. As a consequence the Umtali refinery was shut down on 15 January 1966.[26] Twelve years later, the white settlers' regime under premier Ian Smith was still in place, and the country was still being provided with oil products.

In 1976 the English economist Bernard Rivers found secret documents, which revealed that Mobil subsidiaries had been involved in a scheme to supply Rhodesia with oil. These were published in his report *The Oil Conspiracy*. At the same time the publication of the Dutch pressure group Kairos *Shell in South Africa* appeared in Britain in the English language. Both inspired the journalist Martin Bailey to dig further into the flows of oil and oil products in Southern Africa. In 1977 he published the report *Shell and BP in South Africa*, based to a large extent on the earlier Kairos report. He argued that Shell and BP, together with the three other major international petroleum companies operating in South Africa (Mobil, Caltex, and Total) had played a crucial role in helping to break the oil embargo.[27] Shell repeated its earlier statements that 'although no company in which there was a Shell interest was supplying oil to Rhodesia and although Shell companies feel they have done everything practicable to comply with the UK Second Order in Council of 1968, there can be no guarantee that products emanating from crude oil supplied to South Africa have not found, or will not find their way to Rhodesia'. The explanation Shell gave ran as follows: Shell companies operate under the laws of countries in which they exist. It happened that under South African law companies were unable to refuse to supply customers or to control the ultimate destination of products sold to their customers.[28]

Following the allegations in the various reports and articles in the press, the Zambian Attorney General commenced proceedings in Lusaka against Royal Dutch, Shell Transport, BP, Mobil, Caltex and Total and their respective subsidiaries with a number of essentially political allegations, including conspiring to install an illegal minority racist regime in Rhodesia and sustaining that regime in power, as well as cutting off oil supplies to Zambia in December 1965. The same group of oil companies were also

[20]

In 1979 Britain organized a conference in London to end the violence in Rhodesia and negotiate independence for that country. Protestors in London made it clear that they wanted Ian Smith to go. Key players at the conference were Robert Mugabe and Joshua Nkomo, founders of the

Zimbabwe African People's Union (ZAPU). After an interim return to British responsibility, elections were held in 1980. Robert Mugabe and his Popular Front won a decisive victory and the country reverted to the name Zimbabwe.

[21]

In late 1979 the campaigners against the white settler regime in Rhodesia demanded an oil boycott against South Africa, which supported Rhodesia and clung to its own apartheid policy. In the Netherlands some people returned Shell's promotional leaflets 'Shell helpt' scornfully cut into pieces or with angry comments written upon them. Some sent in cartoons, such as the one suggesting that the regime of Ian Smith was kept alive by oil deliveries. The sales of gasoline in the Netherlands, however, were not affected.

[22]

[23]

Campaign for oil sanctions against
South Africa and Rhodesia by the anti-
apartheid movement, London 1977.

[24]

charged in Britain by the British-based company Lonrho, which
claimed unspecified damages for itself and its associated company
CPMR in their capacities as owners and operators of the Beira –
Umtali crude oil pipeline.[29] The allegations that certain oil
companies had been evading the UK embargo on trade with
Rhodesia, led in Britain to a judicial enquiry ordered by the British
Foreign Secretary and chaired by Thomas Bingham QC.[30] At the
same time, Shell started its own internal enquiry.

From the Bingham inquiry, supported by internal Shell
sources, the following story emerged. Shell companies had fully
cooperated in stopping supplies of crude oil to Beira and made an
effort to ensure that Zambia continued to obtain oil products after
the closure of the Umtali refinery. At that time Shell and BP still had
combined marketing operations in Southern Africa, and these had
delivered oil products to Rhodesia via South African intermediaries
and Shell Mozambique. In 1968 these deliveries had been discussed
with the UK Foreign Office. Shell and BP representatives had
explained that they could never guarantee that petroleum
supplies to South Africa would not reach Rhodesia unless the UK
government would boycott supplies to South Africa, because the
South African government had officially directed South African
companies not to withhold supplies from any South African
customer or to attach conditions as to destination or re-sale. The
British government, however, was not prepared to implement
sanctions against South Africa. To resolve this conflict of interests,
the British government went along with a swap arrangement in
which the South African subsidiary of the French company Total
delivered the supplies to Rhodesia via Mozambique in exchange for
supplies to traders in South Africa by the local Shell and BP
marketing organizations. This arrangement lasted for a few years,
after which the Shell and BP marketing organizations resumed
supplies through South African intermediaries, in this case the
company Freight Services.

In 1974 two developments coincided. First, the regimes in
Portugal and Mozambique changed, and the newly independent
Mozambique immediately stopped the oil trade with Rhodesia.
Second, and unrelated, Shell and BP unravelled their joint
marketing organization in South Africa. During this split the two
South African subsidiaries of Shell and BP discussed the division of
their share in the trade with Rhodesia and copies of these papers,
which started to circulate, seemed to suggest that the two
subsidiaries were directly involved with deliveries to Rhodesia.
Further inspection, however, revealed that after the closure of the
border between Rhodesia and Mozambique the South African
company SASOL had taken over the trade with Freight Services,

while Shell South Africa had increased its supply to its depots in the Transvaal as a replacement for supplies from SASOL.[31]

The Bingham report, when it appeared in 1978, was equally embarrassing for the British government as for the oil companies, because it made clear that both parties had acted perhaps not against the law but certainly against the intentions of the oil sanctions against Rhodesia. The Bingham report was followed by an investigation by the Director of Public Prosecutions. However, in January 1980 the Attorney General Sir Michael Havers announced that there would be no prosecutions arising from the findings of the Bingham Enquiry.[32] By this time the sanctions against Rhodesia had lapsed in the UN, the UK, and the Netherlands, because of the regime change there. After an interim return to British responsibility elections were held in 1980. Robert Mugabe with his Popular Front won a decisive victory and the country reverted to the name Zimbabwe.[33] After the regime change, Mugabe asked the international oil companies to start up the refinery in Umtali again, which had been shut for fifteen years. Repair work would take at least eighteen months and cost $60 million. Shell, which had a 20.75 per cent share in the refinery, doubted whether the investment would make economic sense, but it was clear that the government of Zimbabwe wanted to reduce its dependence on South Africa in oil products. Church leaders in France, the Netherlands, UK, and USA wrote that there was a moral case for reparation to be made by the oil companies with regard to Zimbabwe, an opinion not shared by Shell. Nonetheless, it felt that it would be difficult not to support the rehabilitation of the refinery.[34]

The Zambian government assured Shell and BP that it had no intention of dropping its lawsuit against them because of the independence of Zimbabwe, though in practice that is what happened.[35] The case of Lonrho and CPMR, the owners and operators of the Beira – Umtali pipeline, against Shell and BP continued for another two years. Both parties had agreed to arbitration, but Lonrho had taken two preliminary issues to court. One of the two issues related to the more general question whether documents of subsidiaries in South Africa, Zimbabwe and Mozambique were in the power of the holding companies (i.e. The Shell Petroleum Company Limited and BP), so that they must be produced. The answer in court was negative. The English High Court ruled in favour of Shell and BP on all claims, and this decision was upheld in the House of Lords. The Arbitration Tribunal then dismissed the Lonrho claim in its entirety in 1981 and ordered the claimants to pay the costs of the respondent oil companies.[36] Here ended the Rhodesian saga. Gerrit Wagner remarked in the Conference that the Rhodesian issue had set Shell companies' reputation back years. In his view the weak spot had been the fact that top management had not always been fully aware of the facts, and this would have to be avoided in respect of the South African issue. Top management should be fully informed so that it could be quite open and candid with the public.[37]

To anyone thinking of quitting South Africa: why is Shell Chemicals coming in with R100-million?

Rand Daily Mail, 27 January 1976

[25]

In 1979 campaigners against race discrimination tried to convince the Dutch government to declare an oil embargo against South Africa, design by Jan Koperdraat. The Second Chamber of the Dutch Parliament passed a motion supporting an oil boycott on South Africa, but the government rejected it. This closed the subject, as the cartoon by the Dutch cartoonist Opland shows.

[26]

Shell in South Africa

While public attention on the oil supplies to Rhodesia subsided after the regime change in that country in 1979, the issue of Shell's presence in South Africa returned with renewed vigour. Shell had already been subjected to the persistent activities of a large number of pressure groups during the 1970s, in particular in the Netherlands. In 1973 Cor Groenendijk, spokesman for the Dutch pressure group Kairos, attended the annual general meeting of shareholders of the Royal Dutch Petroleum Company for the first time to ask top management and shareholders to break the ties with the apartheid regime in South Africa.[38] Kairos was a small Dutch group of Christians against apartheid, inspired by the 'Programme to Combat Racism' from the World Council of Churches. In 1972 the World Council called for actions to encourage disinvestments from South Africa. Following this appeal, Kairos decided to single out Shell by raising the more general issue that the economic ties between South Africa and the Netherlands should be severed. Why did they target Shell? Kairos considered the oil industry of strategic importance for the survival of the South African regime, and it reasoned that Shell's investments in South Africa were substantial. Furthermore the oil industry was not labour-intensive and for that reason few jobs would be lost if Shell withdrew from South Africa.[39] Wagner responded by inviting the critics for talks with Shell management. Though the talks took place in a friendly atmosphere, neither party was able to convince the other. Shell argued that it had worked in South Africa for decades. It was a consistent policy of the international Group not to be involved in local politics and to abide by the national laws in the countries in which they operated. Furthermore, its subsidiary Shell South Africa followed a progressive social policy. Leaving the country would have no positive effect for the population, because their facilities would simply be taken over by others, and those could easily follow a less progressive social policy, making the situation worse rather than better. Kairos stuck to its requests to Shell to withdraw from South Africa and stop the oil deliveries. Shell declined to meet those requests. As previously noted, in 1976 Kairos brought its campaign into the open by publishing the report *Shell in Zuid-Afrika*.[40] Other organizations joined the campaign against Shell's presence in South Africa, including Pax Christi Nederland and Komitee Zuidelijk Afrika (Holland Committee on Southern Africa). More importantly, the movement formed international alliances, which enabled them to put pressure on Shell companies in many countries.[41]

Shell was not keen on seeking publicity, because it believed in a strategy of quiet diplomacy. For instance, in 1977 eleven major American companies (including Mobil and Caltex) submitted to the South African government a document detailing the conditions on

A licence to operate: company response to public scrutiny

'...Shell South Africa is unequivocally opposed to Apartheid and believes it to be morally indefensible. This viewpoint is supported by the parent companies of the Royal Dutch/Shell Group.'

(Wilson, executive chairman Shell South Africa / *Business Day*, 11 January 1986)

which these companies wished to employ their black workers. Though Shell South Africa had already implemented nearly all the improvements sought by the American companies, it was still reluctant to sign the document. It had become a leading employer of black people through quiet and diligent efforts, and it felt that the low profile but active Shell approach would continue to be more effective than a public challenge to the South African government.[42] By 1977 there was virtually no segregation left in Shell South African companies or the refinery SAPREF, and what little segregation remained, was expected to be removed quickly. Shell adhered to the EEC's Code of Conduct for companies with affiliates in South Africa.[43]

In 1978 more discussions about Shell's presence in South Africa followed, including those between Shell managers and leaders of the Netherlands' Council of Churches. Shell underlined the good social performance of Shell South Africa. According to Shell minutes of these discussions, the church leaders were of the opinion that the efforts of Shell South Africa would not bring about any significant change in the South African government's policy, and more aggressive action, including disinvestment, was needed. The church leaders expected that changes in South Africa would not be achieved by peaceful methods only. Shell managers argued that if they were to abandon their activities in South Africa, the Government would step in and run the activities itself as it was fully capable of doing. The church leaders, however, pointed out that the black leaders in South Africa were now in favour of disinvestments, and so were they.[44]

The role of South Africa and the subsidiaries of some of the oil majors in providing Rhodesia with oil during the period of the UN oil embargo, as discussed above, damaged the reputation of Shell and other oil majors involved. The pressure groups stopped their

dialogue with Shell and began to demand firm action, including an oil embargo against South Africa. The Arab producers already had a boycott against South Africa in place since 1973, but this had little effect because Iran continued to deliver oil to South Africa. However, when the Shah was overthrown in 1979 and Ayatollah Khomeini took office, Iran joined the oil boycott. Suddenly an oil embargo of South Africa had a chance of being effective. Therefore pressure groups intensified their campaign for sanctions. In 1979 the General Assembly of the United Nations approved a resolution calling specifically for an oil embargo. These General Assembly resolutions, however, were recommendations only and each country still could make up its own mind.[45] In the Netherlands the second chamber of the Dutch parliament passed a motion supporting an oil boycott on South Africa in 1980, but the government rejected the motion and barely survived a motion of no confidence. It was, however, willing to seek support for the boycott from other European countries.[46] In the same year, the anti-apartheid action groups set up a research group, the Shipping Research Bureau, to monitor the movement of tankers supplying crude oil to South Africa. In 1981 Shell was attacked for delivering crude via the Netherlands Antilles and from Oman. The Netherlands Antilles government denied any involvement in supplying crude to South Africa. With regard to the deliveries of crude oil from Oman, Shell could point out that this country had no destination restrictions towards South Africa. After consultation

Protest in the US against apartheid in South Africa, 1985.

[28]

Bishop (later Archbishop) Desmond
Tutu, General Secretary of the South
African Council of Churches, received
the Nobel Peace Prize in 1984 for his
actions against apartheid in South
Africa. Churches worldwide played an
important role in the campaigns to
boycott South Africa and urge western
companies to withdraw their
investments from the country.

with the Omani government, however, Shell concluded that the
country preferred Shell to stop supplying South Africa with Omani
crude.[47] The Shipping Research Bureau continued monitoring all oil
deliveries to South Africa until December 1993. After mid-1981 it did
not register any Shell companies either as ship-owner or cargo-
owner in the trade with South Africa.[48] Shell South Africa continued
to import crude oil, but the company was not allowed by South
African law to disclose its sources of oil. According to confidential
South African documents from the country's energy bureaucracy,
however, Shell South Africa and Total South Africa both declared in
1983 that they were able to import their necessary crude oil
through the intermediation of the parent companies.[49] The figures
of the Shipping Research Bureau show that from 1981 onwards
independent traders such as Transworld Oil and Marc Rich became
important suppliers to South Africa.[50] In 1986 Lo van Wachem,
chairman of the CMD, mentioned that in recent years Shell South
Africa obtained all its crude oil requirements from third parties. To
this information he added: 'The obsession in some quarters with
the question of where South Africa gets its oil implies that there is a
"ban" on oil supplies. There is no such ban – although there are
destination restrictions imposed by certain oil-exporting countries.
In addition there have been resolutions by the UN General
Assembly calling on its members for such a ban. However, such
resolutions have no binding force, not even on those countries
which have voted for them.'[51]

[29]

The President of the American labour
union the UAW (United Auto Workers)
cut up a Shell credit card to announce a
labour-sponsored nationwide
consumer boycott against Shell
products, January 1986.

During the years of economic recession in the early 1980s, the anti-apartheid movement was less active, though they continued to be present during every annual general meeting of Royal Dutch and Shell Transport. Unfortunately the situation in South Africa did not improve but worsened instead. In 1985 the then president P. W. Botha proclaimed a state of emergency. This gave a new impetus to the anti-apartheid movement. The working group 'Programme to Combat Racism' of the World Council of Churches decided in the spring of 1985 to start an international campaign against Shell.[52] In particular in the USA pressure mounted on companies to withdraw from South Africa. Shell Oil received a letter from TransAfrica, an important pressure group in the USA against apartheid in South Africa, to withdraw from the country.[53] A labour dispute at the Rietspruit coal mine, of which Shell South Africa was a 50 per cent owner though not the operator, set in motion a consumer boycott

against Shell Oil in the USA by the United Mine Workers of America (UMWA). This was followed in January 1986 by a broader boycott of Shell service stations and Shell products by TransAfrica, the Free South African Movement and many other institutions, ranging from labour unions to churches and civil rights movements. During a successful media campaign consumers were encouraged to cut up their Shell credit card. Some even acquired such a card in order to cut it again as a demonstration.[54] Similar calls for action followed against Shell companies in the Netherlands, UK, Denmark, Norway, Sweden, Switzerland, and Australia. Though by mid-1986 Shell had noticed no effect on the business, management nevertheless became concerned over the onslaught of negative news.[55]

To counter the many attacks Shell reconsidered its customary policy of reticence, and decided to be more active in explaining its reasons for maintaining business activities in South Africa. Van Wachem gave an interview for two Shell publications, *Shell World* and *Shell Venster,* in which he underlined Shell's rejection of apartheid: 'Every form of discrimination is contrary to human dignity and must therefore be rejected. That is not only my personal view, but as long as I can remember – and I have been working in the Group for some thirty-two years – we have always followed a policy of equal opportunities and equal rights.' In his view, apartheid was not only morally indefensible but also economically counter-productive: 'It is an unworkable and hopeless system.' In the interview the following statement of Bishop Desmond Tutu was quoted: 'Foreign companies in South Africa must stop fooling themselves by saying that their presence is to our advantage. That is nonsense. Whether they like it or not, they are supporting a wicked system.' Asked for his comment, Van Wachem replied that underlying the request for disinvestments was the

[30]

notion that if Shell withdrew from South Africa all this 'support' for the regime would evaporate. 'But the reality would be that only the Shell emblem would disappear. The business as such would carry on as usual.' Nonetheless, he expected that leaving would be a blow to the 2,500 employees of Shell South Africa, and that the company itself was convinced that a peaceful solution required changes from within. 'South Africans, white and black, will have to learn together to create a society which respects the human dignity of all', he argued. 'It would be unwise at this particular moment to reject and isolate the very companies that have a personnel policy giving living proof of how things can and should be done.' The interviewer wanted to know what would happen if the international pressure on Shell should increase. Van Wachem replied: 'We would then ultimately be faced with having to make a very unhappy choice: between our responsibilities with regard to Shell South Africa and its employees, on the one hand, and the other Group companies and their employees on the other hand. But I hope and believe that things will not get that far; I am confident that the "ordinary" man in the street, wherever he may be, our customer, will not allow himself to be taken for a ride by a completely misplaced boycott campaign.'[56]

In their discussions with the anti-apartheid movement, the Group faced one serious dilemma. On the one hand, top management wished to send out a strong message that it was against apartheid and the apartheid regime, but on the other hand it also wanted to stick to the Group philosophy of not interfering in the political system of any country. As McFadzean pointed out: 'it could be very dangerous for the future of the Group to depart from this philosophy'.[57] As a compromise, the managing director of Shell South Africa, John Wilson, became more active and outspoken in the South African business community to promote

changes from within, because the South African business community had the best chance of influencing the policies of the South African government. The company added to the Shell Statement of General Business Principles the clause that 'Shell South Africa has resolved to promote and actively contribute to the elimination of racial intolerance, unjust laws and unacceptable human rights practices.'[58]

Shell faced another more general problem: its structure was decentralized, but suddenly operating companies in a wide range of countries were getting difficult questions to answer on the activities of another Shell operating company, in this case Shell South Africa. It was not the custom in Shell for one operating company to give information about another operating company within the Group. The question arose in the Conference whether it would be opportune to adopt a stronger central management of certain public affairs issues. Van Wachem argued that the decentralized organization had served the Group very well and that it was difficult to make exceptions for particular activities.[59]

During the second half of the 1980s actions in the USA and Europe increased. Action groups enlisted the support of municipalities, which excluded companies working in South Africa from invitations to tender. This pressure instrument was first used in the USA and then introduced in Europe, in particular in Britain, the Netherlands, and the Scandinavian countries. The Shell lawyers

During the 1980s the public pressure on Shell to leave South Africa mounted. Pressure groups used the slogans and advertisements of Shell itself to make their point clear, in this way using the familiarity of the public with the Shell images.

The Dutch advertisement for lubricating with Shell Super Plus Motorolie was used to tell Shell to move out of South Africa. The cartoon, 'You can be sure it's Shell' referred to the slogan in the famous Shell campaign from the 1930s (see volume 1), but in this case with a negative message.

YOU CAN BE SURE IT'S Shell

Rich Cowley 85.

P. W. Botha, South African President from 1984 to 1989, pictured in 1986. He was and remained a staunch defender of the apartheid system.

[32]

took municipalities to court, and with some success. For instance, the decision of the city of Hilversum to exclude Shell from the supply of heating oil was annulled by the Crown, ruling that foreign policy was the exclusive domain of the Ministry of Foreign Affairs. The municipalities then devised a 'preference policy'.[60] In the UK the proposed boycott of Shell by Lewisham council was declared invalid by the English High Court.[61] In the USA the senators Dellums and Wise proposed legislation in 1988 to forbid direct or indirect investment in the petroleum industry in South Africa by United States entities or foreign companies with interests in the USA. The proposed bill sought to deny federal oil and gas leases to companies with South African connections.[62] European measures to forbid further investment in South Africa had little impact on Shell South Africa, because the company could finance itself. In 1988 Shell PA staff concluded that the morale of the employees within Shell companies, particularly in the Netherlands, was being affected by the 'slow drip process of vilification', and 'while there was little doubt in the minds of most employees that the policy of remaining in South Africa was correct, for all the best reasons, there was an increasing feeling that, in practice, it was absorbing too much energy, creating too many risks' and that ultimately Shell anyway would be forced out either commercially or by law.[63]

Anti-apartheid campaigners in Amsterdam distributed stickers in five languages, including Portuguese and French, with the message 'Stop apartheid, boycott Shell'.

[33]

[34]

F. W. de Klerk, South African President
from 1989 to 1994, pictured in 1992.
Under his presidency the system of
apartheid was finally abolished.

The annual general meetings of Royal Dutch and Shell Transport became the focus of demonstrations, with questions asked and freedom songs chanted. In 1980 Werkgroep Kairos and Komitee Zuidelijk Afrika published a leaflet 'Shell, smeer 'em uit Zuid-Afrika' (Shell, move out of South Africa), in which well-known Dutch writers, poets, illustrators, journalists, church leaders, and the leader of FNV trade union Wim Kok, argued for a boycott against South Africa and the withdrawal of Shell from South Africa. Three years later Werkgroep Kairos, Pax Christi-Nederland and Novib 'celebrated' ten years of protests at the annual meetings.[64] Not all shareholders were pleased with the space given to the anti-apartheid movement to make their point. In 1986 the shareholders of Royal Dutch voted to limit this to forty-five minutes, and the same amount of time was given during the next four years.[65] On the streets the campaign to oust Shell from South Africa became more violent with the rise of new and more aggressive action groups. Attacks on Shell property in Europe, in particular the Netherlands, rose from about sixty incidents in 1986 to a peak of nearly 600 in 1989. Service stations were the main targets and the incidents involved mainly the cutting of hoses, pollution of tanks, and the spraying of paint. In a number of cases buildings were set on fire.[66] The anti-apartheid movement in the USA achieved an exodus of American multinationals out of South Africa. In 1989

Mobil joined this group by selling its activities in Southern Africa to the South African company Gencor.[67] Shell, however, decided to stay the course. That same year F. W. de Klerk succeeded P. W. Botha as president, and started negotiations with the ANC (African National Congress). The South African ambassador in The Hague, Albert Nothnagel, later described how in January 1990 he advised his government that Van Wachem wanted to see 'visible results', 'so that the pressure on Shell could ease off a bit'. According to the Dutch newspaper *de Volkskrant*, Foreign Minister Pik Botha telephoned the ambassador and told him: 'Albert, just say that a big announcement is coming.'[68] In February 1990, the government lifted the state of emergency and released all political prisoners, including the most famous prisoner Nelson Mandela, who became the de facto leader of the ANC. It took another four years of negotiations and violent internal strife, before the first multi-racial elections could finally be held in 1994, ending in a resounding victory for the ANC and the presidency of Nelson Mandela.[69]

With hindsight, which party was right: the anti-apartheid movement to put so much pressure on Shell to disinvest, or Shell to hold out and stay the course? The anti-apartheid movement could point to the fact that the regime was overthrown and apartheid as a system brought to an end. No doubt the international pressure on South Africa helped to speed up this process of change. But internal

Chapter 5

A licence to operate: company response to public scrutiny

In February 1990 Nelson Mandela was released from prison. Three years later he received the Nobel Peace Prize, together with President Frederik Willem de Klerk.

[35]

[36]

pressure by the companies that remained had been important too, if only to demonstrate that companies could function effectively without a system of apartheid within their own operations. After the regime change, their programmes of corporate social responsibility, shaped during the years of international pressure, set an example to other foreign companies re-entering the country.

Two observations to conclude: first, the American campaign for consumers to boycott Shell products was never taken up by consumers in South Africa itself. Apparently the people of South Africa had another perception of Shell than those of the United States. Second, Shell South Africa succeeded in building up a good relationship with the ANC. When the ANC bought Shell House for its headquarters, it kept the name in place. During a visit to South Africa in 1992, Van Wachem privately met and discussed matters with De Klerk and the following day with Mandela. Both men received him very amicably, and he thoroughly enjoyed those meetings. In December 1993, though no longer chairman of the Group, he was invited to attend a ceremony in Oslo, Norway, during which Mandela and De Klerk jointly received the Nobel Peace Price.[70]

Why did Shell persevere in its policy to stay in South Africa? After all, it was not an oil-producing country nor were the coal operations very profitable. For both parties important principles were at stake. The anti-apartheid movement strove to end an evil system of apartheid, institutional racism, and white minority rule. The Shell Group wanted to protect its right to have operations in many countries around the globe, in which it sought to do business as a responsible citizen. Desmond Watkins, Regional Coordinator Western Hemisphere and Africa, wrote in 1988 about this issue: 'In my own business career I have seen calls for business not to carry on trade with, amongst others, Israel, Cuba, Chile, Nicaragua, the UK, USSR, Holland, China, Libya, Iran, Vietnam, and Taiwan. International companies are called on to cease trade or supplies to dictatorships, communist countries, one-party states, offenders against human rights, countries which kill whales or ban trade unions or whatever any individual group feels passionate about'.[71] In the confrontation with the anti-apartheid movement, the vision of Shell shifted from the principle that it was enough to observe the national law in each country in which it operated, to the view that Shell companies should be able to follow Shell's own Statement of General Business Principles in their own operations.

Towards a new Public Affairs policy and environmental issues

From the controversy over its presence in South Africa, Shell learned the importance of keeping up with the issues. Never before had the enterprise experienced such vicious attacks in the press and on its properties.[72] The theory and practice of issues management began to play a role in the public affairs activities of Shell companies. Issues management was defined as 'the identification of points of conflict between Shell companies and their public, preparing the appropriate response and communicating this effectively'. The key to combat issues was for the Public Affairs Department to identify potential issues at an early stage and help management to respond in a positive and constructive way.[73] Dealing with issues was important. As Shell's Coordinator Trade Relations had concluded in 1972, 'the ability to operate' relied on Shell's reputation. What companies could do, depended on what legislation and public opinion allowed them to do. Without public acceptance, businesses would suffer and maybe fail. In a talk to staff, Richard Tookey, Coordinator Group Public Affairs, concluded that what Chandler had said in 1972 was still true for 1988, but there were also new elements to take into account. First of all, the scrutiny of business activities was more direct than in the past, and the debate had become very public. Moreover, communications had become global as well as instantaneous, illustrated by the often-used television quote: 'This report comes to you live'.[74] The high speed of communications meant that the media were frequently on to a 'Shell story' before its own Press Office knew about it, as Shell's PA department remarked ruefully.[75]

Activist groups had become very adept at attracting wide international media attention for their causes. They displayed a great ingenuity in creating media events. But it would be wrong to dismiss their message as only representing a small group of activists. Tookey warned that: 'collectively, these groups do reflect the concerns of a society which is becoming less complacent and less compliant, more demanding and more determined to set its own values'.[76] Consumers took ethical concerns into consideration when they made their choices. The young had become more vocal about the world they wished to inherit. Business may sometimes have the feeling that consumers, investors or the public at large simplified complex problems, or were unaware of the fundamental trade-offs involved in the instinctive choices they were making. Nonetheless, it was important to take their concerns seriously. Therefore, if business found that its case was misunderstood by the general public, it had no other choice than to try and bring forward its own point of view with equal sophistication and effort. To do that effectively, Shell managers first had to listen carefully to what the public concerns were.[77] Shell managers in the various operating companies were advised to start a dialogue with the public, the pressure groups, trade unions, church leaders, and university teachers, and also to keep their own staff informed, because they too were under constant pressure from family and friends to answer probing questions. After all, well-informed staff constituted the best ambassadors for the company.

To what extent was this new Public Affairs approach really new? Campaigners in the USA discovered that Shell Oil had hired Pagan International, a Washington-based consulting firm, to advise them how to tackle the boycott of Shell products in the USA. Their report, the Neptune Strategy, came into the hands of church campaigners, who discovered to their dismay that one of the recommendations in the report was for Shell to engage with church people and focus their energy on post-apartheid planning.[78] Indeed, Shell Oil had addressed the threats of the consumer boycott in a very systematic way by engaging with groups it hoped to convince of its own point of view.[79] This was certainly not new, because, as we have seen above, in the 1970s the approach through dialogue with critics was frequently used. Much of the advice given by Pagan was simply common sense anyway. What was new in Shell's PA strategy was the awareness that pressure groups had become very strong with international networks and alliances. This was also illustrated by the fact that some of the more established groups acquired observer status on some important policy-forming committees. Shell noticed, perhaps with some envy, that pressure groups were able to attract young, articulate, energetic, professional, and highly motivated and committed staff who communicated well and appealed to the young. Therefore Shell should make its own points of view more public.[80] The traditional 'low profile' approach could easily be interpreted as weakness. As Shell's PA review of 1989 concluded: 'Pressure groups should be engaged in open debate. After all, they form part of the early warning system, and constructive dialogue may help to avoid a damaging confrontation later with a wider section of the public.'[81]

Not all issues raised by the pressure groups or more generally by the public remained equally alive over time. For instance, in the discussion around the role of multinational enterprise in the Third World, attitudes changed during the 1980s. Shell's PA department had the feeling that governments in the Third World had become more pragmatic in harnessing the energy of foreign companies. As a consequence Third World activists seemed to have developed more appreciation of the market economy and private enterprise.[82] While the presence of private business in Third World countries was no longer contested, their behaviour came under closer scrutiny. Activists from the western world looked critically at the employment of children, the human rights situation, and the effects of production on the environment in Third World countries.

Multinational companies were not only held to account for the activities of their own business units, but were also questioned on the behaviour of their suppliers or contractors. For instance, the Clean Clothes Campaign (Schone Kleren Campagne) pushed for better working conditions in the textile industry worldwide by putting pressure on the big chains, such as European textile company C&A, to improve the working conditions in the establishments of their suppliers, the sweatshops in Asia. Similar pressure was put on the American sports goods company Nike.[83]

The protection of the environment had been a hotly debated topic during the 1960s. After industry and governments had woken up to the problems of air and water pollution and introduced a series of measures and regulations to deal with them, the environment receded somewhat into the background. An analysis of the US trade journals showed that the attention of the chemical and oil industries to environmental matters, measured in the number of environmental articles, peaked in the years 1970-74, and then remained fairly low until the late 1980s, while the 1990s saw once again a steep rise in environmental articles, in particular with regard to the chemical industry.[84] Environmental concerns moved from directly visible damage and the long-term supply of energy to global warming and the survival of the world as we know it.[85] Direct pollution of the environment remained a recurring theme, in particular when disasters befell the oil industry, such as the *Exxon Valdez* oil spill in Alaska in 1989. Also the many small oil spills, emissions, and safety accidents continued to cause local alarm and public outcry.

[37]

[38]

The US army and Shell Oil had both produced chemical products at the Rocky Mountain Arsenal site near Denver, which led to considerable environmental damage. In 1983 the US government filed suit against Shell Oil, resulting in 1988 in a settlement agreement between Shell Oil and the US to clean up the site. Together with the US Fish and Wildlife Service, the army and Shell Oil turned the area into an urban wildlife refuge, where deer, coyotes, and bald eagles took over from the manufacturers.

A major issue for the oil industry as well as the chemical industry was also the clean-up of sites and the possibility that retroactive liability would be enforced. One such case concerned Shell Oil's site in Denver. In December 1983 the US government filed suit against Shell Oil claiming environmental damage at the army's Rocky Mountain Arsenal site near Denver. Though Shell Oil conceded the environmental damage, it considered the claim of some $1.9 billion out of proportion. Shell had leased a portion of the Arsenal for more than thirty years for manufacturing agricultural pesticides, but ceased operation there in December 1982. The army had also used the Arsenal beginning in the Second World War for the manufacture of nerve gas, munitions, and various chemical warfare agents. Moreover, the army had designed, constructed and operated the waste disposal system on the Arsenal, which Shell Oil had been required to use. Shell Oil, therefore, claimed that much of the environmental contamination at the Arsenal was due to failures in the army's waste disposal system.[86] After 1974 the army had asked Shell Oil itself to take care of the disposal of effluent from its Denver chemical plant. Negotiations about the responsibilities of both parties followed, resulting in 1988 in a settlement agreement between Shell Oil and the US to clean up the site. The army had to accept a far greater share in the total costs of the clean-up and redevelopment of the area than Shell Oil.[87] Together with the US Fish and Wildlife Service, the army and Shell Oil turned the area into an urban wildlife refuge, where deer, coyotes, and bald eagles took over from the manufacturers.[88]

In the 1980s environmentalists hotly debated the problem of forests dying because of acid rain, but this issue quietly disappeared. The rain may be acid, but the forests were not dying.[89] As for the disappearance of tropical forests, this was a consequence of forestry, and here the industry was seeking a solution in stricter regulations. At the top of the agenda in the 1990s stood the depletion of the ozone layer, global warming, and the far-reaching consequences of climate change for the whole world population. 'Sustainable development' became a key concept. In the Bruntland report *Our Common Future* sustainable development was defined as 'development that meets the needs of the present without compromising the ability of future generations to meet their own needs'.[90] The Bruntland report sought to persuade nations to work together to tackle the problem of poverty in developing countries while at the same time preserving and protecting the earth. For long-term survival it was essential to find a compromise between the conflicting need for economic growth of the poor countries and the need to preserve and protect the earth. Though environmental problems in developing and developed countries differed, in the end all countries would be affected by global warming. The time had come to break out of past patterns. The report urged governments, non-governmental organizations and industry to take their responsibilities for maintaining the eco-systems and bio-diversity, for optimizing the yield of natural resources and for avoiding pollution.[91] Heeding the appeal, Shell became a member of several committees following up the recommendations of the Bruntland report, including the ICC (International Chamber of Commerce) Working Party on Sustainable Development and the Business Council for Sustainable Development.[92] It also translated the aim of sustainable development into practical guidelines for its operations. For Exploration and Production this meant trying to be increasingly effective and efficient in finding new reserves, maximizing the recovery of reserves, limiting the intrusion into the environment, reducing the effects of waste and rehabilitating the land, and providing technology and knowledge locally. By putting in place a systematic Environmental Management System, achievement of

A licence to operate: company response to public scrutiny

these goals could be monitored.[93] On the issue of climate change, Shell wrote in 1990 that it recognized the substantial gaps in scientific knowledge, but believed that there was enough indication of potential risk to the environment for governments and industry to take action. Shell developed programmes to phase out the use of hard CFCs, to reduce the flaring of natural gas and to improve the efficiency of energy use.[94]

Shell companies were actively involved in policies to preserve the environment.[95] However, the public had a different perception of the company. Clearly, there was a gap between the public's perception of Shell and Shell's own perception of itself. Shell's PA staff wondered 'why is it that we are being misunderstood?' They found that for people in the rich countries quality of life had become more important than just earning a living. Day after day people heard news about the risks of pollution, industrial accidents or the toxicity of certain products. They felt threatened by unknown dangers. These threats led to fear and fear to strong emotions, all the more as people craved a risk-free society. At the same time people began to lose confidence in the traditional safe-keepers of their interests, the governments, the regulatory bodies and traditional industry. In contrast, they saw the environmentalists as the true guardians of the public interest. The public responded easily and eagerly to alleged wrongdoings. For instance, the forestry plans of Shell Thailand were criticized in an article in one environmental magazine. After the criticism was picked up by a UK television programme and a widely read UK newspaper Shell received more letters, mostly from the USA, over a few weeks than it had received in years over South Africa.[96] In the end, Shell did not go ahead with the venture.[97]

Shell's PA staff underlined the importance of public trust in the company, because trust granted legitimacy, a 'licence to operate'.[98] In 1972 reputation was considered necessary to enable Shell to operate, but by 1990 Shell was apparently supposed to need a public consent, permission to operate. Shell top managers expressed their wish to acquire from the public the 'licence to operate' repeatedly during the 1990s.[99] How should Shell try and close the gap between the public and its own perception of the company? Malcolm Williams, head of Group PA's Regional Public Affairs and Training, formulated two challenges for the 1990s: first, to enhance awareness within Shell of external developments and public concerns. Second, to manage the problem of ensuring prompt, cohesive responses to issues in the Group's decentralized matrix organisation.[100] Tookey advised management in 1991 to listen as well as talk, to share the public's concerns, speak its language, demonstrate commitment, and offer reasonable solutions. But most of all, it should address the emotions in people's view and 'be human': 'The public will judge us not by how much we comply but by how much we care.'[101] His successor as the Group's Coordinator Public Affairs, Tony Brak, warned Shell managers in 1994 that corporate reputations could be badly damaged by a single event or issue if not managed effectively, because the media were under constant pressure to publish news and television had become global and instant.[102] A year later, the Group experienced how true these warnings had been. The enterprise came under heavy pressure over the proposed deepwater disposal of the Brent Spar and over its operations in Nigeria.

The proposed sinking of the Brent Spar   When Shell Expro started up production in the Brent field in the North Sea in the mid-1970s, the production facilities were designed to be ready ahead of the pipelines to bring the oil onshore. In the meantime the produced oil would be shipped from the field to the refinery by tanker. Shell Expro could have used a single buoy mooring system, with a floating storage unit and shuttle tankers as proposed by Esso, but instead it developed the large 'Spar storage and tanker loading unit' with specially modified shuttle tankers. The Spar would be more expensive in the short run, but had fewer 'damage prone features'. Therefore there would be less risk of deferred income caused by time lost awaiting repairs, and less risk of pollution of the sea through oil spills.[103] In 1976 the Spar was towed into place. The bulk of the Spar was made up of six segmented storage tanks, which were designed to hold approximately 300,000 barrels of oil. To give some idea of the scale: the content was four times the volume of the clock-tower of Big Ben. The structure included a topside with a helideck and accommodation for twenty-eight people. It was 191 metres high and weighed 14,500 tonnes. After fifteen years in service, Shell Expro decided to decommission the Brent Spar in 1991, because it was no longer needed to handle oil from the Brent field. While the facility remained moored in the Brent field, Shell Expro developed plans for the removal and disposal of the Spar. It was not considered an option to leave it where it was, because without continued maintenance the facility would deteriorate and become a hazard. After taking health, safety, economic, technical, and environmental factors into consideration, Shell UK concluded that deepwater disposal was the best practical environmental option. An independent University of Aberdeen study supported this conclusion. Scrapping onshore would not only be more expensive, but it would also expose personnel to greater risk. Shell UK believed that the sunken Spar would have negligible effect on the deep sea environment. Following UK legislation on abandonment, Shell UK consulted the Scottish Office, the Department of Trade and Industry and other government departments. In February 1995 the Trade and Industry Minister Tim Eggar outlined the government's

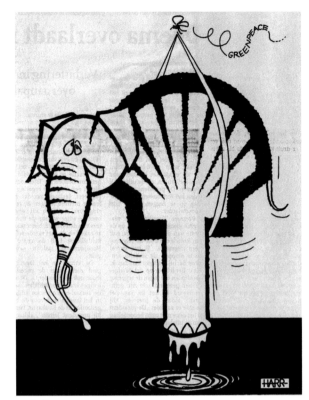

[39]

Advertisement campaign of Greenpeace against the decision of Shell to sink the Brent Spar. The picture refers to the fairy tale of the mosquito and the elephant, with Greenpeace seeing itself as the small mosquito that can drive the big elephant Shell mad. For some Dutch readers it had another connotation, that of turning a mosquito into an elephant – the Dutch equivalent of making a mountain out of a molehill.

abandonment policy at the Institute of Petroleum's conference on abandonment and approved of deepwater disposal of Brent Spar. The Ministry of Agriculture, Fisheries & Food sent a letter and supporting documents to the Secretary General of the OSPAR Commission, the international coordination body for the protection of the marine environment of the North-East Atlantic. The same documentation was sent to European governments at working level. At the same time Shell UK issued its first briefing about the disposal of the Brent Spar. As no objections were raised, Shell UK proceeded with its deepwater disposal plan.[104]

One party, however, felt excluded from Shell UK's round of consultation about the best way of disposing of the Brent Spar, and that was the international non-governmental organization

Greenpeace occupied the Brent Spar, a storage tank and tanker loading unit, on 1 May 1995, to protest against its planned sinking in the deep Atlantic. Shell thought it had solid economic and environmental arguments for decommissioning the structure in this way, but it could not convince the general public of the rightness of this policy.

Greenpeace, which campaigned for a 'green and peaceful' world. Greenpeace had itself commissioned a report on the issue of decommissioning and abandonment of offshore oil and gas platforms, and came to the conclusion that there were 'no grounds for dumping'. Greenpeace was concerned that the disposal of the Brent Spar would be followed by many other disposals, as North Sea oil production was reaching maturity. It thought the environmental damage would be considerable and objected to deepwater disposal in principle. Greenpeace submitted its report to the Department of Trade and Industry, but did not receive an invitation to be included in the consultation process. Therefore, the British, Dutch, and German branches of Greenpeace decided to start a campaign against the principle of disposal with a special focus on Shell UK and the Brent Spar.[105] On 30 April 1995, Greenpeace and a German TV channel boarded the Brent Spar to create Europe-wide publicity.

Greenpeace took the moral high ground with simple, clear messages, telling the public that just as they were not allowed to dump their cars in the local lake, neither should industry be allowed to use the sea as a dumping ground. During the occupation of the Spar, campaigners took samples of its content and claimed that 5,000 tonnes of hydrocarbons were still in the storage tanks. In a briefing issue Shell UK had indicated that at the bottom of the tanks there were around 100 tonnes of 'sludge' consisting of silt, which contained oil residues and small amounts of heavy metals that originated in the Brent field reservoirs. The silt also contained scale, which comprised naturally occurring radioactive salts that were a normal part of the marine environment and which in case of dumping had no implications for health or the food chain. The radioactive salts, however, could have health implications if removed on shore, and therefore formed an extra argument for deep-sea disposal. Greenpeace viewed this 100 tonnes of sludge differently from Shell. It argued initially that the Spar contained 100 tonnes of toxic sludge and more than 30 tonnes of radioactive

scale. In a few weeks of campaigning this transformed into '14,500 tonnes of toxic litter', suggesting that the whole Spar was toxic and that the sinking in deep-sea water would be a major environmental disaster.[106] About the effects of the sludge on the sea environment, opinions differed. The journal *Nature* argued that many deep-sea microbes require heavy metals as electron or energy sources in their metabolism: 'Far from finding heavy-metal residues lethal or even mildly unappetizing, the bacteria of the ocean floor would have greeted the arrival of Brent Spar as if all their Christmases had come at once.'[107] Interestingly, it was the consumers in some continental European countries who most of all responded to the Greenpeace campaign by boycotting Shell petrol stations. During this period, governments in some continental European countries had urged the public to divide their rubbish into different categories and take their empty bottles to bottlebanks for recycling. Against this background it seemed strange that the same governments would allow industry to 'use the sea as dustbin', as Greenpeace phrased it. In Germany protesters damaged fifty service stations, two of which were fire-bombed and one raked with bullets, and they threatened to damage another 150 Shell service stations.[108]

Initially Shell UK decided to continue with its disposal plan for the Brent Spar and explain its reasons more forcefully through press releases and visits to government representatives. On 10 June 1995 the anchor chains of the Spar were cut and a day later the tow to the North Atlantic began. Greenpeace created a second round of worldwide media coverage by landing two activists on the Spar by helicopter. Sales on the continent went down, in particularly in Germany. Part of the Shell staff shared the environmental concerns of the public at large. In Denmark, Germany, the Netherlands, and Sweden government ministers spoke out against the deepwater disposal, despite the fact that they had been formally notified in advance through the OSPAR Commission. At the Esbjerg

[41]

With water cannons Shell tried to
prevent a second occupation of the
Brent Spar in June 1995.

Conference on 8 and 9 June, it became clear that the majority of the
OSPAR governments were opposing the principle of deepwater
disposal. At the same time the British government was unwilling to
delay the disposal operation. Shell's CMD faced a particularly
uncomfortable dilemma. If it decided to go ahead with the offshore
disposal, it would seriously damage Shell's reputation and business
in continental Europe. On the other hand, if it were to abandon the
sinking it would damage its reputation in the UK, in particular with
the UK government, which agreed to the sinking. There appeared a
rift in public opinion between Britain and continental Europe, and
this rift was discernible within Shell as well. Shell UK felt it had to
give in to 'continental pressure'. Under these circumstances, there
was no win, only a choice between the lesser of two evils. Cor
Herkströter, chairman of the CMD, concluded that giving up the
offshore disposal plan would be the less damaging of the two
options. One had to accept that the sinking of structures in
international waters involved a number of stakeholders, and not
just one particular government. On 20 June 1995 Shell UK
announced it had decided to abandon the offshore disposal,
though it remained convinced that the sinking in the deep Atlantic
would have been the most responsible way of disposing of the
Brent Spar. In Britain Prime Minister John Major, who had firmly
supported the deepwater disposal, called Shell 'wimps' for giving
in to public pressure.[109] Also, within the Shell community there
were many bruised feelings to be healed. As Herkströter wrote
afterwards to a number of Shell managers involved with the issue:
'In the UK there was initial incomprehension of the reversal and
our perceived attitude to the UK government; elsewhere in Europe
the decision was widely greeted with relief, although with a
questioning of why deepwater disposal had been contemplated in
the first place. Clearly it affected staff morale.'[110]

The Norwegian government offered a temporary shelter for the Spar in the deepwaters of Erfjorden Fjord near Stavanger. The decision not to sink the Spar gave Shell the opportunity to invite Det Norske Veritas as an independent expert to inspect the content of the Spar. Ahead of the results, Greenpeace admitted that it had overestimated a hundredfold the amount of oil left in the Brent Spar, and apologized to Shell for its mistake. Peter Melchett, Executive Director of Greenpeace UK explained: 'We thought samples had been successfully taken from storage tank 1, but we have realised in the last few days that when the samples were taken the sampling device was still in the pipe leading into the storage tanks, rather than in the tank itself.'[111] Of course that did not change their main argument that it was wrong to dump industrial waste of any sort in the deep oceans. As Greenpeace had underlined their scientific approach in their campaign, news media had the unpleasant feeling that they had been manipulated by them.[112] However, Shell concluded from the uproar over what they had considered to be a fairly technical decision, that public perception counted and that Shell needed to involve the views of external stakeholders in its decision-making. Emotions and beliefs could ultimately have just as much influence on Shell's 'licence to operate' as hard facts and demonstrated performance.[113]

Shell learned another lesson from the Brent Spar. During the debates about how to decommission the Brent Spar the Shell organization had spoken with different voices. While the Managing Director of Shell UK defended the deepwater sinking of the Spar, his counterpart in Germany voiced his doubts about the wisdom of this decision. This was a logical consequence of the decentralized structure and the autonomy of the operating companies, but it made the organization as a whole look weak and internally divided. Therefore the case of the Brent Spar showed Shell that there was a need for a greater internal communication and coordination in important policy decisions. The further implications have already been discussed in chapter 4.

The Brent Spar had also demonstrated how quickly some governments reacted when alarmed by public outcry. There had been no negative reaction when the UK government had notified the OSPAR Commission and the European governments of its plans to sink the Brent Spar. Alarmed by the public outrage over the planned sinking, the governments of the OSPAR Convention opted for a moratorium on deepwater disposal of North Sea oil production structures. Herkströter, while acknowledging the importance of consulting with a wide range of stakeholders, underlined the need for a consistent regulatory framework in order for business to invest: 'Governments' role is to ensure that open debate takes place in accordance with democratic principles through the appropriate institutions. However, once this has taken its course and the proper legislative framework had been agreed it is their task to ensure such agreements are implemented.'[114] However this was a question society had to resolve. After lengthy studies and consultations, Shell decided in 1998 to deconstruct the Brent Spar and use the pieces for the extension of the quay at Mekjarvik, Norway.[115]

Shell hoped to get the opportunity to rebuild its reputation. In July 1995 sales in all European countries had recovered with the exception of those in Germany, where the sales in June 1995 were some 10 per cent down on the levels of June 1994.[116] The public apology of Greenpeace in September 1995 swayed opinion in Shell's favour. However, soon Shell operations once again became the focus of activists, and this time environmentalists and human rights campaigners joined forces to challenge Shell's activities in Nigeria.

In 1998 Shell decided to deconstruct the Brent Spar and use the slices for the extension of the quay at Mekjarvik, Norway.

A licence to operate: company response to public scrutiny

Nigeria

☐ Shell interest
— Gas pipelines
— Oil pipelines
▲ Terminal

In the 1950s a joint-venture company owned by Shell and BP, of which Shell was the operator, discovered oil in commercial quantities in the Niger delta, signalling the start of oil production. The Niger delta turned out to be an oil-rich region, though production was far from easy in this swampy territory.

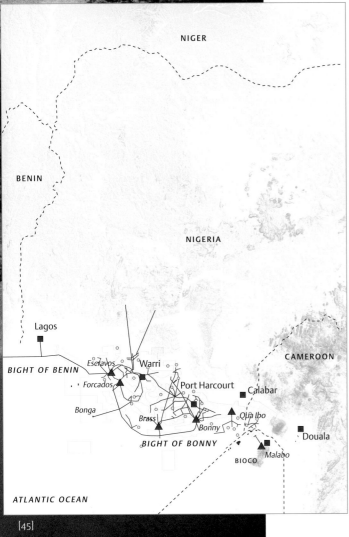

[45]

Shell in Nigeria

Like Shell in South Africa, and in contrast to the Brent Spar issue, the debate about Shell's activities in Nigeria covered a long period of time with regular incidents and accidents drawing intense media attention. In the mid-1990s, the basic issue at stake for Shell was how to operate according to its own business principles under a military regime which used excessive force towards its own people and divided the oil wealth very unequally, leaving out the very people most affected by the oil production. By acting as one of the important operators of oil facilities, Shell worked closely together with the national oil company and it supported the regime indirectly through the oil revenues the state received thanks to the oil production. How the governments used these oil revenues was for them to decide, not for Shell. But the discontent of the local communities in which Shell operated had its impact on Shell. What were the options for the company under these circumstances?

Shell had first entered Nigeria in joint venture with Anglo-Persian (later to be named BP) during the 1930s, when the country was a British colony. In 1956 their joint-venture company of which Shell was the operator discovered oil in commercial quantities in the Niger delta, signalling the start of oil production. After Nigeria acquired independence in 1960, a democratic multi-party government encouraged direct foreign investment. This period, lasting for six years, ended in 1966 with a military coup, followed a year later by a civil war when oil-rich Biafra sought independence. The civil war ended in 1970, after which military regimes alternated with short spells of civil administration. Between 1960 and 1998 Nigeria had seven different military regimes and three civilian governments.[117]

Local people were experiencing the downside of oil production in the form of gas flaring and oil spills without benefiting from the substantial earnings, which mostly went directly to the national government. Above: A woman passing a gas flare from the local flow station in Etelebou; below: Peremabiri, with the plumes of smoke of a Shell-operated flow station in the background.

[47]

[46]

A woman sells gasoline for motor bikes and cars on one of Okrika's main roads, Niger delta, 2005.

[48]

Nigeria joined OPEC shortly after the end of the civil war in July 1971. As in other OPEC countries, the Nigerian government sought to renegotiate the agreements with oil companies, providing for government participation via its Nigerian National Petroleum Corporation (NNPC). Starting with a claim for 35 per cent in 1973, a year later Nigeria raised its participation to 55 per cent.[118] In 1979 Nigeria nationalized BP's marketing activities and BP's 20 per cent stake in the joint venture, alleging that it had violated the boycott against South Africa by transporting Nigerian oil to that country. As a consequence the stake of NNPC in the joint-venture company rose from 60 to 80 per cent, with Shell Petroleum Development Company (Shell Nigeria), holding the remaining 20 per cent.[119] In the 1980s the Nigerian government faced a fall in its oil revenues. For instance, between 1980 and 1983 these revenues fell from $24 billion to $9 billion, a decline which took place even before the oil price collapse in 1985.[120] Therefore it became more difficult for the government to keep up its investments in the joint venture with Shell Nigeria. In 1989 Nigeria reduced its share in the joint venture to 60 per cent, with Shell Nigeria taking an extra 10 per cent, and Agip and Elf both 5 per cent.[121] In 1992 Elf acquired another 5 per cent in the joint venture from the Nigerian government. By 1994 the shares in the unnamed joint venture, the largest producing venture in Nigeria, were divided as follows: the Nigerian National

Petroleum Company owned 55 per cent, Shell Nigeria 30 per cent, Elf 10 per cent and Agip 5 per cent. Shell Nigeria acted as operator for the joint venture. For Shell's oil production Nigeria was an important country. In the years 1991-4 Nigeria produced on average 18 per cent of the Group's equity oil and natural gas liquids. It contributed 12 per cent of the Group's E&P net income over these years.[122]

Nigeria is not only rich in oil but also in natural gas, both associated and non-associated. Most of the associated gas was flared, because of insufficient local demand. However, the flaring of associated gas was both wasteful and bad for the environment. From the late 1960s, the Nigerian government and several oil companies, including Shell, negotiated about an LNG (Liquefied Natural Gas) scheme for Nigeria, including the Bonny Liquefied Natural Gas scheme launched in 1976. In 1981 Phillips Petroleum Company, the technical leader, withdrew, and when BP did the same, the scheme was wound up. The Nigerian government appointed outside consultants to develop a new scheme. One of the options under consideration was a pipeline from Nigeria to Europe, a proposal that seemed to receive heavy encouragement from the US. Peter Holmes did not think the Nigerians would regard the pipeline as a realistic proposal, basically because they lacked trust in their neighbours.[123] The LNG project was interesting for

In the 1990s the Ogoni people demanded political autonomy so as to participate in the affairs of the Federal Republic of Nigeria as a distinct and separate unit, with the use and development of Ogoni languages and culture, and the right to religious freedom. They also asked for the right to protect the Ogoni environment and ecology from further degradation, including protesting against the continued practice of gas flaring.

Shell on it own merits, but also because it offered possibilities to process associated gas and reduce the contested gas flaring. In 1989 the military rulers made moves towards returning to parliamentary democracy, but this process was slow, creating much political uncertainty. When finally the presidential elections were held on 12 June 1993, the military government annulled the result and set up an interim government.

The negotiations about the Nigerian LNG project were equally drawn out, because the government was an important partner. The minutes of Shell's Conference in November 1992 give a glimpse of the difficult negotiations. Considering the best choice for the construction of the project, Shell as technical adviser for the LNG project had recommended consortium A over consortium B on the basis of the overall tender audit. Prior to a decision by the Nigerian LNG board, however, the Minister of Petroleum and Mineral Resources had intervened and recommended that the consortia be combined to 'get the best out of each'. In response, the LNG board convened and agreed that such a combination was not desirable and that Shell's recommendation should be accepted. This decision was sent forth in a memorandum to the Minister. As Henny de Ruiter, Group managing director, explained to the Conference: 'The Memorandum was not favourably received by the Minister's office, and the National Nigerian Petroleum Company had subsequently removed each of its Directors from the Nigerian LNG Board. (..) It was thought that the chances of making a Final Investment Decision by the 16 December 1992, as scheduled, were remote'.[124]

As negotiations were continuing, the media began to scrutinize Shell's activities in Nigeria. Channel 4's television programme 'Heat of the Moment', broadcast in October 1992, accused Shell of double standards in environmental matters and

The writer Ken Saro-Wiwa became spokesperson for the Ogonis and leader of the Movement for the Survival of the Ogoni People (Mosop). He travelled abroad to enlist support for the cause of the Ogonis with great success. In June 1994 he and several others were arrested and accused of having been connected to the murder of four traditional leaders, accusations they vehemently denied. On 31 October 1995 Ken Saro-Wiwa and eight co-defendants were found guilty and sentenced to death in a process that was widely considered unfair. Despite international protests and requests for clemency the executions went ahead.

referred to an incident two years earlier at Umuechem in the Niger delta, during which a peaceful protest had been turned into a bloody confrontation by the intervention of the brutal Mobile Police Force. Shell Nigeria had a different version of the same incident. A group of Umuechem youths occupied a rig location and oil production flow station, operated by Shell Nigeria. The protesters chased out the staff before they had the opportunity to make the locations safe. Complying with its statutory requirement to report any threat to oil production the authorities were informed. But the local police were also driven out by the demonstrators. The Police Commissioner then sent in a contingent of the Mobile Police Force, which attacked the village, causing destruction and killing a number of people. Therefore the police were to blame for the unwarranted attack on the village. Looking deeper into the disturbances, Shell argued that in a number of rural oil-producing areas of Nigeria unease was growing among a group of unemployed but well-educated young people, who were challenging traditional local leadership. Shell Nigeria tried to maintain dialogue with the various groups without becoming caught up in local disputes.[125] The television programme marked the start of an international campaign against Shell and its performance regarding environmental and human rights issues in Nigeria.

The campaign focused on the plight of the Ogoni people and the environmental damage to Ogoniland in the Niger delta by the oil industry. The Ogonis were an ethnic group of over half a million people, who lived by farming and fishing. The oil production in Ogoniland was about 1.5 per cent of oil production in Nigeria. In 1990 a group of five families presented the Ogoni Bill of Rights to the Nigerian government. While reaffirming their wish to remain a part of the Federal Republic of Nigeria, they demanded that the Ogoni people be granted political autonomy to participate in the affairs of the Republic as a distinct and separate unit. Apart from demanding the use and development of Ogoni languages and culture and the right to religious freedom, they asked for the right to protect the Ogoni environment and ecology from further degradation. They also pointed out that the Ogoni people had not profited in any way from the oil revenues: 'It is intolerable that one of the richest areas of Nigeria should wallow in abject poverty and destitution', they wrote.[126] One of the signatories of this Bill of Rights, the writer Ken Saro-Wiwa, became the spokesperson for the Ogonis and leader of the Movement for the Survival of the Ogoni People (Mosop). Saro-Wiwa travelled abroad to enlist support for the cause of the Ogonis with great success.

As the Nigerian government remained unresponsive to the claims of the Ogoni, Mosop decided to focus their campaign on Shell Nigeria instead and claim from it a sum of $10 billion, $6 billion in rent and royalties and $4 billion in compensation for environmental damages. Mosop accused Shell Nigeria of collusion with the government in 'the genocide of the Ogonis'. One might ask why Shell was targeted with the other oil companies seemingly escaping attention. In the first place, Shell Nigeria was the operator of the most important production venture, which controlled half of the Nigerian oil production. Second, it had a larger share in this joint venture than either Elf or Agip. Third, it had a strong position in the onshore oil production, while competitors worked predominantly offshore. In short, Shell Nigeria was an important player in the Nigerian economy and a well-known brand internationally.

In January 1993 Mosop mobilized large groups of Ogonis, who staged a mass protest at oil facilities operated by Shell Nigeria. Though Mosop claimed that their campaign was non-violent, Shell felt it was no longer safe for staff and contractors to work there in the face of growing intimidation from members of the communities. As a consequence, Shell withdrew from Ogoniland, though pipelines still passed through the region.[127] Shell Nigeria acknowledged that the people in the oil-producing areas, including the Ogonis, did not receive their fair share of the oil revenues, but Shell believed that these political issues should be addressed to the government. In negotiations with the Nigerian Head of State, General Sani Abacha, Shell's representative underlined that more money should be allocated to the oil-producing states. Though there were certainly extensive environmental problems, Shell did not think the word devastation applied. Shell agreed that the facilities built in the 1960s and 1970s were no longer acceptable by modern standards, and some were indeed in a poor state. A programme to update these facilities was launched in 1990 and was still ongoing in the mid-1990s. Oil spills took place regularly due to corrosion and in the course of production. However, in the Ogoni area a relatively high percentage of oil spills were caused by sabotage. According to Shell, in the Ogoni area 69 per cent of all oil spills between 1985 and the start of 1993 were caused deliberately to win compensation. The usual methods were hacksaw cuts and opening or tampering with valves. In comparison, in Nigeria as a whole the percentage of sabotage was no more than 25 per cent of all oil spills, while 75 per cent resulted from corrosion in older pipelines and other facilities.[128] A study by the World Bank covering the Nigeria's Delta State found much lower figures for oil spills caused by sabotage during the period 1991-1994: only 43 (that is 15 per cent) of 287 oil spills. In volume the oil spills caused by sabotage, however, counted for 35 per cent of total volume.[129]

In June 1994 Ken Saro-Wiwa and several others were arrested and accused of having been connected to the murder of four traditional leaders, accusations they denied.[130] Human rights campaigners asked Shell companies to intervene in order to gain the release of Ken Saro-Wiwa. Shell, however, argued that commercial organizations should not use their influence to interfere in the legal processes of a sovereign state concerning an alleged criminal matter. In one of its Briefing Notes, Shell made its point of view crystal clear: 'A private company has neither the right nor the competence to become involved or attempt to interfere with those legal processes. (..) Those campaigning on behalf of Mr Saro-Wiwa would be the first to criticise Shell companies if they interfered in the politics of a country on a matter which did not suit their agenda.'[131] Human rights campaigners challenged Shell's point of view in cases where the regime was oppressive and the legal system obviously flawed. Campaigners also questioned Shell's environmental performance. Moving from a defensive towards a more responsive attitude Shell decided to start an independent review of the environment of the Delta region and to increase its community spending. But even an independent scientific assessment of damage to the environment would not have solved the controversy, because the Ogoni had a different perception of their environment. For them it held a cultural and spiritual value that could not be captured in figures and tables but had to be experienced and appreciated.[132]

One of the problems in the Niger delta
is that poor people are driven to use
the oil facilities in ways that were never
intended. For example, Urohobo
women bake their tapioca in the heat
of a gas flare from a Shell operated flow
station in 2004. Though gas itself is a
clean energy source, the burning of
associated gas introduced soot into the
air that over time could cause serious
health problems.

At the beginning of the twenty-first
century the situation in the Niger
delta remained difficult and complex
for people working in the oil industry
as well as for those living there.
Determined to profit from the oil in
their ground, some groups stole
crude oil or gasoline, causing
pollution and creating dangerous
situations themselves. Left below: a
boat used for the theft of oil, moored
in a river near a Shell facility.

From left to right: A member of the Niger Delta Volunteer Force siphons fuel into a jerry can in order to fuel one of their boats.

The national secretary of Orere Uluba village quarrels with Shell employees and Nigerian Federal Security because of their unannounced entry onto village property in 2005. Shell contractors wanted to begin a clean-up operation.

Workers subcontracted by Shell clean up an oil spill from an abandoned well.

On 31 October 1995 Ken Saro-Wiwa and eight co-defendants were found guilty and sentenced to death by a Special Tribunal set up by Sani Abacha outside the normal judicial system. This Tribunal did not allow for the right of judicial appeal to a higher or independent jurisdiction.[133] The trial was widely considered unfair. Shell came under increasing pressure to speak out against their conviction. Up till then Shell had followed a strategy of 'quiet diplomacy', refusing to interfere publicly in the trial. On 8 November 1995, however, the Committee of Managing Directors decided to send a letter to the Head of State to ask for clemency on humanitarian grounds. Shell had tried to get the other oil companies on board, but these had refused to join Shell in making representations to the Head of State.[134] This action did not have the desired effect, and with unseemly haste Ken Saro-Wiwa and the other eight were hanged on 10 November 1995. In his closing address to the tribunal, Saro-Wiwa argued that Shell was more on trial than he and his co-defendants: '...there is no doubt in my mind that the ecological war that the Company has waged in the Delta will be called to question sooner than later and the crimes of that war be duly punished. The crime of the Company's dirty wars against the Ogoni people will also be punished. (..) In my innocence of the false charges I face here, in my utter conviction, I call upon the Ogoni people, the peoples of the Niger Delta, and the oppressed ethnic minorities on Nigeria to stand up now and fight fearlessly and peacefully for their

Chapter 5

A licence to operate: company response to public scrutiny

Congested traffic on a road in Port
Harcourt in Nigeria in 2004.

rights. History is on their side. God is on their side. For the Holy Quran says in Sura 42, verse 41: 'All those that fight when oppressed incur no guilt, but Allah shall punish the oppressor.' Come the day.'[135]

Following the executions Shell companies found themselves under attack from all sides, including the media, NGOs, single issue pressure groups, and even investors. Many critics accused Shell Nigeria of insufficiently distancing itself from the military regime. They found their point of view confirmed by the fact that Shell announced a final investment decision regarding the Nigeria LNG project only a few days later, on 15 November 1995. Indeed, Shell was well aware that the announcement came 'at the worst possible moment'.[136] Having worked on this new LNG project for more than ten years, it was understandable that Shell Nigeria did not want to put it at risk by postponing the investment decision. Furthermore, should the LNG project collapse, then Shell might well experience negative consequences for future business opportunities in upstream activities of which their competitors could be expected to take full advantage. In addition a major opportunity for reducing the flaring of gas would be lost. Therefore the LNG project would help address one of the main demands of the environmental campaigners.[137] Pax Christi and Amnesty International accepted that the Nigerian government was responsible for the deaths of Ken Saro-Wiwa and his fellow activists, but they wanted Shell companies to speak out openly against violations of human rights.[138] Nelson Mandela asked for oil sanctions to be imposed against Nigeria during the Commonwealth Summit in Auckland, but politicians were not very keen to take firm action, despite the public indignation over the human rights situation in the country. Friends of the Earth, Greenpeace and others called for boycotts against Shell petrol stations, but consumers did not respond as eagerly as in the Brent Spar case. The Ogoni issue did not cause an immediate loss in sales as had happened over the Brent Spar controversy, but it had a negative impact on the reputation of Shell companies. As Shell had concluded many times, its 'licence to operate' depended on its reputation. The Group had some hard thinking to do.

Lessons to be learned After the barrage of negative news seriously damaging its reputation Shell began a process of soul-searching. Top managers felt puzzled. Apparently Shell had lost touch with the expectations of a number of its key stakeholders, but why and how? Shell wanted to know what went wrong and which lessons had to be learned. In 1996 the CMD started the project 'Reputation Management' to analyse the problems and develop initiatives to provide solutions. The first step in the review process was a year-long, wide-ranging consultation programme about 'society's changing expectations'. With the help of research among the general public, special groups, and Shell managers, round-table meetings and benchmarking, Shell examined society's rising expectations and Shell's inability to meet them. It turned out that society expected the Group to take responsibility for the significant impact its operations had on global society. It required a demonstrable commitment to sustainable development alongside a strong financial performance. Society expected ethical integrity and concern for human rights. Protestations of commitment had to be backed up by transparency, social accountability, and verifiable performance.[139] Interestingly, all these elements of 'society's changing expectations' had been discussed by Shell's own PA department and published in its magazine *Interchange* in the early 1990s.[140] Therefore, the knowledge had been there, including the awareness that this knowledge had to be spread throughout the enterprise, starting at the very top.

Nonetheless, a poll taken in 1997 by Mori (Market & Opinion Research International) concluded that Shell had failed to match rising societal expectations. In particular young people, women, key media, and legislators did not feel comfortable with the way Shell thought and acted. Both the general public and special groups admired Shell as a competent and professional operator, but suspected it of being aloof, unresponsive, and less interested in environmental or human issues than it should be. Shell was not perceived as being interested in dialogue with local communities or special groups, and too many of its communications reinforced a perception of coldness, according to the Mori poll. Not all countries felt equally negative about Shell. Public opinion in some non-European countries, including Malaysia, Brazil, the USA, and South Africa, was far more favourable towards Shell than in some of its key European countries, in particular the Netherlands and Germany.[141] The chairman of the CMD, Cor Herkströter gave the following analysis of the problem: 'One major reason, from my perspective, was a type of technological arrogance which is rather common in companies with a strong technical base. Most of us in Royal Dutch/Shell come from a scientific, technological background. That type of education, along with our corporate culture, teaches us that we must identify a problem, isolate it and then fix it. That sort of approach works well with a physical problem – but is not so useful when we are faced with, say, a human rights issue. For most engineering problems there is a correct answer. For most social and political dilemmas there is a range of possible answers – almost all compromises. So, starting off with a strong, scientifically grounded mind-set, we tended to misjudge some of the softer issues and consequently made mistakes. We misread some of the situations.'[142]

From the Mori poll and the examination of society's rising expectations, Shell's CMD concluded that it had to take serious action. In fact, it followed the path described by Herkströter: 'identify a problem, isolate it and then fix it'. First the problem had been identified: the enterprise needed to show that it contributed to sustainable development, fostered an open corporate culture, and was willing to engage in dialogue with stakeholders. An

Management is involved in negotiating and balancing demands.

[58]

The Shell magazine *Interchange* underlined in 1992 how managers had to strike a very fine balance between the many different demands posed by the various stakeholders of the company.

essential part of showing its commitment consisted in developing systems to manage, measure, and verify progress and performance. Now it was time to fix it.

To be better prepared for society's changing expectations in the future Shell enhanced its dialogue with external stakeholders. Mark Moody-Stuart, Group managing director, stated in 1996 that the public at large now demanded to be convinced that a company practised what it preached. This had clear implications for how Shell companies put their messages across: 'a fine line had to be steered between a willingness to listen to others and maintaining the courage of one's convictions'.[143] The dialogue with external stakeholders implied that not only the public in general but also specific groups within society had to be targeted. Renaming the function 'Public Affairs' as 'External Affairs' reflected this new approach to stakeholder engagement, which included discussions which were not necessarily in the public eye.[144] The exchanges with external stakeholders took place on Group level as well as local level. For instance, Govert Boeles, director of personnel and social affairs of Shell Pernis, participated in a dialogue with the Dutch

Council of Churches. As a Christian himself he found it refreshing to discover that the churches were prepared to engage in a debate with Shell employees, while in the past as a Shell employee he had felt condemned out of hand. Leen Koster, manager of environmental affairs at Shell Nederland, learned from the discussion about sustainability that people in Shell were inclined to put their trust in new technology, while churches wanted to influence the behaviour of people. The discussions convinced Jan Gruiters, adjunct secretary of Pax Christi, that Shell had undergone a real change in its thinking that went beyond just public relations.[145] In some twenty-five countries Shell engaged in discussion with opinion leaders and organizations such as Amnesty International, Pax Christi, and Human Rights Watch. Tim van Kooten, issue manager of Shell Nederland, organized these encounters not so much to convince the other parties as to find a way of sharing dilemmas.[146] The discussions contributed to the revision of Shell's Statement of General Business Principles.

First formulated in 1976, the Statement had been revised regularly in response to particular issues at the time. For instance, in 1984 it was no longer considered necessary to defend the role of profit and the market economy.[147] The major additions in 1997 included clear references to human rights and sustainable development. The reformulated business principles underlined the responsibility of Shell companies 'to respect the human rights of their employees'. The new statement extended the responsibilities of Shell companies towards society. As in the past, Shell companies were expected to conduct business as responsible corporate members of society and to observe the laws of the countries in which they operated. The new clause asked Shell companies 'to express support for human rights in line with the legitimate role of business and to give proper regard to health, safety and the environment consistent with their commitment to contribute to sustainable development'. The addition 'human rights in line with the legitimate role of business' was chosen with care, because the term 'human rights' covered so many different aspects, ranging from the right to life and liberty to living conditions and the quality of life. Shell companies could not possibly be expected to deal with all those aspects.[148]

Earlier statements had included reference to health, safety, and the conservation of the environment. The new statement referred several times to the wish to contribute to 'sustainable development'. In the conflict with the Ogonis, the refusal of Shell to put pressure on the Nigerian government had been hotly contested by the pressure groups. In the reformulated business principles Shell companies saw their responsibilities extended. Shell companies were, of course, still expected to act within the laws of the countries in which they operated in pursuit of their legitimate commercial objectives, and Shell companies were not supposed to make payments to political parties, organizations or their representatives or take any part in party politics. When dealing with governments, however, Shell companies were given the right and the responsibility to make their position known on any matter which affected themselves, their employees, their customers, or their shareholders or even the community where they had a contribution to make.[149]

Together with a revision of the business principles Shell developed a system of assurances, an internal accounting system to make sure all Shell companies did indeed comply with the business principles. When the business principles were first launched in 1976 local variations according to local customs had been considered acceptable. This was no longer the case in 1997. The Statement of General Business Principles became mandatory for all Shell companies, including Shell Oil in the US. Shell Canada accepted the same principles, and joint-venture partners were also expected to subscribe to them. As the world not only expected words but also proof, an internal and external system of assurances was developed. The external way of showing Shell's good intentions consisted of the publication of the externally audited Shell Health, Safety and Environment report in 1997, followed by the Shell Report for 1997, published in 1998 under the telling title 'Profits and Principles: Does there have to be a choice?' The report was drafted by a small Shell team assisted by consultants, including Arthur D. Little and the environmentalist John Elkington of SustainAbility. Not surprisingly, the Shell Report 1999 borrowed from Elkington the expression 'people, planet & profits' to describe the 'triple bottom line' for responsible companies. The inclusion of external assessments was vital to the credibility of the reports, but here Shell had to explore new territory. The area of environmental auditing was in its infancy, and 'social auditing' was even less advanced. While measuring performance was essential, clear yardsticks had yet to be developed. Also, social criteria were harder to apply and measure than financial ones. Therefore, Shell commissioned Arthur D. Little to propose a social responsibility management system.[150] Though Shell's (social) reports met with considerable approval, some of the environmental critics dismissed the effort as 'greenwash', and some human rights activists remained unimpressed.[151]

Following the custom in the USA and UK, Shell set up a Social Responsibility Committee as a new committee of the boards of the parent companies to review the practices, policies, and procedures of the organization with regard to issues of public concern.[152] This committee, chaired by Lord Oxburgh, oversaw the process of preparing the Shell (social) reports. For instance in 2001 it advised that the report should address explicitly the integration of the different aspects of sustainable development and the necessary trade-off that sometimes had to be made among environmental,

social, and economic concerns.[153] Wind energy offered a striking example of the difficulty of getting it right. Hailed as the perfect renewable energy in the 1980s, wind energy came under attack in the early twenty-first century because wind farms on land changed the landscape and those at sea risked damaging birds.

The Social Responsibility Committee also supported the creation of the Shell Foundation, the Group's flagship social investment scheme. In itself social investment was not new to Shell. Over the years Shell operating companies had been involved with local projects according to local needs. For instance in the early 1990s Group companies' expenditure on charitable grants or donations and social sponsorship amounted to some $40 million per year, representing about 0.6 per cent of the Group's pre-tax profit or 0.9 per cent of post-tax profit. On average 45 per cent of total grants expenditure went to education, and 15 per cent each to

Shell brochures from 1998 with projects to help people build a better world.

A Shell-sponsored elementary school
in the Philippines.

three categories: culture and community, environment, and medical. The remaining 5 per cent were used to 'encourage young people to realize their full potential'.[154] The local companies continued to have their own social investment. The central Shell Foundation made the contribution of the Group more visible and more independent from daily operations. To start with the Foundation received an endowment of $250 million, with additional funding in the next ten years in order to support an annual programme of around $25 million.[155] The Shell Foundation had two main programmes: Sustainable Energy and Sustainable Communities. Initially the long-running LiveWIRE programme counted as a separate third programme. This programme to help young people set up their own business originated in the UK in the 1970s and had been taken up by many other countries as far as it suited local circumstances. Typical of the Foundation's approach was the collaboration with local partners. For instance, the 'Micro-enterprise for women at risk in Romania/Slovakia' was run by the Slovakian NGO Integra. Its main objective was to enable women to break out of the circle of unemployment, dependency, and poverty by helping them set up their own small business. The programme Embarq formed an interesting initiative to combine the two aims of sustainability in energy and community. Embarq, in partnership with the World Resources Institute, aimed to find solutions for cities in developing countries struggling with air pollution, traffic congestion, and lack of access to clean and convenient transport. Both examples illustrate the ambition of the Shell Foundation: 'Helping society build a sustainable future'.

[62]

In its social programmes Shell developed two key areas: sustainable energy and sustainable communities. Providing sustainable energy to local communities served both goals, as seen above at the demonstration of rural solar energy in Hatarekotuwa, Sri Lanka.

Below: In 1998 Shell and Eskom, South Africa's national electricity supplier, started a joint venture project in South Africa to set up solar panels for delivering electricity to circa 50,000 rural villages.

Development grants from Shell Nigeria have funded the construction of homes and schools, and the improvement of roads and infrastructure, including the Mowoe Primary School in Warri, Niger delta, seen here. One huge challenge in corporate community programmes, however, is finding a way of maintaining the facilities after they have been built.

To underline further its commitment to sustainable growth, Shell set up a separate business unit, 'Renewables', in 1997, focusing on solar power, biomass and sustainable forestry. The forestry activities, however, turned out to be more linked with the pulp and paper industry than with biomass. When campaigners began to question the green credentials of forestry, the activity became less attractive from the point of view of sustainable business. Because the link of its forestry business with energy was tenuous, Shell got out of this part of its renewable portfolio but instead included wind power. [156]

The truly sceptical critics were hard to convince with even the most social of programmes or progressive energy plans. In Nigeria, Shell stepped up its spending on local community projects in the Niger delta, but critics found the help inadequate or inappropriate or unequally divided among the various local groups. Local strife and tensions remained. In 2002 the environmentalist campaigner Jack Doyle argued that the British-Dutch enterprise must turn its back on fossil fuels if it were to escape a legacy of well blow-outs, oil spills, chronic air pollution, and polluted rivers. 'Few places and few species, no matter how remote or how special, have escaped the untoward and insinuating effects of oil and petrochemicals', Doyle argued. [157] It was clear that the Group would have to cope with very vocal criticisms as long as it worked in the oil industry.

[63]

[64]

Conclusion   The last quarter of the twentieth century saw the rise of non-governmental organizations (NGOs) putting pressure on companies to pay attention to specific issues they particularly cared about, and a public increasingly willing to respond as consumer to allegations of company wrongdoings. At the same time, communications became more global and much faster, enabling the media to feed the public with daily events from all over the world. In the 1970s the left-wing public in the western world was critical of companies, in particular multinationals, but still had faith in governments and international institutions to act on behalf of the general cause and keep companies in check. In the 1980s this confidence in the role of governments disappeared. Only the NGOs still seemed to have the trust of the public. The attitude of the public towards companies became contradictory. On the one hand, large parts of the public remained suspicious of big companies, on the other they expected them to find solutions for problems governments had failed to solve. Shell, as a very visible and large organization, fully experienced the pressure of these contradictory demands.

Shell companies were well aware of the importance of a good reputation for their ability to operate. They realized that ultimately a good reputation depended on good behaviour. In large international enterprises such as Shell it was inevitable that sometimes managers did not act appropriately. Therefore Shell formulated business principles to set out the standards it expected of its staff and devised internal systems to deal with those who did not comply with the rules. The public also expected higher standards from companies and governments than in the past. The handling of the boycott of Rhodesia, though undeniably complicated by different sets of national legislation in Britain and South Africa, did not show the oil companies or the British government in a very positive light.

More difficult to deal with, however, were issues where Shell companies and the public had different views or different perceptions. This was the case with Shell's presence in South Africa. While critics wanted Shell to leave the country to help undermine the apartheid regime, Shell remained convinced of the importance of political neutrality, though eventually it openly condemned the apartheid system. In the 1970s Shell expected that it could sway public opinion by providing extensive information and explaining the trade-offs that had to be made when dealing with complex issues. From the long-running dispute about South Africa, Shell learned that it also had to show emotions, making clear that it cared about the people it worked with and shared concerns about the environment. Understanding the importance of being more in tune with public expectations, however, was not the same as being able to forestall new issues coming up and making the headlines. In the dispute about the sinking of the Brent Spar, Shell experienced how action by professional NGOs combined with spectacular media coverage unleashed so much public emotion that it could upset its own careful planning founded on sound scientific evidence. It was attacked over its environmental performance in its operation and over the use of violence against local people by the Nigerian government. Many critics simply did not accept Shell's point of view that it could not interfere with the way the government ran the country or with the way the legal system functioned.

In response to rising criticism Shell decided on a very public overhaul of its reputation management in 1996. NGOs were invited to enter into a dialogue with Shell and find solutions for complex issues. In the process Shell accepted a greater responsibility for human rights issues and sustainable development. In their interaction between company and public both the pressure groups and Shell became increasingly professional and sophisticated. As a result staggering amounts of information, some of it externally certified, became available about the company, amounts that would have appalled Henri Deterding and Marcus Samuel.[158] The public, however, remained sceptical.

The merger of 1907 taken to its logical conclusion: the birth of Royal Dutch Shell plc

After a decade of low oil prices, the oil industry started a process of consolidation in 1998. Already one of the super majors, Royal Dutch/Shell did not participate in the mega-mergers, though its rivals Exxon and BP did. Expecting oil prices to remain low in the near future, Shell concentrated on lowering costs. Belatedly, it also looked for acquisitions, however with modest results. From the consolidation in the oil industry Shell concluded that size mattered after all. Therefore it focused on various ways of benefiting more from its size. Devising processes and structures to operate on a truly global basis was one way of benefiting from size. Managing large and complicated projects was another. Ever since the reorganization of 1995 the structure of two parent companies had been under discussion, but it needed the impact of the overbooked proved reserves finally to tackle this complex issue and take the merger of 1907 to its logical conclusion by creating Royal Dutch Shell plc.

At the Royal Dutch AGM on 28 June 2005, ninety-eight years after the merger of the operations of Royal Dutch and Shell Transport, shareholders had to vote on the far-reaching proposal that the parents companies should finally be united.

Two meetings On 28 June 2005 two meetings took place, one in The Hague, or rather in the nearby seaside resort of Scheveningen, and the other in London. These were the Annual General Meetings (AGMs) of shareholders of the Royal Dutch Petroleum Company and the Shell Transport and Trading Company, which were going to decide the future of their companies. The two meetings had much in common, because they were discussing the same enterprise and the same results at the same time. For the shareholders these were historic meetings, but for the NGOs it was business as usual. Though the Group had been engaging with NGOs since the mid-1990s, the criticisms of the Friends of the Earth and Milieudefensie were as severe as ever. They confronted the shareholders outside the buildings with displays and pamphlets. Inside were assembled the traditional shareholders for whom the meeting was as much a day out as an opportunity to be informed about their company. The representatives of institutional investors were eager to defend the interests of their companies and clients. On the table was the proposal to bring together Royal Dutch and Shell Transport under a single parent company, Royal Dutch Shell, which would mean that after ninety-eight years the two parent companies would finally merge. Royal Dutch Shell plc, incorporated in England and Wales, would have its registered office in Britain, but its headquarters and tax residence in the Netherlands. It would have listings on the London, Amsterdam, and New York stock exchanges.

The historic meeting of Royal Dutch, chaired by Aad Jacobs, chairman of Royal Dutch, started at 10.30 with the presentation of the results of 2004 by the president of Royal Dutch, Jeroen van der Veer. He underlined that 2004 had been a year of extremes with on the one hand the reserves issue and on the other an excellent operational and financial performance. He went on to highlight the successes of the year and to outline plans for the future. Shareholders were given the opportunity to ask questions and many made extensive use of it. A representative of Milieudefensie introduced to the shareholders a group of people who were living in the neighbourhood of Shell companies to testify about the bad health situation in the places where they were living as a consequence of oil production and refining. Many of the measures Shell had taken so far to improve the situation were seen as insufficient or inadequate. Though Shell people were talking with community groups, they were accused of not talking with the right groups, or not setting up the right kind of community support. Other representatives of NGOs challenged Shell about the local impact of their activities and the relationships between 'fence-line communities' and local management. Since the 1970s they had used the platform of the AGMs to make their voice heard, and they did so this time, seemingly unaware of the historic importance of the decisions to be taken later that day.

Not all shareholders came to criticize the company. Some asked for more information. Others had detailed questions about possible discrepancies between information on different pages in the *Annual Report*. The representatives of shareholders and institutional investors asked questions about the booking of reserves, class action suits in the US, the targets of the company, the remuneration of board members, the dividend policy and corporate governance. Slowly the meeting proceeded with ballots and more questions asked, until finally at 14.20 the key point of the unification came under discussion, the establishment of one company with one board and one CEO. Shareholders had a few questions about the venue and the language of the future annual meetings, and about whether in the structure of a British plc the

The merger of 1907 taken to its logical conclusion: the birth of Royal Dutch Shell plc

Over the years, campaigners had used the platform of the AGMs to criticize the company, and the historic meeting on 28 June 2005 formed no exception. Friends of the Earth had organized a number of people living in the neighbourhood of Shell facilities to personally voice their grievances at the Royal Dutch and Shell Transport AGMs. This particular group was present at the Royal Dutch AGM.

Sludgelake
Cura

Milieudefensie, the Dutch partner of Friends of the Earth International, had set up a display outside the venue of the AGM to convince shareholders of the disappointing environmental performance of their company. One shareholder engaged in debate with a campaigner standing before a display about the issue of the bitumen lake at the Curaçao refinery, dating back to the Second World War, which in 2005 was still waiting to be worked up into valuable oil products.

long-term interests of all stakeholders would be sufficiently guaranteed. There was also a sceptical question on how long the headquarters would remain in the Netherlands, but the whole discussion took less than half an hour. When shareholders were asked to approve of the 'implementation agreement' between NV Royal Dutch, Shell Transport plc and the new parent company Royal Dutch Shell plc., they voted overwhelmingly for the proposal with a majority of 98.4 per cent of voters and 99.8 per cent of the votes. The meeting continued till 17.00 with further discussions on priority shares, remuneration of executives and a hotly contested proposal to indemnify board members from bearing the cost of legal cases brought against them. The historic decision to end the unique dual nationality structure of the enterprise had been taken without any pomp and circumstance.[1]

The same was true for the other meeting in London. It took place in a modern building in the Docklands that even one of the board members described as a 'ghastly dungeon'. Here the AGM was equally dominated by environmental campaigners asking detailed questions about leaking pipelines and gas flaring. Asked to give his comments on the report of Friends of the Earth, 'Lessons not learned – the other Shell Report 2004', the Shell Transport chairman, Lord Oxburgh, commented that it would be very useful to both Friends of the Earth and their supporters, and indeed to the Shell shareholders, if the Friends of the Earth were willing to have whatever they produced verified by external independent assessors, in the same way as Shell had the Shell Report assessed. To this comment the Friends of the Earth representative replied that 'our verifiers live 10, 20 or 30 metres from your refineries. They are the fence-line communities that we have brought here today. I would suggest that it would be wrong to dismiss that form of verification as if it was worthless'.[2]

The decision about the proposal for unification called 'the scheme of arrangement' took place in a separate meeting, the Court Meeting, directly following the AGM. Despite the fact that the new parent company Royal Dutch Shell would be a British plc, with a listing on the London stock exchange and the registered office in London, one British shareholder was flatly against the proposal: 'I don't buy this scheme at all, not at all. First of all, it does a

At the same time shareholders of Shell Transport voted on the same unification proposal in London under the chairmanship of Lord Oxburgh, chairman of Shell Transport.

[5]

disservice to the British nation. What is happening is that we have Shell Transport and Trading, which is a very important company in the scheme of things within the United Kingdom. Lo and behold, here we have a Board who are prepared to send it over to the other side. I have nothing against our Dutch friends; on the contrary, I have worked hard with them for many years, nearly 20 years, and also as a Member of the European Parliament, I have worked with my Dutch colleagues. But we have to consider the national interest as well.'.[3]

His view was very much a minority view. Declaring the dividends in euros was another sore point for some of the shareholders, as was the fact that future AGMs would take place in the Netherlands, though there would be a video link with London. Finally, as the board member Lord Kerr commented, there would come an end to the bizarre situation that 'we have two very brilliant directors here in Malcolm [Brinded] and Peter [Voser]; we do not have the CEO here. The Royal Dutch AGM is taking place today and they don't have the Finance Director of the Group present, because we have pinched him – he is here. It is bizarre'.[4] From the outset of

the meeting it was clear that the proposal would be accepted, because the proxy voters had already voted in large majority in favour of the scheme. When all votes were counted there turned out to be almost unanimous support of 96.4 per cent of the voters and 99.8 per cent of the votes.[5] The merger of 1907 was at long last taken to its logical conclusion. The new shares in Royal Dutch Shell plc started trading on 20 July 2005.

This chapter will deal with the events leading up to this final merger. It was the conclusion of a reorganization process started in the mid 1990s, which was the logical response to the globalization of the 1990s and the tougher competitive environment of low oil prices, in which companies could no longer afford a lot of red tape. The commotion over the overstatement of the proved reserves, which will be discussed later, made it possible to act at that particular moment.

[6]

The dot.com bubble and beyond

The last decade of the twentieth century was a boom period with rising share prices and mega-mergers, which came to halt after a series of crises. First, in 1997 Japan and the 'Asian tigers', a number of smaller Asian economies that had shown a spectacular growth in the 1990s, were hit by a banking crisis, which then spread to South America. In the wake of the Asian crisis, oil demand dropped and oil prices collapsed to below $10 per barrel. Finally, in 1999, the stock markets crashed when it became clear that the shares of many recently floated internet companies had been hugely overvalued. The

investors had expected internet sales to grow much faster than they actually did, leaving the newly created internet companies with a huge share capital but no profits to pay dividends. When the dot.com bubble burst, the shares of other companies that had profited from the general atmosphere of optimism came down as well.

The sobering mood in the western world deepened when the US was hit by the terrorist attack on 11 September 2001. The shock of the attack was followed by a shock of an entirely different nature: the American energy company Enron, praised in recent years for its

On 11 September 2001, terrorists hijacked four passenger airlines, and used two of them to attack the World Trade Center in New York. The famous Twin Towers collapsed completely, stunning the world by the extent of the damage. Together with the simultaneous attack on the Pentagon and the crashing of a fourth hijacked passenger airliner, some 3,000 people lost their lives.

A few months later the financial world experienced a nasty shock, when the highly rated innovative energy company Enron filed for bankruptcy. It appeared that investors had been misled by the executives of the company. Court cases followed and on 25 May 2006 the jury in Houston, Texas, found two former Enron bosses, Jeffrey Skilling and Kenneth Lay, guilty of fraud.

[7]

high growth rates and its innovative schemes that seemed to revolutionize the industry, turned out to have grossly misled investors. In December 2001 Enron filed for bankruptcy. The auditor of Enron, the accounting firm Arthur Anderson, seemed to have had an active role in devising the schemes that misled investors. Worse, email messages came to light that suggested relevant papers had been wilfully destroyed by Arthur Anderson. As the very rationale for an auditing firm is the trust of the public in the reliability of its audits, the scandal at Enron also led to the downfall of Arthur Anderson. More bankruptcies and critical questions about the accounts followed.[6]

While America was wrestling with its accounting practices, at the other end of the globe China and India were experiencing a growth spurt. Two hugely populated countries were hungry for raw materials, in particular oil. The big question was: how long would oil be available? Old discussions resurfaced about when oil production would peak. Pessimists like the geologist Colin Campbell, trustee of the Oil Depletion Analysis Centre, warned that conventional oil would reach its peak during the first decade of the twenty-first century. He argued that the annual growth in reserves shown by the oil industry on the basis of Security and Exchange Commission (SEC) rules misrepresented the real situation. The SEC had a very strict definition of proved reserves. As fields were further developed more of the reserves could be moved from the possible

and probable categories to that of proved reserves. Such additions to the proven reserves, according to Campbell, were in fact only corrections of previous understatements and should be backdated to the discovery date of the field. If that happened, it would show how much the current oil production depended on much earlier discoveries.[7] Not only that, but the big oil discoveries of the past would not be repeated in the future, as for instance revealed by Figure 6.1 (see page 376). The annual discovered volumes of oil and gas showed a downward trend after 1980, and this was expected to continue in the future.[8]

Another seemingly successful company, the internet company Worldcom, found itself in trouble. From left to right: Breaking News announced the Worldcom $3.85 billion accounting scandal; US deputy attorney General Larry Thompson announced the filing of criminal charges against former executives at Worldcom in 2002.
Campaigners outside the Federal Hall in New York on 11 June 2003.
Traders on the trading floor at the Stock Exchange in New York in the summer of 2004.

Figure 6.1
Annual discovered volumes of oil and gas, 1900-2000/2040 (figures for 2010-2040 are based on stochastic simulation).

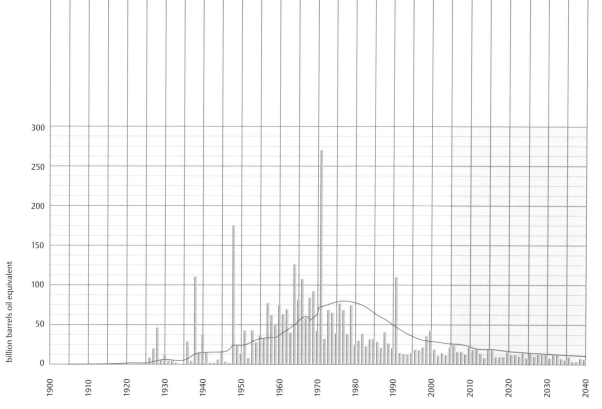

billion barrels oil equivalent

Annual discovered volumes
20-year average

The optimists did not deny the downward trend, but expected the production peak to materialize later, and were more hopeful that economic and technological developments could slow down the rate of post-peak decline. The US Energy Agency forecasted world oil production capacity to rise from 80 million barrels per day in 2002 to 122.2 million in 2025.[9] The Shell vision was that 'easy' oil had probably passed its peak, but that other resources, such as unconventional oil and gas, were still a long way from their peak. With the right technology it would be possible to increase production of oil and gas while at the same time keeping the environmental impact in check.[10] In the short run, however, the oil industry had a hard time meeting the rising energy demand in the early 2000s after a decade of low oil prices and modest investments. All oil majors struggled with production increases.

And Shell was one of them. After a decade of liberalization and privatization governments became painfully aware that the world's energy supply could not be taken for granted. They wondered whether after all they might be wise to continue playing a role in assuring energy security. This reduced the appetite for further privatization and in some cases led to renationalization. For instance, the government of Venezuela, having encouraged the international oil companies to return to its country in the 1990s, after nationalization of the oil concessions in 1975, changed tack again in 2006 by increasing state participation in joint ventures with international oil companies.[11]

With the oil majors struggling to increase their production and with demand for oil rising, the OPEC countries reasserted themselves. For the first time in twenty-five years they organized a summit, this time in Caracas and hosted by Hugo Chavez, President of Venezuela. The previous summit had taken place in 1975 in Algiers.

(From left) The Emir of Qatar Hamad Ibn Khalifa Al-Thani, Iraqi Vice Prime Minister Taha Yassin Ramadan, Iranian President Muhammad Khatami, Libyan Housing Secretary Mustapha Al Kharrubi, Algerian President Abdelaziz Bouteflika, Sheik Hamad Ibn Muhammad Al-Sharqi of the United Arab Emirates, Venezuelan President Hugo Chavez, Crown Prince of Saudi Arabia Abdullah Ibn Abdul Aziz Al-Saud, Indonesian President Abdurrahman Wahid, Crown Prince of Kuwait Jaber Al-Ahmad Al-Sabah and Nigerian President Olesegun Obasanjo.

The merger of 1907 taken to its logical conclusion: the birth of Royal Dutch Shell plc

Consolidation in the oil industry

In the Annual Report of 1997 Philip Carroll, president and CEO of Shell Oil Company, wrote with enthusiasm about 'moving to a networked community': 'As our businesses have transformed to meet the patterns of change, the face of Shell Oil is becoming quite different. In 1998, over half of Shell's capital employed will be in joint ventures and global alliances. This leaves less than half of our capital in traditionally wholly owned business structures. (...) As businesses restructure to meet the pressures of competition, we believe that networks will increasingly replace conventional hierarchical organizations.'[12] Joint ventures were supposed to bundle complementary capabilities, increase the speed of new technologies, create synergies, and reduce the costs of operations.[13] Shell Oil had concluded joint ventures with Mobil in the upstream business, with Texaco in the downstream business and with Tejas Gas in the midstream (pipelines) sector.

In their analysis of the oil sector, consultants of McKinsey went a step further. With reference to the situation in the USA, they prophesied the 'atomization of Big Oil': 'The vertically integrated international oil company no longer represents the winning formula in the petroleum business. Instead, a new breed of tightly focused and vertically specialized 'petropreneurs' are capturing most of the industry's growth and shareholder value'.[14] The consultants added that the oil majors tended to dismiss or downplay the competitive implications of the successes of the petropreneurs, arguing that these upstarts were producing unsustainable results through smoke and mirrors. McKinsey, however, advised the oil majors that skills were becoming more important than scale or scope, and strategic insight and foresight more important than structural position. Legacy assets, vertical integration or the sheer size of their balance sheet would not insulate the majors from industry changes and new forms of competition. The petropreneurs, as yet mainly active in the USA, would move abroad and challenge the majors in their international activities. Only by a process of self-atomization could the majors hope to compete successfully against these specialist energy companies. Growth ambitions should be realized through alliances with third parties rather than relying on traditional ownership models: 'The new world will put influence before ownership, outsourcing before integration, and relationship networks before hierarchies.'[15]

In its Group Plan for 1998 Shell cited this McKinsey article with approval: 'Many of the traditional advantages of Big Oil – the ability to provide a range of technical skills, in-house access to finance, the size to absorb risk, special relationships – are being eroded in a world where specialist skills are bought, capital markets are prepared to lend to pure plays as willingly as to Majors, sophisticated risk management tools are widely available, and freer markets reduce the benefits of connections'.[16] Ironically, the petropreneurs had been able to enter the market through the purchase of assets the oil majors sold as being too marginal for their operations. Having acquired these assets, they could then develop them further by buying specialist skills from oilfield service companies such as Schlumberger and Halliburton, which in the 1990s had grown in knowledge and skills thanks to the policy of outsourcing of the same oil majors. Therefore, the policy of the oil majors to shed marginal assets and outsource specialist expertise had created the new competitors they were now urged to emulate. Jeff Skilling, the CEO of Enron, believed that the industry was on the brink of a revolution in which market forces would dictate the splitting up of Big Oil into lots of specialist firms, each with its own niche. He believed that oil companies would be 'virtually' integrated, by companies like Enron. And he could have a point, wrote Ann St John-Hall, a freelance writer specializing in technology in *Shell World* in 2001: 'over the last ten years, Enron has increased its revenues 20-fold, to over US$100 billion last year. If there wasn't a market for the kind of thing they do, this wouldn't have happened'.[17]

EXXON Mobil

[13]

Most oil majors, however, had another idea of how they wanted to build their strength: consolidation rather than fragmentation of the industry was the response of the oil majors to a decade of low oil prices. BP and Amoco announced their merger in August 1998 and Exxon and Mobil followed in December 1998. In the same month Total announced that it was buying Belgium's Petrofina. Having exhausted the options for slashing costs in their own operations, the oil majors turned to mergers in the search for further efficiency gains and cost savings. Mergers also were a way of showing growth. *The Economist* commented that 'it is now cheaper to buy oil reserves on Wall Street than by drilling your own well'.[18] Two researchers from the Oxford Institute for Energy Studies, Nick Antill and Robert Arnott, concluded in 2003 that: 'In the aftermath of a long period of cost cutting, the oil companies were left with little

choice but to embark on a wave of mergers to rekindle growth aspirations.'[19]

Shell did not take part in the mega-mergers. There were discussions with Mobil prior to its merger with Exxon and ideas of creating a third parent company in the USA, but the CEO of Mobil, Lucio Noto, considered the suggested structure too complicated.[20] An added complication for a possible merger with Mobil was that Shell Oil had already merged its downstream activities with Texaco. This illustrates how decisions taken locally could influence global outcomes. Shell had examined Texaco data in 2000, but a total merger was a bridge too far for Shell because it did not consider the assets of Texaco as valuable as those of Mobil. In any case Texaco was already negotiating a merger with Chevron.[21] In 1998 Shell was struggling with poor results as a consequence of the low oil price

[14]

[15]   [16]

The merger of 1907 taken to its logical conclusion: the birth of Royal Dutch Shell plc

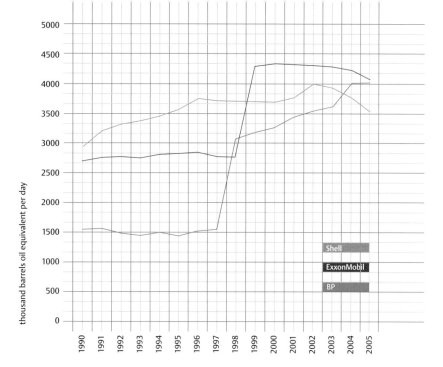

Figure 6.2

Oil and gas production, Shell,

ExxonMobil, and BP, 1990-2005.

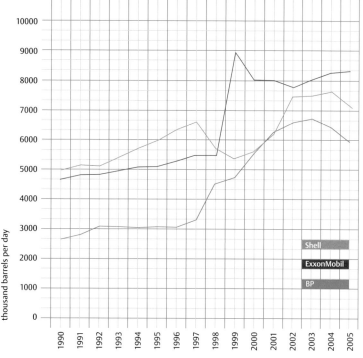

Figure 6.3

Sales oil products, Shell, ExxonMobil,

and BP, 1990-2005.

and because the alliance strategy of Shell Oil had created heavy losses. This was particularly true for the association of Shell Oil with Tejas Gas. In 1997 this company was hailed by McKinsey as one of the fast-growing petropreneurs, which had created by 31 December 1996 a return to shareholders of $4.91 per $1 invested at 1 January 1991. In comparison Royal Dutch Shell had a cumulative return over the same period of only $2.87.[22] However, as discussed in chapter 3, Shell took over the company Tejas Gas at a much inflated price boosted by the atmosphere of optimism at the end of the 1990s and had to write off parts of the acquisition immediately. Shell Oil's joint venture with Texaco in the downstream business in the US did not create the hoped for synergies either. Lack of funding was only one of the reasons why Shell hesitated to participate in the process of mega-mergers. The Group's dual structure made a deal with payment in shares instead of cash not impossible, but certainly more complicated. Moreover, management was not entirely convinced of the benefits of mergers.[23]

In 1999 the Shell people who wrote monthly memos for the Conference, the so-called 'Economic Signals', presented a

discussion on the question: 'Does Size Matter?' First they offered the argument why size did not matter. Technical economies of scale were small compared to the size of super majors, as economists were eager to show. The benefits of spreading best practice and innovative ideas across a large number of businesses were more difficult to calculate, as were the benefits of exploitation of brand and reputation. Being medium-sized was probably just as good as being super-sized. As to wielding market power, here the size of the market was relevant and for the oil industry this market was global. Even the super majors together had no more than half the global market, which was not enough for profiting from market power. Nor were there any benefits in vertical integration because since 1980 there were liquid markets between the various stages in the supply chain. The idea that upstream and downstream margins would compensate each other was no longer convincing either, because those margins seemed largely uncorrelated as a consequence of the competitive conditions in the relevant markets. However, as markets seemed to value size, there should be some advantage somewhere. While some smaller companies might

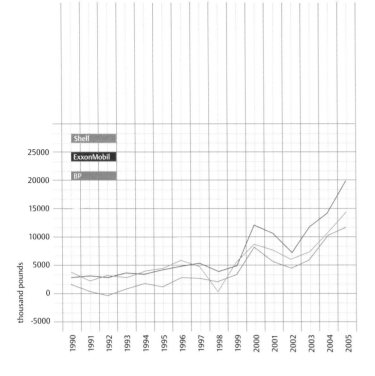

Figure 6.4
Net income Shell, ExxonMobil, and BP,
1990-2005.

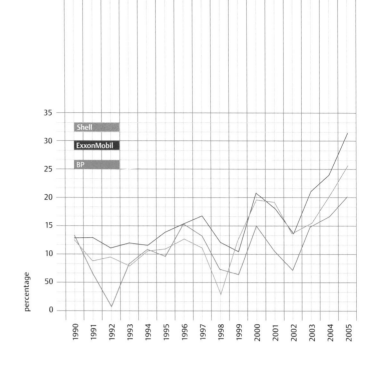

Figure 6.5
Return on capital employed Shell,
ExxonMobil, and BP, 1990-2005.

achieve the highest growth rates and profit rates, many others
failed. In the large companies, which could be seen as a collection
of smaller firms, the high and low growth rates and profits of the
various subsidiaries tended to balance each other. Therefore the
large companies showed more stable results. How should the large
companies make the best use of their size? In an industry that was
constantly changing, physical assets, organizational units,
managers, funds, and ideas had to be reallocated all the time. Large
companies might perform the restructuring process internally
more efficiently than markets via bankruptcy or takeovers. Super
majors could gain advantage by operating a better internal 'market
for corporate control'. This led to the conclusion that size did
matter, 'if management knows how to use it'. Yet, there was no
reason to suppose that the majors would remain vertically
integrated. Perhaps the future would see large upstream
companies and separate, but equally large downstream
companies.[24]

More mega-mergers in the oil industry followed,
strengthening the position of the traditional vertically integrated

companies: TotalFina added Elf Aquitaine in 1999, while Chevron
and Texaco announced their intention to merge in October 2000.
Despite these mergers, the traditional oil majors were no longer
the largest players in the international oil industry. Measured in
access to reserves some national oil companies, such as Saudi
Aramco and Gazprom, were far larger. These players became more
dangerous competitors, because they no longer restricted their
activities to their home countries.

The consolidation in the oil industry had a substantial
influence on the position of Shell in relation to its main rivals Exxon
and BP, as Figure 6.2 on equity oil and gas production, Figure 6.3
on oil product sales, and Figure 6.4 on net income show.
ExxonMobil and BP moved ahead after their mergers in 1998 and
1999 respectively. In all cases, Shell lost its first position to become
either second or third.[25] In return on capital ExxonMobil remained
on top (Figure 6.5), with Shell in second position, and BP in third, as
had been the case most of the time in the past. BP Amoco data
have been merged from 1998, Exxon Mobil from 1999, and BP Arco
from 2000.

Shell in search of acquisitions

After the mega-mergers between BP and Amoco and between Exxon and Mobil, Shell had slipped from first to third position among the oil majors. As a consequence, it felt the need to show some initiatives of its own to regain its top position in the industry. The CMD studied long lists of smaller and larger companies which might be attractive acquisition targets, but very few options seemed attractive if oil prices remained low. The Shell view on oil prices at that time was that long-term, sustainable oil prices would reflect the marginal production cost of non-Opec supplies. And these costs were believed to be around $14 per barrel.[26] New projects were screened for real-terms earning power of 15 per cent at $14 per barrel and at least 8 per cent at $10. When in 2001 the business sectors Exploration & Production and Gas & Power put forward the suggestion to raise the project screening value by 2 dollars, the CMD decided to postpone the decision and continue with the long-term $14 per barrel oil price assumption.[27]

Acquisitions became even more urgent when Shell E&P began to realize its growth targets were unachievable through natural growth. In its presentations to analysts, Shell E&P had forecast 5 per cent growth since 1996 and in 2000 it had repeated this forecast for the 2000-5 period. The pace of winning new business, however, turned out to be slower than expected.[28] Between 2000 and 2002 Shell was involved in three high-profile bids to merge with or acquire companies in Oceania and America: the New Zealand oil and gas company Fletcher Challenge Energy (FCE), the Australian oil and gas company Woodside Petroleum, and the US independent oil and gas exploration company Barrett Resources Corporation.[29] The first bid was accepted and went ahead, but the two others did not. In particular the outcome of the merger bid for Woodside Petroleum was a disappointment for Shell.

Shell had owned a 33 per cent share in Woodside since 1964, and had increased that share to 40 per cent in 1985.[30] In 2000 Shell had come to the conclusion that it wanted to merge Shell Development Australia with Woodside Petroleum. The merger would create the foremost Australian exploration, production, gas and power company with a market capitalization of $9 billion, in which Shell would own a 60 per cent equity interest with majority representation on the board. However, the Woodside board rejected the proposal. They did not think the merger would add to Woodside's future earnings per share, nor would it create strategic diversity or increase the proportion of oil to gas in the company's asset base. Neither did the proposal include adequate premium for control of Woodside, in other words, the price on offer was considered too low. Shell had the feeling that the Woodside board was against the proposal because certain members wanted to retain their independence. Phil Watts did not accept no for an answer and started work on an outright cash takeover proposal. From meetings with the institutional shareholders in Woodside in Australia, Europe, and the US it became clear that the response from the institutions was mixed. Some gave cautious support, but others were totally opposed to such a transaction. All wanted to know what Shell's strategy for Woodside would be. Few of the institutions seemed to think 'national interest' or actions from the Western Australian government would be an issue. However, in this respect their assumptions were wrong. The Woodside bid failed to secure government approval.[31] The Federal Treasurer rejected the proposal because it was concerned that Shell, controlling the North West Shelf operations, would be able to determine the pace of future Liquefied Natural Gas (LNG) developments according to its own global agenda. This decision reflected the public concern about globalization and the power of multinationals, fuelled by

[17]

negative media coverage of the proposal.[32] Shell was accused of heavy-handedness, a 'miserable' offer and a complex bidding structure. Though Shell had the feeling that perhaps with hindsight it might have better explained the rationale behind the offer, it did not think this would have changed the outcome as in the end national feelings had upset their plans.[33]

'Sometimes it works. Sometimes it doesn't, but that shouldn't stop you from trying again when the right opportunity comes along', commented Group managing director Walter van de Vijver in 2001.[34] That right opportunity came along in the form of Enterprise Oil, which Shell acquired in 2002. Enterprise was one of the few remaining independent European oil companies. It provided Shell with additional portfolio to enhance Shell's core North Sea position but it also offered access to growth opportunities, including the Tahiti field in the Gulf of Mexico and a recently discovered gas field off Ireland. The assets in the North Sea offered scope for synergies through applying Shell practices and sharing overhead expenditures with Shell Expro.[35] The financial press was rather critical about the Enterprise Oil deal, which was considered a 'poor deal, badly explained'.[36] Analysts remarked that this deal would only pay off if the oil price rose. Fortunately for Shell the oil price did indeed go up.

Shell did not limit its acquisitions to the upstream business. In the downstream business joint ventures and acquisitions were seen as instruments to improve profitability. Often the one led to the other. This happened with the Texaco joint ventures. The two joint ventures with Texaco in the downstream in the US, Equilon and Motiva in which Saudi Refining Inc was the third party, gave disappointing results, in part caused by the complex governance structure. In early 2000 Shell Oil began to wonder whether it might not be better to buy out Texaco.[37] As mentioned above, in the merger mania of the late 1990s Shell examined the Texaco data with regard to a merger or takeover of Texaco by Shell, but Shell was only interested in taking over the Texaco part in its US downstream joint ventures.[38] When Texaco and Chevron decided to merge, Shell and the third partner in Motiva, Saudi Refining Inc, a subsidiary of Saudi Aramco, agreed to try and buy out Texaco from these two joint ventures. In September 2001 the Federal Trade Commission gave permission for the merger between Texaco and Chevron under certain conditions, including the condition that Texaco sold its US downstream joint ventures. Soon after, Shell, Saudi Aramco, and Texaco were able to strike a deal. The joint venture Equilon became Shell Oil Products US, while the joint venture with Saudi Refining Inc kept the name of Motiva.[39] Immediately after the deal was agreed, Shell started a massive re-branding programme, turning many of the US Texaco service stations into Shell-branded stations. At the same time Shell rationalized the network of service stations in the US, closing down the less profitable ones. Because refining reliability left much to be desired, it took some time for the benefits of the Texaco deal to materialize.

[18]

Shell further strengthened its position in the US market by acquiring the lubricants company Pennzoil Quaker State in 2002. Two years earlier Shell had been interested in acquiring Burmah Castrol, but Texaco was against the acquisition as far as the US was concerned. Instead Burmah Castrol was taken over by BP.[40] In reaction Shell decided to advertise its Helix brand more vigorously. Furthermore, it looked for opportunities to take over another lubricants company. This chance arose in 2002. The Pennzoil brand was particularly strong in the US, Canada, and Mexico. Following the acquisition of Pennzoil Quaker State, Shell decided to build a global lubricants business along the lines of Shell Marine Products, Shell Aviation, and Shell LPG.[41]

The third acquisition concerned DEA's downstream activities in Germany, which were acquired in 2002. The aim was to turn around the declining German retail business. After the unification of East and West Germany in 1990 the relative share of Shell in the German market had decreased. The acquisition strengthened Shell's position in the largest market for oil products in Europe. Shell's transaction team consisting of German-speaking expatriates and German staff succeeded in quickly and smoothly integrating the two companies. This acquisition gave Shell in Germany a market share in the German retail market of 20 per cent in 2003. This was substantial, but not quite as good as the 22 per cent share of BP, after its takeover of the German company Aral. Both acquisitions illustrated the trend for the super majors to pick up smaller pieces in specific markets contributing to the further consolidation in the oil industry.[42] However, of all these deals, none constituted the step change that would give Shell suddenly a different and stronger competitive position.

In 2002 Shell acquired the lubricants company Pennzoil Quaker State. The Pennzoil brand was particularly strong in the US.

Reserves recategorization

On 9 January 2004 Shell announced to the financial world that, 'following internal reviews, some proved hydrocarbon reserves will be recategorized'. Reading the announcement further it became clear that 20 per cent of proved reserves were to be removed from the stock of proved reserves. Over 90 per cent of these reserves belonged to the category of proved undeveloped reserves, while the remaining 10 per cent came from the proved developed category. Shell explained that these findings were the results of their own internal studies. To reassure shareholders the company underlined that this recategorization had no material effect on the financial statements for 2003 and previous years or on the production in the coming years, which was already expected to remain flat. The company anticipated that most of these reserves would be rebooked in the proved category over time as field developments matured.[43] What this message basically meant was that 20 per cent of the proved reserves had to be reclassified to be in line with the regulations of the US Securities and Exchange Commission (SEC).

The British press immediately reacted very negatively. 'Shell hit by move on reserves', wrote the *Financial Times* and it added that the surprise cut would 'put pressure on beleaguered chief.'[44] Phil Watts had become chairman of the CMD in 2001, after a career of thirty-two years at Shell in the upstream side of the business. In between his bachelor's degree in physics and master's degree in geophysics he had taught in a secondary school in Sierra Leone for two years, which gave him a taste for the expat's life and a lasting attachment to Africa. He worked in Indonesia, Norway, and Nigeria as well as Shell's central offices in London and The Hague. In 1997 he

Figure 6.6
Movement in Shell Transport shares,
April 2003-July 2004.

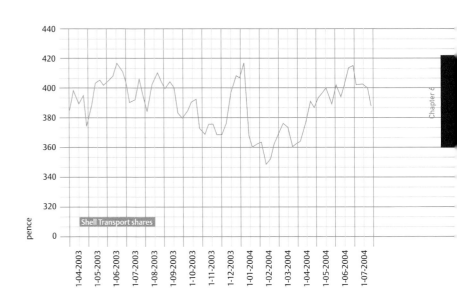

The merger of 1907 taken to its logical conclusion: the birth of Royal Dutch Shell plc

[19]

was appointed Group managing director with E&P as his area of responsibility, and shortly after becoming chairman of the CMD in 2001, Watts had been criticized by the press for announcing that Shell would not be able to attain its production growth of 5 per cent. The takeover of Enterprise Oil was considered a bad deal and the City found him a 'poor communicator'.[45] The recategorization also cast doubts on earlier figures of reserve replacement ratios and finding costs. The financial markets reacted strongly: the share prices of Royal Dutch and Shell Transport dropped more than 7 per cent, although they recovered within a few weeks. Figure 6.6 (see page 06|387) shows the movements of the shares of Shell Transport during the 2003-4 period.[46]

Why this strong reaction? Obviously 20 per cent was a huge amount to remove from the stock of proven reserves. But reserves were always supposed to be estimates. As knowledge of an oil field improved, the estimates of future oil production evolved accordingly. Therefore, it was normal practice in the industry to change reserves estimates. The Annual Reports of Shell included the following remark: 'Oil and gas reserves cannot be measured exactly since estimation of reserves involves subjective judgement and arbitrary determinations. Estimates remain subject to revision.'[47] To reduce uncertainty for investors, the US Securities and Exchange Commission had set rules to determine when reserves could be booked as proved in 1978. Companies listed on the New York stock exchange had to abide by these rules. However, the reporting of reserves was supplemental to, but not part of, the financial statements. Interestingly, it took some time before analysts used these figures to compare competitiveness between the oil majors. The journal *Petroleum Economist* did not use these figures in its industry comparisons until May 1984. Equally, Shell did not use reserves figures for internal comparisons with competitors until 1982. Though the reserves were one way of looking at future growth perspectives, they were not necessarily seen as the most important measure at that point in time, because oil companies

Shell hit by move on reserves *Financial Times, 11 January 2004*

[20]

were busy following diversification programmes. In the 1990s, however, most oil companies shelved their diversification programmes, focusing more and more on their core business of oil and gas production. Reserves were seen as more relevant in comparing the performance of oil companies.

At the same time shareholders became more vocal and more critical. They kept an eye on all figures, including reserves, but most of all on shareholder value and return on capital employed. When share prices collapsed in 2000, financial analysts were accused of having been too focused on short-term indicators during the 1990s. This encouraged them to look more precisely at reserves, because these were a way of measuring long-term growth prospects.

The shareholders at the Royal Dutch AGM of June 2004, the first after the announcement of reserves re-categorization, asked tough questions but gave the new Shell executives their backing.

stery ctices

THE LEX COLUMN
Shell shock

It seems the oil major with the reputation for conservatism was not so prudent after all. In its second public relations disaster within a month Shell has owned up to overbooking a staggering 20 per cent of proved oil and gas reserves.

Shell already had a problem relative to some of its peers. For the last three years it has failed to replenish organically all of its reserves. In 2002, excluding the acquisition of Enterprise Oil, the replacement ratio was only about 57 per cent.

Moreover, in recent years upward revisions have played a significant role in adding to proved reserves at Shell. For 1996-2002 some estimates put this contribution at 5.7bn barrels of oil equivalent, or 60 per cent of organic additions. In yesterday's "grand old Duke of York" move, that figure has been revised down by 3.9bn barrels.

Investors can take comfort from Shell's greater realism and a more consistent approach to booking reserves. This holds out some hope that the share price fall-out could be confined to yesterday's sharp drop.

But the re-categorisation throws the problem of reserve replacement into even starker relief, calling growth prospects into question. Management credibility, questioned by some, has been further dented. The revision, for reserves booked in 1996-2002, would be tough for any company head to explain. Sir Philip Watts, chairman, also has to contend with the fact he was in charge of exploration and production from 1997-2001.

Salmon

If you thought salmon farmers might benefit from the discovery of a first case of mad cow disease in the US, think again. Sales of farmed Atlantic salmon had been growing rapidly in North America. Nutreco, the biggest fish in the aquaculture pond, was predicting a further 16 per cent increase in US sales volumes this year. That projection will now have to be revised down, after the publication of research showing uncomfortably high levels of contaminants such as dioxins and PCBs. The study – published in Science, a serious magazine – suggests some Scottish farmed salmon is so contaminated that you would be crazy to eat it more than three times a year.

The fish-farming industry has, predictably, leapt to the barricades. Its apologists argue that the concentrations of contaminants fall well below levels viewed as acceptable

Shell
Share price relative to the FTSE World Oil & Gas sector

[chart: y-axis 75 to 105, x-axis 2001, 02, 03, 04]

Source: Thomson Datastream

by food safety agencies. They also argue the risks are, in any case, outweighed by the health benefits of eating fish rich in fatty acids. When a product tastes as grim as most farmed salmon, however, consumers are going to be willing to believe the worst.

The research may not stop customers from eating farmed salmon, but it will certainly limit the scope to raise prices from the rock-bottom levels that have helped fuel consumption. That means that any hopes for the emergence of Nutreco, or smaller fry such as Fjord Seafood, from their prolonged slump seem likely to be dashed.

UK retailing

Sir Ken Morrison must be wondering what all the fuss is about. While many UK retailers are still singing the Christmas blues, his grocery chain has swung into 2004 on a high. The British Retail Consortium this week painted a picture of tough December trading, with same-store retail sales down 0.2 per cent. In contrast, Morrison's like-for-like growth accelerated to 10.2 per cent in the six weeks to January 4. There will be a number of other Christmas winners, but leading grocers, including Tesco and Wal-Mart/Asda, are likely to set the pace.

That partly reflects the speed at which they are taking market share from industry laggards in their core food offering. The turbo charge, however, is from non-food. At Morrison, growth from music, DVDs and books far outstripped an already impressive food performance. Traditional high street retailers have much to fear. Tesco and Asda between them are probably increasing non-food sales by more than £1bn a year. That close to adding a new WH Smith chain – that company's high street sales to £1.2bn – to the scene every 12 months

In electronics, health and beauty, music and even clothing, the supermarkets are putting on enough weight to have a real impact. High street rivals will feel the pain both in their sales growth and margins. They should expect little respite. With leading supermarkets focused on value, the pressure will only increase during leaner times.

US economy

The US labour market has once again confounded the forecasting community's hopes. Following a string of strong economic data, payroll employment rose by just 1,000 in December, compared with the consensus forecast of 150,000. Worse still, the November payroll count was revised downwards, leaving the average monthly gain for fourth quarter at a sickly 50,000 compared with the monthly gain of 150,000 needed to keep pace with population growth. The silver cloud is that the unemployment rate dropped from 5.9 per cent to 5.7 per cent; the dark lining is that this reflects people continuing to drop out of the labour market.

Dec... manu... hopes... For t... empl... job g... anot... Dec... one... ref... rat... ma... se... in... b...

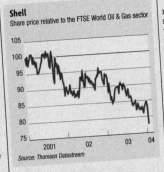

was said to have died
AP/El País

Elections last November swept away the political status quo in Catalonia. Unió Democrática and its coalition partner, Convergencia Democrática, were ousted after 23 years in power.

A new regional government – a coalition of Socialists, Greens and radical Catalan nationalists – has promised to do away with the nepotism of the previous regime.

Mr Cogul's trial was only one of the cases of political

The Daily Telegraph, page 27

Sept 22, 2002 Walter van de Vijver to committee of managing directors (copy to Judith Boynton)

'Given the external visibility of our issues... the market can only be 'fooled' if 1) credibility of the company is high, 2) medium and long-term portfolio refreshment is real and/or 3) positive trends can be shown on key indicators.'

Oct 22, 2002 Van de Vijver's response to Sir Philip Watts' defence of business plan targets, including reserves.

'I must admit that I become sick and tired about arguing about the hard facts and also cannot perform miracles given where we are today.'

Nov 15, 2002 Van de Vijver outlining business plan to exploration and production (EP) staff.

'We finalized our plan submission and could easily leave the impression that everything is fine... The reality is however that we would not have submitted this plan if we 1) were not trying to protect the Group reputation externally (promises made) and 2) could have been honest about past failures.'

Feb 28, 2003 Van de Vijver e-mails to Sir Philip, copy of e-mail to EP staff:

'We know we have been walking a fine line recently on external messages... Promising that future reserves additions are expected in 2003... whilst we know that [th]ere is some real uncertainty around this.'

[N]ov 9 2003 Van de Vijver to Sir Philip:

[I] am becoming sick and tired about lying about the [e]xtent of our reserves issues and the downward [r]evisions that need to be done because of far too [a]ggressive/optimistic bookings.'

[D]ec 2 2003 from memo entitled "Script for Walter [van [d]e Vijver] on the proved reserves position" prepared [b]y EP staff.

[N]ot to disclose it would constitute a violation of US [s]ecurities law and the multiple listing requirements. It [w]ould also increase any potential exposure to liability [w]ithin and outside the US.'

[V]an de Vijver e-mail to one of "script's" authors

[T]his is absolute dynamite, not at all what I expected [a]nd needs to be destroyed.'

[V]an de Vijver e-mail to colleague on timing and reason [f]or January's reserves cut:

[We] are heading towards a watershed reputational [d]isaster...'

March 22, 2004 Van de Vijver excuses his own conduct

Throughout this entire process, my attempts to brin[g]

LLER EVERY DAY

Telegraph

FINAL

‘This is absolute dynamite, not at all what I expected and needs to be destroyed’

Oil chief Walter van de Vijver's reaction to a damning report exposing the true state of the company's oil and gas reserves

BUSINESS Page 27

LING QUALITY DAILY

Tuesday, April 20, 2004   No. 46,2[ ]9   60p

However, since the SEC set up its rules in 1978 the industry had changed. As a consequence, within the industry there were grave doubts about the usefulness of the SEC rules.[48] Cambridge Energy Research Associates (CERA) argued that the interpretation and application of the SEC system was inconsistent with the way in which managements of oil and gas companies themselves made investment decisions. Some of the most important assets in the companies' portfolios for meeting future energy needs did not register in their mandatory disclosures. For instance, discoveries for which development plans had not yet been approved could not be included in the proved reserves, and oil sands did not count as oil reserves at all. CERA concluded that: 'The current system is being pushed de facto from its original principle of "reasonable certainty" to one of "absolute certainty"– which makes reporting so conservative as to distort the message by presenting only a portion of the overall picture and excluding any volumes that are the subject of even limited uncertainty.'[49] Whatever the limitations of the SEC regulations, companies that were listed on the New York stock exchange had to follow them. Shell had always been seen as a conservative company, and for that reason it came as a surprise to the investor community that it had not complied with the rules, and that its chairman had not even been present to explain this problem to the financial world. What made matters worse was that the dubious accounts of Enron, Worldcom, and Ahold, to name a few, had made the financial world very suspicious of company behaviour.

The reactions to the reserves recategorization of Shell differed between Britain and the Netherlands. The Dutch newspaper *NRC Handelsblad* commented that a 'greener Shell should not lead to a lack of commercial focus'.[50] To this Amnesty International reacted by saying that commercial focus and corporate social responsibility could go together very well, and were in fact, inextricably bound up with each other.[51] The Dutch newspaper *de Volkskrant* analysed Shell's problem as one of contrasting interests between those who cared for the environment and those who demanded shareholder value. In the past years Shell had paid a lot of attention to the environment and human rights, and as a consequence had focused less on raising shareholder value. According to *de Volkskrant* British shareholders in particular were seeking to redress what they saw as an imbalance.[52] The discussions in the British press were of a different nature. *The Observer* wrote that 'shareholders want to know where Shell's reserves went', and 'many investors want explanations; some want Watts head'.[53] *The Independent* cited a shareholder complaining about the dual structure of the enterprise: 'Shell should not be Anglo-Dutch, but you can't go back to 1907 and rewrite history'.[54] Some financial analysts were less worried: Deutsche Bank wrote that if the proved and the probable reserves were added up, Shell still had a good portfolio.[55]

On 3 February 2004 the Group Audit Committee hired the American law firm Davis Polk & Wardwell (or Davis Polk) to lead an investigation into the facts and circumstances of the recategorization. Two days later, the Group gave its scheduled presentation of the financial results. Phil Watts, chairman of the CMD, Walter van de Vijver, CEO of E&P, and Judy Boynton, CFO, were all present in London to answer the probing questions of the journalists. Trying to stem the flood of negative news, Watts underlined the handsome profits Shell had made over 2003 and apologized for not presenting the reserves downgrade himself. He explained that extra controls had been put in place to make sure this would not happen again. Walter van de Vijver explained that the hydrocarbons were still there, and in due time most of them would return to the category of proved reserves. He explained that proved reserves were all about the reasonable certainty that the relevant quantities of oil were recoverable in future years from known reservoirs under existing economic and operating conditions. This reasonable certainty depended not only on the technical engineering and geological information around the resource base, but also on the ability to deliver in time and have the associated commitment and understanding about these resources. Of the 3.9 billion barrels oil equivalent that had been recategorized, 2.3 billion related to current producing areas and some 1.2 billion to new projects. As an illustration of problems in mature producing fields he discussed Oman and Nigeria. In Oman the sudden production declines made management realize that more water flooding and enhanced oil recovery techniques had to be put in place to recover more of the remaining oil. The onshore oil production in Nigeria, where Shell had more than 300 fields, faced serious delays because of the need to build an associated gas infrastructure to discontinue gas flaring. New projects associated with the rebooking included Ormen Lange in Norway, Kashagan in Kazakhstan and Gorgon in Australia. Of those three, the Gorgon field really stood out, because Shell was not the operator and none of the partners had booked the reserves as proved. There was no doubt that this was a hugely attractive resource. The decision in 1997 to book the reserves reflected discussions on gas sales, and the expected development timetable. However, the developments did not work out as planned, because the Asian crisis negatively impacted the demand for LNG. Apparently, the reserves had not been revised back into the probable category when the sales contract did not materialize. When questioned over this field, Watts had to admit to some further embarrassing circumstances. In 1994 Gorgon was booked as a probable reserve. Then in 1997 the

resource was moved from the probable into the proved category and this change appeared in the Group filing as a revision rather than as a proper new extension discovery. This explanation was all the more embarrassing, as Watts had become head of E&P in 1997 and headed this business until he became chairman of the CMD in 2001 and Van de Vijver took over as head of E&P. The assembled press asked many questions about the reserves, and wanted to know whether Phil Watts was going to step down, and whether the Group was going to review its dual-listed structure.[56]

On 3 March the supervisory board of Royal Dutch and the non-executive members of the board of Shell Transport acted on the first findings of Davis Polk. They asked the two most senior men responsible for Exploration & Production, Phil Watts and Walter van de Vijver, to resign because the boards had lost confidence in them. At the same time Jeroen van der Veer was nominated as the new chairman of the CMD. About six weeks later, the Chief Financial Officer, Judy Boynton, was asked to step aside as CFO, but invited to remain in Group service.[57] Never before in the history of the enterprise had one of its senior executives been asked to resign so publicly. Though sacking senior executives had become fairly common in business during the 1990s, even in Europe, it was still a novel experience for Royal Dutch and Shell Transport. Losing three senior executives within six weeks made this occasion even more dramatic.

As lawsuits began to pile up, a partly renewed CMD, consisting of chairman Jeroen van der Veer, Malcolm Brinded, CEO Exploration and Production, Rob Routs, CEO Oil Products and Chemicals, Linda Cook, CEO Gas and Power, and Peter Voser, CFO, worked hard to deal with the reserves issue and keep the business focused. In the meantime the inspection of all the proved reserves continued, and more reserves had to be rebooked, until 25 per cent

The five members of the last CMD, also the executive members of the first Royal Dutch Shell board, showed some of the diversity in staffing that Shell found important. Jeroen van der Veer and Rob Routs were Dutch, Linda Cook was an American and a woman, Malcolm Brinded was British and Peter Voser was Swiss.

Jeroen van der Veer, becoming chairman of the CMD in a period of crisis, sent out a clear message of his priorities. He regained the confidence of the financial community by unifying the two parent companies. After the unification he became the first CEO of Royal Dutch Shell plc.

Rob Routs, CEO Oil products and Chemicals.

of the originally reported proved reserves had been recategorized. Figure 6.7 highlights the effect of the recategorization on the position of Shell in relation to ExxonMobil and BP. The figures for Shell have been restated from 2000 onwards.[58]

To tackle the reserves issue, Shell hired external reserves experts to get to the bottom of the problem. It also improved the internal systems and controls to prevent similar events happening again, and it cooperated fully with the investigations of the financial watchdogs, including the United Kingdom Financial Services Authority (FSA) and the United States Securities and Exchange Commission (SEC). In August 2004 Shell announced that it had settled 'without admitting or denying the findings and conclusion in the FSA's Final Notice and the SEC's Cease and Desist Order'. The company agreed to pay penalties of £17 million in the FSA settlement and $120 million in the SEC settlements and to spend an additional $5 million for the development and implementation of a comprehensive internal compliance programme.[59] The US Department of Justice reported on 30 June 2005 that it had concluded its investigation of the recategorizations of Shell's proved oil and gas reserves and would not take any further action

against Shell.[60] The FSA in the UK announced in November 2005 that it had completed its inquiries into the roles of a number of Shell staff and that the FSA would be taking no further action. Phil Watts saw this decision as a vindication of his position that he had acted properly and in good faith.[61] In 2006 the SEC also decided to take no further action against Phil Watts, Walter van de Vijver or Judy Boynton.[62] Earlier that year AFM (Autoriteit Financiële Markten) and Euronext concluded that there were no grounds to continue their investigations.[63] The settlements with the FSA and SEC were important steps for Shell in moving forward after the upheaval caused by the reserves recategorization. Writing in 2006, it was still too early fully to judge the events leading up to the reserves recategorization. Because Shell was still involved in a number of lawsuits, it was not possible for the author to get access to the relevant documents and interview the people involved regarding the matter. The rest of this chapter will discuss the developments in the main business sectors, before turning to the cultural and structural changes.

Linda Cook, CEO Gas and Power.

Malcolm Brinded, CEO Exploration and Production.

Peter Voser, Chief Financial Officer.

More Upstream   By nominating the vice-chairman of the CMD, Jeroen van der Veer, as the next chairman, the boards chose an internal candidate with long experience in the company. Like most of his predecessors, Van der Veer had spent his whole career at Shell, starting in 1971. But unlike his two immediate predecessors, Moody-Stuart and Watts, he was not an upstream man but had moved through the ranks via manufacturing and marketing, including posts at the refineries in Pernis and Curaçao. In 1992 he became a managing director of Shell Nederland, followed in 1996 by the position of president and CEO of Shell Chemical Company in the US. In 1997 he became Group managing director and three years later president of Royal Dutch and vice-chairman of the CMD. When asked what he considered to be the essence of leadership, he underlined that first of all a leader had to listen carefully to what people thought about the company and its weaknesses, and what motivated them. Secondly he had to give a clear message of where the company should be heading. That message should be honest, to the point, and consistent.[64]

Becoming chairman of the CMD in a time of crisis, Jeroen van der Veer indeed sent out a clear message of what his priorities were going to be. First he wanted to get over the reserves issue, second he wanted the business to continue, keeping an eye on the ball as

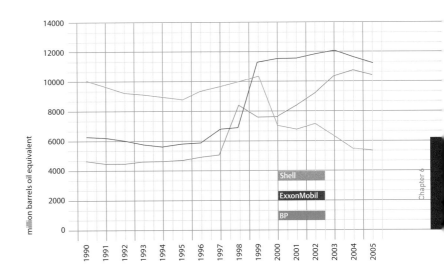

Figure 6.7
Proved oil and gas reserves of Shell, ExxonMobil, and BP, 1990-2005.

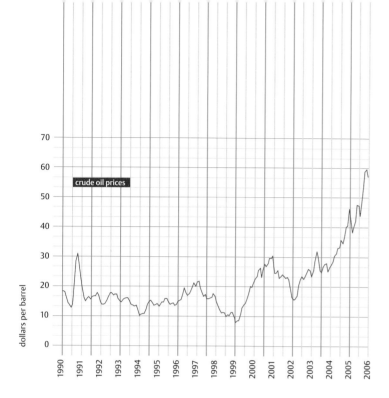

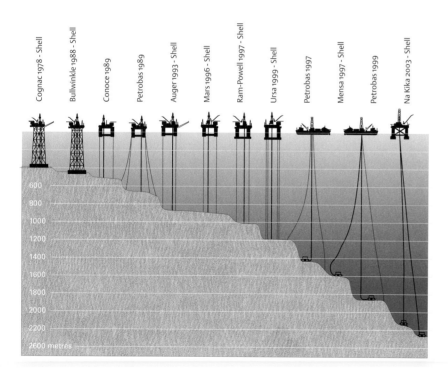

Figure 6.8
Monthly crude oil prices, 1990-2005.

Figure 6.9
Production in ever deeper water.

well as looking for new opportunities. His third priority was the company culture and structure.[65] In his speech to staff during the Business Week in May 2004 in Houston he summarized his priorities in two slogans: 'more upstream and profitable downstream', and 'Enterprise First'.[66]

The strategy of 'more upstream', as Jeroen van der Veer formulated it succinctly, was music to the ears of the E&P staff, all the more as it was accompanied by higher budgets for their business sector. During the 1990s cost cutting had been the message. The nadir for E&P (at least before the reserves crisis) was the year 1998, when the oil price dropped below $10 per barrel. While Shell's top management had reacted in a fairly restrained manner during the oil price collapse of 1986, cutting down on some projects but by and large staying on course, in 1999 it stepped on the brakes heavily. E&P ranked its portfolio of assets globally, and all assets that were not expected to deliver a real-term earning power of 15 per cent at $14 per barrel or 8 per cent at $10, were up for divestment. In 1999 Shell reduced its total E&P workforce worldwide by 7 per cent. About 17 per cent of the expatriates were offered 'VSP', voluntary severance packages. These packages were increasingly involuntary, because resignation rates among international staff continued to be very low.[67] After 2000, however, the oil prices began to increase as a consequence of growing demand in China and the US, creating new opportunities. Figure 6.8 shows the steep rise in oil prices from less than $10 per barrel in 1999 to $60 per barrel in 2005.[68]

Shell remained active in its traditional areas. The government of Oman agreed to extend the concession agreement of Petroleum Development Oman till 2044. In Brunei Shell made a new discovery in the Seria North flank, even after having worked in the Seria field since 1929. In the North Sea the Goldeneye gas field was brought into production in 2004. The Goldeneye field had been discovered

in 1996, but at that time it was considered only marginally economical, because of its long distance from the existing infrastructure. Not until Shell designed an innovative solution could production be considered. The solution consisted of transferring gas and condensate at reservoir pressure directly from an unmanned platform to the onshore processing facilities at St. Fergus in Scotland.[69]

In Shell's core activity of deepwater exploration and production, more achievements were possible. In the Gulf of Mexico the Group built its fifth successful tension leg platform for production from the Brutus field, and a floating hub to produce from the NaKika field. Fixed structures made way for floating platforms, which made it possible to produce in water depths of more than two kilometres. In developing deepwater production Petrobras was a very active competitor, as Figure 6.9 makes clear.

Offshore production continued to reach deeper waters, too deep for steel jackets or concrete structures. The TLP platforms allowed for production at even deeper levels. Another option was the use of floating structures, which also had the advantage that they could be moved when the oil and gas production came to an end. For the first deepwater project in the Bonga field, Nigeria Shell used a floating production, storage and offloading vessel, seen here under construction.

28

With the rise of national oil companies in resource-rich countries, Shell sought its competitive advantage in managing large and complex projects, the so-called elephant projects. One of those was the integrated oil and gas project Sakhalin II, which included the construction of Russia's first LNG plant. In the summer of 2006 the Lunskoye-A topside was installed. The topside was not lifted on the concrete columns by a huge crane, as was the usual procedure, but the ship with the topside steered between the columns of the platform and after that the topside was lowered onto the columns, after which the ship withdrew from underneath the topside and sailed away.

29

Shell's second deepwater play, the Bonga field, was developed off the coast of Nigeria – its first such project there. For this, Shell used one of the largest oil and gas production facilities in the world, which, even more remarkably, was put on board a vessel.

A significant discovery south-west of the Bonga field in Nigeria made this production area even more important. Shell's third deepwater play took place in the Malampaya gas field off the coast of the Philippines. The gas had to be extracted from a depth of 3,000 metres below in water depths of 850 metres. Again, technology played an important role in accessing new gas and oil fields economically.[70]

During the period of low oil prices in the 1990s, Shell had tried to access the major resource-holding countries, preferably those with low cost oil. A number of initiatives had been taken, but developments were disappointingly slow. However, in the twenty-first century earlier efforts began to pay off. In Russia Shell's major investment consisted of its participation in the consortium Sakhalin II, an oil and major gas project. In 2000 Shell took over operatorship from Marathon Oil. As often with projects in new challenging regions, there were delays. For instance, it was necessary to reroute the offshore pipeline to protect the endangered western grey whales. The costs of building the platforms in this extreme climate turned out to be much higher than budgeted. However, steady progress was made. In 2006 Shell and its partners in Sakhalin Energy negotiated with the Russian state company Gazprom about the latter's entry into the partnership. In Siberia Shell developed the Salym oil fields in a joint venture with a Russian partner. Production from Upper Salym field started in 2003, and from the larger West Salym in 2004. In Kazakhstan Shell participated in the North Caspian Sea consortium to explore the Kashagan field, operated by Agip. Shell took a 16.7 per cent interest in 1997. Oil was

discovered in 2000. The field was declared commercial in 2002 and the final investment decision was taken in 2004. Oil production was expected at the end of the decade. This example illustrates the long lead times in the oil industry and why it is not easy to increase oil production instantly in response to higher demand.

Shell's efforts to enter Middle Eastern countries met with some success. In 2003 the company finalized an agreement with Qatar to build a Gas to Liquids plant (see Gas and Power, page 407). Particularly exciting for Shell was the chance to enter Saudi Arabia. In 2003 Shell signed an agreement in Saudi Arabia to explore for natural gas in the South Rub Al Khali (Empty Quarter). In 2005 the Nowrooz/Soroosh project in Iran came on stream. Another milestone was the agreement signed with Libya, in North Africa, to renew and develop LNG facilities and explore for gas.[71]

With the understanding that the major oil and gas fields, the 'easy oil', had long ago been discovered the oil majors began to show renewed interest in unconventional oil resources such as tar sands, leading to the production of synthetic oil. During the period of high oil prices in the 1970s, tar sands had seen a first rush of developments, but the cost of oil production was still considered too high in comparison with the low oil prices of that period. However, by the end of the 1990s production costs had declined through technical innovations. Even before the oil price started to rise, Shell showed a renewed interest in the tar sands.

The merger of 1907 taken to its logical conclusion: the birth of Royal Dutch Shell plc

The Athabasca Oil Sands Project in Canada, a joint venture project which Shell operated, consisted of three stages. First oil sands had to be excavated in surface mining and transported to an separation plant. Here the sands were mixed with warm water to separate the bitumen (heavy oil) from the sand. The heavy bituminous materials were then sent down a corridor pipeline to the site of the Scotford refinery, where Shell built a very large-scale upgrader to transform the feedstock to a synthetic crude oil. In 2001 there were cost overruns, as happened with the tar sands project of its competitor Suncor. However, the project would still be attractive at an oil price of $20 per barrel.[72] The first synthetic oil was produced in 2003. The initial project was built to produce 155,000 barrels of bitumen per day for the next thirty years. In response to the high oil price Shell decided in 2005 to increase production capacity.

The higher investments in upstream went hand in hand with a new organizational structure, which would enable Shell to take better advantage of its large size. By removing the regional structure during the mid-1990s, some of the former coherence in E&P was lost. Moreover, in filling positions Shell had introduced a system of 'open resourcing'. All jobs were placed on the internal Shell web and employees could apply according to their own preferences. This system had ended the former coordination through the system of 'godfathers'. More generally, in the 1990s the trend had been towards fragmentation and lowering responsibilities in the organization: this led to some successes locally, but also to developments that were ill-aligned. According to Malcolm Brinded, local decision-making encouraged a reduction in risk-taking, because the risk was measured against the local budget, not the international budget of Shell. As a consequence, the various operating companies and business units did not profit sufficiently from the combined strengths of Shell.[73] To counter these negative effects of fragmentation, E&P introduced a new global business operating model from 1 January 2004. Walter van de Vijver explained the rationale: 'There is an enormous opportunity for standardising and simplifying our business processes, to increase our learning and act more quickly. We are far too fragmented and lack a sense of direction.'[74] At the same time the Human Resources department introduced the concept of a 'Global Staff Pool' and of 'Managed Open Resourcing'. Though staff could still apply for jobs via the Shell web, top management took a more active role in the allocation of international staff to ensure that they would develop the skills and capabilities needed in the organization and that the various operations would be staffed optimally with people having the right kind of skills and competencies.[75]

In addition, the global model made it easier to tackle huge, complicated and expensive projects, the kinds of multi-billion dollar projects that only large integrated oil companies could undertake. These large projects often required collaboration within Shell between its main business sectors. In 2005 Shell had three 'elephant' projects and the ambition was to have ten such projects in 2015.[76] Initiating cross-business 'elephant' projects signified another way in which Shell could benefit from its size.

Map of the province Alberta in Canada. Improved technology and rising oil prices made the tar sands of Canada into hot spots for oil companies. Shell Canada stepped up its investment in the Athabasca Oil Sands Project in Alberta, Canada, of which it was operator and joint venture partner.

▲ Shell oil projects
■ Shell gas projects

[32]   [31]

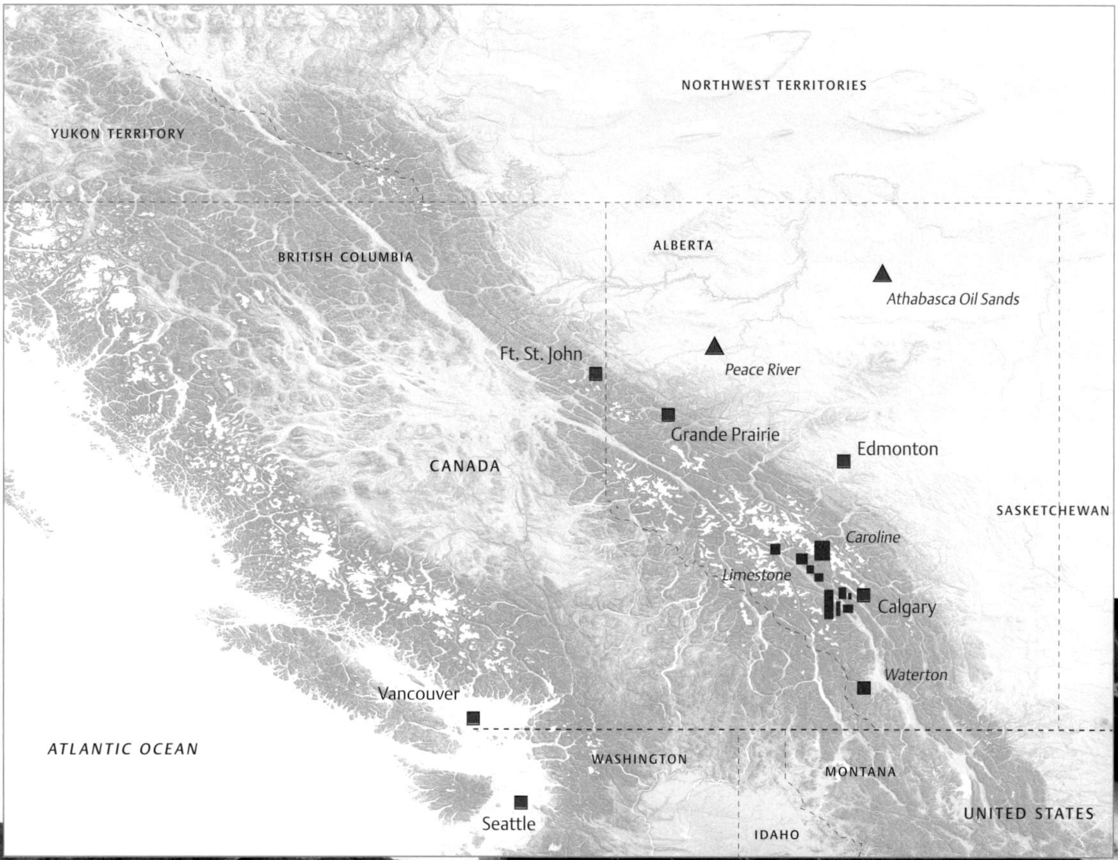

NORTHWEST TERRITORIES

YUKON TERRITORY

BRITISH COLUMBIA

ALBERTA

▲ Athabasca Oil Sands

Ft. St. John

▲ Peace River

Grande Prairie

Edmonton

CANADA

SASKETCHEWAN

Caroline

Limestone

Calgary

Vancouver

Waterton

ATLANTIC OCEAN

WASHINGTON

MONTANA

Seattle

IDAHO

UNITED STATES

Shell played a leading role in the development of LNG plants and ships, and in the beginning of the twenty-first century it remained committed to this clean energy source. Apart from building LNG plants it also participated in a number of regasification projects, such as the LNG terminal in Altamira, Mexico, here seen under construction in 2004. Two years later the first LNG cargo arrived and commercial operations began.

[34]

Gas and Power   The strategy of 'more upstream' implied more gas as well as more oil production, and was therefore also good news for Shell's business sector Gas and Power. Compared to oil gas had two advantages. It was a cleaner energy source, and therefore better for the environment. Also, the world's gas reserves were expected to last longer than oil reserves. However, gas had the disadvantage that it was more difficult to transport than oil, making gas markets country-specific or regional. Gas that was found far away from any infrastructure, so-called stranded gas, could only be brought to value if specific schemes were developed. Pipelines presented some help in covering distances from source to market, but LNG technology, first developed in the early 1960s, offered a more flexible solution to the transport problem. However, it was an expensive solution. Shell had played a leading role in the development of LNG plants and ships. It had also succeeded in substantially lowering the cost of the LNG infrastructure.[77] In the early 2000s Shell continued to grow its LNG business. It extended its LNG plants in Nigeria, Malaysia, and Australia, while setting up new plants in Sakhalin (Russia), Iran, and Qatar. Assessing its competitive position in 2003, Shell concluded that it was still a clear leader in LNG thanks to cost leadership, access to gas reserves, and access to attractive markets. About half of the volume committed under signed sales purchase agreements in 2002 was captured by projects in which Shell had an interest. However, the competitors had stepped up their commitment to LNG and were busy closing the gap.[78]

In the 1970s Japan had been the main country interested in importing LNG. Gradually this interest spread to other countries in Asia, such as Korea and Taiwan. In Europe LNG made its entrance in 1965 with Algerian gas exports to Britain and France. During the 1970s and 1980s LNG supplies grew steadily. But the market for LNG really became global when China, India, and the United States became importers of natural gas. LNG technology made globalization of gas markets possible. Shell became involved in the building of LNG import terminals in North America and India. With the development of Sakhalin II, for the first time Russian gas would be sold to North American consumers. In contrast to the oil market, the gas market was still organized on the basis of long-term contracts. The 'spot market' for gas may arrive if many more LNG projects come on stream, but that stage had not been reached in 2005 to any major extent.

Detail of the SMDS, later renamed Gas to Liquids, plant at Bintulu, Malaysia. In a world that was increasingly concerned about the future availability of oil products, including gasoline, this technology offered the reassuring possibility of making oil products from gas.

Bintulu, Malaysia, by night.

In 2004 Shell in the person of Malcolm Brinded (right) and Qatar Petroleum in the person of Abdullah Bin Hamad Al-Attiyah, Minister of Energy and Industry in Qatar, signed an agreement to develop the offshore natural gas from Qatar's North field and construct the world's largest integrated gas to liquids complex in Ras Laffan Industrial City.

LNG was not the only way of making money out of natural gas. Another interesting option was turning gas into ultra clean fuel. As discussed in chapter 3, Shell set up a pilot plant at Bintulu in Malaysia using its Shell Middle Distillate Synthesis process, later renamed as Gas to Liquids (GTL), for making oil out of gas.[79] The pilot plant at Bintulu enabled Shell to learn from its experiences and achieve cost savings and efficiency improvements for the next generation of Gas to Liquids plants. During the period of low prices it was not advantageous to build more GTL plants. However, when oil prices went up again after 1999 the prospects for turning natural gas into oil products increased dramatically. Shell stepped up its research efforts in this field in order to increase the scale of production, lower costs and improve efficiency. Thus it wanted to

continue its co-leadership position in GTL technology, which it enjoyed with the South African company Sasol as its main competitor. It also devoted research time and money to search for ways of using the unique characteristics of the synthetic products for enhancing its premium oil products. Shell looked for partners in the development of GTL projects among the Middle East countries with an abundance of low-cost gas resources and no infrastructure in place as yet to develop them. One of the countries that showed a clear interest was Qatar.[80] In 2004 Shell and Qatar Petroleum signed an agreement to develop the Pearl GTL project, combining upstream gas development with the building of a GTL plant that would ultimately produce 140,000 barrels per day of GTL products, from two trains each producing 70,000 barrels per day.[81]

[36]

[37]

Compared to the Bintulu pilot plant, which produced 15,000 barrels per day, this was a huge step forward. In developing the GTL business all three main business sectors of Shell were involved. E&P had the task of finding the gas and producing it, Gas and Power operated the plants in which gas was turned into ultra-clean oil products and Oil Products used these products to enhance its range of premium fuels.

Related to the GTL technology was the Coal to Liquids technology, already discussed in chapter 2. Though Shell ended its involvement with the coal sector in 2000, it did not withdraw from its coal gasification technology. The commercial application of this technology in Buggenum, the Netherlands, had proved the technical reliability of the process. In 2003 Shell decided to try to recover some of the large R&D spending in the 1970s and 1980s, through licensing and selected investment in this technology. This strategy resulted in a joint venture with the Chinese company Sinopec to set up a plant to convert coal to synthetic gas (syngas) with the use of Shell's coal gasification technology. The next step could be to turn the syngas into oil products with the GTL technology. Though this whole process was still too expensive to be competitive with oil products from crude oil, both China and the USA showed interest in this technology for strategic reasons. In

particular for China, with its large coal reserves, coal gasification offered interesting prospects for covering its energy needs. However, the use of coal also had the potential disadvantage of releasing large amounts of CO_2, which could have a negative impact on the environment. Therefore Shell at the same time developed schemes for capturing the CO_2 for instance by re-injecting it underground or using it in the building industry.[82]

While developing new gas activities in China, Shell found itself under increasing pressure in its existing markets in Europe. In the 1990s the EU had decided to liberalize the energy markets in order to give new competitors a chance of entering these markets. In the European Gas Directive, accepted by the European Council in 1997, member states were required to reorganize their national gas sector in such a way that consumers would have a choice between different suppliers.[83] Third-party access to pipelines and storage was considered the key to a competitive gas market. Member states had the choice between negotiated or regulated third-party access. To determine its strategy with regard to north-west European gas, Shell used the two scenarios developed by Cambridge Energy Research Associates. In the 'Patchwork Europe' scenario the liberalization would be slow and patchy, while in the 'Blue Gold' scenario third-party access would be widespread with low tariffs based on depreciated asset value. Anticipating losses under both scenarios, Shell formulated three possible responses: 'Do anyway', 'Defensive-Hold the Fort', and 'Downstream Leadership'. As long it was unclear what the European governments would really do, Shell decided to follow the strategy of 'have your cake and eat it'. On the one hand it defended its existing position, stressing price over volume on the continent; on the other hand it set up Shell Energy to grow in gas and power in liberalized markets and it divested midstream assets when returns were being

Chapter 6

The merger of 1907 taken to its logical conclusion: the birth of Royal Dutch Shell plc

regulated. It took good care not to undermine Shell's business value in markets that had not been changed as yet.[84] The pressure for liberalization of the European gas markets would make the link between upstream and downstream gas in each country weaker, but offered Shell some interesting opportunities to seek closer cooperation between its European national gas companies.[85]

When energy prices rose and access to energy became an issue again, national governments showed less willingness to liberalize the energy markets. This became clear in the Dutch situation. The Dutch government and Shell, together with Esso (Exxon), had lengthy negotiations about the new gas structure for the Netherlands, which involved restructuring Gasunie. Initially the Dutch government intended to take possession of the gas infrastructure, while Shell and Esso would end their collaboration and become competing users of the gas network. However, during the negotiations their views evolved. The Dutch government indeed took over the share of Shell and Esso in the gas infrastructure, becoming the sole owner of Gasunie Transport. The trading and supply of gas were brought together in a new company, Gasunie Trade & Supply, in which Shell and Esso each owned 25 per cent, but in which the Dutch government kept its 50 per cent share, as had been the case in the old Gasunie.[86] The result was that the involvement of the Dutch government in the national gas business became larger, not smaller.

Though it was a producer of oil and gas, Shell had not for most of its history been involved in the generation of power. This situation changed in 1997, when Shell acquired 50 per cent ownership of InterGen, a joint venture with Bechtel Enterprises. At the same time Shell renamed its Gas and Coal business sector as Gas and Power, with the idea that in developing countries it would be able to sell stranded gas to a power structure which the Group

would help to build. However, in 2000 the CMD concluded that none of the InterGen power stations actually used Shell equity gas.[87] In the late 1990s Shell Oil took several other initiatives to increase its presence in the downstream gas business, including the transportation, processing, and marketing of gas to profit from the liberalization of gas and electricity markets. The costly takeover of Tejas Gas Company, a US company owning and operating interstate gas pipelines, has already been mentioned. After divesting parts of Tejas Gas Shell continued operating the remaining parts under the name Coral Energy.

Coral experimented with the innovative device of 'tolling transactions'. A tolling deal was a contract under the terms of which the toller supplied the gas, sold the electricity and paid a fee to the tollee who invested, constructed, and operated the power plant. This construction formed part of a strategy to keep the assets of a company low, so that the return on capital invested could seem higher. According to the US accounting rules, a tolling deal did not have to appear on the balance sheet. According to Dutch accounting rules, however, the deals were treated as capital leases that had to be included in the accounts. This Dutch rule made the whole construction far less attractive. For that reason the CMD discouraged Coral from proceeding in this direction.[88] After the collapse of Enron in 2001 the power market in the US deteriorated. Together Shell and Bechtel decided to gradually divest themselves of InterGen, and the last assets were sold in 2005. This divestment did not mean that Shell entirely gave up its ambition to be involved in power stations, but for future projects it wanted to have good local partners in place and a clear link to Shell gas deliveries.[89]

Profitable Downstream: From Oil Products to Downstream One

In contrast to Exploration & Production and Gas & Power, the mission for the downstream oil business was not necessarily to show growth. Its first priority was to become profitable. One might expect this mission to have been an uphill struggle. After all, in the earlier period of high oil prices in the mid-1970s to the mid-1980s it had been difficult for the downstream business to show good results. Therefore, what initiatives did Shell take to bring about profits for the downstream business?

During the 1990s, with low oil prices and fragmentation in the industry, the oil majors faced tough competition from newcomers and supermarkets, because oil was in abundant supply. It seemed that for consumers gasoline had become a commodity, to be bought as cheaply as possible at the most convenient location. Consumers no longer seemed to appreciate the difference between the various kinds of gasoline on offer. Therefore, in 1996 Shell had launched a major effort to raise the stakes in non-fuel retailing, making better use of its service stations, as discussed in Chapter 3. Despite considerable investments, the results were rather mixed, with more success in less mature markets, where the general level of retailing was lower, than in rich countries. To increase scale and acquire new skills in non-fuel retailing, Shell sought collaboration with large retailers with well-known brands in a number of countries. For instance, in the Netherlands Shell teamed up with Albert Heijn. By way of a pilot, some sixty Shell shops were rebranded and operated by Albert Heijn. However, the alliance was quickly dissolved with the Shell shops returning to the Shell Select brand, because profits did not meet the expectations of either party. More promising was the collaboration with Sainsbury in the UK. An instant hit was the alliance with the major Australian retail group Coles Myer. In 2003 Coles Myer took over the

[38]

In non-fuel retailing Shell sometimes sought collaboration with large retailers with well-known brand names, such as Sainsbury in the UK, and at this station the fuel of choice was: Optimax.

management of all Shell's retail sites in the Australian state of Victoria, while Shell contained site control and ownership, together with the Shell brand. The alliance brought Shell rising fuel volumes against reduced costs, because it could concentrate on fuel supply and management of the network.[90]

While the non-fuel retailing tried to make more money by extending the product range at service stations, at the other end of the spectrum efforts were made to reduce costs by limiting the services available and in response to the challenges of low-cost competitors Shell introduced 'Shell Express' – unmanned retail stations with somewhat lower prices than its manned stations and with main-grade fuels only. In 2003 the first series of Shell Express

For customers who were interested in high performance from their cars, Shell developed V-Power. Naturally V-Power was used by Ferrari at the Grand Prix of 2006.

[39]

service stations was introduced in Europe, and these performed better than expected.[91] Apparently, for consumers the fuels themselves still remained the core business.

'The days are long gone when the fuels market was a static one where some people thought that the only way to add value was to sell more sandwiches!' concluded Rob Routs, Shell's CEO Downstream in 2005.[92] When Shell's efforts to sell more additional products at the service stations met with a mixed response from consumers, the Group reconsidered its strategy and decided to refocus instead on its core business, the fuels themselves, and once again to launch a programme of differentiated fuels. This implied the need for persuasive and accurate scientific information to bring back the public perception that gasoline was not one single product but could have different characteristics, and that consumers should make a considered selection according to their own needs and desires. Of course, this also implied that they were expected to pay somewhat more for Shell's new special products, the 'Choice Fuels'. For these, not only different additives were used, as was traditionally the case with premium gasoline, but the fuels

themselves differed, for instance with the amount of ultra-clean fuels included. In developing the Choice programme, Shell used marketing techniques based on insight into the wishes of consumers and the principles of brand management in the same way that consumer product marketers in companies such as Unilever and Proctor & Gamble did. In addition, Shell backed up these principles with its own expertise in fuel formulation and supply-chain management; and together these combined to create a return to Shell's two traditional areas of excellence, namely marketing and technical development.[93]

Shell developed a number of new and different fuels, alongside the competitively priced main grade fuels for the majority of customers. V-Power was designed for motorists who wanted high performance from their cars, and the Group's claims about this product were underlined by its relationship with Ferrari as technical partner and its sponsorship of Ferrari in racing. Optimax was an especially responsive fuel, enabling any car to start better, accelerate faster, and gain more mileage per litre. After being piloted in Singapore, the successful launch of Optimax in

Britain earned Shell UK the prestigious 'New Brand of the Year' industry award in 2003. Defenda had special characteristics that protected the engine, and these were expected to be particularly appreciated in developing countries, where drivers tended to keep their cars much longer than in rich countries. Last but not least, for the environmentally conscious consumers, Shell introduced Pura, a gasoline with lower carbon emissions.[94] By 2003 the Choice fuels had been introduced in fifty markets and a successful start was made to launch V-Power in the US.

The next step was to extend the Choice formula to diesel, which was particularly interesting for the European markets. In marketing this did not require too much effort, because it could latch onto the earlier marketing successes: for instance the slogan 'Shell V-Power, now available in diesel' was very effective in selling this new diesel.[95] Logistically, however, it required a major effort, because most service stations were not set up to offer consumers a choice in diesel. Meanwhile, Group scientists maintained their research on lowering sulphur levels in all Shell gasolines, and the options for using biofuels continued to be examined. Shell Brazil had a long tradition of using ethanol from cane sugar, and in 2004 Shell Global Biofuels explored the possibilities of making ethanol from cellulose produced from straw, the advantage of this technique being that it used a waste product rather than food.[96]

The strategy of creating a profitable downstream business meant the Group had to decide where it wished to have a presence and where it wished to withdraw. On the one hand it withdrew from small markets that had not been sufficiently profitable over the years, or markets where it had a small market share. For instance, in Europe Shell sold its network of service stations in Portugal and Spain, and in Latin America it withdrew from Peru, Ecuador, Uruguay, Paraguay, and from retail stations in Colombia

and Venezuela. On the other hand, it expanded in markets with growth perspectives, and was very eager to have a renewed presence in both India and China. In 1976, when the oil and gas distribution industry in India was nationalized, Burmah-Shell and the pecten logo had left the country. Twenty-eight years passed before Shell fuel retailing returned to India with the opening in November 2004 of the first Shell station in Bangalore. As retail manager Shairan Huzani Husain discovered, the sight of the once-familiar pecten was an emotional experience for some people. One man stared at the pecten for a long time and then told the manager how he knew this brand from his youth: 'When I was young it was everywhere and then one day it just disappeared.'[97] China too signified an important comeback, where the oil majors entered the retail market through joint ventures. Shell formed a joint venture with the Chinese company Sinopec to develop the retail business in Jiangsu province, which started operations in 2002. BP set up a pilot retail joint venture with China National Petroleum Company in Guangdong, while Exxon opted for a refinery project in Fujian province, together with Aramco and Sinopec.[98]

During the 1970s and early 1980s high oil prices had brought lower margins in the downstream business, and therefore lower profitability. At the start of the twenty-first century, however, high oil prices did not automatically mean lower profitability for the downstream business, because in the intervening years the industry had reorganized drastically. In particular refining capacity was reduced as less efficient plants were closed, with the consequence that there was hardly any spare capacity. The refining margins, therefore, started to rise after 2002 in response to the growing demand for oil products.[99]

As was the case with E&P, the downstream business adjusted its organizational structure in order to become more global. The

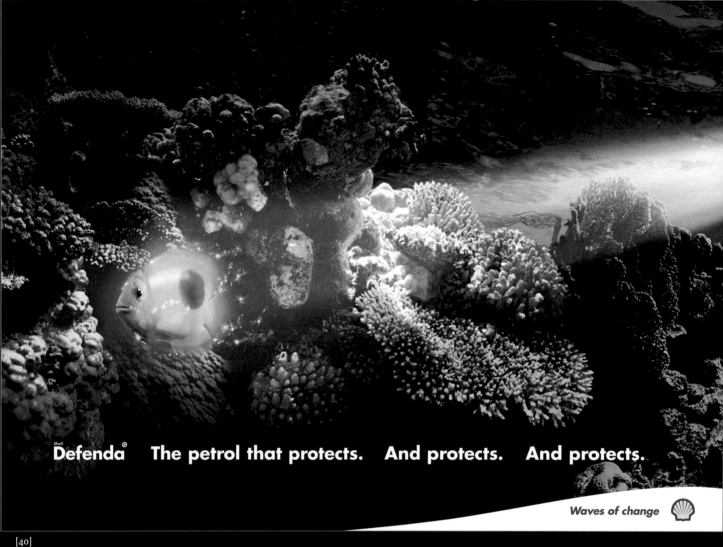

Shell
Defenda®   The petrol that protects.   And protects.   And protects.

Waves of change

Series of Shell advertisements with the
sea as main theme, promoting the
various choice fuels, from left to right:
Defenda, Optimax, Pura (in Thailand)
and V Power. A Chinese service station
announces that it is open 24 hours.

globalization of Oil Products took place in two stages. First Shell set up a number of regional organizations such as Shell Europe Oil Products. The formation of regional organizations made it easier to coordinate the closure of small refineries. Next the regional organizations were integrated in one global organization. This integration included the US after Shell had taken over the Texaco share in the US downstream joint ventures. The trading of crude oil and oil products was brought together in Shell Global Trading, and for the sale of lubricants and aviation fuels Shell also set up global organizations, including Shell Oil. Part of the globalization process consisted of streamlining the supply chain through standardization of processes and systems. The local embeddedness of Shell's retail organization had led to the mushrooming of different ways in which Shell and those who owned or operated the service stations ran their business. In 2005 Shell calculated that it had around fifty different business models and the aim was to reduce that number to four. The number of IT applications involved in business-to-business transactions should be reduced from 460 to around 50. Russel Caplan, senior vice-president of Globalisation warned Shell people: 'Pleading for exceptions is a thing of the past.'[100] This round of integration included the Chemicals, which were combined with Oil Products into one organization, Downstream One in 2005.

The integration of Chemicals into Oil Products followed a process, begun in 1998, of focusing Shell Chemicals on basic petrochemicals. In this strategy the synergy had to come from the interaction between oil refining and petrochemicals, the so-called Oil-Chemicals interface. Practically all speciality chemicals were sold. By 2000 Shell Chemicals had divested 40 per cent of its assets and cut the number of manufacturing sites from fifty-four to seventeen.[101] However, more was to follow. During the divestment process Shell created a 50:50 joint venture with BASF in which both parties combined their polypropylene and polyethylene activities. The new company Basell, though market leader in polyolefins, struggled to achieve acceptable returns. For that reason both parents came to the conclusion that Basell no longer belonged to their core business and they sold it in 2005 to a consortium led by New York-based Access Industries.[102]

Chinese employees on the way to their work at the construction site of the coal gasification plant at Yueyang in 2005, a joint venture between Shell and Sinopec. The plant was built to turn coal into clean synthetic gas with the use of Shell technology. The billboard proudly announces 'Let's build up, hand in hand, the project "Coal replaces Oil"'.

Alongside the divestment process, new business in petrochemicals was undertaken. Shell Chemicals wanted to move the focus of its business from Europe and the US to the fast-growing markets in Asia. From the late 1980s onwards Shell had developed a major petrochemical complex in Singapore, as discussed in chapter 2. In 2002 Shell and its Chinese joint venture partner China National Offshore Oil Corporation (CNOOC) approved the building of a major petrochemical plant in Huizhou, southern China. The construction of the Nanhai petrochemical plant signified Shell's largest single investment in China to date. Before approval had been given, the joint venture had studied engineering designs, bid packages for engineering and the financing, but the social and environmental impact of the plant also had to be taken into consideration. For instance, more than 8,000 people from villages on the site had to be resettled. During construction the number of contract workers was expected to grow to 20,000. Once the plant went on stream, the complex would employ 1,500 people, of whom 95 per cent would be citizens of the People's Republic of China. The plant was set up to serve the Chinese market. When it was finished it should be able to supply between 5 and 10 per cent of the Chinese market at that period in time.[103] The plant was ready for start up in January 2006, after the construction had been completed within the expected schedule and budget.

The merger of 1907 taken to its logical conclusion: the birth of Royal Dutch Shell plc

Expecting rising demand for petrochemical products in China, Shell and its Chinese joint venture partner CNOOC agreed to build a large petrochemical plant in Huizhou, southern China in 2002. The Nanhai plant started production in 2006.

Western business men have been fascinated by the potentially huge consumer markets in China. This was particularly true during the last two decades of the twentieth century, when China's gross domestic product increased at the average rate of 10 per cent per year.[1] Shell first entered mainland China at the end of the nineteenth century, and stayed there with ups and downs until 1966, when its head office in Shanghai was closed following the Cultural Revolution of Mao Zedong.[2] When the American President Nixon relaxed various US trade restrictions in order to improve relations between the US and the People's Republic of China in early 1971, Shell immediately responded by accepting the invitation to attend the Guangzhou (Canton) Trade Fair with representatives of Shell Chemicals in the autumn of that year. Shell returned in the following years, even though the trading levels were rather poor as a consequence of the disruptions in production caused by the Cultural Revolution. With a change in China's leadership following the death of Mao Zedong in 1976 the prospects for western companies began to look more promising. To demonstrate the Group's strengths in trading and technology, Shell launched an E&P symposium in Peking in January 1977 and another symposium on oil additives and lubricants later that year. All Shell businesses suddenly started negotiations in China, for example about the delivery of Shell know-how for a natural gas separation plant, about the purchase of Chinese tin, about the Shell coal gasification process, and about offshore exploration. When Shell discussed the concept of risk-sharing, such as a production sharing system, it discovered that Chinese officials were not eager for the concept. As Peter Baxendell reported: 'the phrase "risk sharing" seemed to upset them as being redolent of capitalism and was therefore to be avoided'. And he continued: 'Apart from the problem of getting the right terms for any arrangements, the labyrinthine nature of Chinese bureaucracy seemed to prevent any coordinated overall discussion of the possibilities.'[3] At the same time Shell management was aware of the fact that Shell itself was not an easy organization to explain to outsiders.

People reading the wall papers in a street in Peking. Some posters suggest a peaceful unification of Taiwan and the People's Republic of China. Others tell the story of the resumption of diplomatic relations between China and US from 1 January 1979. This marked the starting point for western companies to try their luck in China.

Western politicians hoped and expected that economic growth in China would go hand in hand with greater democracy, but of the two economic growth moved considerably faster. Right: Students, demonstrating for democracy and the protection of human rights in Beijing, May 1989, found tanks in their way.

[44]

[45]

In 1978 the People's Republic of China closed a trade agreement with the European Community, followed in 1979 by the establishment of diplomatic relations between China and the US. It was time for Shell to set up office in Beijing. As there were no modern offices available, Shell's China representative, Roger Williams, rented the 'Clouds Gathering' Pavilion in the Summer Palace, a huge historic royal garden with pavilions. Though the Shell office stood out because of its unusual location, Shell only stayed there for two years and then moved to an office above a well-known restaurant, the Roast Duck, before ending up in the more predictable location of the World Trade Centre in 1990.[4]

In 1979 China first opened up offshore acreage in the South China Sea to foreign companies. After having contributed to the seismic work, the companies could apply for exploration acreage. The Chinese officials seemed to have accepted the concept of some form of risk-sharing. Shell participated in two joint ventures, one consisting of Esso and Shell International, and one of Phillips and Shell Oil in the US, which used the name Pecten for its foreign subsidiaries. In neither was Shell the operator. Not being familiar with the precise relationship between Royal Dutch, Shell Transport and their US subsidiary Shell Oil, the Chinese were rather puzzled by those different faces of Shell, and the fact that the activities of Shell and Pecten were divided by 'Chinese walls'.[5] The results of the offshore exploration by the international oil companies were on the whole rather disappointing. Though in a number of cases oil or gas in commercial quantities was discovered, no major fields came to light.[6] Nevertheless, with growing

[46]

When Shell decided to set up office in
Beijing in 1979, it rented office space in
the 'Clouds Gathering Pavilion' in the
Summer Palace, a huge historical royal
garden with pavilions. Shell stayed
there for two years.

local demand for energy, it was well worth following up the discoveries. The Phillips/Pecten partnership developed the Xijiang fields in the Pearl River Mouth Basin together with China National Offshore Oil Corporation (CNOOC). Production started up in 1994.

In the meantime a process of industrialization took place in China. The country followed the classical path from agriculture to industry.[7] This brought more openness and higher standards of living, but also dislocation between town and country and huge environmental problems. Chinese business people outside China played an important role in the industrialization process, because they moved production from Hong Kong, Taiwan and Singapore to mainland China in order to make use of the cheaper labour force there. Initially the production of consumer goods was intended for US and European markets, but with the high growth rates of the 1980s and 1990s China itself became the world's largest consumer market.[8] In that market Shell wanted to be present with its main products and its brand. The latter was not easy to achieve, because the Shell brand was relatively unknown in China and special permission was

needed to set up branded retail sites. To re-enter China, Shell worked at two levels. On the one hand, it undertook small initiatives in partnership with Chinese firms to learn about the country and its possibilities. For instance, investments were made in retail stations and in joint marketing depots in the Shenzhen Special Economic Zone near Hong Kong, and in a joint venture lubricant oil blending plant in Shanghai. More fuel depots and lubricant oil blending plants followed in other regions. On the other hand, Shell looked for big projects with a strong technological flavour that would make full use of Shell's competitive advantage and would demonstrate Shell's commitment to the country. In this context, Shell started a feasibility study for an integrated oil and petrochemical complex in Guangdong Province in joint venture with Chinese partners. For Shell it was important that the project would give the company the right to establish Shell-branded retail sites in the Guangdong Province. The feasibility study, finished in 1993, concluded that the project was technically feasible though probably not sufficiently economic to justify the huge investment. In the ensuing negotiations Shell proposed building

in the first phase only a simple refinery, but the Chinese government preferred the opposite: deferring the refinery and building a world-class petro-chemical complex.[9] On this basis negotiations continued, until finally in 2000 the decision was taken to proceed with the project with CNOOC as 50 per cent partner.

Having local partners turned out to be an essential part of doing business in China. In 2000 Shell signed strategic alliances with two important Chinese companies, CNOOC and China Petroleum and Chemical Corporation (Sinopec). Following the joint venture contract between Shell and CNOOC regarding Nanhai, Shell participated in the initial public offering of CNOOC with a share of 20 per cent, when it listed in overseas markets. The alliance with Sinopec included joint ventures in retail marketing, the development of gas fields, and several coal gasification projects. In addition, Shell supported Sinopec's initial public offering by participating for 14 per cent. Shell made it clear from the start that those participations were intended to help the companies establish themselves on overseas stock markets and would be sold in an orderly manner in due time.[10]

In recent years all Shell's businesses – E&P, Gas and Power, Oil Products, Chemicals, and Renewables – developed activities in China with special focus on cleaner fuels. The air pollution in and around major cities was fast becoming one of the major environmental concerns in China. Therefore, Shell paid special attention to the possibilities for gas. These included the development of the Changbei natural gas field in joint venture with PetroChina, the support for an LNG terminal in Guangdong, and projects for the gasification of coal. To support the coherence between all future Shell activities in the country Malaysian-born Lim Haw Kuang was appointed Executive Chairman of Shell Companies in China in 2005. By that time Shell had some nineteen wholly-owned or joint venture companies employing about 1,600 staff and joint venture staff in China. Almost 90 per cent of their employees were citizens of the People's Republic of China. The flagship Nanhai project was finished on time and within budget in December 2005.

In collaboration with the Dutch Ministry of Economic Affairs, Shell and the Dutch energy company Nuon started the construction of the NoordzeeWind Farm in 2005. Nuon contributed its experience in energy distribution and Shell its knowledge of offshore production. From the harbour of Scheveningen the various parts were shipped to the offshore site, 10 km off the town of Egmond aan Zee. The wind farm consisted of 36 windmills, with a capacity of 3 MW, considered to be enough to supply 100,000 households with electricity.

Renewable energy   In 1997 Shell launched a fifth core business, named Shell International Renewables. Under this new umbrella three existing businesses were brought together: solar power, biomass (wood-based) power, and forestry. Shell had two main reasons for underlining its commitment to renewable energy. According to the Shell scenarios, energy demand in the coming half-century would continue to rise, though somewhat faster in the 'Sustained Growth' than in the 'Dematerialization' scenario. On the other hand, the production of fossil fuels would reach a plateau in 2020. In assessing future energy production, Shell's scenarios were more optimistic than those of Colin Campbell, but they also foresaw a future energy gap. To fill this gap, renewable energies would become increasingly important. Their share in the energy mix could reach, depending on the scenario, 5 to 10 per cent in 2025 and as much as 50 per cent by 2050. Therefore Shell wanted to participate in developing the new energy sources needed to meet future demand. Moreover, renewable energies would satisfy that demand in a sustainable way.[104] In 1995 *Shell World* discussed the global warming issue, and the Shell response was cautious. There was no cause for alarm, but in order to have 'no regret' later on if the case for global warming was proven, some measures should be taken by governments.[105] Increasingly, however, Shell became convinced that there was cause for alarm, and that Shell should play a role in mitigating the problem. Solar and wind energy, for instance, would help reduce CO_2 levels. Though Shell was prepared to invest $500 million over the course of five years in developing renewable energy, it had the view that ultimately, the expansion of renewable energy should be driven by market forces.[106]

Initially, Shell's strategy consisted of finding market niches where renewable energy, though far more expensive than oil or gas, had special value for other reasons. Shell Solar therefore focused on sustainably meeting customer needs for small power and heat supply in 'stand alone' applications, in particular in rural markets in developing countries.[107] Soon after establishing the new core business of Renewables, Shell concluded that the link between renewables and forestry was not very strong. Also, its forestry activities delivered only modest returns and they were too small for Shell to play an important role in that market. Therefore Shell exited this business, as mentioned in chapter 2. The biomass business was discontinued in 2001. Instead Shell focused its efforts on solar and wind energy. To speed up the development of solar energy Shell acquired the Siemens solar business in 2001. However, it soon became clear that the production of photovoltaic cells outpaced the demand, and Shell slowed down the development. With the investment in wind energy Shell used a different business model, which included full ownership in the start-up of projects and partial withdrawal for profits once the projects were partly established. Shell remained committed to developing wind farm projects, including a joint venture with NUON in NoordzeeWind, an offshore project off the coast of the Netherlands.[108]

A woman who is passionate about windsurfing explains why she thinks she can live on the wind: by using wind energy. Shell Renewables agrees with her and invests hundred of millions in the development of wind energy. In May 2006, this Shell advertisement won the monthly prize of the feminist magazine *Opzij* for the most emancipatory advertisement.

[47]

[48]

Kun je van de wind leven?

Deze windsurfer uit IJmuiden vindt van wel.

Surfen op open zee niet, pak 'm beet, windkracht zeven kost behoorlijk wat inspanning en energie. Kijk maar naar Linde, die geeft echt alles wat ze in huis heeft. Thuis is ze heel wat bewuster met energie. Ze is dan ook een groot voorstander van bijvoorbeeld windenergie. Net als Shell trouwens. Voor Shell is de wind een onuitputtelijke bron van energie. Niet voor niets investeert Shell honderden miljoenen in de ontwikkeling van windenergie. Samen met Nuon bouwen we aan een windmolenpark in zee, ongeveer tien kilometer uit de kust bij Egmond aan Zee. Daar is het praktisch nooit windstil. Het park gaat duurzame energie leveren aan ruim honderdduizend huishoudens. Ook voor het huis van Linde. Ontdek hoe wij mensen nu en in de toekomst van brandstof voorzien. Kijk op **www.shell.nl**

The merger of 1907 taken to its logical conclusion: the birth of Royal Dutch Shell plc

Shell Renewables' first wind farm was the Rock River Wind farm in Carbon County in Wyoming, with a capacity of 50MW, supposed to be sufficient to supply 25,000 American households with electricity. Apparently, an American household needed twice as much electricity as a Dutch one. Shell also participated in a wind farm in Colorado, pictured here.

50

THANKS TO HIS STUBBORNNESS, THE WASTE ON THIS TRUCK CAN BE USED TO FUEL IT.

Patrick Foody Sr. is a determined man. Some 30 years ago, he had a visionary idea. He would produce ethanol, a vital ingredient in transportation fuels, from agricultural wastes like cereal straws and cornstalks. Contemporaries doubted him. Initial attempts were costly. Still, Pat and his colleagues at Iogen Corporation pressed on. After much dogged persistence, and with help from Shell, they found ways to make large-scale production a commercial reality. It may be a while yet before alternatives such as EcoEthanol™ can become a major source of energy. But by seeking out partners like Pat, we're hoping to bring that day a step closer. Visit www.shell.com/biofuels for more information.

This Shell advertisement explains how Patric Foody Sr. and his colleagues at Iogen Corporation succeeded in producing ethanol from agricultural wastes after much dogged persistence and with help from Shell.

Though Shell exited biomass (wood-based) forestry activities, it remained interested in biofuels, but in particular on the basis of non-food materials.

In the late 1990s Shell Sweden opened a trial retail site selling biogas and ethanol.

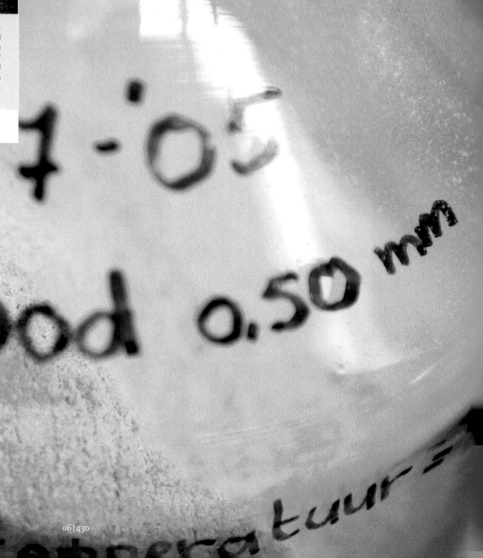

51

[52]

Though Shell exited the biomass activities, it remained interested in biofuels. Shell teamed up with Volkswagen and the biotechnology firm Iogen to study the feasibility of producing cellulose ethanol from the non-food portion of agriculture, such as cereal straw.[109] Shell considered its investments in renewable energy predominantly as efforts to get the various technologies along the learning curve. The amounts devoted to renewable energy were still modest compared to investment in oil and gas, because it was not yet clear which of the technologies would be a winning one and producing renewable energy was still considered too costly to proceed on a large scale at this point in time.

The commercialization of technology In bringing costs down, in finding new sources of energy, and in developing new business, research and technology played an important role. How much was it worth to the company? How much could the company afford to spend on research and development? How efficiently did it organize the process from invention to technical application? During the period of low oil prices in the 1990s, expenditures on research and development had come under continuous pressure. In the reorganization of the service companies in 1995, Shell decided to integrate research and technical services and bring them into closer contact with the end users, the operating companies. This led to two new organizations, Shell Global Solutions for servicing the downstream sector, and, at a later stage, EP Technology for the upstream sector. The reorganization meant a huge upheaval for staff working in the laboratories and technical services, all the more so as staff reductions were part of the restructuring process. Not only that, but also doubt was cast over the commercial value of their previous work. Did they provide value for money? To prove their value to the business they had to become more commercially oriented.

For Shell Global Solutions it meant a change from a dependent cost centre into a (semi-autonomous) commercial company. The traditional knowledge workers had to become service-oriented business people. The director of Shell Global Solutions, Hans van Luijk, developed the vision that the new organization should be truly open to market exposure to show its worth. The usual complaints of managers from operating companies included: 'we have to reduce costs, but Head Office increases charges' and 'no clue what those people in R&D do with our money'. To end these complaints and create a new relationship between the research and technical services organization and the operating companies, services would be priced on a market basis. Shell clients were free to use the open market, while Shell Global Solutions would be free to seek new third-party/non-Shell clients. Cor Herkströter hailed the transformation as extremely positive: 'It's highly innovative, splendid'.[110] Two things are interesting about the new direction. The first is that Shell did not want to

EU sets industry target of reducing carbon dioxide emissions by 6%

Moving to the really long-term future was the business unit Shell Hydrogen. With the support of the Icelandic government it opened the first Shell-branded hydrogen station in Reykjavik to fuel three DaimlerChrysler fuel cell buses. One of the key features of the Icelandic project was that the hydrogen could be produced by electrolysing water using electricity generated from renewable energy, producing almost no carbon dioxide.

[53]

reserve the right to have exclusive access to the technology and innovation that was present in its own service companies. Shell Global Solutions was asked to become customer oriented, and to find customers outside as well as inside the company. The second is that the experiment was a success. As it turned out, there were enough customers inside and outside Shell willing to pay for the services Shell Global Solutions could offer. Apparently, their services were of value after all.[111] In fact, in 2001 Conference began to voice concern that Shell Global Solutions was providing support to Shell's competitors. The CMD chairman Mark Moody-Stuart, however, pointed to the advantage that third parties helped pay for the Group's in-house technology, and he reassured Conference that the best of the in-house technology would not be disclosed to competitors.[112]

EP Technology, the in-house technology service provider for Shell's upstream sector, became a global organization after integrating the research and technical services provided by Shell Oil in 1998. EP Technology faced similar discussions to Shell Global Solutions about how to commercialize the Shell technology and which technology to share and which not. Separate companies, such as Shell Technology Ventures, were set up to commercialize technology.[113] In 2000 Shell EP Technology felt it had a lot of excellent ideas and a number of very promising technologies, but the pace of deploying these new technologies should be speeded up. Its vision was that the 'Difference is Technology' and the aspiration was to become 'too fast to follow'. Therefore EP Technology put forward two proposals. The first was to create joint

ventures with the International Service Companies, in particular Halliburton and Schlumberger. The rationale behind this proposal was that these contractors did the actual drilling and building work in the first place. In the past Shell had shared its knowledge with them for free. Shell could keep the knowledge to itself, but it did not have the ambition to do the work of the contractors. Therefore it seemed more logical to develop the technology together and recapture some of the costs. The second proposal was to start discussions with potential external financial partners to set up a joint entity that would invest in commercialization of certain Shell technologies. For a cash-rich company this second proposal did not seem to make much sense. Though the CMD supported both proposals, only the joint venture with Halliburton with regard to well technologies materialized.[114] This led to the company WellDynamics, in which the Smart Well concept of Halliburton and Shell's 'intelligent' well concept were combined.[115]

Even after more than a century R&D still played a significant role at the core of the oil business, the drilling for oil, accelerating production and bringing costs down. In the 1980s horizontal drilling pushed up production level, while in the 1990s, the slim-hole drilling reduced costs. The big expected innovation of the 2000s was the 'Expandable Tubulars'. Normally, an oil and gas well looks like an upside-down telescope, with the thicker end at the top. The telescopic effect is caused by the way drilling takes place. For various technical and geological reasons, the drilling process has to be regularly interrupted to insert a tube (casing) into the well and cement it in place. Drilling then resumes using a smaller bit size

The merger of 1907 taken to its logical conclusion: the birth of Royal Dutch Shell plc

to fit inside the casing. This cycle is repeated several times and as a consequence the bit hole become smaller and smaller. The technology of 'expandable tubulars' solves this problem of having to drill a large hole at the beginning in order to end up with only a small hole at the end by making it possible for the casing to expand inside the hole. This technique reduces the narrowing effect as the well goes deeper. At the start the holes can remain smaller, so the drilling is faster and cheaper, but has less of an impact on the environment. A forecast new area for development was the 'smart field'. This would embrace new technology and integrate new developments in Information Technology, but most of all it was intended to be a new holistic way of looking at production, reservoir management and other core technical processes.[116]

Having worked very hard at getting money out of technology, Shell took advantage of the high oil prices of the early 2000s to put money back in. The expenditures for research and development increased from $389 million in 2000 to $588 million in 2005.[117] To reinforce Shell's commitment to science, technology and innovation, the company created the role of 'chief scientist' and nominated eight internationally recognized experts in different fields to act as such. Also in 2006 the senior role of a Chief Technology Officer was created, reporting directly to an executive board member. In the new Shell of the twenty-first century technology has once again to play a vital role in helping to provide more energy for future generations without affecting the environment negatively. The real challenge is not only finding new technologies but also integrating technologies from different parts of the company, underlining the importance of structuring collaboration within the company.

Enterprise First 'March/April [2004] was the nadir… with more debookings, press articles on "who knew what", Shell leaking like a sieve… which still makes me very angry… problems with the SEC, annual report delayed, AGM delayed, hammerings from all the media and financial markets. Dark days, indeed. Perhaps some of you even started to take French lessons… with all the rumours around Total.' Thus Jeroen van de Veer opened his speech to the top 100 of Royal Dutch/Shell in The Hague, 15 December 2004.[118] When he was still in the midst of that crisis in May 2004 he had set out his ideas on what had to be done with regard to management, posing a number of probing questions: 'I wonder: has excessive job movement created too many gifted amateurs in a world that needs more professionalism, commitment to performance and discipline? The reserves issue was not caused by our scorecard or bonus system. Nevertheless, we need to consider whether our scorecards and pay system do drive desired behaviours. (..) I do want all of our leaders to be competitively rewarded – but I also want to ensure we have the remuneration structure that builds cohesion, loyalty and commitment to the long-term good of the company. Over the past months, all of us have been in situations in which we had to defend our enterprise. But if I look over the past years, I wonder, has the balance between "Enterprise first" and "Self first" moved too much to "Self First"? (..) Do we understand humility? (..) Do we fix our problems by making a plan full of overstretch or unattainable targets?'[119]

In response to these questions he proposed to change the company culture into an 'Enterprise First' mindset.[120] Keywords were leadership, accountability, and teamwork. Leadership included the standardization, simplification, and globalization of the operations and processes. During the 1990s Shell had introduced the system of 'open resourcing' for its higher management. This had encouraged swift moves from one place to the next every two or three years. Managers became all-round but lost some of their professional expertise. It was expected that with the introduction of longer job tenures the performance would become more professional and disciplined. Targets should be achievable, with neither overstretch nor complacency. Thinking back to the many consultants hired during the 1990s, Van der Veer said emphatically: 'No new gurus; we will do it ourselves and we lead by example.' It was particularly important that Shell managers should comply with external and internal standards and with those of regulators. Scorecards and remuneration plans had to drive preferred behaviour, and preferred behaviour included teamwork.[121]

The company moved from a focus on asset management, where decisions were taken very low in the organization on the basis of (stretch) targets and individual rewards to a more integrated approach where the impact of local decisions on the company as a whole was taken into careful consideration. A consequence of this approach was that the extensive scorecards for each business unit, introduced in the late 1990s, became redundant. Instead, one scorecard for everybody reflected the progress of the company as a whole. Success of the company would be measured in first quartile comparisons with the competition in areas such as operational excellence, project delivery, unit costs, return on capital, cash and reputation. Added to these measurements were total shareholder return and the results of the annual Shell People Survey.[122]

Enterprise First was a staff policy, but was also related to teamwork within and between business units and business sectors. The globalization process had already introduced closer collaboration within the business sectors. For instance, in 2002 Gas & Power began with the ranking of projects on a global – rather than a regional – level, and distributing the funds according to the best outcome for the sector as a whole. This process was taken further with Gas & Power ranking projects together with Exploration & Production to make sure that the one party was not shedding projects that might have been worthwhile for the other.[123]

The 'Enterprise First' way of thinking also led to a revaluation of the position of the Shell country chairs. During the reorganization of the 1990s, the role of the national representatives had become more modest because the business units became responsible for the coordination of operations worldwide. At the local level this could incidentally lead to suboptimal investment decisions, and for that reason the position of the country chairs was strengthened again. They had to take care that investment decisions in their countries meshed with one another. Moreover, with rising oil prices the security of energy became once again an important geopolitical issue, and in that context it was essential for Shell to have the position of country chair filled by senior managers, who could discuss energy issues with the national governments with authority.[124]

One company, one board, one CEO   When Shell announced the need to recategorize its reserves, the financial press and some of the shareholders, particularly those in Britain, responded to the news by pointing to the dual structure as the underlying problem. The 'Byzantine structure' was one of the oft-used expressions to describe Royal Dutch/Shell's dual nationality. Changing the structure of the two parent companies had been studied in the late 1990s, but it was a very complicated issue, not least because of national differences in taxation. The reserves crisis created the sense of urgency needed to look again at the possibilities for a radical change. Shell set up a Steering Group to review the structure and overall governance of the Group. When the AGM of June 2004 arrived and the Steering Group was still studying the problem the financial press became somewhat impatient. However, on 28 October 2004 the Royal Dutch Boards and the Shell Transport and Trading Board announced that they had unanimously agreed, in principle, to propose to shareholders the unification of Royal Dutch and Shell Transport under a single parent company, Royal Dutch Shell. At long last it would be possible to write Royal Dutch Shell without a slash.

The new company was incorporated in England and Wales, and headquartered and resident in the Netherlands for Dutch and UK tax purposes. Royal Dutch Shell plc would get a single-tier board headed by a non-executive chairman. This board would have a majority of independent non-executive directors. The executive management would be led by a single Chief Executive. The boards had tried to strike the right balance between the Dutch and the British legacies and the future interests of the company. While the incorporation and the single-tier board structure reflected the British tradition and the preference of the financial markets, the headquarters in the Netherlands paid tribute to the historical position of the Dutch side in the Group and offered tax advantages as well. For once the financial press was impressed. Shell had moved faster and further than the analysts had expected.

How did the unification take place in practical terms? Royal Dutch shareholders were offered 60 per cent of the issued share capital of Royal Dutch Shell plc and Shell Transport shareholders received 40 per cent. To preserve the existing tax treatment of dividends for all shareholders, Royal Dutch Shell created 'A' and 'B' shares. The Royal Dutch shareholders received 'A' shares and Dutch-sourced dividends, while Shell Transport shareholders received 'B' shares and UK-sourced dividends. In all other respects, these two shares are identical, vote together as a single class on all matters, and have dividends of the same amount declared on them. For the two original parent companies different ways of implementation were chosen. The new parent company Royal Dutch Shell made a public exchange offer for the Royal Dutch ordinary shares (the Tender Offer) and it acquired Shell Transport & Trading following a Scheme of Arrangement of ST&T under section 425 of the Companies Act 1985.[125] As mentioned at the start of this chapter, the shareholders of both parent companies agreed to the proposals at their respective annual meetings on 28 June 2005.

After ninety-eight years the Group finally abolished its long-cherished dual structure with two different national parents and two central offices. Though the reserves issue triggered this change, it was not the reason why the Group was prepared to give up its traditional structure. Earlier in its history the question whether the Group could afford two central offices had already been discussed, for instance in the 1960s. Then the conclusion had been that in the long run the enterprise could not afford two central offices, but that at the present there were no viable alternatives.[126] During the reorganizations of the mid-1990s the

[54]

Aad Jacobs, first non-executive chairman of Royal Dutch Shell plc, opened the Stock Exchange in Amsterdam on the first day of trading in Royal Dutch Shell plc shares.

structure of two parent companies had been studied. Issues such as a clearer governance structure, a structure allowing for mergers, the collective versus individual accountability, and the size of the CMD and Conference had been identified.[127] These were also the overriding themes to motivate the final change. Of course, the new structure would not only allow for mergers but would at the same time increase the risk of an acquisition. Moving to one company, one board, and one CEO would give the Group a simpler and clearer structure. Decision-making would be more efficient with clear lines of authority and a more powerful CEO to implement strategy, and one central office. The responsibilities and accountability would be better identified, with clear roles for the non-executive Chairman, the CEO, and the CFO. The new structure would also provide greater financial flexibility with regard to debt and equity issuance.[128]

The final moment came on 20 July 2005, when trading began in Royal Dutch Shell shares. The Amsterdam stock market (Euronext Amsterdam) was concerned that the trading of RDS shares would move to London, because this was the largest financial market. However, during 2005 Amsterdam remained the main focus for trade in RDS 'A' shares.[129] Even more importantly, the shares' price moved upward, helped by the rising oil prices. In fact, during the first-year start of the twenty-first century, the financial results had been very good. Net income rose from the abnormally low point of $350 million in 1998 to $12,719 million in 2000 and a record of $26,261 million in 2005.

The merger of 1907 taken to its logical conclusion: the birth of Royal Dutch Shell plc

Jeroen van der Veer and Peter Voser on
their way to a press conference on 27
June 2006.

Conclusion   The first years of the twenty-first century gave
Royal Dutch Shell some sobering experiences as well as good
opportunities. Having missed out on the merger movement of the
late 1990s, Shell's position in relation to the other western oil
majors had considerably weakened. Measured in stock market
capitalization, it was relegated to the third position, behind
ExxonMobil and BP. Catching up, however, was difficult. Shell did
consider many takeover opportunities but because it was
expecting oil prices to remain low, nearly all options seemed too
expensive. When oil prices started to rise, the window of
opportunity closed, because oil companies only became even more
expensive. While struggling with a loss of stature, the enterprise
also had to admit in 2001 that it would not meet its target of 5 per
cent production growth in the coming years, though this problem
was mitigated by the fact that other oil majors found it equally
difficult to show production growth. The nadir came in January
2004, when Shell had to explain to the financial markets that the
accounting of the proved oil and gas reserves did not comply with
the rules of the SEC. Uniquely in the history of the enterprise, the
boards asked three senior executives to resign. One negative article
after another appeared in the press. Often negative press coverage
is the result of disappointing financial results. In Shell's case
nothing was further from the truth. The enterprise was doing
extremely well, making very high profits, both in its upstream and
downstream business, helped by high oil prices. Having focused
heavily on profitability during the 1990s, shedding under-
performing assets, the enterprise had become extremely
profitable. The other oil majors showed good results as well.

In order to regain the trust of the financial markets, Shell
introduced tough measures, including the overhaul of its
governance structure. The unique dual nationality structure was
exchanged for the simpler structure of a British plc. The situation of
having two central offices in London and The Hague with equal
standing was finally ended by appointing The Hague as the formal
headquarters of the company. Simpler and clearer governance
structures were one part of the rebuilding process. The other part
consisted of making the downstream more profitable, while
investing heavily in finding new oil and gas fields and bringing them
into production. This strategy was perfectly aligned to the renewed
public concern about future energy supplies. Overall Shell wanted
to make more use of the advantages it enjoyed in being one large
integrated company.

The merger of 1907 taken to its logical conclusion: the birth of Royal Dutch Shell plc

Conclusion

During this period of its history, from 1973 until approaching 2007, the Group faced many challenges great and small, of which two stand out as unusually large and important. First in the early 1970s came the development of a new international oil regime, in response to the increasingly organized demands of the oil-producing countries; and second came the rising demands of shareholders, coupled with the globalization of international markets from the mid-1980s. From these comes one key question: How successful was the Group in addressing those two large challenges and responding to the turbulent markets that accompanied them?

Before answering that question it is important to remember what 'success' meant for the Group itself, because its ambitions changed over time. From 1973 until the late 1980s senior management focused on creating growth and employment, including challenging jobs for its international managers. During the 1990s, in response to the more exacting demands of financial markets, the emphasis shifted to profitability, increasing return on capital, and delivering shareholder value; and as the twenty-first century opened, the Group underlined the need to strike a balance between growth and profits. This was at times a very stormy journey. The Group succeeded in meeting its goal for growth, only to discover that to the rest of the industry and the outside world that goal had become less desirable. Then it succeeded in meeting its new goal for return and value, only to find in doing so that certain of its decisions had reduced its short-term growth perspectives.

Managing any company requires finding the right balance between conflicting demands. Shell managers faced many of these conflicting demands. While managers wanted to be in control, they knew they had to delegate responsibilities to those working for them in order to get the best out of them. The same was true for business units, which had to be empowered to take decisions at their level in order to take quick advantages of opportunities. However, compared to any smaller organization, the potential advantage of large enterprises consisted of creating synergy between their business units, but doing so set limits to the power of the individual parts. In addition, international companies had to deal with the tensions between central and local decision-making. Furthermore, central management had to look at the short term as well as the long term and to satisfy shareholders as well as other stakeholders. As it was impossible to reconcile all these conflicting demands (and there were many more), companies tended to shift emphasis from one side to the other and back again in response to new challenges. As we will see in this conclusion, this was certainly true for Shell in the period discussed in this volume.

Creating growth and employment in the face of the OPEC challenge

In the first phase of this period, during the early 1970s, Shell's management was haunted by doubts about the future of the oil industry. Easy access to oil was diminishing not only geographically but also economically, as the governments of oil-producing countries were looking for ways of increasing their income from the oil in their ground. In most cases these efforts led to total or partial nationalization of the local oil industry. It was not the first time the oil industry had been threatened by nationalizations, and from earlier experiences Shell had learned to be flexible, knowing that even without owning the concessions it could still remain involved and make money out of oil. Meeting these challenges was made much easier by the swift rises in oil prices after OPEC's actions in 1973. To remain involved, it was important for the Group to become an attractive partner for governments and national oil companies, and Shell's organization and business culture were well suited to make the necessary adjustments.

The Group's dual British-Dutch nationality required from its management an understanding of national cultural differences, in order to develop adaptability to local circumstances and local ways of doing business. From the start its management had included a mix of nationalities, and over the years it had increasingly sought to identify with national interests in the many countries in which it worked, creating an elaborate system of moving expatriates around the world to foster internal coherence while managing overseas operations. It was Group policy to promote local management to run the local companies alongside expatriates, with some of the local managers becoming part of the group of expatriates and themselves going to work in countries other than their own. These internationalist policies were beneficial in the face of rising nationalism. The matrix organization, introduced in the 1950s, aimed to combine the perspectives of nations, business units, and capabilities, and was based on coordination rather than subordination. The collective responsibility in the CMD added to the culture of consultation and consensus-seeking, and the position of the managing directors of the national companies became stronger. Each country had its 'Mr Shell' (or sometimes 'Ms Shell') who represented Shell nationally and was empowered to reach local decisions quickly. With rising oil prices, and helped by the persuasive international Shell brand, the Group's traditional strength in marketing was of particular value. Strong local management also had advantages in gaining permission to build refineries or petrochemical complexes or in adjusting to local markets for selling oil products. It turned out to be more difficult, however, to close refineries or petrochemical complexes when they became obsolete or superfluous.

At this time, when pursuing growth over profitability, the Group's business culture had a distinct focus on leading-edge technology and hands-on management. The engineers naturally loved to build plants and run them, and it seems that the feeling of achievement came from finishing projects on time and within budget, not from making money per se. Again, this culture helped in becoming partners of governments. It was also the right approach for exploration and production in new, tougher and previously uneconomic environments such as the Gulf of Mexico and the North Sea. The focus on technology continued to play an important role in the Group's diversification strategy of the late 1960s and early 1970s, when it engaged in other sources of energy (nuclear and coal) as well as in the metals business. In its chemical activities Shell followed a similar strategy of diversifying in products and processes, focusing on products with high added value, which required specialized research and marketing but promised high profit margins. Promises, however, that were not fulfilled.

When the oil price collapsed in 1986, Shell reacted in a more restrained manner than its competiors. Some projects were cancelled or postponed, but by and large exploration and production remained on course. With a business culture concentrated on internal growth it was natural to keep going. The lower oil prices made life for the downstream business easier, though the overcapacity in refining that had become apparent in the 1970s remained, and in the everlasting rivalry with Exxon, Shell finally moved ahead to become the world's largest oil company in 1989. The strategy of growth over profitability appeared to be vindicated by this success. However, by then, the financial markets were no longer particularly interested in size for its own sake. What mattered to them now was profitability and return on capital, and in this respect, Exxon still surpassed Shell.

To have worked long and hard towards a goal and to have achieved it, only to realize that it was no longer valued by others, was an experience that was very likely to produce a marked change in strategy. It did, and in a manner which profoundly affected the Group's view of itself. Hitherto Shell had for many years been seen internally, and to some extent externally, as a community of people, where employees had rights at least equal to those of the shareholders and other stakeholders. Purposely developed, Shell's 'family feeling' encouraged loyalty from its employees, who believed that their bosses saw the Group as more than a bundle of assets to be bought or sold following the latest mission statement. But by the 1990s those traditional strengths started to be considered weaknesses, expensive habits Shell could no longer afford, leftovers from a time when competitive pressure was not so relentless, and moves began to improve shareholder value and the return on capital.

Shareholders were not the only group to put pressure on the Group. All through the 1970s and 1980s the company had been followed critically by non-governmental organizations and the international media, and this continued undiminished during the 1990s. Following its decentralized strategy, the Group aimed at being a good corporate citizen, operating within existing national laws in a socially responsible manner but avoiding involvement in politics. However, national laws and rules of behaviour were not necessarily the same worldwide, and this could create tensions between operating companies in different countries, and actions by international pressure groups made that abundantly clear. The CMD learned from the critical questions regarding Shell's handling of the boycott of Rhodesia that it should be better informed about the policies of their local operating companies. From the long-lasting actions of pressure groups, in particular in Europe and the US, against Shell's presence in South Africa, the company learned that observing national laws was not enough. In order to remain active in a country it was important that Shell companies could fully apply the Shell business principles in their own operations. More complex was the situation in Nigeria, where campaigners against the regime and the way the oil wealth was distributed in Nigerian society implicated Shell and attacked it on its environ-mental performance. In the process, environmental and human rights issues became inextricably linked. Though Shell continued to believe that it should avoid any involvement in party politics, it realized that it had the right and duty to make its position known if human rights were at stake. The situation in Nigeria combined with the public outcry following the decision to sink the Brent Spar made it clear to Shell that it should enter into dialogue with NGOs and provide more information about its environmental footprint and other social aspects of its operations. NGOs continued to challenge Shell on its performances, demanding higher standards in health, safety and the environment. In the 1980s and 1990s Shell experienced more criticism than for instance its rival BP, possibly because during that period it was by far the largest operator, and because its company symbol, the pecten, was so well known and therefore an attractive target.

Increasing return on capital and shareholder value in a period of globalization

With hindsight it is clear that Shell was well positioned to respond to the first challenge of nationalizations in the oil industry in the 1970s, but had to stretch itself to counter the second challenge of globalization and rising demands from investors. It is important to keep in mind that the adjustment to the first challenge was made easy by the rising oil prices, while after 1986 oil prices remained basically low for the rest of the century. During the 1990s, in a strenuous effort to increase return on capital and become more efficient, Shell changed its organizational structure. For such a large enterprise to do so required an enormous effort, and the fact that the senior management succeeded in realizing drastic changes is testament to their determination. Among numerous factors pushing them on, the globalization of markets and the possibilities of connecting worldwide thanks to new information technologies seemed to make the Group's traditional focus on national companies less relevant. Though the decentralized decision-making remained, the focus shifted from the national companies to the business units. Simultaneously, the opportunities offered by globalization meant that many of the talented younger in-coming generation of managers saw the existing structure of checks and balances, of steady promotion and of 'godfathers', as a suffocating blanket which left too little room for individual initiatives. Hungry for personal success and less enamoured of the 'family feeling', they wished to move more quickly up the career ladder, and were willing to sacrifice job security in favour of faster advancement, seeking other employers if Shell could not satisfy them.

Some industry advisors argued that the vertically integrated international oil company no longer represented the winning formula, and Shell senior managers seemed to act on that belief.

Perhaps it was inevitable that in redressing the existing organizational problems, they overshot in the other direction. A number of misdirected initiatives were taken that had to be wound down, and while individual initiatives were encouraged by delegating responsibilities to lower levels, the previously powerful concept of 'the Group' as a whole receded into the background. Projects that were allowed to go ahead (and there were quite a few big ones in hand) were those with very high profit potential in due time, even at low oil prices. However, assets that were seen to be underperforming were summarily disposed of. Diversification largely came to an end with the sales of the metals and coal businesses and a large part of the chemicals operations. Oil fields that were not delivering at the low prices of the 1990s had to go as well. Shell turned out to be better in selling assets than buying them back. Buying did not comply with its traditional business culture, with its focus on internal growth, doing things yourself, inventing things yourself. While concentrating on profitability, growth prospects became endangered. Moreover, core activities were identified more and more narrowly. Even technological development ceased to be seen as a core activity, and although it still played an important role in cutting costs (for instance in innovations such a slim-hole drilling and lighter platforms) Shell no longer insisted that technological innovations must be exclusive. In-house knowledge was shared or outsourced to reduce costs.

In 1997 Shell reached its new goal and became the most profitable company on earth. Unfortunately, as with going for growth over profitability, this top position did not last long. This time, however, it was not so much because of outside factors. In 1998, profits dropped dramatically, for two main reasons, both originating within Shell. First, many of the new activities were generating losses, and second, Group management had rigorously written down oil assets in the conviction that oil prices would remain low for a long time to come. Despite its long tradition of working with scenario planning to 'think the unthinkable' and envision different futures, Shell firmly believed that oil prices would remain low. From that conviction it followed that there was no obvious benefit in buying those competitors that seemed to be available, as their portfolio would not be sufficiently robust in a prolonged period of low oil prices. The Group wanted to reinvent itself, and engage in new activities which – like the alchemist's stone – held out the prospect of delivering profits without assets. In contrast, Exxon and BP had a different view of the future and merged with other oil majors, putting Shell temporarily back to third position in the industry rankings.

Trying to regain its position, Shell discovered that its internal growth was not as healthy as it had believed. This emerged with the reserves recategorization of 2004, in which Shell had to admit that according to the SEC rules it had overbooked its proved reserves to the extent of 25 per cent. Three senior executives lost office, because the boards had lost confidence in them. Whether the SEC rules were still fully valid became a matter of considerable debate, but they were the rules, and the ensuing litigation meant that at the time of writing, although parts of this issue had been resolved, as a whole it was still sub judice. It is therefore not possible in these pages to determine what went wrong. For many investors and employees, who had always considered Shell to be reliable in its figures and conservative in its estimates, the fact that such an event had occurred at all was a huge disappointment. Rebuilding Shell's reputation was not an easy task, a process that was still ongoing in 2006-07; but one part of that process swiftly met with market approval. Rounding off the reorganization that had started in the mid-1990s, the crisis triggered in 2005 a thorough and profoundly historic overhaul of the Group's two-parent structure, by then ninety-eight years old and increasingly seen by outsiders as archaic and redundant. Royal Dutch Shell plc was born and the Group's dual nationality was given a new expression, by combining a British company structure and registered office in London with a headquarters and tax residence in The Hague.

Redressing issues of growth, profits and company strengths

At the start of the twenty-first century the perspectives for the oil industry changed dramatically once again. After a decade of low oil prices, stagnating world production had led to renewed speculation about the 'end of oil'. At the same time, however, very rapidly increasing demand – both from emerging economies such as China and India as well as long-established economies such as the US – caused oil prices to rise to previously unheard-of levels. Uncertain political circumstances added to the problems. With high prices and concerns about security of supply, governments altered their involvement in the oil and gas industries, in some cases reversing previous privatizations. Confronted by new challenges and some old problems, Shell decided to rebuild some of the traditional competitive strengths that it had allowed to slip during the 1990s.

Technology, treasured historically, but no longer considered a core capability during the 1990s, came back on the agenda. Illustrative of this renewed focus were the appointments of chief scientists for eight disciplines and a chief technology officer to oversee it all. With higher energy prices the work on alternative energy also regained momentum. Though the business units remain the basis of the organization, the position of the national representatives of Shell was enhanced. Profitability for some considerable time, perhaps even for the foreseeable future, seemed reasonably well assured by prices that gave no hint of slipping to any significant degree, and top management started to reconsider the competitive advantage of size, for instance by creating greater synergy between the business units. That process of rethinking included more focus on the Group as a whole, once more promoting loyalty to the Group and collaboration between managers instead of focusing on individual performance. A new consistent strategy of creating growth in oil and gas production as well as enhancing downstream profitability sent a clear message to investors. Thus the company was regaining competitiveness in markets that remained turbulent.

Joint conclusion:
the first centenary of Royal Dutch Shell

By Jan Luiten van Zanden, Stephen Howarth,

Joost Jonker and Keetie Sluyterman

The century of oil From its formation in 1907 the Royal Dutch/Shell Group of Companies was a leading player in the international oil industry, and throughout the Group's first century, oil was a booming business for most of the time. The industry as a whole developed in a way typical for a young and successful activity, with early and very rapid growth in crude oil production being followed by a gradual transition towards a lower growth regime in the second half of the cycle. The industry's sales of oil products followed a similar trajectory but grew even more quickly than the production of crude oil, because during the first decades of the twentieth century the fractions of the barrel that could be used for commercial purposes increased dramatically. At first only kerosene had a high sales value, as a cheap and easy provider of artificial light. Other fractions were usually thrown out or burned as waste. However, the progress of motor technology increased the commercially viable fractions and encouraged the development of products such as gasoline, fuel oil and diesel. Moreover, from the 1920s, the petrochemical era began, as other fractions of crude oil and natural gas began to be employed for producing chemicals which had scarcely been imagined just a generation earlier. All these developments meant that the international oil industry became an increasingly efficient provider of key products for economic growth. In addition the period after the Second World War saw the gradual emergence of natural gas as a closely related business. So the actual growth of the industry was even more spectacular than the already high growth rates of the production of crude oil suggest.

The overall growth pattern is clear from the long-term development of crude oil production, which grew very rapidly until the early 1970s and subsequently slowed down considerably (Figure 1).[1] Oil experts currently debate vigorously when global oil production will peak before starting to decline: during the next fifteen years, perhaps much later. But nobody doubts that the peak and decline will come. Few experts would disagree with the observation that the production break in the early 1970s, although exaggerated by the role of OPEC and the voluntary cap on Saudi Arabia's crude output, was the most important break in the long-term trend. In recent decades, the industry has become a mature one, characterized by low growth, increasingly scarce resources, and steeply rising costs of exploration and development.

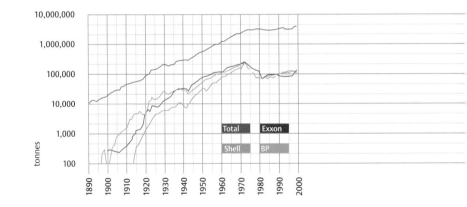

Figure 1

Crude oil production of the world,

Shell, Exxon, and BP in tonnes,

1890-2000, semi-logarithmic scale.

The Group had the advantage of being present close to the beginning of the industry's growth cycle, and it succeeded in remaining a top player for the rest of the century. Insofar as longevity can be seen as a measure of success, it was a very successful enterprise. That in itself was no mean feat, because there were many moments in its history that could have caused serious disruption. Even before the creation of the Group in 1907, Royal Dutch faced a difficult period when its main source of crude oil suddenly dried up. Shell Transport faced financial collapse before its merger with Royal Dutch. The cross-border venture could have become unstuck during the First World War, and the Second World War posed another challenge to the binational enterprise. The Group profited from the strong leadership of Henri Deterding, but his long reign also created serious managerial problems, culminating in a difficult transition period upon his succession. The nationalization of the oil industry in many producing countries during the 1970s posed another threat to the major oil companies, including the Group. In all these cases the Group found solutions, and adapted to new circumstances.

The general statement about the achievement of longevity requires some qualification, however. Compared to its main rivals the Group was very successful at some times, but at others it struggled to keep pace. Figure 2 compares the capitalized values of Exxon and BP with that of Shell.[2] Although admittedly market capitalization is a fairly limited way of looking at the business, this serves well as an indication of what were the good and the bad times for Shell.

Between 1907 and 1920, Royal Dutch/Shell established itself as the main rival to Standard Oil of New Jersey (Jersey Standard, later Exxon). During the interwar years the differences between these two top players remained small. Shell consolidated its

position in the 1920s and for most of the time Jersey Standard was the largest company in terms of market capitalization, though not in terms of crude production. At some times, around 1920 and again during the second half of the 1930s, the Group's market capitalization overtook Jersey Standard's. Until the 1990s Anglo-Persian (later Anglo-Iranian and subsequently BP) remained much smaller than either Jersey or Shell. After the Second World War a sudden divergence occurred between Shell and Jersey, leaving Shell very much behind its main American rival, despite Shell's rapid operational expansion. But the Group showed considerable resilience, and managed to close the gap during the 1980s. In the meantime BP gradually became a serious competitor.

From about 1980 onwards, Shell's capitalized value increased strongly in comparison to that of Exxon and BP, until by the middle of the 1990s Shell was arguably back where it had been in the 1920s, as the most successful oil company in the world. However, Exxon and BP participated in the merger wave of the late 1990s, while Shell did not. In 1998 BP merged with Amoco and in 1999 Exxon with Mobil. The jump in their share capitalization brought Exxon well ahead of Shell and made BP a close contender for the second position among the western oil majors. This concluding chapter seeks to explain the relative successes and failures.

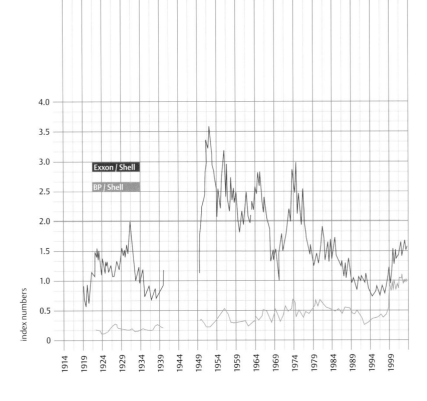

Access to crude oil: from expansion to consolidation

Royal Dutch/Shell was the first fully integrated and global oil enterprise, and from the start was strong in both upstream and downstream activities. Soon after the merger of 1907, in what was perhaps one of the most spectacular growth spurts in modern business history, it expanded to incorporate production, transport, refining and marketing in all inhabited continents. Having access both to cheap sources of crude oil and a vast transport and marketing apparatus was its most obvious strength in the early days. These gave it the competitive edge, enabling it to take over other oil companies in the Dutch East Indies, and proved vital in the 1910/11 price war, when Standard Oil tested the perseverance of the new combination. Figure 3 highlights the steep rise in the Group's share of world crude oil production, from about 9 per cent before the First World War to about 12 per cent in the early 1920s, and that in spite of the loss of its Russian oil fields after the revolution.[3] By contrast, Standard had traditionally based its strength on transport and refining, and had been relatively weak in exploration and production. Moreover, Standard had been greatly dependent on American sources of supply, whereas the Group controlled sources of supply around the world. The dissolution of the Standard Oil trust in 1911 forced its successor companies to change strategy. Jersey Standard copied Shell's success and reorganized itself into a comparably integrated company with a similar global spread of upstream operations.

Royal Dutch/Shell's rapid and spectacular rise was to a large extent the result of the commercial and strategic genius of Henri Deterding. He not only created the Group, by engineering the 1902 marketing alliance and the merger of 1907, but he also laid down the structure yoking together the two companies from different countries. His first overriding aim was to build a concern to

Figure 2
Capitalized value of Exxon, and BP compared with Shell (Shell = 1), 1914-2004.

index numbers

compete on a global scale with the Standard Oil trust. When he had realized this aim, and had in fact overtaken Standard by some measures, he turned to consolidating the Group's position within the oil industry. This intention led Deterding to mastermind the famous Achnacarry agreement in 1928, intended as the blueprint for a worldwide cartel by the framing of general rules for respecting each other's market shares. Achnacarry stabilized relationships within the oil industry, and in particular Jersey and the Group accepted each other as approximate equals with whom risks and profits could be shared as and when practicable.

As a consequence of this turn towards the stabilization of market shares, Shell became distinctly less adventurous. Until the mid-1920s the company had rarely passed a commercial opportunity, taking a leading role in Russia, Romania, in Iraq through the Turkish Petroleum Company, in Mexico, and in Venezuela. Now, however, Shell began to miss a few chances,

Figure 3
Share of Shell, Exxon, and BP in world
crude oil production, 1900-2000.

most notably the opportunity to participate in the development of Bahrain and Saudi Arabia. During the Depression of the 1930s the Group also operated more cautiously than its competitors, probably because it took the fragile instruments of the Achnacarry agreement more seriously than the other majors, including Jersey. This led to a loss of market share and to Jersey overtaking the Group as the biggest producer of crude oil from the early 1930s.

After 1945, regaining parity with Jersey Standard proved to be difficult. Shell's share in crude oil production remained below the peak of the 1920s (Figure 3) due to the loss of its resources in Indonesia and Romania, and the missed opportunities in the Middle East. In this respect BP, and some of the American independents not included in the figure, were much more successful during the middle decades of the twentieth century. Shell did participate in some of the joint ventures with which the majors divided the Middle Eastern oil between them, but not in the most important one, Aramco in Saudi Arabia. Throughout the 1950s and 1960s the Group conducted intensive exploration operations, typically drilling over a thousand onshore wells a year in the US alone, and with enough success to keep it in the running overall. The Group followed a strategy of balancing supply regions so as not to become too dependent on any single one. In addition it eagerly adopted the post-war move to offshore drilling, contributing much to the development of the technology required. In 1960 Shell discovered oil off Qatar: a valuable addition to its Middle East interests which was enhanced by a subsequent exclusive agreement to develop offshore Kuwaiti oil. However, while it was true that the willingness to explore and produce in difficult areas represented one of the Group's traditional strengths, it also expressed one of its more recent weaknesses: a comparative lack of easy access to cheap oil. Moreover, Shell was not uniformly successful, finding oil in Oman after the competition had given up, but exploring for years in Alaska and then missing Prudhoe Bay by a few miles.

The first oil crisis of 1973 brought a severe loss of share in crude oil production for Shell, Exxon, and BP (Figure 3). Nonetheless they continued to play leading roles in the oil business, a remarkable achievement given the complete change in circumstances. Though none of them afterward came even close to their former share in world's crude oil production, they did regain some lost ground. Shell now reaped the benefits of its previous E&P strategy, spreading supply regions and developing offshore positions. The Group was particularly successful during the 1970s and 1980s in finding and producing crude oil from new sources of equity oil in the Gulf of Mexico, the North Sea, and Nigeria, high oil prices enabling it (in line with the other majors) to explore in these more difficult territories. Shell also showed a remarkable flexibility in adjusting to the new situation of more demanding governments in oil-producing countries. During the long period of low oil prices in the 1990s, Shell focused on finding oil close to its existing operations. By the end of the twentieth century it had also succeeded in gaining (or regaining) access to Middle Eastern countries and to Russia. It continued to have a global spread of oil production balancing geographical risks. By showing only oil production, Figure 3 omits gas, which became more and more important during the second half of the twentieth century, notably outside North America. Shell helped to pioneer the technique of refrigerating gas in order to transport it as liquefied natural gas (LNG) in purpose-built LNG tankers, to be turned back from liquid form into gas at its destination. During the 1980s and 1990s Shell was a more important player in natural gas than either Exxon or BP. In the 1990s Shell extended its activities in gas further, because the company expected gas, as a cleaner energy source, to have the future. However, it lost its lead after the consolidation of its rivals in the late 1990s.

Changing fortunes downstream   The Group's early success was built on the fact that it expanded in both upstream and downstream, pioneering the model of the integrated company. Gasoline became the Group's most prominent product – sold to the largest customer constituency, namely motorists – and, though Royal Dutch was the dominant partner, 'Shell' became the Group's dominant brand-name, promoted during the interwar years with top-rank innovative advertising. During the 1920s the Group's refineries developed into producers of a wide variety of different products, creating in the 1930s and early 1940s a strong position that was a great support in rebuilding after the Second World War.

After the war the combination of an abundant supply of crude oil and eager consumers for oil products should have meant an ideal situation for Shell's downstream business. However, circumstances were not as rosy as they looked. Many competitors used their upstream business to generate profits and their downstream business to offload the crude oil at cost price, creating a vicious competition at the pump. Shell resisted the pressure to compete on price and preferred to uphold profits, partly because the downstream expansion already stretched financial and managerial resources to their limits, and partly because the relative lack of cheap Middle Eastern oil prevented the Group from fully competing on price. Shell also considered its downstream operations as a long-term asset not to be squandered. As a consequence, marketing policy continued to centre on brand imaging and product differentiation sustained by promotional campaigns rather than keen pricing, at the cost of losing market share.

In the 1950s and 1960s the Group demonstrated the viability of being a leading company yet crude short. For a variety of reasons, it started shifting manufacturing capacity from producing

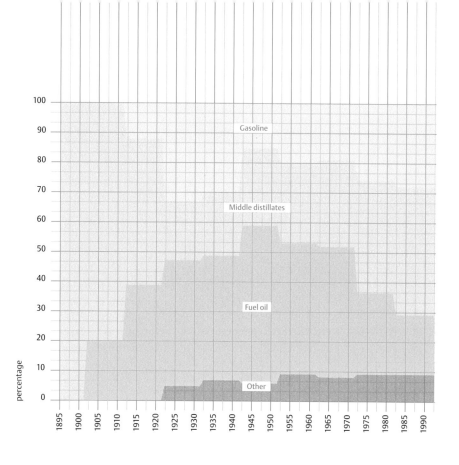

percentage

Figure 4
Barrel cut of the Group (outside
North America), 1895-1990.

Figure 5
Oil products sales of Shell, Exxon,
and BP, 1967-2005.

countries to consuming countries, building a large number of comparatively small refineries. Once that had been achieved, marketing policy shifted to regaining market share by a more aggressive sales policy.

However, during the 1970s the forecast growth in consumption failed to materialize, causing a sudden overcapacity in manufacturing. The situation was made infinitely more complex and confusing by the nationalization of oil assets by the oil-producing countries. With OPEC's quadrupling of crude prices after 1973 the Group considered selling some of its downstream operations to the producing nations in exchange for access to crude. However, these transactions did not come about, and instead the Group came to see its access to consumers as some-thing to be treasured as a way of keeping a strong presence in the oil industry. In response to the higher crude oil prices, Shell's European refineries adopted a strategy of 'whitening the barrel', i.e. upgrading its refineries to produce higher value oil products, a strategy Shell Oil in the US had followed from the 1950s. Figure 4 (above) shows the Group's marked change in policy, reducing its

traditionally large fuel oil sales and increasing the production of gasoline and middle distillates.[4] Although very successful in its own terms, this strategy worsened the refinery overcapacity. Despite rising sales of oil products during the 1980s and 1990s, the industry in general continued to struggle with overcapacity in refining during the entire last quarter of the twentieth century.

As for sales, Shell's revenues and volume were normally more or less on a par with Exxon, and considerably higher than those of BP. However, during the 1980s the Group's volume overtook Exxon's, underlining Shell's strong overall performance during that decade (Figure 5).[5] The low oil prices of the 1990s helped the downstream business to become more profitable. Not until the early years of the twenty-first century did demand for oil products increase sufficiently for refining margins to increase substantially. Though normally downstream profits go down when upstream profits go up, and vice versa, the high demand for oil products in those years made both the upstream and downstream business of Shell very profitable, all the more as it once again preferred profitability over sales volume.

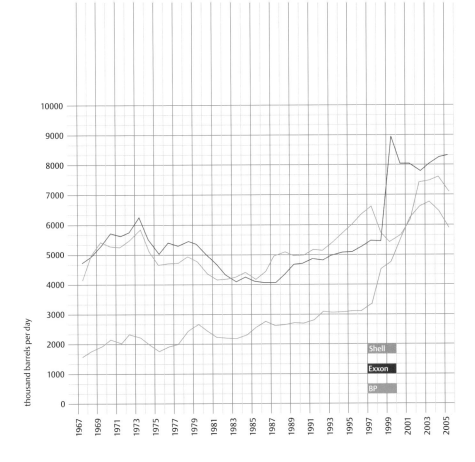

Technology and innovation

Technological innovation was one of the Group's lasting strengths. From early on, managers such as Bob Waley Cohen, Josef Erb, Dan Pyzel, Frits de Kok, and Guus Kessler took a keen interest in up-to-date technology and convinced their colleagues of the need to invest heavily in R & D. Earlier than most oil companies, Shell employed geologists in the search for oil to reduce the factor of chance. Moreover, the range of innovations sponsored by the Group even during its early decades is impressive: from Edeleanu installations and toluol extraction to the development of Diesel engines, hydrogenation, and synthetic chemicals from petroleum. In the more recent past their spiritual descendants have been just as strongly attracted by cutting-edge sciences such as 3-D imaging and gas-to-liquids technologies. This absorbing interest for new technology repeatedly helped to create competitive advantages for Shell during its first century, but at times it stood at cross purposes with the Group's overall commercial and financial objectives. The best example is its early and lasting commitment to petrochemicals which, although supported through thick and thin by the

engineers and scientists at the top, failed to produce the expected benefits.

Nor did the other diversification attempts of the 1960s and 1970s lead to lasting success, whether they concerned metals, nuclear, or coal. These attempts were rooted in the belief that the oil industry had reached its mature phase, and that therefore the Group needed to branch out into other industries, preferably on the strength of its managerial and technical know-how, in order to sustain its growth performance. The Group predominantly looked at diversification opportunities with a clear link to its range of available technology, but Shell chose to diversify mainly through acquisitions rather than through developing new activities in-house.

Continuous investment in the research infrastructure of the Group's three main sources of new technology, the Netherlands, the UK, and the US, were part of the same story. Shell definitely found opening new horizons one of the main reasons for its existence. Managers nursed a strong conviction, indeed a firm belief, in technology as the solution to the world's problems.

Discovering new sources of oil and gas and new means to produce them, however deep the water or remote the environment, provided strong motives for pouring large amounts of money into research and development. This policy was rewarded by the Group's successes in developing the technology to chart underground reservoirs and to draw oil from undersea fields in water more than two kilometres deep. Similarly, Shell engineers were confident that in due time research would provide solutions to environmental problems, a confidence that was not justified in the case of pesticides. They were also convinced that future energy needs would be solved by new technologies that could get more oil out of the ground, or turn gas into oil, or coal into gas.

The Group's strong commitment to technology was a key factor in making the company an attractive and sometimes inevitable partner for national oil companies in producing countries and for the other oil majors alike. Shell was an industry leader in technology and in some cases, such as deepwater and LNG, the leader. Moreover, Group engineers also wanted to be closely involved in actual operations, partly out of their love for technology, partly because of their experience in managing difficult projects. During the 1980s Shell was not the largest producer of oil, but it became by far the largest operator of the oil majors and kept that position during the 1990s and into the twenty-first century, until BP and Exxon closed the gap by 2005.

Management and staff   For a long time the Group's management was composed out of two distinct groups. Royal Dutch supplied mostly graduates, as often as not engineers from Delft, and Shell Transport marketers, who had usually joined the business straight from a public school, occasionally from Oxbridge. As a result British managers tended to focus on marketing and finance, while Dutch managers concentrated on research and technology. Both countries provided eager expatriates, and the two groups mixed very well. Sealed as it was by the practical split of managerial tasks between The Hague and London central offices, the marked difference between these two groups began to fade only with the introduction of uniform management courses during the 1950s.

During the first decades of the twentieth century, the Group was a major source of employment growth in the countries in which it operated. Reliable figures for the first fifty years are not available, but the number of its employees grew from perhaps a few thousand Indonesians and a few hundred Europeans in 1907 to approximately 240,000 in 1929.

The numbers of employees of the three oil majors declined steadily from the 1950s onwards, as one would expect in a mature industry (Figure 6).[6] However, different factors pushed down staff numbers during the last quarter of the twentieth century. Oil-producing countries took hold of the industry in their territory, reducing the number of people employed by the oil majors. Slow growth in oil product sales forced the companies to cut jobs. Likewise, the increasing practices of using contractors and of outsourcing non-core functions all reduced the number of people directly employed. On the other hand, mergers could substantially increase the workforce of a specific company. This explains the jump in the number of employees for BP and Exxon at the end of

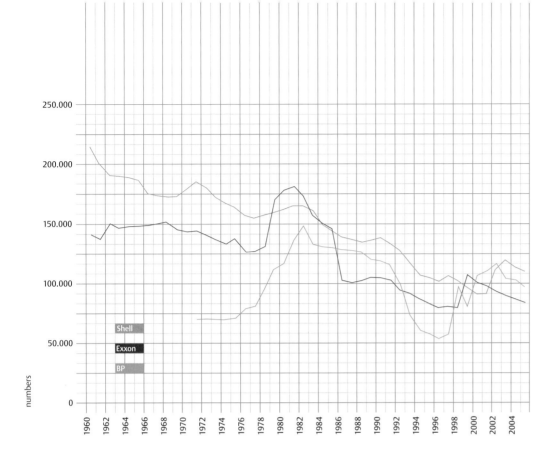

Figure 6
Numbers of employees at Shell, Exxon, and BP, 1960-2005.

the 1990s, while Shell's rise in 2002 resulted largely from an active takeover policy in its downstream operations.

There were, obviously, large differences in the employment terms offered, and in the salaries paid. Top managers were remunerated quite handsomely, in particular during the Group's first decades, when Deterding and his team were considered to be among the world's highest paid businessmen, mainly because they received a percentage of Royal Dutch's burgeoning profits. A core group of employees, numbering a few thousand Europeans and Americans, also received fairly favourable terms. On top of relatively high earnings the Group developed a package of services for this core group, ranging from sports facilities to insurance benefits, which helped to strengthen corporate identity and culture. In return, Shell demanded a very high degree of loyalty: in particular, staff had to accept postings to any part of the world, however remote, that the company considered in its best interest. The earnings of this core group stood in stark contrast with the low wages of the local workforces abroad, even if these wages were quite acceptable by local standards.

Shell's liking for science and technology was reflected in its academic outlook towards staff policy. In the 1950s business management came to be regarded as a skill to be taught to new generations on the basis of systematic analysis. Accordingly, the Group set up a uniform system of recruitment, assessment, and promotion for its core staff, including the expatriates. Local staff working for the operating companies received salaries in accordance with local standards, though Shell tended to pay at the higher end of what markets offered. During the booming 1950s and 1960s a job with the Group meant a job for life and Shell tended to be 'nice to a fault' to its staff, though always within the context of local circumstances. The singular importance attached to staff interests also manifested itself in the diversification debate, a prominent argument in favour pointing to the continuing need to offer challenging jobs to Group managers.

When during the 1970s staff cuts became inevitable in some operations, Shell tried to limit the number of redundancies as much as possible. However, the 1990s witnessed a fundamental change in attitude towards employees. The Group no longer considered it a duty to provide jobs for life, or to plan careers for its staff. Employees were expected to take their own responsibility, to become flexible, to apply for jobs within the business, or else to find a job outside if their services were no longer needed. This policy also applied to the core staff from which the expatriates were recruited. The changed attitude towards terms of employment followed a power shift within the Group's management. If the investors' interests appeared to require the cutting of costs and the shedding of jobs, then people had to go. Even top managers risked losing their jobs if they failed to satisfy the shareholders.

Relationships with shareholders   This power shift was the latest in several changes in the Group's relationship with its shareholders between 1907 and 2007. During the first expansionary phase, until the mid-1920s, managers kept a close watch over the share prices, because takeovers were usually paid with shares. As this need disappeared, the Group's attitude towards investors became less attentive and considerate, as is clear from legal proceedings between dissatisfied investors and Royal Dutch and Bataafsche during the 1930s. To some extent the changing relationship between shareholders and the Group is reflected in the return on shares, though crude oil prices also played a key role. The return on shares is defined as the sum of dividends (and bonus shares) received and the increase in share price during a given year, divided by the share price at the beginning of that year. We have no reliable data on share prices for Shell Transport before 1906, but Royal Dutch was one of the best investments one could make during the first quarter of the twentieth century, when returns on its shares were more than 24 per cent annually on average, and slightly less for Shell (Figure 7).[7] The next twenty-five years were rather meagre: the average investor acquired a 7.7 per cent average return from shares in Royal Dutch, and 6.3 per cent on Shell Transport. The depression of the 1930s and the Second World War inevitably damaged the companies' results.

During the post-war era, the relations with employees had priority above those with investors, but the listing of Royal Dutch shares on the New York Stock Exchange in 1954 showed a clear need to improve the relationship with the shareholders through better communication. The 1950s were again very good for investors in the two parent companies, but then there followed fifteen years of relatively low results caused by low oil prices and accelerating inflation, which depressed returns in real terms.

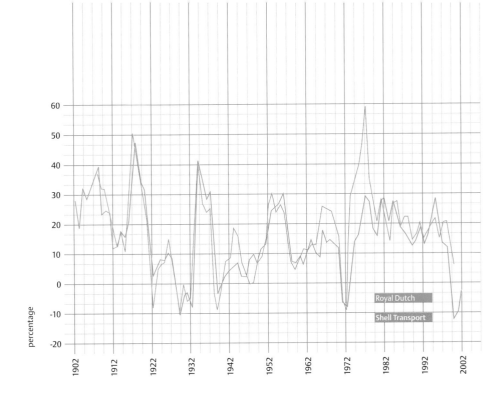

The effect of the steep rise in oil prices in 1973 did not translate into a similar rise in returns, probably because of the huge investments made to develop new oil and gas producing areas. The rest of the Group's first century was very good for investors in either of the Group parent companies, especially during the 1980s and 1990s, with low inflation and high real results. One might have expected investors to have suffered during the period of low oil prices in the 1990s, but that did not happen. Perhaps as a consequence of shareholder pressure, the Group continued to make high profits and to pay matching dividends, though, as it turned out, at the cost of future production growth.

In the very long run the shareholder results have been impressive. Despite the many ups and downs in the course of the Group's first century, the average annual return on Royal Dutch shares from the foundation of the company was 15.7 per cent, and on Shell Transport shares (over the period 1906-2000) 17.5 per cent, with the difference between the parent companies entirely due to exchange rate fluctuations. By comparison, an investment in government bonds either in Britain or the Netherlands would have yielded three to four per cent annually. It is easy to see why stockbrokers for many decades routinely advised their clients that they should 'Never sell Shell.'

The Group, governments and NGOs   The 1907 merger deliberately left the parent companies Royal Dutch and Shell Transport intact as separate corporations. This enabled the Group to operate as a single organization and yet keep all the advantages gained in its two countries of origin: Royal Dutch's very close links with the Dutch colonial elite and its unchallenged position in the Dutch East Indies, the Group's main source of profits until the mid-1920s; and Shell Transport's status as a prominent British company, with access not only to markets and concessions in the British Empire, but also in countries considered to be within the British sphere of influence, such as Mexico and Venezuela. Deterding realized that creating a truly global enterprise capable of challenging Standard Oil required the protection of the British Empire, the only body that could counterbalance the growing economic and political power of the United States. By establishing himself and the Group's de facto headquarters in London, by using Shell as the main brand, and by carefully coaxing Marcus Samuel back to an active role, Deterding succeeded in positioning the Group as a British company in the public eye. At the same time he took care to keep Royal Dutch's base in the Netherlands strong, thus building an exceptional combination that drew on the joint strengths of the two countries – in fact, of the two empires. Having dual nationality also enabled the Group to move subsidiaries from one parent company to another for fiscal or political expedience.

If in creating the dual structure Deterding had showed himself to be sensitive to the importance of politics and national power, his astuteness began to fail him after the First World War. He could simply not come to terms with the political changes wrought by the war, notably the rising importance of economic nationalism which the Group first encountered when the Soviet Union nationalized its oil industry after the revolution there. As a result, he became emotionally charged and inflexible in his dealing with governments. Meanwhile other Group managing directors developed a more practical attitude towards national aspirations. Kessler, for instance, argued that it was important to look after the company's interest, but at the same time the business should also benefit the host country. This pragmatic approach was also inspired by the experience that Shell's power to force issues was closely circumscribed by the fact that governments could always find rival oil companies willing to take over, even if Shell cooperated with Standard Jersey in trying to impose a boycott. This led managers to adopt a policy of tenacious flexibility: standing firm on principles while always keeping negotiations open in the hope of finding a solution. If the policy failed in the face of governments determined to take control, such as the Hitler government, then at least it succeeded in the Group obtaining a better price for its assets, as happened following the nationalization of oil assets in Mexico in 1938.

Shell showed a similar open-minded and flexible attitude towards the rise of OPEC during the 1960s and 1970s, preferring an open dialogue over confrontation. It probably could afford to be more flexible than the other oil majors, because it had a better regional spread of oil production. Moreover, the Group's emphasis on operational decentralization and a delegation of authority to the lowest level practicable, which was enhanced after 1973, enabled the company to adjust quickly to the ambitions of governments in oil producing countries. These two tenets stimulated local managers to align Shell's interest with that of their host countries, enabling them to deploy a great political sensitivity which in turn made their operating companies into attractive partners for governments.

Such an identification with local national interests, however, sometimes landed the Group in difficulties. This happened, for instance, when Shell companies in Mozambique and South Africa used their subjection to the laws of their host country to break the oil boycott against Rhodesia. Moreover, the evolution of international relations began to impose limits on the leeway of local operating companies. With the rise of non-governmental organizations in the US and Europe, events in one country easily became a focus of attention in another, the media providing ever faster coverage from around the world. During the 1970s and 1980s the Group came under attack over political issues, in particular its presence in South Africa under the apartheid regime. Shell responded by taking a close look at its business aims and principles, first drafted in 1962 and restated in 1976 as a formal document entitled 'Statement of Business Principles'. Initially intended as guidelines for the local operating companies, these principles developed into a set of criteria to judge whether the Group could continue working in a certain country. The Group felt that, as long as an operating company could follow the Shell business principles in its own operations, it had a right to stay in that country. For that reason Shell stayed in South Africa, despite having to face, for the first time, a – not very effective – consumer boycott in the US.

NGOs also challenged the Group on its environmental policies, and here the company could get caught in the crossfire of different national viewpoints. In 1995, for instance, when Greenpeace attacked Shell over the announced sinking of the Brent Spar, Britain agreed with the sinking, but some continental European countries were against it. NGOs also accused the Group of having double standards in protecting the environment. Following national regulations was not considered enough; the Group ought to have global standards, and very much higher ones. Other NGOs supported inhabitants of the Niger delta in their protests against Shell's oil production there, and against the fact that the population suffered from the negative effects of the oil production on their environment without benefiting from the profits. The continuing serious problems in the Niger delta had a very negative impact on the Group's reputation. Under the influence of the NGOs, Shell reformulated its business principles, in 1997 for the first time including human rights.

At the beginning of the twenty-first century rising oil prices and mounting concern for energy safety combined in a tougher attitude of national governments towards the oil industry in their countries, which led to a number of nationalizations. Shell responded with the same practical and flexible approach it had used so effectively in the past.

Running a cross-border business   The Group's dual nationality had political and fiscal advantages, but it also posed formidable managerial challenges. Initially, Shell's organization was held together by a fairly small team of top managers with interlocking directorships on the boards of parent companies, holding companies, and main operating companies. Around them a wider group of internationally active managers developed, running operating companies or concentrating on specific topics of vital interest to the business, such as geology in the case of Erb, or technology in the case of Pyzel. These managers moved from one subsidiary to the next, creating a close network within the Group. This simple hierarchical model worked well enough in the globalized world before 1914, with its highly integrated markets. However, the structure came under serious strain from the Group's rapid expansion and then the economic disintegration caused by the First World War. Restrictive legislation, rising taxation, tariff barriers, protectionism, and the appearance of national oil companies all worked to disrupt the Group's global strategy and challenge the organization built to execute it. Asiatic Petroleum, for instance, now had to form separate marketing subsidiaries for the countries in which it operated, creating an additional layer in the organization. Moreover, Asiatic needed managers versed in local circumstances to run them. The proliferation of operating companies altered the managerial balance within the Group, central offices finding it increasingly difficult to retain their grip. The growing number of agreements and joint ventures with other oil companies which followed in the wake of Achnacarry added further complexity.

This fundamental problem should have been addressed much earlier than it was. During the 1920s, Deterding resisted changes, wanting to keep close control over the whole enterprise.

Then the conflict between British and Dutch managers which flared up after his resignation in 1936 prevented any managerial reform for another decade. It was only after the resolution of this conflict culminating in the installation of the de facto committee of managing directors in 1946 that Shell could embark on re-engineering its organization. This took another decade and more, underlining the sheer difficulty of finding a structure reconciling the need for local flexibility with central control. Exercising control through a core group of top managers made for bloated central offices, while keeping a tight rein on operating companies stifled local enterprise. Moreover, managing individual operating companies rather than business functions blunted the economic purposes of integration, i.e. maximizing coordination and building economies of scale. In 1954 the committee of managing directors (not yet formalized as CMD) took the first step towards what became known as the matrix organization by the appointment of functional coordinators to balance the regional coordinators at central offices. However, the required complete overhaul came about only after the determined push delivered by McKinsey & Co. during 1958-59. This reorganization was a remarkable accomplishment in every way, for its speed and scope, for the cost savings and achieved aims, but perhaps most notably for the balance which it created between functional versus regional interests on the one hand, and between central coordination and control versus local operational responsibility on the other.

The matrix organization served the company well during the 1960s and 1970s. When the oil-producing countries took control over their own resources, Shell responded by another round of decentralization, giving general managers more power over their operating companies. However, this devolution of power had its costs as well. General managers would take decisions on the basis of local interests, rather than those of Shell as a whole. In the downstream sector, decentralization created a duplication of refineries and an endless variety of sales conditions. Consequently, the Group failed to reap some of the economies which its scale ought to have generated. Nor could Shell capitalize on the new opportunities created by the internet and e-mail, because the power of local executives cancelled out the benefits of rapid and easy communication between central offices and operating companies. Finally, the elaborate structure of checks and balances was also expensive. This became a serious problem when the globalization of capital markets increased the pressure on companies to raise their return on capital, which the oil companies found particularly difficult to do at a time of low oil prices.

For these reasons the CMD decided on another radical overhaul of the organization in the mid-1990s. The managers of the business sectors changed from 'coordinators' into CEOs, while the national chairs became representatives. This structure was meant to be cheaper and more responsive to economic globalization, but it remained to be seen whether it would show itself as politically sensitive as the old one. This became all the more important when in the beginning of the twenty-first century national interests stirred again.

British-Dutch collaboration In order to work properly, the Group's dual nationality also required keeping a balance between the two national groups, an issue seldom openly discussed yet always present in the background. With its 60 per cent share in the Group, Royal Dutch had the upper hand, but Shell Transport was located in the larger and politically more powerful country. As early as 1914, Marcus Samuel unsuccessfully tried to renegotiate the merger. After the First World War, the British government considered various schemes to obtain control of the Group, including a transfer of all main operating companies to a British company, and even a merger of Shell Transport with Anglo-Persian, all designed to lessen the participation of Royal Dutch. However, none of these plans went ahead.

From 1938 Shell Transport directors once again sought to achieve an equal partnership between Royal Dutch and Shell Transport. In 1945 the boards of the parent companies endorsed a change of the 60-40 ratio to 50-50, as part of a deal involving Shell Transport's acceptance of a management reform transferring the Group's top management to a committee of managing directors. However, the Dutch government, anxious to safeguard national assets at a time of economic hardship, blocked this change. After that, the 60-40 discussion resurfaced occasionally, but Royal Dutch did not see any reason to relinquish its majority. The globalizing world blunted the chauvinist edges of the ownership ratio anyway. Royal Dutch no longer represented Dutch shareholders' interests alone, or even predominantly. With the introduction of its shares on various stock exchanges abroad, the company obtained a very wide spread of ownership. During the latter half of the twentieth century, the Dutch share varied between nearly half to a little less than a third of the total. The Group's top management also became increasingly internationalized, rendering British-Dutch discussions a little provincial.

Nor was there a sufficient incentive for change. With the CMD and the Conference in essence acting as Shell's executive committee and board respectively, the management structure – Byzantine to the outside world – did not in effect differ all that much from common corporate arrangements, perhaps only in having more checks and balances. Consequently, when during the 1990s financial markets exercised pressure for greater corporate transparency, the Group examined the options for a simplification of its structure by a merger between the parent companies, only to relent in the face of the expected legal and fiscal complications.

In 2005, the commotion over the reserves recategorization and the need to restore public and private confidence finally provided the catalyst to abolish the two parent companies and transform the dual nationality into a different yet equally unique form, a company with a British corporate structure and its legal seat in the UK, but with its headquarters and tax residence in the Netherlands. The financial world welcomed this major restructuring, not just because it had happened, but because the Group's effort to restore public and private trust had gone beyond what analysts had expected. By embarking on its second century in an entirely reconstructed form, Shell demonstrated that it still had the power to adapt and to surprise.

Notes

Introduction

1   SLA SC91/1/1, introduction.

2   SLA, *Personnel Management Review*, no. 11, March 1971.

Chapter 1

1   Hartshorn, *Oil trade*, 2-3: From 1913 to 1948 its long-run growth rate was around 6.5 per cent annually, doubling the world production every twelve years. In the next twenty-five years production growth was even faster, increasing by more than 7.5 per cent annually.

2   Levy, 'World oil marketing in transition', 113-33, 117 and 121.

3   Amuzegar, *Managing the Oil Wealth*, 29-30; Shell Oil Archive, Box ID: 163055271, OPEC reference book, January 1981.

4   SLA SC91/b/2, 2 of 2, interviews with senior staff.

5   Yergin, *Prize*, 580.

6   The National Archives UK (former Public Record Office), PREM 15, 505, Sir David Barran of Shell gave PM exposition of study of future energy supply and demand, 1971; Teheran treaty: *Petroleum Intelligence Weekly (PIW)*, 22 February 1971.

7   SLA, SC91/a/2; also SC91/b/19, Shell warnings to Governments.

8   The National Archives UK, POWE 63/828, a report by J. Atkins of the US Department of State in 1971.

9   Odell pointed out how inconsistent this policy was. If the future energy supply was at stake, the Americans could better have imported more oil in order to keep more oil in the ground for future consumption: Odell, *Olie en macht*, 39.

10   Yergin, *Prize*, 567, 589-99.

11   SLA, SC91/b/20, Bénard's material 1968-76.

12   Adelman, *Genie out of the Bottle*, 99-105, and Adelman, 'Is the oil shortage real?', 69-108.

13   The industry uses the expression 'host government take' for the combination of royalties, income taxes imposed on production of oil company equity crude oil, and the income out of equity for which

the governments did not pay. Host government take on equity volume of Arabian light increased from $0.91 in 1 January 1971 to $8.26 in 1 October 1974. 'Investment in oil', *Shell Briefing Service (SBS)* (1974), 4.

14 Amuzegar, *Managing the Oil Wealth*, 30; *RD Annual Report*, 1973.

15 The National Archives UK, POWE 63/828, speech to the 26**th** annual conference of the Middle East Institute, 30 September 1972.

16 The National Archives UK, POWE 63/828.

17 Meadows et al., *The Limits to Growth*.

18 Adelman, *Genie out of the Bottle*, 109.

19 Ibid. 109-12.

20 The National Archives UK, CAB 186, 15, report nr. 34, 5 December 1973.

21 The National Archives UK, CAB 164/1199, discussion between Lord Carrington, McFadzean and Baxendell, 5 Nov. 1973.

22 SLA, SC91/a/2, Shell and the oil crisis.

23 The National Archives UK, PREM 15/1838, note of a discussion at Chequers on the evening of Sunday 21 October on supply and price of oil. This meeting took place after the OAPEC countries had announced the first of several cuts in production and two days before they announced an embargo on shipments to the Netherlands.

24 Yergin, *Prize*, 623-4: the remarks about the nationality of the companies are not included in the official minutes of this meeting, but could have been made during the 'off the record' talks.

25 Bamberg, *BP and global oil*, 483-4.

26 *Petroleum Intelligence Weekly*, 8 December 1973.

27 Hellema, Wiebes, and Witte, *Doelwit Rotterdam*, 55-71: On 21 October 1973 the OAPEC called for a boycott of the Netherlands and in the following weeks

Algeria, Kuwait, Abu Dhabi, Qatar, Libya, and Saudi Arabia responded. Iraq nationalized the Dutch share of Shell in the Basrah Petroleum Company, but did not follow the embargo. Nor did Iran participate in the embargo.

28 Hellema, Wiebes, and Witte, *Doelwit Rotterdam*, 114-20.

29 Adelman, *Genie out of the Bottle*, 110-2.

30 SHA, Minutes Conference, 14 April 1974 and 12 June 1974.

31 SLA, SC91/b/6: memo May 1975.

32 'Report by the Commission on the behaviour of the oil companies in the Community during the period from October 1973 to March 1974' (Brussels, 1975), 3, 154-62.

33 Yergin, *Prize*, 656-9.

34 *Shell News*, 1975, nr. 1, 30-4; nr. 2, 12-3.

35 In 1976 the oil expert M.A. Adelman, Professor of Economics at MIT, wrote in the Washington Post: 'Vertical divestiture would keep Congress and the oil industry busy for years, spinning their wheels, going no place, postponing investment decisions, losing a chance for active defense against the [OPEC] cartel, admitting finally: "wasted time, and now doth time waste me".' *Shell News*, 1976, nr. 4, 4-6 and nr. 6, 21-5.

36 SHA, 282, E&P report 1973; Minutes Conference, 15 May 1974.

37 SHA, Minutes Conference, 10 April 1974.

38 SHA, Minutes Conference, 15 Jan. 1975; *RD Annual Report*, 1974.

39 *RD Annual Reports*, 1972 1976, SHA, E&P reports 1973-75.

40 SLA, CMD files, DCS, C31, minutes CMD, 8-9 Jan. 1974 and 12 Nov. 1974 (quotation); SHA, Minutes Conference, memorandum for Conference at 16 Jan 1974; *RD Annual Report*, 1975.

41 SLA, CMD files, DCS, C30, Venezuela 1969-

74: presentation Wetherell and Quiros to CMD on strategy in Venezuela.

42 SLA, CMD files, DCS, C33, Venezuela 1975, minutes CMD, 9, 16 and 30 Sept. 1975, Shell Brief, 31 October 1975; *RD Annual Reports*, 1971-76; Yergin, *Prize*, 650.

43 *RD Annual Reports*, 1973, 1974; SHA, E&P report 1979.

44 SHA, E&P report 1973; Minutes Conference, 16 May 1979, and 14 May 1980, E&P report 1979; Yergin, *Prize*, 696.

45 SHA, Minutes Conference, 6 Feb. 1974, 15 Jan. 1975; SLA, IT 42, Kuwait Agreement.

46 SHA, Minutes Conference, 10 April 1974, 10 July 1974, 11 Dec. 1974; Yergin, *Prize*, 651-652.

47 Sources: *Oil and Gas International Yearbook*, vols. 63-67 (1973-77); *Financial Times Oil and Gas International Yearbook*, vols. 68-89 (1978-99); Walter E. Skinner, eds., *Oil and Petroleum Yearbook*, vol. 19-62 (1928-72), *RD Annual Reports*, 1960-86.

48 Levy, 'World oil marketing in transition', 117.

49 Taverne, *Petroleum, Industry and Governments*, 154-5.

50 *Shell World*, Oct./Nov. 1979, 10.

51 *Shell Magazine*, 1975, nr. 1, 10, speech in October 1974.

52 *Shell World*, July/August 1977; Who's Who 1995; Wagner chaired an advisory governmental committee that published the following report: Adviescommissie inzake het industriebeleid, 'Een nieuw industrieel elan', (1981).

53 SHA, Minutes Conference, 18 May 1973.

54 Amuzegar, *Managing the Oil Wealth*, preface; SHA, Minutes Conference, 16 Jan. 1974, memorandum on the impact of rising oil prices on the world economic situation.

55 Shell Oil Archives, minutes Board of Directors, 27 Nov. 1973-24 April 1974; SLA,

PL 64/2. In 1975 it was remarked that Shell policy was not to facilitate OPEC countries' entry into the better markets: SHA, Minutes Conference, 9 April 1975.

56 'The Shifting Balance', *Petroleum Economist* (1975): 162-3, quotation 163.

57 SHA, E&P reports 1974-78; Interview of author with Pieter Folmer, Group Legal Director, 1997-2003, 4 November 2003.

58 *RD Annual Report*, 1976.

59 SHA, 202 A/1 and 2, Shell Expro 25 years, interview with William Bell, 13 April 1988. This and other interviews about Shell Expro were taken by David Jeremy and Francis Goodall from the Business History Unit of the London School of Economics in the cause of preparing a history of Shell Expro. This history was not published, though a manuscript is present in the The Hague Archives.

60 Veldman and Lagers, *50 Years Offshore*, 95-7, 105-11.

61 Bamberg, *BP and Global Oil*, 202-3; Yergin, *Prize*, 667-70.

62 SHA, 202 A/1 and 2, Shell Expro 25 years, interview with John Jennings by David Jeremy and Francis Goodall, 2 March 1988.

63 SHA, 202 A/1 and 2, Shell Expro 25 years, interview with David Frowd (interviewer unknown), 29 Jan. 1988; Adelman, *Genie out of the Bottle*, 152-3.

64 SHA, 202 A/1 and 2, Shell Expro 25 years, interview with Fred Chate by Francis Goodall, 23 Feb. 1988.

65 SHA, 202 A/1 and 2, Shell Expro 25 years, interview with William Bell by Francis Goodall and David Jeremy, 13 April 1988.

66 Interview of author with Jack Little, CEO Shell Oil 1998-99, 7 Feb. 2006.

67 SHA, 202 A/1 and 2, Shell Expro 25 years, interview with Jan Memelink by Francis Goodall, 9 March 1988.

68 SHA, Minutes Conference, 19 May 1976, 16

Nov. 1977; SHA, E&P report, 1977.

69 SHA, 202 A/1 and 2, Shell Expro 25 years, interview with Jan Memelink by Francis Goodall, 9 March 1988.

70 SHA, Minutes Conference, 21 May 1975, 14 April 1976, 14 Feb. 1979, and 13 June 1979.

71 RD, *Annual Reports*, 1974, 1975; SHA, MC, 15 Sept. 1976; SHA, Shell Expro 25 years, interviews with David Frowd (29 Jan. 1988), William Bell (13 April 1988), and John Jennings (2 March 1988), by Francis Goodall and David Jeremy.

72 SHA, Minutes Conference, 9 Feb. 1977, 12 April 1978, 12 Sept. 1979.

73 SHA, Minutes Conference, 18 May 1977, E&P report 1976; SHA, Shell Expro 25 years, interview with William Bell by Francis Goodall and David Jeremy, 13 April 1979.

74 *RD Annual Reports*, 1981 and 1982; SHA, Shell Expro, 25 years, interview with Jan Memelink by Francis Goodall, 9 March 1988.

75 *RD Annual Reports*, 1976, 1977, 1979, 1982.

76 SHA, Shell Expro 25 years, interview with Ian Henderson by Francis Goodall, 24 June 1988.

77 *RD Annual Reports*, 1978-1986: for earlier years no data were given in the reports.

78 SHA, Minutes Conference, 9 June 1976, 12 Jan. 1977; *RD Annual Reports*, 1976 and 1977

79 Bamberg, *BP and Global Oil*, 199-200; SHA, Shell Expro 25 years, manuscript.

80 SLA, SC33/49; Lerøen, *Troll*, 23-4.

81 Adelman, *Genie out of the Bottle*, 160-7; Levy, 'Years that the locust hath eaten'.

82 SHA, Minutes Conference, 13 Sept. 1978.

83 *OPEC* Official resolutions, 159; Adelman, *Genie out of the Bottle*, 169.

84 Yergin, *Prize*, 674-98; SHA, Minutes Conference, 10 Jan. 1979.

85 SLA, SC91/b/12 Sitco.

86 Source: website Energy Information Administration *www.eia.doe.gov/*, BP crude oil prices; 1945-85: Arabian light posted at Ras Tanura, 1986-99: Brent Spot.

87 SHA, Minutes Conference, 6 Feb. 1974.

88 Shell World, July/August 1976 and Dec. 1979.

89 Bamberg, *BP and Global Oil*, 258-60; *RD Annual Report*, 1975; SHA, Minutes Conference, 10 December 1975, memorandum 3 December 1975.

90 *RD Annual Report*, 1975; SHA, Minutes Conference, 15 Jan. 1975, SHA, Minutes Conference, 11 Sept. 1974, 9 Oct. 1974, 9 Feb. 1977.

91 Wesseling, *Fuelling the War*, 30: 'As for fuel being delivered to the enemy through Vietnamese army and civilian channels, we knew that trading of hard wood or rice with the North Vietnamese or Vietcong was a common occurrence, given the intermingling of the two opponents. Oil was no exception.'

92 *Life on the Move*, 123; SHA, Minutes Conference, 9 April 1978.

93 *Shell Magazine*, 1975, no. 2, 'The art of the possible'.

94 *RD/S, Financial and Operational Information*, 1960-86.

95 SHA, Minutes Conference, 10 Jan. 1975, 12 Feb. 1975, 13 July 1977; SLA, SC91/c/1, development of Sitco; *Shell Magazine*, 1975, Vol. 3, Introducing Sitco.

96 Levy, 'World oil marketing in transition', 121.

97 SLA, SC91/b/12, Sitco.

98 Yergin, *Prize*, 699-714; Columbia Encyclopaedia, **6th** edn. 2001.

99 SHA, Minutes Conference, 14 May and 19 June 1980.

100 'Oil prices', *Shell Briefing Service (SBS)* (1987).

101 SHA, Minutes Conference, 10 July 1974.

102 SHA, Minutes Conference, 21 May 1975.

103 SHA, Minutes Conference, 21 May 1975; SLC, SC22/27, supply position; *RD Annual Report*, 1975.

104 SHA, Minutes Conference, 14 June 1978, Marine Report; Howarth, *Sea Shell*, 171.

105 SHA, Minutes Conference, 14 June 1978.

106 SHA, 190Y, dossier 79; Minutes Conference, 13 June 1979; Wouters, *Shell Tankers*, 166-7.

107 SHA, Minutes Conference, 12 April 1978; Howarth, *Sea Shell*, 174.

108 SHA, Minutes Conference, 16 May 1979.

109 Source: Skinner, ed., *Oil and Petroleum Year Book*, Vols. 19-62 (1928-71/2); *Oil and Gas International Year Book*, Vols. 63-7 (1973-77); *Financial Times Oil and Gas International Year Book*, Vols. 68-69 (1978-86).

110 SLA, IT 49 Gulf War: tanker disruptions.

111 See Vol. 2, Ch. 4.; *Manufacturing. One hundred years of Shell refining, 1891-1991* (The Hague: Shell Internationale Maatschappij, 1991).

112 SHA, Minutes Conference, 12 June 1974 plus manufacturing oil report, May 1974.

113 Source: Skinner, ed., *Oil and Petroleum Year Book*, vols. 19-62 (1928-71/2); *Oil and Gas International Year Book*, Vols. 63-7 (1973-77); *Financial Times Oil and Gas International Year Book*, Vols. 68-9 (1978-86).

114 Minard and Curtis, 'Exxon, move over', 130.

115 *Shell World*, Jan./Feb. 1980 and July/Aug. 1982.

116 'Issues in refining', *Shell Briefing Service (SBS)* (1989), 2-3.

117 *RD Annual Reports*, 1974 and 1975.

118 SHA, Minutes Conference, 9 July 1975; *RD Annual Reports*, 1975-85.

119 SLA, 120/46/76, Minutes Conference, 11 July 1984: Downstream Oil Sector Report; 120/46/82, Minutes Conference, 9 July 1986, Downstream Oil Sector Report; 'Issues in refining' .

120 *Manufacturing*, 8

121 SHA, Minutes Conference, 10 April 1985 till 9 October 1985.

122 SLA, Conference Minutes, 9 Oct. 1974, Marketing Oil report for 1974.

123 SHA, Minutes Conference, 13 June 1973.

124 Adelman, *Genie out of the Bottle*, 82.

125 SHA, Minutes Conference, 10 July 1974, Supply Oil Report.

126 SHA, Minutes Conference, 13 July 1977.

127 SHA, Marketing Oil Report for 1975, Minutes Conference, 8 Oct. 1975

128 SHA, MOR 795, Franchising and the automotive retail market, Dec. 1978.

129 *Shell Magazine*, 2/1973.

130 SHA, SHOP investment study, MOR 843, January 1983.

131 SLA, Downstream Oil Sector Report, 10 Sept. 1980, Minutes Conference, 8 Oct. 1980; *RD Annual Report*, 1978; SHA, Possible Options for retail outlet operations, MOR 802, April 1979.

132 Source: *Petroleum Economist*, annual overviews of the majors in May or June, 1973-87.

133 SLA, Marketing Oil Report for 1973, Minutes Conference, 13 June 1973; Minutes Conference, 11 Sept. 1974; *RD Annual Report*, 1974.

134 *Shell News*, 1979, nr. 4, 12-6.

135 'Modern automotive retail', *Shell Briefing Service (SBS)* (1989).

136 SHA, MOR 797, LPG in the Automotive Retail Network, Jan. 1979; MOR 804, Automotive retail long-term look.

137 SHA, MOR 876, Ethanol as a gasoline supplement, Feb. 1986.

138 SLA, CMD files, DCS C28, UK, 1971-72; SHA, Minutes Conference, 11 Sept. 1974.

139 Bamberg, *BP and Global Oil*, 238-40, 260-3.

140 SHA, Minutes Conference, 9 July 1986; *RD Annual Report*, 1985.

141 Jones and Gálvez-Muñoz, *Foreign Multinationals*, 10-13.

142 Vol. 2, Ch.2.

143 Priest, '"Americanization"', 188-205, 199-200; See also Vol. 2, Ch.2; about the law suit: SLA, CMD files, DSC, C46, Shell Oil, 1982/83.

144 Interview of author with Alan Lacky, General Counsel Shell Oil (1987-2000), 10 Feb. 2006 and Phil Carroll, CEO Shell Oil (1993-1998), 14 Feb. 2006 .

145 Shell Oil Archive, Minutes Board of Directors SOC, 26 October 1972.

146 *Shell News*, 1980, nr. 4, 1-4; Priest, '"Americanization"', 200.

147 *Shell News*, 1977, nr. 1, 23-5; *Shell News*, 1977, nr. 6, 2-5; Veldman and Lagers, *50 Years Offshore*, 90-1.

148 *Shell News*, 1975, nr.1, 6-7; 'A new life for an old oil field', *Shell Magazine* (1973): 159.

149 *Shell News*, 1975, nr. 1, 9.

150 Archive Shell Oil, Box 224888, Belridge, vols. I –IV; Minutes Board of Directors, Shell Oil, 14 Sept. and 25 Oct. 1979; Shell Oil Annual Reports, 1979-83; SLA, CMD files, DCS, C 39, USA 1979.

151 Minard and Curtis, 'Exxon, move over', 129.

152 SLA, CMD files, DSC, C 39, note from J. F. K. Hinde, 23 November 1979.

153 SLA, CMD files, DSC, C 46, Shell Oil Co. 1982/83 and C 48, Shell Oil Company 1982 to 1984: statement by Sir Peter Baxendell.

154 SLA, CMD files, DSC, C 48, Shell Oil Company 1982-1984, notes used by Sir Peter Baxendell in speaking at the Board Meeting of SOC in Houston on 26 January 1984.

155 SHA, Minutes Conference, 8 Feb. 1984 and press releases.

156 *Shell World* Sept/Oct. 1982 and June/July 1985.

157 Yergin, *Prize*, 734-40.

158 Priest, '"Americanization"', 202.

159 Yergin, *Prize*, 734-735.

160 SHA, Minutes Conference, 13 June 1984, 11 Oct. 1984, 13 Feb. 1985, 10 April 1985.

161 SLA, CMD files, DSC, C50, Shell Oil 1985, CMD minutes 10 June and 17 June 1985.

Notes *Come to Shell for answers*

1 *Shell News*, 1979, nr 3.

2 *Shell News*, 1990/1.

3 *Shell Venster*, 1977/10

4 *Shell World*, Jan./Feb. 1979; *Shell News*, 1990/1.

Chapter 2

1 Chambers, Mullick, and Smith, 'How to choose the right forecasting technique'.

2 Ansoff, *Corporate Strategy*; Chandler jr., *Strategy and Structure*.

3 Drucker, *Practice of Management*.

4 Fast, *Rise and Fall*.

5 Fast, *Rise and Fall*, 1-4, 129-71.

6 De Geus, *Living Company*, 52-89; *Financial Times*, 4 March 1980.

7 SLA, CMD files, DCS, S 84, NTB 1975-79, 'The Exxon enterprises approach to diversification', report of NTB/Group Planning, January 1979, by Michael Kesztenbaum.

8 Goold and Lucks, 'Why diversify?', 7-25.

9 Haspeslagh, 'Portfolio planning', 58-73.

10 SLA, CMD files, DSC, S 65, New Enterprises, note from K. Swart to CMD, 28 April 1971.

11 Sluyterman, *Dutch Enterprise*, 191-200.

12 Porter, 'From competitive advantage to corporate strategy'.

13 SLA, CMD files, DCS, S 65, New Enterprises, Annual Review, April 1970-March 1971.

14 SLA, CMD files, DCS, S 65, Note of A. Bénard, 24 Sept. 1971.

15 Vogel, 'NTB, 1968-1984', 1-2;

16 SHA, Minutes Conference, 12 June 1974: memorandum to the boards of Shell Petroleum NV and Shell Petroleum Company Limited.

17 SLA, CMD files, DCS, S84, NTB report 'Non-Traditional Business highlights', March 1977.

18 Shell, Intellectual Property Department, 2005: Figure 2.2 shows the number of inventions per year for which a patent application was filed. An invention is a new development, and can include a small step forward as well as a major breakthrough. Often breakthrough inventions are made up of a number of small steps. For Figure

2.2 the inventions are counted, not the number of applications, because for one invention Shell often applies for patent protection in a number of countries.

19 SHA, Shell Research Report 1975 and 1976; Minutes Conference, 18 May 1983 and 14 May 1974

20 *RD Annual Reports* 1973-1995; two brochures Shell Research [1986] and Shell Research 1992.

21 SHA, Shell Research Reports, 1973-94. Similar figures for the period after 1994 were not available.

22 SHA, Minutes Conference, 8 Feb. 1995. The expenditures on R&D decreased from the top of US$ 845 m. in 1990 to the low point of US$ 389 m. in 2000. After 2001 the expenditures were stepped up again to reach US$ 584 m. in 2004: *RD/S Financial and Operational Information*, 1990-2004.

23 Flavin, *Nuclear Power*, 9.

24 Flavin, *Nuclear Power*, 9-11.

25 Pringle and Spiegelman, *Nuclear Barons*, 266-73.

26 *Nuclear Power Issues and Choices*, 389-405.

27 Pringle and Spiegelman, *Nuclear Barons*, 273, 336.

28 SHA, Minutes Conference, 18 May, 13 June, 12 Sept. and 14 November 1973.

29 SHA, Minutes Conference, 27 Feb. 1974, 15 May 1974; *RD Annual Report*, 1974.

30 *RD Annual Report*, 1975; *Nuclear Power Issues and Choices*, 396.

31 SHA, Minutes Conference, 11 Feb. 1976, 14 July 1976.

32 SHA, Minutes Conference, 9 Feb. 1977, 8 Feb. 1978.

33 *RD Annual Reports*, 1973-1980; SHA, Minutes Conference, 11 Sept. 1974, 9 April 1975, 11 Feb. 1975, 11 April 1979.

34 SHA, Minutes Conference, 11 Feb. 1976, 16 Nov. 1977, 12 Oct. 1978.

35 Pringle and Spiegelman, *Nuclear Barons*, 336-42.

36 Flavin, *Nuclear Power*, 13.

37 Ibid., 12-28.

38 *RD Annual Reports*, 1979-82; SHA, Minutes Conference, 11 April 1979.

39 Broersma, *Eene zaak van regt en billijkheid*, 79-85; SHA, Minutes Conference, 10 June and 9 Sept. 1970: see also Volume 2, Ch.5.

40 SLA, PL4, Billiton NV, review of long-term plans, 1971-72.

41 SHA, Minutes Conference, 11 April 1973.

42 *RD Annual Reports*, 1970-1980.

43 SHA, Minutes Conference, 14 April 1976.

44 SLA, publications collections, 272, About Billiton, 1977/8.

45 SHA, Minutes Conference, 12 April 1976, 14 April 1978.

46 *RD Annual Report*, 1980-5.

47 SHA, Minutes Conference, 13 Sept. 1995, metals sector review, 1970-1995: The share of bauxite, alumina and aluminium in total sector NCE grew from 48 per cent in 1982 to 85 per cent in 1986.

48 *RD Annual Report*, 1985.

49 *RD/S Financial and Operational Information*, 1979-94.

50 SHA, Minutes Conference, 8 April 1987, metals sector review 1986.

51 Murray, *Go Well*, 245-6.

52 SHA, Minutes Conference, 1 March 1989, metals sector review, 1988.

53 SHA, Minutes Conference, 12 Feb. 1992.

54 SHA, Minutes Conference, 14 October 1992.

55 SHA, Minutes Conference, 13 Sept. 1995, metals sector review, 1970-95.

56 SHA, Minutes Conference, 13 Sept. 1995.

57 SLA, Shell Reports 'Major Oil Companies Performance', 1975-2000.

58 SLA, SCO 1, Group planning diversification, extract from proposed CMD policy statement concerning coal, 1 Nov. 1971; CMD files, DCS, S 58, Coal 1971-73, Preliminary Planning Review , 30 May 1972.

59 SLA, SCO 19, coal marketing and Shell identity.

60 *Shell Information Handbook*, 1976-77, 159-71; Shell Coal Review 1982.

61 SLA, 120/46/42, Minutes Conference, 9 October 1974.

62 *Shell Information Handbook*, 1976-77, 162-71.

63 SHA, Minutes Conference, 9 Oct. 1974; *Shell Information Handbook*; *RD Annual Reports*, 1974-77, 1982-85.

64 Murray, *Go Well* , 238-9.

65 SHA, Minutes Conference, 12 Feb. 1975, 14 Jan. 1976, 9 Feb. 1977, Coal report 1976.

66 The Group's affiliate Shell Oil had acquired a portfolio of coal leases and producing mines from the early 1970s onwards. In addition to these activities, the Group wanted to buy a substantial stake in coal mining via its Scallop subsidiary in the US. After the acquisition of the minority shares in Shell Oil by the Group in 1984, the Group's US coal activities were transferred to Shell Oil.

67 SHA, Minutes Conference, 5 March 1980; *Shell World*, April/May 1981. The extensive financial, technical, social, and legal reports could not prevent heavy losses for Shell, in 1982 resulting from offtake obligations and in 1985 as a consequence of lengthy strikes and the disposal or closure of certain subsidiaries. SHA, Minutes Conference, 13 April 1983; SLA, 120/46/81, Coal Report 1985.

68 SLA, 120/46/66, 11 Feb. 1981, Coal Report 1980.

69 SLA, 120/46/72, Minutes Conference, 13 April 1983, Coal report 1982.

70 SLA, 120/46/72, Minutes Conference, 13 April 1983 and 120/46/75, Coal Report 1983.

71 SHA, Minutes Conference, 9 April 1986.

72 Murray, *Go Well* , 238-9.

73 *RD/S, Financial and Operational Information*, 1979-2000.

74 SHA, Minutes Conference, 14 May 1993, Coal Report 1992/93.

75 *Shell Oil Company Annual Report*, 1992. *RD Annual Report*, 1994.

76 *RD Annual Reports*, 1993 and 1994.

77 SHA, Minutes Conference, 9 April 1997, project IKE.

78 SHA, Minutes Conference, 14 July 1999, divestment of Shell's coal business; *Economist*, 1 Feb. 1997: Digging for trouble.

79 NTB Newsletter, no. 1, 1985.

80 SLA, NTB, 21-1, meeting 23 Jan. 1978 and 21-2, note 14 July 1978; SHA, MC, 13 Feb. 1980.

81 *Shell World*, February/March 1985, 28.

82 Ibid., 31.

83 NTB Newsletter, no. 7/1988: Shell's first venture into pulp manufacture.

84 NTB Newsletter, no. 9/1989; NTB Newsletter, no.10/1990.

85 SHA, Folders Conference, 11 Dec. 1991.

86 SHA, Folders Conference, 13 September 2000: Group divestment and financing proposal.

87 In ascending order of boiling point, the main fractions into which crude oil can be separated are petroleum gases, gasoline, naphtha, kerosene, gasoil (or diesel), lubricating oil and waxes, fuel oil and bitumen.

88 Crone, *Chemicals & Society*, 3-10.

89 *Chemicals Information Handbook*, (London: Shell International Chemical Company, 1992)1982/82-1998/99. Figures based on *Chemical Insight*.

90 *RD Annual Reports*, 1974-75; sales figures: *RD/S, Financial and Operational Information*, 1975-98.

91 'Petroleum-based chemicals the

feedstock problem', *Shell Briefing Service* (1973), 4.

92　SLA,120/45/44, MC 9 April 1975, Chemical review 1974; see also Vol. 2, Ch. 5.

93　Fast, *Rise and Fall*, 134.

94　*RD Annual Reports* 1972 and 1973; SLA, 120/46/44, MC 11 April 1973, Chemicals review 1973. The fertilizer company Shellstar in the UK was sold to the UKF (Unie van Kunstmest Fabrieken) and the Shell interest in UKF was increased from 16 per cent to 25 per cent. This 25 per cent equity shareholding in UKF was sold to DSM in 1979, because this commodity had little affinity with other parts of the chemical business: SHA, Minutes Conference, 10 Oct. 1979.

95　'Planning a chemical company's prospects', *Shell Briefing Service (SBS)* (1975).

96　SHA, Minutes Conference, 13 April 1977; 'Shell in base chemicals', *Shell Briefing Service (SBS)* (1977).

97　Rozendaal, Van Bekkum, and Reewijk, *Chemie achter de dijken*, 104-5.

98　SLA, *Shell Technology*, 3/1982, 5-6; *Shell Petrochemicals*, no. 6, 1987; *Detergents Half Century*, Shell Chemicals UK, 1987; *Shell World*, Oct. 1983.

99　*RD Annual Report* 1974; SHA, Research Report, 1976 and 1977; Bamberg, *BP and Global Oil*, 424-44.

100　SLA, 120/45/44, Minutes Conference, 9 April 1975, Chemical review 1974.

101　SHA, Minutes Conference, 12 April 1978; 12 July 1978.

102　*Shell News*, 1974, no. 3, 10-3; *Shell Oil, Annual Report* 1974.

103　SLA, CMD files, DCS, C36, Shell Oil, 2 December 1975.

104　*Shell Deer Park. Celebrating 75 Years*, (no place: no publisher, 2004), 119.

105　*Shell Oil Annual Reports*, 1975-79; *Shell News*, 1979, no. 6, 21-3 and 1983, no. 4, 11-4.

106　SHA, Minutes Conference, 8 April 1981.

107　*RD/S Financial and Operational Information, 1979-1982*.

108　SHA, Minutes Conference, 9 March 1983.

109　Steenbakkers, *Dynamics*, 166-7.

110　Spitz, *Petrochemicals*, XIV (quotation), 541-3.

111　Lowe, 'Business strategies for the eighties'.

112　Lowe, 'Investment strategies for the petrochemical industry'.

113　Stobaugh, *Innovation and Competition*, 153-5.

114　SHA, Minutes Conference, 14 April 1982, Chemicals Report 1982, 9 March 1983, Chemicals Report 1983.

115　*RD Annual Reports*, 1976-84; *Shell News*, 1985, no. 6, 1-7.

116　Aftalion, *History of the International Chemical Industry*, 330.

117　SHA, Minutes Conference, 14 March 1984.

118　Eckstut and Spitz, 'Strategy Development in the Chemical Industry', 111-44.

119　*Shell World*, July/Aug. 1981, no. 5.

120　See Vol. 2, Ch. 6.

121　*Shell World*, June/July 1985, no. 3, Vol. 10: Agrochemicals, the sense of balance.

122　SHA, Minutes Conference, 9 April 1986.

123　Shell figures: *RD/S, Financial and operational information*, 1979-2000; industry figures: *Petroleum Economist*, July 2000 and July 2003.

124　SHA, Minutes Conference, 13 April 1988, 8 April 1992, 14 April 1993.

125　*Shell Petrochemicals*, number 25, 1994.

126　*Shell World*, Oct. 1996.

127　*The Economist*, 15 Feb. 1997.

128　SLA, Minutes Conference, 8 April 1992, 14 April 1993, 8 June 1994.

129　SHA, Minutes Conference, 11 April 1979.

130　SHA, Minutes Conference, 10 Jan. 1996.

131　*RD Annual Report* 1993.

132　SHA, Minutes Conference, 10 April, 10 July 1996, 11 Sept. 1996.

133　SHA, Minutes Conference, 8 June 1994.

134　SHA, Minutes Conference, 10 April 1996.

135　SHA, Minutes Conference, 9 Sept. 1992.

136　*Shell News*, 1988, no. 4, 6-11.

137　SHA, Minutes Conference, 10 Feb. 1993, 8 Sept. 1993, 14 Jan. 1994, 14 Sept. 1994, 14 Dec. 1994, 8 March 1995; *RD Annual Reports*, 1992-1995; *Economist*, 4 Dec. 1993.

138　Interview of author with Peter Vogtländer, 17 December 2003.

139　SLA, CMD files, meeting 12 September 1997, minutes and Shell Chemicals business plan 'Building on basics'.

140　See Vol. 2, Ch.5.

141　SHA, Minutes Conference, 9 December 1998.

142　SHA, Minutes Conference, 9 July 1997, 10 Sept. 1997, 14 Jan. 1998, 9 Dec. 1998, 3 Nov. 1999, 9 Dec. 1999; *RD Annual Reports*, 1997-99.

143　SHA, Minutes Conference, 9 July 1997, 10 Dec. 1997, 10 June 1998, 12 July 2000.

144　SHA, Minutes Conference, 8 Nov. 1989, 10 Dec. 1997, 8 April 1998, 9 Dec. 1999; *RD Annual Reports*, 1989, 1992-95.

145　SHA, Minutes Conference, 8 April 1992, 8 June 1994, 13 July 1994, 11 Dec. 1996, 8 April 1998, 9 Feb. 2000; *RD Annual Reports*, 1990 and 1994.

146　Shell Chemicals Europe Magazine, no. 1, Oct. 1994.

147　*RD/S Financial and Operational Information, 1997-2001*.

148　*RD Annual Report*, 1999.

149　Steenbakkers, *Dynamics*, 118 and 226.

150　SHA, Minutes Conference, 8 June 1994, 12 Oct. 1994; interview of author with Ed Vogelzang, 17 February 2004.

151　Chapman, 'Agents of Change', 16.

152　Sim and Westervelt, 'Recovery comes into focus', 21-6.

153　SHA, Minutes Conference, 8 July 1987, 9 Sept. 1987, 12 Oct. 1988, 3 May 1989; *RD Annual Reports*, 1987-89.

154　SHA, Minutes Conference, 9 Feb. 1994, 10 July 1996, 12 March 1997.

155　SHA, Minutes Conference, 8 April 1992, 9 April 1997, 11 Feb. 1998, 13 Sept. 2000.

156　*RD/S Financial and Operational Information, 1970-2000*.

157　*RD/S Financial and Operational Information, 1975-2000*.

158　*Shell World*, June 1994.

159　SLA, Minutes CMD, 3 Aug. 1971 and note to managing directors from E. G. G. Werner, 6 Aug. 1971; see also Vol. 2. Ch. 5.

Note *From coal to gas to oil*

1　*Shell Information Handbook*, 1976-77; *RD Annual Reports*, 1974-94; *Shell World*, June/July 1987 and Oct. 1994; *Shell Chemicals Handbook*, 1998-99; quotation *Financial Times*, 25 April 1980.

Chapter 3

1 Sources for Figure 3.1: Walter E. Skinner (ed.), *Oil and Petroleum Year Book*, vols. 19-62 (1928-72); *Oil and Gas International Year Book*, vols. 63-67 (1973-77); *Financial Times Oil and Gas International Year Book*, vols. 68-9 (1978-99).

2 Yergin, *Prize*, 745-50.

3 SLA, 120/46/85, E&P report 1986.

4 SLA, Group planning, Note from A. P. de Geus, 19 December 1985.

5 Yergin, *Prize*, 751-61.

6 Levitt, 'The globalization of markets'. *Harvard Business Review* (1983).

7 See e.g. the discussion about Levitt's original article in: Quelch and Deshpande, *The Global Market*. About the rise of global capitalism, see also: Jones, Multinationals and Global Capitalism, 31-42.

8 Interview with John Jennings, *Shell World*, February 1994.

9 Sources for Figure 3.2: Walter E. Skinner (ed.), *Oil and Petroleum Year Book*, Vols. 19-62 (1928-72); *Oil and Gas International Year Book*, Vols. 63-7 (1973-77); *Financial Times Oil and Gas International Year Book*, Vols. 68-9 (1978-99); *RDS Financial and Operational Information*, 1960-97.

10 *Financial Times*, 16 Oct. 1989.

11 Pink, 'Exploration and appraisal technology', 6.

12 Pink, 'Exploration and appraisal technology', 10.

13 SHA, Minutes Conference, 6 May 1992, E&P report 1991.

14 SHA, Minutes Conference, 3 May 1989, E&P report 1988.

15 *Shell World*, June 2001.

16 Sources for Figure 3.3: *RD/S Financial and Operational Information*, 1986-1998.

17 This selection only partially covers Shell's E&P activities. For instance in 1994, Shell E&P worked in 45 countries and had equity oil production in 28 countries, of which the US, UK, Oman, Nigeria, and Malaysia were the most important. Gas was produced in 17 countries with the Netherlands and the US as leaders: *RD Annual Report* 1994.

18 Pink, 'Exploration and appraisal technology', 12-3.

19 SLA, Shell press cuttings, *Lloyds List*, 19 July 1989. *RD Annual Report*, 1992.

20 SHA, Minutes Conference, 9 Nov. 1988.

21 Steven Butler, 'Accidents bedevil the North Sea', *Financial Times*, 20 April 1989.

22 SHA, Minutes Conference, 6 May 1998 and 19 Oct. 2000: Expro review note: Shell Expro in middle age getting fit, staying healthy.

23 SHA, Minutes Conference, 12 Feb. 1997 and 19 Oct. 2000: Expro review note.

24 Annual Reports Petroleum Development Oman (PDO), 1970-2000.

25 Source Figure 3.4: PDO powerpoint slide pack, 2003.

26 Archives PDO, Development in Oman, 1970; Annual Reports PDO, 1970-80.

27 Archives PDO, Annual Reports PDO, 1981-83; EOR Chemicals, Shell brochure 1982, SLA, 229.

28 Archives PDO, Annual Reports PDO, 1986-1997; SHA, Minutes Conference, 8 May 1991.

29 Archives PDO, Annual reports PDO, 1998-2005.

30 *RD Annual Report*, 1987.

31 Annual Report Shell Oil Company, 1986 and 1987; SHA, Minutes Conference, 11 Feb. 1987.

32 SHA, Minutes Conference, 9 March 1994.

33 SHA, Minutes Conference, 11 Oct. 1995; Annual Report Shell Oil Company, 1995-97; In 1995 Shell Oil had brought the oil fields in California under a separate subsidiary, CalResources, to give employees a greater sense of ownership and accountability.

34 Annual Reports Shell Oil Company, 1986-92.

35 'The offshore challenge', *Shell Briefing Service (SBS)* (1993), 6-7

36 *RD Annual Report*, 1997; SHA, Minutes Conference, 11 June 1997.

37 SHA, Minutes Conference, 7 May 1986.

38 SHA, Minutes Conference, 10 May 1995, E&P report 1995, 12 June 1996, E&P Self appraisal, 11 June 1997, discussion note South Pars Gas to Pakistan, Minutes Conference July 1997.

39 C116, Iran 1998, note for information, 15 Dec. 1998.

40 *RD Annual Report* 1992.

41 *Life now; Shell Ladies' Project 1996*, (1996), 185.

42 SHA, Minutes Conference, 13 April 1994.

43 SHA, Minutes Conference, 9 April 1997.

44 Taverne, *Petroleum, Industry and Governments*, 270-274.

45 SHA, Minutes Conference, 11 Jan. 1998, 8 April 1998, 10 June 1998; *RD Annual Report* 1997; Philip Watts, 'Russia: Building on the past, looking to the future', (paper presented at the Russia Economic Forum, London, 18 April 2002).

46 SLA, CDM files, DCS, C92B, Russia 1995. From the files it is not quite clear why the deal did not go ahead. Perhaps competitors were prepared to offer a higher price.

47 SHA, Minutes Conference, 12 June 1996.

48 SHA, Minutes Conference, 12 Nov. 1997.

49 Sources for Figure 3.5: as in n. 1 above. Also: *Annual Reports Royal Dutch, Exxon, BP*, various issues.

50 Sources for Figure 3.6: 1982-1994: *Petroleum Economist*, Annual overviews of the oil majors in May or June (1971-94); 1995-1997: SHA, Major Oil Companies: performance in ..., Shell internal overviews. Measured is crude and natural

51 SHA, Minutes Conference, 10 May 1995, E&P report.

52 SLA, CMD files, DCS, C94, E&P 1995, CMD minutes 25 April, 31 Oct. and 1 Nov. 1995.

53 SHA, Minutes Conference, 12 June 1996.

54 Sources for Figure 3.7: Shell Financial and operational data, 1980-97.

55 SHA, Minutes Conference, 8 June 1988.

56 SHA, Minutes Conference, 10 June 1987.

57 *Manufacturing. One hundred years of Shell refining, 1891-1991* (The Hague: Shell Internationale Maatschappij, 1991), 8-9.

58 SHA, Minutes Conference, 10 June 1992.

59 Blom, *Honderd jaar Shell Pernis*, 307: 'een super-nieuwe badkamer in een verouderd grachtenhuis'.

60 Ibid., 57

61 Skinner, 'Changing oil markets', 2.

62 Skinner, 'Changing oil markets', 3.

63 SLA, 120/46/130, Oil Products presentation to conference, 9 Oct. 1996.

64 Source Figure 3.8: *Petroleum Economist*, Annual overviews of the oil majors in May or June (1971-94); *Annual Reports, Shell, Exxon and BP*, 1995-8.

65 SHA, Minutes Conference, 9 July 1986.

66 Porter, *Competitive advantage*.

67 Prahalad and Hamel, 'The core competence of the corporation', 79-91.

68 *Shell World*, Feb. 1989, 8-9.

69 Ibid.; *Financial Times*, 20 May 1986.

70 SHA, Minutes Conference, 9 Sept. 1987, 8 June 1988, 13 June 1990; SHA, Research Reports, 1986-88; *RD Annual Report* 1996.

71 *Shell News*, 1988, no. 4, 1-5.

72 SHA, Minutes Conference, 9 July 1986, 13 June 1990 with Downstream Oil Report [1989], 10 July 1991 with Downstream Oil Report 1990 and 10 June 1992 with Downstream Oil Report 1991.

73 *Shell World*, August 1993.

74 SLA, Shell Downstream Oil Report 1993,

75 *Shell World*, February 1994.

76 SHA, Minutes Conference, 10 June 1992, 11 Dec. 1996.

77 Interview of author with Adrian Loader, 7 May 2004.

78 SHA, Minutes Conference, 13 Nov. and 11 Dec. 1996, 8 Jan. 1997.

79 SHA, Minutes Conference, 13 Dec. 2000.

80 Annual Reports Shell Oil Company, 1986-90.

81 SHA, Minutes Conference, 8 Jan. 1997.

82 Annual Reports Shell Oil Company, 1997-98; SHA, Minutes Conference, 2 Aug. 2000.

83 SHA, Minutes Conference, 11 July 1990 and 10 July 1991, Downstream Oil Report 1990.

84 *RD Annual Reports*, 1988-1997; Shell in the CIS, central and east Europe, *Shell Briefing Note* [August 1994].

85 SLA, CMD files, DCS 35, China 1971/75 and 43, China 1977-1981.

86 *Shell World*, June 1997.

87 Interview of author with Adrian Loader, 7 May 2004.

88 Yergin, *Prize*, 724.

89 *Shell World*, Feb/March 1986, 12-16.

90 Interview of author with Mike Warwick, head of Stasco, 29 April 2004.

91 *Shell World*, April 1993, 7-9.

92 Ibid., 7.

93 SHA, Minutes Conference, 4 May 1988.

94 Howarth, *Sea Shell*, 188-91.

95 *Marine News*, Sept. 1986,

96 SHA, Minutes Conference, 10 April 1991, Marine review 1989/90.

97 *Shell World*, August 1991.

98 Stasco Archives: Marine the next decade. Strategy study carried out from July 1990 to March 1991 to examine the role of the Marine Sector, 1991.

99 *Marine News*, July 1993

100 Stasco Archives: Shipping strategy review, 1995.

101 Interview of author with Jan Kopernicki, vice president Shipping, 5 May 2004.

102 *Ship & Shore*, 2 Sept. 1994, interview of author with Jan Kopernicki.

103 Correljé, Van der Linde, and Westerwoudt, *Natural Gas in the Netherlands*, 30-7, 157. A third company, NAM/Gas Export exported the gas on behalf of Gasunie until 1975, after which date Gasunie took over the exports.

104 Correljé, Van der Linde, and Westerwoudt, *Natural Gas in the Netherlands*, 94.

105 Ibid., 88-99.

106 Howarth, *A Century in Oil,* 280.

107 *RD Annual Report*, 1972; SHA, Minutes Conference, 27 Feb. 1974.

108 Brinded, 'Using associated gas the Climate Double Dividend', 1.

109 SHA, Minutes Conference, 16 April 1989; 'Gas from the Southern North Sea', (1984), 4.

110 Lerøen, *Troll, Gas for Generations*, 9-30.

111 SHA, Minutes Conference, 10 Sept. 1986.

112 Lerøen, *Troll, Gas for Generations*, 127-211; *RD Annual Report*, 1996; Cook, 'Serving customers in diverse markets', 5.

113 SHA, Minutes Conference, 13 April 1977, 11 April 1979. For Nigerian LNG projects: see Ch. 5.

114 SHA, Minutes Conference, 13 April 1977, 12 April 1978: Van der Linde, *Time Bomb*.

115 SHA, Minutes Conference, 8 April 1981; Bull and Stachan, 'Liquefied natural gas safety research', 11.

116 Murray, *Go Well*, 250-60, SHA, Minutes Conference, 10 April 1985.

117 *RD Annual Reports*, 1989-93.

118 SLA, NGB/FF/B2, Natural gas expansion how fast? Natural Gas scenarios, March 1992.

119 SHA, Minutes Conference, 11 June 1986 and 8 July 1987.

120 Moody-Stuart, 'Shaping the future of

energy in industries', figure 13.

121 Long-term scenarios oil, Group Planning, October 1986.

122 Van der Veer, 'Fuelling the future: the shift to gas'.

123 SLA, NGB/FF/B2, Natural gas expansion how fast? Natural Gas scenarios, March 1992; World Commission of Environment and Development, *Our Common Future*.

124 Source Figure 3.9: *Petroleum Economist*, Annual overviews of the oil majors in May or June (1971-1994); *Annual Reports Shell, Exxon, BP*, 1995-97.

125 SHA, Minutes Conference, 11 May 1983, 13 July 1988, 12 July 1989 and 12 Sept. 1990; Gainey, 'Natural gas for power generation'.

126 SHA, Minutes Conference 9 July 1997 and 10 Dec. 1997, Downstream Gas, 1997 Business Plan, December 1997; *RD Annual Report* 1997.

127 SHA, Minutes Conference, 14 Sept. 1994.

128 Williams, 'Natural gas the world supply challenge', 5-6.

129 Interview of author with Paul Skinner, 16 June 2004. Shell Oil Archive, Box ID 232175, McKinsey report: Enhancing Shell's position in the natural gas industry, Feb. 1986.

130 *The Economist*, 12 February 1994, and 28 February 1998.

131 SHA, Minutes Conference, 12 July 1995.

132 *Shell World*, special on the US, October 1997.

133 SHA, Minutes Conference, 4 November 1998; *RD Annual Report* 1998; SLA, CMD files, DCS C138 C, Tejas legacy, 30 August 2001.

134 Interview of author with Adrian Loader, 7 May 2004.

135 *Fortune*, 4 August 1997, 53.

gas liquids. Natural gas is not included.

120/46/117; *RD Annual Reports*, 1993-96.

Notes *Guarding the Shell brand*

1   Kapferer, *[Re]inventing the Brand*, 3-10.
    Jones, *Renewing Unilever*, 115-51.
2   SLA, MK 64-67, Shell Emblem Research
    Recognition Study, Jan. 1971 and Shell
    Emblem Study Report; SHA, Instructie
    Visuele Manifestatie, Dec. 1974; *Shell
    Venster*, March/April 1991.
3   SLA, CMD files, DCS, S 65, CMD, 10 June
    1975, motor gasoline and the Shell brand
    and 23 Sept. 1975, Marketing Oil report for
    1975; the update of the new emblem of
    Shell Oil was a gradual process as well:
    Shell News, 1979, no. 2.
4   Riezebos, *Merkenmanagement*,
    introduction.
5   *Shell News*, 1984, no. 1; *Shell World*, April
    1990.
6   SLA, CMD files, DCS, C113A, Brand
    Workshop, 3 Nov. 1997.
7   SLA, Oil Products, Global brands: report
    GCT Q1, '06, KPI Global: based on
    different criteria from the 1996 brand
    tracking, the 2005 research found global
    brand preference scores for Shell of 18 per
    cent, for BP of 17 moving to 14 per cent, for
    Esso of 9 per cent and for Mobil of 10-8 per
    cent. The scores for global spontaneous
    brand awareness was in the range of 61-4
    per cent for Shell, 53-5 per cent for BP, 44-
    6 per cent for Esso and 39-43 for Mobil.
8   Holt, Quelch, and Taylor, 'Managing the
    global brand',180-201.
9   *Shell World*, April 1990.

Notes *Scenario planning in Shell*

1   SLA, Reflections on the Evolution of
    Scenario Planning in Shell, 1971 to 1992,
    Group Planning, November 1995. This
    overview has been very helpful in drawing
    up this cameo on Shell's scenario
    planning.
2   SLA, Scenario, 'Individual producer
    government take/production strategies',
    May 1972.
3   SLA, Shell's collection of scenarios from
    1972 to 2002.
4   De Geus, *The Living Company*, Ch. 4.
5   Schwartz, *The Art of the Long View*.
6   Interview of author with Ged Davies, 8
    June 2004; SLA, New medium term
    scenarios, 1981-1985, 13 April 1981: 'In
    societies already characterized by rising
    frustration, a rapidly growing young
    population that is both educated and
    under/unemployed adds a volatile
    ingredient to the mixture. If combined
    with the potentially self-destructive
    fervour of Islamic fundamentalism, the
    result could be an eruption even more
    violent than the "Paris Spring" of 1968.'

Chapter 4

1   Source Figure 4.1: Annual Reports Shell,
    Exxon, and BP; SHA, internal Shell report
    Major Oil Companies' Performance in ...
    (1972-96), included in the conference
    folders.
2   'The Human Resource', *Shell Briefing
    Service (SBS)* (1981).
3   Personnel Management Guides, Social
    Performance, Nov. 1977.
4   From 1968 till 1984 Shell Personnel
    published its own periodical Personnel
    Management Review, in which outside
    experts were invited regularly to discuss
    recent developments in human relations.
5   SLA, Boxes HR, Report long range
    planning of managers, December 1962.
6   SLA, 120/46/ 46, Group Personnel Report
    for 1975; 120/46/82, Group Personnel
    report 1986.
7   SLA, Boxes HR, foreword by G.A. Wagner
    to the Shell copy of Muller's dissertation:
    Muller, *Search for Qualities*.
8   Muller, *Search for Qualities*, 107-9.
9   *Shell World*, no. 2, 1977: 'Picking
    tomorrow's managers', 6-7.
10 *Shell World*, no. 3, 1977: 'Developing
    tomorrow's managers', 10-2.
11 SLA, PN 48, no. 1, May-Sept. 1970.
12 SLA, PN 48, no. 3, Feb. 1971 Feb. 1972.
13 SLA, Minutes AGM Shell Transport, 20
    April 1972 and 26 April 1973.
14 SHA, Minutes Conference, 11 Sept. 1974:
    Group Personnel Report for 1974.
15 SHA, Minutes Conference, 11 Jan. 1978.
16 See e.g. the description of the
    Technostructure in: Galbraith, *New
    Industrial State*, chs. 5 and 6.
17 In case of a tied vote, the Chairman of the
    Board (elected by shareholder
    representatives) has the deciding vote.
    Fürstenberg, 'West German experience
    with industrial democracy', 44-53.
18 SHA, Minutes Conference, 12 Sept. 1974.

19 Schut, 'Ontwikkeling van het ondernemingsrecht in Nederland', 65-84.

20 Davies, 'European experience with worker representation on the board', 51-83.

21 *RD Annual Report*, 1976.

22 Davies, 'European experience', preface.

23 Ibid., 160-2.

24 Ibid., 142-4.

25 SLA, AGM ST&T, 12 May 1977, 141/9/20.

26 SHA, Minutes Conference, 9 May 1990.

27 SLA, 120/46/38, Group Personnel Report for 1973.

28 SLA, Boxes HR, A stepping stone to a new Shell culture, September 1978.

29 Ibid.

30 SLA, 120/46/46, Shell Personnel Report for 1975; 120/46/62, Shell Personnel Report 1980.

31 Peters and Waterman, *In Search of Excellence.*

32 SLA, Boxes HR, Report Corporate Culture and Corporate Strategies, 19 April 1982, and cover letter, 17 May 1982. The Dutch 'analyst Peereboom' mentioned in the report is probably Ed Peereboom, editor of the book *Management en arbeid nieuwe stijl* (Amsterdam, Elsevier 1984).

33 SLA, Boxes HR, Report Corporate Culture and Corporate Strategies, 19 April 1982

34 *Petroleum Economist*, May 1990, 147-8. Shell surpassed Exxon on a large number of counts, including income, reserves, oil production and sales of oil products.

35 SLA, Boxes HR, Personnel, The Management of Change, May 1989.

36 SLA, PN 35, memo 1 Jan. 1968

37 SLA, PN 34, note from I. P. Bruce to C. C. Pocock, 21 Oct. 1970.

38 SLA, PN 36, 16 March 1973.

39 Boyle, 'Equal opportunity for women is smart business', 85-95.

40 SLA, PN 36. Shell people studied Boyle's article (n. 39 above).

41 SLA, PN 34, Report 29 April 1974.

42 SLA, PN 36, Career opportunities for women in Shell, 31 May 1973.

43 Ibid.

44 SHA, Minutes Conference, 12 Sept. 1973 and 12 Sept. 1974.

45 SHA, Minutes Conference, 19 Sept. 1975 and Personnel Report 1975; Minutes Conference 15 Sept. 1976 and Personnel Report 1976; SLA, Boxes HR, Equal Opportunities workshop, 17 November 1980.

46 SLA, Boxes HR, Extracts from Equal Opportunities Audit of Shell International's Graduate Recruitment Programme, by Dr. L. Mee-Yan Cheung-Judge.

47 *Shell Venster*, Sept./Oct. 2001.

48 *Shell World*, Jan./Feb. 1981.

49 SLA, 120/46/82, Group Personnel Report 1986: In 1985 Shell had 4930 expatriates on overseas assignments in Shell and other companies; in comparison this number was 4750 for IBM, 2300 for Exxon, 1500 for BP, 1100 for Unilever and 1100 for Philips. See also: Jones, *Renewing Unilever*, 232-3.

50 SHA, Minutes Conference, 11 April 1984: A study in expatriation had suggested shorter term assignments on a bachelor basis (that is sending the employees abroad without their families). However Group Personnel considered it preferable to keep families united.

51 *Life on the move; Shell Ladies' Project 1993*, (1993), 34, 36, 26-7.

52 SLA, PN43, file 2, meeting 1 March 1977.

53 *Life on the move; Shell Ladies' Project 1993*, 58-9.

54 Ibid. 54-5.

55 SHA, Minutes Conference, 11 Jan. 1978.

56 SLA, Hofstede, 'Motivation, leadership, and organisation'; See also: Hofstede, *Culture's Consequences.*

57 Trompenaars, *Riding the Waves of Culture.*

58 SLA, Boxes HR, Shell and its Staff. The evolution of an international service, Blair report, Jan. 1959.

59 SLA, Boxes HR, Report on Internationalisation, Nov. 1980, Appendix I.

60 SLA, Boxes HR, Regional and international staffing study, undated (around 1989).

61 SHA, Minutes Conference 7 May 1986 and Group Personnel Report 1986.

62 Baxendell, 'Human resource management in practice'.

63 Source Table 4.1: *RD Annual Reports*, 1970-1999 and *RD/S Financial and operational information*, 1970-99; after 1999 a different breakdown of the geographical distribution was used.

64 SLA, CMD files, DCS, S 65, Minutes CMD, 4 May 1971; see also Vol. 2, Ch.5.

65 *RD Annual Report*, 1979.

66 SHA, Leaflet inserted in the RD Annual Report 1976.

67 Fruhan, 'Corporate Raiders', 63-8.

68 Ibid.

69 *RD Annual Reports*, 1973-2000.

70 Source Figure 4.2: Walter E. Skinner (ed.), *Oil and Petroleum Year Book*, 19-62 (1928-71/2) *Oil and Gas International Year Book*, 63-67 (1973-77); *Financial Times Oil and Gas International Year Book*, 68-9 (1978-99); *RD/S Financial and Operational Information*, 1960-97.

71 Source Figure 4.3: *Annual Reports RD, Exxon and BP.*

72 *RD Annual Report* 1998; Shell Oil Annual Report 1998.

73 SHA, internal Shell report Major Oil Companies' Performance in... (1972-99), included in the Conference folders.

74 SLA, CMD files, DCS, S62, competitors 1975/76.

75 SHA, Minutes Conference, 14 October 1994.

76 SHA, Minutes Conference, 8 June 1983.

77 SLA, Personnel Management Review (PMR), 58, Nov. 1983, 'Taking a new look at overheads', 44-9.

78 SHA, Score 1983/1984, 358 A B36f. Notes and letters, 26 April 1983 till 7 March 1984.

79 SLA, PMR 59, July 1984.

80 SHA, Minutes Conference, 8 June 1983.

81 SLA, unnumbered file, 1986, note from Van Wachem, 19 June 1986 and note from R. H. T. Hingston to Van Wachem and others, 12 Aug. 1986, ibid., 29 August 1986.

82 Shell Centre, CMD Files, S 90: Organization 1976/79, Minutes CMD, 12 April 1977.

83 SLA, unnumbered file, Note from R. H. T. Hingston to Coordinators, 21 August 1986.

84 Ibid.

85 SLA, unnumbered file, memo De Geus, 26 August 1986.

86 SLA, SC 98, The matrix organization in the service companies, undated, around 1987.

87 Van Wachem, 'Unity in diversity'.

88 Ibid.

89 Ibid.

90 *Shell World*, June 1992; Archives Shell Oil, Minutes Board of Directors, Shell Oil Company, 25 June 1992.

91 *The Independent*, 18 March 2002.

92 SLA, Boxes HR, An investigation of the system of staff appraisal used in Shell by Dr P. Bramley (undated, around 1990).

93 SHA, Minutes Conference, 7 May 1986.

94 SHA, Minutes Conference, 7 May 1986: Group Personnel Report 1986.

95 SHA, Minutes Conference, Group Personnel Report 1988 and 1990.

96 SLA, Group Resources Review, Jan. 1995.

97 Shell Global Scenarios 1992-2020 and Global Scenarios 1995-2020.

98 SLA, Files CMD, DSC, C106, minutes Senior Executives' Meeting, Hartwell House, 27-

29 May 1994. About the transformation in Shell Oil Company, see *Shell News*, 1994, nr. 4, The Transformation of Corporate America, 3-5 and the Transformation of Shell Oil Company, 6-13.

99   SLA, SC 98, Service companies review and transformation, 1995-1997; SHA, Minutes Conference, 14 Dec. 1994, 11 Jan. 1995, 8 Feb. 1995.

100 SLA, SC98, Service Companies Review and Transformation, 1995-97, diary by Basil South.

101 SLA, SC98, diary by Basil South.

102 SHA, Minutes Conference, 11 Jan. 1995.

103 SHA, Minutes Conference, 11 Jan. 1995-8 March 1995.

104 SLA, Boxes HR, Senior Executives Meeting, Hanbury Manor, 23-6 Feb. 1995.

105 SLA, SC 98, Speech Herkströter, 29 March 1995.

106 SLA, SC 98, diary by Basil South.

107 SHA, Minutes Conference, 8 Feb. 1995.

108 *Shell World*, April 1995.

109 SLA, SC 98, letter from Herkströter, 20 Dec. 1995.

110 SHA, Minutes Conference, 14 Feb. 1996.

111 *RD Annual Report* 1994.

112 Shell Outpost Family Archive Centre, The Hague, Destinations, no. 12, September 1999.

113 *Shell World*, April 1995, interview with Herkströter.

114 Shell Outpost Family Archive Centre, Outlook Expatriate Survey: summary of findings and summary of changes; *Shell World*, Feb. 1995.

115 Shell Outpost Family Archive Centre, Destinations, 23 September 2005, Special Commemorative issue with focus on Judy Moody-Stuart.

116 *Shell World*, August 1995; Expatriate Spouse Employment Support, May 1995.

117 SLA, Boxes HR, regional & international staffing study (around 1989); *Destinations*, number 21, December 2001.

118 SLA, SC 98, letter from Herkströter, 31 Jan. 1996.

119 *Shell World*, March 1997, interview with Steve Miller, Group Managing Director.

120 SLA, Files, Files CMD, DCS, C106, Draft Shell Transformation Survey.

121 'Why is the world's most profitable company turning itself inside out?' *Fortune* (4 August, 1997): 52-7. People within Shell, including Pieter Folmer, commented that Hans van Luijk had never been a cold technocrat to start with.

122 Interview of author with Mike Warwick, Head of Stasco, 29 April 2004.

123 *Shell World*, Dec. 1997.

124 *Shell World*, July 1998.

125 *Shell World*, Sept. 1998: Letter by R. A. Blake.

126 Interview of author with Mark Moody-Stuart, 13 December 2005; *Shell World*, July 1998; Moody-Stuart, 'Meeting needs, offering choices'.

127 SHA, Minutes Conference, 14 Oct. 1998.

128 Ibid.

129 SHA, Minutes Conference, 4 Nov. 1998.

130 *Shell World*, June/July 2000, 'Facing the findings'.

131 SLA, Files CMD, DCS, C129B, Human Resources 1999, People Survey Results, March 1999.

132 SLA, Files CMD, DCS, C136A, Human Resources, 2000, minutes CMD, 2/5 Dec. 2000.

133 *Financial Times*, 9 August 1997, interview of Mark Moody-Stuart by Robert Corzine.

134 Interview of author with Malcolm Brinded, 3 November 2006.

135 SLA, 141/13/19-22, Minutes Board Shell Transport, 16 Sept., 28 Oct. and 17 Nov. 1976 and 12 Jan. 1977; SHA, Minutes Supervisory Board Royal Dutch, 10 March 1976, 16 Sept. 1976, 13 Oct. 1976.

136 SHA, Minutes Supervisory Board Royal Dutch, 9 Feb. 1977.

137 RD *Annual Report*, 1998, 6.

138 SHA, Minutes Conference, 10 Feb. 1999.

139 SHA, Minutes Conference, 8 Dec. 1999 and note about the Group Structure, 1 December 1999.

140 Interview of author with Mark Moody-Stuart, 13 December 2005.

141 The only arrangement discussed between the Boards was in 1972 when it was agreed that one of the offices of Chairman and Vice Chairman of the CMD should be held by the President of Royal Dutch and the other by the Chairman of Shell Transport.

142 SHA, Minutes Conference, 13 Dec. 2000.

143 Interview of author with Jeroen van der Veer, 18 Oct. 2006.

144 See Ch. 4, section 'expats: life on the move'.

Notes *Dutch-British relations*

1   *Shell World*, Jan./Feb. 1982, 26.

2   ibid.

3   Interview of author with Rob Routs, 16 Oct. 2006 and Malcolm Brinded, 3 Nov. 2006.

4   Information given to author by Mark Moody-Stuart, 14 Oct. 2006.

Notes *Men at the top*

1   *Fortune*, 3 August 1987.

2   Our Way Forward, Speech by Jeroen van der Veer to the top 100 of Royal Dutch/Shell, The Hague, 15 December 2004; 'Ik ben van het lange volhouden': *Het Financieele Dagblad*, 3 March 2005.

Chapter 5

1   SHA, Minutes Conference, 27 Feb. 1974: quote from G. A.Wagner.

2   Shell's reputation, *Interchange*, 62, Jan./Feb. 1972.

3   Galbraith, *The New Industrial State*, 1-10, 60-85, 296-317.

4   Vance Packard in *The Hidden Persuaders* argued that companies were employing professional persuaders, who used the insights from psychiatry and the social sciences to sell the company's products to an unsuspecting public, which reacted like the Pavlov Dog.

5   Mandel, *From Class Society to Communism*, 43-72.

6   Blomström and Hettne, *Development Theory in Transition*.

7   SHA, Minutes Conference, 8 June 1977.

8   Chandler, 'Transnational Corporations'.

9   Homburg, 'Chemie', 269-408, 400-1.

10 *RD Annual Report*, 1974; Shell Oil Company, Annual Report 1978.

11 *RD Annual Report*, 1976.

12 Meadows et al., *The Limits to Growth*, 23-4.

13 Report by the Commission on the behaviour of the oil companies in the Community during the period from October 1973 to March 1974 (Brussels, 1975).

14 Unander, *Oil Crises & Climate Challenge*, 13-9.

15 SLA, PA 12/9, Review of Public Affairs, May 1980; SHA, Minutes Conference, 14 May 1980. President Carter had stoked up the fire of public hostility by proposing a windfall profits tax to push his energy programme through Congress.

16 Annual Report Shell Oil Company, 1978, 3.

17 SLA, PA 12/4, Review of Trade Relations January 1975.

18 SLA, PA 34, draft letter to Shell companies, 1976.

19 Ibid.

20 SLA, PA 34, Statement of General Business Principles, November 1976.

21 SLA, PA, 36, 1: Ethics and responsible behavior, Exxon Corporation, January 1979.

22 SHA, Minutes Conference, 14 September 1977; *RD Annual Reports*, 1975-78.

23 SLA, PA 12-5, Review Trade Relations, Jan. 1976.

24 *RD Annual Reports*, 1978-80.

25 Fage, *History of Africa*, 487-8.

26 Bailey, 'Enforcing Oil Sanctions', 225-7.

27 Hengeveld, 'Part A: Embargo', 17-8.

28 SHA, Minutes Conference, 14 July 1976, 9 March 1977.

29 SHA, Minutes Conference, 14 Sept. 1977.

30 Bingham and Gray, *Report on the Supply of Petroleum and Petroleum Products to Rhodesia*.

31 Ibid., 212-23. See also: SHA, Minutes Conference, 14 Sept. 1977, 12 Oct. 1977, 17 May 1978, 14 June 1978, 13 Sept. 1978, 9 January 1980; Bamberg, *British Petroleum and Global Oil*, 266-7.

32 SHA, Minutes Conference, 12 July 1978, 13 Sept. 1978, 11 Oct. 1978; SLA, CMD files, DCS, C39, Attorney-General's Statement about the Bingham Report: one of the arguments for not proceeding further was that many of the companies and their officials were subject to the laws of States deeply hostile to the sanctions policy and were liable to penalties for any refusal or failure to supply oil on demand.

33 Fage, *History of Africa*, 489-90.

34 SHA, Minutes Conference, 10 March 1981, 8 April 1981, 13 May 1981.

35 SHA, Minutes Conference, 11 July 1979.

36 SHA, Minutes Conference, 13 May 1981, 8 July 1981.

37 SHA, Minutes Conference, 8 July 1981.

38 SHA, Woordelijk verslag aandeelhouders-vergadering Koninklijke, 26 April 1973.

39 Van den Bergh, 'Dutch Campaign against Shell', 306-24.

40 Van Riemsdijk, *Actie of dialoog*, 76-9.

41 Van den Bergh, 'Dutch Campaign against Shell', 313-15; Woordelijk verslag aandeelhoudersvergadering Koninklijke, 1977-80.

42 SHA, Minutes Conference, 9 March 1977.

43 SHA, Minutes Conference, 14 Dec. 1977.

44 SHA, Minutes Conference, 8 Feb. 1978.

45 Bailey, 'Enforcing Oil Sanctions'.

46 SHA, Minutes Conference, 9 July 1980.

47 SHA, Minutes Conference, 14 Jan. 1981 and 11 Feb. 1981; SLA, CMD files, C 24, CMD Minutes, 20 Jan. and 3 Feb. 1981: The Omani government had decided to cut off commercial links with South Africa in 1973, but it had not given instructions to Shell or PDO not to deliver Omani oil to South Africa.

48 Hengeveld, 'Part A: Embargo', 206-21.

49 'Stop Press!' in: *Embargo*, 325-6.

50 Hengeveld, 'Part A: Embargo', 206-21.

51 Shell in South Africa, an interview with Lo van Wachem, *Shell World*, April/May 1986, 10-2.

52 Van Riemsdijk, *Actie of dialoog*, 86-8;

53 SHA, Minutes Conference, 9 Oct. 1985.

54 Katzin, 'Anatomy of a boycott', 327-37; Archives Shell Oil Company, Box ID, 263240, Shell Oil boycott chronology update, 11 December 1986.

55 SHA, Minutes Conference, 9 July 1986.

56 Shell in South Africa, an interview with Lo van Wachem, *Shell World*, April/May 1986, 10-2.

57 SHA, Minutes Conference, 12 March 1986.

58 Watkins, 'Business and South Africa', 3; *Shell South Africa Social Report*, 1985-86.

59 SHA, Minutes Conference, 15 Jan. 1986.

60 Van Riemsdijk, *Actie of dialoog*.

61 SHA, Minutes Conference, 9 Sept. 1987 and 13 Jan. 1988.

62 SHA, Minutes Conference, 13 April 1988; SHA, Minutes Conference, 14 Feb. 1990, PA Review 1989: 'Reputation: a common bond', Dec. 1989.

63 SHA, Minutes Conference, 13 April 1988.

64 *Shell smeer 'em uit Zuid-Afrika*, (1980); *De aan(deel)houder wint* (1983).

65 SHA, minutes AGM Royal Dutch, 1985-90. In 1988 and 1989 the shareholders were given the opportunity to give their opinion on the policy of the board via an informal polling, and 99 per cent of the shareholders supported the Shell policy.

66 SLA, 'Management Brief, South Africa', November 1990; SHA, Minutes Conference, 14 Nov. 1990; SHA, Minutes Conference, 13 Jan. 1988, Review of Public Affairs, December 1987.

67 SHA, Minutes Conference, 3 May 1989.

68 *Volkskrant*, 25 November 1994, as cited in: Van den Bergh, 'Dutch Campaign against Shell', 323.

69 Fage, *History of Africa* , 538-41.

70 Interview Lo van Wachem in *Shell World*, June 2002, and in *Shell Venster*, July/August 2002.

71 Watkins, 'Business and South Africa', 5.

72 'The vitriolic campaign and violence against Shell were, for many of us, a new and unpleasant experience.' (Tookey, 'Reflections of a coordinator', 11-3).

73 'Keeping up with the issues', *Interchange* (1986).

74 Tookey, 'PA is good business'.

75 SLA, Minutes Conference, 15 Jan. 1986, Review of Public Affairs, Dec. 1985.

76 Tookey, 'PA is good business', 2-3.

77 Ibid. 6-7: 'We have to impart facts and improve knowledge, deal with issues and dispel misconceptions and misunderstandings in the countless places and in the countless ways that Shell companies touch the community.'

78 Katzin, 'Anatomy of a boycott', 332-3: 'To engage the ecumenical institution, churches and critical spokespersons in post-apartheid planning should deflect their attention away from the boycott and disinvestments efforts and direct their vision and energy into productive channels.'

79 Archives Shell Oil Company, Box ID, 263238; SLA, CMD files, DCS, C 54, memo about boycott strategy Shell Oil.

80 SHA, Minutes Conference, 12 March 1986; SLA, Management Brief, August 1989: International pressure groups: a challenge to management?

81 SHA, Minutes Conference, 14 Feb. 1990, PA Review 1989: 'Reputation: a common bond', Dec. 1989.

82 SLA, Management Brief, August 1989: 'International pressure groups: a challenge to management?', 2.

83 Van Tulder and Van der Zwart, *Reputaties op het spel*, 167-71, 195-202.

84 Hoffman, *From Heresy to Dogma*, 114-17.

85 Van Zanden and Verstegen, *Groene geschiedenis van Nederland*, 204.

86 SLA, CMD files, DCS, C 48, Shell Oil Company 1982 to 1984: SOC, 4th quarterly report 1983.

87 Shell Oil Annual Report, 1987: Shell Oil would pay 50 per cent of any amount expended for remedial costs and natural damages up to $500 million, 35 per cent for such expenditures between $500 and $700 million and 20 per cent of any amount expended in excess of $700 million. The court approved the settlement in 1992: Shell Oil Annual Report 1992; Shell Oil Archives, Box ID: MOR 213705, Rocky Mountain Arsenal.

88 *Shell News*, Spring 1999.

89 Verstegen, *Vervuiling van het milieudebat*, 50-9.

90 World Commission of Environment and Development, *Our Common Future*, 43.

91 Ibid. 308-43.

92 SHA, Minutes Conference, 12 Feb. 1992, PA review 'Profit with responsibility'.

93 Visser, 'The test of tomorrow'.

94 'Global climate change', *Shell Briefing Service (SBS)* (1990).

95 'Shell and the environment', (London: Shell International Petroleum Company Limited, 1992).

96 Tookey, 'Public opinion in the 90s', 1-4.

97 SHA, Minutes Conference, 12 February 1992.

98 Ibid., PA Review 'Profit with responsibility'.

99 Van der Veer, 'Inzicht door doorzicht'; At the beginning of the twenty-first century the 'licence to operate' was no longer considered enough. Shell needed a 'licence to grow': Van der Veer, 'Meeting society's needs through collaborative innovation', 2.

100 'Refocus for PA training', *Interchange* (December, 1990), 6-7.

101 Tookey, 'Public opinion in the 90s', 4-6.

102 'Interview with Tony Brak', *Shell World* (1994).

103 SLA, MR 81, Brent field. A comparison of two field offtake systems.

104 SLA, Minutes Conference, 12 July 1995, including attachments: Shell UK Issues Brief: North Sea abandonment- Brent Spar disposal, February 1995.

105 Zyglidopoulos, 'The Social and Environmental Responsibilities of Multinationals, 141-51.

106 Jordan, 'Indirect causes and effects in policy change: the Brent Spar case', 614-5; Jordan, *Shell, Greenpeace and the Brent Spar*.

107 'Brent Spar, broken spur', *Nature* 375 (29 June, 1995): 708.; Nisbet and Fowler, 'Is metal disposal toxic to deep oceans?'

108 Zyglidopoulos, 'Social and environmental responsibilities', 144.

109 SLA, Minutes Conference, 12 July 1995, including attachments; Interview of author with Herkströter, 14 December 2004.

110 SLA, Minutes Conference 13 September 1995, letter C. A. J. Herkströter, 31 July 1995.

111 *Financial Times*, 6 September 1995; Letter Peter Melchett to Shell UK, 4 September 1995, *www.archive.greenpeace.org*. (checked 6 January 2005).

112 'Greenpeace under fire on Brent Spar coverage', *Nature* 377 (1995), 6.

113 SLA, Minutes Conference 13 September 1995, letter C. A. J. Herkströter, 31 July 1995.

114 'Brent Spar the wider perspective', *Shell Management Brief* (August, 1995).

115 'Brent Spar: see and hear the solution', *Interchange* (1998), 17.

116 SHA, Minutes Conference, 12 July 1995.

117 Frynas, 'Political instability and business', 457-79.

118 Bamberg, *BP and Global Oil* , 109-13, 169-70, 473-86.

119 SHA, Minutes Conference, 12 Sept. 1979, 10 Oct. 1979; SLA, CMD files, DCS, C 92A, Nigeria LNG Project, October 1995.

120 SHA, Minutes Conference, 10 Oct. 1984.

121 SHA, Minutes Conference, 3 May 1989 and 14 Oct. 1992.

122 SHA, E&P reviews, 1992-4 (Minutes Conference 5 May 1993 and 10 May 1995.)

123 SHA, Minutes Conference, 11 Nov. 1981, 11 May 1983.

124 SHA, Minutes Conference, 11 Nov. 1992.

125 SHA, Minutes Conference, 14 Oct. 1992; 'The Heat of the Moment', *Shell Brief* (October, 1992): 3; SLA, CMD files, DCS, 59, CMD Minutes, 6 November 1990.

126 ANSD (Association of Nigerian Scholars for Dialogue) Documents: Ogoni Bill of Rights, November 1990.

127 Manby, 'The role and responsibility of oil multinationals in Nigeria', 281-302; 'Operations in Nigeria', *Shell Briefing Note* (1994).

128 'The Ogoni Issue', *Shell Nigeria Brief* (January, 1995); SLA, CMD files, C84, CMD Minutes 20 December 1994, C 92A, Fax Brian Anderson, 1 Aug. 1995.

129 Frynas, 'Political instability and business'.

130 Manby, 'The role and responsibility of oil multinationals in Nigeria'.

131 'Developments in Nigeria', *Shell Briefing Note* (March, 1995).

132 Wheeler, Fabig, and Boele, 'Paradoxes and dilemmas for stakeholder responsive firms in the extractive sector, 306.

133 *http://web.amnesty.org*: Nigeria, a Summary of Human Rights Concerns, March 1996.

134 SLA, CMD files, DCS, C 92A, CMD Minutes 7-8 November 1995; SHA, Minutes Conference, 8 Nov. 1995.

135 http:/archive.greenpeace.org/comms/ken.murder.html, checked 16 Jan. 2005.

136 SHA, Minutes Conference, 13 December 1995.

137 SLA, CMD files, DCS, C 92A, Nigeria LNG Project, October 1995; SHA, Minutes Conference, 8 Nov. 1995, 13 Dec. 1995.

138 'Multinational Enterprises and Human Rights'.

139 SLA, 390/l, External Affairs Review 2001.

140 *Interchange*, see e.g. August 1988; no. 1, 1991; no. 2, 1993.

141 SHA, Minutes Conference, 9 July 1997, including 'Shell's global reputation management summary'.

142 Herkströter, 'Dealing with contradictory expectations'.

143 SHA, Minutes Conference, 10 April 1996.

144 SLA, 390/l, External Affairs Review, 2001.

145 Van Woerkum, *Shell en de Raad van Kerken in gesprek*, 10-11, 18-19; Gruiters, 'De stille revolutie', 140-53.

146 Interview of Tim van Kooten by author, 6 June 2006.

147 SLA, PA 34 and 36.

148 SHA, Minutes Conference 8 January 1997.

149 Statement of General Business Principles, 1997.

150 SHA, Minutes Conference, 7 May 1997, 11 March 1998, plus memo The Shell Report.

151 Rowell, 'Het gevaar van de dialoog', 44-57.

152 SHA, Minutes Conference, 12 November 1997. Van Wachem felt that the experience of such committees in the USA had been somewhat mixed.

153 SHA, Minutes Conference, 31 October 2001.

154 'Dear Mister Shell...' *Interchange* (1992): 10-11.

155 SHA, Minutes Conference, 13 December 2000.

156 *RD Annual Reports*, 1997-2003.

157 Doyle, *Riding the Dragon*.

158 The Shell website, *www.Shell.com*, has corporate information, but also links to non-governmental organizations.

Chapter 6

1 Shell The Hague, Notarieel verslag Algemene vergadering van aandeelhouders NV Koninklijke Nederlandsche Petroleum Maatschappij, 28 June 2005; for number of votes: Shell website (*www.shell.com*), investor centre, 29 Nov. 2005.

2 Shell Centre London, The Shell Transport and Trading Company, plc, 107th Annual General Meeting, Tuesday 28 June 2002.

3 Shell Centre London, Court Meeting, following the AGM, 28 June 2005, 13 and 24: comment made by shareholder and former Shell employee James Moorhouse.

4 Shell Centre London, Court Meeting, following the AGM, 28 June 2005, 5 and 10.

5 Shell website (*www.shell.com*), investor centre, 29 Nov. 2005.

6 Lowenstein, *Origins of the Crash.* 157-87; 192-3. Global Crossing, WorldCom, and Adelphia Communications were among the companies under the spotlight.

7 Campbell, 'Proving the unprovable', 27-30; also: *www.oilcrisis.com*: C. J. Campbell, Oil depletion the heart of the matter, Oct. 2003.

8 Source of Figure 6.1: www.shell.com: Shell Global Scenarios to 2025. Executive Summary and Excerpts., 31: IHC Energy/Shell

9 *www.eia.doe.gov*, US Energy Agency, report International Energy Outlook 2005.

10 Jeroen van der Veer, 'A vision for meeting energy needs beyond oil', *Financial Times* (25 January 2006).

11 For recent developments: *Financial Times*, 6 January 2006.

12 SHA, Annual Report Shell Oil Company, 1997.

13 'In search of the perfect partner', *Shell World* (2000): 26-7.

14 Bleakley, Gee, and Hulme, 'The

atomization of big oil', 123.

15 Bleakley, Gee, and Hulme, 'The atomization of big oil', 142.

16 SHA, Minutes Conference, 10 Dec. 1997: Group Plan.

17 *Shell World,* Sept. 2001, 20-2.

18 *The Economist*, 5 December 1998.

19 Antill and Arnott, *Oil Company Crisis*, cover.

20 Mobil: interviews of author with Mark Moody-Stuart, 13 December 2005 and Jeroen van der Veer, 19 December 2005.

21 For the discussions with Texaco, see: SLA, CMD files, DCS C 135A, E&P 2000, Minutes Conference, 2 August 2000. Against the transaction were the facts that it would be expensive, many of the assets were considered of relatively poor quality and the assets did not fit easily with the Group's existing portfolio and strategy. On balance, the negatives appeared to outweigh the positives.

22 Bleakley, Gee, and Hulme, 'The atomization of big oil', 124.

23 Interview of author with Maarten van den Bergh, retired president of Royal Dutch, and supervisory director of Royal Dutch, 17 June 2004.

24 SHA, Folders Conference, Economic Signals, Nov. 1999 and Dec. 1999.

25 Sources for figures 6.2-6.5: *Annual Reports* Shell, Exxon, and BP. Also: 6.2: Deutsche Bank, oil majors report 2004; 6.3: *Petroleum Economist*, 1990-4 May-June issues, 6.4: *Oil and Gas Yearbook*, 1990-2000 and 6.5: internal Shell reports: Major Oil Companies Performance in 1990-2002.

26 Mark Moody-Stuart, 'Prospering in uncertainty – the North Sea industry in evolving energy markets', (paper presented at the Offshore Europe conference, Aberdeen, 7 September 1999).

27 SLA, CMD files, DCS, C 137 E, note from Lorin Brass to CMD, 10 April 2001.

28 SLA, CMD files, DCS, C 137 E, note from Walter van de Vijver to CMD, 24 August 2001.

29 *Shell World,* Sept. 2001, 20.

30 Murray, *Go Well*, 202, 251.

31 SHA, Minutes Conference, 12 July 2000, 1 Nov. 2000, and 2 May 2001.

32 *Shell World,* Sept. 2001, 20-2, explanations given by Shell Australia's Alan Parsley.

33 SHA, Minutes Conference, 12 Sept. 2001.

34 SHA, Minutes Conference, 30 Dec. 2000 till 2 May 2001; SLA, CDM files, Box 137C, USA 2001; *Shell World*, Sept. 2001.

35 SHA, Minutes Conference, 1 May 2002 and 5 Feb. 2003; SLA, CMD files, DCS, Box C137, E&P 2001, Minutes CMD, 11 Sept. 2001, Box C145, E&P 2002, CMD minutes 19 Feb. 2002.

36 *Independent on Sunday* 7 April 2002; *Observer*, 7 April 2002.

37 SHA, Minutes Conference, 9 Feb. 2000.

38 SLA, CMD files, DCS, C 136B Oil Products 2000, 24 July 2000, CMD minutes.

39 SHA, Minutes Conference, 12 September 2001, 31 October 2001.

40 SLA, CMD files, DCS, C 136 B, Oil Products, CMD minutes, 17-18 April 2000.

41 SHA, Minutes Conference, 1 May 2002, 12 June 2002 and 11 September 2002.

42 SHA, Minutes Conference, 13 June 2001, 1 May 2002, 13 July 2002; SLA, CMD files, DCS, C 150, Shell Oil Products 2002, OP Strategy review, 22/23 April 2002, CMD Minutes; DCS, C166 Shell Oil Products, OP Acquisition overview, 8-9 December 2003.

43 Shell website: www.Shell.com: news and media releases, release 9 January 2004; Shell Centre, minutes of investor and media teleconference, 9 January 2004.

44 *Financial Times*, 10/11 Jan. 2004.

45 *The Independent*, 23 August 2002: City attacks Shell's 'brusque' chairman.

46 *www.uk.finance-yahoo.com*, December 2005.

47 *RD Annual Reports*, 2000-02.

48 Campbell, 'Proving the unprovable'.

49 CERA, 'In Search of Reasonable Certainty' (Cambridge: Cambridge Energy Research Associates, 2005), 7. Companies, investors, and technical experts are increasingly questioning whether the current US system provides an accurate understanding of a company's position or whether, on the contrary, it results in a view of reality that diverges from the one used by a company or, in aggregate, by the industry for making investment decisions.

50 *NRC Handelsblad*, 10 Jan. 2004.

51 *NRC Handelsblad*, 22 Jan. 2004.

52 *Volkskrant*, 5 Feb. 2004.

53 *Observer*, 18 Jan. 2004.

54 *Independent*, 3 Feb. 2004.

55 Deutsche Bank, Global Equity Research, Company Update 18 January 2004.

56 Shell Centre London, Q4 and 2003 Full Year Results Presentation, London 5 Feb. 2005, 'Delivering performance with a long term view.'

57 SHA, Minutes Conference, 16 April 2004: interview of author with Aad Jacobs, chairman Royal Dutch, 8 Dec. 2006.

58 Source for figure 6.7: Annual Reports Royal Dutch, ExxonMobil, and BP.

59 *www.Shell.com*: News & Media releases, 24 August 2004.

60 *www.Shell.com*: News & Media releases, 30 June 2005.

61 *The Guardian*, 10 November 2005.

62 *International Oil Daily*, 31 August 2006.

63 Information Michiel Brandjes, Company Secretary: letter AFM, 2 May 2006; Press release Euronext, 13 April 2006.

64 Interview of Jeroen van der Veer for the Buitenhof programme, 18 December 2005: www.vpro.nl/buitenhof.

65 Shell Centre, Press Conference, 5 March 2004.

66 SWW: Shell Business Week 2004, Opening address by Jeroen van der Veer (May 2004).

67 SLA, CMD files, DCS, Box 127 A, E&P 1999, 2 Dec. 1999, EP HR Review 1999/Plan 2000.

68 *www.eia.com*: Energy Information Administration: monthly crude US domestic first purchase price, dollars per barrel.

69 *RD Annual Reports*, 2000-4; Goldeneye: *www.Shell.com*: media & press releases, 18 October 2004.

70 *RD Annual Reports*, 2000-04.

71 *RD Annual Reports,* 2000-05 and press releases on www.shell.com

72 SHA, Minutes Conference, 31 Oct. 2001.

73 Interview of author with Malcolm Brinded, CEO E&P, 16 Sept. 2005.

74 *Shell World*, July 2003, 19-21.

75 SLA, CMD files, DCS, C160, E&P 2003, Minutes CMD, 14 Jan. 2003.

76 Jeroen van der Veer, 'Shell's strategy to fuel the future' (paper presented at the IMD CEO Roundtable, Lausanne, 11 November 2005).

77 'Shell designers had cut the cost of LNG plants by more than half since 1969', explained Mark Moody-Stuart in 2000: Mark Moody-Stuart, 'Meeting needs, offering choices, providing solutions - challenges and opportunities for energy companies' (paper presented at the Institute of Petroleum, London, 14 February 2000).

78 SHA, Conference 3 Dec. 2003, report GP Technology Strategy.

79 In 2000 the SMDS plant at Bintulu

produced up to 15,000 b/d of middle distillates such as naphtha, gas oil, and kerosene. Because the products were virtually free of nitrogen and sulphur, they possessed excellent combustion properties. Linda Cook, 'Globalising, growing, changing. Globalisation of natural gas in the 21st century' (paper presented at the World Petroleum Congress, Calgary, 15 June 2000).

80 SLA, CMD files, DCS C138 C, Gas and Power 2001, 13 March 2001: report SMDS portfolio development and way forward; DCS C148, Gas and Power 2002, 12 March 2002 and 25 June 2002; SHA, conference minutes 3 Dec. 2003, including report GP Technology Strategy.

81 www.Shell.com, news & media releases, 8 July 2004.

82 SHA, Minutes Conference 3 Dec. 2003, including report GP Technology Strategy.

83 Correljé, Van der Linde, and Westerwoudt, Natural Gas in the Netherland, 186-210.

84 SLA, CMD files, DCS C135, Gas and Power 2000, CMD minutes, 24-25 January 2000; DCS C138 C, Gas and Power 2001, CMD minutes, 13 March 2001.

85 SHA, Minutes Conference 12 July 2000.

86 www.Shell.com: press release 1 July 2005.

87 SHA, Minutes Conference 8 March 2000; SLA, CMD files, DCS, C 135 Gas and Power 2000, CMD minutes 17-18 April 2000.

88 SLA, CMD files, DCS, C 138C, Gas & Power, 2001, CMD minutes, 22 May 2001, 23/24 July 2001, 28 August 2001; DCS, C148, Gas & Power, 2002, minutes CMD, 4/5 March 2002.

89 Interview of author with Linda Cook, 26 July 2005.

90 SHA, Minutes Conference, 9 Feb. 2000 and 2 May 2001; Globe, The international business magazine of Shell Oil Products, 2, 2004.

91 SLA, CMD files, DCS, C166, Shell Oil Products 2003, CMD minutes 25 Nov. 2003.

92 Rob Routs, 'Seizing opportunities in the future fuels market', (paper presented at the National Ethanol Conference, Arizona, 8 February 2005).

93 Shell World, June 2001, 11-3.

94 Ibid.; SLA, CMD files, DCS, C166, Shell Oil Products 2003, Oil Products Choice Fuels Strategy, 25 Nov. 2003.

95 SLA, CMD files, DCS, C166, Shell Oil Products 2003, Oil Products Choice Fuels Strategy, 25 Nov. 2003.

96 Shell World, October 2004, 22.

97 Shell World, May 2005, 28: letter from Shairan Huzani Husain.

98 SLA, CMD files, DCS, C 150, Shell Oil Products 2002, 22/23 April 2002, CMD minutes.

99 RD Annual Report, 2004.

100 Shell World, May 2005, 10.

101 RD Annual Report, 2000.

102 Shell website, www.Shell.com: news releases 5 May 2005.

103 Shell World, Dec./Jan. 2000 and May 2004.

104 SHA, Minutes Conference, 10 Sept. 1997; Jeroen van der Veer, 'Shell International Renewables. Bringing together the Group's activities in solar power, biomass and forestry' (paper presented at the Press conference, London, 6 October 1997).

105 Shell World, Feb.1995.

106 Van der Veer, 'Shell International Renewables'.

107 SHA, Minutes Conference, 10 Sept. 1997.

108 SHA, Minutes Conference, 12 July 2000, 12 Dec. 2001, 11 Dec. 2002, 3 Dec. 2003; RD Annual Reports, 2000-2004.

109 www.Shell.com, news and media releases, 9 January 2006.

110 Booklet: Lessons from Shell Global Solutions; Transformation into a commercial knowledge company', 2 April 2000.

111 SHA, conference minutes, 14 March 2001: Shell Global Solutions also showed a very strong performance with significant earnings growth in the markets it is pursuing as it commercializes technology.

112 SHA, Minutes Conference, 14 March 2001.

113 SHA, Minutes Conference, 10 Feb. 1999.

114 SLA, DCS, C 135A, E&P 2000, Note for information to CMD, EP Technology Strategy, January 2000; SHA, Minutes Conference, 9 Feb. 2000; Interview author with Mark Moody-Stuart, 13 December 2005.

115 EP Technology, information map September 2004, EP GameChanger.

116 Ibid., Expandable Tubulars and Smart Fields.

117 RD/S, Financial and Operational Information 2000-4; RDS Annual Report 2005.

118 'Our Way Forward', Speech by Jeroen van der Veer to the top 100 of Royal Dutch Shell, The Hague, 15 December 2004. The mention of the oil company Total was a reference to rumours in the newspapers that Total was considering taking over Shell. He also mentioned: 'Your wholehearted support gave me and my colleagues new reserves of energy to get us through the rest of the crisis. Unfortunately the SEC doesn't recognise such reserves... but they are important nonetheless'.

119 SWW: Shell Business Week 2004, Opening address by Jeroen van der Veer (May 2004).

120 Van der Veer had already included the Enterprise First mindset in the Targets and Resources Plan of Shell Chemicals from 1998: SLA, DCS, C118A, Chemicals 1998, CMD meeting 26, 27, 28 Oct. 1998.

121 SWW: Shell Business Week 2004, Opening address by Jeroen van der Veer (May 2004).

122 SWW, Shell Business Week, Houston 25 May 2005, second Houston speech by J. van der Veer; Shell World, 15 Oct. 2005, 9-13.

123 Shell World, 15 Oct. 2004, 9-13.

124 Interview of author with Rein Willems, president-directeur Shell Nederland, 22 Dec. 2006.

125 Press release, 28 October 2004; M. C. M. Brandjes and Josien Vegter, 'Een Koninklijke Plc Royal Dutch Shell', Nederlands juristenblad (2006): 369-75.

126 See Vol. 2, Ch. 2.

127 Collection M.M-S: conference presentation, 10 Feb. 1999: Mark Moody-Stuart had proposed finding a solution in a single board or twin boards with identical membership and with an independent chairman. He suggested changing the CMD into an Executive Committee with the CEO and CEOs of the larger businesses. He wanted to clarify the individual accountability of each member. These changes were also intended to include Shell Oil as a normal operating unit, but allow it to retain a 'US' face.

128 Press release, 28 October 2004.

129 Financieele Dagblad, 17 November 2005.

Notes *Shell in mainland China*

1   Dutta, 'China's Industrial Revolution, 1169-1202.

2   When Shell pulled out of Shanghai in 1966, its special advisor Nien Cheng, whose husband had served as general manager before his death in 1957, was imprisoned for ten years on the accusation of being the 'running dog of imperialism'. She was released and rehabilitated in 1976 and later wrote a moving account of the events: Nien Cheng, *Life and Death in Shanghai* (New York: Penguin Books, 1988).

3   SLA, CMD files, DCS, C43, Note China, 29 November 1977; CMD minutes, 31 Oct. - 2 Nov. 1978 and 6 Feb. 1979.

4   *Looking to the Long Term. The Story of Shell in China* (Shell China Beijing Office, 1997).

5   SLA, CMD files, DCS, C44, CMD minutes, 14 July 1982; DCS, C55, Note from Jennings to CMD, 17 January 1989; Minutes CMD, 24 January 1989.

6   SLA, CMD files, DCS, C55, Note from Jennings to CMD, 17 January 1989 and China Upstream position paper.

7   Dutta, 'China's Industrial Revolution', table 3, 1173.

8   Hamilton, *Commerce and Capitalism in Chinese Societies*, 140-9, 171-80, and 237-44.

9   SLA, CMD files, DCS, C82, CMD minutes, 6 Sept. 1994.

10 SLA, CMD files, DCS, C70, CMD minutes 8 June 1993; DCS, C99B, CMD minutes, 1 and 2 Oct. 1996.

11 SLA, CMD files, DCS, C137A, Memo to Board of Shell Petroleum NV, 4 Oct. 2001; *www.shell.com*, Shell China, media releases 2000 (consulted September 2006).

Joint conclusion: the first centenary of Royal Dutch Shell

1   See Volume 4, Appendix Statistical Tables 1890-2000, in particular Table 1.1

2   See Volume 4, Appendix Statistical Tables 1890-2000, Tables 2.4-2.9.

3   See Volume 4, Appendix Statistical Tables 1890-2000, Tables 1.1 and 1.3.

4   *Manufacturing. One Hundred Years of Shell Refining*.

5   *Petroleum Economist*, Annual overviews of the oil majors in May or June (1971-94); *Annual Reports Shell, Exxon and BP*, 1995-2005.

6   SHA, Internal Shell reports Major Oil Companies' Performance in... (1972-96); *Annual Reports Shell, Exxon, and BP* 1997-2005.

7   See Volume 4, Appendix Statistical Tables 1890-2000, Tables 2.3-2.9.

List of figures

List of interviewees

Mundhir Al Barwany	21 October 2003	Peter Kwant	11 April 2005
Peter Baxendell	23 November 2005	Alan Lackey	10 February 2006
Maarten van den Bergh	17 June 2004	Tom Lawson	16 September 2005
Renger Bierema	3 November 2006	Jack Little	7 February 2006
C. J. F. Böttcher	24 January 2006	Adrian Loader	7 May 2004
Karen Brakel	20 October 2003	George Loudon	19 February 2004
Michiel Brandjes	2 June 2006	Garmt Louw	11 April 2005
Malcolm Brinded	16 September 2005 and	Keith Mackrell	24 April 2006
	3 November 2006	John Malcolm	21 October 2003
Phil Carroll	14 February 2006	Hugh Mitchell	11 April 2005
Linda Cook	26 July 2005	Mark Moody-Stuart	13 December 2005
John Darley	16 September 2005	Michiel Noorduyn	10 Maart 2004
Ged Davis	8 June 2004	Raoul Pinnell	26 May 2006
Gerard Drenth	27 April 2004	Rob Routs	3 June 2004
Pieter Folmer	4 November 2003	Sven Royall	10 May 2004
Arie de Geus	20 June 2005	Karen de Segundo	19 May 2004
Tim Hanagan	26 May 2006	Paul Skinner	16 June 2004
Cor Herkströter	14 December 2004	J. J. Traynor	30 June 2006
John Hinde	2 March 2005	Mark Turner	21 April 2004
John Hofmeister	9 July 2004	Jeroen van der Veer	19 December 2005
Venetia Howes	18 July 2003	Ed Vogelzang	17 February 2004
Mary Jo Jacobi	15 June 2004	Peter Vogtländer	17 December 2003
Aad Jacobs	8 December 2006	Lo van Wachem	10 February 2004
Peter J. Jones	26 April 2004	Mike Warwick	29 April 2004
Tim van Kooten	6 June 2006	Rein Willems	22 December 2006
Jan Kopernicki	5 May 2004	Mark Williams	15 June 2004

Abbreviations

A

AG	Aktien Gesellschaft (joint-stock company)
AGIP	Azienda Generali Italiana di Petroli
AGM	annual general meeting of shareholders
AGNS	Allied General Nuclear Services
AIOC	Anglo-Iranian Oil Company
AN CAMT	Archives Nationaux, Centre des Archives du Monde du Travail (Roubaix, France)
API	American Petroleum Institute
APOC	Anglo-Persian Oil Company
Avgas	aviation fuel

B

B/d, bpd	barrels per day
BASF	Badische Anilin- und Soda-Fabriken
BB RWM	Bundesarchiv Berlin, Reichswirtschaftsministerium
BB	Bundesarchiv Berlin
BEA	Bank of England Archives, London (UK)
BEF	British Expeditionary Force
BHP	Broken Hill Proprietary Company
BIM	Bataafsche Import Maatschappij
BNOC	British National Oil Corporation
BP	British Petroleum
BPC	Basrah Petroleum Company
BPM	Bataafsche Petroleum Maatschappij

C

CBE	Commander of the Order of the British Empire
CEI	Compagnie d'Esthétique Industrielle
CEO	chief executive officer
CEP	Current Estimated Potential
CERA	Cambridge Energy Research Associates
CFCs	chlorofluorocarbons
CFO	Chief Financial Offices
CFP	Compagnie Française des Pétroles
CIF	cost, insurance, freight
CMD	Committee of Managing Directors
CNOOC	China National Offshore Oil Corporation
CONCAWE	Conservation of Clean Air and Water, Western Europe
COT	Curaçao Oil Terminal
CPIM	Curaçaosche Petroleum Industrie Maatschappij
CPMR	Pipeline Mozambique Rhodesia Company
CSM	Curaçaosche Scheepvaart Maatschappij
CSV	Compañia Shell de Venezuela

D

DAPG	Deutsch-Amerikänische Petroleum Gesellschaft
DEA	Deutsche Erdöl Aktiengesellschaft
DNB	Nederlandsche Bank, Amsterdam (Netherlands)
DSM	Dutch State Mines
DWT	Deadweight Tonnes

E

E&P	exploration and production
EC	European Community
EEC	European Economic Community
EGM	extraordinary general meeting
Elf	Essence et Lubrifiants français
ENI	Ente Nazionali Indrocarburi
EP, E&P	Exploration and Production
EPU	Europäische Petroleum Union
ERAP	Entreprise de Recherches et d'Activités Pétrolières
Expro	Exploration and Production

F

FCE	Fletcher Challenge Energy
FIH	free in harbour
FOB	free on board
FSA	Financial Services Authority
FTC	Federal Trade Commission

G

GRT	Gross Registered Tonnes
GTL	Gas to Liquids

H

HDNP	Historisch Documentatiecentrum voor het Nederlands Protestantisme (Vrije Universiteit, Amsterdam, the Netherlands)
HMG	His/Her Majesty's Government
HR	Human Resources
HTGR	High Temperature Gas-cooled Reactor

I

ICC	International Chamber of Commerce
IHECC	International Hydrogenation Engineering and Chemical Company
IHP	International Hydrogenation Patents Company
IMCO	Intergovernmental Maritime Consultative Organisation
INOC	Iraq National Oil Company
IPC	Iraq Petroleum Company

K

KBE	Knigt Commander of the Order of the British Empire
KNPM	Koninklijke Nederlandse Petroleum Maatschappij
KOC	Kuwait Oil Company
KPM	Koninklijke Paketvaart Maatschappij
KSLA	Koninklijke Shell Laboratorium Amsterdam

L

LEAP	Leadership and Performance
LNG	Liquid Natural Gas
LPG	Liquified Petroleum Gas
LWR	Light Water Reactor

M

Mekog	Maatschappij tot Exploitatie van Kooks-Oven Gassen
MFH	Ministry of Finance, The Hague (the Netherlands)
Mogas	automobile fuel
Mori	Market & Opinion Research International
Mosop	Movement for the Survival of the Ogoni People

N

NA Kew	National Archives, Kew (UK)
NA The Hague	National Archives, The Hague (the Netherlands)
NAM	Nederlandse Aardolie Maatschappij
NGO	Non-governmental organization
NHM	Nederlandsche Handel-Maatschappij
NIIHM	Nederlandsch-Indische Industrie- en Handel-Maatschappij
NIOC	National Iranian Oil Company
NIOD	Nederlands Instituut voor Oorlogsdocumentatie (Amsterdam, the Netherlands)
NIT	Nederlandsch-Indische Tankstoomboot Maatschappij
NKPM	Nederlandsche Koloniale Petroleum Maatschappij
NNPC	Nigerian National Petroleum Corporation
NSB	Nationaal Socialistische Beweging
NT	New Technology Ventures Division
NTB	Non-Traditional Business
NV	Naamloze Vennootschap (joint-stock company)
NVD	New Venture Divisions

O

OAPEC	Organization of Arab Petroleum Exporting Countries
OBE	Officer of the Order of the British Empire
OECD	Organization for Economic Cooperation and Development
OPC	Oil Price Collapse
OPEC	Organizaton of Petroleum Exporting Countries
OVA	Overhead Value Analysis

P

PA	Public Affairs
PDO	Petroleum Development Oman
PDVSA	Petróleos de Venezuela S.A.
Pemex	Petróleos Mexicanos
PET	Polyethylene Terephthalate
PPAG	Petroleum Produkte Aktien Gesellschaft
PVC	Polyvinyl Chloride

R

R&D	Research and Development
RA Alkmaar	Regionaal Archief Alkmaar (the Netherlands)
RAF	Royal Air Force
RD	Royal Dutch
RD/S	Royal Dutch/Shell
RDS	Royal Dutch Shell plc
RIS	Republik Indonesia Serikat
RM	Reichsmark
ROACE	Return on Average Capital Employed
RTZ	Rio Tinto-Zinc Corporation
RVI	Retail Visual Identity
RWM	Reichswirtschaftsministerium

S

SAPREF	Shell and BP South African Petroleum Refineries
SASOL	South African Synthetic Oil Ltd
SCORE	Service Companies Operations Review Exercise
SEC	Securities and Exchange Commission
SHA	Shell Archives, The Hague (the Netherlands)
SHAC	Shell High Activity Catalyst
SHOP	Shell Higher Olefins Process
SIEP	Shell International E&P
Sietco	Shell International Eastern Trading Company
SIMEX	Singapore International Monetary Exchange
Sinopec	China Petroleum & Chemical Corporation
SIPC	Shell International Petroleum Company Ltd.
SIPM	Shell Internationale Petroleum Maatschappij NV
SIS	Shell International Shipping
Sitco	Shell International Trading Company
SLA	Shell Archives, London (UK)
SM/PO	Styrene Monomer/Propylene Oxide
SMBP	Shell-Mex & BP Ltd.

SMDS	Shell Middle Distillate Synthesis
SOC	Standard Oil Company
SOCAR	State Oil Company of Azerbaijan Republic
Socony	Standard Oil Company of New York
Stanvac	Standard-Vacuum Oil Company

T

TBA	Tyres, Batteries, and Accessories
TCP	Tri-chresyl Phospate
TEL	Tetra-Ethyl Lead
TINA	There Is No Alternative
TNT	Tri-Nitro Toluene
TPC	Turkish Petroleum Company
TVP	True Vapour Phase

U

UMWA	United Mine Workers of America
UNC	United Nuclear Corporation
UOP	Universal Oil Products

V

VLCC	Very Large Crude Carrier
VOC	Venezuelan Oil Concessions Ltd.
VU HDNP	Historisch Documentatiecentrum voor het Nederlands Protestantisme (Vrije Universiteit, Amsterdam, the Netherlands)

W

WOCANA	World outside the Communist area and North America
WTI	West Texas Intermediate

Y

YPF	Yacimientos Petroliferos Fiscales

Bibliography

Adelman, M. A., 'Is the oil shortage real? Oil companies as OPEC tax collectors', *Foreign Policy* (winter 1972/3), 69-108.

—— *The Genie out of the Bottle: World Oil since 1970* (Cambridge, Mass., and London: MIT Press, 1995).

Aftalion, F., *A History of the International Chemical Industry: From the 'Early Days' to 2000* (Philadelphia: Chemical Heritage Press, 2001).

Amuzegar, J., *Managing the Oil Wealth; OPEC's Windfalls and Pitfalls* (London, 1999).

Antill, N., and Arnott, R., *Oil Company Crisis: Managing Structure, Profitability and Growth* (Oxford Institute for Energy Studies, 2003).

Bailey, M., 'Enforcing oil sanctions: A comparison of the Rhodesian and South African embargoes', in J. Rodenburg (ed.), *Embargo: Apartheid's Oil Secrets Revealed* (Amsterdam: Amsterdam University Press, 1995), 225-33.

Bamberg, J. H., *British Petroleum and Global Oil, 1950-1975: The Challenge of Nationalism* (Cambridge: Cambridge University Press, 2000).

Baxendell, P., 'Human resource management in practice'. Paper presented at the INSEAD International Human Resource Management Symposium, Fontainebleau, 26 February 1986.

Bergh, E. van den, 'The Dutch Campaign against Shell', in in J. Rodenburg (ed.), *Embargo. Apartheid's Oil Secrets Revealed* (Amsterdam: Amsterdam University Press, 1995), 306-24.

Bingham, T. H., and Gray, S. M., *Report on the Supply of Petroleum and Petroleum Products to Rhodesia* (London: Foreign and Commonwealth Office, 1978).

Bleakley, T., Gee, D S., and Hulme, R., 'The atomization of big oil', *The McKinsey Quarterly*, 2 (1997), 123-42.

Blom, W. (ed.), *Honderd jaar Shell Pernis – een eeuw raffinage in de Rotterdamse haven. One Hundred Years of Shell Pernis – A Century of Refining and Petrochemicals in the Port of Rotterdam* (Rotterdam, 2002).

Blomström, M., and Hettne, B., *Development Theory in Transition: The Dependency Debate and Beyond: Third World Responses* (London: Zed Books, 1984).

Boyle, B. M., 'Equal opportunity for women is smart business', *Harvard Business Review* (May/June, 1973), 85-95.

Brinded, M., 'Using associated gas – the Climate Doube Dividend'. Paper presented at the Global Gas Flaring Reduction Initiative Conference, Oslo, 16 April 2002.

Broersma, K. E., *Eene zaak van regt en billijk-heid. Enkele episoden uit de enerverende Billiton-geschiedenis 1860-1985* (Leidschendam: Billiton, 1985).

Bull, D., and Stachan, D. 'Liquefied natural gas safety research', *Shell Selected Papers* (March, 1992).

Butler, S., 'Accidents bedevil the North Sea', *Financial Times*, 20 April 1989.

Campbell, C., 'Proving the unprovable', *Petroleum Economist* (1995), 27-30.

Carson, R., *Silent Spring* (Boston: Houghton Mifflin, 1962).

CERA, 'In Search of Reasonable Certainty'. Cambridge: Cambridge Energy Research Associates, 2005.

Chambers, J. C., Mullick, S. K., and Smith, D. D., 'How to choose the right forecasting technique', *Harvard Business Review* (July/August, 1971)

Chandler, A. D., jr. *Strategy and Structure: Chapters in the History of the Industrial Enterprise* (Cambridge, Mass.: MIT Press, 1962).

Chandler, G., 'Transnational Corporations'. Paper presented at the World Council of Churches Consultation of Transnational Corporations, Geneva, 13-18 June 1977.

Chapman, K., 'Agents of change in the internationalization of the petrochemical industry', *Geoforum*, 23 (1992), 13-27.

Chemicals Information Handbook (London: Shell International Chemical Company, 1992).

Cook, L. 'Globalising, growing, changing. Globalisation of natural gas in the 21st century'. Paper presented at the World Petroleum Congress, Calgary, 15 June 2000.

——, 'Serving customers in diverse markets', Paper presented at the 20th CERA Annual Executive Conference, Houston, 14 February 2001.

Correljé, A., van der Linde, C., and Westerwoudt, T., *Natural Gas in the Netherlands: From Cooperation to Competition?* (Amsterdam: Oranje-Nassau Group, 2003).

Crone, H. D., *Chemicals & Society: A Guide to the New Chemical Age* (Cambridge: Cambridge University Press, 1986).

Dankers, J. J., and Verheul, J., *Hoogovens 1945-1993. Van staalbedrijf tot twee-metalenconcern. Een studie in industriële strategie* (The Hague: SDU, 1993).

Davies, P. L., 'European experience with worker representation on the board', in Industrial Democracy Committee (eds.), *Industrial Democracy. European Experience: Two Research Reports* (London: Her Majesty's Stationery Office, 1976), 51-83.

De aan(deel)houder wint; 10 jaar protest tegen steun Shell aan Zuid-Afrika (Utrecht/Den Haag: Werkgroep Kairos, Pax Christi-Nederland, Novib, 1983).

Doyle, J., *Riding the Dragon. Royal Dutch Shell & the Fossil Fire* (Boston, Mass.: Environmental Health Fund, 2002).

Drucker, P. F., *The Practice of Management* (New York, 1954).

Dutta, M., 'China's industrial revolution: Challenges for a macroeconomic agenda', *Journal of Asian Economics*, 15 (2005): 1169-1202.

Eckstut, M., and Spitz, P. H., 'Strategy development in the chemical industry', in P. H. Spitz (ed.), *The Chemical Industry at the Millenium: Maturity, Restructuring, and Globalization* (Philadephia: Chemical Heritage Press, 2003), 111-44.

Fage, J. D., *History of Africa*, 3rd edn. (London and New York. Routledge, 1995).

Financial Times Oil and Gas International Yearbook, vols. 68-89 (1978-99).

Fast, N. D., *The Rise and Fall of Corporate New Venture Divisions*, vol. III, Research for Business Decisions (UMI Research Press, 1978).

Flavin, C., *Nuclear Power: The Market Test*, Worldwatch Paper 57, 1983.

Fruhan, W. E. Jr., 'Corporate raiders: Head 'em off at value gap', *Harvard Business Review* (1988): 63-8.

Fürstenberg, F., 'West German experience with industrial democracy', in J. P. Windmuller (ed.), *Industrial Democracy in International Perspective*, Special edition of The Annals of the American Academy of Political and Social Science (Philadelphia, 1977), 44-53.

Gainey, B. W., 'Natural gas for power generation', *Shell Selected Papers* (1991).

Galbraith, J. K., *The New Industrial State* (London: Hamish Hamilton, 1967).

Geus, A. de, *The Living Company: Growth, Learning and Longevity in Business* (London: Nicholas Brealy, 1997).

Goold, M., and Lucks, K., 'Why diversify? Four decades of management thinking', *Academy of Management Executive*, 7: 3 (1993), 7-25.

Gruiters, J., 'De stille revolutie. Internationale ondernemingen en mensenrechten', in J. van Workum (ed.), *Maatschappelijk verantwoord ondernemen. Een nieuwe fase in het kapitalisme* (Kampen: Kok, 2000), 140-153.

Hamel, G., and Prahalad, C. K., *Competing for the Future* (Boston, Mass.: Harvard Business School Press, 1994).

Hamilton, Gary G., *Commerce and Capitalism in Chinese Societies* (London and New York: Routledge, 2006).

Hammer, M., and Champy, J., *Reengineering the Corporation: A Manifestato for Business Revolution* (New York, 1993).

Hartshorn, J. E., *Oil Trade: Politics and Prospects* (Cambridge: Cambridge University Press, 1993).

Haspeslagh, P., 'Portfolio planning: uses and limits', *Harvard Business Review* (January/February, 1982), 58-73.

Hellema, D., Wiebes, C., and Witte, T., *Doelwit Rotterdam. Nederland en de oliecrisis 1973-1974*, Den Haag: SDU Uitgevers, 1998.

Hengeveld, R., 'Part A: Embargo: Apartheid's oil secrets revealed', in J. Rodenburg (ed.), *Embargo: Apartheid's Oil Secrets Revealed* (Amsterdam: Amsterdam University Press, 1995), 6-221.

Herkströter, C. A. J., 'Dealing with contradictory expectations – the dilemmas facing multinationals', *www.shell.com (media centre, speeches, 1/26/2005)* (1996).

Hoffman, A. J., *From Heresy to Dogma: An Institutional History of Corporate Environmentalism* (San Francisco: New Lexington Press, 1997), 114-7.

Hofstede, G., 'Motivation, leadership, and organisation: do American theories apply elsewhere?' *Personnel Management Review (PMR)*, 51 (1981).

—— *Culture's Consequences, International Differences in Work-Related Values* (London: Sage Publications, 1984).

Holt, Douglas B., Quelch, John A., and Taylor, Earl L., 'Managing the global brand. A typology of consumer perceptions', in *The Global Market. Developing a Strategy to Manage Across Borders*, ed. John Quelch and Rohit Deshpande (San Francisco: Jossey-Bass, 2004), 180-201.

Homburg, E., 'Chemie', in A. A. Albert de la Bruheze (ed.), *Techniek in Nederland in de twintigste eeuw*, vol. ii, *Delfstoffen, energie, chemie* (Zutphen: Walburg Pers, 2000), 269-408.

Howarth, S., *Sea Shell: The Story of Shell's British Tanker Fleets, 1892-1992* (London, 1992).

—— *A Century in Oil. The "Shell" Transport and Trading Company, 1897-1997* (London: Weidenfeld & Nicolson, 1997).

Jones, G., Renewing Unilever. Transformation and Tradition (Oxford: Oxford University Press, 2005).

Jones, G., Multinationals and Global Capitalism. From the Nineteenth to the Twenty First Century (Oxford: Oxford University Press, 2005).

Jones, G., and Gálvez-Muñoz (eds.), *Foreign Multinationals in the United States: Management and Performance* (London and New York: Routledge, 2002).

Jordan, G., 'Indirect causes and effects in policy change: the Brent Spar case', *Public Administration*, 76 (Winter, 1998), 601-28.

—— *Shell, Greenpeace and the Brent Spar* (Basingstoke: Palgrave, 2001).

Kamp, A. F., *De standvastige tinnen soldaat, 1860-1960*, ('s Gravenhage: NV Billiton Maatschappij, 1960).

Kapferer, Jean-Noël, *[Re]inventing the Brand. Can Top Brands Survive the New Market Realities?* (London: Kogan Page, 2001).

Katzin, Donna, 'Anatomy of a boycott. The Royal Dutch/Shell Campaign in the US', in **J. Rodenburg** (ed.), *Embargo. Apartheid's Oil Secrets Revealed* (Amsterdam: Amsterdam University Press, 1995), 327-37.

Lerøen, B. V., *Troll, Gas for Generations*: A/S Norske Shell and Statoil, no year.

Levitt, Th., 'The globalization of markets', *Harvard Business Review* (May/June, 1983).

Levy, B., 'World oil marketing in transition', *International Organization*, 36: 1 (1982), 113-33.

Levy, W. J., 'The years that the locust hath eaten: oil policy and OPEC development prospects', *Foreign Affairs* (winter, 1978/9).

Life Now: Shell Ladies' Project 1996 (1996).

Life on the Move: Shell Ladies' Project 1993 (1993).

Linde, P. van der, *Time Bomb: LNG, the Truth about our Newest and Most Dangerous Energy Source* (New York: Doubleday & Co, 1978).

Lowe, A., 'Business strategies for the eighties'. Paper presented at the SCI London section, 5 November 1979.

——, 'Investment strategies for the petrochemical industry'. Paper presented at the European Chemical market Research Association, Cannes, 19 October 1981.

Lowenstein, R., *Origins of the Crash:The Great Bubble and Its Undoing* (New York: The Penguin Press, 2004).

Manby, B., 'The role and responsibility of oil multinationals in Nigeria', *Journal of International Affairs*, 53: 1 (1999), 281-302.

Mandel, E., *From Class Society to Communism: An Introduction to Marxism* (London: Ink Links, 1977).

Manufacturing: One hundred years of Shell Refining, 1891-1991 (The Hague: Shell Internationale Maatschappij, 1991).

Meadows, D. H., Meadows, D. L., Randers, J., et al., *The Limits to Growth* (New York/London: Potomac Associates, 1972).

Minard, L., and Curtis, C. E., 'Exxon, move over', *Forbes*, 24 (November, 1980), 129-40.

'Modern automotive retail', *Shell Briefing Service (SBS)*, 5 (1989).

Moody-Stuart, M., 'Prospering in uncertainty – the North Sea industry in evolving energy markets'. Paper presented at the Offshore Europe conference, Aberdeen, 7 September 1999.

——, 'Meeting needs, offering choices, providing solutions – challenges and opportunities for energy companies'. Paper presented at the Institute of Petroleum, London, 14 February 2000.

——, 'Shaping the future of energy in industries – an energy company perspective'. Paper presented at the Offshore Northern Seas conference, Stavanger, 22 August 2000.

Muller, H., *The Search for the Qualities Essential to Advancement in a Large Industrial Group. An Exploratory Study* (Dissertation Utrecht University, 1970).

'Multinational Enterprises and Human Rights. A Documentation of the Dialogue between Amnesty International/Pax Christi and Shell' (Utrecht: Pax Christi Netherlands, 1998).

Murray, R., *Go Well: One Hundred Years of Shell in Australia* (Melbourne: Hargreen Publishing Company, 2001).

Nisbet, E. G., and Fowler, C. M. R., 'Is metal disposal toxic to deep oceans', *Nature*, 375 (1995).

Nuclear Power Issues and Choices (Cambridge Mass.: Ballinger Publishing Company, 1977).

Odell, P.R., *Olie en macht (Oil and World Power)* (Utrecht and Antwerp: Het Spectrum, 1970).

Oil and Gas International Yearbook, vols. 63-7 (1973-7).

OPEC Official resolutions and price releases, 1960-1990 (Vienna: OPEC, 1990).

'Operations in Nigeria', *Shell Briefing Note* (May, 1994).

Packard, V., *The Hidden Persuaders* (New York: Longmans, 1957).

Peters, T. J., and Waterman, R. H., jr., *In Search of Excellence: Lessons from America's Best Run Companies* (New York: Harper and Row, 1982).

Pink, M. J., 'Exploration and appraisal technology – maximising rewards by integration', *Shell Selected Papers* (January, 1992).

Porter, M. E., *Competitive advantage* (New York: Free Press, 1985).

—— 'From competitive advantage to corporate strategy', *Harvard Business Review* (May/June, 1987), 43-54.

Prahalad, C. K., and Hamel, G., 'The core competence of the corporation', *Harvard Business Review* (May/June, 1990), 79-91.

Priest, T., 'The "Americanization" of Shell Oil', in Gálvez-Muñoz (ed.), *Foreign Multinationals in the United States: Management and Performance*, 188-205 (London and New York: Routledge, 2002).

Pringle, P., and Spiegelman, J., *The Nuclear Barons* (New York: Avon Books, 1983).

Quelch, J., and Deshpande, R. (eds.), *The Global Market. Developing a Strategy to Manage Across Borders* (San Francisco: Jossey-Bass, 2004).

'Report by the Commission on the behaviour of the oil companies in the Community during the period from October 1973 to March 1974' (Brussels, 1975).

Riemsdijk, M. J. van, *Actie of dialoog. Over de betrekkingen tussen maatschappij en onderneming* (Proefschrift Universiteit Twente, 1994).

Riezebos, Rik, *Merkenmanagement. Theorie en toepassing van het ontwikkelen, beheren en beschermen van merken en merkenportfolio's*, 2nd edn. (Groningen: Wolters-Noordhoff, 2002).

Routs, R., 'Seizing opportunities in the future fuels market'. Paper presented at the National Ethanol Conference, Arizona, 8 February 2005

Rowell, A., 'Het gevaar van de dialoog', in E. Lubbers (ed.), *Schone schijn. Smerige streken in de strijd tussen burgers en bedrijven* (Amsterdam: Fagel, 2002), 44-57.

Rozendaal, S., Bekkum, H. van, and Reewijk, J. (eds.), *Chemie achter de dijken. Uitvindingen en uitvinders in de eeuw na van 't Hoff* (KNAW, KNCV, 2001).

St John-Hall, A., 'Saddled with uncertainty', *Shell World* (September, 2001), 20-?

Schut, G. H. A., 'De ontwikkeling van het ondernemingsrecht in Nederland', in *Economische orde en beleid. Twintig jaren sociaal-economisch beleid. Bundel ter gelegenheid van het aftreden van dr. J.W. de Pous als voorzitter van de Sociaal-Economische Raad (1964-1984)* (Den Haag: Kluwer, SER, 1985), 65-84.

Schwartz, P., *The Art of the Long View* (New York: Doubleday, 1992).

Shell smeer 'em uit Zuid-Afrika (Werkgroep Kairos: Komitee Zuidelijk Afrika, 1980).

Skinner, P., 'Changing oil markets – impacts and strategies'. Paper presented at the Cera 19th Annual Executive Conference, Houston 2000.

Skinner, W. E. (ed.), *Oil and Petroleum Yearbook*, vols. 19-62 (London: Skinner, 1928-72).

Sluyterman, K. E., *Driekwart eeuw CSM: cash flow, strategie en mensen* (Diemen: CSM, 1995).

—— *Dutch Enterprise in the Twentieth Century. Business strategies in a small open economy* (London and New York: Routledge, 2005).

Spitz, P. H., *Petrochemicals: The Rise of an Industry* (New York: Wiley & Sons, 1988).

Steenbakkers, K. B. J., *Dynamics of the European Refining and Petrochemcial Industry: Strategies, Structure and Change* (KU Nijmegen, 1997).

Stobaugh, R., *Innovation and Competition: The Global Management of Petrochemical Products* (Boston, Mass.: Harvard Business School Press, 1988).

'Stop Press!' in J. Rodenburg (ed.), *Embargo. Apartheid's Oil Secrets Revealed* (Amsterdam: Amsterdam University Press, 1995), 325-6.

Taverne, B., *Petroleum, Industry and Governments. An Introduction to Petroleum Regulation, Economics and Government Policies* (The Hague, London, and Boston: Kluwer, 1999).

Tookey, R., 'PA is good business', *Interchange*, 19 (August, 1988).

—— 'Public opinion in the 90s: threat or opportunity?' *Interchange*, 1 (extra, 1991).

——, 'Reflections of a coordinator', *Interchange*, 2 (1993), 11-13.

Trompenaars, F., *Riding the Waves of Culture: Understanding Cultural Diversity in Business* (London: Nicholas Brealey, 1993).

Tulder, R. van, and Zwart, A. van der, *Reputaties op het spel. Maatschappelijk verantwoord ondernemen in een onderhandelingssamenleving* (Utrecht: Het Spectrum, 2003).

Unander, F., *Oil Crises & Climate Challenge: 30 Years of Energy Use in IEA Countries* (Paris: OECD/IEA, 2004).

Veer, J. van der, 'Inzicht door doorzicht'. Paper presented at the Verzekeringskamer, Apeldoorn, 19 November 1998.

—— 'Profits and Principles, the Experience of an Industry Leader'. Paper presented at the Greenport '99 conference 1999.

—— 'Fuelling the future: the shift to gas'. Paper presented at the Finance and investment In Qatar conference, London, 19 September 2002.

—— 'Meeting society's needs through collaborative innovation'. Paper presented at the EIRMA Conference, Vienna, 29 May 2002.

—— 'Shell's strategy to fuel the future'. Paper presented at the IMD CEO Roundtable, Lausanne, 11 November 2005.

—— 'A vision for meeting energy needs beyond oil', *Financial Times* (2006)

Veldman, H., and Lagers, G., *50 Years Offshore* (Delft: Foundation for Offshore Studies, 1997).

Verstegen, W., *Vervuiling van het milieudebat; een milieusceptisch essay* (Amsterdam: Uitgeverij Nieuwezijds, 1999).

Visser, Koos, 'The test of tomorrow', *Shell Selected Paper* (1993).

Vogel, P. J., 'NTB, 1968-1984. The Group and Non-Traditional Business' (Shell, 1984).

Wachem, L. van, 'Unity in diversity – organisation and people in multinational enterprises'. Paper presented at the German Society for Business Economics conference, Berlin, 13 October 1992.

Watkins, D., 'Business and South Africa: reason and responsibility'. Paper presented at the Business International Conference, London, 3 October 1988.

Watts, P., 'Russia: Building on the past, looking to the future'. Paper presented at the Russia Economic Forum, London, 18 April 2002.

Wesseling, L., *Fuelling the War: Revealing an Oil Company's Role in Vietnam* (London and New York: I. B. Tauris, 2000).

Wheeler, D., Fabig, H., and Boele, R., 'Paradoxes and dilemmas for stakeholder responsive firms in the extractive sector: lessons from the case of Shell and the Ogoni', *Journal of Business Ethics*, 39 (2002), 297-318.

'Why is the world's most profitable company turning Itself inside out?' *Fortune* (1997), 52-7.

Williams, J. R., 'Natural gas – the world supply challenge'. Paper presented at the Gastech 93, Paris, 16 February 1993.

Woerkum, J. van, *Shell en de Raad van Kerken in gesprek* (Driebergen: Kerk en Wereld, 1998).

World Commission of Environment and
Development, *Our Common Future* (Oxford
and New York: Oxford University Press, 1987).

Wouters, W., *Shell Tankers: van koninklijke
afkomst* (Rotterdam: Shell Tankers BV, 1984).

Yergin, D., *The Prize: The Epic Quest for Oil,
Money & Power* (New York: Simon & Schuster,
1991).

Zanden, J. L. van, and **Verstegen, W.**, *Groene
geschiedenis van Nederland* (Utrecht: Het
Spectrum, 1993).

Zyglidopoulos, Stelios C., 'The Social and
Environmental Responsibilities of Multi-
nationals: Evidence from the Brent Spar Case',
Journal of Business Ethics, 36 (2002), 141-51.

Illustration credits

The publisher has made every effort to contact all those with ownership rights pertaining to the illustrations. Nonetheless, should you believe that your rights have not been respected, please contact Boom Publishers, Amsterdam.

ANP: Dutch Press Agency, The Hague
EPA: European Pressphoto Agency
IISG: International Institute of Social History, Amsterdam
NFA: Dutch Photo Archive, Rotterdam
NFM: Dutch Photomuseum, Rotterdam
SHA: Shell Archive, The Hague
SLA: Shell Archive, London

Introduction

1   Corbis/Schlegelmilch

Chapter 1

1   Spaarnestad Photo
2   Corbis
3   Corbis
4   Corbis
5   Spaarnestad Photo
6   Spaarnestad Photo
7   Spaarnestad Photo
8   Arjen van Susteren
9   Corbis
10 Spaarnestad Photo
11 Getty Images
12 Corbis
13 Corbis
14 Spaarnestad Photo/Intercontinental Press Service
15 Spaarnestad Photo/Anefo
16 Spaarnestad Photo
17 SHA, 190F/KON 549
18 Getty Images
19 Spaarnestad Photo/ANP
20 Shell Photographic Services/Shell Int. Ltd.
21 Arjen van Susteren, based on: *Annual Report* 1975
22 Paul Maas/Eric van Rootselaar, based on: SHA, 190Y/387
23 Arjen van Susteren, based on: *Financial and Operational Information*, 1998-2002
24 Shell Photographic Services/Shell Int. Ltd.
25 Shell Photographic Services/Shell Int. Ltd.
26 Spaarnestad Photo/ANP
27 Spaarnestad Photo/Ger Dijkstra
28 Shell Photographic Services/Shell Int. Ltd.
29 Shell Photographic Services/Shell Int. Ltd.
30 SHA, 190F/205
31 Shell Photographic Services/Shell Int. Ltd.
32 Spaarnestad Photo
33 Shell Photographic Services/Shell Int. Ltd.
34 Shell Photographic Services/Shell Int. Ltd.
35 Shell Photographic Services/Shell Int. Ltd.
36 Shell Photographic Services/Shell Int. Ltd.
37 Shell Photographic Services/Shell Int. Ltd.
38 Paul Maas/Eric van Rootselaar
39 Spaarnestad Photo/ANP
40 Getty Images
41 Spaarnestad Photo/ANP
42 Shell Photographic Services/Shell Int. Ltd.
43 Shell Photographic Services/Shell Int. Ltd.
44 Shell Photographic Services/Shell Int. Ltd.
45 Shell Photographic Services/Shell Int. Ltd.
46 Hollandse Hoogte/Panos/Brendan Corr
47 Hollandse Hoogte/Magnum
48 Hollandse Hoogte/Magnum/Jean Gaumy
49 IISG/Ernst Volland
50 IISG
51 Getty Images
52 Spaarnestad Photo/ANP
53 Spaarnestad Photo
54 SLA, SC330/B/1
55 Spaarnestad Photo/ANP
56 Spaarnestad Photo/ANP
57 SLA, APDS/ITC/22M
58 Studio Marise Knegtmans, based on: *Issues in refining*
59 Corbis
60 SHA, 190F/100
61 SHA, 190F/100
62 SHA 190F/205
63 SHA, 190F/205
64 Shell Photographic Services/Shell Int. Ltd.
65 Shell Photographic Services/Shell Int. Ltd.
66 Shell Photographic Services/Shell Int. Ltd.
67 SHA,190F/205
68 SHA, 190F/205
69 Shell Photographic Services/Shell Int. Ltd.
70 Studio Marise Knegtmans, based on: *Shell Venster*, 8/1980
71 Shell Photographic Services/Shell Int. Ltd.
72 SHA and Shell Oil, Houston
73 Shell Oil, Houston
74 Paul Maas/Eric van Rootselaar, based on:

Shell News, 1/1977

75   From: *The history of Shell*

76   SHA, 190F/3.81.03.27

Chapter 2

1   SHA, 190F/3.81.03.27

2   Shell Photographic Services/Shell Int. Ltd.

3   Shell Photographic Services/Shell Int. Ltd.

4   Shell Photographic Services/Shell Int. Ltd.

5   Shell Photographic Services/Shell Int. Ltd.

6   Shell Photographic Services/Shell Int. Ltd.

7   Shell Photographic Services/Shell Int. Ltd.

8   Shell Photographic Services/Shell Int. Ltd.

9   Shell Photographic Services/Shell Int. Ltd.

10 Paul Maas/Eric van Rootselaar, based on: SHA

11 Paul Maas/Eric van Rootselaar, based on: SHA

12 Shell Photographic Services/Shell Int. Ltd.

13 Shell Photographic Services/Shell Int. Ltd.

14 Corbis/Owen Franken

15 Corbis/Wally McNamee

16 Getty Images/Ernst Haas

17 Nationaal Archief/Anefo/Bert Verhoeff

18 Hollandse Hoogte

19 Shell Photographic Services/Shell Int. Ltd.

20 Hollandse Hoogte/Roel Burgler

21 Shell Photographic Services/Shell Int. Ltd.

22 Shell Photographic Services/Shell Int. Ltd.

23 SHA, 190F/3.85.10.03A

24 SHA, 190F/3.85.10.28A

25 SHA, 190F/3.81.06.12

26 Shell Australia

27 SHA, 190F/3.85.10.28A

28 Shell Photographic Services/Shell Int. Ltd.

29 Shell Photographic Services/Shell Int. Ltd.

30 Shell Photographic Services/Shell Int. Ltd.

31 Shell Photographic Services/Shell Int. Ltd.

32 Shell Photographic Services/Shell Int. Ltd.

33 Shell Photographic Services/Shell Int. Ltd.

34 Shell Photographic Services/Shell Int. Ltd.

35 Shell Photographic Services/Shell Int. Ltd.

36 Shell Photographic Services/Shell Int. Ltd.

37 Shell Photographic Services/Shell Int. Ltd.

38 Hollandse Hoogte/Magnum/Jean Gaumy

39 Shell Photographic Services/Shell Int. Ltd.

40 Corbis/Marco Cauz

41 Kees Rutten

42 Hollandse Hoogte/Magnum/Ferdinando Scianna

43 Reuters

44 EPA/ANP

45 Shell Photographic Services/Shell Int. Ltd.

46 Hollandse Hoogte/François Goudier

47 Shell Photographic Services/Shell Int. Ltd.

48 Shell Photographic Services/Shell Int. Ltd.

49 Shell Photographic Services/Shell Int. Ltd.

50 Shell Photographic Services/Shell Int. Ltd.

51 Shell Photographic Services/Shell Int. Ltd.

52 Shell Photographic Services/Shell Int. Ltd.

53 Shell Photographic Services/Shell Int. Ltd.

54 Shell Photographic Services/Shell Int. Ltd.

55 Shell Pernis/Ernst Bode

56 Hollandse Hoogte/François Goudier

Chapter 3

1   Shell Photographic Services/Shell Int. Ltd.

2   Hollandse Hoogte

3   Corbis/Bernard Bisson

4   Corbis/Bernard Bisson

5   Corbis/Peter Turnley

6   Getty Images/Allan Tannenbaum

7   Corbis/Najlah Feanny

8   Hollandse Hoogte/Magnum/Peter Marlow

9   SHA, 190F/205

10 Shell Photographic Services/Shell Int. Ltd.

11 Shell Photographic Services/Shell Int. Ltd.

12 Shell Photographic Services/Shell Int. Ltd.

13 Paul Maas/Eric van Rootselaar, based on: SHA, *Shell EP, Global Graphics Team*, 2005.

14 Shell Photographic Services/Shell Int. Ltd.

15 Paul Maas/Eric van Rootselaar, based on: SHA, 190Y/391

16 Shell Photographic Services/Shell Int. Ltd.

17 Shell Photographic Services/Shell Int. Ltd.

18 George Steinmetz

19 ANP

20 Shell Photographic Services/Shell Int. Ltd.

21 Shell Photographic Services/Shell Int. Ltd.

22 SHA, 190F/138

23 SHA, 190F/138

24 Shell Photographic Services/Shell Int. Ltd.

25 Shell Photographic Services/Shell Int. Ltd.

26 Arjen van Susteren, based on: *Financial and Operational Information*, 1998-2002

27 Shell Photographic Services/Shell Int. Ltd.

28 Corbis/Vince Streano

29 Shell Photographic Services/Shell Int. Ltd.

30 Shell Photographic Services/Shell Int. Ltd.

31 Arjen van Susteren, based on: *Financial and Operational Information*, 1998-2002

32 Corbis/Philip Gould

33 Shell Photographic Services/Shell Int. Ltd.

34 Arjen van Susteren, based on: *Financial and Operational Information*, 1998-2002

35 Shell Photographic Services/Shell Int. Ltd.

36 Shell Photographic Services/Shell Int. Ltd.

37 Corbis/Shepard Sherbell

38 Spaarnestad Photo/UPI

39 Hollandse Hoogte/Magnum/Thomas Dworzak

40 Hollandse Hoogte/Magnum/Ian Berry

41 Shell Photographic Services/Shell Int. Ltd.

42 Shell Photographic Services/Shell Int. Ltd.

43 Shell Photographic Services/Shell Int. Ltd.

44 Shell Photographic Services/Shell Int. Ltd.

45 Shell Photographic Services/Shell Int. Ltd.

46 SHA, 190F/205

47 Shell Photographic Services/Shell Int. Ltd.

48 Shell Photographic Services/Shell Int. Ltd.

49 Shell Photographic Services/Shell Int. Ltd.

50 Shell Photographic Services/Shell Int. Ltd.

51 Shell Photographic Services/Shell Int. Ltd.

52 Shell Photographic Services/Shell Int. Ltd.

53 Alamy Images

54 Shell Oil, Houston

55 Shell Photographic Services/Shell Int. Ltd.

56 Shell Photographic Services/Shell Int. Ltd.

57 Shell Photographic Services/Shell Int. Ltd.

58 Shell Photographic Services/Shell Int. Ltd.

59 Shell Photographic Services/Shell Int. Ltd.

60 Studio Marise Knegtmans, based on: SHA, Minutes Conference, 12 July 2000

61 Joost Guntenaar

62 Shell Photographic Services/Shell Int. Ltd.

63 Spaarnestad Photo

64 Spaarnestad Photo/Camera press

65 SHA, 190F/3.81.06.27

66 NFM, Aart Klein

67 SHA, 190F/3.82.05.01

68 SHA, 190F/3.82.05.01

69 Shell Photographic Services/Shell Int. Ltd.

70 Paul Maas/Eric van Rootselaar, based on: SHA, 363/5

71 Shell Photographic Services/Shell Int. Ltd.

72 Arjen van Susteren, based on: *Financial and Operational Information*, 1998-2002

73 Shell Photographic Services/Shell Int. Ltd.

74 Shell Photographic Services/Shell Int. Ltd.

Chapter 4

1   SHA, 190F/110

2   SHA, 190F/205

3   PDO Oman

4   SHA, 190F/205

5   SHA, 190F/205

6   SHA, 190F/205

7   Spaarnestad Photo/ANP

8   Spaarnestad Photo/Anefo

9   From: *Shell Magazine*, 4/1975

10 Hollandse Hoogte/Magnum/Martine Franck

11 Hollandse Hoogte/Magnum/Bob Adelman

12 SHA, 190F/138

13 SHA, 190F/139

14 SHA, 190F/139

15 SHA, 190F/139

16 SHA, 190F/139

17 Shell Photographic Services/Shell Int. Ltd.
18 Shell Photographic Services/Shell Int. Ltd.
19 Shell Photographic Services/Shell Int. Ltd./Heine Gerritsen
20 Shell Beeldbank, Netherlands
21 SHA, *Annual Report*, 1976
22 Hollandse Hoogte/Peter Hilz
23 Hollandse Hoogte/Martijn Beekman
24 SHA, 190F/205
25 SHA, 190F/138
26 Shell Photographic Services/Shell Int. Ltd.
27 Shell Photographic Services/Shell Int. Ltd.
28 SHA, 190F/Portraits
29 Shell Photographic Services/Shell Int. Ltd.
30 Shell Photographic Services/Shell Int. Ltd.
31 Shell Photographic Services/Shell Int. Ltd.
32 Shell Photographic Services/Shell Int. Ltd.
33 Shell Photographic Services/Shell Int. Ltd.
34 Shell Photographic Services/Shell Int. Ltd.
35 Shell Photographic Services/Shell Int. Ltd.
36 Hollandse Hoogte/Camera Press
37 Shell Photographic Services/Shell Int. Ltd.
38 Shell Photographic Services/Shell Int. Ltd.
39 Spaarnestad Photo/ANP
40 SHA, 190F/3.81.03.30
41 Shell Photographic Services/Shell Int. Ltd.
42 Shell Photographic Services/Shell Int. Ltd.
43 From: *Shell World*, May 1998
44 From: *Shell World*, December 1997
45 From: *Shell World*, December 1997
46 Shell Photographic Services/Shell Int. Ltd./Reinier Gerritsen
47 Shell Photographic Services/Shell Int. Ltd./Reinier Gerritsen
48 Shell Photographic Services/Shell Int. Ltd.

Chapter 5

1 Corbis/Greenpeace
2 SHA, 190F/3.81.01.16-B
3 Spaarnestad Photo/Anefo
4 Corbis
5 Shell Photographic Services/Shell Int. Ltd.
6 Getty Images

7 Getty Images/Jamal Nasrallah
8 Shell Photographic Services/Shell Int. Ltd.
9 Shell Photographic Services/Shell Int. Ltd.
10 Shell Photographic Services/Shell Int. Ltd.
11 Shell Photographic Services/Shell Int. Ltd.
12 IISG
13 Shell Photographic Services/Shell Int. Ltd.
14 Shell Photographic Services/Shell Int. Ltd.
15 Shell Photographic Services/Shell Int. Ltd.
16 Shell Photographic Services/Shell Int. Ltd.
17 Shell Australia
18 SHA, 190F/205
19 Corbis
20 Corbis
21 Corbis
22 SHA, 190F/205
23 SHA, 190F/205
24 IISG
25 IISG/designer: Jan Koperdraat
26 IISG/© Opland, 'Debat gesloten', c/o Beeldrecht Amsterdam 2007
27 Corbis/Wally McNamee
28 Corbis/Sygma/Micheline Pelletier
29 Corbis
30 IISG and SHA, 190F/205
31 IISG/designer: Rick Cowley
32 Corbis/David Turnley
33 IISG/Komitee Zuidelijk Afrika
34 Corbis/David Turnley
35 ANP
36 Corbis/Saba/Louise Gubb
37 Corbis
38 Corbis
39 SHA, 190F/205
40 Corbis/Greenpeace
41 Alamy Images
42 Shell Photographic Services/Shell Int. Ltd./Dag Magne Soyland
43 Shell Photographic Services/Shell Int. Ltd./ Dag Magne Soyland
44 Hollandse Hoogte/Magnum/Peter Marlow
45 Arjen van Susteren, based on: *Financial and Operational Information*, 1998-2002

46 Hollandse Hoogte/Kadir van Lohuizen
47 Corbis/Ed Kashi
48 Corbis/Ed Kashi
49 Corbis/Greenpeace
50 Corbis/Greenpeace
51 Corbis/Ed Kashi
52 Panos/Fredrik Naumann
53 Hollandse Hoogte/Panos
54 Corbis/Zuma/Mark Allan Johnson
55 Corbis/Ed Kashi
56 Corbis/Ed Kashi
57 Corbis/Ed Kashi
58 SLA, from: *Interchange*, 3/1992
59 SHA, 190F/205
60 Shell Photographic Services/Shell Int. Ltd.
61 Shell Photographic Services/Shell Int. Ltd.
62 Shell Photographic Services/Shell Int. Ltd.
63 Hollandse Hoogte/Sven Torfinn
64 Panos/Sven Torfinn

Chapter 6

1 Hollandse Hoogte/Gerard Til
2 Shell Beeldbank, Netherlands
3 Shell Beeldbank, Netherlands
4 Bas Czerwinski
5 ANP
6 Hollandse Hoogte/Woodfin Camp
7 Reuters/Tim Johnson
8 Reuters/ Win McNamee
9 Reuters/Peter Morgan
10 Corbis/John Gress
11 Reuters/Peter Morgan
12 Getty Images/AFP/ Adalberto Roque
13 Reuters
14 Reuters/Yves Herman
15 ANP
16 Amoco
17 From: *Shell World*, July 2002.
18 Corbis/Duomo
19 Hollandse Hoogte/Martijn Beekman
20 Hollandse Hoogte/Martijn Beekman
21 Shell Photographic Services/Shell Int. Ltd.
22 Hollandse Hoogte/Peter Hilz

23 Hollandse Hoogte/Peter Hilz
24 Hollandse Hoogte/Peter Hilz
25 Hollandse Hoogte/Peter Hilz
26 Paul Maas/Eric van Rootselaar, based on: SHA, *Shell EP Technology*, 2006
27 Shell Photographic Services/Shell Int. Ltd.
28 Shell Photographic Services/Shell Int. Ltd.
29 Shell Photographic Services/Shell Int. Ltd.
30 Shell Photographic Services/Shell Int. Ltd.
31 Arjen van Susteren, based on: *Financial and Operational Information*, 1998-2002
32 Corbis/Greg Smith
33 Shell Photographic Services/Shell Int. Ltd.
34 Shell Photographic Services/Shell Int. Ltd.
35 Shell Photographic Services/Shell Int. Ltd.
36 Hollandse Hoogte/Magnum/Stuart Franklin
37 ANP
38 Shell Photographic Services/Shell Int. Ltd.
39 Shell Beeldbank, Netherlands
40 Shell Beeldbank, Netherlands
41 Shell Photographic Services/Shell Int. Ltd.
42 Shell Beeldbank, Netherlands
43 Shell Photographic Services/Shell Int. Ltd.
44 Corbis
45 Corbis/Kevin Morris
46 Corbis
47 Shell Beeldbank, Netherlands/Ernst Bode
48 Shell Beeldbank, Netherlands
49 e-Comms & Internal Communication Shell Renewables, Hydrogen, and CO_2
50 Shell Oil
51 Shell Photographic Services/Shell Int. Ltd.
52 Shell Photographic Services/Shell Int. Ltd.
53 Shell Beeldbank, Netherlands
54 ANP
55 ANP

Joint Conclusion

1 Shell Photographic Services/Shell Int. Ltd.

Index

Page references in grey refer to illustrations or maps. Page numbers followed by a slash and a number refer to notes. Names of oil platforms, ships, newspapers and periodicals are in *italics*.

Colophon

Book design

Marise Knegtmans, Amsterdam

Picture research

Nienke Huizinga, Amsterdam

Picture production

Karin Creemers, Nijmegen

Lithography

Colorset, Amsterdam

Map design

Arjen van Susteren, Schiedam

Technical illustrations

Paul Maas & Eric van Rootselaar, Tilburg

Photography cover

Kees Rutten, Amsterdam

Slipcase

Ruimtelijke Zaken, Eindhoven

Print

Drukkerij Wilco, Amersfoort

Binding

Binderij Callenbach, Nijkerk

Index

Hans van der Pauw and Aida van Gelderen

Typeface

DTL Argo

Paper

Absolut mat, Proost & Brandt

Paper cover

Tom & Otto, MoDo van Gelder

Uitgeverij Boom

Geert van der Meulen, Aranka van der Borgh,
Ton van Lierop, Max Dumoulin

Oxford University Press

David Musson, Matthew Derbyshire,
Tanya Dean

With many thanks to

Julia Bate and colleagues (Shell Photographic
Services), Tom Chandler, Veronica Davies
(Shell London), Jack Doherty, Matthew Green,
Johan Holterman, Rob Lawa (Shell The Hague)